THE SELECTED LETTERS OF BERNARD DEVOTO AND KATHARINE STERNE

Katharine Grant Sterne

Bernard DeVoto

THE SELECTED LETTERS OF

BERNARD DEVOTO AND KATHARINE STERNE

EDITED AND ANNOTATED BY

Mark DeVoto

THE UNIVERSITY OF UTAH PRESS

Salt Lake City

The Defiance House Man colophon is a registered trademark of the University of Utah Press. It is based upon a four-foot-tall, Ancient Puebloan pictograph (late PIII) near Glen Canyon, Utah.

16 15 14 13 12 1 2 3 4 5

LIBRARY OF CONGRESS CATALOGING-IN-PUBLICATION DATA

The selected letters of Bernard DeVoto and Katharine Sterne /
edited and annotated by Mark DeVoto.
p. cm.
Includes bibliographical references and index.
ISBN 978-1-60781-188-6 (cloth : alk. paper)
1. DeVoto, Bernard Augustine, 1897–1955—Correspondence.
2. Authors, American—20th century—Correspondence. 3. Historians—United States—Correspondence. 4. Sterne, Katharine—Correspondence.
I. DeVoto, Mark.
PS3507.E867Z48 2012
818'.5209—dc23
[B]

2012021499

Printed and bound by Sheridan Books, Inc., Ann Arbor, Michigan.

CONTENTS

DeVoto at work.

PREFACE

By the year 1933, a critical year in world history, the United States had suffered for more than three years from an economic depression that was already worldwide, and its effects were visible everywhere, with millions of citizens unemployed and unable to find work, the nation's manufacturing industries reduced to a fraction of their peak capacity, and no recovery in sight. The national government that might have initiated important measures to revivify the economy had repeatedly fallen short of decisive action, and President Herbert Hoover, piously asserting that "prosperity is just around the corner" and opposed on principle to government intervention in the business sector, refused all pleas for direct economic relief to citizens. In the summer of 1932 a caravan of some twenty thousand veterans of the Great War, for whom Congress had voted a bonus in 1924 to be paid in 1945, had marched on Washington to demand that they receive the bonus now, when they desperately needed it; they were chased away by the army at the president's order.

But with the new year, America began to experience a swell of hopefulness not felt since the 1920s. The inauguration in March of the new president, Franklin D. Roosevelt, coincided with a desperate crisis in America's money supply, and he moved decisively to meet it by proclaiming a four-day bank holiday and calling Congress into special session. The Emergency Banking Act that resulted was only the first part of a whirlwind of recovery legislation produced during what became known as the Hundred Days of the New Deal. Addressing the entire country by radio on March 12 in the first of the so-called "Fireside Chats," President Roosevelt rallied the spirits of many who for endless months had been certain that the government would never take action to relieve the misery of ordinary people. And while the Democrats' 1932 campaign theme song, "Happy Days Are Here Again," might not ring fully true for many months, optimism was in the air nevertheless, and America's economic recovery was definitely under way, thanks to a visionary program of public works projects and stimulus to the business sector. One particularly favorable sign for the future was the ratification, in December 1933, of the Twenty-first Amendment to the Constitution, repealing the Eighteenth Amendment that had tried and failed to enforce Prohibition on an unwilling public; free manufacture and trade in alcoholic liquor commenced forthwith.

Around the world, there were other signs of tidal change, and many of these were ominous. At the end of January 1933, the faltering Weimar Republic in Germany, already suffering cruelly from the Great Depression, propelled Adolf Hitler and his Nazi Party to power which immediately began an aggressive program of rearmament. Direct confrontations between Germany and the major European powers would begin within three years, and an all-out European war three years after that, into which America was forcibly drawn in 1941. As Josef Stalin consolidated his absolute power in the young Soviet Union, promoting the collectivization of agriculture, millions of Russians starved to death. In 1931 a militarized Japan had already begun invading China, in the initial stage of a plan to dominate all of eastern Asia and Oceania. None of these growing menaces were widely noticed in America in 1933.

The depression variously affected America's colleges and universities, but for the most part students and faculty alike were somewhat shielded from the economic catastrophe. Tuition rates remained modest everywhere, as did faculty pay scales, and as long as enrollments were sustained faculty could be confident that their jobs would not disappear. And when Bernard DeVoto (1897–1955), a busy professional writer who was also a lecturer in the English department at Harvard University, received a fan letter from a young woman named Katharine Sterne in August 1933, neither could have imagined the beginning of a correspondence that would last eleven years and amount to some eight hundred letters before her death at age thirty-seven.

Sterne (1906–1944), a native of New York City, had graduated with honors in 1929 from Wellesley College, where she majored in art history. Returning to her hometown, she worked for a year as a designer before joining the staff of the *New York Times* as an assistant art critic. In 1932 she fell ill with tuberculosis, and following a short stay at Saranac, New York, she transferred to the Samuel and Nettie Bowne Hospital in Poughkeepsie, where, with a few brief detours including hospitalization for surgery, she remained for the rest of her life.

DeVoto, a native of Ogden, Utah, had graduated from Harvard in 1920 following service in the United States Army during the Great War. In 1922 he moved to Illinois to teach English at Northwestern University, and in 1923 married Avis MacVicar, a student in his first freshman class. In 1927 the DeVotos moved to Cambridge, Massachusetts, and in 1930 Gordon, the first of their two sons, was born. At the time of Sterne's first letter, DeVoto was thirty-six years old and had been teaching in the English department at Harvard University for four years. By then increasingly recognized as a gifted and provocative writer and literary critic, he had published numerous articles and reviews in *Harper's Magazine*, the *American Mercury*, and the *Saturday Review of Literature*; popular short stories in the *Saturday Evening Post*, *Redbook*, and *Collier's* magazine; three unsuccessful novels; and most recently, a major literary and historical study, *Mark Twain's America* (1932).

Samuel and Nettie Bowne Hospital, 1956. The Dutchess Community College campus occupies the former hospital site. This building is now known as Bowne Hall. *Courtesy Dutchess Community College.*

Avis DeVoto and Mark DeVoto, 1940.
Mark DeVoto Collection.

Gordon DeVoto and Mark DeVoto, 1940.
Mark DeVoto Collection.

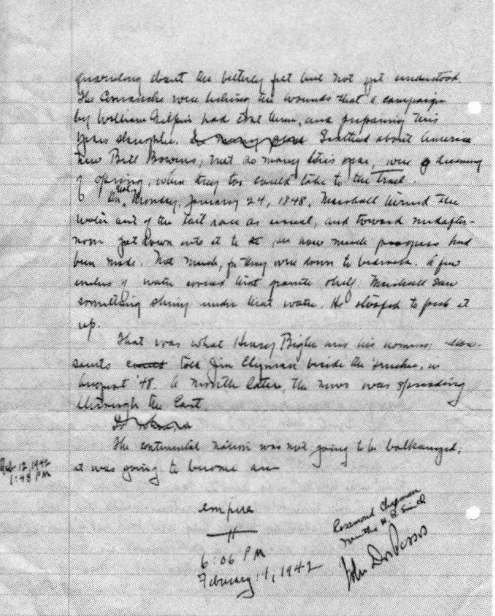

This handwritten enclosure to the letter dated 13 February 1942 contains an early draft of a portion of the text of DeVoto's book *The Year of Decision: 1846*, published in 1943 and the first of DeVoto's three histories of the American West. DeVoto dedicated this book to Sterne.

The correspondence between DeVoto and Sterne rapidly bloomed into a close and wide-ranging literary friendship. Sterne soon showed an uncanny ability, in her letters, to stimulate DeVoto about a great variety of subjects; for his part, DeVoto enjoyed displaying his knowledge and wit, and his letters to Sterne, which he sometimes wrote as often as two or three times a week, were clearly a means of both energizing and relaxation for him, after a hard day of lecturing in the classroom or writing popular fiction. Many letters on both sides reveal a deeply personal vein, each responding to the other's depth of feeling, and to the need for counsel on many different personal matters.

What is perhaps most remarkable about the friendship is that Sterne and DeVoto never met in person. When DeVoto proposed, early in the correspondence, to visit her at the Bowne Hospital, Sterne declined the offer, and he did not press the issue, perhaps sensing that the postal distance between them permitted a psychological closeness in a relationship that was already ideal and that could be upset by a face-to-face meeting.

The entire DeVoto-Sterne correspondence traces a significant cross-section of literary and historical chronology in America of the 1930s and 1940s. His full-time employment on the faculty of the Harvard English department continued for less than three years after the correspondence began, and the transfer to New York, when DeVoto took over the editorship of the struggling *Saturday Review of Literature*, lasted less than two. The years that followed witnessed the DeVoto family's move back to Cambridge, the resumption of

Boone

Dear Benny,

I was touched + excited beyond measure to get The Consummatum est. Only a transient bellyache prevented my toasting "empire" with what remains of the Christmas Scotch... Very many Thanks!.. "Become an empire", yes: but right now I'm scared chartreuse that it ain't gonna stay one. I have the

2/

Japs in Pocatello by Whitsun.

Who, by the way, is Martha H. B. Smith?

You know, I take it, how sorry I am to hear of L. J.'s death. I feel, now, as though Gage Ewing had died twice.

Not arthritis. This is the year my friends are having babies, of assorted sexes. Bill Wilson became a grandfather (a daughter

3/

of a daughter by his first wife) on the same day he had to register for the draft. (He'll be forty-five in May)... Jimmy, our cute little Scotch kitchen-boy, went on a two-days' brannigan to celebrate the occasion (registration, not childbirth), but most of my 36–45 age friends are, I think, quietly hoping that they'll be called up. I don't like being a female zombie, right this minute.

4/

I can't illustrate my state of mind better than by telling you the kind of thing I laugh at these days: Feller on the radio says as how he was drivin' through town the other evenin', + he seen Amnesia Paddock, the local receiver of stolen goods, settin' on Mayor Hardcastle's lap. Shore did give him a turn, seein' a fence settin' on a politician like that...

Yours.

Kate

Letter from Sterne to DeVoto written in response to the previous letter. *Courtesy Department of Special Collections and University Archives, Stanford University Libraries.*

DeVoto's full-time writing career, the birth of his younger son, the beginning of his most important historical writing, and the outbreak of war in Europe that would engulf America in 1941. The first large-scale product of DeVoto's pen from these years was a monument of American historical writing, *The Year of Decision: 1846*, which he published in 1943 and dedicated to Sterne. Sterne herself lived another year to enjoy the esteem of the book and to share in DeVoto's ongoing controversies; the book that he dedicated to her is still in print in 2011.

At a relatively early stage in their correspondence, Sterne expressed fascination with DeVoto's occasional references to his earlier life in Utah and urged him to expand on these. DeVoto warmed to the task immediately. "By God, I learn about autobiography from you," he wrote at the end of April 1935. In many instances in these personal effusions, the reader may guess that DeVoto exaggerated or invented details for Sterne's amusement, and one is just as certain that Sterne understood and accepted these fancies entirely. That same year he sent her, seriatim, segments of a long memoir which he titled *The Bucolics of Decadence*, about his years in Ogden after the Great War, and later he sent her a "Kent Potter Story," about his Harvard friend Kent Hägler, and Hägler's puzzling death in Paris and its psychological aftermath. These two long pieces are included in the Appendices to the letters.

Sterne died on 31 August 1944. The terms of her will directed that all of DeVoto's letters written to her, which she had saved in their original envelopes, were to be returned to him; her executor, her close friend and personal attorney Beatrice Rosenberg, carried out Sterne's wish. DeVoto was surprised to see again what he had written even years before; he flagged various portions of them and had a secretary type these for some possible future use which remains unknown.

In 1956, a few months after DeVoto's death, his personal papers and research library were acquired by Stanford University. Before they went to Stanford, the DeVoto-Sterne letters were sorted and read through by my mother and by DeVoto's editor at Houghton Mifflin, Anne Barrett, who also made a rough attempt at dating them. It was apparent to my mother and Barrett that the correspondence offered rich possibilities for publication, not only for their vivid expression but for their historical and chronological record of the literary and artistic scene in New York and Boston during the 1930s and 1940s. At the same time, the frank and personal expression could be embarrassing or painful to people still living who are mentioned in the letters. My mother therefore stipulated that the Sterne-DeVoto correspondence in the DeVoto Archive at Stanford should remain indefinitely closed to research; she granted exceptions to Wallace Stegner when he worked on his biography of DeVoto, *The Uneasy Chair* (1974), and later to me when, a few years before her own death in 1989, I began to assume the formal function of my father's literary executor. It was my mother's hope that eventually the entire correspondence would be published when persons mentioned in the letters are no longer living; by now (2011), sixty-seven years after the last letters, this is nearly the case except for some of the youngest.

I began cataloguing and transcribing the letters from photocopies in 1992, a task that even with assistance took four years. The two most important problems from the start were establishing dates, because both DeVoto and Sterne dated their letters only rarely. Barrett's provisional dating depended chiefly on postmarks on DeVoto's envelopes, and on Bernard DeVoto's penciled jottings on some of the letters when he reread them; internal evidence clearly shows that some of these dates are incorrect. I have several times revised Barrett's dating, relying almost entirely on internal evidence. Sometimes this is specific and conclusive, as when DeVoto notes the fifth birthday (7 August 1935) of my brother Gordon ("Bunny"); more often the evidence is vague or conjectural, usually when one correspondent replies to something the other has written. Dates given in [square brackets] should normally be understood as referring to a postmark unless there is specific reference to a different date. An unbracketed date is the actual date indicated by DeVoto on the letter, whether correct or not.

The majority of DeVoto's letters are handwritten, at least in the earlier years, and all of Sterne's are handwritten. Sterne often wrote several drafts of her letters before copying them out for DeVoto, but whether this is true of all of them cannot be determined for certain. In the transcription, I have followed the writers' habits of underlining or not underlining titles or putting them in quotation marks, even where these practices are not consistent; for this volume, titles have been regularly given in italics. I have corrected a few errors in DeVoto's typing where these are clearly slips of the fingers, but I have mostly let stand the very rare errors in spelling.

The letters of 1934 constitute a special case in the collection. When DeVoto's letters were returned to him in 1944, two notebooks came with them. In these notebooks, Sterne had drafted not only a number of letters to DeVoto but also many other letters, to family and friends, apparently all from the year 1934. In many instances, the drafts of the letters to DeVoto are significantly different from the versions that were finally sent to him. I have included some of the drafts of Sterne's letters to DeVoto but also to others as well, for these help to enlarge our view of the careful and sensitive writer that was Sterne herself.

EDITORIAL REMARKS

When my mother, Avis DeVoto (1904–1989), expressed the hope that the correspondence of Bernard DeVoto and Katharine Grant Sterne would be published one day, she did not expect that that might happen soon, and this was doubtless the reason for her insistence that the correspondence be closed to research for the foreseeable future. Nor did she expect that her younger son would be the one who would eventually be in charge of the editing job. Wallace Stegner had made use of the letters for his biography of DeVoto, *The Uneasy Chair* (1974), but steered clear of publishing any of them when his selection, *The Letters of Bernard DeVoto*, appeared in 1975, in which he expressed his feeling that DeVoto himself would not have published them. Stegner's reluctance may have been well motivated; yet DeVoto had read through his own letters to Sterne after these were returned to him following her death in 1944, and he had flagged portions of a number of them; these portions were separately typed by a secretary—when, or for what purpose, we do not know.

My own involvement with the letters began in 1987, when with my mother's permission I examined them for several days at the Green Library at Stanford, where they were housed in the Bernard DeVoto Archive in Special Collections. At that same time I met Stegner, then an emeritus professor at Stanford, and we discussed what might be done with the letters. My own active work began in 1992, three years after my mother's death, when I obtained photocopies of the complete letters and began to transcribe them; the transcription alone took four years of miscellaneous spare time, even with the assistance of several friends. The task of annotation began in 1999 and was essentially finished nine years later, except for the inevitable updating and correction.

During all the editing process I have always realized that I was hardly the most able or authoritative editor that might have been chosen for what has been a massive and complex task, but at the same time, I was likely the only one available for it. I have also been aware that while DeVoto was certainly a literary expert, I am certainly not; though an academic by profession, I am trained as a musician, one accustomed by trade to writing about classical music. The reader who expects more in literary knowledge than I have demonstrated will have to be content with what is offered. A more responsible editor, for example, might be expected to have read, or at least known something about, all of the hundreds of books mentioned by DeVoto and Sterne; dedicated readers will have to dig these out for themselves, and life is short.

When I consulted with Stegner, seeking advice about how the letters might be published, I wondered, as I do still, whether the entire collection of eight hundred letters, Sterne's letters as well as DeVoto's, would attract as much reader interest as might a simple selection. Eventually I came to feel that the letters as a whole might be useful to students and historical-cultural researchers of the period, simply as a cross-section of the years in which they were written. Thus both choices are offered: the selection offering significant interest, and the complete correspondence possibly offering more. DeVoto, as Stegner repeatedly emphasized, was a synecdochic historian, who had already written a scintillating historical portrait of the rich cross-currents in the American frontier in *The Year of Decision: 1846*, which is still in print today.

In preparing these letters for publication I had in mind especially their potential audience of readers, which I considered would be twofold: those who would seek historical and cultural information and enlightenment about the years when they were written, and those who would read them purely for pleasure, on their own terms. I remembered the serious counsel of my younger daughter, Marya, who examined some of the letters while she was a graduate student and teaching fellow in English literature: that today's college students cannot be depended upon to know even the most elementary facts about history, science, literature, or the arts. Accordingly I have provided basic informational endnotes about nearly every person, event, and literary or artistic work mentioned in the letters, and I do not apologize for annotating even Lincoln and Shakespeare. But to avoid what would inevitably be exasperatingly frequent repetition, I have done this for each name or term usually only once, normally at its first appearance. Thus the poet Archibald MacLeish, DeVoto's friend who appears abundantly in the letters, is personally annotated only when he is first mentioned.

My usual annotative sources were hardcover reference works, abundantly accessible in the Tisch Library at Tufts University; the principal ones are listed in the bibliography. During the first decade of the present century many databases of the Internet became more available and much more user-friendly than before, and were of indispensable value for my work. The online versions of well-known catalogues, including WorldCat, OCLC, and the various catalogues of Boston-area libraries, including the Boston Library Consortium and HOLLIS at Harvard, were invested with powerful tools that greatly simplified all my searches. Eventually two new sources stood out as particularly useful: the online *New York Times,* containing every word published by the newspaper since its founding in 1851 and fully searchable; and the Google search engine, whose utility is recognized everywhere today. I cite here only one resplendent example of the latter, which I read in one of DeVoto's letters about "the Frederick Law Olmstead [*sic*]–Captain Kidd–John Jacob Astor yarn of a few years back." For two years I was totally puzzled about what kind of story might have brought together Olmsted (American, born 1822) and Captain William Kidd (British, hanged 1701), or any of three named John Jacob Astor in the famous dynasty; every American historian whom I asked drew a complete blank. But a Google search retrieved it at once, including a reference to a 1931 article in *Forum* magazine, which is doubtless where DeVoto heard the story.

The library resources readily accessible to me did not include some that I wish I might have used. Most notable among these were microfilmed issues of the New York *Herald Tribune*, a newspaper that DeVoto preferred to the *Times* and that he referred to often; in fact, he published several reviews in the *Weekly Book Review* of the Sunday edition. I was unable to reach a library that might have had back issues of *Town and Country*. In these instances and in several others, time, travel, and effort would have been required that I could not spare when occupied with full-time teaching and other activities, and when mindful of my natural laziness. On the other hand, communication via e-mail obviated many similar expenditures, and I am grateful to countless information sources, especially those that made personal replies to my queries, in any number of institutions, among which I especially note the Harry Elkins Widener Library at Harvard University, the Boston Public Library, the New York Historical Society, the Countway Library of Harvard

Medical School, the Huntington Library, libraries at Northwestern University, Middlebury College, Kenyon College, and Amherst College, and the office of the Massachusetts Attorney General.

In any work of this size there are bound to be numerous undetected errors. I will be happy, even when sometimes nettled, to be informed of any that are found. Sharper or more imaginative eyes than mine might have deciphered the few illegible places indicated by [illegible] in transcription, and those who want to consult the original letters will be pleased to find that the DeVoto-Sterne letters at Stanford University are no longer a closed collection but are accessible to all.

This book is dedicated to those who will find it useful or enlightening or both: namely, dedicated readers.

ACKNOWLEDGMENTS

In editing the DeVoto-Sterne correspondence over a period of nineteen years, during hours casual and concentrated for many days at a stretch, I have had casual and concentrated assistance from many persons. Though I cannot sufficiently thank all of them here, I did want to single out a few names for special recognition.

Peter DeLafosse of the University of Utah Press has been an ideal supervisor of the long and varied process of publication of this large book. I am grateful for his friendship, his advice, and his outstanding judgment in bringing Bernard DeVoto back to his native state.

The facilities of Special Collections at the Green Library of Stanford University are expertly equipped and have withstood even major earthquakes without difficulty. Margaret Kimball and Linda Long gave me repeated and unstinting assistance during my several trips to Palo Alto to work with original documents, as well as by correspondence via e-mail and snailmail for over a decade.

I will never be able to sufficiently repay my debt to the Tisch Library of Tufts University, especially to JoAnne Michalak, director of the Tufts University Libraries; to Cathy DiPerna, who arranged for me to use a faculty study for several years; and to the reference and acquisitions staff, especially Christopher Barbour, Pauline Boucher, Margaret Gooch, Edward Oberholtzer, Regina Raboin, Constance Reik, Laurie Sabol, and Laura Walters. These were the colleagues and friends who cheerfully, day after day for years, made my life in the library as effective as it was efficient.

Several physicians gave me valuable information relating to DeVoto's interest in medicine generally and in psychiatry and psychoanalysis in particular. Among these I thank Leon Balter, Sanford Gifford, Edward Gross, and the late I. Herbert Scheinberg, who was also DeVoto's personal physician. Ancillary to these I am grateful to Jack Eckert of the Countway Library at the Harvard Medical School.

Patrick Quinn of the Libraries at Northwestern University provided valuable information relating to DeVoto's days at that institution. Another librarian who gave encouragement as well as assistance is Kevin O'Kelly of the Somerville Public Library in Massachusetts. He wrote the note about Jessie Costello (see chapter 1, letter dated 17 October 1933), assisted by my younger daughter, Marya, when both were graduate students in English literature at the University of North Carolina. Emily, my older daughter, who lives in England, has done some oblique investigations into DeVoto's Hertfordshire forebears.

Among my colleagues in the Arts and Sciences faculty at Tufts University I thank Liz Ammons, John Brooke, John Fyler, Sol Gittleman, Evan Haefeli, and Michael Ullman for miscellaneous details and consolation. Jeff Todd Titon, formerly of Tufts and now at Brown University, helped me to connect with strategic historians of the American West.

A major portion of the task of transcribing the letters from photocopies of handwritten originals was undertaken by Eve Bowen and Vickie Ray. My hat's off to them for their expert work, especially when they had to read difficult handwriting.

I enjoyed two semesters coordinating sections of "Windows on Research" for Tufts College freshmen, who found "The DeVoto-Sterne Correspondence" an interesting introduction to the world of university libraries and research tools. These students have long since graduated to the world at large, but perhaps some of them will remember their experience with documents of their grandparents' civilization: Julia Arazi, Allison Archambault, Laura Bennett, Molly DeCock, Martha Douglas, Melissa Fiorenza, Gregory Hawley, Kate Holohan, Catherine Jett, Jamila Moore, Emi Norris, Brittany Perham, Blair Rainsford, Sarah Sandison, Jacqueline Silva, Luis Sirotzky Jr., Jeremy Sueker, Jeffrey Theobald, and Hillary Tisman.

I am grateful to Jerry Bartholomew and George Blaustein for reading some of the letters during the editing process, and especially to another interested reader, Joan Allen Smith, colleague and friend for nearly half a century amid our collaborative study of Alban Berg. Donald Lamm, president of W. W. Norton and Company, and Margaretta Fulton of the Harvard University Press read and commented on much of the material.

Thanks to Nathaniel Smith of Franklin and Marshall College, I was able to learn much about his father, DeVoto's friend Melville Smith, who was also my teacher.

And my lasting and loving gratitude goes to Lois Grossman, who has lived with this book as long as I have.

PUBLISHER'S NOTE

The selection of letters offered in this volume represents about one-sixth of the total exchange of letters between Bernard DeVoto and Katharine Sterne. The complete eleven-year correspondence, transcribed and annotated, amounts to the equivalent of approximately 2,500 single-spaced typewritten pages. The serious student of Americana, not to mention many an interested general reader, will sooner or later want to examine the entire correspondence. It is available, absent the letters printed in this volume of selected letters, as part of the University of Utah Press's Open Access Collection, hosted by the J. Willard Marriott Library, at the Press's website, www.UofUpress.com.

The letters on the website are individually numbered in chronological order by successive year from 1933 to 1944, each number beginning with an @ character to facilitate searching and cross-referencing. Each letter is separately annotated with endnotes; otherwise, the letters in the Open Access Collection are unformatted and unindexed, but available as fully searchable PDFs.

1

1933 LETTERS

Several of the earliest letters from Sterne to DeVoto and from DeVoto to Sterne seem to be missing from the surviving correspondence of 1933, but the friendly and easygoing tone was established on both sides from the start, and likewise the extensive detail about topics of mutual interest—literature and art. Politics, history, journalism, criticism, music, and the techniques of fiction writing were added to these in short order. Relatively little personal information is exchanged at first; a letter in which Sterne mentions that she is a tuberculosis patient at Saranac Lake presumably existed but has not been found, nor has Sterne's letter praising *Mark Twain's America* which DeVoto appreciated. But Sterne's predictable future became ominously shadowed in October 1933 as she prepared for major surgery even while in a physically weakened condition. Emerging from this trauma "much to my surprise," Sterne hoped to resume the correspondence while still at Mount Sinai Hospital; DeVoto's response to Sterne's recuperation, "Thank God," was followed immediately by four dense pages about current literature, including his own novel, *Second Gentleman*, at the time less than half finished in draft. Sterne's next letter found her established at the Samuel and Nettie Bowne Hospital in Poughkeepsie, New York, where, with one four-month exception in 1940, she remained for the rest of her life.

⁂

17 St. Bernard St.
Saranac Lake
New York

[BEFORE 23 AUGUST 1933]

Dear Bernard de Voto —

I realize, of course, that you weren't trying to prove anything very much in your SEP story, "The Home-Town Mind."[1] Certainly, you weren't trying to prove that it is necessarily higher or nobler to pound a 1918 Oliver on a "tank town sheet" than a 1931 Remington on the Washington Bureau of the *New York Globe*. Your masterly stalling in your fifth-last paragraph clinches that.[2]

However, there is a moral involved. If all the metropolitan newspapermen who nurse a secret nostalgia for the dirt and camaraderie of their first city-rooms were to take the next train home, would there be any New York papers?

Why don't you do a sequel? (Do you remember the F. Scott Fitzgerald piece about the expatriate who made a fortune doing sad, wistful tales of Virginia; came back to Virginia and made a fortune doing sad, wistful tales of the Paris boulevards?)[3]

Well, anyway, why don't you write a story about John Hoyt in Custis[4]—how he got to hankering after the great swinging steel doors of the morgue, and the feel of *City News* flimsy; how he went back to New York and took a job on a super-super-sheet, made twenty-six copies of each story on twenty-seven different colored papers; knew, not merely Anne Darcy, but the entire Carroll chorus, got together and established the Exclusively-for-John-Hoyt Harem?

With deep admiration,
K. G. Sterne

BREADLOAF WRITERS' CONFERENCE
Bread Loaf, Vermont

[23 AUGUST 1933]

No, my dear—just my conviction that if one hour of a house party can be said to be worse than another, it's the one when they sit round and shine. Cocktails, unless they are on a strictly man to man basis, should be à deux. Then it's the best hour in New York or anywhere.[5]

John Hoyt exists in one more yarn, a pretty lousy one. The *Post* has three of my jobs in type but shows a reluctance, quite understandable, to give them to the world. My stuff is pretty awful these days. So much so that I'm going rural & when I get back to Massachusetts I'm going to be sweet, Yankee, and quiet in two or three stories to see if the change of scene will improve the product. Did you ever hear of the seven houses of Orford (New Hampshire)? I'm going to affront them with fiction.... Why do you read this tripe? I'm sending you a book which does make clear that I have written intelligently.[6] Expect it as soon as I can get off a note to Little, Brown.

I'm sorry you're disabled. What you need is the mountain air that John Hoyt is breathing. But that's what we all need. Christ, I'm lecturing to old women in the Green Mountains. Did some one say mountains?

Yours,
DV

Lincoln, Massachusetts

[7 September 1933]

Dear K

It's damned handsome to say such pleasant things about M T's A, and much handsomer to think them.[7] I think it's a pretty good book; I know it's an honest one. It's going to catch Hell next month when a Ph.D. brings out a Mark Twain and has already brought the intellectuals down on it in groups. Not, however, in matters of fact.

Writers don't confer—outside of speakeasies—I believe. But the wishful and the earnest and the devout gather at Bread Loaf for the last two weeks of August and listen to Robert Hillyer, Walter Eaton, Gorham Munson, Janet Fairbank, Archie MacLeish, Sinclair Lewis, Ted Weeks and me.[8] Listen, open-mouthed, gaping, as in the presence of Jesus or at least Bruce Barton.[9] The phenomenon, I have decided, is associated with the menopause. They were all women of a certain age. But the curious thing is they think they're professionals. They get intense about markets, inspiration, whether it's best to have an agent, should one keep a notebook, and what the typewriter does to one's style. If ever, even on liquor, I could manage to feel for 30 seconds as confident that I'm a writer as they are all the time, life would offer me fewer off days.... God knows why I go there—this is my second year. Except that Ted Morrison who runs the place is a persuasive friend and it is fun to load half the staff in my Chevrolet and get the hell out of there for an afternoon, which seems a curious pleasure to work so hard for.[10]

I know the Huffman photographs of the West but not Paul Strand's.[11] Where does one see them? But the bit you quoted sounded terribly like Lewis Mumford, which would be discouraging or worse.[12]... Curiously, or shamefully enough I don't know whether Benton is related to Benton, and I should—God knows I should.[13] I'll find out. There's a lot of good work, pictorially I mean, coming out of the West these days. Seven years ago when I wrote a kind of survey of the West I had to lower my sights to name anyone.[14] Now the very sagebrush breeds them in swarms. Someone has just sent me a lithograph from my home state and it's damned good and the dealer who found it for me wanted the lithographer's address. It doesn't seem to be the Utah I was born to—and thrown out of. Getting sissy, maybe. But then the damnedest people get born out there anyway. Ezra Pound, for instance.[15] Born between the sage and the lava on the slopes of an Idaho desert. I said so in print once and at once he wrote from Rapallo, declaring me one of the 12 Americans capable of general ideas and asking me to write a letter denouncing the American Academy.[16] The Western manner.

Oh, I'll send you MacLeish's *Frescoes for Mr. Rockefeller's City* when I can get hold of a copy.[17] It's not only fine poetry, it's great stuff. It will reinforce your Americana. But speaking of that, for God's sake don't think about work while you've still got a limping lung. Another thing about the Western heritage—it has accomplished much for your special problems but the real answer is to sit on your fanny and think the kind of thoughts you ought to think. It's just about as easy as being religious, but it has to be done. I don't think, even, that you should read fiction more exciting than Trollope's.[18] My *Post* stuff is O K, of course.... I'm sorry as hell you're on your fanny, especially since your soul is as obviously hungry for the inkpots and fleshpots of your profession. But: Wry Reflection, Series B—Did you ever know anybody worth a damn that didn't have to learn to take it, in some such way? God has the loveliest imagination.

Maybe I'm not writing about the Seven Houses of Orford.

I've plunged into a story and it has that horrible crackling sound.

Yours,

DV

17 St. Bernard St.
Saranac Lake

[AFTER 18 SEPTEMBER 1933]

Dear DV,

Who is Gustavus Myers,[19] & why does John Chamberlain name him as your alternate?[20] Have you been baying the moon on that subject in print? Seems to me he (J.C.) might have been allotted a few of those two grand for research into such topics as Why All Art Museums Have Terrible Cafeterias; A Short History of Modern Art, With Special Reference to Mass Hysteria and the Popular Confusion of Ethics and Aesthetics; The Economic Interpretation of Journalism or Gotta Have a New Hat Don't I; or, as you suggest, The Impulse to Authorship as a Psycho-physical Corollary of the Female Climacteric.

A New York scout reports that "the hoary & becaned book critics of this town are hoping that J. Chamberlain's preoccupation with sociology will bore his readers to tears & John's undoing."[21] I fear they may get their wish.

Confiteor.[22] It occurred to me, when your letter was in the post, how ungracious, not to say downright feline, was that crack about the Penrose book. Let me retract it. Let me, if possible, efface it. A dark magenta rage, plus the circumstance that I have never known any creative writing worth a damn to be produced without a certain amount of agony and misgiving, betrayed me into that meanness. I hope it is a swell book. I hope it makes a million dollars. I hope you greet it in the *Atlantic* with trumpets and flugelhorns. I am an envious and unbelieving bitch....

misereator [*sic*] mei omnipotens Deus et dismissis [*sic*] peccatis meis.[23] Amen

Kate

Lincoln, Massachusetts

[PROBABLY LATE SEPTEMBER 1933]

Dear Kate,

Gustavus Myers is—he may be preterite for all I know—an elderly and bilious gent who labored some years back in the Socialist vineyard.[24] Very acute and painstaking mind but indications of rabies around the jowls and preeminent for solemnity as the liberal brethren so soon get to be. He wrote a lot of stuff of which I remember only two, "Ye Olde Puritan Blue Laws"[25]—you read it right, my dear, and it's lousy—and the one Chamberlain was talking about, *History*, or *Origins*, I forget which, *of the Great American Fortunes*. A good book and first-rate stuff, exciting and satisfying reading too although written in an English that makes Veblen seem like a stylist and puts the Book of Mormon in a new & favorable light.[26] But it would have been so much better if I'd done it, for Myers suffers from chronic indignation and sometimes the facts don't come through the blood pressure and all the man's irony was just glue. I haven't seen Chamberlain's crack in the *Times*—I'm a Bostonian, dear—but it's been mentioned to me and I gather he was alluding to an exchange in print we put on a month or so ago. During the spring and summer the *Sat Rev of Lit* was practically a one-man show, with me alternating as the autopsist & the remains. At one time Chamberlain devoted a column to announcing that I ought to rewrite M T's A to show cause why the steamboat age which I had painted pretty black wasn't "pioneering materialism."[27] I answered (a) I didn't say it wasn't, (b) because I put separate things in separate chapters didn't mean I was carelessly contradicting myself, (c) after fasting & meditation I remained unable to perceive any difference between pioneering materialism & any other kind, & would John kindly look into the competing English, Dutch and Scandinavian transatlantic lines of the 40's & conclude that materialism in the carrying trade wasn't specifically a pioneer or even an American characteristic.[28] This, I gather, is what he wants to subsidize me to elaborate. No thanks.... I don't know—. He's enough younger than I to be a boy's image in my thinking. Out of Yale 5 or 6 years ago. Bright, alert, honest as honesty goes in the literary business, semi-realistic (which is 108% more realistic than most of the young literary minds), and sufficiently confused in mind to make an excellent understudy for Canby.[29] It has pleased him to write me up quite large, which also sets him off from the gang, and he wrote a quite good book last fall, "Farewell to Reform."[30] I gather that he's a typical college liberal who recovered earlier than most & had too much intelligence to join the belated stampede of the speakeasy liberals into Communism. Probably Cowley or Calverton will be calling him a black shirt before the year is out.[31] ... My black shirt was manufactured by one Novack in the *New Republic* six or eight weeks ago.[32] ... It will be too bad if anything does cut the boy's job short on the *Times*, for the spectacle of any kind of intelligence reviewing books for the N Y press has had a kind of awe and wonder. The newspaper business does not change. It remains an assumption of editors—all & all degrees of editors—that anyone can review books or music. Even I have filled in as a music critic many a time. They brought Harry Hansen east on the simple grounds that he had lifted the *Daily News* from last to first in book ads in Chicago, and it was true, & till Hansen's legs started to go he hadn't ever read a book.[33] Broken down war correspondent whom they didn't want to let go and wouldn't pension. Genesis of the literary critic. So far as I've been able to follow his career he's never said an unfavorable thing about any book whatsoever, or any favorable thing that made clear he knew what he was talking about. Or Heywood Broun.[34] From the sports desk to the mantle of Dr. Johnson.[35] My capacity for surprise has been at a minimum ever since I was two—for I grew up in the Wasatch—but I cannot yet keep my jaw from dropping at the spectacle of Heywood Broun expressing an opinion about a book, or for that matter expressing an opinion. They'd better bring reviewing under the blue eagle damn quick or else fire John.[36] This is all ungenerous of me for I'm unquestionably the least sold writer in America and just about the best reviewed. But the fact lends peculiar authority to my analysis of fake in reviewing. But alas, God bless us, I wouldn't change it a bit. The world is much more reassuring this way, for an era that produces immortal masterpieces with the rapidity of ours must be sound. And productive of lineage.

You're not a bitch, darling—or no more of a bitch than is appropriate to your interests. Hell, if we were to develop qualms over every remark made about some one else's book—don't set up so high a standard for the race. I don't know anything about this attempt to go God one better by making fiction out of Penrose but I can promise you it won't make a million dollars. Nothing will except the Bible and *Anthony Adverse*.[37]

I don't know whether Simon Cameron ever said it—for that matter I don't know whether Zinc Barnes did, having only the fragrant tradition of the Great Basin & the memory of C.C. Goodwin—but Simon was certainly in a position to know.[38] My surest weapon in my occasional invasions of the Adams family hereabouts is my ability to point out that when Henry had finished rejecting America in the name of its failure to recognize a dynasty of Adamses in high places he then sought round for the one place & time in the US where the state & people were indissoluble & life flowered in the purity dreamed of by great-grandfather John when he created America, and pointed out Pennsylvania under the Camerons.[39] Somehow joy overflows me at that realization—as when, a day or two ago, setting out to do some more surgery on the intellectual, I discovered that Mary Austin had misquoted the Gettysburg Address four times in eight passionate lines.[40] God has his moments. The good Mumford and his wild strawberries is another.[41] It will be in print sometime.

But speaking of Pennsylvania, would you be the daughter of that Stern [*sic*] who rehabilitated a Springfield Illinois paper, moved on to do the same thing in New Jersey, & is now shocking the good people of Philadelphia by printing this century's news?[42] If you are, I respectfully commend your father and extend my sympathies for a brother who at Harvard a couple of years ago set an all-time high in pests. And if you are, how this Arizona interlude? On the strength of Arizona you should read about Grandfather Dye in the Sept. *Harper's*, which I'll be glad to send on application.

Not kicked out of U. U. Appalled out, if you prefer.[43] Some chapters in *Second Gentleman* will be autobiographical, within limits.[44]

A keen reportorial sense for the observed fact will have shown you that this is accompanied by Archie MacLeish's *Frescoes*, my shipment having at last arrived. I hope you like it. For my part, it's the first poem that has stirred me since the brave days of 1915 when nearly anything you might pick up had something momentarily noteworthy in it. When one stumbled over the Everlasting Mercy much as one runs on an Ogden Nash jingle these days, when the world was younger and Gordon Abbey & I were witnessing a Renaissance.[45]

Yours,
Benny

Saranac

SATURDAY [BEFORE 17 OCTOBER 1933]

Dear Benny,
Oh, decidedly, God has his moments,[46] & I must admit that one of them was when (with perfect logic & from false premises generously supplied by me) you deduced that I was a daughter of J. David Stern. My idea of J. D. is based entirely on the bitter & slightly bawdy reminiscences of a couple of ex-*Record*-reporters &, naturally, is far from fragrant.[47]

Soon I shall be urban again. How often—sipping egg noggs on an icy porch, listening to the soughing of the pines—I have wondered what it would be like to sit once more on an armchair, in a well-heated apartment, fully clothed, clutching a martini, and listening, say, to the Toccata & Fugue in D Minor.[48]

Sometimes, in the old days, when I had covered—in a manner of speaking—fifteen or sixteen galleries from Flatbush to Fordham, or made over the Sunday pages four times, I used to fall exhausted into people's *chaises longues*, exhaling a pious wish that I might be, like Irita Van Doren, a lady in the country.[49] (Chalk that sentence up to Proust.)[50] I would wander in fancy over gorse*-strewn moors, with my Dobermann Pinscher. I would cultivate my garden. I would sit down, before a blazing wood fire, to an early supper of honey, eggs & tea. In the evening I would write, in violet ink & a fine Spencerian hand, long letters to whoever happened to be the analog of Stuart Sherman.[51] Maybe then my exile is poetic justice.

Suddenly, in the teeth of my ineffable post-adolescent conceit, I grasp the fact that I am a person of no possible importance. A congenital floppiness of character was only aggravated by being subjected, at closely spaced intervals, to such diverse influences as: the pious conservatism of three unmarried aunts; the rowdy & slightly lesbian atmosphere of a small girls' boarding school; the aggressive "broadmindedness" of one of my father's mistresses; the pragmatic discipline of the School Sisters of Notre Dame.[52]

Intellectually, I am nothing to get excited about. I have a good memory & a fairly well-oiled collative faculty, but I am quite incapable of original, or even strictly logical thought; I have no creative gift that exceeds the dimensions of an accomplishment. So you see...

The occasion for this spiritual strip-act (God knows why I should burden you, but I hope you will pardon it with the charity you have shown on other occasions) is that I am going down to New York to-night to have eleven of my ribs cut out. My father arrived this morning with Miss Child, my pneumonia nurse, & we are going down to-night on the 9:50. Neuhoff of Mt. Sinai will do the operation, probably Wednesday of next week. I shall not be able to write for a couple of months anyway. I shall miss your letters.

*what in hell is gorse?

Yours,

Kate

Private Pavilion
The Mount Sinai Hospital
Fifth Avenue & One Hundredth Street
New York City

[BEFORE 17 OCTOBER 1933]

Dear Benny,

Here I am, much to my surprise and, I suspect, the surprise of the surgeon.

A thoracoplasty is a lovely little party, complete with delirium and fancy retchings.

I don't know why you're so damn generous, but if you really meant what you said, the above address will be good for some time.[53]

When can I hope to see "Second Gentleman"?

What did you think of "The Proselyte"?[54]

Yours,

Kate

K.S./V.B.

Lincoln, Massachusetts

[17 October 1933]

Dear Kate:

Thank God.

But you stump me with "The Proselyte." Again, I remind you that I live in Boston. Picture, play, movie, novel? If the allusion is an oblique Manhattan remark about Mrs. Costello's teaming up with Sister Aimee, I am unwrung.[55] The Costello case achieved the Euripidean climax,[56] and anything further could be mere gruel, when the gent whom our profession had christened the Kiss and Tell Cop was employed by…the Lydia E. Pinkham Company.[57]

You must be patient with an aging mind resident in, much in love with, & enormously exasperated by Boston. If you were to go to work for the *Transcript*, for instance, all your ideas about the velocity of news would undergo revulsion. You understand, of course, that no music has its premiere until it has been played in Boston, in fact not until H T P[58] has heard it, so that an allusion to something which someone might have thought he heard at Carnegie Hall could conceivably have no meaning for me. Similar principles from the circulation of other items, especially among the intellectuals, pedagogues, artists, neurotics, scientists, and—I believe the word is—publicists of Cambridge, from whom I fled these twelve miles into the country but who remain my chief deliverance from solipsism. Child, you may think residence in New York has given you authority about madhouses. It hasn't: I can tell you so as one who knew the Village in 1920, too late for its distinguished imbecility but, all things considered, quite early enough. One who has never lived in Cambridge will well hold his tongue when one who has begins to speak of madhouses. Any good definition of acute mania would only be a bystander's description of Beyond Brattle Street. You were a Wellesley girl. Doubtless you glimpsed the exterior aspects of the ward. It may be that you were enough of a Wellesley girl to mistake those aspects for amusement. It would make a good novel, if one had time to write it.

Kaufman and Ryskind & Gershwin brought up their nice show a while back.[59] I attended the baptism and it was amusing, less so than the first but not so much less as one anticipated. I hear they've amended it to make Shuttlebottom [*sic*] President at the end which was so obviously right that I don't see how they missed it. I'll try to go back and review the changes before they take it away. The music was rather better than before, but on the whole I left the theater, after the last broadcast back stage, with the same feeling the other gave me, the same feeling one gets so damn often. Why didn't they have the guts to do the job they started? Earlier in this show even than in the last they decided not to risk the satirical thing, not to let it stay in its own terms, but to fall back into the dependable arms of burlesque. A damn shame. They have Broadway licked. The city of your admiration would take anything that Kaufman offered, and call it genius. Why didn't he go through with it? I doubt that it's his intelligence that fails. A mind that can Put Love in the White House doesn't go soft by the end of Act I.[60] If it isn't intelligence, three guesses what fails. But that is the—one of the—defect of the American intellectual. Who will, large groups of him, find *Let Them Eat Cake* in very poor taste, I think, when it makes New York, for it burlesques the Revolutionists this time, and an intellectual knows that whatever cows can not be held sacred from derision, the Revolution must be. Maybe the affront will be sufficient to ensure the membership among potential thinkers which the *Nation* awarded George and Morrie after the last show.[61] Which was one of the funniest awards since the Pulitzer Committee read *Years of Grace*.[62] ... Oh, I meant no offense to Heywood Broun. He's a good guy and you could carve porterhouses off his heart. But, whether by act of the legislature or extra-legal boycott, something should be done about his tendency to think he has ideas.

Watch out how you tell me anecdotes, when you're able to resume the pen. I am again a novelist and suddenly my mind has acquired the faculty of flypaper. The other morning I found myself incorporating a story that I had heard at dinner the night before and casting round for a way to use another. The first was only the remark of an elderly Bostonian who was taken to see Isadora Duncan and sat unmoved throughout the evening, only to find his glasses at the end and say that Isadora "looked just like any naked Cabot."[63] It's in *Second Gentleman* now, but whether I shall use the incident of the daughter of a great brain surgeon, to disguise her most effectively, remains to be seen.[64] At a deb dinner, she stood up suddenly, looked with some feeling at her champagne glass, and said, "Christ, how the stuff goes through you."

S G will be out a year from last month or not at all. I say, I'm a novelist again and I expect to be for the next four months, but who knows? At intervals during the last year I've contemplated throwing the thing away, and I may yet. One gets fed up with breaking off in mid-flight, agonizing over a hunk of tripe for Uncle George for a month, and then going back cold and slowly gathering momentum again, achieving it about the time it's obligatory to go back and produce some more tripe.[65] The process damn near strangled M T's A in the womb and it had kept S G to about 100 ms. pages—until 2 weeks ago.... I should perhaps explain, in view of the *Post*'s known willingness to pay outrageous sums for tripe, that the last years have gone hard with an assortment of relatives, and I have no fleece to cover them with except what I got from the *Post*.... Three weeks ago, I mailed off a story to Uncle George—didn't I tell you about the Federalist houses at Orford?—and pulled out the neglected ms., confident that I and all my army corps could rest for 6 or 8 weeks. Ten days of false starts and the thing showed signs of breathing again, and the *Post*, usually wounded by my attempt to pass off a semi-literary offering, dumped it back on my doorstep with demands of a peculiarly annoying sort. Was it Cousin Hugo who could be pushed just so far?[66] The prospect was two or three weeks of cursing while I did the job over, followed by 2 or 3 weeks of the sort of footless backing & filling I'd just got over. And Cousin Hugo had been pushed too far.[67] My dear, it's the first gesture in the direction of Art I've made since the summer of 1927 when I finally decided, at Chatham, Cape Cod, that as for me, between pedagogy and Prostitution, they could have my virtue every time—and I'd laugh my head off at any one who told me he was contemplating a similar gesture. But I went novelist—hard. First I added up my check book; second I notified the army corps that reducing diets would be well thought of for a while; and third, I went in to Little-Brown, called up my recollections of Duse and Red Lewis in a rage, did an Artist in Alfred McIntyre's office, demanded four times the advance they paid me on the book a year ago, got it without a quiver, drove back to Lincoln, and told the *Post* that my soul has been so wounded by their Philistinism that it wasn't likely they could expect anything from me before April.[68] . . . Along about February either the death rate or the crime wave is due to pick up in the American hinterland, and shortly thereafter I'll have to put on my lace pants and take to the streets again, but I'm turning out upwards of 15000 words a week now and contemplating a velvet rest. As always, after these seizures of nobility, I have two regrets, both poignant. 1) A couple of days ago Collier's offered me $550 above my present price, which, these days, is an interesting raise, and 2) when I last went to Canada I brought back only one case of Scotch.[69] I don't know which steel goes deeper, but I think the latter. Rob me of all honor, all capacity, all future, all reputation, but it's a good world if I can keep my palate—and if Art brings me to drinking gin, may the Marxist state extirpate it as a bourgeois menace.

What gives all this richness is the fact that S G is going to be a lousy novel. All mine are and there isn't much to be done about it, except on the part of my friends, who are patient and dogged. To forsake the fleshpots for a bum novel is about as funny as can be conceived—in fact, I think I'll put it into S G. The amount of needless sacrifice on behalf of dull books makes an enormous turnover every year—it's some kind of trend, some kind of aberration, and it's a damn queer feeling to realize that one has been drawn into it. As if I should find myself taking part in a marathon dance or seized with belief in spiritualism or Christian Science. . . . Oh, a question in an earlier letter. Gordon Abbey is the center of my first and lousiest novel.[70] I thought it would amuse you and then discovered that I have only one copy, which has to stay here. I've sent out a call to the 2nd hand market, and if it shows up I'll send it to you. Provided that you promise to read it purely as a joke book and provided further that it doesn't arrive until you have built up sufficient convalescence to make immoderate laughter no menace to you.

Hell, I'll even send you a carbon of S G when the first draft's done. Interest in it is the first sign of morbidity you've shown. So you can make marks on the margin. But look out: an artist has his sore spots.

Don't acknowledge this. I'll fire off another dose after a while. For God's sake watch your step and love your nurse and do what the doctors tell you to do. It's hell to be in New York on your back.

Yours

Benny

NOTES

1. *Saturday Evening Post* 205, 1 April 1933.
2. "There would always be a bitter sense of something given up, a painful wonder about the possibilities abandoned. He would have troubled hours, regretting the offstage excitement, the public greatness, the fictitious brilliance and achievement that, perhaps, were not altogether fictitious. Pauses would come, and John Hoyt would be wondering about a gayer, surer John Hoyt who might have gone straight to Washington and flamed like a bonfire. No matter. All that had already receded." (*op. cit.* p. 45).
3. (1896–1940), author of novels and short stories; *This Side of Paradise*, 1920; *The Great Gatsby*, 1925; *Tender is the Night*, 1934. What Sterne (hereafter refered to as KS) was thinking of is unknown; no story or article of this description by Fitzgerald is known to exist. DeVoto's (hereafter refered to as BDV) final treatment of the return-to-hometown theme is *Mountain Time* (1947), his last and most successful novel.
4. The fictional town of Custis appears as early as BDV's short story "In Search of Bergamot," *Harper's* 155/3 (August 1927), and also turns up in *Mountain Time*. BDV doubtless remembered the family name of Martha Dandridge Custis (1731–1802), who married George Washington (1732–1799) in 1759, two years after the death of her first husband, Daniel Parke Custis; or Peter Custis, naturalist and explorer of the American Southwest in 1804.
5. See BDV's *The Hour*, 1951.
6. BDV's *Mark Twain's America*, 1932.
7. Ibid.
8. Hillyer (1895–1961), poet, novelist, critic; Boylston Professor at Harvard; Pulitzer Prize in poetry, 1934. Eaton (1878–1957), playwright, professor at Yale. Munson (1896–1969), critic. Fairbank (1878–1951), novelist. MacLeish (1892–1982), poet, diplomat; Boylston Professor at Harvard; Librarian of Congress, 1939–1944; assistant secretary of state, 1944–1945; Pulitzer Prize in poetry, 1933 and 1953. Lewis (1885–1951), author; *Main Street*, 1920; *Babbitt*, 1922; *Arrowsmith*, 1925; Nobel Prize in literature, 1930. Weeks (1898–1989), editor, *Atlantic Monthly*, 1928–1966.
9. (1886–1967), writer, advertising executive, newspaper editor, congressman from New York.
10. (1901–1988), poet, teacher of writing at Harvard, close friend of BDV; director of the Bread Loaf Writers' Conference, 1932–1955. Most of those named in this paragraph are identified in Morrison, *Middlebury College/Bread Loaf Writers' Conference: The First Thirty Years (1926–1955)*, Middlebury College Press, 1976; see also David Haward Bain and Mary Smyth Duffy, *Whose Woods These Are: A History of the Bread Loaf Writers' Conference/1926–1992*, 1993.
11. Laton Alton Huffman (1854–1931), photographer of the American West. Strand (1890–1976), photographer, produced studies in Colorado (1926), New Mexico (1930–1932), and Mexico (1932–1933). See *Paul Strand: A Retrospective Monograph/The Years 1915–1946*, 1971.
12. (1895–1990), historian and social critic.
13. Thomas Hart Benton (1782–1858), U.S. senator from Missouri, father-in-law of the adventurer John C. Frémont (1813–1890), army officer, adventurer, and first Republican candidate for

president, in 1856; and Thomas Hart Benton (1889–1975), grandnephew of the foregoing, artist and writer, called by President Harry S. Truman "the best damned painter in America."

14. "Utah," *American Mercury* 7 (March 1926); "Ogden: The Underwriters of Salvation," in Duncan Aikman (ed.), *The Taming of the Frontier*, 1925. These articles were BDV's first published nonfiction to achieve national circulation; they provoked controversy and considerable indignation in his native state. BDV later referred to them as "ignorant, brash, prejudiced, malicious, and, what is worst of all, irresponsible"; see his letter of 24 May 1943 to Jarvis Thurston, in Wallace Stegner (ed.), *The Letters of Bernard DeVoto* (hereafter referred to as *LBDV*), 1975.
15. Ezra Pound (1885–1972), born in Hailey, Idaho; brilliant poet, critic, expatriate fascist; became mentally unbalanced.
16. Probably the American Academy of Arts and Letters, possibly the American Academy in Rome.
17. *Frescoes for Mr. Rockefeller's City: Six New Poems*, pamphlet, 1933.
18. Anthony Trollope (1815–1882), British serial novelist.
19. See the next letter.
20. Chamberlain (1903–1995), assistant editor, *Saturday Review of Literature* (hereafter refered to as *SRL*); founding editor of "Books of the Times," a daily review in the *New York Times* from 6 September 1933. In the latter, on 18 September, he wrote: "Bernard De Voto, for example, has been baying the moon because American intellectuals such as Lewis Mumford, H.L. Mencken and Van Wyck Brooks have been scarifying this country because of its 'materialism.'...Why not a grant of money to Mr. De Voto, or to Gustavus Myers, in order that they may prove to the culpable intellectuals that 'materialism' in America is only part of a pattern....Another $2,000 grant might go to George Novack to undertake an economic interpretation of American philosophy."
21. Probably a friend of KS.
22. (Latin) I confess.
23. (Latin, correctly), *misereatur mei omnipotens Deus et dimittat peccatis meis*, (freely) may almighty God have mercy on me and forgive my sins.
24. Myers (1872–1942), historian; *History of Tammany Hall*, 1901; *History of the Great American Fortunes*, 1909–1910.
25. Correctly, *Ye Olden Blue Laws*, 1921.
26. Thorstein Veblen (1857–1929), economist and sociologist, best known for *The Theory of the Leisure Class*, 1899.
27. *SRL* 9/51 (8 July 1933), editorial, "A List for Revision."
28. *SRL* 10/1 (22 July 1933), "Mr. DeVoto Wins."
29. Henry Seidel Canby (1878–1961), author, founding editor of *SRL*, 1924–1936.
30. 1932.
31. Malcolm Cowley (1898–1989), writer, editor, literary editor of *New Republic*. BDV scorched Cowley's *Exile's Return*, just published, in *SRL* 10/46 (2 June 1934). Cowley published a memoir of these years in several articles, gathered and reprinted as *The Dream of the Golden Mountains: Remembering the 1930s*, 1980. See BDV's letters to him in *LBDV*. Victor Francis Calverton (1900–1940), author of *The Liberation of American Literature* (1932).
32. George E. Novack, "Vilfredo Pareto: The Marx of the Middle Class," *New Republic* 75/972 (19 July 1933), pp. 258–61: "With the tide of fascism rising higher in Europe and threatening our shores, it is significant that an extravagant estimate of Pareto's work should appear in this country at this time," with footnote referring to BDV's "A Primer for Intellectuals," *SRL*, 22 April 1933. See also notes to the previous letter.
33. Hansen (1884–1977), editor, writer; reviewer for *Harper's*, 1923–1939.

34. (1888–1939), American journalist, essayist, and novelist. Wrote a column, "It Seems to Me," for the New York *Tribune and World*; champion of Sacco and Vanzetti. Socialist candidate for Congress, 1930; founded American Newspaper Guild, 1933.
35. Samuel Johnson (1709–1784), outstanding British essayist, lexicographer, biographer, translator, and poet; compiler and author of the first great dictionary of the English language, 1755.
36. The blue eagle was the symbol and logo of the National Recovery Act, 1933–1935.
37. Huge bestselling novel by Hervey Allen, 1933.
38. Charles Carroll Goodwin (1832–1917), Western newspaperman and writer; *Why Silver Should Be Remonetized*, 1890; *The Comstock Club*, 1891; *Steel Rails on the Old Trails in the Western Pacific Country*, 1913; etc.
39. Henry Adams (1838–1918), Harvard '58, author, philosopher and historian; grandson of president John Quincy Adams; *Mont-Saint-Michel and Chartres*, 1913; *The Education of Henry Adams*, 1918; *History of the United States during the Administrations of Jefferson and Madison*, 1885–1891, and many other works. Simon Cameron and his son, James Donald Cameron (1833–1918), U.S. secretary of war, 1876–1877; senator from Pennsylvania, 1877–1897.
40. Austin (1868–1934), novelist. The reference is to *The American Rhythm: Studies and Reëxpressions of Amerindian Songs*, new and enlarged edition, 1930. See BDV's "How Not to Write History," *Harper's* 118/2 (January 1934), reprinted as "Thinking about America" in *Forays and Rebuttals*, 1936.
41. Lewis Mumford, "Prophet, Pedant and Pioneer," *SRL* 9/42 (6 May 1933), review of revision of Van Wyck Brooks, *The Ordeal of Mark Twain*, rebutting BDV's *Mark Twain's America*; BDV's reply, ibid., 9/44, 20 May 1933.
42. Julius David Stern (1886–1971), newspaper publisher; *Memoirs of a Maverick Publisher*, 1962.
43. BDV spent his freshman year, 1914–1915, at the University of Utah in Salt Lake City. After his freshman English instructor was fired in an academic-freedom controversy, BDV applied for transfer to Harvard College and was accepted.
44. BDV's fourth and best novel, then in progress; before publication it was retitled *We Accept with Pleasure*.
45. Nash (1902–1971), poet and humorist. Gordon Abbey was a character in BDV's first published novel, *The Crooked Mile*, 1924.
46. See previous letter.
47. Probably the Philadelphia *Record*; possibly the Boston *Record*, tabloid newspaper, later the *Record-American*, finally merged with the Boston *Herald*.
48. By J. S. Bach, for organ, one of his most popular compositions.
49. (1891–1966), literary editor of New York *Herald Tribune*, 1926–1963; married to Carl Van Doren.
50. Marcel Proust (1871–1922), outstanding French author; author of a massive novel, *Á la recherché du temps perdu*, in seven sections (1913–1917).
51. Spencerian was a style of eighteenth-century copperplate calligraphy, with loops and flourishes. Sherman (1881–1926), critic, professor of English at the University of Illinois, literary editor of New York *Herald Tribune*.
52. Founded in Bavaria, 1833; American order, from 1847.
53. Not identified; this suggests that a letter from BDV is missing.
54. A novel about the Mormons, by Susan Ertz (1894–1985), just published.
55. Mrs. Jessie B. Costello, the "poison widow" of Peabody, Massachusetts, was tried in 1933 for the murder of her husband, whose body contained traces of cyanide. Press coverage of the trial struck notes of religion and lucre that no doubt reminded many of the evangelist Aimee Semple McPherson (1890–1944), who once had as many as forty-five legal actions pending against her. The prosecution pointed out that Mrs. Costello was the beneficiary

of her husband's five-thousand-dollar life insurance policy. The defense asserted that Mr. Costello had been depressed and fanatically religious since the death of one of their children, implying he may have committed suicide. The jury apparently accepted the defense with irony: they entertained themselves in the jury room by singing "Abide with Me" and "Till We Meet Again." Mrs. Costello celebrated her acquittal by signing a contract for her life story and beginning a ten-week, twenty-five-thousand-dollar vaudeville tour (*Newsweek* 2/24, 26 August 1933). For McPherson, see Lately Thomas, *Storming Heaven: The Lives and Times of Minnie Kennedy and Aimee Semple McPherson*, 1970.

56. Reference to Euripides (480–406 BCE), great Athenian dramatist and playwright.
57. Lydia E. Pinkham (1819–1883), evangelist; Lydia E. Pinkham's Vegetable Compound was first marketed in 1875; Lydia Pinkham's Pink Pills for Pale People originated in Canada in 1876.
58. Henry Taylor Parker (1867–1934), music critic for the *Boston Transcript*.
59. George S. Kaufman (1889–1961), playwright and director. Morrie Ryskind (1895–1985), librettist, screenwriter, political writer. George Gershwin (1898–1937), incomparable American composer of songs, musicals, orchestral music (*Rhapsody in Blue*, 1923), and opera (*Porgy and Bess*, 1935). The show, *Let 'Em Eat Cake*, opened at the Imperial Theatre in New York on October 21, 1933. In the finale, President John P. Wintergreen is succeeded by Vice-President Alexander Throttlebottom. *Let 'Em Eat Cake* was a sequel to *Of Thee I Sing* (1931, by the same authors), about a presidential campaign.
60. Slogan of John P. Wintergreen in *Of Thee I Sing*.
61. *Nation* is a liberal weekly magazine, published since 1865; the oldest continuously published weekly in the United States.
62. By Margaret Ayer Barnes; Pulitzer Prize for fiction, 1931.
63. Duncan (1878–1927), great American dancer, one of the founders of modern dance. The Cabots were and still are an ancient and honorable family of Massachusetts patricians ("Here's to good old Boston/The home of the bean and the cod,/Where the Cabots speak only to Lowells/And the Lowells speak only to God").
64. Possibly Harvey Cushing (1869–1939).
65. George Horace Lorimer (1868–1937), editor of *The Saturday Evening Post*, 1899–1936.
66. Unidentified.
67. "The Bulfinch House," by John August, *Harper's* 169:156–70 (August 1934). Orford (New Hampshire) appears as "Collamore."
68. Eleonora Duse (1859–1924), Italian tragic actress. Red Lewis is Sinclair Lewis. McIntyre (1886–1948), president of Little, Brown and Company, 1926–1948.
69. See BDV, "My Career as a Lawbreaker," Easy Chair, *Harper's* 208/1 (January 1954). BDV's taste for Scotch whiskey disappeared in the 1940s.
70. *The Crooked Mile*, 1924, was BDV's first published novel; an unpublished novel, *Cock Crow*, preceded it.

2

1934 LETTERS

In 1934 Sterne had recovered from her drastic surgery and was restored, more or less, to her previous state of invalided health at the Bowne Hospital, and was able to resume intense activity as a letter writer. Sterne's surviving notebooks of her draft letters add extra dimension to her many friendships that are only obliquely mentioned in her letters to DeVoto. At the same time, the notebooks show clearly that her letters to and from DeVoto dominated all of her writing. It is obvious even without the draft letters included here that 1934 was one of the most productive years in an increasingly rich and personal relationship with DeVoto; the epistolary intensity was sustained through 1936 and diminished only slightly thereafter, as the new friendship ripened into old friendship.

Much of the 1934 correspondence is about literature. The literary year began with newly published works by Hemingway and Scott Fitzgerald among many others. DeVoto's novel-in-progress, *We Accept with Pleasure*, under its original title *Second Gentleman*, occupies much of the earlier letters, as he sent parts of the draft typescript to Sterne and solicited her comments, and later again when the book was published in September. With this major publication secured, DeVoto wrote more freely about his Harvard teaching and his friends in Cambridge and Lincoln. It was also in 1934 that Sterne and DeVoto exchanged information about their religious upbringing; DeVoto is alternately sarcastic and serious about his mixed Catholic-Mormon parentage, and Sterne is affectionate about her own Catholic origins, without any direct indication that her father was Jewish. Sterne revealed at some length her academic background as an art historian, which eventually landed her the assistant art critic's position on the *New York Times*, and in a poignant letter described the devastating onset, two years before, of the illness that resulted in her permanent hospitalization. DeVoto, prodded by Sterne, began writing a series of long and somewhat fanciful reminiscences about his youth in Utah both before and after his Harvard and army years (see also *The Bucolics of Decadence* and "Kent Potter Story" in Appendices); these would continue into 1935.

Lincoln, Massachusetts

[29 January 1934]

Dear Kate:

If you have the low down on the fornication in *Farewell to A.*[1] for God's sake convey it to me, verbally or graphically, at once. Few problems in the history of literature have balked me as obstinately and infuriatingly as that one. With an imagination which, I must insist, is neither defective nor unwilling, with an adequate background, with a sympathetic intellectual constructiveness, I have remained utterly baffled. Even granting that there was no cast.... Speaking of Hemingway, is it worth doing to insert in SG, at an appropriate place, a slight snoot at the natural history of death?[2] The passage seems to me one of the most snivelling in any literature.... I seem to be mostly allusive to your letter tonight—my dear, you know nothing whatever about the mores of nurses until you've spent some time in a negro hospital. That happened to me once in the days of my wanderjahre,[3] and ever since then I've had an absorbing interest in the human animal's capacity for extremes. But nurses aren't the most extreme, even of the polite professions—it's medical students. I remain unable to decide what transforms a medico into a ~~practo~~—I can't spell it—into a G P apparently sober & trustworthy enough to receive one's private confidences. And I never saw anybody go West very picturesquely, though I've been ex post facto.[4] I'm still saving for a story an occasion when, as a newspaper reporter in my home town, I accompanied a coroner *pro tem*,[5] he being the Judge of the District Court & having to function as coroner because the real one was drunk & the Municipal Judge out of town—to the scene of a reported suicide. Picture an August full moon just above the Wasatch. A viaduct where one railroad crossed another, with the girders making angular, futuristic shadows on the ground. White cement abutments graduated like the steps to a temple. And, on the lowest step, just in that overpowering moonlight, with deep shadows behind him, a chap sitting with his head meditatively held in his hands. All except the top of it, which was nowhere any more. We look at him, the judge & the cops & I, and someone turns a flashlight on him. And it's the judge's son.... Again, there was the best friend I ever had who died of a cerebral hemmorhage [*sic*] the night before the day on which he had carefully, minutely, perfectly planned to kill a man. You'll see something of that, it may be, in SG.[6]

Of course I'm going to send you that ms.—first draft bulls and all.[7] What you interpret as reluctance is only my black bile at being unable to go on with it until I've filled the till again and my neurosis which is the result of frustration, inability to get beyond p. 146 in the typing. My aversion to the pt of view of the professional novelist, though, is real enough. I was probably a yearner in some earlier existence for God has made me serve a long sentence this time in the company of fictioneers. No, I don't care to know what a writer of novels thinks about it till it's safely in print.

You seem to get most of the dope: have you heard anything about Red Lewis's play?[8] I've heard nothing since the last drunken farewell in September and he was still in the throes of secrecy then. Secrecy with Red consisting of hour-long improvisations. He hadn't yet got together with Lloyd Lewis, but even then there was talk of calling in Marc Connolly, which was always a good idea.[9] Red had, during the summer, when I saw him frequently, discovered the Civil War. It hit him with all the impact of a new Marxism on G. Hicks.[10] He yammered about it for hours at a time—to me, who hold copyright & patents on the Civil War. To sit there & hear Lewis inform me about the Battle of Chancellorsville, the generalship of U. S. Grant, or the ride round Meade of J. E. B. Stuart was as poignant a torture as I've ever experienced.[11] By the way, it is not true that I have talked Lewis into silence. I claim great achievements but not that one. I have made Ernest Boyd give up and go home, I have even been found still talking after Felix Frankfurter went to sleep in his chair, but I can only be runner-up while Lewis still lives.[12]

My Americana gets into Yankeedom only by way of crank religions and communisms. I hold proprietary rights in the frontier beyond the Alleghenies, in the Civil War, and in Mormonism, but not in the Fathers. If you have a Yankee ancestor who saw God on the top of Monadnock or Wachusett or who set out to regenerate the world by living on bran and with or without females, I can probably tell you all about him. But S^ml^ Grant, storekeeper, I know not.[13] I'll drop in on Sam Morison and see where he can direct me.[14] Have you, by the way, read his *Builders of the Bay Colony*? A rich book. He even spits information about the Bostonians—he should be able to show me what there is practically offhand.... That, incidentally, is my proved recipe for knowledge: go to an expert & be helpless. My career in history—oh yes, I have one, cf. Lewis Mumford—has been bought [*sic*] at no greater labor than a few dinners, with liquor, to the Harvard department. I am, even, in Fred Merk's & Arthur Schlesinger's bibliographies.[15] As a result of no more than bringing my own liquor in person from Quebec during the drouth.

Notes from the cellarette:[16] FD's quotes continue to promote temperance by making liquor cheaper & more available than wine.[17] As a result my pantry shelf now contains a number of distillates unsavored for 14 years. How they bring back one's vanished youth! Here is, for example, sloe gin. I was in my first year at Harvard and experimenting with sin at—by God—Revere Beach, when I first tasted that subtle sweetness.[18]... Apricot brandy—one Kate, now the mother of three, and a summer moon in the Berkshires, and the earliest nostalgia I can remember.[19]... I have bought a cocktail book—with this confession, exit my pretence that I have a palate—and have been amusing myself with the new freedom by trying them out. 99% are inconceivably nauseous. I am more than confirmed in my elderly conviction that there are Dry Martinis, Manhattans, and no other cocktails—a conviction that should at least nominate me for the Somerset.[20] Except that one novelty has proved worthy. In my book it calls itself a Chauncey. It is made of equal parts sweet vermouth, dry gin, cognac, and rye. It has suavity and sophistication and its impact, as you may conclude, is all that can be desired...But, melancholy reflection of an Americanist, what hogs the forefathers were. We frontiersmen are apt to remember the stillhouse, corn liquor, apricot & especially peach brandy, applejack, & rum. Fair enough all, and it may be that the frontier was pure. But in the centers of civilization—well, read the flips, the cups, the punches, the coolers, the cobblers, the sangrías—read them and gasp. They didn't have stomachs, those gents, they only had receptacles....The Parker House has as yet been unable to get a Premier Cru, but it has found a '24 Château Pontet Cavet and that is something.[21] Even Something. Also it has a liquid which it calls Hospice de Beaune. It was made in Brooklyn I'm sure and not, I'm even surer, out of grapes. Thank God it was an editor's $8 that paid for it—I'd have to confess to the priest if I'd been victimized....Being brought up on the single standard, I was taught that only whores drank crême de menthe and only pretty awful whores poured cream in it. I have seen that mixture twice in one week, once at a restaurant, once in private, both times by women of unimpeachable, hitherto, reputation.

What, by the way, has happened to the whore? In fiction, I mean—I know the ready explanation of her actual obsolescence. I was once set to restore the bastard to the American novel but for some reason gave it up. Must I leave the whore to Faulkner?[22]

Your address, you say, will be Poughkeepsie till spring. When is spring? Outside, I mean, of Middlesex County, where it's from 10:15 to 11:30 AM every third day. Was I recently telling you about our sub-arctic spell? Pussy willows have been picked in my yard and the chipmunks have come out of hibernation, which is a hell of a good joke on the squirrels, whose fur, all the weatherwise noted, was thicker this year than at any time since the harbor froze in 1674. I have collegiate duties *nach*[23] Poughkeepsie in late May. Would you receive a caller? And, for Christ's sweet sake, how many ribs are you parting with? My anatomy is mostly hearsay, but I've understood that the supply was limited.

Is Fitzgerald's novel worth reading?[24] And is T. Wolfe writing another? The first was 3/5 great stuff & 2/5 first novel even worse than usual.[25]...The word from Wellesley

I can't, at the moment, recall what the word from Wellesley was. The ink will show you that I was interrupted some time ago, interruptions, dear, being what the literary life consists of. Among them was Mr. Littauer from *Collier's*, something novel, by the way, in editors for he drinks only vermouth and has no scandal to retail.[26] I don't know whether we did business or not. What he wants is my last remaining virginity, one I've chastely retained against wear and tear and gold. That being my way—while it was worth a lot of money I was too Fine to sell it, and now I'm thinking of doing so at 60% off par.

In the meantime I've read *Work of Art*—and Isabel Patterson's praise of it in today's H-T.[27] It's a lousy book, although, after 80 oz. of Scotch at Barnard last summer, Lewis assured me it was a good one. I dropped in on him with Hillyer and a car full of Canadian booze the day he finished the last revision, and I'm happy to say there were 5 snootfuls in celebration of it that night. It's too bad, for I happen to think he's a damn fine novelist and I don't like to see him fire a dud. Are there any good novels? I may have to know that answer soon, for I am he who has retired from teaching several times, each time forever, and now Harvard is suggesting how pleasant it would be for all of us if I were to lecture for a semester next year on contemporary American literature and I, having now at least 4 times as much work as there'll be time to do, am prone to agree.... There would be some amusement in going back over the immortal masterpieces I've helped to honor and finding out again just what their names were. *Pars fui*[28]—almost—of that Great and ended Age. At least I've lived through it. I was learning to write sports on the Ogden *Standard-Examiner* and sometimes glancing at a weekly called the St. Louis *Mirror* which my father subscribed to because it was single tax.[29] So opening it one autumn day I read something in shredded prose which called itself *Spoon River Anthology*.[30] And no leaf fell. So, sometime later—how long? I'll know if I do lecture—the Harvard boys were playing *The Moon of the Caribees*.[31] I collect no rarities, and yet here's a first of Winesburg—that was the summer after the war and I was city-editing the S-E before coming back to Harvard—and the only known first of *Main Street*—I bought it in NY at the Pennsylvania Station, read it in San Francisco, and wrote a note for the *Nation* (I was once a Liberal) prophesying about what happened.[32] December 1918, Lt. DeVoto with a discharge in his pocket takes the ferry to Governor's Island to call on Lt. King, as yet undischarged.[33] Lt. King is reading a thick Crown octavo which makes him furious because, he says, it's anti-democratic and snotty as hell. So Lt. DeVoto first glimpses the *Education of Henry Adams*.[34] A copy of *Poetry* falls open. "Darling, Darling, Darling, Darling said the Chinese Nightingale."[35] It had a music then that it curiously lacks now. Declaration of B. DeVoto in Fairfax Hall, Cambridge, winter of 1919: "The bastard that writes a play like *Beyond the Horizon* will never amount to anything."[36] Well, has he? The same: "This guy Mencken who writes *The American Language* is the best humorist since Mark Twain."[37] Stet OK...Child, child, you were in diapers—how can a veteran tell you about it? Did you know that *This Side of Paradise* was once smart, dangerous, and risqué?[38] You never heard of Ben Hecht, you have to think twice to remember that Floyd Dell was once a Promise, you never heard Jack Reed, you didn't see the little magazines which were just as hot, in my day, for Beauty as they are in yours for Social Justice.[39] And had still An Immortal

Sophomore for editor, contributor, audience & inspiration. I doubt that you remember the Little Blue Books—how should you know that the Haldeman-Julius pair wrote a novel called *Dust* which was once important, for a reason that escapes me.[40] How should you know there was once a Midland School of Fiction?[41] I can remember that Ruth Suckow belonged to it, but my fingers grope in vain for the others.[42] And battles long ago, the judging of *Jurgen*, and an issue of the *Mercury* 80,000 copies, burned in New Jersey because the Hatrack noise burst just before it was to come out with an article "Sex and the Co-Ed" by one Prof. John August, né DeVoto, and the Dunster House affair, and Aphrodite and Fantazius Mallari.[43] The Spectrists, but you wouldn't ever, possibly, have heard of the Spectrists.[44] Once, the intellectuals got word that a young English Armenian was doing an amazing kind of short story, <u>intime</u>, recondite, exotic, for the few: it was too bad that *The Green Hat* came out.[45] Another inspiration was Katherine Mansfield, and that was even worse.[46] But let us not raise up the ghosts of the Geniuses from abroad of that vanished day.... My God, I should write my reminiscences. I <u>am</u> doting. Still, on the morning of my recent birthday, age-old & bowed down, bare ruined choir,[47] I found in my mail a blank and a flowing letter bespeaking my name for some new booby-trap to be called... "America's Young Men."[48]

Yours
Benny

S & N Bowne Hospital
Poughkeepsie, N.Y.

[3–4 February 1934]

Dear Benny,

I've read only the first installment of the Fitzgerald book, but it seems pretty sleazy. I don't go for the fastidious pearl-casting of the Woolf-Boyle school of fiction,[49] at best, & F.S.J. [*sic*] gets so damned oblique in this introduction that he doesn't come within a mile of his point, granting—which I doubt—that he has one. It consists, in about equal parts, of pseudo-subtle intimations of character, strained figures, and bright conversation that doesn't come off. Cast of characters: young virgin, beautiful & damned, with a virulent mother-complex; young matron, also beautiful & damned ("Viking madonna") who, apparently, has what it takes. Also all the sad young men, to wit, ye Adroit Host-cum Satyr-cum underdone medico; thwarted musician with a playful penchant for sawing waiters in two; Franco-American condottiere by Hemingway out of H. James;[50] he-man movie actor. Also merry widow; brash American couple who think Joyce & Antheil are still news[51] (wasn't it H.T.P. who once made a mountain out of an antheil?);[52] two particularly obnoxious pansies. Also busboys, nannies, lesbians, children, chauffeurs & villagers. Plot: usual tri-lateral mish-mash, heated with intra- &

extra-marital encounters, seasoned with homosexual hysterics, interlarded with parties obviously thought up by Elsa Maxwell & William Lyon Phelps—Christ![53]

That "Farewell to Arms" problem has given me many a thoughtful moment, too... but you never know with Hemingway, he's so ingenious. Harry Hansen, in *Harper's*, misconstrued every damn one of the *WTN* stories that he mentioned... or maybe HH is Krafft-Ebing *en pantoufles*[54] & I'm Elsie Dinsmore.[55] I would not have you make sport of "A Natural History of the Dead," either. Think of that definition of a humanist! Besides, the passage has, for me, a certain baroc beauty—although H's necrophilia and his necrophobia seem to me singularly exaggerated for one who has had repeated, first-hand contact with death.

Speaking of medical students, so you know that Harvard classic, the "Ballad of Chambers Street"?[56]

Oh, I've a good fistful of ribs left—I lost only six in that skirmish—and it looks as though I might keep 'em all. Neuhof was up here last Thursday & he said pretty definitely that a second stage will not be necessary. I have an almost total collapse of the right lung, which is what he was after. I'm inclined to take Neuhof literally. He is not given to euphemism. The afternoon of the third day at Mt. Sinai he walked into my room, helped himself to one of my cigarettes (medical bravado), settled elaborately into the leather arm-chair & spoke: "I've just been looking at the x-rays... this is a much more unfavorable case than I had any idea of... frankly, the results are on the knees of the gods... do you still want me to operate?" He then rang the bell for the nurse & asked for saltines & orange juice. Odd duck.

It is damned good of you to want to visit the sick—one of the seven works of mercy, isn't it—but I couldn't allow it.[57] Like Hem's Mr. Frazer my nerves are shot, & I dislike seeing people when I'm in this condition.[58] I'm such a foul egotist that I can't bear to have my diminished person & personality exposed to public, or private, view. I do hope you will condone this, my major neurosis.

There doesn't seem to be much hope on the Lewis piece.[59] Walter Huston is starring in it, Howard Benedict handling the publicity.[60] Opens in Philly to-night (Saturday), comes to New York at an unnamed & undetermined theatre & date, respectively (about Feb. 15). My informant adds that "Lewis comes to rehearsals & sobs boozily a good deal of the time at the sheer beauty of his own devising—Huston says it is first rate stuff—a sure fire hit"—so—

Yours,
Kate

SUNDAY [4 FEBRUARY 1934]

Thanks, thanks for the Harvard Graduates' Magazine. Was much taken with your remarks & with T. Morrison's misgivings about research.[61] Also Mather on Babbitt.[62]

What could be less "Humanistic" than that bouncing, exuberant, Kris Kringleish little man (F.J.M. Jr.)?[63]

Somehow "Four Saints" with Harlem bucks impersonating Teresa of Avila, Ignatius Loyola, & other 33rd degree members of the R.C. hagiology is a little too-too, even for me.[64] I understand they are planning four performances; must have it mixed up with "Abie's Irish Rose."[65]

Second take of "Tender Is the Night" makes the Grand Guignol look like a Christmas pantomime—murder, incest, schizophrenia, pederasty, miscegenation...[66]

Did you see Martha Gruening's animadversions on regionalists, proletarians et al. in current *Hound & Horn*?[67] & R Blackmur's ditto on Granville Hicks?[68]

Charlie Poore says nice words about A. MacLeish's pomes [*sic*] in to-day's book review.[69] Charlie, who inherited the Chamberlain burberry last Summer, was, in my day, the wag, wit, pride & pet of the Sunday Dept. Shortly after his apotheosis to the 10th floor, Uppie, of the Sunday, sent him a little card decorated like this:

[*drawing of a door:*]		[*drawing of a tombstone:*]
C. G. Poore	→→→→	Ci-gît[70] Poore
Private		

Oh, why should The Spirit of Mortal be Proud?[71]

Charlie, rumor says, was not amused.

Kate

Lincoln, Massachusetts

[27 March 1934]

Dear Kate:

Ms. will leave Lincoln as soon as I can find some wrapping paper. Read it until you begin to get bored, then don't read any more. You are under no obligation to read it, still less to like it.

Disregard a certain uncorrected quality in the writing—looseness of phrase, overemphasis, clogged sentences, heaped-up adjectives, frequent insecurity of phrase. All of that can be eliminated and all I detect will be—and I'll detect most of it. It's very much in first draft and, stylistically, will improve in second draft.

Ch IV & V to be rewritten entire. Especially to differentiate the dialogue, to throw a certain naïveté and directness into an oblique and I hope less ingenuous manner, to remake Ric and give what he says more point & less noise, to improve on Beatrice, to get Jonathan <u>into</u> the passages to which he is now just affixed, to crowd a decent fig-leaf over the resoundingly announced theme—to keep that one straight I suppose I should say put the drawers on with the woodwind instead of the brass.

The fact that Julian was a literary gent will come forward sooner than it now does.

Most contradictions have been caught, I think—as Beatrice's shift from peroxide to dark lady,[72] Libby's naturally-permanently-waved hair, a repetition of speeches, etc.

Ch VI may be cut down, maybe not. Any vote?

Little-Brown has been agitating for a different title.

Now, my dear, you need not write me anything about the ms. If you feel moved to, I'd be glad to hear what you think of it. You need not pull any punches. What I want to know is just that: how it strikes you. In any detail you can go into. If you want to, tell me what parts in particular click for you, & which ones don't—especially, any passages that seem silly or flat and most especially any that are soft, sickly, gelatinous. And, with the ms., will be a sealed question which I hope you won't read till after you've read the ms. It bears on the most important technical matter in the book and I don't want to sensitize you to it in advance.

℞:

Keep Glauber's salts, digitalis, and tartar emetic close at hand and remember your first communion instructions.[73]

God give you a quick reaction.

Oh, since I have no copy in the house, the sooner you can conveniently get this back to me the easier my nervous system will be.

Yours

Benny

Original estimate was badly calculated. 219 pages will be nearer ½ than ⅓.

Bowne

[AFTER 27 MARCH 1934]

Dear Benny,

I shall probably laugh. I shall probably cry. But I know damned well I'll not be bored!

Thanks!

Yours,

Kate

Lincoln, Massachusetts

[6 SEPTEMBER 1934]

FEAST OF SAINT LAWRENCE JUSTINIAN[74]

Dear Kate:

The third Martini of two hours ago dies in a violet petal-fall and muted French horns sounding the land-motif in *Tristan*.[75] I'll be hung in a half-hour, I'm afraid. Now I'm faintly iridescent, much at ease, without vocabulary, and desirous of saying that I'm glad you like the book. I got a distinct lift from mailing it to you: the Catholic was ever a symbolist. I had four of them made up, one to the dedicatee, two mere formalities, and the one I sent you—sent you with a vivid if hardly to be verbalized feeling that you had buoyed me up while I was writing it and had said the only useful things that were said about it.

So it will issue to the world on the 21st, and L-B have again increased their advertising allotment. Alfred is grimly determined to get back the twenty-five hundred he advanced me on it, and who am I to stand on his toes?[76] He was yesterday much bucked up by a letter from the president of the Booksellers Association, which said the usual things, and by the trade-release of the American News Company, which said that DeVoto had gone to town with this one and added "it's in the bag." Publishers, dear, are the quaintest people.... Let's get this on the record before the 21st. I am informed that the scene beginning on page 102 has a distinct resemblance to one in "Little Man, What Now?," one which is repeated in the movie.[77] Well, I haven't read "Little Man, What Now?" or seen the movie. Also, Henry Dart Reck, a most educated though Dartmouth man, took down a copy of Galsworthy's "Beyond" from my shelves yesterday, searched through it, found a page and had me read it.[78] It wasn't as uncomfortable an experience as he expected it to be. It did undertake to do my page 347 but I reluctantly assert that I did the job much better than Mr. Galsworthy, and that isn't saying any too much about my page, either. I have never read "Beyond" and now I'm not likely to, though when I remember the impression "The Dark Flower" made on me at the age of eighteen I'm a little hesitant to go back to it and investigate. Well, literatoor is simply wonderful: all I can say is, multiple invention is a fact.

Bread Loaf was highly amusing this year. The conference clicked most enjoyably. I assign three causes: the four fellowships, the fact that there were some twenty professional writers besides the forty-five elderly ladies, and the DeVoto Dry Martini.[79] It took me three years to perfect the system, but the place was no oasis this year. Two years ago it was simply dreadful, and poor Lee Dodd was driving as far as Yaddo for a couple of pints of dubious liquor. Last year, warned by experience, I went up with a carload of QLC[80] stuff but forgot about Hillyer and in three days faced a drought that was ended only when, sixty miles away, I found a native who sold me the godawfulest liquor since my Legion days, honest Vermont applejack which had been flavored with rye extract. But this year we were all equipped and the State of Vermont had also opened stores in Rutland and Burlington which could be tapped at need. And every day promptly at five o'clock the staff and the fellowship people broke firmly away from the gasping and assembled in the cottage that Gorham Munson and I occupied, where Ray Everitt and I made as expert a team as you could get together.[81] How that hour grew and how it did transform Bread Loaf Mountain. I had bought a dozen cocktail glasses in Rutland on the way up, Hervey Allen went to Middlebury for another dozen on the third day, and I wired my wife to bring another dozen when she came on the eighth day.[82] When we swam into the dining hall at ten minutes to seven nightly, the literary and intense learned that our private lives had Another Side.... Alex Laing came up from Hanover to bring Owen Lattimore back into my life.[83] (Lattimore has a Mongolian tobacco which he insists on smoking. Even if you have smelled beet pulp, you can't imagine it. Quite seriously, till I tumbled to it, I thought a rat had died and fallen in the fireplace.) Alex rolled out of his car and emitted this:

Benny DeVoto
A writer of note-o
Went down to defeat-o
Because of Pareto[84]

Then he had several of my cocktails. So we went over to dinner. They were at another table—I was doing the lecturing that evening—and presently Owen noticed that Alex had gone to sleep in his plate. He helped him up and out and got almost to their cottage, but then the DeVoto Martini crept up on Owen and he went away, but first he leaned Alex at an acute angle against a larch. Sometime later Johnny Farrar found him there and put him away, Alex waking up just long enough to wail "This is the Thirties and I'm acting like the Twenties."[85] This being made known to me, Alex found another quatrain about Pareto on his plate at breakfast.... Johnny and I got along quite well, for us marvelously. Margaret was there and she probably soothed him. Anyway, he only once screamed.... Hervey was jovial but very tired, and that announces itself. Anne was there, a charming girl whom I'd never got to know before.[86] It's Hervey's notion that he, Archie MacLeish, Gorham and I should form a vendetta. The principle appears to be that we aren't a clique—but this is old stuff with him and I've probably given you the by-laws before. I'm against it—how do I know when it may get hellish good fun to shoot holes in Hervey or Archie?... Once I got adapted to South Carolinian Gullah, I liked Julia Peterkin.[87] But she was accompanied by a couple of young girls and Lord, Lord, I hadn't met the southern belle since 1918 and the Richmond Country Club, and I was younger then.... All the literary were there, My dear, it's such a privilege to know writers. On some days they came through in swarms. I couldn't begin to list them, Archie, Maxwell Aley, Irving Fineman, Teddy Hill, Doc Lewis–Red didn't get over, the ballad woman (accompanied by a Vermonter who, when we separated him from her and poured Scotch into him, sang a selection that have never got into Child or Kittredge), Christ I forget them, dozens, scores of them.[88] Bill Upson came over and gassed to my gang, though I couldn't get him to repeat the lecture on How To Write

Stories Though Ignorant of two years ago, which remains the high point of my service there.[89] Fanny Butcher turned up to see what was going on and was promptly put to work helping me out, for all the customers wanted to write short stories, and for the first time I'll probably get a decent review from the Chicago *Tribune*.[90] Fanny found out that I wasn't so coarse as she'd heard, though awfully drunken.

The point about the twenty-odd professional writers who registered was that you could really say something to them, which is distinctly an innovation. The point about the four fellowships was that Ted and I did an uncanny job of picking them out. Scott O'Dell, who did a novel about California I never got round to reading, was more appreciated by the customers than by the staff.[91] He's a handsome young man and was kept so busy by ladies of a certain age that I felt for him sincerely. Lauren Gilfillan, the Pit College girl, proved to be about four-feet-ten and full of wild Irish aberrations, but was extremely amusing.[92] She helped, she distinctly helped. I set myself the job of winning her from the Comrades and I think I pretty well did it; on her part, she read my hand and announced that I'm a romantic idealist. She reads heads, too, and handwriting, but we didn't get round to that. Frances Prentice proved to be one of the most charming women of America—about forty, prematurely gray, devilishly good looking, with a tongue as barbed as any I've ever heard.[93] At cocktail hour, the conference seemed to center in her. Josephine Johnson was something else.[94] In the first place, she is as pretty a child as ever lived, twenty-four, dark, gray-eyed, slender, shy but poised—God, my elderly heart chinned itself at my first glimpse. So did every other heart on the Mountain—the place was sighing like a spruce forest in a gale. In the second place, her novel is distinctly something. I'll send you a copy as soon as I can get one. "Now in November." Exquisitely written—a precarious skirting of the literary that always and most memorably keeps this side of it. And it has a combined intensity and economy of emotion that simply dazzles me. And others. Clifton Fadiman wrote up that it was going to be a hard book to put over and wouldn't we get behind it.[95] We fell all over ourselves getting behind it. All of us wrote blurbs—the first I've done in years, and I even drove home by way of Elizabethtown, primarily to put Louis Untermeyer behind it.[96] Do I convey the impression that Josephine scored? She has one very vicious habit: we couldn't get a drink into her and day by day had to watch her at cocktail time corroding her interior with ginger ale.

I'll have a copy of George Homans' Pareto book for you before long.[97] And now I don't need to know anything more about John Chamberlain. He treated it a couple of days ago.[98] The Utahns say: you can't fool them horse-flies. What's more, my earlier suspicion that John can't even read is now abundantly, redundantly, confirmed. I knew he had great confidence in the right ideas, but it was an open question whether he knew the English language. He doesn't, and I think I'll have to say so in print.

You have a taste for the bizarre, you study editors. O.K. The two stories I wrote before leaving for Bread Loaf were expertly tailored for *Collier's*. They were the worst possible kind of tripe—if I knew my trade, and I ought to, they were sure-fire for *Collier's*. *Collier's* turned them both down. Before I knew it, my agent offered one of them to *Liberty*, which turned it down. She then phoned me that she had sent them to the *Post* and I spent four dollars overtime—Cora reverses her charges—calling her a damned fool and announcing that she'd ruined my plans for this fall's invasion of the *Post*.[99] The *Post* bought both of them. I don't know anything about the magazine game.... In a couple of weeks, the *Post* is publishing the last John Hoyt story, which they've been hoarding for God knows how long.[100] Probably they'll also shoot the other co-ed story they have on hand, but I hope to God the Revolution arrives before they publish the two they've just bought. Some of my friends read the *Post*. I'm laying elaborate ground plans for a new series—I'll send you specifications in due time. Furthermore, I've decided to sign up with Ray Everitt if I can muster up enough guts to fire Cora, and Ray swears to put me into the serial game. I've been ducking a college serial for five years. Ray says pooh, quite right to duck the college serial, but why not a literary detective story for the *Post*? Walk round that one and look it over from all the angles. Benny Roberts Rinehart, or S. DeVoto Wright.[101] I'd rather write Freckles.[102]

Just a year ago, I remember, I was issuing prophecies about the fiscal year then beginning. You must have had a nice laugh as the year developed. No prophecies this time, even with a series gestating and Harvard about to open. Besides, I'm in the depressive phases. Either I should avoid the literary in concentration or else I'm growing old too fast. All I know about the fiscal year is that it will be awful and I'll belch the usual amount of type. Belch? What's happening to my stylistic precision?

Well, anyway, we can get back to Bob Major.[103]... Out of the silences, suddenly a letter from Fitz. He tells me that my one-time room-mate has moved back to Ogden, given up the practice of medicine, and become a director of the brewery. Fitz never liked Arthur either, and I've probably set down what he thought of Katy. Yes, I think we'll see them in fiction before long.

Yours,
Benny

NOTES

1. *A Farewell to Arms*, by Ernest Hemingway (1899–1961), 1929.
2. Hemingway, "A Natural History of the Dead," gruesome passage originally in *Death in the Afternoon* (1932), reprinted with changes in *Winner Take Nothing*, 1933.
3. (German) years of wandering.
4. (Latin) after the deed.

5. From (Latin) *pro tempore*, for the time being, temporary.
6. BDV's Harvard classmate Kent Hägler, who died in Paris under mysterious circumstances in 1920; see Stegner, *The Uneasy Chair*; see also "Kent Potter Story," in Appendix B.
7. Bull, "a grotesque blunder in language" (*WNCD9*).
8. *The Jayhawker*, 1935, written in collaboration with Lloyd Lewis.
9. Lewis (1891–1949), a writer, no relation to Sinclair Lewis. Marc (Marcus Cook) Connelly (1890–1980), playwright; *The Green Pastures*, 1930.
10. Granville Hicks (1901–1982), Marxist novelist and literary critic; literary editor, *New Masses*.
11. May 2–4, 1863, north of Richmond, Virginia, where Confederate forces under General Lee defeated a much larger Union army under General Hooker. Confederate General Thomas "Stonewall" Jackson was killed in this battle. (Hiram) Ulysses Simpson Grant (1822–1885), Union general, eighteenth president of the United States (1869–1877). George Gordon Meade (1815–1872), Union general. Stuart (1833–1864), Confederate general.
12. Boyd (1887–1946), author and translator. Frankfurter (1882–1965), jurist, professor at Harvard Law School (1914–1939), associate justice of U.S. Supreme Court (1939–1962).
13. Samuel Grant (1705–1784). KS had asked BDV for information about him. KS's mother's family was named Grant, and Ulysses S. Grant was distantly related. Further confusion arises from the name of KS's father, Samuel Grant Sterne.
14. Samuel Eliot Morison (1887–1976), professor of American history at Harvard; Rear Admiral, USNR, 1942–1951; *Oxford History of the United States*, 1927; *Builders of the Bay Colony*, 1930; *Tercentennial History of Harvard University*, 5 vols., 1936.
15. Frederick Merk (1887–1977), professor of American history at Harvard, specialist in nineteenth century. Arthur Meier Schlesinger (1888–1965), professor of American history at Harvard, specialist in eighteenth century; his son, Arthur M. Schlesinger Jr. (1917–2007), Harvard '38, was a favorite student of BDV.
16. BDV's pronouncements on mixed drinks are settled for all time in *The Hour* (1951).
17. Probably Franklin D. Roosevelt.
18. A few miles north of Boston Harbor.
19. Kate is unidentified.
20. Somerset Club, private club on Beacon Street in Boston. BDV, in *The Hour*, wrote that "the Manhattan is an offense against piety."
21. The Parker House was an elegant restaurant on Tremont Street in Boston, now part of the Omni Parker House Hotel.
22. William Faulkner (1897–1962), Mississippi-born novelist; *The Sound and the Fury*, 1929; *As I Lay Dying*, 1930; *Light in August*, 1932; *Absalom, Absalom!*, 1936; Pulitzer Prize in fiction, 1955, 1963; Nobel Prize, 1949.
23. (German) towards.
24. F. Scott Fitzgerald (1896–1940), *Tender is the Night*, then appearing serially in *Scribner's*; now generally regarded as his masterpiece.
25. *Look Homeward, Angel*, 1929. See BDV, "Genius Is Not Enough," *SRL* 13/26 (25 April 1936); reprinted in *Forays and Rebuttals*, 1936.
26. Kenneth Littauer (1894?–1968), fiction editor of *Collier's*; an army flier in World War I, he served again in World War II.
27. *Work of Art*, by Sinclair Lewis, 1934, reviewed by columnist Isabel Paterson (1885–1961) in the New York *Herald Tribune*.
28. (Latin) I have been a part. Vergil, *Aeneid*, Book II, 6: "et quorum magna pars fui."
29. Also known as *Reedy's Mirror*.
30. Very popular collection of poems by Edgar Lee Masters (1868–1950), 1916.

31. Play by Eugene O'Neill, 1919.
32. *Winesburg, Ohio*, short stories by Sherwood Anderson (1876–1941), 1919. *Main Street*, by Sinclair Lewis, 1920.
33. Gordon King (1893–1930), writer, Harvard '17, close friend of BDV. BDV's older son was named after him. King taught comparative literature in 1925–1926 at the Curtis Institute of Music; published a novel, *Horatio's Story*, 1924, and a play, *The Ostriches*, 1926, and wrote occasionally for the New York *Evening Post* and *SRL*.
34. By Henry Adams (1838–1918), historian and writer, 1918.
35. From "The Chinese Nightingale" by Vachel Lindsay (1879–1931), *Poetry: A Magazine of Verse*, 5/5 (February 1915).
36. By Eugene O'Neill, 1920.
37. First edition, 1919; Mencken oversaw it through the fourth edition (1936) and two supplements.
38. F. Scott Fitzgerald's first novel, 1920.
39. Floyd Dell (1887–1969), novelist and critic; *Love in the Machine Age: A Study of the Transition from Patriarchal Society*, 1930; *Homecoming*, autobiography, 1933. John Reed (1887–1920), journalist, poet, revolutionist; *Ten Days That Shook the World*, 1919, about the Bolshevik Revolution in Russia.
40. Series of inexpensive books, published in Girard, Kansas, by E. A. and Marcet Haldeman-Julius; nearly two thousand titles appeared between 1919 and 1951. Emanuel Haldeman-Julius (1889–1951), editor, author, and publisher, with his wife, Marcet Haldeman (1887–1941); *Dust*, 1922; *My First 25 Years*, autobiography, 1949.
41. *The Midland: A National Literary Magazine*, 20 vols. published 1915–1933; founded by John Towner Frederick (1893–1975), professor, University of Iowa.
42. (1892–1950), novelist; *Country People*, 1924; *Iowa Interiors*, 1926; *The Folks*, 1934.
43. *Jurgen: A Comedy of Justice*, controversial novel by James Branch Cabell (1879–1958), 1919, banned as licentious, 1920; exonerated, 1922. "Hatrack," a short story about an endearing prostitute, by Herbert Asbury, *American Mercury* (April 1926), caused the issue to be banned in Boston, where Mencken, the editor, as a test case, personally sold a copy to the director of the New England Watch & Ward Society and was arrested in a well-publicized confrontation. "Sex and the Co-ed" was never published. The Dunster House affair refers to Al DeLacey's Dunster House bookshop. *Aphrodite* is an erotic novel by Pierre Louÿs (French, 1870–1925); BDV's copy was published in 1932 by Illustrated Editions, New York. *Fantazius Mallare, a Mysterious Oath*, is a novel by Ben Hecht, illustrated, 1922.
44. A literary hoax by Witter Bynner and Arthur Davison Ficke, *Spectra: A Book of Poetic Experiments*, 1916. See William Jay Smith, *The Spectra Hoax*, 1961.
45. *The Green Hat: A Romance for a Few People*, by Michael Arlen (1895–1956), Armenian-British writer, 1924.
46. Katherine Mansfield (1888–1923), writer.
47. BDV was thirty-seven years old on 11 January 1934. The reference is to Shakespeare's Sonnet 73: "Bare ruin'd choirs where late the sweet birds sang."
48. First published 1934; BDV declined.
49. Probably ref. to Virginia Woolf (1882–1941), British writer, and Kay Boyle (1902–1992), American writer.
50. Henry James (1843–1916), American-born British author; *Portrait of a Lady*, 1881; *The Spoils of Poynton*, 1897; *The Awkward Age*, 1899; *The Wings of a Dove*, 1902; *The Ambassadors*, 1903.
51. James Joyce (1882–1941), great Irish author; *Chamber Music*, poems, 1907; *Dubliners*, short stories, 1914; *A Portrait of the Artist as a Young Man*, 1916; *Ulysses*, 1922; *Pomes Penyeach*, 1927;

Finnegans Wake, 1939; the most path-breaking and influential stylist in twentieth-century literature in any language. George Antheil (1900–1959), American pianist and *enfant terrible* composer; *Bad Boy of Music*, autobiography, 1945.

52. H. Taylor Parker.
53. Maxwell (1883–1963), actress and columnist. Phelps (1865–1943), author, professor of English at Yale.
54. (French) in slippers.
55. Hansen is not found. *WTN* is Hemingway's *Winner Take Nothing*, 1933. Richard Baron von Krafft-Ebing (1840–1902), German neurologist and psychiatrist, specialist in psychology of criminal behavior; *Psychopathia Sexualis* (1885). Dinsmore was the pious heroine of twenty-eight works of juvenile fiction by Martha Finley (1828–1909), Indiana writer.
56. A clever, highly indecent, anti-Semitic poem in nine stanzas of iambic heptameter, beginning "Now in the East the gleaming wheel of Phoebus' car is turning,/High on [*sic*] a suite in Chambers' Street the gas is dimly burning." Authorship, though he disclaimed it, has been traced to Frederick C. ("Fritz") Irving (1883–1957), Harvard '06, and Harvard Medical School '10, where he was Richardson Professor of obstetrics; grandfather of the New Hampshire author John Irving (*The Cider House Rules: A Novel*, 1985). See H MS Misc. B in the Harvard Medical Library Collection at the Francis A. Countway Library of Medicine.
57. The Seven Works of Mercy, corporal, are: (1) tend the sick; (2) feed the hungry; (3) give drink to the thirsty; (4) clothe the naked; (5) harbor the stranger; (6) minister to prisoners; and (7) bury the dead.
58. In *Winner Take Nothing*, "The Gambler, the Nun, and the Radio."
59. *Jayhawker* eventually opened in New York at the Cort Theater on 5 November 1934 and ran for twenty-four performances.
60. Huston (1884–1950), actor. Benedict, publicist.
61. BDV's "The Faculty First," *HGM* 42 (December 1933), pp. 90–97. [Theodore Morrison]: "The Editor's View" (ibid., pp. 156–60): "Misgivings about Research," questions the balance of research versus teaching as a measure of academic professionalism. BDV had anonymously expounded like sentiments in "Grace Before Teaching: Letter to a Young Doctor of Literature," *HGM* 40 (March 1932), 261–75; reprinted with revisions in *Forays and Rebuttals*.
62. *HGM* 42 (December 1933), "Irving Babbitt," by Frank Jewett Mather Jr. (1868–1953), writer, editor, art critic; professor of art and archaeology at Princeton. Irving Babbitt (1865–1933), professor of French at Harvard, critic, founder of the "New Humanism"; *The New Laokoön*, 1910; *Rousseau and Romanticism*, 1919.
63. "Kris Kringle," the sobriquet of the Christ child in German folklore, analogous in function to Santa Claus.
64. *Four Saints in Three Acts*, opera by Virgil Thomson (1896–1989), libretto by Gertrude Stein (1874–1946), first produced Hartford, 8 February 1934. Saint Teresa of Avila (1515–1582), Spanish Carmelite nun. Saint Ignatius of Loyola (1491–1556), founder, Society of Jesus.
65. Comedy by Anne Nichols (1891–1966), ran for 2,327 consecutive Broadway performances, 1922–1927.
66. Theater in Paris, 1897–1962, famous for over-the-top horror shows.
67. Gruening (1889–1937), Smith College '09, suffragist and civil-rights activist, occasional writer for *SRL*, associated with Emma Goldman and W. E. B. du Bois; worked for the NAACP and the No-Conscription League. *Hound & Horn* was a short-lived but influential literary periodical, 1927–1934, founded at Harvard by Lincoln Kirstein and Varian Fry; see Edward E. Chielens (ed.), *American Literary Magazines: The Twentieth Century*, 1992.

68. Richard P. Blackmur (1904–1965), author, professor of English at Princeton; one of the founders of the "New Criticism."
69. Charles Poore (1902–1971), staff writer, *New York Times*, 1929–1971. Probably a reference to Joyce's *Pomes Penyeach*, 1927.
70. (French) here lies.
71. From *Songs of Israel* (1824) by William Knox (1789–1825), Scottish poet.
72. Oblique reference to Shakespeare's sonnets.
73. Salts refers to sodium sulfate, a purgative. Tartar emetic is potassium antimony tartrate, a toxic substance formerly used as a vermifuge and amebicide.
74. (1381–1456), teacher and mystic, patriarch of Venice; feast, 5 September.
75. *Tristan und Isolde*, ponderous but passionately expressive opera by Richard Wagner (German, 1813–1883), 1859.
76. Alfred McIntyre (1886–1948), president of Little, Brown, 1926–1948.
77. *Kleiner Mann, was nun?*, novel by Hans Fallada (German, 1893–1947), 1932.
78. Reck (1911–1973), BDV's occasional editorial assistant and a close family friend; a lieutenant commander in the navy during World War II, he was assistant to Captain (later Admiral) Samuel E. Morison in the Office of Naval History. Later he taught American history at City College of New York. John Galsworthy (1867–1933), English novelist, author of the Forsyte novels; Nobel Prize 1932. *Beyond*, 1917; *The Dark Flower*, 1913.
79. BDV extolled the dry martini as the only admissible mixed drink in *The Hour*, 1951, and provided precise instructions.
80. Quebec Liquor Commission.
81. Raymond Everitt (1901–1947), publisher, editor at Little, Brown after 1936.
82. Allen (1889–1949), author of long historical novels; *Anthony Adverse*, 1933; *Action at Aquila*, 1937; biography of Edgar Allan Poe, *Israfel*, 1926.
83. Alexander K. Laing (1900–1976), author, professor at Dartmouth College. Lattimore (1900–1989), author, historian, expert on China; *Ordeal by Slander*, 1950.
84. Vilfredo Pareto (1848–1923), Italian sociologist.
85. John Farrar (1896–1974), publisher, writer, editor; Farrar & Rinehart, 1929–1944; Farrar, Straus, then Farrar, Straus & Giroux, 1946–1974.
86. Annette Andrews Allen.
87. (1880–1961), author; Pulitzer Prize, 1928; Bread Loaf faculty, 1935, 1936.
88. Aley (1889–1953), editor, publicist, writer, literary agent. Fineman (1893–1976), author, engineer, screenwriter; Bennington College. Hill is unidentified. Doc Lewis-Red is Sinclair Lewis. The ballad woman is probably Helen Hartness Flanders (1890–1972), collector and editor; *Vermont Folk-Songs and Ballads*, 2nd edition (with George Brown), 1932, and seven other collections; in a long career she collected some nine thousand ballads. Her recordings and other materials were given to Middlebury College. Her husband, Ralph Flanders (1880–1970), was U.S. senator from Vermont, 1947–1959. Francis James Child (1825–1896), professor of English at Harvard, pioneering collector and redactor of folksong and balladry; *English and Scottish Popular Ballads*, 5 vols., 1883–1898. George Lyman Kittredge (1860–1941), professor of English at Harvard, renowned Shakespearean scholar; *English and Scottish Popular Ballads*, with Helen Child Sargent, 1904.
89. William Hazlett Upson (1891–1975), author of perennially popular Alexander Botts stories in *SEP*.
90. Butcher (1888–1987), critic, literary editor, Chicago *Tribune*; *Many Lives—One Love*, 1972.
91. O'Dell (1898–1989), novelist; *Woman of Spain*, 1934.
92. Pseudonym of Harriet Gilfillan (1909–1978); *I Went to Pit College*, 1934, about coal mining.

93. Frances Woodward Prentice (1894–1961), short-story writer and editor; later married to Charles P. Curtis, BDV's attorney.
94. (1910–1990); *Now in November*, Pulitzer Prize in fiction, 1935. See David Haward Bain, *Whose Woods These Are: A History of the Bread Loaf Writers' Conference, 1926–1992*, pp. 180–81.
95. (1904–1999), writer, critic, editor.
96. (1885–1977), poet, editor.
97. Homans (1910–1989), student of BDV, later professor of sociology at Harvard; *An Introduction to Pareto: His Sociology*, by George C. Homans and Charles P. Curtis, 1934.
98. *New York Times*, 4 September 1934.
99. Cora Wilkening, BDV's literary agent.
100. Probably "The Obvious Thing," *SEP*, 29 September.
101. Reference to Mary Roberts Rinehart (1876–1958), novelist. Wright is unidentified.
102. Novel by Gene Stratton Porter, 1904.
103. For Bob Major and Fitz, see *The Bucolics of Decadence* in Appendix A.

3

1935 LETTERS

DeVoto's autobiographical serial installments, begun in 1934, continued through the earlier part of 1935, included in segments with occasional letters to Sterne. Other letters illustrate DeVoto's friends, not in chronological sequence, with the Ogden and Kent Potter stories, with the portrait of DeVoto's Northwestern colleague Ney McMinn the most elaborate, and those of "Theodora," Betty White, and "Dorinda" ranging from the affectionate to the sarcastic. The long letter about Donald Born and his wife reveals the depth of DeVoto's concern for his admiring student. In his August 17 letter DeVoto's enthusiasm for his new friend, the poet Robert Frost, is complete, showing no hint of the tragic disaffection the friendship would encounter only three years later.

The letters of 1935 are as abundantly saturated with discussions of literature, art, music, and the theater as were those of the previous year, but are also marked by external events: the death of DeVoto's father; Sterne's major surgery; and the first stirrings of major changes in DeVoto's professional life: his appointment to the "Easy Chair" at *Harper's*, which lasted until his death twenty years later, and his reluctance to accept the editorship of the *Saturday Review of Literature*, which was nevertheless finally consummated in 1936. DeVoto and Sterne both enjoy writing *portraits-mémoires* during this year: DeVoto's about his aunt Rose Devoto Coffman and her son-in-law Jean-Marie Guislain, and Sterne's about her Wellesley professors.

Lincoln, Massachusetts

[13 January 1935]

Dear Kate:

I welcome the establishment of the Oursler Prize and will read your entries.[1] I grant you that Wilbur Steele and Elsie Singmaster enter the competition under odds that put practically all competitors out of the race. Let us, however, humbly keep an open mind. Fiction is a succession of apparent nadirs, and it is the nature of writers constantly to surpass themselves. Such a natural as "Heaven's My Destination" will hardly be come upon thrice in lifetime.[2]

If any quirk of your personality would be morbidly attracted to "Joshua Todd" which the jacket describes as "A novel by Fulton Oursler," I shall be happy to send you a copy which the psychotic Johnny Farrar sent me but yesterday.[3] I know, and shall know, no more than what this deposition contains.... The son of its author has been since September a bewildered and protesting member of English 31.[4] I can say of him that before long he will certainly be publishing in *Liberty* a succession of stories, all of them high up in the rating for the Oursler prize. He has been most unhappy among a group mostly composed of young Faulkners and Eliots where it is not composed of young Vicos who regard *Work in Progress* as *vieux jeu*,[5] and passionately irked by my reception of his creations. Nor have I been able to explain to him just why I so receive them. His ears catch no vibrations within the compass of my instrument. One afternoon, after failing completely to suggest to him what I meant by sensationalism, sentimentality and vulgarity, I said wearily, "Put it this way: You write like a tabloid reporter." A blank look followed by the introspective gaze of one examining himself at a confessor's direction. "Why shouldn't I?" he said, "I work for the *Record*."[6]

The debate with Zinsser will reach no end till he leaves for the Sorbonne, it seems, and then will suffer only a recess.[7] Nor can Hans be made to see why it is not bad taste to mention a physician's mention of Hester's menstruation and is bad taste to interpolate the expression "Oh, boy!" in his account of the sex life of the louse. He was talking about epidemics at Winthrop House the other night and we adjourned to Ronald Ferry's quarters where Hans insisted on fighting the old battle over again.[8] And I begin to wonder if some amendment isn't necessary in my reverence for the scientific mind. Ronald, it then developed, was genuinely shocked and horrified by Libby's reference to "the foetus." The term, Ronald says, is scientific, technical and professional and, in the mouth of a layman, especially a woman, disgusting.

To the projects he has in store for my pen, Arthur Hill[9] has now added a biography of the Honorable Governor of the Commonwealth and Senator in Waiting, James M. Curley.[10] At lunch the other day he was both eloquent and persuasive. Under the spell of that mind, I'd do it like a shot if he'd collaborate with me. I explained, however, that though I knew the Bostonians I could never hope to know the Irish, and he agreed. They are, he said, a society far more exclusive than the Brahmins and infinitely harder to crash.[11] Hill was Peters' corporation counsel and held over to help Jim get started in one of his administrations.[12] He had a dozen stories you would love, provided you have ever heard Jim swing from a more than Beacon Hill austerity of speech to a rich brogue as the circumstances dictated. The city was preparing a parade in celebration of something or other, doubtless the founding of that Puritan commonwealth which the Catholics have so competently taken over, and Jim was adjusting his hat and smile preparatory to taking his place in it, when entered a breathless messenger saying that the delegation of Jews were protesting about the place allotted to them in line. Jim turns to another aide: "Shaughnessey, do you go out and satisfy the Jews." Then, as Shaughnessey goes through the door, "And that, Patrick, is more than ever our Blessed Savior was able to do." Or Hill once asked him about a member of the Board of Aldermen, inquiring why he was so unpopular. Says Jim, "I'll tell you, Arthur-r. Reagan don't know how to behave and the bhoys won't talk to him for that he will not observe the etiquette of his place. We were sittin' round the aldermanic table once when Reagan comes in. He goes up to Ryan of the Fourth and he says to him, 'Ye voted for the Fenway contracts, and ye were bought.' He goes on to Gilhooley of the Ninth and he says to him, 'Gilhooley, ye voted for the Fenway contracts, and ye were bought.' I picked up an inkwell and I was sittin' there, askin' the Blessed Mother of God should I let Reagan have just the ink alone or should I give him both the ink and the inkwell, when he comes up to me. 'Jim Curley,' Reagan says to me, 'ye voted for the Fenway contracts an', Jim Curley, ye were bought, an', Jim Curley, ye got twice as much as anyone else.' So, f'r the compliment, I put down the inkwell."

Well, belatedly, I got round to finding you in *Time*.[13] I found other points of orientation in that number.... The Charles A. Spoerl of page 4 is half a genius and ⁵⁄₇ a maniac.[14] An actuary for the Aetna Life, he practices mathematical necromancy on all occasions. He has some kind of fixation on eclipses. Let any of us announce a party and Charlie must, to legitimate it, calculate where, on the announced day, an eclipse occurs or, failing that, has occurred on that date in historic times. He fills the mails with insane correlations, the relation of the wave-length of sodium in Sirius to the tax on virgins in Thibet, the per capita value of the individual hair lost at the barber's and its bearing on the annual rise in the frequency of diabetes—that sort of thing. He is a self-taught and pretty competent pianist, banjoist and composer, and has a side-splitting and really amazing flare for parody. And a mind like the sewers of Paris. If ever I become a person of dignity in the land, be very sure that Charlie will unearth and give to the public the text of a musical comedy we once drunkenly collaborated on. It is, I believe, the first Freudian revue ever written and, I am certain, the filthiest.... P. 11. Under an alias, the late Secretary of the Navy wrote to Mrs. Dall that he had got so much pleasure from "Sistie in the White House," that he wanted to give a copy to his big sister for Christmas.[15] In due time, Mrs. Abigail Adams Homans received an autographed copy.[16]... Anguished cry (p. 12) of Johnny Farrar's partner, on learning that "American Outpost" was in preparation, "But there is no autobiography left for Upton to write."[17]... P. 14. It was in an interview when the Overland Limited stopped at Ogden that I learned from Mr. McAdoo that all the maxims of politics are not dependable.[18] One basic aphorism holds that no newspaper man is ever insulted by a politician. Still, some years later, his brother-in-law, Mr. Sayre, made that interview seem sweet. I wonder if there was something about marriage to a Wilson girl.... P. 17. Geraldine is—and the recent broadcasts affirm it once more—one of the most remarkable women of our time. Yet I can't help reflecting that her Carmen was one of the few completed orgasms ever presented on the stage and that, with Caruso, it was either bite or rape and he should not be blamed for biting. Also remembering that the movie version of *Carmen* made its premiere in Boston a couple of weeks after the Crown Prince's dear friend had scandalized New York by refusing to stand when the national anthem was played (this would be circa December 1916), and that Geraldine added to my education when, at the premiere, she was confused to be discovered in a box, stood up, and sang the Star Spangled Banner.[19]... P. 34. Of all possible adjectives that might be applied to your state of mind upon/if completing *The House of Sun-Goes-Down*, "shocked" is not among the number.[20] Somewhere among my papers is one of the most curious letters of this century. Acting upon one of the bizarre impulses that occur only in The Macmillan Company, Latham sent the manuscript to E. L. Thorndike to be read.[21] The professor had a complete and violent thrombosis. It was, he said, a disgusting and reiterated offence to decency.... Neither Bennington College nor Mr. Leigh impressed me very much.[22] The place looked phony from the first poster on the bulletin board and though its president seemed too much an opportunist and too little a crank to rouse my suspicion of all educational experiments, I never even let him mention the stipend he wanted to pay me to be a professor of English there. I should not be deeply enthralled if he winked at me, and none of the three instructors I know has more intellectual skepticism than enables him to undertake the conversion of the Junior League to the life of the mind.[23]... P. 38.[24] On 52d Street, just back of DePinna's, is a small, I think four-story building, the bottom floor of which used to be occupied by one of Valentino's ex-wives in the millinery business.[25] The top floor is a charming apartment. The whisper used to be that it was maintained by Barney Baruch for the war-time President's ventures into amour.[26] That, dear, is one of the aspects of the newspaper business in time of national crisis.... Cornelia Lunt, the aunt of Valleyhead's director, was the leading exponent of Evanston culture.[27] Evanston is the home of, yes, the cradle of, the Women's Christian Temperance Union and the American Federation of Women's Clubs. I used to occupy the apartment above a garage just round the corner from her palace, and though it is not true that the villagers genuflected when she passed, still that frail, unworldly ancient did part the town's traffic when her companion took her out in the last surviving electric runabout in America.... I was going (p. 39) to quote Maxwell Bodenheim's limerick about Peggy Wood but on the whole, no, let it join the unrepeated.[28] I offer instead two or three sentences which have charmed me from the letters of Mr. Bodenheim in the Braithewaite [*sic*] Collection now at Widener.[29] "...a copy of my second novel, entitled 'Crazy Man.'[30] I believe that you will find this book to be dramatic and challenging and perhaps you can secure an early review for it in The Transcript."[31] "...wonder if you know of any organization in Boston that would like to engage me. I am a very excellent reader of my poetry." "...but I am sorry you did not select poems more representative of my powers and originality. I also regret that you did not care to include more than two poems of mine." "I have never, in any sense, been a follower of (Ezra Pound). I think, rightly or wrongly, that my work has an individuality of its own, not dependant [*sic*] upon Mr. Pound, or any other man."...(I am having God's own bliss with that collection. The era was even more cockeyed than I remembered it. A bit by Mary Austin on the spirituality of commas was certainly a forecast of Stein's recent tour and I shall take, next week, to Hervey Allen this sentence from a letter of his of 1923, "I have been living in Charleston for some years, taking an active interest in the renaissance which I think was started by me and Mr. Heyward from there.")[32]...P. 46. I hope sometime to get round to telling you about the nudists of Belmont Hill.[33]...P. 53. The final quotation from Earnest Hooton—and you will please spell his name that way—acquires a rather sharp poignancy when one knows that two members of his family, one of them a son, are definitely halfwitted.[34] Ernie is an amusing chap, a clever talker, an amusing writer, a fine teacher, a sound anthropologist. Very good company. Moreover, as the photograph suggests, he is almost incredibly myopic, blind as a bat without his glasses....Among the profession, Mr. Millikan is held to be, on all matters outside his specialty, crazier than any coot.[35]...P. 54. The Marquis de Caussade controls more Armagnac than all the other proprietors put together.[36] He will not allow his name to go on any but vintage years and will permit only those years to be exported to America. Park-Benziger are going to offer an 1834 at $45 a bottle, not in the hope of selling any but in hope that the price will overcome the local skepticism and guarantee the authenticity of the later vintages, which are, by the way, authentic.[37] The Marquis left America convinced that it is and will always be a barbarism. Les Americains wholly failed to equip their pissoirs with toilet paper....P. 55. The most amazing statement I have seen recently in the public prints is Neal O'Hara's remark that Dorothy Canfield Fisher looks like a twin sister of Katharine Hepburn.[38]...P. 56. Anyone who found a pearl in the food at the Ranch Cafe is quadruply fortunate.[39] In my time, it was more customary to find cockroaches and even mice....I offer you page 73, all three columns of it, as an amazing exhibit even in a field where all capacity for amazement should be excised from any who desire to frequent it.[40]

Reverting to Arthur Hill. Discussing Jim Curley, he dismissed him from all consideration and, as innocently as succinctly, summed up the Bostonian when he said "He doesn't know the difference between principal and interest." As the tree from the acorn, you may draw all Boston, past, present and to come, out of that sentence.

All the Logan Eccleses are handsome.[41] And, following their heritage from Dave, virile. A tennis-playing younger brother of Marriner's ranged through Ogden like a bull through a convent of heifers. The Ogden branch were runty, in my time, and given to ambiguities. The males, that is; the females were not in the least ambiguous.... I exercise a peculiar function at Harvard, which the faculty had not legitimated, that of angel to the literary. This year two graduate students of faintly purple quality are from Utah and both are emeritus Mormons. In the writings of one of them, who comes from the hierarchy and should know, I have read the most hair-raising stories of incest I've ever seen. Polygamy loosened a number of taboos.... Oh, shortly I shall send you the chapter of reminiscence you are unquestionably responsible for.[42] And, as time permits, I'm working on a Brigham Young for the DAB.

I go on tour, the middle of the week. I seem to have been working rather hard and there's no likelihood I'll stop before June, so I'm taking a week off. The return engagement in Philadelphia supplies a convenient take-off—I'm going on down to the Eastern Shore and spend a couple of days with Hervey, then back to Baltimore and Mencken.[43]

It was this Friday. I rose yesterday a year older than I had gone to bed, being awakened by Bunny running in and yelling, "Daddy, I'm 38 today." He has not since abandoned the idea and he celebrated the day by composing a gorgeous fantasy in which he fell off a sleeping-boat, caught a whale on a whale-pole, gave it a long handkerchief to blow its nose on and took it to Dr. Porter for cold shots. The future sets strongly toward romance.

Yours,
Benny

Lincoln, Massachusetts

[28 January 1935]

Dear Kate:

This would have been along sooner if I had not been shocked by the death, on Friday evening, of a man who meant a good deal to me.[44] His heart, which nobody seems to have known was bad, failed while he was dancing at a party. I casually broke a casual engagement with him Friday afternoon.

But what an extraordinary person your great-aunt was![45] I have seen variants of the same emotion, but I can't remember Holy Church's sacred masochism so nakedly exhibited in modern times at least. Uncle Pierce, on the whole, though, makes better material for fiction—what a novel one could make out of the two of them. No Freudian would be stumped by Pierce's discovery of his vocation three months after his wife conceived. Something of that guilt shines through his conversion to the Faith following his marriage. He was certain to make a bad priest for just that reason, too, and I must say it looks as if he were belatedly maturing when he finally left the Church and invoked the House of Commons. That, right there, is the part of the novel I'd like to write, swinging back and forth between him and Cornelia. Religious fiction has jammed the stacks but it isn't too at home with reverse English on its commonest theme—if enough of my one-time spirituality were left I'd like to try it sometime.

The conscientious historian, however, holding the pious chronicler to the same standards he enforces on the ungodly, points out that John McCloskey was only bishop coadjutor of New York when Cornelia consulted him, and wasn't elevated to the cardinalate till thirty years later.[46] ... Incidentally, what about the author? My guess is that if she didn't write in English she at least thought in it. And has the *Vie*[47] appeared? I'd like to read it.

... And here occurs one of the mortifying discoveries I occasionally make, as when I found out that this forcing-bed of literature contained no copy of Aristotle's *Poetics*, and, even worse, that this hive of native Americanism had no copy of the Constitution of the United States.[48] It has been in my mind that either you remember something else or that your memory goes back further than you think, for if those battleships were truly of the Hudson-Fulton celebration, then you were not yet two. So, making sure of my ground, I started to look up Hendrik Hudson—and if it hadn't been for the DAB and the new Webster's, I'd have been out of luck.[49] The north wall of this room—beyond it for a half-hour the best northern lights of some years have been jumping about like the searchlights of your fleet—is packed from floor to ceiling with profound treatises on American history. And none of them date the Half-Moon's voyage and only one of them alludes to it. Which shows, among other things, what Beard, Turner and Arthur Schlesinger have done to the writing of American history.[50] Happily the 2d edition of the New International again renders all other books superfluous: you were wheeled along the drive between Sept. 25 and Oct. 9, 1909.[51]

You also started me wondering what was the first play I saw. With this result: it was an antique thriller, probably by Owen Davis, called *The Eleventh Hour*.[52] At that hour the switch was thrown just in time and the limited roared safely by. But Bernardo was borne out shrieking and that night had bad dreams.

Well, the literary were more amusing than usual or else I grow tolerant—or senile. The Chris Morley–Tom Daly act in Philadelphia lasted for at least three hours and I enjoyed it.[53] Bonfield Manor was fogbound and half flooded, but Hervey was genial and genially morose. He really expects the system to crack and dissolve, and he's making Bonfield a self-maintaining unit.[54] A mill for the grinding of Bonfield wheat arrived the same day I did and when he slaughters his first calf he'll have rennet to begin cheese-making. A smoke-house is already started.... I wonder just how these intensely mechanized withdrawals from the machine age are going to get gasoline and distillate to run their engines when the disorganization they're fleeing from begins to happen.... So on to Baltimore where it developed, at Dr. Bordley's, that my hearing is quite all right after all, and then to dinner with Mencken. About Mencken I've seen nothing or heard nothing to change my mind in ten years: he's the wittiest man in America, one of the most intelligent, probably the friendliest, the foremost stylist and, so far as my wanderings go, the finest host. It occurs to me that there has never been a time since I first spilled ink that I wouldn't have immediately given up whatever I was doing to do anything that Mencken might want me to.

So we came home and it was another blizzard. Last year I could hire people to shovel my drive out. This year they're all working for Ickes.[55] Henry and I shoveled for eight hours on Thursday. Then after dinner an oil truck got stuck just outside my drive and I went out and shoveled for two hours more. That being done, I did this year's good deed by bringing in the driver and feeding him the first meal he'd had since six that morning, but human service got stopped short: I couldn't get a drop of liquor into him. He said, regretfully, that he couldn't hold it.

Well, my religious aunt was quite different.[56] Not to put a fine point on it, she was, and for all I know is, the blackest-souled bitch who ever entertained an archbishop.... In that pleasant period when we received ten-million-dollar bequests just as sleep blots us out, I customarily write novels. Ever and anon I have played with the notion of a novel about Victoria's[57] high tide in interior, though not transalpine, America. A sweet subject for someone, sometime. My opening scene has usually been the girls going back home when school is over, crushing their hoops against each other and weeping while John brings up the carryall to take them to the train and writing furiously, writing in each other's autograph albums. "Dear Rose," an entry ran in my aunt's, "in Life's showers may you always have Love's umbrella." That would do, I think, nicely. Or, after supper, she sits on a hassock doing petit-point when a guitar is strummed outside on the lawn and male voices softly sing "Come where my love lies dreaming."[58] A serenade! She runs—no, she flits—out on the iron balcony, waving her handkerchief and kissing her fingers. But that is not enough. They have come to hear her sing and they will not go until she does. So we will raise our curtain on her there—standing on the balcony, pressing that handkerchief to her breast and singing "I dreamt that I dwelt in marble halls."[59]... The Runyans [*sic*] and Peglers of the trade, not to mention the Studebaker company, have let you know that, somewhere near South Bend, Indiana, exists an educational institution called Notre Dame.[60] You may not know that, a few miles away, is St. Mary's Academy, now, I believe, a college, called St. Mary's of the Lake and ruled over by a talented scholar, a poet of some quality, an accomplished critic, a woman of wit and urbanity, Sister Mary Madeleva.[61] It is there that we first encounter Rose Devoto.

So far as I can remember, my father has told me only two things about his father: one was disturbing and both were discreditable. What I more or less believe about the origin of my line on this side of the Atlantic rests on my aunt's statements; and though she has spent a good deal of money propagating these particular ones, I have found few of her statements that were worth one cent on the dollar. Anyway, her story is that the De Rosas were of the small Italian nobility and the DeVotos of the military caste that came up, I suppose, with Cavour's bourgeoisie, and that the thought of a daughter's marrying even a well-heeled commoner was more than the Countess DeRosa could abide.[62] They could marry, finally, but they could not stay in Italy, so behold the ex-colonel operating a prosperous commission business in St. Louis a couple of years before the Civil War, with connections all the way down the Mississippi and up the Ohio. He seems to have thriftily utilized the necessities of both armies when the war came, and he had a realism of his own for, on my father's statement, he was in Cincinnati when Covington was raided and escaped the draft for the home-guard by donning my grandmother's clothes and walking out of town. Anyway, both of my grandparents died and Rose and my father—she is the older by three or four years—were left, with a sizable nest egg, to the care of the church. Notre Dame acquired my father at about the age of seven, I imagine. Rose went to St. Mary's under the care of a nun who was or eventually became Mother Superior of the Sisters of the Holy Cross, Sister Mary Augusta. Or is it Agusta? She lived into this century, for I have a memory of her in Washington in 1901 and I believe she even took notice of my first communion.

Some people have a gift for messing up the lives of others. When it was finally apparent that I wouldn't be a priest, my aunt gave up working on mine, but she has managed to raise hell with everyone else I know to have been related to her. She did a lovely job on my father, who was a pupil of Puvis de Chavannes but became a Utah abstractor.[63]...However, I began this with some intention of linking up her state of grace and the libido. She told me once that the only thing she couldn't reconcile with God's goodness was the way children were brought into the world, and I had no trouble believing her. She married a brilliant surgeon in Omaha who put his fees into real estate and became very rich.[64] She had four children, one of whom died in infancy. The only boy, named Weir after her husband's friend Weir Mitchell, died in his early manhood—by the infinite kindness of God.[65] It is in the two daughters that her difficulty with that reconciliation shows up, though it is probably not without significance that her husband developed an inexplicable paralysis which kept him in bed for the last fifteen years of his life and all his reflexes sound and functioning. The older one, Marie (both of them were educated in a convent), developed one of the grand romances that were current among the gently born about 1905. You know, the Alice Roosevelt sort of thing, Delmonico, the Gibson Girl, George Barr McCutcheon.[66] It sang itself to mandolins and orchestrelles for a few months and Marie's veil was to be twelve feet long. Then her mother commanded her to break off the match, not to marry at all. Marie obeyed and my aunt was very happy, though a little puzzled when the girl's health broke and she went to bed for six months, her father being already bedridden. Then there was a period when Marie was going to enter the sisterhood and my aunt was ecstatic, but she couldn't survive the apprenticeship and came out again into the world. I remember her—wan, ossified, brilliant-eyed. Once or twice young men called on Marie and all hell seethed in the old girl. Then Marie's health failed again. It mended somewhat when she met an elderly gent, a couple of years older than my aunt, who had a physical deformity—a curiously misshapen head. Suddenly he wanted to marry the girl and, not quite so curiously as it seems at first glance, my aunt was strong for the match. So Marie married him and bore him four children in three and half years. I last saw her about 1919. She looked older than my aunt, who thought that, if there had to be marriages, this was a really excellent one. That is the first term in your equation.... We pass now to the younger girl, Rose.[67] She was a beautiful girl, as Marie wasn't. Rose was tall, very dark, with the enormous brown eyes and the soft, dark but distinctively tinted skin of mid-Italy. A genuine beauty. Omaha grew metropolitan in the three or four years between Marie and Rose, and Rose was a debutante and all the inconceivable rituals of midwestern gentility were spun round her. So one of the Northern Pacific Hills came a-courting and Rose fell head over heels in love with him. Rose had the passion that I've supposed Marie didn't, and when she fell in love she fell in love. This too got about as far as the wedding veil, and then my aunt commanded Rose to break it off. Rose did. Somehow, with the Italian tradition and the convent education and the remaining folkways of genteel America, when one's mother said not to marry, one obeyed. But my aunt lived to see her ecstasy curdle. For Rose was not Marie.

Sorry, I've got to quit. This is the story of Jean-Marie Guislain. I've just had a letter from him for the first time in ten years. It's amusing. I'll come back to it.

Yours,
Benny

Lincoln, Massachusetts

[11 February 1935]

Dear Kate:

To the historian & collector of American sentiments the most important aspect of the D'Oyly Carte tour is the reassurance that an ancient principle is still lively and the aggregate is therefore, in all these frantic modern days, unimpaired.[68] When the reviewers of America can still stretch out in rigid and unanimous ecstasy on the ground that it's perfect because it's English we need have little apprehension about the convincing soundness of these times. Well it is, God knows, English. It's a Rolls-Royce with all that that implies. It will run forever and it weighs eight tons. The strong who bear up under it are enormously rewarded but, no weakling in these matters, I've had my moments of fearing it would prove too much for me. Not a word against the principals. Well, yes, one word. This Martyn Green is a star and no mistake, he's almost as good as he's being said to be, but he isn't the Lord Chancellor that Frank Moulan was and he never will be.[69] But any group of principals is better than any American group I've ever seen, and Muriel Dickson's voice would be useful to the Metropolitan.[70] And when that has been said—it's, I grant you, quite a bit—the rest is disconcerting if not downright painful. I don't know whether the British jaw or the British thoroughness irks me the worse. The dentition of the chorus is bad, the hips, thighs, calves, insteps, feet, breasts, shoulders and throats are also massive and empire-building, but the jaws are beyond all toleration. Why does every collection of English women look like studies for Piltdown or even the Horse Show?[71] And they don't sing—the sacred Savoy tradition doesn't run to ensemble numbers that take your mind off the program. As for the Savoy direction—it's damn near lethal. We don't get let off the slightest bit. No sir, those girls are going to take every step the script called for under gas light, and every phrase that Sullivan wrote is going to be punched out clear and strong before we get on to the next one.[72] Which may be tradition but is damn stupid, for where the parodist and the exercise-book joined hands Sir Arthur could be quite as tiresome as the next one. What those scores need is just what American directors have been giving them for forty years—intelligent but firm scissors work in all overtures, ensembles and finales, especially first-act finales. If our ancestors didn't frequently yawn at the originals, so much the worse for ancestry—God knows there was room to yawn. And I say this as probably America's leading Sullivan maniac. . . . As for that, my slowly growing conviction that the good Gilbert slipped badly at times was this year increased by a startling feeling of sympathy for the lampooned in Patience.[73] It's as enchanting music as anything out of the Savoy, but—it may be I grow older than I think—this year it was just a little revolting to listen to some of Gilbert's hearty beef-eating no damn nonsense about it bluff Philistine division. He doesn't show up well on the side of God's Englishmen. . . . Further note: nothing diminishes my conviction that *Iolanthe* is the best of it and None Shall Part Us the best of *Iolanthe*.[74] . . . And once more: what the gilt-edged tradition needs most is a sense of pace.

Judging by the opening reviews of Zinsser's book, the blurb I was going to write would be conspicuous waste. Wasn't *Time* a little solemn to run it under Medicine?

If my correspondence these days is episodic, blame the initial effort to tell the young about recent American literature and the developments which make this, besides the Year When Marriages Collapsed, the Year When People Had Babies. My services as a photographer of children are in steady demand and, photographs once taken, no man can tell a Young Mother, Sorry, I wasn't thinking of working in the dark room this week. And yet, it's the repeat orders that depress me. God forbid I should be small minded about a hobby, but no one considers that I occasionally like to work on my own pictures or for that matter, if a friend of mine should ever send me a dozen sheets of bromide on the theory that Eastman doesn't give it away the experience would unsettle me.

Observe the current rehabilitation of Veblen. It was bound to happen. The perfect theorist. A sociologist completely unembarrassed by factual knowledge, an economist who never touched reality at any point. For that large and alas increasing group of American thinkers who derive knowledge from pure navel-gazing he is certain to become the Holy Ghost.... He will always be, in my mind, an *Ur*-nudist, a shadow in a G-string flitting among the bushes of Washington Island.

Yet this deeply comforts me: the New Democracy groups have found an angel in California, the moulting-ground of angels—whose simple program is to sell the Douglas Credit Plan to the Republican Party.

Well, to Rose Coffman.[75] My uncle's death helped my aunt keep her in seclusion for a while. She was, besides, a Catholic, convent-reared, at least partially influenced by Italian notions of family authority. A docile girl, lovely as a dream, but without intelligence. Her life was given over to good works throughout the diocese and to the faint and decorous gentilities that lingered on in Omaha from Victoria's hey-day: a shudderful tinkling of Chopin and Chaminade, painting on china, convent embroidery.[76] My aunt—who has never been out of mourning since her son died about 1904—bloomed and flourished, serenely confident that this perfect mother-love and daughter-love could never be [?] darkly blown across by those fiery winds. Her husband's death put her in possession of a large estate which helped out a good deal with the expansion of Creighton College and numerous other Intentions of the Bishop of Omaha.[77]

So one day a trusted friend introduced a Belgian who was painting her portrait. Jean-Marie Guislain was—is—an Artist in the grand tradition. He came from an eminently respectable diplomatic family, but, unhappily for Harold Stearns, there are Babbitts to the eastward as well as locally and when it was finally clear that Jean could not be turned from his namby-pamby painting, he was chucked out.[78] Going to Paris, he lived the Murger life, sometimes living for months on turnips and coffee.[79] He so undermined his health, then, that several times tuberculosis has flattened him. From Paris, he wandered widely, painting as he went. To Italy, to Spain, to South America where, in Bolivia, a couple of his brothers were doing the old man proud as ranchers, and to California, where he stayed for a couple of years exchanging lessons in painting for permission to attend lectures at the University and so on. Now, in my worthless judgment, he has never been a very good painter but he is one of the most charming men in the world. A brilliant talker, heart-warming manners, an enthusiastic and wide knowledge of four literatures, something of a poet (he has published five or six volumes of verse in Paris), quick-witted, highly intelligent, mercurial, chock full of the romantic properties of the fin-de-siècle Bohemia that had not yet put in the slot machines. One imagines the impact on the pious, unworldly, Victorian-midwife atmosphere of pre-war Omaha.

Rose was tall and dark and beautifully made. To her mother's infinite rejoicing, she had, following the shattered romance, looked with abhorrence on the men who occasionally dared face my Gorgon aunt. She was certainly unaware what was happening to her now. What happened was merely a boiling up of the despised hormones that suffered to break her neurosis, overcome her heritage, flout her traditions, cancel the teaching of her church, and, most astonishing of all, defy her mother.

For, of course, my aunt rapidly went crazy. Just that—from the time that Rose married him she has been, from any satisfactory clinical standard, insane. I assume that excessively religious people have an infection to begin with, and she now met a frustration of a desire she did not understand and had reanimated a terror which she had assumed was laid forever. The combination produced an alteration of values that would be called insane if it occurred in a public character or a person who had to earn his living. But it must have been amusing—from a distance. She developed God knows how many delusions. Jean is an extremely emotional person. At one interview she so worked on him that he had a nosebleed. She has described to me in full detail the process by which he got those chemicals into his nose, so that he might work on Rose's sympathies.

Driven by these unguessed frenzies in her blood, Rose acted on instinct. When my aunt closed the house to him, Rose met him at the family friend's. When my aunt worked on the friend, she met him on the street. She went to her favorite priest and got an official ruling: it was not sin to meet him so long as they kept walking. It would, however, be sin to stop.

And now one of the violent tornadoes that make the prairies adventurous from April to October tore its way across Omaha, killing several hundred people and levelling a good many houses.[80] Marie, in bed with her fourth child, saw the wall lifted from beside her bed and blown through the far wall of the next room in which two children were not so much as wakened. Her husband, starting upstairs, had the stairway blown out from under his feet. The piano was carried some two miles. Three or four blocks away, my aunt's house was blown in. She and Rose were imprisoned under it—bruised and shaken but not damaged, but unable to move. Jean-Marie, a couple of miles away, was unharmed and so desperately prevailed upon one rescue crew that they went with him to the ruins. In four or five hours they were able to get the two women out. In the course of the rescue, a fireman drove his axe through my aunt's hand. It was a clean wound that healed neatly and she was lucky—as some dozens of us were unlucky—that it was her hand and not her head. But she knew, and has told hundreds, that it was Jean who swung that axe and did so with malice perpense but poor aim. She fails to take into account the fact that anyone who knew her would swing again if he had to.

The tornado finished matters. A few months later, Rose married him. In the house of the family friend, in the absence of my aunt. Ceremony by a heretic, since my aunt had prevailed on the Bishop to forbid the priests to perform it. Note on the curiosities of the pious mind: why was she willing to let her daughter live in mortal sin but not in holy matrimony? Rose accepted the sin, but determined to amend it when they got to Belgium, and did amend it.

My aunt's delusions now quadrupled. She had set detectives to looking up what they could find, which was nothing at all. She had written to Jean's father and got back a letter from the ambassador which read like an address to an uncouth fungus. The family, he said, had walked out on Jean but he supposed the man could marry an American girl if he liked, certainly the family was no longer interested in any of his depravities. So Omaha now began to fill with stories about Jean's past. To my certain knowledge she has accused him of every crime under the statutes, the common law and the Code Napoléon, with eyewitness, circumstantial detail.

My chronology is uncertain but the marriage was either seven or nineteen months before August, 1914. They went to Belgium—to Brussels. Jean set up as a portrait painter. And presently von Kluck occupied Brussels.[81] They had something over a year of it before Whitlock on that side, stirred up by Rose, and Hitchcock on this side, stirred up by my aunt and paralyzed by her demand that he get Rose out but see to it that Jean stayed in captivity, succeeded in delivering.[82] Delivering, that is, their persons. What money they had, Jean's canvases and brushes—and books, their furniture—everything, naturally, was gone. My aunt promptly told the world that the reason they were able to escape was that Jean sold military information about his country to the Germans in return for freedom. Or, J.-M. Guislain, Spy and Traitor.

The boat landed at Boston. They took a small apartment in Cambridge and Jean undertook to become known here. Boston, you may have observed, is a damned queer place for any painter, even a La Valle or a Hopkinson.[83] Presently Rose heard that I was in Cambridge and so I saw her for the first time in about five years. Promptly I formed a deep friendship with Jean, one of the most satisfying of my life. It lasted till I quarreled violently with Rose just after the war. Practically all I know about French literature and absolutely all I know about painting and the French language I learned from afternoons when I went sketching with Jean or evenings when we drank a bottle of beer after one of Rose's dinners—she had become a magnificent cook. I sharpened most of my ideas about the world—especially about writing—on Jean's strop.

The old girl had half the money in the Great West, but never a penny would she contribute to those pinched days. At six-month intervals she would send Rose the fare west, for the breathless beatitude of a visit with her, during which she would steadily pour into Rose's ears the latest details of her delusions. On my way east & west through Omaha she would tell me. And she would, in the meantime, write them to my father—who hadn't written to her in twenty years or more. Jean, the defaulter and absconder; Jean, the traitor & spy; Jean, the deadbeat; Jean, the rapist and seducer; Jean, for all I know, the murderer.

Jean made a little headway here and rather more than that in New York, whither they removed just before the war ended. His portraits, which he respected, were rather patronized, but his water colors, which he thought frivolous, had something of a small vogue. Anyway, he made some money and before long they went to Paris. In the meantime I had quarrelled with Rose, her mother having, in recompense for my friendship with & defence of Jean, told her an astonishing assortment of lies about me. In Paris, Jean's lungs went bad and for two years—I found out through Gordon King—while my aunt put another window in the cathedral and supported a new establishment of nuns, Rose supported him by sewing—at the Paris wages of a seamstress. He crawled back, made a little headway again, collapsed again. And so on, two or three times through the cycle.

I had a letter from Jean a month ago, the first one in about ten years. He had just read S.G. Well, he seems to be doing fairly well, although a friend through whom I have kept an eye on him recently wrote me asking if for God's sake I couldn't buy one of his canvases. But the word from Omaha is that the poor of the diocese regard Mrs. Coffman as a saint and Father Somebody does also, who has a new car. But the old girl seems to be breaking up. At least I hear, also through my friend, that she didn't interfere when a couple of years ago, Marie, the widow of a multi-millionaire, sent her sister an old coat and fifty dollars.

Yours

Benny

Lincoln, Massachusetts

[EARLY JUNE 1935]

Dear Kate:

Sorry I miscued on the Dana verdict.[84] But, by God, if ever prophecy is safe, I give you a Brahmin who is also a fairy and also a declared radical up before an Irish Catholic judge. My agents have not yet reported what occurred on the inside, but the obvious inference is that State Street decided to play with Brattle Street and so made a deal with City Hall.[85] Ultimately, the Cardinal must have got some advantage.[86] . . . Or, pensively, according to the rumors of twenty years ago, may have felt a certain fellowship. . . . Anyway, the honorable judge was obviously under great pressure.[87] He threw out the indictment with the sour remark that whenever the alleged act took place, the State had offered no evidence that it took place on the alleged night. . . . The net result is to increase an already quite intolerable martyr complex. Dana is sure that Hearst framed him.[88] Framed! With Craigie House all but openly a house of assignation.[89] And Hearst had less to do with this indictment than I did—I, at any rate, live on the road down which the boys were speeding in Dana's nephew's car when apprehended by the Concord militia, who had got the number as stolen over the teletype, the nephew unhappily not remembering all the intricacies of the relationships.

An illustrious fellow-townsman once remarked that some circumstantial evidence is pretty strong, as when you find a minnow in the milk.[90] . . . Going up and down the world and to and fro therein, I long ago adopted a policy toward the glib allegation of homosexuality that is so entertaining in the circles of (a) the intellectual, and (b) the nautical. The policy: I would entertain no idea that any given gent was a nance unless he solicited me or unless I saw him in bed with a man. One by one friends, students and cocktail acquaintances of mine told me highly circumstantial stories about the Craigie House. Over a good many years I disregarded them, thinking of them, when I thought at all, as picturesque forms of the outrage suffered by Brattle Street in the treason of one who was both a Longfellow and a Dana in turning Red. Meanwhile, he was, and is, one of the most charming of men, gracious, beautifully mannered, really kind, immensely learned in the drama and especially the experimental drama—a man also who has suffered a good deal on behalf of his opinions, though with a more patient pleasure in such suffering than a psychiatrist could pass over, and though the opinions seem to be sheer nonsense, and, for a Brahmin, sidesplitting. Dr. DeVoto perceived in him, apart from that pleasure in martyrdom, only one quality that suggested any imbalance, a certain tyrannical and even despotic behavior when he was in circumstances or among people that allowed him to get away with it. But God bless us all, a little sadism never meant much, and if it did might have any of a hundred explanations.

The first New Year's Eve I spent in this house I was summoned to the phone by one who represented himself as a writer in great and pressing distress. His name meant nothing to him [*sic*] but I did know that such a novel as the one he named as his had been published. He had, he said, just reached Boston, was in flight from the police, was broke, and needed shelter and food. He was bringing me word from friends of mine at Northwestern. He mentioned several of those friends. One was a man who reached

NW after I left and whom I had never met—wherefore I was a little canny. I told him there was no way of reaching me that night but directed him to a student of mine for dinner and a bed and went in to interview him the next day. It's a long and complex story, and probably I've already told you all or parts of it. The point is, he was a complete criminal, a petty racketeer, engaged in three different rackets, literary, psychiatric, and homosexual. He made a good living at it, from a hundred to two hundred dollars a week. He would breeze into town and first he would milk whatever literary people were about, being either a helpless unfortunate in a scrape or the frank immoralist as seemed most promising. Then he would move on to the psychiatrists and get some small sums from them as a neurote who was bound for hospitalization. Then he would move on to the really remunerative field and blackmail the local fairies. He was a fairy himself and he was letter-perfect in the grapevine lore of that curious world. The fellowship is international—they all know, or hear about, or can hear about whenever they want to, everyone else.

Well, he got five dollars from me before I decided that the best thing was to warn him out of town. He got similar sums from a number of other writers hereabouts. He got fifty cents from Jack Wheelwright, but whether it was a poetic or a homosexual donation I don't know—I do know that it represents, certainly, the highest achievement of his career.[91] And ... he had told me that he was going to call on Dana, since Dana was a homo and would be kind. He also told my student a number of vivid stories. My policy swung into operation and I decided that he had alertly picked up some of the local gossip.... He spoke of wanting to get to Detroit where, alone among the major cities of America, the police were not after him for check-raising and blackmail, and where his sweetheart was, "a young man whom I love ~~daily~~ (!) dearly." ... Then I began to hear about the other donations and decided to investigate. I was closeted with Hillyer, who had also contributed five dollars to an artist in distress, when Dana telephoned. A couple of questions brought out the fact that he had given our artist eighty-five dollars for a ticket to Detroit and other sums not specified. Canvassing the local patrons of literature, I achieved a mathematical expression: above five dollars and you had a minnow.

The Consulting-Room Notebook. I have been reading her ms. for a long time, fiction and verse, but it was not till a few months ago that I knew any but the most casual, surface facts about her as a person. Not too good as writing, though fairly publishable, they interested me greatly as the most naked betrayal of the creative faculty as a function of fantasy I have ever encountered. I spent above four adolescent years mooning about Mattie Guernsey. So many-cylindered and highly compressed is my faculty of fantasy that Mattie has contributed to my written work just two things, the bit about climbing a fence in my last *Harper's* article and a wisecrack which I never uttered to

Mattie but thought up afterward and which reappeared in the first of the John Hoyt stories.[92] But this girl, oh, my God. Let her meet and dance with an Englishman at some party and a week later I would be poring over a story in which a transfigured but all too recognizable beauty met a young Englishman, plunged him into a turmoil of doubt about his English love, and finally plumbed either his or her better nature in either marriage or renunciation. It was therefore no great labor to reconstruct her past from her fiction. There was one recurrent theme, the young girl with whom a much older, married man falls in love. Once this father-image slept with a seventeen year old girl, but quite platonically. Once a somewhat older girl brought out the noblest in a man when he wanted to leave wife and child. Once a still older girl fled abroad rather than produce or lest she might consent to such a debacle. Then, some months ago, she got jittery and I made a bet with myself that the same pattern was preparing to shape up again. It did and half-way through it, my God, Benny, she couldn't tell such things to anyone but me and I got the whole story. A man much older than she wanted to abandon wife and children and marry her and she wanted him to. I like the girl and she was obviously suffering badly. I tried, besides the expected role of friendly ear, only one thing, to induce her to go through with it this time, to suffer a fractured hymen, to make one pass at the taboo of her father. Whether I had a casting vote or not, she at any rate did suffer that fracture, but of course the romance came to nothing. I don't know—a pattern that firm and vivid is not likely to get broken short of analysis, and I doubt that she'll ever get out of it. Anyway, I had the satisfaction of checking my guesses and finding out that every single story I had had a hunch about was a literal recording. The girl has been preserved, since her earliest impulses, from ever falling in love with, even from appealing to, any man who could conceivably marry her. Even any man who could conceivably menace the dearest treasure of papa's little girl. Which is why the violence to that treasure achieved in the last affair is an omen of hope. I want to tell you, no young buck was going to get what papa couldn't have. The beauties of rationalization: young men have always been dull, stupid, unintellectual, uncultivated, lacking the riches of the ripened personality, the interest that comes with experience and philosophy.... Sigmund is a great man. The purest theory holds that when a fixation occurs at that level there are strong incursions of narcism shading toward homosexuality. This girl abnormally adores the field and woodlands and what the clouds whisper to the birds. And I met her a week or so ago when I was fresh from a Ph.D. exam at Radcliffe and had just crossed the quadrangle. It was a viciously hot day and all the young things were stretched out on the grass with nothing much on. I told her about the display, with due critical appreciation. So she went home and wrote a poem about girls lying in the sun. Most fleshly. "... They court with insolence of nudity the sun fire's welting, tense/Embrace on breast and buttock, face and thigh..../Hunching their hips to tan their under sides,/Stretching their legs in great immobile strides to catch the stain even behind the knees..." I used to write that way when I was twenty and poetic and tumescent.

I saw the same hook-up with Dorinda, only much more pronounced, Dorinda never having grown up to the level where any kind of man made any kind of appeal to her. Still that isn't absolutely accurate, for she once had some dates with a Chinaman and told us she might marry him, the original of Evelyn Kron whooping up the match with a ribaldry that makes me laugh as I remember it. I've told you parts of the Dorinda saga? She was, among a great many other things that made for amusement, the complete narcist. On the eve of her birthday she would bathe very late, laving Her Body with unguents and ointments. When the city grew late and silent she would sit down at her desk and write a letter from the dying Dorinda to the Dorinda who was being born, a letter, I promise you, of the most heartfelt and poetic adoration, page upon multiplied page. That finished, she would commune with beauty till the stroke of midnight, whereupon, all the lights turned out, holding a lighted candle in one hand, she would go to the mirror and there, swooning with the loveliness of it all and I dare say with something else as well, she would press Dorinda's lips against the mirrored lips and say, "Good-bye, Dorinda dear."...And if you think I invented that, I ask you if it's something anyone could invent....And my God, how that wench loved nature, Freud's simplest index of narcism. That summer we rented a farm near Harvard Village and she came out sometimes for week-ends, remaining practically orgasmic for hours on end because willow leaves trembled or browntail moths made nests of what she described as gossamer.[93] She inquired what certain little green clumps were and was considerably dished when I told her juniper. She had thought, she said, that they were the pine tree's babies and had congratulated the pine tree, with a kiss so help me St. Bernard, on having such a beautiful family. I am happy to say that, against my advice, she rose at dawn and wandered barelegged—probably barearsed too, for she believed that we should not be ashamed of our bodies and she had one that no one need be ashamed of, which she bared for anyone's gaze but primarily her own—through some woods and hayfields which were ripe with dew, and came down with such a case of ivy poisoning as I had never seen before....Freud's observation was exact and from time to time she was struck with the beauty of some girl. The commission she worked for toured some woolen mills on a survey that interested me a good deal. I could get nothing about it from Dorinda except the luscious fact that in certain rooms the operators worked in their panties. When Betty White came to stay with us, Dorinda, meeting her, was plunged into such an ecstasy of aesthetic appreciation that I told Betty she had a chance to do a great human service and raise the emotional age level of Dorinda some six years, but Betty was too occupied trying to induce a hard guy to come on from

Chicago and shoot pistols at her. Avis swears that when she drove Dorinda to the Harvard station she opened wide her arms and carolled "Farewell, country!" but Avis is a malicious wench and was sore because Dorinda had taken a nude I'd made of her, Avis, and framed it and set it up on her office desk.... The psyche is God's most ingenious creation.

Incidentally, Betty did induce that gent to come on. That's a longer story than there's enough of tonight left to tell, but it had its moments.... That was a crowded summer, the first half of it at Harvard, the rest at Bob Almy's place at Hix Bridge. There was everything in that summer, including a poltergeist. That was also the time when Henry Reck's sister, Virginia, stayed with us for a week just before she got married, and having little to occupy her time took a series of sunbaths that sent her to the altar a red and pulpy mass of water blisters. Evelyn Kron rushed back from England, deserting her second husband, had a series of hysterical fits of conscience, rushed back to England, and took the next boat home again, deserting him for good, by way of a siege of insomnia that required all Harvard Village to hold it within bounds. A lady graphologist with a chin decided she was going to marry Bob. A Harvard boy was the 1001st victim to Betty's beauty. Another Harvard boy and a Boston deb took a neighboring camp for an experiment in the companionate marriage and consulted my wife about a dilemma that had them stopped, neither of them having informed himself about the mechanism of copulation. I was escorted off a golf links at night for necking my own wife. There was a horrible week when Betty decided that her real destiny was to become a writer of popular songs.... And suddenly I realize why all evening I've been under an impulse to tell you, apropos of nothing, about the time when my cousin Rhoda was afflicted most intimately with stinging nettle, while we were on a camping trip. It was, of course, apropos of your remarks about allergies, for another item of that summer of 1928 was Evelyn Kron's sudden and neurotic inability to stand water on her skin and the linked bronchitis that broke out in her—a woman as sound and healthy as any horse—as symbols of the disrupted marriage relation. Though why, that being so, she hadn't spent the last three years in a coughing fit I don't know. But if you don't think that water can make an arresting allergy, reflect a while.

It seems to me that I have explored the minor psychopathia quite enough for one sitting. Next time I address you, suppose I simply discuss gardening. But no, for in my current mood, the earth and the implements it is worked with are all too symbolic.... Fred Deknatel cut a minute gash in his finger with my axe. Ginny was all for having him take anti-tetanus treatment... until I told her it was accompanied by injections of horse serum.

Yours,
Benny

Bowne

[EARLY JUNE 1935]

Att. Dr. DeVoto:

All right, now tell me what polisphilia is an index of.[94] (I bare my soul to you, Benny.) One of the few verses I've ever done that seemed to me even at the time of writing infinitesimally above the level of a Sophomore literary magazine, was a piece on New York, written in the greyness of a Saranac dawn, with the damned birds chittering in the hawthorn thicket, & a truck rumbling on distant asphalt the very *leit-motif*[95] of loneliness.

I have another one, too—I love to play poker, & smoke little cigars, & drink straight rye, & set type, & swear, & indulge in a good many other supposedly strictly masculine pursuits. I love to wear tailored suits & put my feet on the desk, & yet I'm damned if, after intrusive & merciless soul-searching, I can find any homosexual tendencies. So what, Herr Ebing?

I see by the papers that my second cousin, Eleanor Grant, is being married to James Auchincloss next Saturday.[96] By the papers is the only way that I would know it, for the Rye Grants & the New York Grants have not spoken to each other for nigh twenty years. I've been trying all morning to remember what the feud was about. It's pretty hazy, but it had something to do with a silver cup which Aunt Cornie Broome gave to my grandfather, Edward, & which Eleanor's great-grandfather, James, thought should have been given to him. Don't ask me what were the special virtues of the damned cup—maybe it was the Holy Grail—but I do know that when my grandfather died he left it to the Holy Child Convent at Sharon Hill, Pennsylvania, secure in the knowledge that no Rye Grant was going to get anything away from the S.H.C.J.

Bunny's umbilical observation put me in mind of the only childish saying of mine I'm ever likely to retail to you. At the age of five or thereabouts my favorite reading material was the *Evening Globe*: especially Thornton Burgess's *Bedtime Stories* & the display ads.[97] Lane Bryant's maternity corset (illustrated with a line cut) I not unnaturally took to be a girth control device for stout women.... So one day when my father was complaining that he had put on five pounds & would certainly have to have a couple of good workouts on the river & lay off sugar & potatoes for a while, I looked up from my building blocks & said: "Daddy, why don't you just get a pair of maternity pants?" For years I wondered why Shef & Kent & Mr. Kinney & my father threw down their cards & rolled on the floor.

Yours,
Kate

Lincoln, Massachusetts

[July 1935]

Dear Kate:

The only literary Boyd I know is Ernest, and pansy is about the only epithet that I've never heard Madeline apply to him—a woman of magnificent vituperation, though she was usually under reasonable provocation, usually in the form of blondes.[98] I don't know James or any of his friends, unless Julia Peterkin is a friend of his—I've never heard her mention him.[99] But I've heard no rumor that he was. *Who's Who* gives him a wife and three children, which is the best evidence though not necessarily conclusive.... What, in particular, gave you the idea? The datum in *Roll River* that tugged most strongly at the impulse to go beyond the book which I resolutely refuse to yield to except in flagrant cases like Wolfe, was the fact that nobody seemed to get his screwing.[100] If we were to take that as fantasy and not fiction—I, probably too vehemently, insist that usually it's wrong to—the analyst rushes up in me and pronounces it not homosexuality but probably a part of the involved impotence-fantasies attached to the Oedipus complex.

The best of Freud is in occasional papers on highly technical matters. The best book, the only one unless you embark on a prolonged and intensive study, is *A General Introduction to Psychoanalysis*, and make very sure that you get either the English edition of last year or the American edition of this year—make sure that it's an edition introduced by Ernest Jones.[101] All other editions are (I'm speaking of translations—I take it you don't propose to tunnel through the German) reprints of the 1920 edition, which was a god-awful translation and is notorious in the profession for having tremendously misrepresented Freud. Joan Riviere is the translator you're after. I'd say it's worse than a waste of time to read any other of Freud's books, except the collected papers in the complete works. Especially don't read *The Interpretation of Dreams*, which is practically incomprehensible, or *Totem and Taboo*, which is practically nonsense.[102] Oh, the little one of two or three years ago, I forget the name (!), about civilization and especially war, is great stuff.[103] A handy gloss to have at your elbow is Healy, Bronner and Bowers, *The Structure and Meaning of Psychoanalysis*.[104]

Bear in mind, while reading the Introduction, that a lot of water has flowed under the bridges since those lectures were written nearly twenty years ago, thousands of analyses have been reported and studied, and the theory has grown quite a bit and changed a little.

It is by a self-control almost unparalleled that I am restraining myself from an introductory lecture of my own right now. The truth is, for a long while now I've been spoiling to write a chapter on The Method of Scientific Thought and I'll probably do it for the helpless subscribers of *Harper's* some day. Using either Pareto or Freud to make my points, or quite possibly both of them.... Again, I propose to do a job on the neat dovetailing of Freud and Pareto.... I can be fairly eloquent, I believe, on the notion of a conceptual scheme.

Well, hell, I will give you this much of that lecture. (1) Be as skeptical as you care to be while reading the book, but watch how the wildly incredible of the first quarter appears to be a demonstrated thing by the end of the book. (2) Bear in mind that you are watching an induction unfold, not a deduction ~~building up~~ [*handwritten:* proliferating, I mean.] (3) The great difficulty everyone has with scientific theory is the insatiable and incurable tendency of the mind to regard concepts, and specifically hypotheses, as things. The commonest barrier to Pareto is people's insisting on thinking of the Residues as instincts. They are not instincts. They are precisely what the ether is to the theory of radio waves. So with Freud. Everybody sometimes and most people always fall into thinking of the Oedipus complex, the castration complex, the censor, the ego, the id, etc., as material, or tangible, or apparent entities. They are and must be taken as hypotheses, a conceptual scheme, a modus operandi. They are a frame of reference for psychoanalytical material—emotions, behavior, drifts. When Pete Bridgman said that light was corpuscular on Mondays, Wednesdays and Fridays and a form of wave motion on the alternate days he put the whole thing in a nutshell.[105] The hypotheses are merely useful ways of thinking about the material, and they do no more than lead from fact to new fact. (4) Bear in mind that Freud is a genius first and a scientist second. As a friend of mine once put it, he has never been wrong in clinical interpretation—what has seemed to be the wildest and most insupportable stuff has always, in the consulting room, been subsequently justified and vindicated by the people who were wariest of it when he announced it.

Your analyst pleads that, please, dreams don't mean anything except in the associations they give rise to. The next time you have one, spend five minutes being Molly Bloom and see where you end up.[106] The best thought these days, I take it, is that, whatever else a dream may be, it is also, in one way or another, in one part or another, a wish-fulfillment. Lacking the associations, even a willing amateur can't make anything of your acid night, but the manifest content of the alkaline dreams would appear to fulfill a wish. A wish to have children is probably not censorable in any woman and would go as is. To have a lot of children would obviously be to be a strong, triumphant, victoriously physical person, something which I take it you can't be while you're battling tuberculosis. To have small children would be to have them easily—which goes a little deeper into the ego. You'd like to have them at no great cost in pain. We could maybe get some more from the manifest content if you'd note what the kids are like. What do they look like? Whom do they resemble? What are they doing? Etc. But the latent content is what gives a dream point, and the associative path is the only way to get at that.

I took one glance at *The Fountain* and told Alfred[107] he needn't give it to me, and the Chips book was effectively stopped when I heard it was about an English schoolmaster—I don't think I could read one of those if faced with the traditional alternative. I have read *Of Human Bondage*, but so long ago that my opinion is worth nothing. I thought it was pretty good in 1920 or thereabouts, but when I read *Cakes and Ale* I thought that was much the best he'd ever done.[108] I still think it was the greatest service that Thomas Hardy ever did to English letters.[109] There is a fruitful place to exercise your aberrations, dear, if you're fascinated by the very bad in art. At the moment the only worse novelists I can think of are Dreiser and D.H. Lawrence, and I'm not sure that Dreiser is worse.[110] The only novel in the language that's worse than *The Return of the Native* is—well, make it *A Pair of Blue Eyes*, or *Desperate Remedies*, or *The Mayor of Casterbridge*, or possibly *Jude*. I'm fairly sure that *Tess* is a better book.

Before the year is out the public may be getting the inestimable privilege of my literary views once a month. This is for your ear alone, since negotiations are by no means conclusive, but I may be bellowing from a platform you won't have much trouble guessing.[111] Then if, as has been suggested, Mencken gets the other department, it ought to be an amusing magazine. But the Mencken lead is even more hush-hush than mine.

Another rumor I've heard is that Bruce Gould has been made editor of the *Ladies' Home Journal*.[112] Affairs in the Curtis publications appear to be growing steadily more chaotic, but whatever this does to the *Journal* it makes the *Post* better than it's been for just about a year. If someone will now poison Graeme Lorimer I can probably visit Philadelphia both in comfort and without homicidal impulses.[113] Graeme's papa has made fewer mistakes than any other editor in American history, but when he let Tom Costain go he made one that has already been infinitely costly and may prove, before or after George Horace dies, damned near fatal. Costain was the only conceivable successor to Lorimer, and he came closer to making the *Post* than Lorimer realized. Erd Brandt is a nice guy and, I gather, a good man, but he and Gould and any half-dozen others don't add up to any five minutes of Tom. At the moment, Stout is the only editor left and the *Post* needs a lot more than one.[114]

The hot weather that delights you has been, in these parts, just a southwesterly steam bath that would take the scale off a boiler and did take off repressions of mine as far back as the diaper. It arrived in the final stage of some sixteen hour days in which I wrote a short story and the tentative first installment of a serial. I did get away for Saturday and Sunday, but only to Easthampton. The Connecticut valley is an induction coil to all the heat in the east and the air was of a consistency that allowed it to cling to my car like a sponge.... Oh, sponges. A friend of Ted Morrison's fed one to a horse, on the theory that horses are too intelligent to eat them. He now pays the Angell Memorial a weekly sum to keep the horse, which contracts and expands with each drink.[115] . . . The woodchucks at the bottom of my garden are now reduced to one. He is the totem of the whole damn tribe and amuses himself twice a day by showing up my woodscraft. . . . A folk tale that will reach Woollcott eventually and always happened to your friend's friend[116] tells about the man who, in the woods, zippered himself into his sleeping bag when the rain came up and then couldn't un-zip the next morning and had to bump several miles downhill and across streams till he ended in a boy's camp. Jesus, I mean girls' camp. I've met the damn story in four different places in three different towns in the last fortnight. . . . A Dartmouth story that hasn't reached the *New Yorker* yet exhibits the young man, at the railroad station, unwinding himself from an intricate and prolonged embrace, then shaking the girl's hand and saying he certainly is glad to have met her. . . . I wish your guild would make up its mind about Orozco in the Dartmouth library.[117] Me, I humbly accept all your cheerleaders have been telling me about how nice it is to have the artist integrate the experience of his land, race, time and tradition, and still I don't see just how Mexican subjects and the gent's idiom fit in with the only really effective monumental bit of twentieth century Georgian in the whole damn world. . . . Hostels are swell, except those which seem to be bringing a youth movement to the Berkshires. I was ever a set-up for a piano like that, but something in me fiercely repudiates a field-stone fireplace, I know not why. Probably a hangover from the Brewer's Daughter. Do they speed the parting guest, at Graymoor, with the skin of wine that Zinsser attributes to a monastery on Mount Athos?[118] Have you, by the way, seen or heard about the wormholing at Avon Farms?[119] . . . Zinsser was recently in a seizure, denouncing my trash (see enc.) as keeping me from occupying what he described as my place in the culture of my times. Quite apart from the typically bacteriological nonsense, I get just a trifle fed up with gents like him, and Charlie Curtis, who from the eminence of an enormous trust fund are superior to the workingman. Hans had just bought an old circus horse so that his guests could come out with juleps in their hands and watch it play basketball, count its age and kiss the ladies. . . . The boys think that Pasteur's anti-rabies serum is shot to hell. If it is, what happens to bacteriology? . . . A Very Prominent Official was recently saved from a disgrace when a medic cured him of advanced drunkenness with an injection of apomorphine. . . . Are we all changing our phase? At this moment a wire from Frances Prentice imploring me to come to Stonington and tell her what's wrong with the half of a serial she has written. I'd heard nothing of a serial. Kitty Bowen, on the other hand, has forsaken the lowly and is doing a book about Tschaikowski.[120] . . . (It seems I understated the novels of our Mr. Fast. Two have been published, and there are twenty-two, not twelve, in ms; and he is twenty, not nineteen.) But my God the picture he sends us. One more footnote on the art of Gertrude Stein. . . . Proposed: to make a book out of John Hoyt. Vetoed. But the temptation was strong to carry out the project I'd always had to wish one of my Katherines on him and do that curious series of events that followed a performance of *Thais* at the Boston Opera House in the winter of 1916–17. For story purposes it would better be *Die* [*sic*] *Rosenkavalier*.[121] That was one story in which I needn't exhibit myself to you as the man who fell some distance short.... I also always wanted to do John Hoyt and a Harvard esthete who wrote poetry about Faustine. What this country needs is a magazine that will combine the *Post* and Uncle Billy's Whizzbang.[122]... But the *Post* has had a curious vindication. I once got the word "drawers" into it, whereas Ken Littauer has just told me I mustn't in *Collier's*. I wonder what they changed it to.

Yours,

Benny

Lincoln, Massachusetts

[19 July 1935]

Dear Kate:

Gyneco-thaumaturgical note, or Planck's principle of indeterminism:[123] the Deknatel baby, which was to be conceived next October, will be born on the 28th of next February, or rather since it is Leap Year, the 29th.

Analytical prophecy on which I nevertheless stake my reputation for tick-counting: Ginnie will now be racked to her dowel pins with a subliminal conflict, the issue of which will be can an infant bear an infant? She will presently solve this in the negative, give up her luxuriating in Oedipus guilt, and go noble. Woman's patient acceptance of her destiny is due for a new high.

Generalization: there are topics of conversation which can hold me from the chimney corner longer than obstetrics.

Random observation: millions of babies are born every year.

The new Harvard story isn't much but you have to have it in your files. I condense what is acted out with much mouthing, goggling and drooling. It has to do with the census-taker who gets to the far end of the farthest draw in the most remote of the Kentucky hills and finally succeeds in luring a sixteen year old imbecile to the door. A long interrogatory follows. Father? No, no father, he fell down a well. Mother? No, no mother—she ran off with a lightning-rod salesman. Sisters? No, no sisters. Brothers? Yes, one brother. Name? Ain't got no name but he's at Harvard. Harvard, for Christ's sake? Yeah, Harvard. What class is he in? Huh? What class is he in? Ain't in no class—in a bottle—two heads.

Unverified rumor has Archie MacLeish as the new head of the Harvard Press. Charlie Curtis was here last night but I hadn't heard the rumor and he said nothing about it, as I tend to think he would if there is much in it, for he's as fond of Archie as I am. Nothing could give me greater delight than to have Archie and Ada here, and I know that he's restive in the Fortune job (for which he was destined by Almighty God) on the ground that it takes too much of his time. At the same time, he isn't the man for the job that Ted Morrison would be. I simply can't sell Ted to the authorities. Charlie Curtis and others boomed me for the job when it fell vacant a year and a half ago but I killed the boom as soon as I heard of it and undertook to put Ted in. No go. Charlie thinks he hasn't got iron enough in him to fight the Syndics, which is the first job the new head must undertake, and Ken Murdock vehemently refuses to consider his quitting the faculty.[124] As a matter of fact Ted is one of the few men in my generation with a genuine talent for editing and has the fierce, instinctive loyalty that is the first qualification for these largely anonymous, altogether unhonored and absolutely indispensable and invaluable services in which Harvard University tends to specialize.... I think the job was offered, once, to Fred Allen. Most jobs of that sort are sooner or later, on just what grounds I don't know, for though he's a talented guy and one of the pleasantest people in the world I've never been able to see that, as an editor, he was anything but Lee Hartman's stand-in.

Editorial miscellany. Gorham Munson has resigned the editorship of "Controversy," why I know not, but it was always the world's lousiest idea anyhow. He has also sent me, in his capacity as an editor at Crowell, the galleys of Ted Morrison's new book for a blurb, thus putting me in a nice box.[125] I don't mind the blurb, any friend of mine can have a blurb from me any time, but Ted and I are, in literary tastes and practices, poles apart and he knows it as well as I do and he'll be uncomfortable if I blurb his poetry and I'll be uncomfortable knowing that he is.... Little-Brown's latest caper is to send me the ms. of a novel by a gent who was for twenty years a prison guard on Deer Island.[126] For advice, counsel and, it is suggested (by Scaife—Alfred and Jenkins, who know better, are both out of Boston) possible collaboration.[127] The gent is simply spilling over with good dope which he could make into swell articles if he could write swell, but imagine the novel.... But, well grounded in the Sermon on the Mount, I have, I am fairly sure, snared for them the manuscript of what ought to be the Pulitzer prize [for] history of 1936 and, whether or no, will certainly be the best history in the U.S. field since *The Rise of the Cities* [*sic*].[128] You will hear more of this. It is—badly—called "Reconciliation, North and South," is by Paul Buck, and is a honey.[129] ... The *Harper's* situation is still for your ears alone but can now be identified by name. For several years there has been vague talk of making me a monthly adjunct of the magazine. The original dope was to give me the Editor's Easy Chair when the long-senile Martin should die—it has been his only hold on life for practically forty years.[130] The situation began to bubble a couple of months ago, but in the meantime I had decided that Lee could get plenty of other people who could do that job better than I, whereas there was one job I could probably shine in. I therefore proposed that he put someone else in the Easy

Chair, preferably Mencken, and give me Harry Hansen's literary column, with leave to transform it from a bad and quite useless column of reviews and chit-chat to a revival of the once honorable practice of literary criticism. I was to treat one book a month, at great length, in relation to the writer's earlier work and to the literary currents of the time. The idea was greeted with salvos of applause, and I freely admit it's a good idea: both for *Harper's Magazine* and for the literary scene. The idea of a reviewer's knowing what he is talking about is almost as brilliant as it is revolutionary. And I still think that with Mencken in the Easy Chair, belching about the world in general and the New Deal in particular, and with me in the book column telling the boys that they're all wrong, we'd have something nice in family journals. A couple of weeks ago it looked as if that was going to happen right off. Since I wrote to you, however, something has broken—I can't make out what, Lee being the sort of bird who erases the drawings he makes in phone booths. Anyway, Mencken is out and it looks as if I'm offered the Easy Chair first, with some reluctant consent to my taking the literary column if I insist on that. He won't put it on paper or breathe it over copper, but I'm going down next week to consult with him and Canfield.[131] I still think that he could get better men for the Easy Chair but would be stumped if he tried to go Beyond DeVoto for the other, but I may be the successor of William Dean Howells when I come home, for I'd rather have that forum than no forum.[132] The fact that John Chamberlain will once more perceive my heirship is a serious drawback. On the other hand, a chance to correct John's political ideas as well as his literary ones is worth a big deposit in advance.

Which brings me, by an obscure nexus, to the only boast about my first novel you'll ever hear me make: say that it is style-less if you will, for it is, but by God it's not full of other men's styles. The matter was in my mind when I was reading the early Dos Passos, and now I've moved on to Faulkner. I turned him over to my assistant this spring on the very ground that I hadn't read those books but I want to talk about him next year. And he had written and published three novels before, in his fourth, he began to write like Faulkner.[133] That is, of course, subject to the perfectly understandable view that there are three Faulkners, one a Hemingway, one a Joyce, and one, God help us, a Dreiser. That is, if you're bilious, the formula of *The Sound and the Fury* entire and parts of the others. But the Faulkner-Faulkner, however compounded, is not visible in the first three books. A curious pastiche of a dozen styles, notably the Crane-Beer, the Fitzgerald, and the Hergesheimer.[134] I don't mean resemblances, I mean long, sustained applications of the sedulously aped. I don't know which of the three is the most surprising. On the whole, I guess, the Hergesheimer.... An amusing thing is the romantic nobility of two characters in "Soldier's Pay," who might have come from Maurice Hewlett or even Mary Pickford, who, I note, is about to be a novelist.[135] The same book has also the war-weariest characters outside of John Riddell's works, and the first adumbration of the ultimate Faulkner character, the man of Gargantuan and never identified evil.[136] He is named Januarius Jones.... I remember when the book came into the News-Index office. It was after Avis had taken over my page. Neither of us had ever heard of Faulkner, so she gave it to Ney McMinn, who, I remember, brought in a verdict that it was obscure.

Here is an essay on Faulkner which I will sometime publish in forty pages: the basic fact about him is a sick mysticism, far sicker than the type that knocked over Aubrey Beardsley and a lot of his friends.[137]

At that, I can't make out why the comrades regard him as decadent offal, whereas Erskine Caldwell sees through to the noble heart of the proletariat.

Coming back to Hemingway, don't you think that the Esquire letters have by now extracted all the humor there is composing arch euphemisms for the six monosyllables?

Add historians. Walter Webb, of the University of Texas, is lecturing at the Harvard Summer School.[138] His "The Great Plains" is one of the few original and permanent contributions to American history in twenty years. The gentle schoolmarms who compose the summer audience can't take him. He lectured for an hour on the cactus, the theory being that, never having seen the plant, they couldn't appreciate its importance in our culture. Then, half-way through a lecture on the importance of the Colt's revolver in the conquest of the West, he pulled out of his pants a horn-handled, seven and a half inch barrel Frontiersman model and waved it at the screaming class. I don't know whether he was emitting Rebel yells or the Comanche screech. He's coming out here to dinner Monday. Both the windmill and the prairie dog were also important in the era he treats but if he's moved to a demonstration I'd rather have him put on the technological feat I always considered folklore till satisfied by an overwhelming weight of documentary evidence that it was fact—grabbing a rattlesnake by the tail and snapping its head off.

We had quite a chapter meeting last week—I was chin-deep in historians gathered to welcome Dumas Malone, the editor of the D.A.B. An excessively handsome Virginian with an amusing, malicious mind. He alluded to a document I'd like to see, the Dictionary's blacklist—I did, gratefully, find out (purely by deduction) that J.T. Adams heads it—and had some hair-curling stories about sabotage, suits and social pressure by Christian Scientists, osteopaths, professional Southerners, the D.A.R., the Daughters of the Confederacy, etc.[139] Writing the biographies of the great Americans has its charm. It costs thirty-five thousand dollars to bring out a volume of the D.A.B. When all other resources failed, the Christian Science Church, through channels, offered to bring out Vol. VI all over again, with the Truth about Mother Eddy substituted for mortal error.[140] ... The Dean of American Historians is Worthington Ford. About a year ago I printed a short review of J.T. Adams's "Henry Adams" in the *New*

England Quarterly.[141] I did it with a crowbar for it was [a] lousy potboiling job, which was all right with me, except that Adams has time after time talked, in potboiling articles, about the vicious quality in American life that leads scholars and literary men to debase their integrity with potboilers once they have become eminent. Adams is the author of *The Epic of America* and even more vulgar jobs.[142] Well, I went after him dornicks[143] and creosote and the Adams audience rose up from Tia Juan [*sic*] to Bombay and called me a son of a bitch, and Worthington Ford sat down in London and foamed at me with a document that I thought of turning over to the Psychiatric Hospital for never have I seen such rabies in ink.[144] I felt, if anything, flattered—for after all he is the Dean. But, at this luncheon, Stewart Mitchell, the editor, said plaintively that Ford has sent him such a document every three weeks since the review.[145] So the science of history, which I have always respected, seems to be more properly classified under the heading of literature.

All this in weather that has probably made you fat and obscenely self-satisfied. It hasn't made me fat. It has taken lard off me till I look like Andy Gump.[146] I arrive up from Stonington at 2 A.M. Monday and even at that hour there was no pleasure in motoring. Sometime I must tell you about the Battle of New Bohemia. There was a spell of weather you would have enjoyed.

But who killed Eugene Fifield?[147] Was it Paula Traggas or Tommy Pierce? Or did he do the job himself? Or did Paula's husband avenge his own horns? You know quite as much about this as I do, but I'll have the answer within another week. All I know now is that he's going to be dead as hell at the end of installment five. And a good job, too, the bastard.

Yours,
Benny

Bowne

[BEFORE 25 JULY 1935]

Dear Benny,

As a matter of fact, the weather lifted me from 95 to 97 lbs., the first weight I've gained in a coon's age. The third chin now threatens, and the roll at the back of the neck. What I'd really like would be to be plump *comme un pigeon*.[148] Even to waddle a little.

Subject for Dissertation:—the Relation of Short Marital Separations (as College Art Association Annual Meetings, May 22, 23, 24, 25) to the Theory & Practice of Contraception in the American Home....

I am minded to send you a ms. of the "Ballad of Chambers Street."[149] Please let me know if you have it, as it is something of a chore to write out. On second thought, maybe better not.

Mary & I think it would be amusing for someone to manufacture fruit essences:[150] the lush perfume of peaches, the tang of apples so favored by farm novelists, the fragrance of grapes, the delicate scents of pineapples & melons, the fresh odor of raspberries, the spicy smell of kumquats... yes, we have no banana.[151]

There's a questionnaire on English & American letters on pp. 36-37 of the August *Vanity Fair* that has me gasping.[152] Out of fifty questions I answered eight, and four of these I'm not sure of. Not that I set up to know anything about English & American letters, but even so.

In the same mail with your Hardy animadversions came a letter from V. Whitehill who is gestating peacefully in Philadelphia.[153] Excerpt: "I'm rereading *Jude* & is it lousy![154] Tame & ridiculous. Does nothing survive except war & the pyramids?" Mr. HC seems to be voted out, but I still think *Tess* is a pretty good book.[155]... One of my father's earliest memories—which he will trot out on request, or even without it—is of Mrs. Fiske (who at that time was imitating Duse's style) as Tess, coming out the door & saying, "I've killed him," just as though she were saying that the milkman had forgotten to leave cream.[156]

Well, hell, that's pretty serious.

Yours,

Kate

[from *Vanity Fair*]

THE PERMANENT QUESTIONNAIRE

No man is living who can answer all of the questions on these two pages. There are fifty questions—each with a literary humdinger—, and the test is to see how many you can master by dint of much brain-wracking in the quiet of your August cabaña. All except one of the queries pertain to English or American literature, between 1600 and the present time. If one (or more) of them looks answer-proof, don't blame VANITY FAIR, because we didn't ask them. They were maliciously hatched by twenty-five distinguished writers, columnists, educators, and critics. When the dead and missing are counted, three prizes will be awarded: $50., in cash to the contestant who turns in the greatest number of correct answers; $25., as second prize; and a copy of VANITY FAIR's Portfolio of Modern French Art, as third prize. Contenders must have their answers in our hands no later than August 21st, next. The correct answers, as well as the names of the winners, will be announced in the October issue.

SINCLAIR LEWIS

1. Who was the first author to use the realistic-policemen-Hammett type of detective, in contrast to the Poe-Doyle school of amateur detectives?
2. What is the most popular literary work of Theodore Dreiser?

Damon Runyon

3. What American baseball reporter wrote a poem which had nothing to do with sport, but is one of the best-known pieces of verse in the English language and is almost rated as a classic?
4. What English poet was patron, pal, and pupil of a famous heavyweight fighter of his time, and mentions his boxing lessons in his works?

Edmund Pearson

5. Which two heroines of English literature suffered death by hanging?
6. What is the name of the English authoress of whom it can be said: her parents were literary people; her husband was an illustrious author; she took part in a celebrated elopement; her fame rests on one novel—her first; she once had a mild flirtation with a celebrated New York author; and her work, after more than a century, is still, in this present year, inspiring Hollywood?

Joseph Hergesheimer

7. What two heroic legends of the Civil War, celebrated in American verse and history were actually inglorious?
8. What minor poet was employed by the United States government to cover the attack of a new deal on Federal sanctity?

H. L. Mencken

9. To the funeral of which American metaphysician did the Elks of Boston send a floral piece in the form of a book four feet high, made of carnations, daisies and tea-roses?
10. Which eminent American poet is buried in the red-light district of a great American city?

Aldous Huxley

11. What American poet wrote: "You are the living cuspidors of day"?
12. What Poet Laureate of England translated into heroic couplets a Latin poem on venereal disease?

Carl Van Doren

13. What episode of what famous American novel is a backwoods version of the story of *Romeo and Juliet*?
14. Who wrote the novel and who the play about Serena Blandish?

John Van Druten

15. What happened to Barnes' Gander and when?
16. Who, upon hearing someone say that he was a member of the Church of England, asked what the subscription was?

Manuel Komroff

17. What was the source of Hearn's first name, Lafcadio?

18. A great many books have been written about Napoleon, but how many would you imagine?

HENRY SEIDEL CANBY

19. What great American writer liked pie for breakfast?
20. What great American war story was written by a man who had never seen a battle?

HARRY HANSEN

21. In what book and in what year did Sherlock Holmes arrive on the scene?
22. What famous story by an English author was used as a theme for an orchestral suite by a living American composer?

CLIFTON FADIMAN

23. What have the following literary figures in common: Stirling, Simple, Grimm, Bell, Whiffle, Paltock, Fleming, Wimsey, Quince, Belloc, and Rabbit?
24. Name two authors, both of whom wrote *The City of Dreadful Night*.

GEORGE JEAN NATHAN

25. Who wrote the *Belle of Bowling Green*?
26. What American writer was arrested as a spy during the early days of the late War and lodged briefly in the hoosegow because he had been seen lounging-about a mile and a half from an Atlantic seaboard light-house?

WILLIAM LYON PHELPS

27. What American historian is buried in the Protestant Cemetery in Florence, Italy?
28. Where did the late William De Morgan obtain the title for his novel, *Somehow Good*?

BOOTH TARKINGTON

29. In what book by what American writer is a "solitary oesophagus" seen floating high in the air?
30. In what American book is a slave fattened for use as an ottoman?

EDMUND WILSON

31. What extremely improper scene did Shakespeare write in French?
32. What famous quotations, from one of Shakespeare's plays, are really interpolations by someone else?

STARK YOUNG

33. What celebrated author was said by the wife of what author to be always within sound of her dinner bell?
34. What famous author complicated his financial budget through the urge he felt to dig for buried treasure?

CHARLES HANSON TOWNE

35. What American literary society expelled a member for his alleged pro-German sympathies during the World War, and what was the member's name?

36. What magazine, in 1915, made certain editorial changes in the last installment of what American author's serial, and was forced by the author to print, in the following issue, his own version of the manuscript?

Charles T. Copeland

37. Truth resides in the statement, which I quote from memory: "A little dinner, not more than the Muses, with all the guests clever and some of them pretty, offers human life and human nature under very favorable circumstances." Who first made the statement?

38. What celebrated English poet and letter-writer wrote the story of *The Three Bears* commonly placed among the anonymous classics of the nursery?

John Erskine

39. How many days before the Battle of Lexington did Paul Revere really make his famous ride?

40. Who gave Longfellow the plot of *Evangeline*?

Robert Cantwell

41. From what religious writer did Stephen Dedalus quote—without giving proper credit—when he characterized Shakespeare's London life: "Twenty years he dallied there between conjugal love and its chaste delights and scortatory love and its foul pleasures"?

42. Who was the first American novelist to try a sympathetic portrait of a revolutionary terrorist?

Corey Ford

43. Who said that who was only a part of whose dream, and if he woke up "you'd go out—bang!—just like a candle!"

44. Who put salt in her tea and what did the lady from Philadelphia do to help her out of her difficulties?

S. S. Van Dine

45. Of what American detective novel was a "memorial" edition published—fifty-six years after its initial appearance—during the author's lifetime?

46. And who (solemnly believing the publisher's report that the author was dead) wrote the introduction to this "memorial" edition?

Tess Slesinger

47. Who wrote *The Portrait of the Artist as an American*?

48. What great American short-story writer went to Mexico, disappeared, and was never heard of again?

John Held, Junior

49. What author was a prize-fighter in Galveston, Texas, known as "Nig"?

50. What author used a pair of strange spectacles in order to translate part of a famous book?

[*Vanity Fair*, 43/12, August 1935, pp. 36–37]
Answers to the Great Vanity Fair Questionnaire

• Here, on this page, are the long-awaited answers to VANITY FAIR's *Permanent Literary Questionnaire*, which has broken the hearts and destroyed the homes of many Americans during the past two months. Most of our foremost citizens—editors, bankers, publishers, and housewives—gave up their summer for this inquisition, and have now been put away for the fall.

We print the answers exactly as we got them from the renowned writers who hatched them originally. [. . .] Fidelity to *these* answers is all that counted in the final reckoning; but even so, the judges have left town. [. . .]

The Editor himself was able to answer only six of the queries. And the winner, after weeks of research, mastered not many more than two-thirds of them. But the difficulty of the questions has not kept this from being the most successful questionnaire in Vanity Fair's history. And now we are happy to announce that the three *Croix de Questionnaire*—$50, $25, and a copy of Vanity Fair's *Portfolio of Modern French Art*—go, respectively and with everlasting acclaim, to:

THE WINNERS
David A. Randall, New York City, First Prize
Manter Q. Hall, Cambridge, Mass., Second Prize
Betsy M. Fleet, Richmond, Virginia, Third Prize

[the answers:]

1. Charles Dickens, with Inspector Bucket, in *Bleak House*.
2. His lyric for the song, "The Banks of the Wabash."
3. "Denver" Langdon Smith, who wrote *Evolution*.
4. Lord Byron, who mentions, in the 11th Canto of Don Juan, "My friend and corporeal pastor and master, John Jackson, Esquire, Professor of Pugilism . . ."
5. Cordelia in *King Lear* and *Tess of the d'Urbervilles*.
6. Mary Godwin, daughter of William Godwin and Mary Wollstonecraft; wife of Shelley, with whom she eloped; she had a tender friendship, when a young widow, with Washington Irving; and she was the author of *Frankenstein*.
7. Sheridan's Ride and Pickett's Charge.
8. Philip Freneau.
9. Ralph Waldo Emerson.

10. Edgar Allan Poe, in Baltimore.
11. Maxwell Bodenheim.
12. Nahum Tate, who translated Fracastoro's poem, "Syphilis, sive morbi Gallici."
13. The Shepherdson-Grangerford feud in *Huckleberry Finn*.
14. Enid Bagnold and S. N. Behrman.
15. "When we lived at Henley, Barnes' gander was stole by tinkers," said Mrs. F.'s aunt in "Little Dorrit." [by Dickens, 1857]
16. Dolly Clandon, in Act II of *You Never Can Tell*. [by Shaw, 1896]
17. Lafcadio comes from Leucadia (pronounced Lefcadia), which is the name of the Greek-Ionian island where he was born.
18. A bibliography by F. M. Kircheisen (1911) lists 100,000 titles. It is by no means complete, and since then, many more thousands have appeared.
19. Ralph Waldo Emerson.
20. Stephen Crane's "The Red Badge of Courage."
21. *A Study in Scarlet*, 1887.
22. *Through the Looking Glass*, by Lewis Carroll, for Deems Taylor's *Through the Looking Glass*.
23. The name Peter.
24. James Thomson and Rudyard Kipling.
25. Amelia Barr.
26. Eugene O'Neill.
27. Richard Hildreth.
28. Tennyson's "In Memoriam," stanza LIV.
29. In Mark Twain's *A Double-Barreled Detective Story*.
30. In Herman Melville's *Moby Dick*.
31. *Henry V*, Act III, scene iv.
32. "Off with his head! So much for Buckingham!", and "Richard is himself again!", in the last act of *Richard III*—lines which Colley Cibber wrote into his acting version of the play.
33. Mrs. Emerson said this of Thoreau.
34. O. Henry.
35. The Poetry Society of America; George Sylvester Viereck.
36. *Everybody's Magazine*; Owen Johnson's "Making Money."
37. Disraeli in Coningsby.
38. Robert Southey.
39. The Battle of Lexington happened on a Wednesday morning, and Paul Revere rode through all the towns on the preceding Sunday, warned them, and promised to ride out Tuesday night to say whether the British were coming by river or by

road. He had advance information, but, unluckily, so had the British, and when he started on the Tuesday ride he was promptly arrested. He got to Lexington on foot after the battle was over. He told all this in a letter which ought to be famous. It is published in *Old South Leaflets*.

40. Nathaniel Hawthorne. The plot is published in Hawthorne's *Notebooks*.
41. Swedenborg, who wrote, "Deliciae sapientiae de amore conjugiali; voluptates insaniae de amore scortatorio."
42. Henry James.
43. Tweedledee said Alice was part of the Red King's dream, in *Through the Looking Glass*. Tweedledum said that if he woke up, Alice would go out like a candle.
44. Mrs. Peterkin of *The Peterkin Papers* [by Lucretia Hale, 1880]. The lady from Philadelphia suggested that she pour herself a new cup of tea. (The hard part about this question is that it was not tea, but coffee.—The Eds.)
45. *The Leavenworth Case*, by Anna Katharine Green.
46. S. S. Van Dine.
47. Matthew Josephson.
48. Ambrose Bierce.
49. Roark Bradford.
50. Joseph Smith. The spectacles were the Urim and Thummim. The famous book: The Book of Mormon.

[*Vanity Fair*, October 1935, pp. 54–62. A total of 103 names were listed, KS's among them, of those who answered 40 percent or more correctly. The editor of these letters, without looking anything up, answered six correctly.]

Lincoln, Massachusetts

[1 August 1935]

Dear Kate:

God knows what I'll do when they tear down the Murray Hill. It's half way between Curtis Brown & Harper's, and I'm a Harper's editor now.[157] Beginning with the November or December issue I run the Easy Chair in succession to Mr. Martin, Henry Mills Alden, Wm Dean Howells, George Wm Curtis and what have you.[158] This isn't under a release yet—I had to leave too fast to find out when they'll announce it. One reason, of several, for the speed: a wine-tasting party by Frank Schoon~~over~~maker of some hours before caught up with me.[159] But what wines! He's opening a business on damned sound principles. It will be in the press.

So I got another job and it takes hard thinking to locate one I haven't got. Well, in this mail go notifications to Canby & Ted Weeks that this time I mean it, no more reviews in any circumstances whatever. And tomorrow I go in and tell Alfred McIntyre, who is back, that the perfect friendship which can't be sullied by any low commercialism in the way of reader's fees can't even be sullied by reading any more. Never, never, never. But the last one, Paul Buck's ms., was a honey. If they don't take it they're just crazy. I've drawn up a two-page report on the theory & practice of the footnote and offered to straighten out some sentences. A book, an important book even. And just how many important books are there?

So in two weeks I've got to write one and revise three serial installments, in order to get off to Bread Loaf. Then I send in the four of them and if they like it I get a contract & advance, finish the damn thing by Oct 15, and give up hack writing for at least two years. If they don't like it, God help us all.

By God your home town was like the mud room at Utah Hot Springs. If the wind doesn't change before long I'll be just an item in the quincennial [*sic*] catalogue & you'll be incorporated at 25¢ a look in a side show. How's to make this weight change efficient. If you can canalize the solid flesh I melt away while serializing in a south wind you won't have any metabolical apprehension thereafter.[160] Even my kid sees I'm thin.

So what shall I write about in the Easy Chair?

Yours

Benny

Bread Loaf Inn
Bread Loaf, Vermont

[17 AUGUST 1935]

Dear Kate:

1. Inspector Bucket—*Bleak House*[161]

2. "The Banks of the Wabash"[162]

The second, I think, is really good. Red is a moral guy. He wouldn't tell me till I swore an oath not to compete for money.

Inc. on your hunch, thus vindicating the inquiring mind.

Lewis has just finished a novel called *It Never Could Happen Here*.[163] Fascist America 1936–7–8. Sounds godawful to me but Red is enormously steamed up over it. So is Dorothy, which makes me even more dubious. No doubt she's responsible for the book. He mentioned one rather good jape: a vegetarian hot dog.

Things I never knew till Red told me: Robert Forsythe of the *New Masses* is Kyle Crichton of *Collier's*.[164]

The Green Mts are hot as hell's furnace door but infinitely silent—away from this dog-fight.

Random observation: Robert Frost is not only the best poet of all U. S. lit, he is also the swellest gent that walks the earth.[165]

Would you know Hart Crane's limerick about Edna Millay?[166]

Yours,

Benny

Lincoln, Massachusetts

[3 SEPTEMBER 1935]

Dear Kate:

Now in September I can see the holes in our Conference. A good time: not so gay as last year but a little more congenial and lots drunkener. At the moment I've postponed my motor trip in order to be a newspaperman for a while, and I take back some of the harder things I've said about my past, for it seems I'm a pretty good one. If I could have had the handling of this story when it was news it would have rated more than the ed-3 it got in the *Herald-Tribune* last November. I spent a couple of days in interior New Hampshire digging it out and I'm going back tomorrow to get the last interviews, then back here and make the first Easy Chair out of it.[167] It makes a nice launching party for my new venture but in a way I'm sorry to use it in that restricted space, for it's a honey and worth a lot of display type and at least 7 thousand words of thoughtful feature writing. It's the story of how the town of Alexandria, New Hampshire, got its back up and declined to be adjudged sub-marginal, shifted out and resettled, and lent money for the more abundant life elsewhere. I've had an absorbing and really stirring time. It's something to be told, in a bleak farm kitchen, eight miles beyond Hellandgone, by a woman who has come straight from milling flour in a hand-mill: "As one of those old fellers said, eternal vigilance is the price of liberty."[168] It's something to hear two philosophies summarized in one sentence: "We don't want to let them put us on relief so we can buy their radios." And, I promise you, it's something to hear the measured judgment of a Yankee grandma: "All these fields need is more manure and a little loving." Free text for anyone who wants to write a Pulitzer Prize editorial, representing a feeling I've vividly experienced: America is not more than ten minutes' drive away.[169]

Well, the Conference. We sorely missed Frances Prentice and Kitty Bowen—except for Shirley Barker and Isabel Wilder this year's Fellows were godawful busts, and the literary aspect of the place depends on the Fellows.[170] One of them, the Sokoloff girl, didn't show up at all: diagnosis, temperament. I may have confided my foreboding when Ted overrode me and appointed a young genius who had written some sixteen novels by the age of twenty and, if that wasn't enough, was recommended by both Gertrude Stein and the *New Republic*. He was even worse than was to be assumed. A dreadful fog of last generation's Village notions, he announced the first evening that as for him, he wrote for Immortality, and thereafter he did nothing but take the staff women and wives aside, separately, and describe his unhappy childhood and his suffering as an artist. He addressed no word to any man, except to tell me, when he saw me swimming, that he hadn't supposed I was man enough. (There was also something about the Holy Body. His, he meant.) After some five days he suddenly announced that we had wounded him, and took a bus home. I don't know whether this was cumulative or overt. When it came Helen Everitt's turn to take that psychic stroll, she told him for God's sake to stop trying to crawl back into the womb. Or it may be that, when he showed signs of forsaking the staff for the customers and sidled up to a pretty little sorority blonde, one of the commercials took a poke at him. I hope so. There was also a poet from Chicago, one Stallman, who came recommended by Harriet Monroe.[171] Is it enough to say that, because of him, Vicky Lincoln's psychoses attracted no attention whatever?[172]

The staff was, both humanly and professionally, the best that Ted has so far assembled. The mere omission of Walter Eaton humanized it, and John Mason Brown, who took his place, was swell, I'd never met him before—a gay and witty young man who puts on a fine show and drinks like the old issue.[173] George Stevens helped a good deal, it was pleasant to have both the Everitts on hand, and Vicky Lincoln, besides captivating the customers, filled my clinical notebook with material it will take months to digest.[174] Not many visiting firemen this year. Red and Dorothy went to England instead, Steve Benét pulled a Joseph Wood Krutch on us, Carl Carmer was hastily voted down as a substitute, and only Gilbert Seldes really pitched.[175] He pitched okay. Best story: Norma Shearer, overwhelmed by the wedding present of her bridesmaid, Marion Davies, fondling the foot-wide strap of diamonds, pearls, emeralds, etc., "Marion, I'm speechless, I don't know what to say, you make me feel like a kept woman."[176] He had a dozen Sam Goldwyn stories but I never can remember Sam Goldwyn stories.[177] ... This was produced by my earth-shaking psycho-analytical lecture on Fantasy as the Genesis of Fiction. Gorham Munson got [to] telling about a gent who consulted an analyst in regard to his unhappy tendency to premature ejaculation. He was told that he was too single-minded, that he concentrated too much on his pleasures, and advised to divide his attention by keeping in mind any impersonal, trivial, accustomed thing that might occur to him. Greatly encouraged, he hurried out to apply the teaching, only to find his old trouble overtaking him. "Darling," he whispers frantically, "think of that old rain barrel outside the window, the one with the hoops—Whoops!" Well, neither do I, but few of the anecdotes we heard were up to it.... Gorham put on one of the most awe-inspiring shows I've ever witnessed. He thought that I had been announced to deliver the evening lecture whereas he had been. At six-forty-five, when it was borne in on him that he was to talk, he couldn't say three words consecutively. At seven-thirty he mounted the rostrum and began to come together like a jigsaw puzzle in a Mickey Mouse movie. The customers were absolutely ignorant of his condition and never did get a hint, whereas the first half-hour nearly annihilated the staff with vicarious suffering. Except for difficulty with words like "corroborate"—whereat Gorham would pause and smile with a sort of beatific apology—he sailed through all the intricacies of *The Artist and the Social Revolution* with yards of open water on each side. It was magnificent.

Gladys Hasty Carroll is just what you would suppose.[178] She thinks just the way she writes. But for all her Christian sweetness, and for all that pair of elegant pins, she's feline if I know cats. There'll be indrawn breaths at South Berwick, especially about Gorham and Ray Everitt and me, the drinkingest of the lot. But Julia Peterkin, I insist, is a fine art. She says absolutely nothing but, year by year, she's the only one who gives the customers what they come there for—inspiration. Beside any hour of Julia any DeMille spectacle is just impromptu.[179] . . . Vicky Lincoln is plain cuckoo, and if she does go to Hollywood, she'll make millions. Her mind works that way. This is the first time I've ever spent more than a few hours in her vicinity. Hitherto when she's confessed herself manic-depressive I've written off at least forty percent of it as a good joke. But it isn't; it's the only triumph of understatement Vicky will ever achieve. She's the only existent challenge to my mother-in-law for non-consecutiveness.

The customers were, mostly, as always. The place is just a function of the menopause. (Which seems a pity, for no university in the country could put on as intelligent a selection of lectures on literature as we did this year.) This year we didn't even get the five or six semi-professionals who can be developed that we usually get. The stuff they submitted in ms was godawful. About forty-five grandmothers, about fifteen schoolteachers (including one Miss Hamilton who now becomes the reason why I can't send my daughter to Wellesley), and about ten plain neurotes but young.

There was one thoroughly sound wench, as lovely a sight as these eyes have ever gazed upon. Would you know an Eleanor Van Alen of Roslyn?[180] My God, she's beautiful. She was there, I gather, because Jimmy, a hefty husband who plays court tennis and polo and once captained the Cambridge tennis team, has put some money into the *North American Review*, and she wants to influence its policy.[181] Christ, she doesn't need to study writing to influence it.

A couple of cases definitely over the line. A most youthful father and a daughter of some nineteen or twenty years with queer eyes, who were never out of each other's arms and kissed each other with a passion that, on the first day, had us thinking that at last we'd bought some honeymooners. Then there was a Lesbian lady of about thirty, a rejoined expatriate, with Left Bank clothes and ways. Gaunt, rapt, given to ecstasies; hair to her shoulders, bare feet, stained toenails, soft sandals, white serge trousers. And an act. It pleased her to tell us that she had starved for weeks to put aside the tuition, whereas the one dress she exhibited must have cost twice what we charged her. She had to have her ms. read word by word to her, and by us all. Most customers got half an hour: she wanted three hours from each of us. When Helen Everitt dismissed her at the end of three hours she burst into tears, wailing, "I go without my meals to come here, and then I have to see you knocking balls around a tennis court."[182] But she was making passes at Helen. Also at Avis. And she was heard threatening to beat down a door if one of the few personable girls in the Inn didn't kick through. Ted didn't quite know what to make of her; he'd just read about these things in a book. She also told me, after my farewell talk (an institution: I'm the one who tells them they can't be taught to write) that she'd starved in order to come here and look, how could I bear to say such depressing things. I told her if she was damned fool enough to go without her meals she ought to go to a sanitarium, not a writer's conference, so she cried some for me too.

The wives, mostly there for the first time, stymied the principal diversion of the customers, which has hitherto been deciding who was sleeping with who. Last year I was popularly awarded Frances Prentice, her bitterest enemy, and one of the Middlebury girls who waited on table, but that wasn't a patch on the year when Peggy Widdemer was observed emerging from my room, but was not seen to be carrying a bottle of citrate of magnesia.[183] This year there was quite a flutter when a whole veranda-full of customers saw a window emit first a bottle of whiskey, then Julia Peterkin's leg, then Julia, then a man...It was only that Mr. Fast, the Stein genius, had just knocked on Julia's door.[184]

Well, we drank a lot of gin (something over three cases) and a lot of whisky, and sang a lot of songs. One horse-faced pulp-writer from what she called Deetroit informed me that I was a disappointment as a teacher, as a writer and as a man, though just how the last she didn't make clear. Ray Everitt's new game consisted of finding out just what the country needed for five cents. Allene Corliss, our one great alumna and a swell girl, confessed she had made thirty thousand dollars between October and May and, getting tight, begged us all never to write serials and spoil her racket.[185] One of the ms submitted to John Brown was a play about the germs and the bits of food not brushed away from the teeth. Shirley Barker's new volume of verse is damned good.[186] Ted Morrison hung up a conference record, by reading from his own verse for two hours and twenty minutes. John Crowe Ransom decided that everything he'd ever heard about the North was a lie, and decided it more vehemently with every drink.[187] And I have not yet, after four sessions, learned to play poker when a baby-faced grandma with white hair and a corset asks me, Mr. DeVoto, <u>must</u> I write about Young Love?

And so to the Granville Mfg Co, where Avis once more filled the car with wooden bowls, and on to Perry Miller and André Morize in New Hampshire, and the Alexandria story.[188] Mr. Martin has now been told, so I gather it's no longer a secret I'm to run the Easy Chair. And this morning Mr. Spivak of the *Mercury* writes asking if I want a magazine connection.[189] If it's Laurence Stallings' job I'm going to be just a little sore, for what I really wanted was to be a Critic, not a Thinker.[190] At Bread Loaf we never did decide whether the hundred thousand dollars Stallings gets for going to Abyssinia is big pay or cut-rate.... Elinor Glyn wasn't on my mind.[191] I can't make out what was—but I was at Bread Loaf, dear, and can't be held accountable. I think that Nancy Cunard died in 1932, but I wouldn't know.[192] She's just an item in Harold Cook's* stories so far as I'm concerned. But it's an open secret that she was Brett and the others, except for that nebulous other entry that I thought I remembered. Some British photographer made a magnificent study of her some ten years ago. It ran through the salons.

As of last Wednesday Frank Simonds promises me (a) it will be confined to Italy and Abyssinia, (b) unless Hitler begins the Anschluss—oh, hell, you spell it—which isn't likely for at least two more years, and in any case (c) the U.S. will keep out.[193]

Why is there a monument to Gen. Thomas in Rochester, Vermont?[194]

Back to New Hampshire. That done and the story written, I am going to the battlefields and the Hill Cumorah. I saw the prophet's birthplace on my way to Red Lewis's. This seems to be the year when the angel of the Lord is letting me by.

Latest rumor for the Harvard Press: Dumas Malone.[195] Most appalling item in the literary gossip: Johnny Farrar is writing a play. Weighty thought: Hervey Allen is writing two novels—one U.S., 1840, in the DeVoto preserve, the other Roman Britain.

* announced: a book by him on Edna Millay.[196] Clearly not autobiographical.

Yours,

Benny

[picture postcard: The mountains round about Peacham]

PEACHAM, VT.,
12 SEPTEMBER 1935

Pleased to report the Republic still lives.

DV

Lincoln, Massachusetts

[7 OCTOBER 1935]

Dear Kate:

My father died a week ago yesterday. It has been many years since we had much in common and he had been so ill for so long that the kindest thing to wish him was the easy and comparatively quick end he had—I can't say that I was grieved. At the same time, no one loses a father without a shock.

This for the Freudian—although you never said whether you'd read the *Introductory Lectures*: I have been much interested in watching Bunny's reactions. Happily, my father died at night, while Bunny was asleep, and the nurse and the body were out of the house before he woke up. We told him merely that Grampa was dead and, since he had some childish acquaintance with the phenomenon, said nothing more except a couple of generalizations to the effect that it was good for Grampa to have a long rest, since he was very old and very sick. He accepted it as a matter of fact without much interest. A week ago today, Sunday, I took him over to Concord in the afternoon for a release from the discipline he had been under and was called back to sign some of the certificates, etc. Bunny demanded to know why we had to go back so soon and I told him that Mr. Reed was at the house and wanted to talk to me, explaining that Mr. Reed was the man who had come and taken Grampa away when he died. The first time Bunny recurred to the subject was a couple of days later, when he said "Now I can make all the noise I want—Grampa's dead." That may all be on the surface, the necessary reaction of a child who had been shushed pretty consistently for a couple of weeks—or it may be much deeper. A day or so after that, though, he suddenly stopped some game he was playing and said to me, "What did Mr. Reed give Grampa to eat when he died?" The idea of poison is at the very core of infantile sex, and in fact the association of food, death and begetting is so intricate and so fundamental that folklore, and the sacraments, bristles with it from the other side of history. And last night when he got up to go to the can he said, only twenty percent awake, "What is poison water?" and, a moment later, burst into tears and ordered me out of the bathroom. He has also referred to me as an old man oftener in the last week than in all the rest of his talking life put together.... What made the first question the more striking was the fact that, in my own irrational moments, I had found myself full of remorse, believing that the drugs given my father had killed him. And, the second night after he died, I had the most vivid dreams full of the most unmistakable symbols of intercourse.

The jazz age, diminuendo. Don't I recall summarizing the career of Theodora, six foot daughter of a bankrupt Lee-Higginson partner, poet, child of the inflation, mad presser with joyous feet of all the grapes the Twenties offered in America? When I did, she had sold her Wianno house and was off to Europe with her second husband, an amiable alcoholic weak as water whom she had married after living with him for a year or so in selective succession to a miscellany the most outrageous. Well, Theodora is back. She shed her husband in Munich, thereby fulfilling all the prophecies of all her friends, and thereafter passed through a period of hysterics and depression that duplicated her condition following the severance from her first husband. At the end she achieved the only plan of action she has ever been known to pursue. Since the middle of August she has been up in Pinkham Notch, flattening her stomach muscles on the trails, acting as impromptu cook, hostess or mechanic in A.M.C. huts, and writing poetry.[197] She is in Boston now to abandon her Beacon St. house to the bank and the Commonwealth, store a few antiques which no conversion can induce a Bostonian to abandon, outfit her child with parkas and hobnails, and close out everything. In a couple of weeks she goes back to the Notch to live in a hut, continue her activities there, and write poetry. And that she proposes to do for the rest of time. And by God I think she'll do it. It's the queerest form of flight I've ever happened upon, but I think 'twill serve[198] and God!, how the blessed age of Hardingand Coolidge fades in the west.[199]

Preparations are under way to equip Boston with a psycho-analytical clinic, but under whose auspices, Harvard Medic or the Mass Gen is still a little obscure. It will be a fine way of keeping up to date. Already from the gathering analysts, I have gleaned two pleasant items. One that the Kyle Crichton fear of revolution which I alluded to recently has become, these last years, so common in the milder paranoid conditions as to be practically diagnostic. The other I should have guessed but didn't: that the castration linkages are showing themselves in dreams as Ethiopian symbols or, at the next remove, Pullman porters.

I face the hard job of telling a very pleasant woman that I won't finish and revise her son's novel. I'm going to plead antipathy of style which would require me to force it altogether out of its shape. But the truth is that it's a poor job. Written throughout with the ecstatic lushness of musicians (I suppose I should have foreseen that, but I always think maybe they'll write better than they ever do), intolerably romantic and idealistic in the worst senses of both terms, full of highfalutin motives I've never seen in human beings and characters I couldn't take even if drunk, and so inflated as to be altogether out of my line. Neither the emotions nor the action would have made up to more than five pages of S.G., and young Mr. Hutchinson blows them up to nearly five hundred pages. It's the first, and will be the last, proposal ever to get this far.

In the living room Born and some chorus are singing some arted-up version of All Through the Night.[200] Not even artiness can make that anything less than a very great song, but it needs a contralto. On a good many occasions it has shaken me loose from all my pride and vainglory. If I had ever worked the Jessie theme into that autobiography…For some time I've been meaning to ask you why, when you're passing out cordons, you don't confer one on Andre Kostalanetz's (sp?) orchestra.[201]

I had no chance to get to the new Deems Taylor, but I did manage to catch a performance of *Jubilee*.[202] It goes, if not quite so well as your venturesome pals made out when they came up to look at it, a damn sight better than the Bea Lillie show and with a better chance to last the winter out on Broadway.[203] Nobody in it is superlative but they're all good enough and the long first act is gay and light and fast—the second half drags pretty badly and is only saved by some amusing routines. The dancing is better throughout than I've seen for quite a while, June Knight is pretty and, surprisingly, pretty good, and the sets can only be described as spectacular.[204] My suspicion that another Ziegfeld age is upon us are heightened.

Report on what looks like a promising and cockeyed year at Harvard, on Lucius Beebe's book, and on seasonal wear in literature will follow in due time.[205]

Yours,
Benny

Lincoln, Massachusetts

[21 OCTOBER 1935]

Dear Kate:

Sure you will, and the event will make Mt. Sinai seem almost sweet. Good luck to you, my dear: luck is all you need, you've got the guts, the malice, and the morale they make men and women out of sometimes—but only sometimes. Do you realize that, by ink & a shared exasperation, we've become damned good friends? Well, as before, have someone tell me when the last ether-pocket is far enough behind you so that you can face more of these witless reports of mine with only a normal risk of retching. Since I can't shake your hand, to hell with it: I'm damned fond of you, Kate, and I wish I was sitting outside your door.

Yours,
Benny

Lincoln, Massachusetts

[26 NOVEMBER 1935]

Dear Kate:

I expect to get an evening before I leave & so cleanse my stuff'd bosom.[206] If I don't here's the dope:

Dec. 3 & 4, Palmer House, Chicago

Dec. 5 & 6, Hotel Tiger (sic), Columbia, Mo.

Dec. 7, 8 & 9, J. Lesser Goldman, 386 North Euclid, St. Louis

Dec. 10 & 11, Robert F. Almy, 126 West High St., Oxford, Ohio

I may stay another day with Bob Almy but in any event I'll be home by the 14th, with nothing to do before the 30th except read two sets of fortnightly masterpieces by Harvard boys, revise & replot the whole course in Am Lit Since I Can Remember, read proof on S S, & write a learned paper called Mark Twain & the Limits of Criticism to be torn apart at Cincinnati on New Year's Day.[207] Oh yes, I will—another Easy Chair.

Well, the damndest things: I come home from the Yale game & find the managing editor of a celebrated magazine at my house—& sober—& he thereupon, on behalf of himself, the publisher & the national culture, offers me the editorship thereof.[208] How far the *Harvard Graduates' Magazine* shines in a naughty world.

Also Alfred McIntyre has decided to bring out next fall a collection of my magazine articles.[209]

He has S S at this moment, having demanded a reading. He'll mail it to you Tuesday or Wednesday.... Christ, it's lousy. It's so lousy that *Collier's* threaten to circus it. If some of these bastards now clamorous for my personal charm & dignity had made me offers say last June, when any maidenhead of mine could have been had for a nickel, & that mortgaged, I wouldn't have had to write the damn thing.

But at any rate the magazine offer is going to have its chance to give George D. Birkhoff, Acting Dean of the Faculty, his chance to sweat or shut up.[210] I've already refused it but there's no reason why George should know that, with the budget for next year still unsettled.

No, youth is over. I left a Yale game half way through the 3rd quarter. And, II A[(a)], I had only a cocktail & half a bottle of Chambertin that night.

I had a newspaper story for you but it seems to have taken wings. Bunny, probably. But there was a *Bertha the Sewing Machine Girl* ending in Lincoln during the week.[211] I'll do it myself if I can't find the clipping.

Yours,

Benny

NOTES

1. KS offered two nominations, by Steele and Singmaster, for "the most nauseating short story of 1935."
2. By Thornton Wilder (1897–1975), 1935. Wilder was three times a winner of the Pulitzer Prize, notably for the eternally popular play *Our Town* (1938) as well as for *The Skin of Our Teeth* (1942), a less successful play that BDV admired.
3. *Joshua Todd*, published 1933.
4. William (Will) Oursler (1913–1985), Harvard '37.
5. (French, freely) old hat. Reference to T.S. Eliot (1888–1965), Harvard '09, A.M. '10, American-born British poet, critic, and essayist; *The Waste Land*, 1922; *The Hollow Men*, 1925; *Ash Wednesday*, 1930; Nobel Prize, 1948. Reference to Giovanni Battista Vico (1668–1744), Italian philosopher of history. *Work in Progress* was the working title of James Joyce's last novel, composed 1922–1938 and published in various segments before its first complete appearance in 1939 as *Finnegans Wake*.
6. The Boston *Record*, a tabloid, later merged with the *American*, which in turn was absorbed by the Boston *Herald*.
7. Hans Zinsser (1878–1940), professor of bacteriology, Harvard Medical School, and a close friend of BDV; *Rats, Lice and History*, 1935, about typhus, and a memoir, *As I Remember Him*, 1940, in which BDV appears. See BDV's letter to him in *LBDV*, pp. 331–35.
8. Ferry (1891–1970), professor of biochemistry and master of John Winthrop House.

9. (1869–1947), attorney, professor at the Harvard Law School.
10. James Michael Curley (1874–1958), congressman (1910–1914, 1943–1945), mayor of Boston (1914–1918, 1922–1926, 1930–1934, 1945–1949), governor of Massachusetts (1935–1939), the brilliant, colorful, and controversial architect of Irish Catholic predominance in Massachusetts politics; *I'd Do It Again*, autobiography, 1957.
11. Epithet of Boston natives of ancient Protestant pedigree.
12. Andrew J. Peters (1872–1938), mayor of Boston, 1918–1922, between Curley's first and second terms.
13. *Time Magazine* 25/1 (7 January 1935). KS's telegram to the Editor, "WHERE IS EDWARD HOPPER THE NOBLEST AMERICANA PAINTER OF THEM ALL?" was in response to a cover story in *Time* 24/26 about Thomas Hart Benton and other American painters; the editor agreed that Hopper merited a place on *Time*'s list.
14. Spoerl (1901–1969), Harvard '22, mathematician; his letter mentions the then largest known prime number.
15. Charles Francis Adams (1866–1954) was President Hoover's secretary of the navy (1929–1933). Mrs. Curtis (Anna) Dall, daughter of President Roosevelt, mother of Sistie and Buzzie; Anna Roosevelt Dall married John Boettiger in January 1935.
16. Homans (1879?–1974), mother of George Caspar Homans.
17. Farrar's partner was presumably Stanley M. Rinehart Jr. (1897–1969), publisher.
18. William G. McAdoo (1863–1941), attorney and businessman, secretary of the treasury, 1913–1918; senator from California, 1933–1938. In 1914 he married President Wilson's daughter, Eleanor Randolph Wilson, whose sister Jessie married Francis B. Sayre (1885–1972), Harvard professor and diplomat.
19. *Carmen*, a naturalistic opera by Georges Bizet (French, 1838–1875), 1875, after a novel by Prosper Merimée. Regarded as a failure by its composer, *Carmen* rapidly became and has remained one of the most popular stage works of all time, and was repeatedly adapted for the screen. The version BDV saw was probably the silent film of 1915, with Theda Bara in the title role. Geraldine Farrar (1882–1967), American operatic soprano, sang at the Metropolitan Opera 1906–1922, and later was a storyteller for Met broadcasts. An outstanding performer of German music, Farrar was long assumed to have had a romantic relationship with Crown Prince Wilhelm of Germany and Prussia (1882–1951), son of Kaiser Wilhelm II; Farrar understated but did not deny this in her autobiography, *Such Sweet Compulsion* (2nd edition, 1938). Her fondness for German culture was an issue when her allegiance to the Allied cause was challenged during the Great War. Neither of the incidents BDV alleges can be found reported in the *New York Times*, but the issue of 26 March 1917 reports a testimonial dinner under this headline: "Geraldine Farrar Exhibits Loyalty."
20. BDV's third novel, published 1928.
21. Harold S. Latham (1887–1969), vice-president at Macmillan. Edward Lee Thorndike (1874–1949), professor of educational psychology at Columbia.
22. Robert DeVore Leigh (1890–1961), president of Bennington College, 1928–1941.
23. The Junior League of the City of New York for the Promotion of Settlement Movements (NYJL) was founded in 1901 by Mary Harriman, then a nineteen-year-old student at Barnard College, to secure volunteers from society debutantes for community service along the lines of Chicago's Settlement Movement. Eleanor Roosevelt was an early member. The Junior League today has 294 chapters with a membership of more than 170,000 women.
24. Mentions the engagement of Bernard Baruch's daughter, and the death of Cornelia Lunt.
25. DePinna's was a department store at 650 Fifth Avenue, now the site of the Piaget Building. Rudolph Valentino (1895–1926), Italian-born movie star and heartthrob, was married twice.

26. Bernard Baruch (1870–1965), financier, government advisor, "elder statesman." The wartime president was Wilson.
27. Cornelia Lunt died at the age of ninety-one. She was the daughter of John Evans, one of the city founders of Evanston. Valleyhead, a psychiatric retreat in Carlisle, Massachusetts, was headed by Lawrence Kirby Lunt.
28. Bodenheim (1893?–1954), poet and essayist, forerunner of the Beat Generation writers. Wood (1892–1978), actress, then appearing in *Birthday*, a new play by Aimée and Philip Stuart; thirteen performances.
29. William Stanley Braithwaite (1878–1962), black poet and editor; professor at Atlanta University; *The House of Falling Leaves*, 1908. His *Anthology of Magazine Verse*, 1920, contains two poems by Bodenheim.
30. 1924.
31. The Boston *Evening Transcript*, published from 1854 through 1941.
32. DuBose Heyward (1885–1940), poet and playwright, organized the Poetry Society of South Carolina with Allen in the early 1920s. His novel *Porgy* (1925) was adapted for the libretto of Gershwin's opera *Porgy and Bess*, 1935.
33. About a court decision involving nudists in New York.
34. Hooton (1887–1954), professor of anthropology at Harvard; *Up from the Ape*, 1931. A specialist in research on criminal populations, he called for sterilization of criminals and mental defectives.
35. Robert Andrews Millikan (1868–1953), physicist, public spokesman, professor at the University of Chicago and California Institute of Technology, studied the origin of cosmic rays; his classic "oil-drop experiment" for measuring the charge of the electron earned him the Nobel Prize in 1922.
36. With an ad for the Marquis de Caussade's armagnac.
37. Park-Benziger, importers, founded 1933 in New York.
38. O'Hara (1893–1962), writer, columnist for the McNaught Syndicate since 1931. Fisher (1879–1958), novelist and translator; *The Deepening Stream*, 1930; *Bonfire*, 1933. The comment concerns Hepburn's role in *The Little Minister*.
39. About a lawsuit involving oysters at the Ranch Café.
40. Reviews of Wilder's *Heaven's My Destination* and Mark Van Doren's first novel, *The Transients*.
41. Prominent Mormon family in Utah.
42. See *The Bucolics of Decadence*.
43. Henry Louis (H. L.) Mencken (1880–1956), Baltimore-born journalist, critic, pundit, and editor, an early supporter of BDV; cofounder of *The American Mercury*; *The American Language*, 1918 (with many subsequent editions).
44. William Herman (1893–1935), M.D. Harvard '20, Boston psychiatrist whom BDV consulted for an unknown period. See *The Uneasy Chair*, p. 401. Herman died on 25 January 1935.
45. Cornelia Peacock, born 1809 in Philadelphia, married Pierce Connelly, an Episcopalian minister, in 1831; both converted to Roman Catholicism four years later. After they had five children, they took vows of separation and permanent chastity in 1845. Following Pierce Connelly's ordination to the Catholic priesthood, Cornelia established the Society of the Holy Child Jesus for the education of Catholic girls (*DAB*).
46. McCloskey (1810–1885); cardinal archbishop, 1875.
47. (French) life.
48. Aristotle (384–322 BCE), Greek philosopher, disciple of Plato; *Poetics*, on the nature, structure, and expressive values of literature, especially poetry and drama.
49. Henry Hudson (d. 1611), navigator and explorer, "never [called] Hendrick" (*DAB*).

50. Charles A. Beard (1874–1948), historian, professor of political science at Columbia, later cofounder of the New School for Social Research in New York; *The Rise of American Civilization*, with his wife, Mary Ritter Beard (1876–1958), 1930; revised edition, 1956. Frederick Jackson Turner (1861–1932), historian, professor at the University of Wisconsin and Harvard; *The Frontier in American History*, 1920.
51. *Webster's New International Dictionary*, second edition, 1934.
52. Davis (1874–1956), playwright. The play was probably by R. J. Raymond, melodrama in 3 acts, 1826.
53. Probably *The House of Dooner*, 1928. Thomas Augustine Daly (1871–1948), Philadelphia newspaperman and poet.
54. Hervey Allen's estate near Oxford, Maryland; possibly referred to in BDV's "Homily for a Troubled Time," *Woman's Day*, January 1951.
55. Harold L. Ickes (1874–1952), secretary of the interior and head of the Public Works Administration.
56. Rose Devoto Coffman, older sister of BDV's father, Florian Devoto. See BDV's letter of 6 October 1927 to Robert S. Forsythe, in *LBDV*, pp. 14–19.
57. Queen Victoria.
58. Song by Stephen Foster (1826–1864).
59. "I dreamt I dwelt in marble halls," song from *The Bohemian Girl*, opera by Michael Balfe (Irish, 1808–1870), 1843.
60. Reference to Damon Runyon (1880–1946), New York journalist and author; and Westbrook Pegler (1894–1969), newspaper columnist and sportswriter. University of Notre Dame, Catholic university founded in 1842 in Notre Dame, Indiana, near South Bend. BDV's father, Florian Devoto, had five degrees from Notre Dame and taught mathematics and engineering drawing there for several years beginning in the 1870s.
61. St. Mary's College for women, Notre Dame, Indiana, founded 1855; sister college to the University of Notre Dame. Mary Madeleva Wolff, CSC (1887–1964), poet and medievalist; principal, Sacred Heart Academy, Ogden, Utah; president of St. Mary's College, 1934–1961.
62. No one by the name De Rosa appears in BDV's immediate Italian ancestry. His paternal grandmother was born Maria Marré, to Italian nobility of German ancestry; a collateral branch of this family was named De Rossi. Camillo di Cavour (1810–1861), prime minister of Sardinian kingdom, 1852; together with Giuseppe Garibaldi the architect of the Risorgimento and Italian unification in 1861.
63. Pierre Puvis de Chavannes (1824–1898), French painter and muralist. BDV's information is incorrect; Florian Devoto, a talented painter, was supposed to have been apprenticed to Luigi Gregori (1819–1896), director of the art department at Notre Dame, whose murals adorned the walls of the chapel, but there is no evidence for this. Puvis de Chavannes never visited America, although he executed several murals for the Boston Public Library in Copley Square.
64. Victor H. Coffman (1839–?), Lieutenant Colonel, 34th Iowa Infantry Volunteers, served in the Civil War; professor at Omaha Medical College from 1881; married Rose Devoto 10 September 1879 in Chicago.
65. Weir, born 1880, died ca. 1904. After Weir Mitchell (1829–1914), neurologist, novelist, poet.
66. Alice Roosevelt (1884–1980), daughter of Theodore Roosevelt, married Nicholas Longworth (1869–1931; Speaker of the U.S. House of Representatives, 1925–1931) in 1906. She was famous for her witty remarks. Delmonico is presumably Lorenzo Delmonico (Swiss, 1813–1881), famous New York restaurateur. The Gibson Girl was drawn by Charles Dana Gibson (1867–1944), illustrator. McCutcheon (1866–1928), reporter and prolific novelist; *Graustark*, 1901; *Brewster's Millions*, 1903.

67. BDV's cousin Rose Devoto Guislain.
68. Richard d'Oyly Carte (1844–1901), English producer, founder of the Savoy Theatre and d'Oyly Carte touring company that produced the immortal Gilbert and Sullivan operettas, from *Trial By Jury*, 1881, to *The Grand Duke*, 1896.
69. Green (1899–1975), actor, made a long and very successful career in Gilbert and Sullivan performances. Lord Chancellor, in *Iolanthe; or The Peer and the Peri*, 1882. Moulan (1875–1939).
70. Dickson (1903–1990), Scottish singer, with d'Oyly Carte 1928–1935, then at the Metropolitan Opera, 1935–1940.
71. Piltdown, site in Sussex, England, where skull fragments of a previously unknown species of prehistoric man were unearthed in 1911. In 1954 these fragments were proved to be spurious, and "Piltdown man" was exposed as a hoax.
72. Sir Arthur Sullivan (1842–1900), British composer; in addition to the eternally popular Gilbert and Sullivan operettas, he composed a grand opera, *Ivanhoe* (1891), much church music, including such well-known hymns as "Onward, Christian Soldiers," songs ("The Lost Chord"), and concert music.
73. Sir William Schwenck Gilbert (1836–1911), British poet (*The Bab Ballads*, 1869), playwright, and peerless librettist of thirteen Gilbert and Sullivan operettas. The character of Bunthorne in *Patience or Bunthorne's Bride* (1881) is a lampoon of Oscar Wilde (1854–1900), Irish poet, playwright, and wit.
74. Duet between Phyllis and Strephon in *Iolanthe*.
75. BDV's first cousin.
76. Cécile Chaminade (1857–1944), French pianist, composer of agreeable salon music, including the famous *Scarf Dance* and *La Lisonjera* (The Flatterer).
77. Founded in 1875 in Omaha under the sponsorship of the Society of Jesus; now Creighton University.
78. Stearns (1891–1943), Harvard '13, journalist, social critic, editor of *Dial*, lived in France during the 1920s; *Rediscovering America*, 1934. Reference to Sinclair Lewis's *Babbitt*, 1922.
79. Henry Murger (1822–1861), French writer; *Scènes de la Vie de Bohème*, 1849, was the source for Giacomo Puccini's immortal opera *La Bohème*, 1896.
80. The great tornado of Omaha was on Easter Sunday, 23 March 1913. There were ninety-four deaths recorded, and property damage then estimated at $3.5 million. See Snowden D. Flora, *Tornadoes of the United States*, 1953.
81. General Heinrich Rudolph Alexander von Kluck (1846–1934), commander of the German First Army.
82. Brand Whitlock (1869–1934), writer, politician, American minister to Belgium. Gilbert Monell Hitchcock (1859–1934), attorney, newspaperman, U.S. senator from Nebraska, 1911–1922.
83. John La Valle (1896–1971). Charles Hopkinson (1869–1962).
84. Henry Wadsworth Longfellow Dana (1881–1950), writer; grandson of H. W. Longfellow. Four boys allegedly stole an automobile belonging to Dana's nephew; when they were prosecuted, one of them brought a morals charge against Dana. Following a trial that lasted a week, Dana was acquitted on 29 May.
85. State Street in Boston; Brattle Street in Cambridge; Craigie House and Longfellow Park are situated on Brattle Street.
86. William Henry O'Connell (1859–1944), archbishop of Boston since 1911; *Recollections of Seventy Years*, 1934.
87. Nelson P. Brown.
88. William Randolph Hearst (1863–1951), newspaper publisher.

89. Also known as Craigie-Longfellow House. Built in 1759, this mansion was given to Henry Wadsworth Longfellow in 1843 as a wedding present by the father of Frances Appleton, his second wife.
90. Henry David Thoreau (1817–1862), of Lincoln, Massachusetts. *Journal*, 11 November 1854: "Some circumstantial evidence is very strong, as when you find a trout in the milk."
91. Wheelwright (1897–1940), Harvard '20, poet and architect; brother of George Wheelwright.
92. "Fossil Remnants of the Frontier: Notes on a Utah Boyhood," *Harper's* 170/5 (April 1935), reprinted in *Forays and Rebuttals*. "Helen stopped and modestly bade me look the other way lest I glimpse her calf when she climbed the fence."
93. The summer of 1928. See *The Uneasy Chair*, p. 84.
94. Not in the OED; presumably "love of the city."
95. (German, Leitmotiv), leading motive; roughly, psychological theme.
96. Grant was the daughter of James Pierce Grant.
97. Burgess (1874–1965), author of children's stories.
98. Madeline Boyd.
99. James Boyd (1888–1944), author; *Drums*, 1925; *Roll River*, 1935; *Bitter Creek*, 1939.
100. Thomas Wolfe (1900–1938), North Carolina-born author of large-scale novels.
101. 1920, first English translation of *Vorlesungen zur Einführung in die Psychoanalyse*, 1916–1918; *Neue Folge der Vorlesungen zur Einführung*, 1932, in English as *New Introductory Lectures in Psychoanalysis*, 1933. Jones (1879–1958), British psychoanalyst, pupil of Freud; wrote *Sigmund Freud: Life and Work*, 3 vols., 1953–1957.
102. *Die Traumdeutung*, 1900; *Totem und Tabu*, 1913.
103. *Civilization and Its Discontents*, English translation of *Das Unbehagen in der Kultur*.
104. *The Structure and Meaning of Psychoanalysis as Related to Personality and Behavior*, by William Healy, Augusta F. Bronner, and Anna Mae Bowers; this book is one of the first important interpretations of Freud's work published in English. Healy (1869–1963), psychologist and psychiatrist in Chicago and at the Judge Baker Guidance Center, Boston, had Bronner as his assistant, whom he later married.
105. Percy Williams Bridgman (1882–1961), Harvard '04, Ph.D. '08, professor of physics, received the Nobel Prize in 1946 for his research on the behavior of matter at ultrahigh pressures.
106. Reference to the long stream-of-consciousness chapter at the end of Joyce's *Ulysses*.
107. Alfred Knopf.
108. By Somerset Maugham, 1930.
109. Hardy (1840–1928), beloved British novelist and poet; *The Return of the Native*, 1878; *A Pair of Blue Eyes*, 1873; *Desperate Remedies*, 1891; *The Mayor of Casterbridge*, 1886; *Jude the Obscure*, 1895; *Tess of the d'Urbervilles*, 1891.
110. Theodore Dreiser (1871–1945), ponderous novelist and editor; *Sister Carrie*, 1900; *Jennie Gerhardt*, 1911; *An American Tragedy*, 1925.
111. *Harper's*. The negotiations culminated in BDV's succession to "The Easy Chair," which he continued to write every month until his death. Mencken did not join the *Harper's* team.
112. Gould (1898–1989), co-edited *Ladies' Home Journal* with his wife, Beatrice Blackmur.
113. Lorimer (1903–1981), author, assistant editor *SEP*, son of George Horace Lorimer.
114. Wesley Stout (1889–1971), associate editor, *SEP*; editor, 1937–1942.
115. MSPCA Angell Memorial Hospital in Boston, founded 1915.
116. The term "foaf" (friend of a friend) originates in several books by the folklorist Jan Harold Brunvand, beginning with *The Vanishing Hitchhiker: American Urban Legends and Their Meanings*, 1981.

117. José Clemente Orozco (1883–1949), Mexican painter and muralist, executed 24 panels, a panoramic depiction of history and the American experience, on the walls of the Baker Library at Dartmouth College, beginning in 1932 when he was artist in residence.
118. Graymoor Monastery in Garrison, New York, established 1898, originally within the Episcopal Church; reconstituted 1909 as Roman Catholic, and now within the Franciscan order. A founding sister was a member of the Society of the Holy Child Jesus. Mount Athos in Greece is the site of some twenty Orthodox monasteries, seventeen of them Greek Orthodox, which have been all-male since the eleventh century.
119. Probably the Avon Old Farms School, private boys' school in Avon, Connecticut, founded 1927.
120. *"Beloved Friend": The Story of Tchaikowsky and Nadjeda von Meck*, by Catherine Drinker Bowen and Barbara von Meck, 1937. Peter Ilyich Tchaikovsky (usual American spelling; 1840–1893), the greatest and most prolific of the Russian romantic composers, is best known for three ballets, *Swan Lake*, *Sleeping Beauty*, and *Nutcracker*, and much concert music, including Symphony No. 6 in B minor ("Pathétique," his last work).
121. *Der Rosenkavalier*, beloved opera by Richard Strauss, 1910; text by Hugo von Hofmannsthal (Austrian, 1874–1929).
122. The expression "the greatest thing since Uncle Billy's Whiz Bang" turns up from time to time during this period, probably in reference to a Fawcett magazine of the 1920s and 1930s, *Captain Billy's Whiz Bang*.
123. Max Planck (1858–1947), great German physicist (Nobel Prize, 1918), formulated the quantum theory of matter in 1900. He is not known for any "principle of indeterminism"; BDV may have been thinking of Heisenberg's Uncertainty Principle.
124. The Syndics are the governing board of the Harvard University Press. Kenneth Ballard Murdock (1895–1975), professor of English and dean of the Faculty of Arts and Sciences.
125. *Notes of Death and Life*, 1935.
126. Deer Island, in Boston Harbor, was the site since 1896 of the Suffolk County House of Correction; today it houses the waste water treatment plant for greater Boston.
127. Roger Scaife (1875–1951), vice president of Little, Brown. Alfred McIntyre, president of Little, Brown. Herbert Franklin Jenkins (1873–1960), vice president and editorial director at Little, Brown.
128. *The Rise of the City, 1878–1898*, by Arthur M. Schlesinger, 1933.
129. Published in 1937 as *The Road to Reunion: 1865–1900*, by Paul Buck (1899–1978), professor of history at Harvard, later Dean of the Faculty; it won the Pulitzer Prize in history in 1938.
130. Edward S. Martin (1856–1939) wrote "The Editor's Easy Chair" in *Harper's* from 1920 to 1935.
131. Cass Canfield (1897–1986), writer, editor, publisher; president of *Harper's*, 1931–1945.
132. Howells wrote the column from 1900 to 1920, succeeded by Martin.
133. *Soldiers' Pay* (1925), *Mosquitoes* (1927), *Sartoris* (1929).
134. Joseph Hergesheimer (1880–1954), author.
135. Hewlett (1861–1923), British novelist and poet.
136. Riddell was a pseudonym of Corey Ford (1902–1969); satires and lampoons for *Vanity Fair*; *The J R Murder Case: a Philo Vance Parody*, 1930; *In the Worst Possible Taste*, 1932.
137. Beardsley (British, 1874–1898), outstanding Art Nouveau illustrator and decadent writer.
138. Walter Prescott Webb (1888–1963), historian of the American West, professor at the University of Texas; *The Great Plains*, 1931; *Divided We Stand*, 1937; *The Great Frontier*, 1952.
139. James Truslow Adams (1878–1949), historian. Daughters of the American Revolution, organized 1890, Washington, D.C., for descendants of those who supported the American Revolution. The D.O.C. was founded in 1890 in Missouri; now the United Daughters of the Confederacy.

140. Mary Baker Eddy (1821–1910), founder of Christian Science.
141. 1933. BDV's short review appeared in *NEQ* 7/1 (March 1934).
142. 1931.
143. Small stones (*OED*).
144. Ford (1858–1941), historian and editor.
145. Mitchell (1892–1957), Harvard '15, managing editor, *The Dial*, 1919–1920; editor, *NEQ*, 1928–1938; Massachusetts Historical Society, 1929–1957; *New Letters of Abigail Adams, 1788–1801*, 1947.
146. Scrawny mustachioed character in *The Gumps* comic strip.
147. Characters in BDV's current potboiler, *Senior Spring*.
148. (French) like a pigeon.
149. See letter from 3–4 February 1934.
150. Such were increasingly adopted in confectionery from the 1960s, and abundantly adopted in cosmetics from the 1980s on.
151. Reference to a very popular song, "Yes! we have no bananas," by Irving Berlin, from *Music Box Revue*, 3rd edition, 1923. See also *Sabrina*, starring William Holden, Humphrey Bogart, and Audrey Hepburn, directed by Billy Wilder, 1954.
152. See 1935 letters.
153. KS's friend Virginia Nirdlinger Whitehill, who wrote under her maiden name, later reviewed books for *SRL*.
154. Thomas Hardy, *Jude the Obscure*, 1895.
155. Thomas Hardy, *Tess of the D'Urbervilles*, 1890.
156. Minnie Maddern-Fiske (1865–1932), actress. *Tess* opened in New York in 1897 and toured; it was filmed in 1913. Eleonora Duse (1859–1924), Italian actress.
157. Curtis Brown Ltd., literary agency.
158. Alden (1836–1919), editor of *Harper's*. Curtis (1824–1892), the first writer of "The Easy Chair." See BDV, "Number 241," *Harper's* 211/5 (November 1955), also in *The Easy Chair*, 1955; and see also the preface to that volume; see further "The Third Floor," *Harper's* 204/3 (March 1952), also in *The Easy Chair*.
159. Schoonmaker (1905–1976), vintner, oenologist.
160. "O, that this too too solid flesh would melt,/Thaw and resolve itself into a dew!" *Hamlet*, Act I, scene 2.
161. By Dickens, 1853.
162. State song of Indiana, 1897; words by Theodore Dreiser, music by Paul Dresser (his brother).
163. *It Can't Happen Here*, novel, 1935; play, 1936.
164. *New Masses*, published between 1926 and 1948 as a successor to Max Eastman's *Masses*; during the 1930s it was chiefly a literary magazine under the sponsorship of the Communist Third International and edited by Granville Hicks. See Jack Alan Robbins (ed.), *Granville Hicks in the New Masses*, 1974. Crichton (1896–1960), author and editor; his pseudonym, "Robert Forsythe," must not be confused with Robert S. Forsythe, BDV's friend from Northwestern University. About Crichton, see Patrick McGilligan and Paul Buhle, *Tender Comrades: A Backstory of the Hollywood Blacklist*, 1997; about Robert S. Forsythe, see BDV's autobiographical note to him (6 October 1927) in *LBDV*.
165. This letter is the first to KS indicating the beginning of BDV's friendship with Frost, which would grow and flourish for three years before suffering ongoing difficulties beginning in 1938. Frost had been one of the founders of the Bread Loaf Writer's Conference, but had not participated for some years before his regular return in 1936.
166. Crane (1899–1932), poet; *White Buildings*, 1926; *The Bridge*, 1930.

167. "Solidarity at Alexandria," *Harper's* 171/12 (November 1935). See also BDV, "Number 241," the twentieth-anniversary Easy Chair, *Harper's* 211/1266 (November 1955): "The first Easy Chair I wrote described some asininities committed by a New Deal agency. (Prophetically, it was a news story, one I had dug out for myself.)"
168. Usually cited thus and attributed to Jefferson; "The condition upon which God hath given liberty to man is eternal vigilance," from John Philpot Curran (1750–1817), 1790, as given in *BFQ*.
169. See also BDV, "New England: There She Stands," *Harper's* 174/4 (March 1932), also in *Forays and Rebuttals*.
170. Barker (1911–1965), poet. Wilder (1899?–1995), novelist, sister of Thornton Wilder; *Mother and Four*, 1933; *Heart Be Still*.
171. Robert Wooster Stallman (1911–1982), critic; professor at the University of Connecticut. Monroe (1860–1936), author, poet; founder of *Poetry* magazine, 1912; autobiography, *A Poet's Life: Seventy Years in a Changing World*, 1935.
172. Victoria Lincoln (1904–1981), novelist.
173. Brown (1900–1969), drama critic and author.
174. Stevens (1904?–1985), managing editor of *SRL* from 1933; succeeded BDV as editor, 1938.
175. Stephen Vincent Benét (1898–1943), author and poet; *John Brown's Body*, Pulitzer Prize in poetry, 1929. Krutch (1893–1970), critic and nature writer, professor of English at Columbia; *Edgar Allan Poe: A Study in Genius*, 1926; *The Desert Year*, 1952. Cramer (1893–1976), poet, historian; *Stars Fell on Alabama*, 1934; *America Sings*, 1942. Seldes (1893–1970), critic, newspaperman, playwright; *The Seven Lively Arts*, 1924; *Against Revolution*, 1932.
176. Norma Shearer (1902–1983), actress; wife of producer Irving Thalberg. Marion Davies (1897–1961), actress, protégée, and mistress of William Randolph Hearst.
177. (1879?–1974), Polish-born American movie producer, founder of Goldwyn Pictures, later Metro-Goldwyn-Mayer (MGM) Corporation; famous for colorfully fumbling phrases ("I'll give you a definite maybe," etc.).
178. (1904–1999), author; *As the Earth Turns*, 1933.
179. Cecil B. DeMille (1881–1959), movie producer, famous for movies on historical subjects on a grand scale; *King of Kings*, 1927 (silent); *Cleopatra*, first version, 1934; *The Ten Commandments*, 1956.
180. (d. 1982), later Eleanor (Langley) Fletcher.
181. James Henry Van Alen (1902–1991), vice president, Farrar, Straus & Co.; founder, International Tennis Hall of Fame. *North American Review*, founded 1821 as *North American Review and Miscellaneous Journal*, sometimes subtitled *Stuff and Nonsense*; editors included Edward Everett (1794–1865), James Russell Lowell, and Henry Cabot Lodge (1850–1924).
182. BDV dedicated *The Course of Empire* to her, 1953.
183. Margaret Widdemer (1884–1978), writer, poet.
184. Howard Fast (1914–2003), highly prolific writer active in American leftist causes; *Citizen Tom Paine*, 1943; *The American*, 1946; *The Naked God*, 1957. *Being Red*, memoir, 1990, mentions his Bread Loaf summer.
185. (1898–1979), writer; *That Girl From New York*, 1932; *Smoke In Her Eyes*, 1935; *Daughter to Diana*, 1935; *It's You I Want*, 1936; *Summer Lightning*, 1936; *I Met My Love Again* (movie), 1938; *Borrowed Husband*, 1943.
186. Probably *The Dark Hills Under*, 1933.
187. Ransom (1888–1974), poet, critic, Carnegie Professor of Poetry at Kenyon College.
188. Granville Mfg., manufacturer of woodenware in Granville, Vermont, since 1857. Morize (1883–1957), professor of French literature at Harvard.

189. Lawrence E. Spivak (1900–1994), publisher of the *American Mercury*; later created "Meet the Press" for NBC television.
190. Stallings (1894–1968), playwright and screenwriter; *What Price Glory?*, with Maxwell Anderson, 1924; literary editor and sometime associate editor of *American Mercury*, 1935–1937; editor for Fox-Movietone.
191. (1864–1943), British novelist and Hollywood scriptwriter; *Three Weeks*, 1924; *It and Other Stories*, 1929.
192. Died 1965.
193. Simonds (1878–1936): journalist and war historian. The Italian dictator Mussolini mobilized troops in Italian Somaliland, adjoining Ethiopia (Abyssinia), invading Ethiopia in October 1935 and completing occupation by spring 1936. Ethiopia protested in vain to the League of Nations. Ethiopia was liberated by British forces in 1941 and the Emperor Haile Selassie was restored to his throne. Anschluss refers to (German) annexation; the term is usually applied to the forced absorption of Austria into the Third Reich in March 1938.
194. Presumably George Henry Thomas (1816–1870), Union general, known as the "Rock of Chickamauga."
195. Headed the Harvard University Press 1937–1943.
196. Karl Yost, *A Bibliography of the Works of Edna St. Vincent Millay, with an Essay in Appreciation by Harold Lewis Cook*, 1937.
197. Appalachian Mountain Club.
198. "... but 'tis enough, 'twill serve": *Romeo and Juliet*, III/1.
199. Warren Gamaliel Harding (1865–1923), twenty-ninth president of the United States, died in office and was succeeded by Calvin Coolidge.
200. Welsh folksong, traced to 1784.
201. André Kostelanetz (1901–1980), conductor of light orchestral classics.
202. Deems Taylor's opera, *Peter Ibbetson*, produced by the Metropolitan Opera, 1931. *Jubilee*, musical by Cole Porter and Moss Hart, 1935.
203. Lady Peel (1894–1989), Canadian actress.
204. Knight (1913?–1987), actress and dancer.
205. Probably *Boston and the Boston Legend*, 1935. Beebe (1902–1966), journalist, historian, was an authority on railroads.
206. *Macbeth*, Act V, scene 3: "And with some sweet oblivious antidote/Cleanse the stuff'd bosom of that perilous stuff/Which weighs upon the heart?"
207. Robert Forbes Almy (1901–1969), Ph.D. Harvard, 1935; Northwestern University, later Miami University of Ohio. The Mark Twain paper was printed in *Forays and Rebuttals*, discussed at the meeting of the Modern Language Association in Cincinnati.
208. Yale 14, Harvard 7; played on 23 November. The editor was George Stevens of the *Saturday Review of Literature*.
209. *Forays and Rebuttals*, 1936.
210. Birkhoff (1884–1944), mathematician.
211. Cover, *New York Weekly*, 25 May 1871; silent movie, 1926.

4

1936 LETTERS

1936 proved to be an exceptionally busy year, full of major changes for DeVoto. Returning from the annual meeting of the Modern Language Association, about which he commented acidly to Sterne, he went on the road again, this time to lecture at the University of Miami at Coral Gables, Florida, at the invitation of Hervey Allen, taking his son Gordon with him. DeVoto had a low opinion of Florida but the trip gave him a fine opportunity to fortify his new friendship with "the greatest living American," Robert Frost. In February he confided to Sterne that he was attempting fruitlessly to negotiate a permanent faculty appointment at Harvard, hoping that he would not be further pressured to accept an editorial job. He enjoyed a special diversion in drafting for Sterne a detailed description of his mother's family and in sending to her the beginning of a long-planned novel, for which Sterne had suggested the title *Mountain Time*.

In April, extended negotiations came to a head. DeVoto asked Sterne whether he should accept an invitation, already made three times, to be the editor of the *Saturday Review of Literature*, in which he had already published frequently for several years. In May, DeVoto accepted *SRL*'s offer and resigned from the Harvard faculty. By September, DeVoto and his family had packed up their household in Lincoln and moved to White Plains, New York. The disruption of the move was accentuated by the discovery that the newly hired Irish maid had syphilis. DeVoto settled rapidly into his new position at *SRL* but immediately noted ongoing problems. Nevertheless in all this disarray DeVoto found time to organize a collection of his published essays, which appeared in October under the title *Forays and Rebuttals*, and to write a potboiler for *Collier's*, which was published in 1938 as *Troubled Star*, by John August.

Lincoln, Massachusetts

[29 JANUARY 1936]

Dear Kate:

With a groan and gesture as of Eugene Gant,[1] I yank out of the machine the caption and five lines I managed to get down of what will be, so help me St. Francis who the gent in question finds had a great deal in common with Huck Finn, the last writing I'll do about Mark Twain till the stonewood trees of the Bonneville Basin give up their silica or it's time to revise MT's A. It was to be, and God help us all probably still is to be, a review for the *NEQ* of Wagenknecht's book more detailed than I did for the *Times*.[2] But by the sainted bones of Parley Pratt I don't have to do it for another 24 hours.[3] I think I'll print one copy on laid paper and send it to you with my compliments. Then, dear, let's you and me read some other humorist for a while, if we're going to write or talk about him anyway. Say Artemus Ward, Kyle Crichton or Malcolm Cowley.[4]

Well, it was Godawful. I grant you, the sun was magnificent but you have my oath that nothing else was. Look, I don't want any of the South, any part of it I've ever seen, anything associated with it, anything that looks, smells, feels and above all tastes of it. Honesty constrains me to admit that this time I was more in touch with Indianapolis and Dubuque than the Sons and Daughters of the Confederacy, but even so I stand my ground. Consulting my memory, I find that this was my fifth sojourn below what one of the San Sebastian guests referred to as the Mason & Hamlin line, and the only pleasant detail that memory returns to me is a few week-ends at the Jefferson Hotel in Richmond, and nearly any hotel anywhere would have seemed pleasant during the war, which is when I used to go to the Jefferson.[5] Where in hell did this notion get started that there's good food in the South? Add to my five sojourns several main line passages en route and I've tried it all from the Jefferson and the old family retainers at the manor house down to the Pass-a-Grille Beach Hotel, Pass-a-Grille Beach, etc., which was my address for the last few days, and all I ask is this: if it's good cooking why are you always so near to tears when you eat your first meal thereafter on a dining car?[6]

And the liquor situation is archaic. They zoned Coral Gables so that the only places you can get a cocktail are the Miami-Biltmore and the other big hotel five miles away, the only places you can get beer are in the business section, *soi-disant*,[7] some four miles away, and no place in between can sell anything at all. If God ever gives me that delusion again, I'll take an automobile with me.

My knowledge of the great state had been confined to the interior, where the oranges grow. That part is filled up with the hopeful who have been sold ten acres of sand as a graceful habitat and a safe investment for their declining years. I now make out the rest of it thus: Gopher Prairie goes to St. Petersburg, Zenith City to Coral Gables and Coconut Grove, opulent Jewry to Miami Beach, and the people Hergesheimer gapes at to Palm Beach. There must be another classification for I now learn that there's a book store in Tampa. No verification.

Congregations of the bemused that carried me back to old Los Angeles. This is typical. I'm called to the phone one morning.

Female Voice: Good-morning, Mr. DeVoto. I see by the paper that you live in Lincoln, Massachusetts.

DV: Yes.

Voice, tensely: Have you ever visited the Slipe house?

DV: Slipe?

Voice: Yes, the Slipe house.

DV: No, I never have. Is it in Lincoln?

Voice: Yes, of course. My mother's family lived there once. It's an old house.

DV: Yes, there are a good many 18th Century houses there and one that's supposed to be 17th Century. I don't believe it is.

Voice: My mother's family lived there once. It's an old house.

DV: Did you want me to find out something about it?

Voice: No, my mother's family lived there once. It's an old house.

DV: Yes. Did you want to ask me or tell me something about it?

Voice: Oh, no. My mother's family lived there once. I think it's so nice you live there. I thought you'd like to know.

My God, though, that was hyper-normal. I was always being called to the phone or stopped in the patio for far more cock-eyed conversations. One woman said she'd always wanted to hear a writer's voice. One elderly—and fat—gent who spent his daylight hours in a sun-helmet and a pair of long woollen drawers got me off under a palm and let me listen to his involuntary belches, drinking his morning glass of hot water. He was as full of kindness as of wind—he knew that he was a remarkable belcher and he wanted me to enjoy a unique experience. He told me so. A newspaper gal came to interview me—I was interviewed at least a dozen times—, took a slug of the bourbon I had walked four miles to get, and began the interview by asking me whether she ought to break off with this slicker she'd taken up with.

Still, I can't kick. I spent an average of five hours a day with the greatest living American. And the more I see of Frost the more I'm convinced he's just that. I go tearful whenever I talk about him, so I won't try here—but whatever are the profoundest and most searching adjectives, those are the adjectives to use on Frost. He talks along, moderately, aimlessly, quietly, rather slowly, and you listen and pretty soon you notice some sparks, then a glow, then a blaze, then the incandescence of the interior of a new star. He is the quintessence of everything I respect and even love in the American heritage.... If he redeemed the place for me, I can fairly claim to have saved his health and maybe his life. He'd been in Florida for a couple of weeks, with nobody to talk to. The place had got him, as it gets us all. When I got in, he'd gone to bed, turned his face to the wall and was ready to give up his soul to God. He had a temper like a spoiled Kerry Blue,[8] a bad cold and a bilious Weltanschauung[9] that was rapidly becoming an eschatology. The rheum left his eyes at sight of me, he swung his feet over the side of the bed, croaked a few words that took up the argument where we left it off in Amherst in November, cleared his throat, and began to speak out loud and strong. An hour later he had no cold, he had cleared the professors out of Washington and the obscurantists out of poetry, and had found a new title (Poetry as Prowess) and sufficient reason for living out his stay. Thereafter everything went sublimely. I am not an inordinately silent man, dear, but I hold my peace so long as Robert Frost is willing to so much as grunt, and I've never heard him reach the heights he did down there.... One of my lectures was on Red Lewis. It griped Frost so hard that he couldn't sleep for the ensuing eighteen hours and was constantly driving over or phoning over to convey new rebuttals. He was like the sound of a horse shoe on iron. He was superb. And I got the lead I've been half-consciously looking for into my chapter on Frost when, if ever, I turn my English 70 notes into a book. Just this: Lewis, the Sauk Center boy, in flight to the metropolitan point of view, turning on Sauk Center the lens of his own insufficiencies and finding *Main Street*—and Frost, the San Francisco boy retiring of his own will to Salem Depot, New Hampshire, and finding...*North of Boston*.[10] I can drive that point pretty deep into the literature of Our Times, or I'm not half as hot as I pretend to be when I get up and tell Harvard College what our better minds are reading and writing.... As a boy, Frost once picked up an amiable drunk and drove him safely home. Listening to the talk of the amiable drunk, he devised on his own hook a comprehensive and intelligible theory of free association and the stream of consciousness that checks with Freud at every point and a theory about their use in literature that nobody, to my knowledge, has yet improved upon or even quite equalled. Common sense raised to genius—which, somehow, is the formula that sums up all my wistful hopes about the world and mankind. Some argument with some painter unknown to me, one of these idea boys. The painter had a theory: the human retina sees everything double except at the exact center of focus, which is quite true. Therefore, why not paint canvases in which there would be double images everywhere except in the visual center? So he did. Frost, inquiring in that patient, quintessential Yankee courtesy: but wouldn't that be seeing everything quadruple?... By one of those gracious inspirations that Harvard pulls off every so often, and usually just at the moment when you're deciding that the place has gone to hell once and for all, he has been invited here to do the Charles Eliot Norton lectures this year.[11] The most brilliant appointment ever made to that chair. And, gratefully, perhaps even significantly, the first American—if you decide, as I do, that Mr. Eliot isn't quite. There's going to be a lot of pinched fingers. The local chapter of the Amalgamated Adorers of Ezra Pound are already howling. He's also to do the Phi Beta Kappa poem this year. Which is better than I dared to hope for the Tercentenary. Things are looking up, on Charleside.

Well, I mean to imply that Frost took the curse off Florida. But it was swell for the kid. He is as brown as he was in August and he's had a million new experiences—yanked at the controls of a transport plane, seen a shark brought in, watched an enormous jellyfish quiver through the spectrum, realized for the first time that there are negroes, learned fascinating words like palmetto—he damn near justifies the trip.... My word of hope for you is that spring is on the way. They're making turpentine in the Georgia pineries, and you may meditate on that when the cold wave forecast by tonight's *Transcript* reaches us.

So I come back and find that Hillyer has broken an arm, the story is while skating but when did Hillyer ever skate, that the juicy homosexual scandal which has hovered over Louisburg Square for the last year and has already allowed a couple of precinct captains to retire in affluence has lost by death the most exalted name of all, that Ken Murdock brings back sciatica and mumps from the British Museum, and that John Chamberlain has printed Alec Laing's boozy jingle about me and Pareto with the solemn announcement that that puts an end to the Pareto movement—Jesus, aren't the literary wonderful?

I tramped the second hand bookshops of Boston to pick up that Beckwourth. I was relying on Alfred Knopf's word that he had remaindered that series long ago. I then found that he hadn't remaindered it—he had only reduced the price. I suppose it isn't worth while sending you a cleaner copy, but I am sending you another item from the series that may amuse you. It faintly amused me here and there when we were doing it.... Nobody has to like Indians, but if you do like Indians there are some good bits in that book. When Jim used his eyes, he sometimes saw something quite clearly. But I reprinted it for scholarship, not for literature. It was almost unobtainable, and it's required reading for anyone who takes up the West. But have I ever been thanked for making it available? The hell I have.... The by now indispensable Mrs. Chapman has just nicely wiped my eye. (We make a really fine research team—I sit on my fanny and figure things out and she goes and looks them up.) I recently put her to work on a hunch of mine, that if we looked in the right places we'd find that there were some Mormons in Great Salt Lake Valley in 1846, which is a year before they're known to have got there. I'd picked up hints of it here and there in the literature. So she goes and looks—the woman has a sixth sense for research. She finds that yes, indeed, there were—six of them, gone out to make a map of the valley so that when God should tell Brigham This Is the Place, God would know what he was talking about.[12] And they were guided there by Jim Beckwourth.

Gene Saxton has vaguely proposed bringing out some Easy Chairs sometime, but I don't know when or how many. I think, just to make it a representative selection, I'll reprint one in the collection Alfred McIntyre is bringing out next fall. I'll print whichever one you choose. My own preference would be the Wm. Miller one. All of them so far have been produced under pressure, hurriedly, at the last possible moment. From now on I'll have time for meditation and planning and I'd like to stir things up now and then. It looks, though, as if the first one in this new leisure (March is on the small college in the sticks)[13] will have to be about education again. Lee has a long article by Louis Adamic,[14] in which Black Mountain College is made out to be the power and the kingdom and the glory, and Lee feels a little bewildered by it all and wonders if I wouldn't like to dissent in the Easy Chair.[15] If I'd like to write about it at all, I'd like to dissent all right.... I'm letting Mrs. Chapman get that collection ready, only reserving the veto power and resolving to rewrite one which was called "The Centennial of Mormonism," which remains an authoritative job, but which can easily be expanded into something quite nice.[16] I find that I have far from a complete collection of my stuff, and Mrs. C's bibliography, compiled from *The Readers' Guide*, astonished and alarmed me.[17] One great luxury: I'm going to restore the titles under which they were originally written. There will be none of this "The Co-ed: The Hope of Liberal Education," "Jonathan Dyer, Frontiersman," Etc.[18] It's seldom that I achieve a good title; no editor has ever been known to achieve one.... I am some three weeks, or thereabouts, short of beginning Theme with Variations or Libido in the Great West. The closer I get to it, the less I know about it. I could use a lot of names that don't sound like people in a book. I could use a good ground plan. I could use about three crucial decisions.... And yet, experience has taught me one thing about writing books: that, once you get started, there are no real problems. Time after time I have lost sleep, weight, digestion and civil disposition worrying about things to come which, from this side, looked to be insoluble problems, insuperable barriers or what-not. And time after time, rising on the morning when the decision had to be made, the problem solved, the barrier broken down, I've found that none existed—that everything was settled and always had been settled. It is literally true that, with SG clearly in my mind for months and even years before I began it, I did not know what had happened between Ted Grayson and Julian till a couple of days before Ted had to tell Loring. Anything in the book that indicates otherwise was put in ex post facto. And so, though at the present moment I couldn't, to save my soul or even yours from hell fire, tell you whether or not the Union Pacific Railroad is going into Rollo Among the Piutes, and if so how much and where, I'm serenely sure that I'll know three weeks some Wednesday.[19] Or if not then, whenever I have to begin writing or not writing about it. In a moment of self-protection I once told an inquiring bore that didn't know what my next book was going to be about, that I wrote books to find out what I knew, and there's more truth in that than I meant to put into it.[20]

The most amusing book I've heard about recently. At Coconut Grove, I resumed my companionship with Collins, Hervey Allen's chauffeur, protector, major domo and—it now appears—biographer. For Collins, in one long wait while Hervey was adding to the complications of his inconceivably complicated existence, confided to me that ever since he started to work for Hervey, which was about as soon as Anthony got to its twentieth thousand, he has been keeping a journal of happenings, observations and personal details. I don't know whether Hervey knows about it: if Johnny Farrar does there must be hourly chills on Madison Avenue. And it ought to have its points, since Collins looks on Ann with a bilious eye, feeling that she is young, flighty and frivolous and not properly appreciative of the dignity of the station to which she has been called.... Ann, incidentally, is pregnant and just recovering—with her customary vigor and enjoyment—from a short but pretty appalling bout with pneumonia. She looked rosy and blooming and carefree, but I guess it was a close thing for the child. Hervey was pretty close-mouthed about his book, in spite of the fact that I got tight and injudiciously spilled the story of my recent editorial offer.[21] But I gather that nothing came of the ancient Britain stuff, that this one is early American, subtitled *A Tale of the Old Republic,* and that he expects to finish it in a few months but intends to keep it back for about a year.[22] Fame and the inquiring public have produced a lot of neuroses in Hervey. Some of them pretty pathetic, as his all but incurable belief that his old friends feel superior to him for having made a lot of money. Some of them pretty amusing, as his checkerboard reflexes about the press. He took me out to the Surf Club, at Miami Beach, an incredible place but blessed with good food and drink and a beach where the water was 75 degrees.[23] Right off the publicity girl wanted to know if she could take a picture of us. Hervey said, what do you say, and I said, it's you that['s] photographically desirable, brother, what do you say? So after due thought he consented. But then he insisted that she must release it only to the A.P., for if she gave it to the local papers there'd be allegations of unfairness.[24]... Archie MacLeish is right: you are on a completely wrong track about Hervey, whatever you think, until you come to realize that he is a force of nature. His mind is as massive as Pike's Peak, and hardly more agile. It's the only mind I ever knew that you could watch maneuvering in echelon.

I seem to have been writing for quite a while. Read it afternoons till you're through. But please return the inclosure, which soothes and comforts me a good deal. It is a conscientious report from a great psychologist at Stanford University.[25] He sent out questionnaires to a lot of writers. And I mean questionnaires—there must have been three hundred questions on it. The purpose was vocational guidance: find out the tastes of writers, then when a young man wanted to be a writer and didn't know whether be could be, ask him what his tastes were. I customarily burn such things but this one was a novelty, in that it promised to tell me what I might have been if I hadn't been a writer.

So I answered it—would you rather run a street car or hear a Brahms symphony?[26] Are you courageous in the presence of danger or do you scream? Is blue more beautiful than E-minor? Would a jail sentence or a social snub seem more disgraceful to you? The correlations and conclusions you may observe for yourself.

Yours,
Benny

Lincoln, Massachusetts

[18 February 1936; probably later]

Dear Kate:

Samuel Dye in Middletown:[27] or, A Study in the Formation of the Small Bourgeoisie Following the Stage of Frontier Society.... The data regarding Samuel and his wife Rhoda have been listed in "Jonathan Dyer, Frontiersman," which you may or may not have read when it came out in *Harper's*. These are relevant here: he was a religious emigrant from England to Deseret; he was a mechanic, not a farmer, who was nevertheless required by the Mormon system to become a farmer; he was docile to religious and political leadership; he reclaimed forty-odd acres of desert; he was tough as a hickory knot, in that life and circumstance were never too much for him.[28]

The study is founded on—dependable—information from Grace Dye, spinster and milliner, of Pocatello, Idaho.

Excuse it, please. I've just realized that I'll never do this again and that I'd like a copy for possible reference. God forbid that I should write letters this way, but, asking your favor, I'm going to insert a carbon.

[beginning on a new page:]

(How appropriate that the radio should be doing barn dances, across the hall.) Well, then listening to Aunt Grace and checking off my interests, I was uneasily struck by the frequency of marital difficulties in the record, amazed by the more explicable prominence of the railroad theme, and quite unable to come to any conclusions about family diseases, as I had hoped to, and unable to make more than one generalization—which will follow in due time.

This is the generation of Samuel and Rhoda, except for one stillborn child.[29]

<u>Samuel</u>: Born in Boston, died in Ogden. Education, country school. Telegrapher for the U.P. in various parts of Wyoming, Utah, and Nevada.[30] Left the railroad and undertook to be a commission merchant in Nevada. Finally got too expansive and went under. Manufactured cleansing powder in a small shop. Went back to U.P. as car inspector. Ended running a filling station. Cause of death: stomach ulcer. Widow still survives.

Married to the daughter of a railroad man, in Wyoming. Her family from Nebraska. One child. She divorced him. She and the child unreported.

Married, 2d, to a (Mormon) daughter of a Scotch immigrant. Children:

Rhoda. High school education. Married to a banker. Four children.

Beatrice. (I think I have referred to her as Rhoda in earlier communiqués, out of some vague notion of disguise.) With the possible exception of Edith, see below, the best looking descendant. One year of college. Married an insurance man; is his business partner. No children.

Maynard. No education. Died of epilepsy at the age of eighteen.

Glenn. High school education. Various jobs—still too young to classify.

Robert. Still younger; no report.

Rhoda: Born in Brooklyn, died in Ogden. Education, "academy" (frontier high school)—by virtue of "hiring out" in Ogden in order to get it. Worked as waitress in a railroad restaurant in Wyoming, before her first marriage; as dressmaker before her second marriage. Cause of death: pernicious anemia.

First married to a New Yorker named DeWolfe, county clerk of Sweetwater County, Wyo. When a shortage of funds was discovered, he held the bag and slipped away to Mexico. She went back to her father's farm, then moved to Ogden and took up dressmaking, divorcing her husband some eight years after the desertion. This experience made a hysteric of her.

Child by this marriage, Cleveland. High school education. Railroad telegrapher in southern Utah, then buccaneer in Mexico, then a secretary, finally a C.P.A. Now lives in Salt Lake City. Has had no communication with his half-brother in twenty years. Two children, one of whom is in his first year at college; the other will probably go that far too, if not beyond.[31] [*marginal note*: Both A.B.]

Second marriage: Florian DeVoto, then a railroad freight agent, later abstractor of title. The only college man who appears in this generation—he held six degrees.[32] A man of great brilliance and completely paralyzed will.

Child by this marriage, Bernard. Artium baccalaureus, cum laude. One child so far. (That A.B. is the only college degree to date.)

Sarah: Born in Uinta, died in Sacramento. Education, country school. She seems to have been the dumbest of the children. Cause of death, undetermined, general debility. First married a Wyoming railroad man named White; details of his occupation unknown, for Aunt Grace dismissed him as a drunken bum. Children of this marriage:

George. Boilermaker, first railroads, now steamboats (California). Married. No children.

Bert. Railroad conductor in California. Married. Two children.

Florence. Died in infancy, of meningitis.

Cora. Two years in some cow college in Idaho. Married to a stock-breeder. Two children. This is one of the romantic parts of the saga. Cora was born just after her father died—of D.T.'s, I gather. Her mother was struggling to support the family, in the semi-cooperative house that my mother's dressmaking establishment had by then become—all the sisters showed up there when widowed, abandoned, or out of work. She gave the child to a childless couple to raise, and Cora grew up as their daughter, not learning her identity till they and her mother were dead. I can remember the histrionic behavior when she came to see my mother after the revelation. If my memory is dependable she was, next to Beatrice, the most intelligent of the grandchildren.

Second marriage: a Scotchman named Kennedy, a railroad mechanic, first in Nevada, then in California. He died before she did, but not much before. Children:

Madeleine. High school. Married. Two children. No dope on her husband's occupation, for Aunt Grace has quarreled with her. She is disliked by the whole family—faintly tartish behavior, followed by some kind of dispute over Samuel's estate, I don't know what it could have been, for her share would have been under a hundred dollars. I remember her at seventeen as mildly pretty and godawful dumb. I only saw her that once.

Donald. High school. Electrician, with particular reference to airplane beacons. Married. No children.

Edward. Couldn't, I believe, finish grammar school. The lowest ebb of the family energy. Aunt Grace describes him as a bum and a damned liar, that being the only oath I ever heard her utter. It coincides with my observations during the month he spent with us when I was in high school. Married. No children. No occupation. Lives with various relatives till they pass him on.

Madeleine: Born in Uinta, lived in Ogden, now lives in Bakersfield. Education, pretty damn vague. The aunt I never could stand. She was neurasthenic and a weeper. She used to weep in our house a good part of the time. Also she was "poor" and that irked me—it meant that she couldn't live on the modest level of the rest of us, and my too ready sympathies were always being aroused when I didn't want them to be.

First marriage: to a big, genial, worthless hulk named Ward, a railroad fireman whom she picked up in Chicago while staying with Martha (q.v.).[33] He was a tough baby, contributed very little to her support, was always in trouble, once shot a man through the cheek, did some high grade swindling, bummed a bit, ran pumping engines, raised chickens, wheedled money from everyone especially my father, and was forever having to be kept or bailed out of jail, again by my father. But I liked him. He was worthless but he was genial and always jolly and kind to me. Except for Samuel, he was the only one of my uncles I ever saw (I think), and the word Uncle has always had a glow because of him. Children:

Grace. Part of high school, I think. A fairly pretty and pleasant dimwit. Married dining-car conductor when she was seventeen. Divorced him. Learned beauty-parlor technique from Martha. Married an insurance salesman. Operates a beauty parlor somewhere in California. No children.

Etta. Practically no education. Pretty and absolutely petrified. Has been married twice, once to a farm-management teacher or superintendent (Aunt Grace is pretty vague, here), now, after divorce, to a gent who does nothing at all. Lives with, and on, her mother. Two children.

[*handwritten omission:*] Albert. About 22 yrs old. RR mechanic—2nd marriage of Madeleine follows later.

Martha: We get on more agreeable ground here—she and Aunt Grace, with Beatrice, Rhoda and Webb, are the ones I have liked. Born in Uinta, lives in Ogden. Education rather hard to make out; some "academy," I think.

~~First marriage~~ (that was pure suggestion—she had only one) She married a railroad man in Chicago named Gray. Aunt Grace says he was an engineer, which is hard to fit in, for his family was on a distinctly higher level, economically, than the family had elsewhere attained. His people were well to do and his father lived to become Governor of the Federal Reserve Bank of Chicago. Anyway, he was too much of a hand with the ladies. He railroaded in Louisiana, Kansas, Mississippi, and finally Mexico. When he went to Mexico, she left him, having had enough of his gayeties. The experience produced the typical Dye crackup—see Rhoda and Grace, not to mention Madeleine. She had herself a beautiful nervous seizure. Once, when I was repeating the theme with brass and percussion, I asked her if she knew anything about it. She said that for over a year she did not dare go into the children's room after they were asleep for fear she might kill them.... But she, together with Rhoda and Grace, had Samuel's toughness. She took training in the Cook County Hospital and became a nurse, then went back to Ogden and worked at her trade. Sometimes she parked the kids with my mother, sometimes she set up a joint household with Grace, sometimes she let them run themselves. But she saw them married. Then she went back to Chicago and took a highly-gadgeted course in beauty-parlor stuff. Going back to Ogden, she worked up from a one-table joint to founding a school in the stuff she had learned. When Edith died, she took the child and has brought him up. She has made a modest competence—which has been damned convenient, along with Grace's, for the Dye descendants. The failure of the Ogden State Bank pretty well wiped her out. But she has expanded her school again and is coming back. This refusal to be downed by circumstance, this ability to meet it head on and subdue it, is the sheer guts that distinguished Samuel. Just three of his children had it. I won't be able to follow the grandchildren, but it would be interesting to see where it appears in them. Rhoda, maybe—I'll tell you about her sometime. Anyway, in Martha and Grace the Dye stock gets its highest expression. Children:

Alice. Two years at the U of Utah, taking kindergarten training. Pretty and fairly clever. Something of a tart, I think, in the first Wilson administration; anyway, a "flirt" and a "belle." Taught kindergarten. If Skinny Browning's oldest brother didn't sleep with her for over a year, he was unlike the other Brownings. Finally married a bank clerk—amiable and worthless. Three kids. Finally had to teach kindergarten again. Now helping her mother run the beauty-parlor school.

Edith. The one who taught my childhood that femininity was beautiful. She was pretty even when I was adolescent and had seen other blondes. High school. Went to Pocatello to learn the millinery business from Aunt Grace. Married a railroad clerk. Died in the influenza epidemic.[34] One child, whom Martha has raised. Martha dreamed of putting him through college (the best evidence that she was consciously joining the bourgeoisie) but Aunt Grace says he has decided otherwise and is a government photographer, recently at Boulder Dam.

Grace: Born in Uinta, lives in Pocatello. Education, "academy." Lived with my mother, clerking in an Ogden store, during the dressmaking period. Learned how to make hats and worked in an Ogden millinery. Had some kind of tragic love affair, about which neither I nor Rhoda, who was closest to her, have ever been able to find out anything.[35] My mother always refused to tell me. Anyway, it gave her the Dye crash pretty early, and she never tried again, she's unmarried. She got together a little money, borrowed a little more from my father and elsewhere, and set up an establishment in Idaho Falls. She laboriously got it out of debt and was prospering a little when it burned down, uninsured. She had another crash, a pretty bad one. She made another start, in Pocatello this time. Little by little she has gone ahead, enlarging the story here, buying a farm mortgage there, salting away a bond elsewhere. Martha has contributed to most of her sisters and some of her nephews and nieces, but Grace has practically supported them all at one time or another. She has become the family's capitalist. She has a lot of Idaho farm land, some bonds, some good stocks, too many bum stocks. She lives the good life, too. She likes traveling about, and goes to California every year (where she is unmercifully milked by the grandchildren) and most years to Chicago or one of the national parks or the Gulf Coast or whatnot. She likes the theater and is an inveterate sightseer. She likes to motor through the mountain country and go on picnics. She faithfully reads everything I publish, without ever understanding it, but is, thank God, completely unimpressed by it—she likes me because I have been a "good son," because people with a claim on me can get money from me, and most of all because I obviously work hard. She saw Sam Dye wrenching a farm from the desert—and that is what counts. I could sell a million copies, get the Nobel Prize, or have a statue erected to me in the Hall of Fame, and she would pay no attention. But she sees me working at my job, long hours, of my own will, every day—and that's what a man should do, that's what counts. She is shrewd, self-contained, tolerant, in every real sense of the word sophisticated. She gives off a curious and memorable aura of mastery. She has dealt with the conditions of her life and subdued them. I'd say she is Samuel's highest reach, and it's a damned shame that it wasn't Sarah or Madeleine who turned out to be the spinster.

Edith: Born in Uinta, lives in ~~Pocatello~~ [*pencil:* Oakland]. Education, not a hell of a lot. She is said to have been the prettiest of the daughters, though Grace is certainly the handsomest now. Appears to have been something of a bright girl, too; at least several of the pious Mormon books I salvaged from Samuel's library were presented to her as prizes. Married a railroad conductor from Nevada. Divorced him some ten years ago. Children:

Webb—or maybe Webster.[36] High school. Several years older than I and the one grandson I liked. Used to spend his summers on the farm. Humorous and naturally sophisticated. Was intelligent but a long sickness affected his eyes and he could not go to college. Was a taxi driver for some time. Now runs a small business of his own. Aunt Grace describes it as a "basket lunch place." I don't know what it is—a California invention probably. Was married but his wife died. No children. Lives in San Francisco.

Martha. 2 years of college. Married an insurance salesman. 1 child.

Madeleine (cont.): I forgot to list her romance. She divorced Bill Ward and some years later, she being fifty or thereabout, married a childhood sweetheart, whose passion had endured through the years. She abruptly ceased to be a charge on Grace and Martha. For the sweetheart, beginning life as a U.P. engineer, ended it as a prosperous orange farmer in California. He ended it pretty soon after exposure to her whines, leaving her a pleasant income.

Well, there's the record. It teaches a little sociology, maybe, but I'll be damned if it teaches me any genetics. Obviously there is a recurrent neuroticism but I can't chart it. I don't know whether it has showed up in any of the third generation except me and the epilept. I can't plot any curve of intelligence, either. Beatrice and Rhoda were conspicuously intelligent; but their brothers are dimwits. Of the rest, only Cora, Webb and I have any brains, and I'm not sure of him, having not seen him since 1919. Sam's tenacious staying power skipped his son, touched my mother, touched Martha a little more and came out full strength in Grace. Nobody else had it. But the others don't show any obvious traces of its counterpart in Sam's wife, who was tireless, even tempered, optimistic. She and Sam were readers and Sam was something of a student, granted his education and his status: of his children, only my mother ever read books, and of his grandchildren, so far as I know only my half-brother and I—and my father was more of an influence on me than my mother. I doubt if Sarah's and Madeleine's children, except

Cora, can read a headline without moving their lips. About half of the grandchildren have shown an ability to maintain themselves in the world; the rest just subsist, with help from Grace and Martha. Cora, Alice, Beatrice, Martha and I go [got?] to college. My half-brother, Martha's other daughter, Sarah's second brood, Edith's son certainly could have gone if they had wanted to, and my father offered to put Rhoda through. They didn't want to; probably most of them couldn't have lasted if they had gone.

Conspicuous respectability, broken in the direct line only by Edward. Conspicuous intellectual mediocrity, broken in the second generation only by Grace and in the third, if I may be so bold, only by me—and that break unquestionably due to genes that had their origin in Genoa. Conspicuous looseness of heel—it doesn't come out here but they have wandered all over the continent, and one of them remains in the occupation of the Founder. There's a kind of progressive deterioration, in that Sam was at least one of Malinowski's earth-people, and only Grace of all that crew is today. But they have, the better half of them, the industry, adaptability and tribe stability of the small bourgeoisie. And they are a cooperative lot. Most of them hate my guts but any of them would take me in, and I suppose I'd take any of them in—which is not a loyalty I get from my father's house. The third generation seems to be staying married better than its parents did. Rhoda has done well for herself by marriage, I've done well for myself, financially I mean. Probably only Beatrice and I have to pay income tax. In the American social hierarchy, only Rhoda as the wife of a banker, Beatrice as the wife of a branch executive, and I as a college professor could sit about [*sic*] the salt.[37] But I'll bet that half the grandchildren own at least an equity in their houses, have savings accounts and life insurance. America seems safe enough, but somehow I think they haven't lived up to Sam.

This has crowded out a lot of flashes and week-end cables from the Harvard sector. I hope it hasn't bored hell out of you. I'll be back on the air after writing lectures on the Muckrakers and Greenwich Village and reviewing the new Wolfe.[38]

Yours,
Benny

Lincoln, Massachusetts

[1 May 1936]

Dear Kate:

Give me—have I not taken shots in the dark at your bidding?—some 6, 8, or 10 lines of answer to this:

Do I, having twice refused the editorship of *The Saturday Review of Literature*, want, on its being offered me still again, to accept it and the probable dictatorship of literary opinion in the US for the next 10 years, an era of much tumult and considerable amusement, at the loss of Harvard, the certainty that I will write no more history, & the probability that I will write no more novels?[39]

Bearing in mind:

That I write the sort of thing represented by that Wolfe job more easily than anything else, can't quite take it seriously, and in fact write it well because I feel contemptuous of it.

That my path of advancement at Harvard has been declared closed by no other than James B. Conant, on the ground that I'm a literary hack...but that this is not so final as it seems, since there is a strong groundswell in my name, the department is solidly behind me and I am a competent scholar and a good teacher...and in fact that it's a 6 to 5 bet Conant about faces.

That the urge to accept what I have twice refused—November and January—comes not only from the omen of the third offer of the crown but also my clear realization that MT[40] is not, as yet, as good as SG, and its involuntary sequel, the fear that maybe I've always been right in fearing that I wasn't a novelist.

That I have also: a complete belief in the virtue & value of MT and a dogged determination to work on it till I bring it up to the conception.

That, on the one hand, I dislike criticism, hate the literary life, and both despise New York and am afraid of it.

That, on the other, there is something in obligation: I can probably do that job, decent people need a spokesman these days, I am a controversialist first of all, and I was the first choice of the boys who run the sheet & they keep coming back to me.

That the literary people who know I turned it down before—Hervey Allen, Zinsser—call me a God damned fool for so doing. That the only other person who knows I did—L.J. Henderson—says I was right.

That, I think, covers it. Do your stuff.

Yours

Benny

Or, more simply: I can be a big-shot in a field I'm not interested in, whereas at best I can be only a 3rd rate novelist, with the present chance of missing 3rd rate.

[telegram]
NE 33 28 DL=POUGHKEEPSIE NY 2 1013A
1936 MAY 2 AM 10:34
BERNARD DEVOTO=
LINCOLN MASS=

I WOULD LIKE TO FIND OUT HOW ONES LIFE CAN HAVE DISTINCTION OR SYMMETRY STOP I WOULD LIKE TO DISCOVER SOMETHING A MAN WOULD WANT TO DO STOP=

KGS.

Lincoln, Massachusetts

[5 May 1936]

Dear Kate:

I can't seem to write—even fiction—while the reverberations go on & on. Cathcart & George Stevens will be here this evening for more negotiation.[41] Meanwhile another exponent has been given a definite value by Mr. Conant's decision that DeVoto on the present basis is one thing but DeVoto on permanent appointment is something else—something that has to be approached with this question, "Would we bring him here from California?", to which the answer is, "He is not the best man in America for his job, and so we would not."

A curious young man, our Mr. Conant. He maintains that my scholarship is deficient. My department says that it is far more than adequate, I being the leading authority in one field of American literature & the discoverer & only authority in another. The department alleges further that I am the best teacher of composition in the US & the only one who can maintain the succession, Hill-Wendell-Briggs-Copeland, for which the University has been noted.[42] Mr. Conant replies with Bob Hillyer's declaration that I have "debased the honorable tradition of composition at Harvard." He tells me that he has many opinions about me, some of which would surprise me. Some of the sources of them certainly have, especially Mr. Canby.

I have little opinion in the matter. Two possibilities are obvious, that I am not as desirable for Harvard as I think, and that Conant is making a mistake. But one curious little incident has acquired meaning for me in the light of another incident that followed it almost at once. What followed it was Conant's letter to Charlie Curtis, dropping him from the Society of Fellows. It was easy enough for Charlie to give up the Harvard Corporation, since he knew, & I realize, that matters of public policy, the Brahmin tradition, & the endowment funds made it wise to get rid of a divorced man. But the Society of Fellows is not bound up with any of those things, is purely private to the interior of Harvard, is an organization with the sole object of intellectual activity—and has been the center of Charlie's life since, with A. L. Lowell, he founded it. Firing him from it could mean absolutely nothing but moral disapproval.... So, when I learned of it, my mind flashed back to that same morning. I'm speaking of the magazine whose editorship I had been offered, Conant referred to it as the *Saturday Evening Post*.

Well, I judge that, whatever else happens, I am out of Harvard. For two years Harvard has been paying me $3200, after paying me $1585 for the preceding five years. The portion of my time & energy it has taken could be justified only on the expectation of the permanent professional appointment which I was in fact promised in writing by the last head of the Dept, Murray, when I accepted my present job, and by the present head, Munn, shortly afterward.[43] I obviously cannot go on—much as Jim Conant feels it would be agreeable for us all—spending 60% of my time & strength on a job that produces only 20% of my income and is leading nowhere. So I will be resigning. Whether I go to NY, or whether I stay here & have more time & ease &, the serial market being what it is, a 33% boost in income.

And, I'm glad to say, released of the obligation to work up a graduate course in "The Literature of the Frontier" for next year, and one in "Pre-Civil War Cultural Forces in America" for the following year. The amiable English dept had imposed them on me.

Well, all you say is absolutely true.[44] Add the centripetal fact that the kind of life I now have is one which I selected for myself, bent my plans & energies to serve, and want to continue in till I die. If there is anything in human choice, it's my life. Then oppose to that an ambiguous fear that, if I turn down the *Review*, the decision may be dictated not by all these rational considerations but by some basic dread of New York, or some even more basic fear to meet a challenge.... You perceive some of the juice in which I now fry.

Well, my best hope is that Cathcart's highest possible salary offer will be much too low for me to afford the job.[45] That would at once relieve me of any further anti-analysis.

Jesus, what a set of stale jokes the literary life is! I'll tell you from day to day what happens. Mr. Lamont, the Angel, sails for Africa—to clean up Addis Ababa?—on May 15 & everything must be settled before then.[46] And if I turn down the job, then George Stevens leaves the *Review* too, for his desire is to make it self-supporting & he feels that I'm the one chance.

As of yesterday it had not been decided whether to award no *Atlantic* Novel Prize this year, or to award it to a mss. from—of all places to get MFH symbolism—Iowa, called *I Am The Fox*, a study of frigidity in women by free association.[47] Curious the persistent influence of James Joyce in 8 Arlington Street.

Be so good as to hold my hand for the next 4 days.

Yours

Benny

Bowne

[BEFORE 13 MAY 1936]

Dear Benny,

Yes, well, I've been stewing in hot oil right along with you.... Enclosure: Nomenclature in the U.S.A. I wonder who the French Broad was. Reminds me, too, of the attractive pet-name that certain newspapermen covering the Scopes trial devised for Alice Warner Milton, wife of George Fort Milton of the Chattanooga *News*.[48] ... "Newspapermen," says Dorothy Thompson, "are incredibly respectable; belong, in fact, to the very nicest people." Oh, yes?

The Whitehills have found a baby. Name: Jon. Age: 7 weeks. Weight: 7 lbs. "He has a good background, blond hair & a temper. And bowels. And yowls." They suspect he is a bit premature, but "the mother is very vague as to dates," so they can't be sure.... Francis & Pamela Taylor's work-in-progress, *A History of American Collecting*, is said to be more amusing than you might suppose.[49] ... Vollard's *Recollections* are lousy: such a damned waste of swell material.[50] ... Edith Wharton's s.s. collection strikes me as a must.[51] I read two of them, *Roman Fever*[52] & the one about the M'divains, in magazines, & the hand does not falter.... Mary Norworth's kid brother Maurice comes up for his Ph.D. oral some time this month & is obviously in an acute state of nerves:

Mary—Ah, well, Mimi, you're far too young to be a Ph.D. anyway.

Maurice (with a grin)—Not if I make it...

What happened to the youth who last summer importuned you from Italy to save his soul & his prose style? Have you a student named John Bainbridge?[53] What kind of a goat is this Conant, anyway? I guess Philip's original estimate was correct:[54]

"They say he's a good chemist..."[55]

Yours,

Kate

Lincoln, Massachusetts

[13 MAY 1936]

Dear Kate:

It's 8:40. At 6:15 I called up George Stevens and accepted his job. At 6:30 I called Jim Munn and resigned from the faculty of Harvard College. I'm afraid this is going to be a dirge.

I settled it in my own mind yesterday but waited for his word that I could keep on with the Easy Chair. Lee said, "Your drawers are too red—you won't get on with Tom Lamont—and you belong at Harvard—but go ahead." Of course I belong at Harvard.

I know that and so does everybody else except James B. Conant.... Word has got out in the last two days. I have been flooded with incredulity & shock. Fred Merk still doesn't believe I'm quitting. Schlesinger believes I'm going to quit Harvard but doesn't believe I'll leave Cambridge. In fact the history dept feels outraged the whole length of its frame, and it's queer how I realize that it's history I'm leaving and not English. Of my own dept, I've respected only Munn, Murdock & Miller, and been able to work only with Murdock & Miller, whereas the historians, from Sam Morison to Paul Buck, from Jim Baxter to the janitor of HW, are all brothers of mine.[56] And it's something of a historian, just above the janitor, that I'm ceasing to be. The first & third volumes of *Empire* will get written all right, but the second one never will for one has to live for years next door to Widener in order to write it and now I won't.[57] That's the one Fred Merk has been moving for, too: the technological one, the frontier as a conditioner of skills, handicrafts, instruments, methods & ways of life. Jesus.... The point has been: Murdock, Miller & I, with H.M. Jones being deliberately brought in to close the ranks, as a sort of half-way house between American literature & American history.[58] Pairing with Morison, Merk, Schlesinger & Buck, historians, and a sociologist always referred to as X, in the hope that some day we'd find him. A kind of unofficial institute in American culture. Merk the historian and me the minister without portfolio to share the frontier between us, all of us realizing that the frontier is the key to all the rest. Well, Merk is a great historian, and I find I've been proud of the linkage. The boys will do a lot in the next ten years. It would be nice to have a hand in it.

My guess is that Buck will be moving on, too. He happens to be the best young historian in the US but no matter.

...I say, it has leaked out in the last 48 hours. Just as I wrote "US" above, the phone rang. Colleague of mine, who has been most poisonous for some time. Yesterday he bade Frost tell me that he had submitted a memorandum to Jim Munn recommending my promotion. This afternoon when I called Jim, my pal had been telling Jim just today the wonders I achieve in English A3. There were no inquiries in this phone call but the liveliest conversation imaginable. He hasn't phoned me in two years.

Well, hell. It narrowed down to quite a simple matter. I can't go on forever writing magazine tripe. It has to be Harvard or an editorship. I can't go on doing two men's work at Harvard (Munn: "I'll have to get two men to take your place, one in composition, one in Am Lit"—Yeah, just who'll pay for them?) for ⅘ the salary of an asst. prof. on an insecure tenure. I'll write the serial I've promised *Collier's*, and then I'm through with tripe forever.[59] I'll tuck most of it away to educate my kid when the time comes—educate him, if God is good, for the public service, a scientific foundation, or something else that doesn't imply the kind of shifts I've had to make. I'll run this sheet 3 years or 5 years. And I'll be in a better position to make my way, my terms, or my peace.

I don't quite understand why I feel Conant's offer somehow insulting. I'm a bargain at cut-rate price—I can stay on indefinitely on the present terms—but no permanent appointment, no promotion. That he was obviously sincere seems to make the insult more sincere. My weak flesh takes satisfaction in Schlesinger's "The honeymoon's over—he's been making mistakes and this is a bad one," in Henderson's "It's a stupid mistake".... That's silly. But it is damn hard to leave Harvard College. Queer what an affection the place inspires in the unlikeliest people, what irrational and tremendous loyalty it has always been able to count on. I read Cushing's book, I come across names like Roger Lee, Arlie Bock, George Derby, George Denny—and I find myself glowing in the damn nonsense of the Harvard fellowship.[60] Though Roger Lee is not the happiest name to glow over. Conant has been leaning on him principally of the Corporation—having fired Charlie Curtis, & Bob Homans, the other of Conant's creators[,?] having died.[61] And the most rational hypothesis of my—call it my discharge—is not that I am deficient in scholarship, that budgetary requirements or the future growth of my dept interfere, or that I don't measure up to the standards that have let worse men by—but simply that I offended what Roger Lee stands for, by writing SG. One does not deal with the Brahmins in such terms.[62] The adulterers shall be dropped from the Corporation, Roger Lee unquestionably evaporating, and the outspoken & upstart shall be stopped short. He's a great doctor. And so was Dr. Holmes.[63]...He examined me for the first of my several inductions into the armed forces of democracy. Thrusting a hand up my groin till he could have pulled out my diaphragm: "Cough." I cough. "Not in the face, please."

Well, hell.... I seem to have said Well, hell as often as Mark Howe stutters for the last 2 weeks.[64]...I wonder how Mark will finish his Overseers Report on Composition Courses.... Well, hell, I'll be writing MT by fall—I'll be writing it & taking over the *Review* on October 1st. And wouldn't you predict that, these last 2 days, I've made pages of notes for it and been unable to see the exterior world or say anything rational to Cambridge or New York, for seeing scenes play themselves out in a kind of red fire.

I feel pretty low, Kate. Or is that evident by now? God knows I did my best to stay here. God knows that if the President had consulted the wishes of my department or had inquired about me of the people I've worked with for 7 years & planned to work with for 26 more, I'd be staying here. I'm being kicked out of the way of life that means most to me. But I'm also being kicked upstairs. In reality, my work is being simplified. No more lecturing. No more reading themes. No more interviewing students. No more working up courses. No more professional chores—the innumerable time-consuming minutiae, which have been all the more common with me because I have been the one Literary Adviser to Young Harvard.

Telephone call from, by God I'll have to start thinking of him as my business manager. Please come to NY on Thursday & have the no longer avoidable interview with Canby. I'll have to pull the damn phone out, to sleep.

But figure it any way—and I've figured it every way you can conceive of and threescore more, I'll have at least as much time to write my own stuff—provided always that I try to write only one book at a time—as I've had these last years at Harvard. Or any other years. With some sense of security. With a lot less on my mind. With less pressure. With less conflict. With fewer balls to keep in the air. That's something.

And if I have to give up my planned economy—all planned economies have to be given up. And if I have to leave Lincoln, Cambridge, and my friends—well, after all, I am stepping into immediate power and an opportunity which, no matter how alien it is to my desires and how much I've tried to avoid it, does remain an opportunity.

And it isn't, I believe, for ever. Five years at the outside. And who in hell do I think I am to suppose it matters?

It strikes me that this letter doesn't sound a hell of a lot like a declaration of policy & confidence by the editor of a literary journal.

Anyway, you'll get your literary gossip from HQ.

I'd say this is enough about my private diseases. Probably you'll have to listen to another wail when I get back from NY. After that, let's recline for a while in the more assuasive material of who has stopped, or begun, sleeping with who.

Yours

Benny

Lincoln, Massachusetts

[September 1936]

Dear Kate:

I find my study papered with wires from Lee demanding an unwritten Easy Chair but before I begin it, a few running heads.... I find that the line which comes back most clearly is John Mason Brown's description of Coca Cola, Josephine's only drink, as tasting like liquid halitosis. He also described George Stevens as given to mustang moods, which is exact, and said that after a conference with an old lady about some work of rare talent, he felt as if his privates had been subjected to a vacuum cleaning, which gives the feeling better than I ever could.... The best yarns of the Conference were related in the rich Tennessee idiom of one O'Donnell, a "Fellow" much given to gab but a nice boy, and so are beyond rendition.[65] I should like to reproduce the one about the weaning of a twelve-year-old po' white boy which ended, "Pappy, git the shotgun, Ma's been into the bitterweed." ... Gorham Munson had one about the balls of a musk-ox which you may not have heard. It has to do with a meeting of Jean and Marcel in a pissoir[66] and Jean's noticing that the letters S and E appear in tattoo in a conspicuous place on Marcel. M explains that Jean observes him in a moment of relaxation and that if conditions were more favorable Jean would understand a bit of sentiment—the whole legend is in reality the name of his mistress, Suzette. Some years pass and again chance brings them together in a pissoir. Marcel is not astounded and somewhat angered to observe the same letters tattooed on the anatomy of Jean. Jean pacifies him: do not anger yourself, my friend; you observe me in a moment of relaxation; I have been gone from France since we met and if conditions were more favorable you would be able to make out my legend, Souvenir de Service militaire avec le Général Chateaubriand-Tissôt en Algérie.... One night argument reverted to a question which you once raised and O'Donnell supplied the following key to *The Sun Also Rises*, which he says was given to Allen Tate by Hemingway himself:[67]

Prentiss—Glenway Wescott |
Bret—Lady Twisdon[68] |
Braddocks—Ford Madox Ford
Bill[69]—Donald Ogden Stewart
Jake—E.H.
Harvey Stone—Harold Stearns |
Robert Cohn—Harold Loeb[70] |
Frances—Kitty Cannell |
Michael—Duff-Gordon

I don't even know whom the last one refers to; I had heard stories that various women of the Duff-Gordons were to be found in Bret. Those marked | are verified by Munson, who is never wrong in things of that sort and has reasons for knowing about Loeb and Kitty Cannell. I looked up Prentiss and the description of Wescott is exact, though just why he should be separated from the fairies I don't make out.... Gorham said that the Kitty Cannell episodes were literal, and then talk wandered off into inquiries about Skipwith Cannell.[71] He seems not to have died, disappeared or been divorced but just to have dissolved. There is no record of him anywhere. My judgment was that his only existence at any time was in the fantasies of Ezra Pound, but then there is Frost's narrative about his arrival in New York, after Pound had written his four poems, and asking "What is America saying about me?"... John Farrar arrived in a pet, grew more pettish when no carpet was laid down for him, and finally had to be spanked. God knows how he feels toward me now: I had never been overt before and still he hated my guts.... An incredible person who has appeared but not by name in these memoirs, one Zoltan Harasty, turned up and got so obnoxious that Ted Morrison had to kick him out.[72] He left calling Ted a beef and threatening to expose him as one, and as a maniac also, to as puzzling a trio as you could name, President Conant, Sam Morison, and Sam Houghton, ex-editor of *The Writer*.[73] ... This year's pest was male, a creature who called himself Colonel Jean-Jacques Rousseau Voorhees, apparently a kind of press agent, who pontificated to women, broke some hearts and it may be some maidenheads as well, and honored us all with notes of appreciation and gratitude the most flatulent.... Both the fellows and the customers set a new high. It was much the best collection we've had. There were a good many good mss, and at least a dozen of them were by customers, including one very good novel and an astonishingly good detective novel (by a granddaughter of John Humphrey Noyes.[74] She is a stunner for looks and has a very high I.Q. The founder of stirpiculture certainly made good. I've signed her for articles and reviews.) ... Best manuscript was probably *The Joppa Gate*, a novel by Hope Sykes, one of the Fellows, a middle-aged Coloradoan whose hearty voice carried me back to the high plains.[75] ... None of the men, outside the Fellows, amounted to anything but both O'Donnell and a Connecticut farmer named Crook will be heard from.[76] .. Our this year's mistake was Marie Luhrs.[77] Ted and I picked her for a fellowship on what seemed sound principles. She was recommended by the Greenberg Press and by *The American Hebrew* and her list of some thirty publications sounded obviously proletarian.[78] We wanted to do our bit for Semitism and the radical press and so we took her, pursuing the inquiry no farther. She turned out to be a pulp-writer, German Catholic and the damnedest dimwit south of the Waterbury hospital. God knows our screen is coarse enough but what came through it was too fine for her comprehension. But an amazing fantasy life. With the story about a beau of hers, the head of a Scottish clan who lives in New York and wears kilts for political reasons. I suggested that he might be the McCohen and Kay Morrison, a native Scot, could go no further. Her pulp stories were all about lords, ladies, daggers and eerie cries by night.... But this was a high life year in the productions of the customers. Helen Everitt got a manuscript set on the Normandie. The author thought deck tennis was played with a racquet and presented chess as a four-handed game. An act of one of the dramas submitted to Johnny Brown began, "My, we certainly are having a formal party tonight, aren't we?" The gentlemen then enter, saying "We have imbibed, ladies, but not too much." ... Hillyer was on his best behavior and some of the heroic couplets that are to follow the not so good ones in the current *Atlantic* are distinctly something.[79] He has had a curious rebirth as a poet; the quality of his conversation is getting into his verse.... Speaking of that, in a syndicated Sunday article Silas Bent is referring to me as, with Dreiser and Elmer Davis, one of the only three writers who have good conversation.[80] To the best of my knowledge all I have ever said to Silas is "Have a drink," but then I've said that quite often.... Josephine is so beautiful that there is now not even a pretence among the women of the staff of being fair to her books. Even Helen Everitt, who has the assurance of Semiramis, was overheard remarking that she couldn't imagine Josephine in love.[81] Curiously, I can. I can imagine Josephine in love with some small, unpretentious, humble person who can never possibly challenge her distinction, and in fact I not only imagine it, I know it. He is, besides, physically small. Which adds up to a most interesting inquiry. I began speculating, once, about her disdain of—well, call us adults or call us talkers or social beings or what you will. Then I began to think that the violence, terror and turbulence of her short stories were an odd kind of fantasy for a young girl to be having. And she told me this year that she always seemed to fall out of love just when it was going to get serious. So... But the contrast she made with Vicky Lincoln, whose last year's function she assumed, was altogether shocking. Not only has Josephine beauty and intelligence, she has warmth and kindness and good humor, she is without envy, she is tranquil and serene, and she is modest.... I derive a considerable, if quiet, satisfaction from seeing my remarks turn up in her stuff. They are invariably on the side of darkness and the fallen angels, but they are there. And at any rate, I have gotten most of the vegetables out of her books. If she has any image of me at all it is as the father of lies and the counselor of corruption, but I have made my point about the hummingbirds and the squashes.... Interesting physiological phenomenon: a week after my sprain, the discoloration of my ankle has in part detached itself and moved down to color three of my toes a magnificent purple.... The Easy Chair being done, I will, when and as, resume this summary.

Yours,
Benny

~~Lincoln, Massachusetts~~

[28 September 1936]

Dear Kate:
Cancel most humbly my remarks on the practice & perspicuity of medicine in Greater New York. And add whatever other adverb will support my state of mind on being informed, yesterday noon, that the report on Louise's Wassermann revealed a ripe +4. Hell, which has been popping since the 10th inst., popped still more from then on. Tension eased a little at noon today when a Kahn test of Bunny's blood was negative. His Wassermann and Avis's and mine won't be in for several more days. As a familiar of Hans Zinsser, I'm aware that the odds against any of us having been infected are astronomical, but that knowledge in no way impedes my phantasy. And as a clinician I know the tests will have to be repeated in 3 months.

The cause of this fortissimo was on her way home to Haverhill within an hour, where, according to the perspicuous physician, she will shortly discover that she is also pregnant. I am happy to say that I acted with no social conscience whatever, bouncing her out on her Canuck fanny at once.... She came to us on the suggestion of the incomparable Hannah, whose aunt lived across the street in Haverhill. Hannah is far too good a Catholic to be aware of the social infections, or even of their common cause. The one ray of light in a dark time is the hope, probably illusory, that Hannah's even more incomparable sister Catherine may soon sail from Ireland to join us. A triumph, if it prove not an illusion, an ultimate triumph over a Wigglesworth for whom Catherine worked for eight years and so vengeance upon the Brahmins may be mine at last.

It would be hard to imagine any ingenuities that could have been added to these 16 days. Doubtless, however, the unimaginable are in preparation. No probable possible doubt no possible doubt [*sic*] whatever remains about a hay fever that has closed me up like a padlocked speak except that I wheeze like a model T Ford with a worn gasket. I have edited in the midst of a total fug & a partial blindness & deafness. The office all but snarls at me awaiting action on one major firing & a major readjustment of powers that I simply have not yet had intelligence to consider on their merits. The house is without order & without service. Except that the nurse will be back tomorrow, Bunny having folded today with what may be another cold, may be a temporary reaction from the second inoculation in the series which he always has to be given this time of year, or may be simple protest against what has been so far a quite intolerable mode of living... Poor kid! It's been a hell of a strain on him & sometimes he speaks plaintively about Lincoln & his possessions & habits & associates there. Did I give the public school two or three weeks? It lasted exactly 2 ½ days & he is now entered at something called "Windward" which isn't as progressive as it might be no doubt but is bad enough.[82] At any rate, it will sometimes be fun for him, he may pick up a little knowledge or skill here & there and he may not lose quite all his morale.

Chaos revealed, out of something or other, Lt. DeVoto's barracks cap, complete with ornament & rain band. Being told that that was Daddy's army hat, my son inquired if I was a messenger boy in the army. Also, note on the word-sense of the modern child: to anything covered by the word "confusing," or by his other synonym "mixedy-uppy," the adjective "static" may be applied with identical effect. Which seems to me a pretty logical analysis.

What book on the world's series by games? I bought half of a 3 to 1 on Roosevelt at the office, and, on your clairvoyance, I have taken quite a bit of 1 to 2 that R will carry Pennsylvania. I think the only way I stand to lose—but that's, alas, a lead pipe & in fact consummated cinch—is from the automobile industry. As a commuter I would be clearly insane to maintain & insure two cars, but alas the Buick was a coupé & I would not drive the Chevrolet so there was nothing to do but turn them in on a family car. I'm getting a new Buick as soon as the '37 models begin to come in, but I've taken a beating that will have me shuddering still when the '47 models are announced.

Oh, my dear, have you forgotten the English novelists, especially the English she-novelists? Consider May Sinclair, consider Rose Macaulay, consider Sheila Kaye-Smith.[83] Consider, for that matter, Dorothy Richardson.[84] And I will not yield you Louis Bromfield while Francis Brett Young is alive.[85] ... Did you, by the way, ever meet his wife? .... There is also Warwick Deeping, though he may come under the migratory bird act, and whichever Waugh wrote *Kept*.[86] In fact, take away Aldous Huxley & the Storm Jamieson [*sic*] of *The Lovely Ship* & *Voyage Home* and the whole field will come down the stretch hard on Louis Bromfield's crupper.[87] Yes, dear, I know V. Woolf is not excepted in the above.[88] It seems to me that you ignore some honeys at home, too. Sherwood Anderson yet lives—and in fact will have a book out in a week.[89] Only the fact that I face a Westbrook Pegler,[90] an Edgar Lee Masters[91] & an Easy Chair[92] restrained me from doing it myself. If the jacket does not lie, it tells how a wood-sprite forsook her high hills & came down to be chauffeuse for a bootlegger.

Experience of the week: a publisher demanded that I review economics strictly from the Republican point of view. Observation of the week: my first Sat Rev lunch, Lin Yutang & Pearl Buck—who resembles Gladys Hasty Carroll but has more brains & fewer looks.[93]

The most esthetic youth who was ever a student of mine, who ran a salon and used lavender paper, a Mr. Victor Rosen, turns up as managing editor of *Furs*: A Journal of the Fur Business.[94]

Word from Cambridge is that the fireworks were swell.

Yours

Benny

333 Ridgeway
White Plains, New York

[21 December 1936]

Dear Kate,

I don't care whether you send the Cather here or to the office. Probably more convenient to leave them all wrapped together, isn't it? Not to mention depriving Jim Farley's outfit of several cents.... I can't—and maybe won't—make out whether it's Farley or the mailing co. that does us dirt. Certainly it's the P O that holds up our New England and Canadian deliveries, but a sprinkling of complaints elsewhere don't seem to be the [?] govt.... [?] New list herewith. I strongly recommend the Lucas, and will send the Marquand in a day or two without order. I can't get the <u>Geo Moore</u> for you without asking the publisher for it and I don't want to do that. But I may be able to steal one from Harry Scherman in due time.

A slack time—thank God—in the literary business. Geo. Stevens is going to Washington for 10 days, Amy to Boston for 4, and I to Providence for 2, after Christmas, and nobody will miss us, except, possibly, Rosy, who may have to suffer illness for a time.[95] I've been able to catch up on my reviews, write my A H A speech, read Charles Crane's fascinating but formless & rather artless ms on Vermont, and even go out to dinner a couple of times. It would be nice to know just why, at my age and in my business, I read a ms. Probably, as a victim to Alfred Knopf's geniality, which is calculated and crafty even though genuine. In the last ten years I must have done several thousand dollars worth of work for him gratis. Or gratis less some excellent lunches & dinners at the very best places. This one is a book I'd like to write myself and I have Paul Moody's word that it would be a better one if I did. Which reminds me, at long last Moody has made me Abernethy Lecturer for next Spring.[96]

Frost stopped off on his way to, of all places, Corpus Christi, for the winter and I had an evening with him. He is certainly the greatest man I've ever known or am likely to know—a wisdom, a subtlety, a serenity, and a massiveness that fairly make me weep to contemplate. Such talk there has surely never been since Lucifer fell out of heaven. I had to leave before midnight and so hadn't rubbed him past the white heat of his normal intelligence to the shooting nuclei he begins to give off before dawn, but even in that stage he is a comet in our dusk. He will be writing the Harvard lectures soon and I can have what I can use of them. He approaches them with his characteristic uneasiness about prose, a foreboding as little justified as any in the history of literature. The few pages he wrote to introduce Robinson's last book might be written on ivory.[97] From a recent letter to me: "I would never have written about the poor if I had thought it would lead to anything's being done about them. Or better: I wrote about the poor as the most permanent subject to hitch onto. I took Christ's word for it that poverty would be abolished." And, "I see Yale is pulling a convention to discuss happiness as a human possibility. One thing is sure: I never enjoyed happiness till it was over." (In regard to my book.) "It strikes me that if the West has been exploited on the economic plane by the East in times past, it is now being exploited by the East on the plane of sentiment in the p[*illegible*]s of Roosevelt and Farley. I guess the West is a sucker." I'm weak enough to add another sentence about F & R: "And the way you lay into the writing with your whole body like an archer rather than a pistolman." . . . . I turned up the interesting fact that there are not only a couple of plays lying around in ms. but even several chapters of a novel. All of them, he says, fumbling toward *North of Boston*. They would be something to see. Maybe I can see them next summer—I hope to be in his part of Vermont, possibly even his neighbor. My inclinations, of course, are to get up into the mountains but Bunny's need for companions may keep us on the plain, and if so, why not Shaftesbury, He wants me to come there—and follow him to Craftsbury for the hay fever season, having been so delighted by what seemed to be my allergy that I shrink from telling him it was just sinus. (It's being rather viciously dealt with from week to week. Yesterday portions of my nose were fried with a high-frequency needle, and I expect to have some bone sawed away almost any time now.) Robert is feeling the farmer surge up in him. He wants to set out some orchards, buy some more woodlots, start raising hay to sell. When he's in that mood, you look at his forearms and realize that they are like a shoemaker's.... There is an affinity between his mind and mine, *mutatis mutandis*,[98] which I begin to realize may make it necessary for me to write his biography. For God's sake, don't even have a dream about this, for I'd prefer anything on earth to writing a book about a friend. But who else is there? Foster Damon?[99] Jesus Christ, no! Van Wyck Brooks? No soft mind should be permitted to try. Well, who? Already the bibliographers are cutting each other's throats, and already literary opportunists like Mildred Boie are clamoring to do the biography.

Buckminster Fuller, the Etzler *de nos jours*,[100] has been using his job with Phelps-Dodge to compile some of the most intricate & amusing charts ever made.[101] They prove everything. He is so completely inarticulate and I'm so bad at figures that I can only divine what it's all about, but if he can find somebody to translate & record him, we'll have a fad that will make the Technocracy uproar seem like dominoes.

The reliable news sense of our British cousins swung into action on Thursday, when every English newspaper that has a representative in N Y called up inside one hour to find out what this was we had about T.E. Lawrence. We sold extracts for 5 pounds & 20 pounds and the article itself for 50 pounds, thus making a nice profit on our expenses.... And learning, incidentally, that the War Office & the Foreign Affairs Office have got to work. People won't be reading *The Mint* any more.

Reading time 37 minutes—I want to catch a symphony.

Well, toward the end of my first year at Harvard, the Met came to town and on the night when Mary Garden did *Thais* I happened to get very tight indeed, so tight that the music, and damned bad music it is too, slipped in through the interstices of my soul, broke down God knows what resistances, piled all my emotions into a quivering heap, and transported me into a kind of ectoplasmic world that was all tears and all ecstasy.[102] An experience of some interest in itself, but that isn't our present point. Anyway, after being minced, pulverized and obliterated, I awoke cold sober & very tearful to find myself in a practically dark & practically empty opera house with the well-bred ushers crashing seats all around me to tell me it was time to get the hell out of there. I stood up and got into my coat and then somebody said, in Boston accents badly blurred by tears, "Oh, excuse me but...... would you help me to my car?" I looked round and there was a girl. You've seen the face in dozens of Copleys—hundreds of times at the Symphony—three or four times at the same dinner. At the time I'd seen some Copleys but no more, but knew enough to recognize Beacon Hill. You know the face—big nose, wide forehead, rather more chin than necessary, nondescript hair, rather pleasant in the ensemble. If any guaranty had been necessary, it was furnished by the ramshackle hat and the sloppy tailored suit. Obviously the Hill had suddenly decided to go to the opera—and more obviously had been knocked for a series of loops as I had been, though without alcohol. She'd been bawling furiously, she was trembling, and she looked faint. She took my arm and leaned on it hard, murmuring something about how silly & how she seemed to be faint. This was in the 2nd balcony. She got heavier, and before we were down the first stairs I had an arm around her and was practically holding her up. At the next balcony she made an ancestral effort of will and got on her own power. We stopped in the lobby while she gathered herself together still more. I made politely casual talk—as well as one could who was [?] calf with the hair side out and awed by Beacon Hill as only Utah can be, and as I've never been since. We went out to Huntington Avenue. No car—the chauffeur having probably swung by once or twice and then decided to smoke a cigarette. There was a moon and though it was something short of spring and much past dusk, I said, fatuously enough, "The pale moon like a petal floats in the pearly dusk of spring."[103] She said, "Sara Teasdale," and came alive.... This, dear, was in the very moment of the Renaissance of American Poetry, and I was up to my ears in all those things, and at that time even Sara Teasdale could unlock the hearts of maidens yearning for beautiful emotions.... She fired Sara at me and I fired Amy back and we exchanged shots from all through the renaissance for a rapid five minutes, and suddenly there was the car with an open door and a heel-clicking chauffeur.[104] A limousine like a hearse and as awkward-looking for those days as a 1921 Pierce is now.[105] In the cool air, she had got back some color and her eyes were snapping. She said, "We can't stop yet," and got a lot more color, got into the car, & impelled me in after her. It isn't a long ride from the Boston Opera House to approximately the corner of Clarendon and Beacon.[106] We talked poetry and Harvard, and before we stopped near that corner I was telling myself, out of my bucolic awe, that I must certainly be wrong, that there couldn't possibly be any such voltage in that car as I thought I felt. The car stopped, the door opened, we sat for a second or two, and she said to the chauffeur, "Go on home. I'll put the car up." (She never, to my knowledge, did.) She climbed out to the open front seat, bidding me bring the robe with me. She said, "If one is going to be crazy, one may as well be thoroughly crazy, and I want to talk poetry." She said no more about the proprieties. In those days Boston had few drives. She headed towards Charlestown, and we covered Chelsea & Everett before we turned back, talking poetry so furiously that I lost all my bucolic awe without noticing it was gone. I seemed to get an idea that what you had learned with the Mormon girls could help you a lot with the white. Or the bluestockings. Back over the bridge, I bade her stop at an all-night lunch and we had some coffee. So now, forsaking poetry, she plunged with the awful frankness of a Bostonian into an account of a quarrel with her fiancé. That quarrel, she seemed to want me to understand, and not the music was responsible for her deplorable lack of control at the Opera House. I got a look at her eyes and felt better. She got morose and silent, back in the car, and I got an idea she was feeling the hangover already. I tried to minister to it. No go. She seemed ready to burst into tears again and desperately, harking back to a chance remark, I said "Can't we have that chess game now?" Two A M on Beacon Street, and she came alive again. We tiptoed in and upstairs to a water-side library. She took off her coat, got out a chess board and set up the men. We played a game.... Jesus! I had no more idea where I was, what was happening, what the [?] clue was, than I'd had in the last act of *Thais*. Chess in a Beacon St. library with an obviously congealed Brahmin—or wasn't she?—or what? And me, a Utah boy, prepared always to commit any breach of morality whatever but always terrified by the possibility that I might breach an amenity. We started another game, and if I so much as touched her fingers, moving a piece, she made me feel as gauche as a Mormon funeral sermon. I could feel as high a voltage as even my own Telluride Company had ever sent out over the wires and if I even looked aware of it I got frozen in my chair.[107] Three o'clock struck, and slippered feet sounded outside on the stairs. Someone said, "Betty?" She said evenly, "I'm here, Aunt Helen, go to bed." Aunt Helen's feet patted upstairs. I thought, they're Mormon girls or they aren't Mormon girls, pushed the table away, and said, "I hope Aunt Helen's deaf." She said, "The maids come down at six-thirty."..... That was my first reception into the homes of the Bostonians. Did I ever tell you that Prexy Lowell's niece told me that she had never heard of immoral relations in the Back Bay?[108]

Yours
Benny

NOTES

1. In Wolfe, *Look Homeward, Angel*.
2. Of Edward Wagenknecht, "Mark Twain: The Man and His Work," *New England Quarterly* 9 (June 1936). "The Greatness of Mark Twain: A New Biography That Silences the Frustration Theory," *NYT Book Review*, 27 October 1935, page 1; cites evolving criticism by Waldo Frank, Van Wyck Brooks, Newton Arvin, and Ludwig Lewisohn, now well rebutted by Wagenknecht's "sane, sound and tolerant" appraisal.
3. Parley Parker Pratt (1807–1857), Mormon apostle and writer.

4. Artemus Ward, pseudonym of Charles Farrar Browne (1834–1867), humorist.
5. Mason & Hamlin, Boston manufacturer of excellent concert grand pianos. The Jefferson Hotel was built by the cigarette manufacturer Louis Ginter, opened 1895, now with 274 rooms; designed by Carrère & Hastings in a polyeclectic Beaux-Arts style.
6. Pass-a-Grille Beach Hotel, near St. Petersburg, Florida.
7. (French) self-styled.
8. Terrier.
9. (German) world view.
10. Frost's second published collection, 1914.
11. At Harvard, usually a series of six public lectures on poetry or music in alternating years.
12. Uttered by Brigham Young, July 1847, when the Mormon emigration reached the valley of the Salt Lake.
13. "Terwillinger in Plato's Dream."
14. "Education on a Mountain: The Story of Black Mountain College," *Harper's* 172/5 (April 1936). Adamic (1899–1951), born in Slovenia, published *A Native's Return* in 1934.
15. "Another Consociate Family," in the same issue; reprinted in *Forays and Rebuttals*, 1936. See also Martin Duberman, *Black Mountain: An Exploration in Community*, 1973, for discussion of ensuing correspondence.
16. BDV published this essay in *American Mercury* 19 (January 1930), revising and expanding it to three times its original size in *Forays and Rebuttals*.
17. *The Readers' Guide to Periodical Literature*, since 1900.
18. The first appeared originally in *Harper's* 155/4 (September 1927); reprinted in *Forays and Rebuttals* as "The Co-Eds: God Bless Them." The second appeared in *Harper's* 167/4 (September 1933); reprinted in *Forays and Rebuttals* as "The Life of Jonathan Dyer."
19. The Rollo books were written by Jacob Abbott (1803–1879), Congregationalist minister, for moral instruction of children; *Rollo Learning to Talk*, 1835, and *Rollo's Travel*, 1839, were followed by twenty-six others.
20. BDV, *The World of Fiction*, p. 79.
21. From the *Saturday Review of Literature*.
22. *Action at Aquila*, 1938, a novel about the Civil War.
23. Luxurious private club, since 1930.
24. Associated Press news network.
25. Probably Lewis M. Terman (1877–1956), author of the Stanford-Binet test, 1916. In 1936 he published a masculinity-femininity test.
26. Johannes Brahms (1833–1897), great German-Viennese composer.
27. Reference to *Middletown, a Study in Contemporary American Culture*, by Robert S. Lynd and Helen Merrell Lynd, sociologists, 1929, 1936; *Middletown in Transitions, a Study in Cultural Conflicts*, 1937.
28. Deseret was a Mormon sobriquet for Utah Territory.
29. Samuel George Dye (1834–1924) and Rhoda Paxman Dye (1830–1919), both natives of Hertfordshire in England, were married in 1856, emigrated to Boston and then New York, and settled in Utah Territory in 1861. Their children were Samuel George Dye Jr. (1859–?); Rhoda Ann Dye (1861–1919), Bernard DeVoto's mother; Sarah Jane Dye (1863–1909); Madeleine Dye (1864–1946); Martha Amanda Dye (1866–1954); Grace Matilda Dye (1868–1950); and Edith Elizabeth Dye (1872–?). The stillborn child, a daughter, was born and died in December 1870. See "The Life of Jonathan Dyer," in *Forays and Rebuttals*, 1936.
30. Union Pacific Railroad.

31. Laprielle DeWolfe, called Dee, married Gerald Boicourt; she died in 1954.
32. See *LBDV*, pp. 14–17; in fact he earned only five degrees, all from the University of Notre Dame.
33. Known as Aunt Matt.
34. The pandemic of 1918–1919 is thought to have killed 60 million people worldwide.
35. Rhodas appear in at least three generations of Dyes. The one referred to here is the daughter of Samuel Dye Jr.
36. Samuel Webster Moore (1895–1958).
37. Correctly, "sit above the salt," i.e., sit in a place of higher social rank or distinction.
38. Muckrakers: reformist journalists and popular historians who attacked the failures of American society and corruption in politics and big business; the best known were Ida Tarbell (1857–1944; *History of the Standard Oil Company*, 1904); Upton Sinclair (1878–1968; *The Jungle*, novel about the meat-packing industry, 1906); and Lincoln Steffens (1866–1936; *The Shame of the Cities*, 1904).
39. BDV later (January 1938) wrote a formal summary of events that led up to the questions posed here, in a letter to a Harvard committee; see *LBDV*, pp. 218–24.
40. *Mountain Time*, not Mark Twain.
41. Noble Cathcart (1898–1988), founding publisher of *SRL*.
42. Adams Sherman Hill (1833–1910), professor of English at Harvard; father of BDV's friend Arthur D. Hill, professor at Harvard Law School. Barrett Wendell (1855–1921), professor of English; *A Literary History of America*, 1900. LeBaron Russell Briggs (1855–1934), professor of English and dean of the faculty of Arts and Sciences, 1902–1925. Charles Townsend Copeland (1860–1952, "Copey"), professor of English.
43. John Tucker Murray (1877–1956), professor of English; James Munn (1890–1967), professor of English.
44. This suggests that KS's reply is missing.
45. Unknown; but family tradition held that it was approximately three times BDV's Harvard salary.
46. Thomas W. Lamont (1870–1948), financier and philanthropist who underwrote the *SRL*.
47. By Winifred Van Etten (1902–1982), 1936, professor of English at Cornell College, Iowa.
48. George Fort Milton (1894–1955), author, editor; his daughter was Alice Fort Milton.
49. This work in progress would seem to be *The Taste of Angels: A History of Art Collecting from Rameses to Napoleon*, vol. 1, 1948.
50. Ambroise Vollard (1867–1939), *Recollections of a Picture Dealer*, 1936.
51. *The World Over*, 1936.
52. In *Liberty*, 10 November 1934.
53. John S. Bainbridge is listed for the class of 1938; not identical with John Bainbridge (1913–1992), staff writer for *The New Yorker*.
54. Probably Philip McMahon.
55. Echo of a famous quip by the philosopher and Harvard professor Alfred North Whitehead (1861–1947), when a colleague declared that Charles William Eliot (1834–1926), often called Harvard's greatest president, had been a chemist: "I know—but Eliot was a *bad* chemist!" James Bryant Conant, before becoming president of Harvard, achieved a distinguished reputation both as an organic chemist and as an author of textbooks.
56. HW, the Harry Elkins Widener Memorial Library, the main library building at Harvard.
57. It was in fact replaced by *Across the Wide Missouri*, 1948.
58. Howard Mumford Jones (1892–1980), professor of English at the universities of Texas, Michigan and North Carolina, and at Harvard; prolific author and editor.

59. *Troubled Star*, 1938.
60. *From a Surgeon's Journal*, by Harvey Cushing, 1936. Lee (1881–1965), '02, physician, member of the Harvard Corporation. Derby (1875–1931), ophthalmologist, professor at the Medical School. Denny, uncertain; possibly (1870–1955), university chancellor.
61. Homans (1873?–1934) '94, Ll.B. '97, Fellow of Harvard College; attorney, Hill, Barlow, and Homans; father of BDV's student George Homans.
62. The elite of wellborn Boston families.
63. Oliver Wendell Holmes (1809–1894), Harvard 1829, physician and poet, professor at the Medical School; columnist for *Atlantic Monthly*: *The Autocrat of the Breakfast Table*; father of Oliver Wendell Holmes Jr. (1841–1935), Harvard 1861, professor at the Law School; associate justice of the U.S. Supreme Court, 1902–1932.
64. Mark Antony DeWolfe Howe (1864–1960), biographer, editor of *Atlantic Monthly*; Overseer at Harvard. See Helen Howe, *The Gentle Americans: Biography of a Breed*, 1965.
65. George Marion O'Donnell (1914–1962), poet.
66. (French) public toilet.
67. Novel by Hemingway, 1925. Tate (1899–1979), poet, professor of English at the University of Minnesota.
68. Duff Twysden.
69. Bill Gordon.
70. Loeb (1891–1974), writer, edited a little magazine, *Broom*, 1921–24, with Alfred Kreymborg; was a partner of Kitty Cannell; *The Professors Like Vodka*, 1927. Cohn was savaged in *The Sun Also Rises*; Loeb, a cousin of Peggy Guggenheim, rebutted Hemingway in *The Way It Was*, 1959.
71. (1887–1957), poet, married to the dancer Kitty Eaton, 1913–1921; published *The King*, 1917; later became a government statistician.
72. Apparently Zoltan Haraszti, curator of manuscripts at the Boston Public Library; *John Adams and the Prophets of Progress*, 1952.
73. G. Samuel Houghton (1902–1975), Harvard 1923, writer; editor of *The Writer*, 1933–1936; *The Writer's Handbook*, 1936, with many subsequent editions.
74. Constance Robertson (1897–1985). Noyes (1811–1886), perfectionist minister, author, and advocate of "complex marriage" (free love), founder of the Bible Communists (Vermont, 1836) and the Oneida Community (New York, 1848).
75. Hope Williams Sykes (1901–?); *Second Hoeing*, 1935; *The Joppa Door*, 1937.
76. Edward Crook, otherwise unknown.
77. (1902–1988), poet and short-story writer.
78. Weekly magazine of Reform Judaism, since 1920.
79. "A Letter to Robert Frost," *Atlantic* 158/2 (August 1936), six pages.
80. Bent (1882–1945), writer, journalist, biographer.
81. In Greek legend, Semiramis was queen of Nineveh and builder of Babylon.
82. Private school in White Plains, founded 1930, 1–12; since 1976 chiefly for students with learning disabilities.
83. Mary Amelia Sinclair (1863–1946), British novelist and biographer. Dame Rose Macaulay (1881–1958), British novelist and columnist. Sheila Kaye-Smith (1887–1956), British writer and biographer; *Rose Deeprose*, 1936.
84. (1873–1957), British novelist.
85. Young (1884–1954), British author of long novels; *Portrait of Clare*, 1927; *My Brother Jonathan*, 1928.
86. Deeping (1877–1950), British physician and prolific author; *Love among the Ruins*, 1904; *Sorrell and Son*, 1925. Alexander (Alec) Waugh (1898–1981), British novelist and travel writer, older

brother of Evelyn Waugh; *The Loom of Youth*, 1917; *Kept: A Story of Post-War London*, 1925; *Jill Somerset*, 1936. Evelyn Waugh (1903–1966), British novelist, satirist and critic; *Black Mischief*, 1932; *The Loved One: an Anglo-American Tragedy*, 1948; *Love among the Ruins: A Romance of the Near Future*, 1953.

87. Huxley (1894–1963), prolific British-American author, poet and critic; *Point Counter Point*, 1928; *Brave New World*, 1932; *Eyeless in Gaza*, 1936; *The Devils of Loudun*, 1952.
88. Virginia Woolf (1882–1941), prominent British novelist, critic, and editor, a leading member of the so-called Bloomsbury Group; *Jacob's Room*, 1922; *Orlando*, 1928; *The Common Reader*, 1925, 1932.
89. (1876–1941), author; *Winesburg, Ohio*, 1919; *Dark Laughter*, 1925; *Tar: A Midwest Childhood*, 1926. The book referenced here is *Kit Brandon: A Portrait*, 1936. It was reviewed (*SRL*, 10 October) by Howard Mumford Jones.
90. *'T Ain't Right*, 1936; BDV reviewed it, "Crackerbox Commentator," *SRL* 14/24 (10 October 1936).
91. BDV's review of *Across Spoon River* appeared as "Delphic Apollo in Illinois," *SRL* 15/3 (14 November 1936).
92. Probably "Seed Corn and Mistletoe," *Harper's* 174/1 (December 1936).
93. Lin Yutang (1895–1976), Chinese writer, translator, and editor, resident in the U.S. from 1936; *My Country and My People*, 1935; *The Importance of Living*, 1937. Pearl Buck (1892–1973), Chinese-born American novelist, very prolific; *East Wind: West Wind*, 1930; *The Good Earth*, 1931, Pulitzer Prize, 1932; Nobel Prize, 1938.
94. (1908–1990), Harvard '31, writer.
95. Amy Loveman (1881–1955), associate editor, *SRL*.
96. At Middlebury College, which in 1937 awarded BDV an honorary degree.
97. *King Jasper: A Poem*, 1935, with an introduction by Frost.
98. (Latin) those things being changed which are to be changed.
99. (1893–1971), Harvard '14, poet, biographer, and critic: *William Blake: His Philosophy and Symbols*, 1921; *Amy Lowell: A Chronicle with Extracts from Her Correspondence*, 1935.
100. (French) of our time.
101. Phelps Dodge Mining Company, from 1834; mining and refining of copper in Arizona and New Mexico; manufacturer of electrical wire.
102. Met: Metropolitan Opera Company of New York.
103. From Sara Teasdale, "Come," *Love Songs*, 1917.
104. Amy Lowell.
105. The Pierce Motorette was first manufactured in 1901 with a three-horsepower engine; from 1909 the Pierce-Arrow was one of the most popular luxury cars. Production ceased in 1938.
106. The Boston Opera House was on Huntington Avenue, a few blocks from Symphony Hall. Built in 1909, it was torn down in 1957.
107. Probably the Ames Hydro-Electric Generating Plant, built by the Westinghouse Corporation in 1891 near Telluride, Colorado; this was the first commercial alternating-current power station in the U.S.
108. Area of filled land at the foot of Beacon Hill, encompassing Copley Square and the Boston Public Garden, extending to Brookline, the Fenway and South End; since 1900, next to Beacon Hill the most fashionable and expensive part of Boston.

5

1937 LETTERS

DeVoto had a much more enjoyable visit to the American Historical Association, meeting in Providence, than he had had a year before with the Modern Language Association. The correspondence of 1937 involves much preoccupation with the *SRL* and specifically literary talk, but DeVoto does write lyrically about his travels in Vermont in search of a summer residence and a later trip to receive an honorary degree at Middlebury College and to lecture at Bennington. In between these Vermont idylls he was deeply moved by a visit to the Gettysburg battlefield, which resulted in a major article in August. Another trip to Vermont that summer was for his annual residence at Bread Loaf, which was preceded by a report on Sinclair Lewis's domestic crisis. DeVoto also found some time for his principal hobby, photography, which he described in detail. Commenting on the national scene he wound up supporting the controversial Supreme Court nomination of Hugo Black. In December, DeVoto returned to Harvard for a successful lecture engagement.

333 Ridgeway
White Plains, New York

[18 January 1937]

Dear Kate,

It wasn't a happy omen that had me, on my fortieth birthday, in bed with a high fever from the current epidemic. I struggle upward, or part of the relic does, and, shakily, prepare to go back to work tomorrow. With that shaggiest of feelings, that I was about to get a haircut when I succumbed.

This year's virus does not affect the nose or sinuses but does appear to get into the central nervous system. I was quite daft for eight or ten hours. It's going to be fun when the boys eventually find out what it's all about. I'd like some explanation of how it contrives to affect, with marked unanimity, different parts of the organism in different epidemics. There was that year when it actually made the hair sore.

I can't tell you much about Marquand. A nice lad, very odd. Eight or nine years ago I resented him a little. For no reason within my comprehension he contrived to inflict on me one of the two genuine affronts I suffered in Boston—C. T. Copeland being the author of the other. But I saw a bit of Marquand when I first went back to Boston and we were a set-up for each other, being the only two people in Massachusetts, if you except Ben Ames Williams, who were actually engaged in literary endeavor.[1] An amusing, witty, self-conscious and very sensitive person, exactly like the kind of hero of all his books until this one. If you've read a *Post* serial called, I believe, Deep Haven, you've got him and his compulsions.[2] He comes from Newburyport and from a family there about which I gather only that it had wealth and glamour in the clipper ship days. Newburyport is the town he always writes about and it's always one of the old merchant families fallen from their high estate and conscious about a conflict between decay and noblesse oblige. He was under great pressure to restore it to its former glory, by the odd expedient of writing *Post* serials. His exact Boston classification was Union Boat Club, and I think he suffered because it wasn't Myopia Hunt.[3] Or rather that does him an injustice: he tried to make it Myopia Hunt but suffered because it wasn't Norfolk Hunt.[4] Very sedulous in all the observances, all the athletic and social ones at least, pertaining to the Union Boat Club—the Commonwealth Avenue arriviste, too sensitive to the gulf between Beacon Street on the one hand and Brookline on the other. My guess is that his own compulsions were feeble and would have quieted except that they led him to marry the niece of Ellery Sedgwick and that did the business. The formula of such a marriage is obvious and the details too painful for my imagination. The process of another thousand years would be required to obliterate the son of a bitch from even the most presentable Sedgwick, and she appears to have been not of the most presentable. She divorced him about three years ago.[5] Eventually she will be buried at Stockbridge in a segment of a circle, her feet pointing toward a kind of Stonehenge monolith in the center of the pie.

John is something of a stick in company, like a good many Bostonians, but very genial and pleasant in the company of one or two. A nice facility at parody, which gets its first expression in this new book. I literally have not seen him since about 1930. Even then, partly in retaliation for the affront alluded to, I had done him a disservice. Merritt Hulburd, then with the *Post*, incautiously lamented that only Marquand appeared to be able to write about the Harvard Gold Coast.[6] So I invented the Jim Wick cycle, with reverberations still going on in the popular press, and did John out of his best market.[7] He thereupon got interested in the Civil War and J. E. B. Stuart. . . . I don't even know what the Marquand Chair is.

Speaking of all this, will you agree with me that *Life*'s photograph of Joseph Hergesheimer put the seal and all necessary comment on one item of contemporary literature?[8]

The dope has been unbroken for three months, a record, that Ted Weeks will be announced as editor of the *Atlantic* next month. The best guess, of course, is that Sedgwick will find himself able to keep his food down and come back again. Even if he doesn't there is always the fact that he is not only a Sedgwick but Ellery Sedgwick as well and therefore there is the large chance that he will knife Weeks, having had about fourteen years of hard work from him on the explicit promise that he would succeed to the chair. If I were in Ted's shoes I would count on that job when I had a signed and delivered contract that Hill, Barlow & Homans had gone over, and when Ellery died.[9] But if I were in Ted's shoes, I would have told Ellery to go to hell, and probably broken his jaw, thirteen years and eleven months ago. But I suppose he has a better chance of getting the job than anyone else, and even a good chance of getting it before Ellery dies. Which illustrates the curious inability of the Boston culture to develop any native successor to James Russell Lowell. Sedgwick comes closer than anyone else, of course, even than Bliss Perry by twenty-odd miles, and a good half of the probable explanation of Sedgwick is his failure to be a Bostonian. But it does seem odd that no one can grow up in Boston town qualified to edit the town pump. If, as I seem to remember, Aldrich was born in Portsmouth, then this is the first time since Howells that they have had to go altogether outside of New England.[10]

And the truth is, it's really a decline from Sedgwick to Weeks. This quite without reference to the fact that, through years of amiable and even genial association with Ted and liking for his wife, I've never quite liked him. He's a harder worker than Sedgwick—he's the hardest working literary gent I know, he works as hard as I do and that's as hard as there is—and he has Ellery's basic lack of intellectual integrity, but he lacks also what Ellery has, an odd, indeterminable, microscopic and free-floating and unpredictable but genuine particle of genius. He will never be the preposterous fool that Ellery has frequently been, and also he will never pull off the undoubted triumphs that Ellery has been able to bring about once in four or five years. And since they are the only justification the *Atlantic* has had this last thirty years, just why should it go on? Ted has a considerable faculty for running with the hare while hunting with the hounds that would qualify him for the *New Republic* but will do him no good on a monthly, especially since writers are just names for him and he will never take a chance, any kind of chance. He has great sagacity, he has mastered the technique of his job and way of life, he has energy and shrewdness. But he has neither subtlety nor guts nor, in the last analysis, intelligence. I'd say that in the course of the next five years Lee Hartman will take over the high school teacher trade, which is all that the *Atlantic* has had for a generation.

All books received. I'd have got the others off to you today but, getting round to it, discovered that there is neither paper nor cord in the house. In due time. Do you want

Guedalla's *The Hundred Years?*[11] Personally, I think it's spinach. Four or five good cracks and a hundred thousand surplus adjectives. Ersatz Tom Beer. On the other hand, Roeder's *Catherine* is good, but a big book.[12] Nothing else is coming out—or was a week ago, when I last took an interest in the question. I refrain from offering the new Josephine Johnson, which I'll have in a couple of weeks, and I can't suppose you'll care for the new Vardis Fisher which will be along about the same time and which, God help me, I've probably got to do myself.[13] I wonder what he'll make of a female neurotic.... Josephine, by the way, has decided I'm a fascist. And your friend V. N. threatens to bring me into social relations with Max Lerner.[14]

I love your southern winters. There were pussy willows above the Kensico dam a week ago yesterday, and word comes from Ted Morrison that it's time to advertise for Bread Loaf fellows, which makes it practically Palm Sunday.

Yours,

Benny

[*with an enclosure, a fragment of a typed letter, presumably from George Homans to BDV, including the following:*]

My mother, who is the femme moyenne sensuelle,[15] thinks that Marquand's book is terribly dull. So does my sister. But A. N. Whitehead agrees with you that it is better than Santayana's, while claiming that it does not do justice to many of the Bostonian's qualities....

[*BDV's handwritten comment:*] The Homans family is now recorded—I hope the sister is Fanny and not Helen, the exception to all one knows about Boston girls. I'm still a little shaky on my feet. B

333 Ridgeway
White Plains, New York

[22 February 1937]

Dear Kate,

Yeah, I was raising hell with the phone girl—who had just cost me $16.00, all I had on me to the last dime, by failing to perceive & tell Rosy that a gent who had to see me was a literary moocher—when Jim Farley's representative dropped your ad on her desk. I had a painful moment of wondering whether you were interfering with one of the customers' love affairs. Your ad, though, gave Noble so much solace that I should have seen it anyway in due time.[16] Well, be eased: I finally got in touch with Sidney Howard and my name has gone out on the summons.[17]

But Jesus, it's hard to be on Dorothy Thompson's side of anything. That girl always did get me down. First she pointedly disliked me because I got Red tight, and he breaking his poor heart for a drink. Then she ignored me as a minor novelist. Next she was respecting me as a Thinker. All those were hard enough, but now I'm both a Force in Literature and a Student of Affairs, I like to gag. She's a damn nice person, too, which makes it all the harder, but she's also the most tireless pick-brain in America, which helps. God knows what I'll be after that June morn when we're made *litterae doctores*[18] in the same batch.

Something's amiss with my psyche, sympathetic nervous system, vasomotor system, gall bladder, or bump of ideality.[19] I gloom by day and lie awake by night and some articles have been writing themselves in those night watches. Books That Have Impressed Me. I trust that beautiful letters have always meant less to me than pleasant living, but, lying awake, I have been remembering some amusing literary hours. I came, the other night, smack into an alcove of remembrance that I swear to God has been closed to me for 23 years. Come June 1914 and me broken hearted over Mattie and an alumnus of O.H.S.[20] and sports reporter on the Ogden *Evening Standard* (which was not yet the *Standard-Examiner*) and the Great War still sleeping in the back rooms of what was then called Servia, I got quite literary. Eddie Higman and Wendell Fitzgerald and I had been occasionally buying an Everyman's Library classic—they then cost 35¢. But Spargo's Book Store, naturally, did not carry them in stock, and we had to order them by catalogue & wait for Fred Scriven to send for them.[21] So one day Fred said to us—look here, I'll bank for you birds, why don't you make out a long list, let me send for them all at once, and take them as you can afford to pay for them. So by God we did, and presently there were about a hundred & fifty Everymans on a book shelf in Spargo's, and all through that summer & the year I spent at the U of U & the next summer, I was giving Fred 35¢ whenever I had it and walking off with another allegedly immortal work. Something of my emotions can be seen in that I had insisted on having one of them in leather, at 70¢. Which one? You'll probably do some heavy analysis before you arrive at—*Sesame & Lilies*.[22] Well, by God, I bought and presumably read, or tried to read, some of the most incredible things. The *Mahabaratta*—oh, spell it yourself.[23] I have the clearest memory of sitting on a boulder, probably to the eastward of Mattie's house, and reading that, whatever it is. I must have been going in for the folk, for I remember the *Mabinogion*, Grimm's fairy tales, Marie de France, Chrétien de Troyes[24]—maybe it was the Siege Perilous & the Table Round, not the folk.[25] I was going to be a highbrow if it killed me, and it probably did for I can remember going back to none of, at least, those. And Stevenson *Across the Plains* had some treacly essays in it and I spouted them for weeks, triple brass, the dark lantern beneath the coat, crabbed age & youth.[26] Ruskin, oh God! I read *The Cestus of Aglaia*, and what in hell could that have been about?[27] I don't know but a year later I was calling a wench Aglaia in some verses. The polite essay had been praised by Mrs. Farnsworth, my English teacher, so I bought Lamb, and got a permanent bellyful of him, and Leigh Hunt, ditto, and Hazlitt, who somehow survived that strain. And Hazlitt & Coleridge on Shakespeare—though all the Shakespeare I had read was *Macbeth* and, because I'd played Shylock on the boards, the *Merchant of Venice*. And Percy's *Reliques*—God only knows why.[28] And Buckle: can you imagine anyone, least of all a high school boy, tackling ~~Butler~~ Buckle?[29] That got written Butler because, by God, I now recall that I tried *The Analogy of Religion*.[30] Some of the dreariest fiction in the world, the early 19th century English. It would be sociologically interesting to know why, at that ripe time, I hadn't heard enough about Tolstoy & the other Russians to try that.[31] Ben Jonson because my father told me it was swell, and I added another reason to scorn the Catholic education. And Lucretius, on my word, and the Anglo-Saxon Chronicle, and Piers Plowman, and the Mirror of Perfection, and, I remember with awe, the Koran.[32] God knows how many more & what else. If I don't start sleeping too early I'll get them.

Well, I don't know what, as a social historian, to say about the exhibit. Democratic education? Persistence of Notre Dame on the frontier? Unsatisfactory sex life of a high school teacher? There was never the slightest infection of Felix Fay in me—when I bayed the moon it was strictly because Mattie Guernsey's endocrine balance was disturbed.[33] I was two years short of Beauty and 23 years plus short of Truth. But, reading the Koran or Marie de France on a boulder on the west slope of the Wasatch, there was something funny—and something ambiguous. I don't get it. But as the nights go on I'm apparently writing an article.[34]

I also tried Ernst Haeckel, in the Carnegie Public Library, and Bergson, and Herbert Spencer.[35] Yet, after the War, & after Harvard, meeting the 16 year old, hellishly homely Phyllis McGinley in the library, I saw that she had one of Shaw's plays & decided she was a lot brighter than I because when I was sixteen I hadn't heard of Shaw.

My God, though, you've got a documentary mind. Or do you just tell lies? Do you swear that you can like either the *Nation* or the *New Republic* better than the other? I can tell them apart, but not by taste.

Your favorite author is beginning her life story in the *L.H.J.* & Bruce Gould is throwing a reception for her.[36] I threw the invitation away, reclaimed it when Avis said she wanted to meet her, & threw it away again when Bruce said it was so exclusive that no additions to the list could be made. There, if you please, is one of the most objectionable editors in the business. But now comes a long, softening letter from Wes Stout, the one human being left in the Curtis publications, & much endeared to my nostalgic soul by long association. I conclude that Helen Everitt is right & the magazines do want stories. Well, the *Post* should not have vulgarized its output during the lean years: the new crop don't know how to write anything else.... Kitty Bowen's party was a godawful crush and damned dull. I endured it by reason of the couple of friends and the satisfaction of watching Ernesta in Action. An international beauty is a dreadful thing. Catherine Whitcomb there—what vicious eyes.[37] She is badly scarred from the celebrated accident but definitely beautiful still. And hellridden to carry it off. She was all but undressing every minute or two & every man in the room was happy, & well able, to complete the process. I wrote Ted that, on the whole, he didn't want her at Bread Loaf. And didn't Frances do a nice job on her book for me? But the feat of the evening was my talking to Isabel Patterson for fifteen minutes without even trying to choke her. It now appears that part of this frontier childhood of hers was spent on the Sand Ridge, two miles southwest of Ogden. So henceforth I came from Colorado.

Yours
Benny

[*newspaper clipping from the* New York Times, *6 March 1937, showing a profile photograph of Miss Elspeth Davies, with headline "4 Student Officers Named at Barnard"*]

[KS:] The Steegmullers say I look like this—nice of 'em—please return—K

[BDV:] A damned good looking wench—congratulations

333 Ridgeway
White Plains, New York

[26 April 1937]

Dear Kate:

Now what the hell. I spend God knows how long changing the ribbon twice—the first one proving to be inkless—so what happens now? She seems to work all right on the lower end but, as yet, not on the upper one. Oh, well.

This is supposed to be the best typewriter that the neotechnic age can produce, too.

I think I may claim to be released from all except the ordinary obligations now. So far as I can foresee there are no more speeches to make before the fall, only the Pulitzer Prize article[38] to write and that not till the evening when the SRL annually behaves like a newspaper, and only a couple of books on Vermont to review unless I am found with my eyes open. At that, it would be nice to have a topic—other than education—for the next Easy Chair.

It was a—oh, well—a pleasant and God knows a welcome trip to Vermont, in spite of two days of deluge. Nothing is in leaf above the Massachusetts line and the whole country has the emptiness of early winter, but the wind was aromatic with spring, the run-off was all but over except in the highest places, and on Monday, on top of Peru Mountain, there was a sun and a wind that might have been half way across the Gulf Stream. A deep drift was making a three-foot brook underfoot and on top of it I had my hat and shirt off. Here and there a sugar-bush was still bearing sap-buckets and the

Adirondacks across from Middlebury were still white, but clearly the season was moving sunwise.

Oh, last winter Charles Crane sent me a bottle of something called Amerind Liqueur, a sickish sweet thing made from maple syrup in Montpelier. It pushes green mule and Egyptian arrack hard for the worst liquor in the world. But this trip I sampled a maple rum distilled in Burlington as Vermont Maple Liquor, and it has its points. It tastes like a middling California cognac and, given time to age it a little, the state may have something.

Finding nothing satisfactory in Peru, Londonderry, or what is best described as the slums of Manchester and Arlington, we recoiled on Bennington and rented a faculty house from the college at a summer's rent just about twenty-five percent of what I had expected to pay. The idea is to coast round this summer and look for a place I can buy, or begin to buy. There are other ideas. At the moment, I have unusual and alarming intentions of trying to lengthen my wind, and the available tennis, badminton, and swimming will help, if they don't scare me into fits. Also, it will be nice to have Bruce Corliss's dark room just a couple miles away.[39] And though there occurred some weeks back what can only be called a slight miscarriage of plans, Avis is hopeful of not wanting to rough it through the summer. God knows how well we will bear up under six weeks of what is called The School of the Dance, but it is only six weeks and the width of the campus away.

So on to Middlebury, where I performed adequately and had a jovial afternoon and evening with Charlotte Moody and her father.[40] The love affair between Paul Moody and me is getting a little scandalous. He has all the ideas a college president ought to have, according to the Easy Chair, and he has decided that I am all that counts in contemporary American letters. I can hardly repay him in kind for the Litt. D. he is giving me in June, but I found myself quite sincerely and even eagerly telling him that he ought to write a book about his father.[41]

We spent a couple of nights with the Corlisses, and I may say that nothing in Vermont astonishes me more than Allene. She's a good kid and I've liked her for years, but with a chin customarily hanging slack at her behavior and ideas. Her stuff brings her in forty or fifty thousand a year, which is fantastic money in Vermont, and she lives just beyond her income, which in Vermont is quite inconceivable. She does it by buying houses, furnishing them in a style modeled on the buyers' pages of *Harper's Bazaar*, and then selling them at a heavy loss so she can buy and furnish new ones. She has been stuck with a heavy acreage that will never sell, but she has also got a couple of the most beautiful houses in America. The one she lives in now, while she meditates one that somebody else started to reclaim and didn't finish, is one of the loveliest in Old Bennington, which is to say one of the loveliest anywhere. She fills it with the most esoteric food, her appetite being the only part of her that has been in the least sophisticated since, seven or eight years ago, she got the notion that it might be nice to write and came to Bread Loaf from St. Albans to find out how to do it. She believes firmly in astrology and has a seer in New York whom she consults at regular intervals and at all periods of conflict or decision. She believes firmly also in the literary splendor of her stuff, and always whips herself into a mood to write by reading morceaux choisis[42] of the very best writers. She went to Mexico last fall and from there to Hollywood, and coming back she found herself in a condition which was at last solved by one of the faculty under no diagnosis I can recognize. Myself, I would have treated it by psychiatry, but he gives her regular injections of adrenal extract and heavy doses of castor oil, which leaves me up in the air. She hasn't written anything for six months, and so has fallen a house or two, several farms, and half a ton of caviar in debt, but is about ready to start again. She will probably have finished a serial by June first and do two or three more at the cluster of islands which she owns in Lake Champlain. Presently Kathleen Norris and Faith Baldwin will pass to their rewards and Allene's income will go up to three or four times what it now is.[43] She'll probably buy Addison County, fence it off, and fill it [with] blini.[44]

Bruce, having graduated from a St. Albans bank to the real estate business and the management of Allene's debts, took up photography a year or so ago, and by now is not only a far worse photographer than I but a far worse goof. And I can't say that my reawakened photographic life has gone any too well. The new Leica is almost as good as I persuaded myself it was while buying it, but nothing else is any good at all. I manage to get a couple of hours on Sunday in the dark room—Howard Auerbach's dark room—and this is the season when shutters leak light, films crack in the camera, or if they don't crack they get spots from a thrice-filtered developer, or if they come through the developer then dust settles on them while drying, or if they escape the sandpaper effect then it turns out that the emulsion was a bit off-center and the regular developer has made them flat. Or what-not. I haven't taken a decent picture since I started up again, or on the few occasions when I had something passable, either it went wrong in processing because I had forgotten my art, or something was wrong to begin with. I had a film-pack the other day that had been packed backwards, and if you'll tell me how you can do that with an automatic machine I'll sell the new era short. But it's partly the season. We threw out a whole page of Disraeli pictures last week, and we nearly threw out Disraeli as well when it turned out that he hadn't bothered to get one of Aldous Huxley standing up, the height being all of Huxley we wanted.

I had lunch with Huxley. He proves to be one of the nicest literary gents I ever met, and I can't tell you a single thing he said.... Probably the order of that sentence is wrong.

Anyway, I'm over the hump. After five days of Vermont I can hold over till summer. And the season is over besides. In a week or so I'll be writing something or other in the hope of selling it, which shows how the publishers are slacking off. There are three out-size volumes of Sorokin on my desk but I know I'll never read them.[45] There are four books about auto-trailers on my shelf, but I know I'll never do the escape-literature feature they were supposed to touch off. Our Ohio project languishes and will certainly go over till fall. Next week Houghton-Mifflin will publish the six New England volumes of the WPA guide, and for my part, that marks the beginning of summer.

You've seen, or will see with the next issue, all of Nathan you'll ever see in my sheet. He was arranged for before I came and I had in decency to give him his year. At least two more departments will presently disappear for good. The sheet has had too many departments and too little editing. Hereafter it's going to have five active editors instead of two. And when I get back in the fall it's going to cease being edited by committee. I've heard too damn much talk this year, and I've deferred to too damn many precedents and institutional habits. I think I've done a pretty good job of face-lifting this year. Next year I'm going to change the intestinal flora.

I forgot to mention the peak of something or other. My agent, Edith Haggard who succeeds Helen, was recently approached by Stanley Walker, who it seems thinks I write beautiful, with a proposal that I write something on New York life for *The New York Woman*.[46] He must have heard about the time I got down to Thirty-second Street[47].

Yours,
Benny

333 Ridgeway
White Plains, New York

[9 May 1937]

Dear Kate:
I'm back about two hours from—as you should know—fighting Gettysburg.[48] As much that is, as one can from 4 to dark on one day and from 8 to 3 on the next, which is quite a bit but just enough to rouse a Godawful hunger for a real job. I suppose I'll have to limit within reasonable bounds the unalterable determination I've now developed, but as it stands it runs to fighting the whole '63 campaign in Virginia, the Valley, & Pennsylvania.[49] Probably it will turn out to be a day at Chancellorsville, another one up the Valley & across the Cumberlands, and 3 or 4 at most at Gettysburg.[50] But by God I'll do that much within a year.... I can't remember when I've had so much fun or when my emotions, imagination, & literary processes have been so much wrought upon.

Avis, who was conscious but puzzled throughout, asked me just why. All I could answer was the typical literary gent's remark that Gettysburg was the reality of which drama is only the fake—that when Longstreet was right & Lee wrong in a decision it carried the destiny of a nation with it & not just some paid admissions, that when Reynolds saw two roads dusty some miles off & wrote a note to Meade he settled things once & for all, that when Hancock waved Webb's gang on the resulting dead didn't get up & go out for a beer five minutes later.[51] I'm a softie, I guess, but it seems to me—quite apart from a good many thousand dead men—the most breathless story in the world, with human intelligence, human will, & human fallibility at white heat, & the stakes just exactly what was to happen in the Western world from then on. And a classic of meeting the unforeseen with emergency ad hoc methods according to empirical knowledge. A battle that neither general wanted to fight, on ground neither wanted to fight on, at a time and in circumstances which neither would have picked. A classic, too, of elapsed times & developing sequences, and of extemporized cooperations & combinations.

God knows I know all this, but I'd never visualized it in relation to the all-conditioning terrain. And when I got a chance to—or found one, rather, suddenly revising every arrangement I'd made & telling Mary Ellen to lie hand over fist—I had myself a time. Jesus, it was swell!

They've done a nice job on the field itself. Say what you will, the govt. runs things well. Compare any national forest with any private recreation center, or Mount Desert[52] with any Maine beauty spot, or this battlefield with, say, the Coney Island at the Crater where guides slug you, beggars skin you, children run over you, & every kind of fake cannonball, [?]mince ball, canteen & haversack is sold you along with hot dogs, pennants, and all the souvenir junk that the East Side can produce.... Faultlessly clean & quiet, no junk, no disfigurement of any kind, guides unobtrusive and—judging by the one I hired for two hours—efficient. The 800-odd monuments get a little monotonous—but not tiresome to one who reflects that after all they arise out of the comradeship of men in battle & are erected to those killed in battle—and the 2000-odd markers are discreet & indispensable. The entire action can be seen piece by piece and in panorama, and when I read about the Peach Orchard or Devils Den again, I'll know what I'm reading.[53] ... Unhappily one marker is conspicuously not there and I still don't know where Pickett, the great Roland of the South, stopped and waved 4100 men on to southern manhood's fulfillment or however the phrase goes.[54] If I have to take the word of the most authoritative gent I talked to, the proprietor of the Cyclorama who claims to have talked to over 20,000 veterans, it was considerably nearer the ultimate stone wall than I've always supposed. Still it was a good 400 yards back of where the survivors of the 4100 got to.... The net effect, if there is any net effect, was to convince me that Pickett's charge really was a decisive action and the most dramatic one. A literary gent in spite of hell, I always supposed that the various actions for & about Little Round Top were really the thing & that Pickett's charge had got the press.

The battle was won—or lost—three times on the Union left, all of them in relation to Little Round Top, twice on the right at Culp's Hill, & finally in the center.[55] The Culp's Hill action is the one that I lost out on yesterday—it's difficult to follow on the maps & there's so much timber you can only see it piecemeal on the ground.

There is no monument to Sickles, so the govt has officially decided that Meade was right.[56] I think I'll read the whole damn controversy this summer & see how I vote.

There are, including the one in the national cemetery—which, by the way, is a genuinely serene, beautiful, & moving place & who the hell says that republics forget?—no less than four to Reynolds. And it's a pleasant thought of someone's to have Meade's & Lee's statues (Lee's much the better) facing each other directly down the axis of Pickett's charge, from the line of CSA artillery to the Angle.[57]

But hell, I'm going back for a week.

Then I'll probably write you 10,000 words about it.

Well, it was my first shot at touring the sovereign state of Pennsylvania and I don't think so much of it. Not, at least, west of Gettysburg & thence north up the Great Valley (again for literary reasons) & obliquely across the anthracite country to Port Jervis.[58] The Harrisburg section is swell & the food fine & the Dutch prosperous & neat. But by God there's no food nor even a bed on the route we took home. It is not, to be sure, the trippers' slum country of New Hampshire, New Jersey, & half of Connecticut, but there were times when I found myself wishing it were, for at least hot-dog stands are reasonably clean these days. I can't remember when I've had worse food than yesterday & today. The countryside—barring the coal country—is lovely & full of memories for the amateur historian, but, probably because I was in a hurry to get home, I found it a bit lifeless. I wish to God the immediate hundred & fifty miles any direction from New York City (except NW by W) could be hurdled.... Don't get on your native ear: I mean road miles, not as the crow flies, and I'll give you the Catskills. But <u>does</u> NY begin before Cooperstown or Troy?

So I lost all told $4 on the Pulitzer awards, including two side bets against G W the W. Those who stuck to the election returns did best. And I'm wondering just how to best raise a loud howl about leaks to the press—& elsewhere. The *Times* had everything in complete detail at 1 PM & the other papers had part of it by 3. Now that two hours & the complete coverage are suggestive as hell. The *Sun* gave it to Macmillan, or rather carefully gave it away. Holt's were tipped off—I don't know yet by whom—that they had a winner, but the damn fools thought it must be Bemis's *Diplomatic History* instead of Frost, & went ahead on that basis.[59] And so on—I'm going to raise a stink when I decide which is the best one.[60]

The awards couldn't possibly be worse—this is the reductio ad absurdum of Pulitzer Prizes. The Mitchell book is just plain lousy. So, when you come down to it, is

Brooks's—an eloquently written adventure of Brooks's gentle soul among the books he hadn't read when he first wrote about them and among the letters & journals of the men who wrote them. If that's history, then so is the journal of Marie Bashkirtseff, and if it's good history then Odd McIntyre is Herodotus.[61] The history prize should have gone to Sam Morison. Giving Frost three Prizes & Nevins two is just plain damn silly. And the drama prize was just absurd—Nathan happily said all that needed to be said about that show in the last column he'll ever write for me.[62]

Shall I write a piece about G W the W?

Well, anyway, I've met a nice guy, this Dr. Agha who art-directs for Condé Nast. Fletcher Pratt, too, though he's damn queer—& full of hot dope that Ellis Parker is holding the bag for Hoffman.[63] Agha said he'd be charmed to do a piece for the S R—he'd also be glad to dance for the American Ballet. I bet I get a good one from him, but the way he endeared himself to me was by telling me how to—well, partially—avoid getting scratches on Leica film.

Yours
Benny

Bennington College
Bennington, Vt

[24 June 1937]

Dear Kate:

I'm damned tired—but not as I was tired in Westchester County. This is a combination of hired men's work settling in and, by Jesus Christ, if you will believe me, tennis. I don't believe it but it seems to be true. And fatigue may be enhanced—I don't know what Henderson would say—by the state of mind produced by the noon mail.[64] I am invited to deliver three lectures on the common field of American literature and American history, at my convenience, next college year—by what President of what college? James Bryant Conant. In the circumstances, I'm between disbelief and obscenity. I give it up. But I expect to see Ken Murdock next week and he may have light... Of course, it's possible that Charlie Curtis sent Conant a Christmas subscription to the *Review*.

Apparently all I need to do to put out an interesting sheet is to get out & leave it in George Stevens's hands. This number seems to me pretty damn good,[65] possibly because I saw little of the mss & none of the proofs and came on Hendrick's piece with complete surprise.[66] That's the kind of idea you can depend on George to have.... I also note that he sent Carlos Williams' novel to someone other than the man I flatly ordered him to send it to after he protested, & you can also depend on him to do that whenever he can.[67] ... The Pegler article was my hunch, after I had lunch with Peg & Chris.[68] We also have a bad one on Steinbeck, which had been sent back for revision when I last heard of it. Everybody needed revising when I left. I had to fire Mari Sandoz's stuff back at her, even, & probably lost her hitherto warm support.[69] . . But of course I'm writing the fiction treatise from here.[70] When the hell would I have got time for it in White Plains? I haven't the slightest idea where it's going. II followed easily enough from I, and if God is amiable, the rest will develop. I have decided, however, that editorials will reappear about August 20, when for two or three weeks they will be written by Amy.

I've moved about so much that I can't remember whether I've written you from here, or from Middlebury, or from the Walloomsac Inn. I better not, anyway, risk repeating myself on the Litt. D., which was most pleasant. I'm always a set-up for ritual.

But Vermont is—Vermont. My nerves sheathe themselves and my soul comes out of the rocks as soon as I cross the line. The inscription on the Middlebury Chapel, "The strength of the hills is his also," has its point, but as a specialist in hills I could find nouns that mean more.[71] What happens to me is, I suppose, what Henderson & the psychiatrists & the philosophers mean by relaxation, but that seems a pretty damn neutral word. Some kind of modulation into a more straightforward key happens to me. My timing suddenly becomes accurate.... This afternoon I set out with Bunny to find a quarry. We got up to Dorset & found a hill road (shun pike) over the mountains to Danby and another one from Danby town to Mt. Tabor, and for my part I could have driven those roads through eternity as [*sic*: and?] if the brain boys are right, perhaps I did.

Here I fell asleep from muscle strain.... The new day brings your word that I didn't tell you about Commencement. The two impressive features were the half-mile procession to the Middlebury meeting house, which is one of the gems of Congregational architecture and the only distinctive one in northern New England, and the feeling that the Latin of Paul Moody & the deans was a genuine language. Perhaps I should add a third, a little blonde who was marshal of the coed seniors, about the loveliest thing I've seen since my adolescence—or else there is an as yet unstudied relationship between learning and the gonads. I was accompanied by a Trustee who is executive financial head of the Macmillan Co. and who contrived to put the hood over my cap without damaging the dignity of either of us—Moody prolonging the handclap the while in the empirical knowledge that the newly honored bolt before the hood is adjusted if he doesn't. He muttered, "There, that wasn't too hellish, was it?" I confess I was too flustered to get his official statement of the alleged grounds on which the degree was awarded. But Charlotte has promised to send them to me & if you're interested I'll send them on. President Park of Wheaton was one of us & made the address; he's good or I was weakened, for I admired the art of oratory for the first time since I heard Bryan in 1908.[72] Then I made a very bad speech at the alumni lunch, Charlotte took me to the Inn for a couple of drinks, and meanwhile my car sprung a hole in the gasoline tank. The decadent mechanics left some lint in it, & I've had the carburetor off five times since then, & this morning's indication is it will have to come off again.

Well, the day after the Supreme Court proposal I told Dorothy Thompson he wouldn't put it over. I also described it as a blunder, not a crime. My point then was that I didn't care much what was done to the Court—no historian can be much upset by that, since every conceivable thing has been done to it with no permanent damage—but I didn't like (a) government by ruse and (b) the obvious menace to what I really believed necessary to the country, Roosevelt's financial & some of his economic reforms. I believed that the Court proposal would frustrate them—primarily by losing him his popular support—and it has. But I hung on still. I'm off now. Not because of the C.I.O. strikes: that situation must eventually be faced by any administration. But because of the govt. reorganization bills. They are obviously going to be defeated, they are obviously the product of bright, intellectual, impractical minds, & they are obviously going to cost the administration its power. If I know my way round, Congress will now reassert itself and will have at best the Taft administration and, at worst, the Andrew Johnson administration.[73] Which is hellish unfortunate. It is more government by ruse and it's going either to force an avoidable crisis or to prepare the way not so much for a reaction, which is certain anyway, but for an unnecessarily savage reaction. At any rate, the ideologues who are advising him have now twice regarded what Pareto describes as a Residue, and the one they are now disregarding happens to be the most important political one in American society. There is already a kind of smash. It can be kept just about where it is or it can be permitted to get worse. In either case, after a smash there must always be someone to pick up the pieces. The concern of people like me, people who believe in ameliorating as much as possible the unavoidable casualties of social warfare, must be with who picks up the pieces & how soon they are picked up. It was once smart to speak of F D as the Karensky [*sic*] of the American revolution.[74] Actually he is the Trotsky. We will presently have a Stalin—someone whose first job will be to make things work and whose first step toward it will be to get rid of the Old Bolsheviks. I do not prophesy beyond that. But I'd make a modest bet, as the field now stands, on Jesse Jones.[75] The figure that dominates my nightmares is Orval Adams.[76] P.S. I know Orval Adams.

In any event, I promise you that it is fifty years too early to despair of the republic. Read the history of Reconstruction.

Oh, the Advocate's double crostic was about the young man from Bengal who declared he had only one ball but some envious bitches pulled off his breeches and found that he had none at all. As puzzles go it was prettily worked out, much the best job in an otherwise fairly inept parody.

Vermont report.... Allene Corliss has started to write again and so has bought another farm. Just to make sure that she keeps on writing under neurotic pressure, she is having Bruce stock it with Ayrshires from the Fillmore farm, hereabouts, which requires all the Colgate money to support it.[77] She flits from here to Lake Champlain & back, & before the summer is out I intend to take the lid off her psyche & look inside.... The Bennington campus is pretty Bohemian and I have not sojourned in Bohemia for a long time. Somehow I derive a reassurance about our American institutions from contemplating the immortal quality of arty talk. And of the palest pink professor. And of the debutante who thinks herself radical. The college is what my intuitions pronounced it when I was offered a job here, amiably "progressive," superficial, dilettante, and altogether without intellectual discipline. The library is quite worthless, even for the limited use my current activities would put it to. Such girls as remain here are like those who go to liberal lectures in N.Y. They run to exophoria and what they suppose is repartee and are painfully plain. One really pretty child is secretary of the college & graduated from Vassar. The cheesecloth army arrives next week & we shall move from an open mind to the empty one, from Bohemia to Hysteria.

Frost has been in and out, smouldering about the govt. His word about Bennington was that he didn't like the way they kept some scholarship girls on as samples of the poor. He has not written the late Norton Lectures and I judge he never will. But he gets his Harvard degree today and I feel better about the whole affair than I did, though if he can stomach the typical Harvard situation that gives it to him this year and not last year, I can't. Harvard, the Boston mind that governs it at least, does so dreadfully strive to do right and so dreadfully hashes things. I venture to believe, however, that Frost's degree is not a decision of the Conant administration, which must have considered it last year, but an act of that other administration which I suspected some months ago of at last beginning to take a hand. I mentioned Ken Murdock's state paper.... Southern Vermont has had a bad plague of tent caterpillars, but it stops at about Rutland. The State is working on it and I suppose will soon reach the Massachusetts policy of planting them here as soon as it has got rid of them there, in order to keep the service fully staffed.... The streams are higher than usual, thus proving that snow is not what the meteorologists call it.... The summer folk are not yet here in force, so I have heard no Vermont stories.... Oh, Frost has bought another farm too, not in North Craftsbury but in, of all places, Concord Corners. From what I can [find out?] here the Peru section is pretty well bought up. The back country in Danby has impressed me and I may start looking there. But among my perquisites as a Doctor of Middlebury is an option to rent a magnificent place in Shrewsbury and that will be investigated.

I left instructions for various things to be sent to you. I don't know whether you have *Factors Affecting Human Behavior* or not. I can send it to you if you haven't, but it is much too late to get sheets. As for me, I now begin to read Civil War & Revolutionary novels, and *So Red the Rose* has got me stopped even as I begin.

Yours

Benny

[*handwritten in pencil, upside down:*]

Well for God's sake—what did I send?

Bowne

[? BEFORE 16 JULY 1937]

Dear Benny,

Hot-Weather Notes: Riding down to the examination room, in a wheel-chair, I pass Mooie Allen lying on top of her bed in a brassière.

KS: Why the bras, Mooie?

MA: Oh, in case somebody (i.e. some man) happens along.

Times visitors report that no work has been done in the Annex since Tuesday, due to the chorines in the Dixie Hotel running around in mules & panties.[78] Of course the extra-marital didoes[79] in the Dixie are always a major source of diversion to the staff of America's greatest newspaper, but I gather that this week's turns were something pretty special. . . . The nudist story in the *New Yorker* recently reminded me of the time when, still young & new to the newspaper business, I was given an interview by Constance Carpenter clad only in a dazzling diamond cross on a platinum chain & a huck towel thrown negligently over her shoulders.[80] P.S.—She had nice shoulders.

A gent of my acquaintance went to see Alfred Barr at the Museum of Modern Art the other day. He was shunted around from bright young assistant to bright young assistant & finally left without having seen Alfred. ". . . Christ, by the time I got out of there, I didn't know whether I was in a museum or a greenhouse!"

I'm finding your Summer Course very interesting & instructive. Only less instructive than reading SG in typescript. . . . By the way, wasn't your reviewer a bit solemn about the Bemelmans book?[81] Dufy is not Dürer & what of it?[82] . . . I'm painfully conscious that my letters get duller & duller, & terribly afraid that answering them must be a chore for you. So, please, don't let noblesse oblige oppress you.

Yours, warmly,

Kate

Bennington College
Bennington, Vermont

[16 July 1937]

Dear Kate:

No, my dear. You certainly know by this time that writing to you and hearing from you are indispensable to my spiritual equilibrium. You know too that it doesn't much matter what either half of the correspondence says, and that I squirm with the frequent knowledge that what I write to you is dull as clabber in an August drouth. But you will have to be patient with me a while. It develops that, after all, I'm forty and have driven myself rather harder than I should have for more years than seems reasonable, and I've run into a streak—I trust not a long one—of paying for it. My physical condition is unbelievably bad, considering that it was only day before yesterday I won tennis tournaments and climbed mountains, and must somehow be built up. My health is not so good. Not so bad, either, but capricious. My spirits are lower than a snake's ass hole. I'm worried about money matters, I'm troubled by the state of the world, and I'm going through an odd phase, a very odd phase for me, of lack of confidence in myself, my mind, my future, and what was once called my pen. And I don't work very well. I came up here intending to write three stories. Now I'll be lucky if I get one written, and may soon abandon hope of doing that much—though if I do only our comrade God knows where next year's $1500 deficit beyond my income will be made up from. And Nelle Forsythe killed herself a couple of weeks ago—she was nothing to me but Stan, her husband, is, and thinking of him has made me extraordinarily somber.[83] And in short my soul is becalmed in the shallows & seaweed beyond Sargasso. I am damned poor company for myself. I have felt I would be worse company for you.

Well, about the Court Bill. Since your barbed question, there has been Sumners's speech in complete exemplification of what I meant, and now poor Joe Robinson's death looks to me like another screw in the coffin lid.[84] I had two points, and still have them both: one that, from the point of view of Roosevelt's first administration, which on the whole I supported though frequently opposed to details, it was worse than a crime, it was a blunder; and two, that it would not pass. It won't pass, I believe, because it gets over the line beyond which the sentiments of the country will go, and it is the sentiments of the country that ultimately will govern it, and expert as Roosevelt is in reading those sentiments he is President after all and nowhere near as skillful, or as quick, at reading them as any Congress. That, in simple terms, has been my prophecy from the beginning. I can give you the Paretan analysis if you want it, as I did to Dorothy Thompson, who rejected it. Well, I may be wrong. If I am, either I have learned the wrong things from the past, or the country has changed more than I can believe it has. But I still tell you, the Bill won't pass. The administration strategy is obvious: to get this

Bill past the Senate & a far more drastic one past the House, so that all the objectives could be objained [*sic*] in the inter-house committee. I don't think it can be done, and my bet is that Sumners's speech shows the wind turning in the House.... God knows the Republic will be badly enough off with the administration defeated & Congress on the loose. It's the immemorial impasse of our government, and I hold it a worse crime of Roosevelt's to have brought it about than to have proposed the Bill in the first place.

For rather more reasons, I predict for you that the Reorganization Bills will end up in the ash can.[85] I don't predict more than that. I don't hope much more. The best hope, of course, is that the administration will make peace with its Congressional leaders, especially in the Senate. I do not see that in F. D.'s eye. There are, after all, certain disadvantages to the state in having in the White House a man who has faced death & licked it.

But I will venture a hunch: watch the fine hand of Jack Garner decide the appointment to Van Devanter's place. The children of light are all predicting Garrison—my classmate and a first class ideologue, practically the Jeff Davis de nos jours[86]—and the wise money has been on Jackson.[87] One gets you five that it's neither. One to two that the appointee comes from Texas, Georgia, or Alabama.[88]

Talk of revolution is no longer fashionable, is no longer even hopeful in the New Republic. Curious that we should now be approaching the only symptom of revolution in this country since 1876, a humanitarian administration discredited and a deficit.

The hell with politics. There isn't one intelligent Republican in public life. There aren't above three intelligent men in public life, of any persuasion. Thank God the Republic is tough.

You must have heard—and may even have written me—about the Lesbian from Khartoum who received a fairy in her room, when they got to bed, the Lesbian said, "Who does which, and with what, and to whom?" Ken Murdock *fecit*.[89] I saw him again over the week-end, after visiting Bunny at New Hampton. He also told me a yarn that horrified me—and reminded me once more that there is a great novel in Harvard College and no one will ever write it. One of Ames's associates in the botany dept. has been, for forty years, the last survivor of a once-great Brahmin family.[90] A bachelor, he has lived in one of those Victorian, nay Regency, warehouses back of Fayerweather Street.[91] No money, no service except one of Corliss Lamont's exploited charwomen.[92] He has lived in a couple of rooms in that enormous barn, the rest of the house shut up, the furniture raddled, the shutters banging, half the windows out. I used to see him sometimes emerging from the place, stooped, other-worldly, unsung, a green bag on his rusty shoulders. He spent his forty years arranging the data of a botanical classification on 3 x 5 cards in numerical sequences. No one ever spoke to him. No one ever saw him anywhere but entering or leaving his house & the laboratory. He had not talked to anyone, gone anywhere, seen anything, done anything in 40 years—just sat there and arranged his 30,000 cards from 1 to 30,000.... Well, Ken says that last winter Fritz Robinson finally got wrought up to a high pitch of charity, and began to cultivate him, and finally prevailed on the poor devil to go out to dinner in Boston.[93] They went out, they had a fine dinner, as Fritz does, they sat and drank Port and talked of 40 years ago. And when he got home he found that some Cambridge muckers had got in and scattered the 30,000 cards and wrecked 40 years. Ken says that he still sits at his desk, and the cards are still scattered on the floor.

Kenneth also told me that some years ago, when he was Dean of the Faculty, a survey he made turned up another Mammoth Cave fish in one of the departments who, it shortly turned out, hadn't heard about the World War.... All this was apropos of my ancient horror: the privations induced by graduate students to no known end. I could chill your blood with some things I've seen. The Spanish instructor with the crippled child & insane wife, who sold his blood to eke out his salary, for instance.

The *Times* would not have enjoyed the heat wave here. There are 120 wenches in the School of the Dance. If there are five who would make me turn my head to observe them in mules & panties or without either, they are kept well concealed. There is one stunning wench, & she turns out to be an Eliot & well known to my Cambridge gang.[94] She would be something else, I grant you.... As for me, I crumpled on the second day, which is two days earlier than my custom, and was revived only by the prospect of seeing Bunny.... That day was not made more pleasurable by seeing a pony run away with Jeff Wyman's kid, but my kid seemed in excellent spirits & condition, rested, quite elderly & protective. He now has the sex life of a farm animal straightened out. And I took him a tape measure, which should make his summer perfect.

I wish someone would give me a plot machine.

Yours

Benny

[from Bennington]

[9 August 1937]

Dear Kate:

I may have told you this the last time I came through Bread Loaf. Well, it's still good—so far this year's best Vt. story. Seems that a circus was coming down the Rutland & St. Albans R.R. when, somewhere in the vicinity of Pittsford, the baboon, who had been ailing, died. He had been a great favorite with the troupe, who were much depressed, the more so because it seemed desirable but inconvenient to give him the obsequies which were his due. Finally, after much heartrending debate, they faced the facts and ended by simply throwing him off the car. The corpse landed in the ditch and a couple of minutes later a truck came down the highway, saw it, and stopped. Three natives stood up, gazed at the phenomenon for quite a while, and thought it over. Finally one of them said, "'Tain't nobody from over Vergennes way." Silence for a space, then the second rendered judgment, "'Tain't none of my kin, over to Burlington." More silence, then, hopefully, the third, "Mebbe it one of the faculty over to Middlebury."

I see already that my typing is going to be impressionistic. I'm just back from camp, via Woodstock and Bread Loaf, and my eyes are about out. They've been that way all summer, and you can imagine how the motorist's life has suffered in consequence. One day is OK but I catch hell the second day—and this was the year I was going to tour all the back country, unimproved roads, and semi-closed gaps. Oh, hell.

Anyway, I've beaten this quarter of the state pretty thoroughly, and I've about decided that, so far as the DeVoto permanent location is concerned, it's out. The best of it's round Rutland, and if it comes to spending a whole year in the State, as I just about may pretty soon now, Rutland would do. Pittsford and Danby are the only other places I'm in a mood to consider at all. But western Vt. isn't comparable with the central valley and East of the Mountains. I don't see why we don't fix on Peacham and let it go at that. If I stay on in New York I'll have my summers off anyway, and any part of the state is really too far for a casual week-end. If I go back to Boston, Peacham will be nearer than any part of the state is to New York, and it's God's loveliest hillside. Unless, of course, I get a brain wave and decide to saddle myself with a farmer. In that case all bets are off anyway. And so are they if I decide to take out my second papers and come here permanently.

But Jesus, this is one swell place. Even Bennington has to be forgiven the college and the New York dudes—it's a beautiful town and, underneath the Old Bennington hooey, it's a community. And even on a day like today, with the sun spots pumping up a hundred percent humidity, all the vistas blocked with mist, and clouds half way down even moderate sized hills, I can't hit the valley from Bethel to Hancock without feeling that I've crossed over into camp ground.[95] There must be something in that verse of Kipling's about hill men desiring the hills.[96]

I'm now in a position to piece together a fairly trustworthy account of the Lewis split. I've stayed away from both of them—in fact I haven't seen either of them, though I've talked to Red over the phone—since the day after the Supreme Court bill was announced. There was one of the regular bust-ups last November when Red refused to make the Palestine trip they'd planned on because he was getting hot with a novel, so Dorothy went to Europe, so Red began to tell everyone she'd run out on him, so that was just one of those things and nobody paid any attention to it. Thus far my own observation, except that I might add one more, that in February Red seemed to me to have changed his line about Dorothy. It used to be proud Rotary statistics about how many papers took her stuff, now it was beginning to be a rather nasty, my wife knows everything, etc. Well, from here on it's my agent's story. Red went off the wagon with a bang when Dorothy went to Europe. (I can confirm that—he called me up that week and had to have Lou come to the phone and tell me what he wanted.[97]) He stayed off and Dorothy couldn't get him back on. (Of course not. She tried to make a total abstainer of Red, which was damn nonsense all these years. If she'd confined herself to holding back his big benders there might have been some sense to it.) He walked in one day, toward the end of March, and told Dorothy he was through. He went to a hotel for some weeks, and about once a week came back and told her he was through, and about as often walked in and proposed a trip to Europe. Dorothy didn't know from moment to moment whether she was supposed to be a grass widow or a second honeymooner. In April Red took Lou and went to Bermuda, where he seems to have been as drunk as possible, which is pretty drunk with Red, all the time. Lou couldn't do anything with him. Getting back to New York, he had to be carried off the boat and was unconscious for a couple of days in a hotel. Some time later he turned up in some Connecticut town, wired Dorothy that he was through forever and demanded that she send him his clothes, etc. (At the time, I heard a different version here, but my agent, well, it's Dale Warren, ought to have the better dope.) Dorothy decided to investigate, went to Connecticut, found Red damn near dead, and bundled him off to the Riggs sanitarium at Stockbridge.[98] Riggs apparently straightened him out temporarily, and Red appears to have done some work. Meanwhile, he was in and out with Dorothy—who, according to Dale, doesn't know where she stands but keeps the latchstring out—and intermittently separating and coming home. But he took a house in Stockbridge and has been there most of the time since. Except when at Barnard, where Dorothy has been when she hasn't been in the hospital for female troubles. It appears to be three weeks divorce and one week honeymoon every month. But Dale says, and my other spies agree with him, that this time Red is down—everyone that knows him has seen him with one shoulder on the mat from liquor but this time it looks like both shoulders.

So that's that. The psychological situation has been obviously getting worse ever since Dorothy set up as a columnist. *It Can't Happen Here* postponed things, but even last summer it wasn't hard to imagine what was going on.[99] Red was obviously slipping and Dorothy was even more obviously on her way up, and obviously Red wasn't going to be able to take that. I dunno. Two years ago, when Dorothy was slipping her guests over to the other house for a cocktail, three and four years ago when she was sweetly trying to kid Red out of a drink, I had the most serious forebodings. I knew you couldn't run Red that way, if she didn't. I'm not one of the old guard—all of his old friends hate her guts, apparently on the ground that she inspired Ann Vickers, which is where he began to crack. I don't. I've always felt deeply sorry for the hopelessness of her job. I don't see why a writer has to be lousy at fifty. I don't think Red would be if—well, I was going to say if he'd do his proper stuff. But his proper stuff is done once and for all and there's no place left in the world for it, and the simple truth is that Red has a naive and child-like mind which cannot possibly be called intelligent, and he'd have to be intelligent as hell to do anything but what he has been doing. And add to that this practical dipsomania, well, what's the answer? Red is as sweet and lovable a gent as ever lived, a heart as big as a ham, an exquisite sensibility, and he's one of the orneriest bastards that ever lived too. He can't endure slipping, and nothing can keep him from slipping. He probably can't endure Dorothy's rise, which is certain to go on. He'll die of the fantods if he stays off liquor, and he'll die of D.T.'s if he keeps on drinking.

Dorothy must have occupied the guest suite in hell this last year. Yes, or any other year. But, my God, where did two people like that get the idea they ought to get married?[100] She's a magnificent person, but she's a good deal less than admirable in lots of ways. For my part, the drive she's got seems perfectly obscene, and the head-on collision of hers and Red's as a daily routine for eight or nine years—well, the thought of it stuns you. Oh well, let it go. God in his laboratory mood again.

There's a different kind of dancer on the local lot now. This Martha Graham gets just as literary as the others in what she says about it in her programs, but she has a world of stuff.[101] For the first time I get some pleasure from angles and contortions. I suppose she'd be humiliated by the notion anyone was getting anything as low as pleasure from her work—with my own ears I heard Horst stop a rehearsal and take a skin off one wench for having been graceful, God's [*sic*] knows it must have been altogether an accident.[102] She is also clearly a great teacher. Just to watch her teach a class has an aesthetic quality. Also, she starts them with fundamentals, whereas Weidman and others started them in the middle of things. She hasn't broken a single damn ankle since she got here.

Short story. A couple of Sundays back Avis and I went to dinner at Overlea Inn, a quiet place with a good cook a mile or so from here. One of those hot, motionless, steamy evenings that this summer has specialized in. There was nobody else at the tables under the trees except a stout, grayish gent who looked hot and depressed. After a while Avis suddenly said, "What do you think about this college anyway?" Thus challenged, I called on my phrases and said, "It seems to me to have the characteristic intellectual vices of a decadent plutocracy and the characteristic emotional vices of an evangelical liberalism." The stout gent crossed his legs and looked more depressed. Avis said, "Do you think it has any importance?" I said, "Only in its own phantasies." And so on for several exchanges. So the inn's hostess came out and said to the stout gent, "Good evening, Mr. Leigh."[103] He's got gray and soft since he offered me a chair in English two or three years ago. But I guess I don't need to fume any more about the outrageous command performance I was supposed to give here during the college year for twenty-five dollars.

I told you Chalmers' yarn of the Bennington girl who found that the inhabitants of New York and the middle western farmers were beginning to make rhythmic movements.

I've found one who went to that German place I can't spell, where they threw the winter Olympics, to do a between-semesters project on—John Donne.[104] . . . The library appalls me almost daily. A day or so ago I wanted to look up Hannibal Hamlin.[105] They did have the D.A.B., but otherwise Abraham Lincoln's vice-president will never exist for the Bennington girls. They have a fairly good collection of art-and-water books, good enough for the purposes of the esthetes at Phillips Exeter Academy, I should imagine, and a thousand-odd volumes of what I can only describe as Chautauqua social service—projects in Social Problems, combined with The Dance or The Theater, are the favorite activity here—but hardly exhaustive enough for a home-study course even from Chautauqua.[106] And the rest would disgrace Ogden High School, even Ogden High School in 1914. When I intimate as much to any of the resident faculty—except Irving Fineman, who chews no betel nut—get told severely that Bennington believes in studying Life, Not Books.[107] What they do during term time I can't figure out. They talk with their instructors and they set up lights in the theater and they deduce rhythms from patterns or vice versa, but how they check up on anything, God knows. I've tried to figure out the project in History. The history teacher is a pleasant and intelligent and well-informed gent, but he must be the sole source of data and verification. The DeVoto Collection, whose proprietor has never been able to get really concerned about the history of them furriners, has at least three times as many books, and they are at least ten times as serviceable for reference, as the library has in European, Oriental, and ancient and mediaeval history. As for American history, compared with what they've got, I've got a research library and could confer Ph.D. degrees. Does the Kilpatrick Plan consist exclusively of conversation, when it reaches the college level?[108] . . . But hell, nobody should get this serious about Educational Frontiers. Let it go with a recent invitation to Ravi Booth, one of the founders of the place and minister of the First Church of Bennington, which has just been magnificently restored.[109] A while back his institution rose up and asked him to conduct a Sunday evening service. It was stipulated that he must not (a) pray, (b) have a hymn, or (c) allude to the Bible.

Yours,
Benny

Cedar Tree Neck
Martha's Vineyard

[6 September 1937]

Dear Kate:

Sea air has got me down—I was never strong for Swinburne's mother[110]—but before I collapse with another nine hours of sleep, which is the equivalent of a forty hour stretch for the merely normal, I ought, considering my lugubrious manifesto of late June, to announce just as formally that the ravel'd sleeve has been pretty well knit up again.[111] I find myself not only in good health and physique but hardened as well to another forty years of the literary life. I am even willing to go back to NY and resume the editorship of our leading literary weekly. I can contemplate without a qualm the prospect of seeing Blanche Knopf again, I feel equal to hours at a time with Leonard Bacon, the thought of lunch at the Harvard Club brings no quiver to my gorge.[112] What is more important, between some midnight and the dawn it came to me that I might still write a book or two before long.

Well, I've found out some more about that promontory when the body and the mind are all together in the dark. I thought I knew quite a bit about it and I still think I did; but it's something one goes on learning about. Just when I made the turn I can't tell you. A few days before I went to BL I was in a mood to wire you some cryptic messages saying there was still a dog or two to hang. I didn't, for I was skeptical. But I've been on the up-grade ever since, and I suppose I must be—rested? redeemed? purged?... A damn near thing, though a half-dozen times at Bennington I found myself phrasing a letter to Tom Lamont telling him he'd better find another editor and one to Curtis Brown telling them they'd lost a client. I went looking, one day, for a house on the outskirts of Rutland. It was closer than that, though—I told Paul Moody I'd give a course for him, and then had to back out when my white-count fell.

With this curious residuum that I'm now spiritually or instinctively or what you will, on leave. I'm not going to live in NY—I've always heard it's a good place to visit. I'm not an editor—I'm just weekending on someone else's job.

So explain to me what happened in the substructure of DeVoto from June to September. It would be nice to know. If the case were referred to me I'd find no words for it in Freud but lots of similarities to it in Rivers's abstracts.[113]

May we now resume this correspondence?

It was a good session at BL. The best club I've ever belonged to. It bathes my soul in perfumed waters to get among old friends. There was less alcohol and more talking—reverted to my college years and talked almost as late as Frost. I can say no more of geniality than I actually enjoyed Herbert Agar, who thinks that words have mass & physiology, and once ganged up with him to convert T. Morrison from 19th century scientific atheism to Holy Church.[114] Poor Ted. I wear him down; our association has been years of his denouncing me as a cynic, a pacifist, a Freudian, etc., and then slowly coming round to my position as of his own initiative. I have no doubt that a month with the Catechism would now make a communicant of him. But I have left an escape open by notifying him that though I preached Holy Church to the infidel I regarded myself, in my innermost thoughts, as more properly belonging to the heresy of Marcion.... There was also an evening of lyric eloquence when I explained the modern world to Eleanor

Chilton, Bob Bailey, Charlotte Moody, and some Fellows who probably thought I was talking about sex in a veiled way, and a long talk with Edith Mirrielees—the one great woman I have known since Clarissa's mother.[115] A great woman, a great person. Now I think of it, if I wasn't on the mend before, I was cured by Edith. She is wiser than the rocks among which she sits. She knows the human heart—and will you tell me how? A spinster, a college professor, she simply can't. But she does.

A quiet session. There was no episode this year, there was hardly a hysterics. We've all done our jobs so long that we do them well enough to absorb the mistakes of any newcomers. Ted slowly improves the quality of the customers, so that year by year more of them have touched the fringes of professional work. Bob Bailey has improved the staff work and relieved me of all responsibility for the bar. The place is already an institution and is becoming a good one. But it was a little humdrum to hear no rumors of how the staff slept with one another, to have no fat lady weep over her ms or pop out at me from behind a tree, not to be led up the road by Kay Morrison and told "Benny, you're beginning to act like a damn fool," not to be denounced as a crass commercial prostitute by some pure artist from the sticks. Dullness gets to be the curse of efficiency.... Paul Green is an amazing soul.[116] I never liked anybody more at first glance and have never known so instantly that I had a complete romantic to deal with. He looks like a 3/4 size copy of T. Wolfe and his ideas are Wolfe plus Byron plus Percy MacKaye plus the Oversoul.[117] I've come to understand that the post-war Southern literary gent may be described as Lord Byron in a flannel shirt. Nevertheless I hope I see a lot of him, which I hope of damned few literary folk.... Our outside importations were the best yet: Elmer Davis, Frost, Louis Untermeyer, Jim Farrell, Archie MacLeish. Farrell was pretty strong meat for the customers, the more so in that he arrived with ten (10) highballs in him, but did a beautiful job. MacLeish burned the place up, as always, but I think he won't soon forget the going-over we gave him about the ΦBK poem I published.[118] My God, though, how the man writes words. Even the radio play, which comes from the phonier 3% of Archie clangs like a sword on stone.[119]

Except for Fletcher Pratt the Fellows were nothing much—good run of the mill stuff, with one total washout and one little southern wench who used her eyes & tail & didn't need to for she wrote surprisingly well. But I've got something in Pratt. He is the super-hack, Dumas in modern dress. Writes from 9 AM to 10 PM. Writes a couple of pulp magazines & 3 books at a time.[120] Writes on everything & is mostly beyond rebuke. Reads such languages as Danish, Icelandic & Japanese. Keeps three monkeys & a Siamese cat. Knows every detective in New York City. Has a thousand ideas a day—if 99% of them are cockeyed, still 1% of 1000 will mount up in time. I'm signing him on a long term contract. Probably I'll sign his wife too, who showed up a couple of days before the end, a nice girl with a swell shape (as he certainly hasn't—he looks like the offspring of John Bakeless & a marmoset) who turns out to be a lesser Bourke-White with a Leica.[121] She left suddenly, receiving a wire that one of the monkeys had gone into a decline because she'd gone. I must certainly see what the inside of that apartment looks like.... Pratt will publish 3 books this next year, certainly, and possibly two more—the last two on Vidocq the detective, and the successors of Alexander the Great.[122] He wants to write a novel about King Arthur. He is a self-made author. A year at some jerkwater college,[123] two years at the Sorbonne—fought as a fly-weight pug for $6 a fight, ran a literary-agency racket, worked for Hearst, edited some contingent-pay pulps. He fascinates me. I'd give much for courage enough to wear his checked suits or his checkered shirts—or to be able to pronounce naivette [*sic*] his way. Or use fundament in the sense he thought it had.

Josephine turned up for a day on her way home from England. I ask leave to report that, whatever may be the dope about that Hope Gale idea of yours, my primary impulse is now that of the psychiatrist. Josephine has got into troubled waters—I don't think she even knows she has. Have I ever remarked to you about the basis in phantasy of her short stories?

Oh well, the hell with BL. You must forgive it as the only active part of my summer. I wonder if I told you about Martha Graham.... Yes.... There was nothing else at Bennington. So we came down here—and before I had been on the island for an hour I had fallen victim to the most ruthless hostess-grabbing act I ever experienced. The woman had never met even a friend of my friends. However, I'm to meet Thos. H. Benton at the party and that may help. But by God I'll yet murder one of these women. And I had supposed that the Vineyard held nothing but Don Born and the Gay Head Indians, and all those at the far end. Nevertheless it has been another magnificent adventure for Bunny and ought, when I finish the Easy Chair, to supply me with a solid week of doing nothing, the longest period of that sort I've ever had. I expect to be on the job on the 13th.... I could like this place, but not for long at a time. It is wider apart than the Cape, which counts for something, but also it would take you a hell of a lot longer to get to Vermont when a longing for free soil came over you. Also in a week or so there'd be nothing left to do. I don't sail—I've never set foot aboard a sail boat—and God knows you can't swim all the time. Furthermore the overhead on cameras would be terrible in this air.

In the once Methodist town of Oak Bluff [*sic*] last night I found a store from which you would have shortly received a package except that my better angel won. There was a pair of silk drawers closed with handcuffs. There was a picture of nuts into which two small chamberpots had been set, labeled "Pe-cans." There was a squatting dog under whose tail you inserted pellets of that firework which we used to call "snakes." There was a miniature tail which you were to pin on a girl's back, captioned "Why ask me?"

There were matches which popped and slivers of the same which you were to insert in cigarettes. Sneeze powder. Stink powder. Back scratchers. Bronx-cheer-blowers. Rubber snakes. Wire spiders. Jumping beans. . . . It's a great nation. Some day I'll probably send you some of them. I confess I bought some.

Yours

Benny

333 Ridgeway
White Plains, New York

[4 October 1937]

Dear Kate:

Jesus, if so I've forgotten a lot. To the best of my knowledge I never heard of Eliphalet Potter till your remark sent me to the D.A.B. (the index volume to which is at last announced, thank God). What with one thing & another my mind has quartered across a lot of Americana in its time, but I'd say that up-state small colleges are, like riding to hounds, one of its barren areas. The conscious story is that I picked out Potter on the same sound ground that commended it to J. P. McAvoy fifteen-odd years ago when he was worth reading and that I went through Biblical names till I found one acceptable.[124] Not without some pangs as a member of KΓX.[125] I expect to use him again. Possibly in the Christmas Chair—which I should be writing at this moment. The November Chair is the lousiest to date.[126]

One wouldn't think that the world held people who considered Frank Sullivan funny, but I've had to read too many periodicals that were sold & bought as funny to assert flatly that they don't exist. All I can say is, I never met one. As for me, I don't find him as lethal as S. J. Perelman, but certainly he is a powerful somnifacient.[127] Why the *New Yorker* maintains him I don't know. Though they feel that the analyst is the proper one to break off a psycho-analysis that has been going on since the year I moved to Mason Street, which would be 1929. And is discussed publicly perhaps a little less often than Alfred Harcourt's kidneys, but only a little. . . . Then again, I'm not supposed to know about, appreciate, or even understand humor. Ask my colleagues, or attend one of the conferences when we pick out our cartoons. We invariably reject the funny ones & run the flops. Except that we have a nice one next week. So you can check on that. . . . But when you mention Coates, you touch on one of the most fascinating minor mysteries of our time. I suppose we must recognize that there is a local Left Bank, populated by conversationalists and completely unproductive of work, which has its ordinances, its hierarchies, its traditions, and even its history. A damned odd one, for it contains Joe Gould and also Alfred Kreymborg, Eugene Jolas and also Harry Kemp, and a winsome one for they are all great men and even equally great men.[128] Well, one of the oddest areas in it is that kingdom of beautiful letters over which Malcolm Cowley is ruler. Coates is one of the satraps under Cowley, and you could substitute his name for Cowley's, or for any other name, in *Exile's Return*. You must understand that these are souls great with art, ideas, and revolution. They almost never write. When they do write, it is *Exile's Return*—or something described as a Dada novel, or a very bad book about the Mississippi authors (and I have long wondered where he/they heard of them), or a masterpiece in little for the *New Yorker*. You must understand that, though little, they are masterpieces. If they seem to you stale, trivial, & even preposterous, that just goes to show. They are conceived in awe & delivered in ecstasy. They are, though you appear not to know it, the only evidence that the creative spirit remains alive west of the Balearics. I try to hold that realization in mind but get betrayed into confusion, for I'm always assuming that Coates is Kenneth Burke or that Burke is Coates.[129] At that, they may be. My essentially critical mind has apparently added them to give them substances, palpable if tenuous & microscopic. If you add the diffused shadow of the reflected shade of a tenth-rate idea to its resorbed twin you get, it may be, enough substance to register. That is the principle of pre-fogging a film. Burke & Coates—the beginning of the H & D curve.

No one told me that one of the pleasures of being 40 was watching one's contemporaries carry their adolescence past that deadline. An adolescent in need of Herpicide is something to look at.[130]

So is the *Nation* explaining that the KKK is no more to be held against one than any similar high jinks like the Rotary Club.[131] ... Black's speech was nothing much, either way, and should, I think, not be counted.[132] In my opinion he was disqualified for the Court by his connection with the Klan, but he's obviously going to sit there. So be a little cautious how you decide he's a bad choice. Obviously the Court is going to be liberalized—if you don't like the adjective quote it—and when you consider some of the liberal agencies that might have been employed instead—Jesus Christ, are we lucky! F.D.R.'s alternative choice was Minton, and the white hope of liberal thinkers was Lloyd Garrison.[133] The first is nothing, rimmed; the second is a YMCA secretary with a touch of Hutchins.[134] Black is, anyway, an intelligent man. Roughly five times as intelligent as Sutherland, J., and fifty times as intelligent as Butler, J.[135] I know direct that Frankfurter was pleased by the choice, and I hear on quite unimpeachable authority, direct through a dependable friend, that Brandeis was. Black knows far more law than either Van Devanter or Sutherland—and he's been out in the world now and then.[136] Add to that the fact that the Court naturally confers sobriety on the wildest sons of the wild jackasses who get appointed to it and the further fact that Black, J. has the present uproar to bear in mind—we could be worse off. When Harlan Stone was Attorney General he found that the best way to get work done in Alabama was to deputize Black to do it.[137] That says something.

Felix, of course, was dead against the Supreme Court Bill. So I take very seriously the rumor, now current in informed places, that he & FDR have irrevocably split. I couldn't find out if I went to Cambridge, but I certainly do have to get up there & start interviewing.

There is no hurry for either Remarque or the Harvard symposium. Keep them as long as you like. Give *The Citadel* to some worthy cause when you're done with it. I expect to send you J. J. Chapman this week, and that ought to come back in, say, a month, for I couldn't loot one from the Book of the Month Club & had to levy on Amy.[138]

The Yale Press is also costive, but I expect to get the Von Steuben biography released pretty soon too.[139] Quiet & cynical people are saying that it's the best book of the fall. I don't know—I'm now just an editor.... At that, we're putting to bed a pretty good book tomorrow night sometime. Its claim on eternity is pretty feeble, but I bet you it makes good reading. I had to pull out of it Edith Hamilton's preface to *The Trojan Women*, but that's something to wait for, and meanwhile we have Zora Hurston on Fanny Hurst.[140] ... Can I yell about the gravure illustrations? *U. S. Camera* looks a hell of [a] lot cheesier than need be. What do I propose? Well, if you want a platform: aquatint.... P.S. Where are the poets of our day?

Yours

Benny

33 Ridgeway
White Plains, New York

[11 October 1937]

Dear Kate:

To demonstrate that I have mastered the first law of prose, I will confine my discussion of the two topics that exhaust my energy these days to one sentence apiece. (1) The Bureau of Internal Revenue, having voluntarily refunded $120.61 of my 1936 income tax, has now decided to give me a thorough going-over and, apparently, a thorough shaking-down, at the precise moment that the Income Tax Division of the Commonwealth of Massachusetts has decided that it made a mistake in my favor, when it computed my 1936 tax. (2) The distemper that has increasingly affected me over the last fifteen months has now been diagnosed: by an otorhinolaryngologist, as a mild chronic sinusitis which cannot be demonstrated by his tests; by an ophthalmologist, as muscular imbalance which various prescriptions have corrected so completely that I can have felt no discomfort for months; by an allergist, as a migrainous syndrome which is due to some food allergy which may or may not be identifiable; by my confessor, as a bad First Communion.

Bunny turned on the radio half an hour ago and got John Barrymore.[141] Hamming all over the place. My God, was he that bad when we used to go to see him? I've always believed that no one could spoil the great soliloquy in *Hamlet*—I mean the great one, "Oh, what a rogue and peasant slave am I"—but I was wrong as hell.[142] John B strewed it in fragment [*sic*] across the starry heavens. Now, I must have been sober when I saw him in *Hamlet*, for I wouldn't go tight to see it, and he must have hammed it there, for there is no reason to suppose that an actor hams only on the air, and even less reason to suppose that he changes his stuff.[143] Yet I have a clear memory of thinking he was pretty good, no Forbes-Robertson certainly, but no Mantell, either.[144] So what? Have I got a bum memory, or did I used to be a literary person?...I'd like to hear him do some of the stuff I've been sneaking off back of the barn to read this last week. It happened that the annual day when I feel good at breakfast time came this year at Bread Loaf and it happened to coincide with a euphoria (I don't know its periodicity) of Edith Mirrielees'. So, some nerve twisting darkly, I said my name was Norval and on the Grampian hills my father fed his flock, to which Edith promptly replied, "Give me three grains of corn, mother, only three grains of corn."[145] That sufficed to set us off and for at least an hour, while the depressed genius came in to gulp coffee from mugs gingerly held in two shaking hands, we spouted such a mess of literature as the geniuses had never heard of or believed in. We made a good team—what I couldn't finish, Edith could, and vice versa. Everything from "Spartacus to the Roman Envoys" to "The Baggage Coach Ahead," by way of "The Face on the Bar Room Floor," "Beautiful Hands," "The Blue and the Gray," "Marco Bozzaris," and "Banished! What's banished but set free?"[146] I had a ripe time, not only spouting the classics of my boyhood but, at lunch, explaining that that was American literature proper and pretty damn near America too. Pretty soon a theory emerged, plentifully eked out with earlier researches of mine: that the ear had the primary function in the creation of American style. I came back resolved to hunt out these masterpieces and the orations too—I couldn't remember the Reply to Hayne or Ingersoll on Blaine, the G.A.R., or Napoleon the First.[147] I haven't got round to the orations yet but I have managed to buy, principally from Mark Mendoza, no less than sixteen series of *One Hundred Choice Selections*.[148] And by God I'd like to hear Jack Barrymore in them. If he couldn't tear the heart of a *New Republic* editor out with "The Brides of Enderby," say, or "The Angels of Buena Vista," or "Somebody's Darling," or "A Child's Dream of a Star."[149] It seeps into my soul, as out of Gilead. I want to spout it—maybe I could substitute "The Basis of American Literature" for "The Present Status of American Fiction," which I'm to take to 3 colleges next winter. And if from the far Pacific, a voice feebler than the feeblest murmur upon its shore may be heard—why not mine? Let Opulence tremble in all his palaces! Let Cruelty turn pale at thought of redder hands than his....I wonder if this stuff can't be useful in some of the wars

I get into? Properly served up, couldn't it seduce some of the literary into incautious remarks? I'm loaded, from other sources, with stuff the literary may be supposed to have written—couldn't they be supposed not to have liked but to still public acclaim this sort of stuff? Malcolm Cowley has handsomely contributed to the Christmas Easy Chair—I have a strong hunch that Granville Hicks can be smoked into supporting Felicia Hemans.[150] . . . As for me, I confess I love it. I can turn over the very pages that shaped and colored my childhood—my father chortling over "Nick Vanstann" & "The Frenchman & the Flea" till tears ran down his cheeks—my own phantasies of the noble engineer who stopped the train in time, the drummer boy of Ratisbon, the beautiful maiden frozen in the snow—the G.A.R. quartermaster-sergeant next door declaiming "Welcome them, cheer them, crown them with flowers," my mother histrionically weeping over "There's But One Pair of Stockings to Mend Tonight."[151] My God, how many ways there are of revisiting one's past! And, for that matter, how much excuse, these days. . . .

All this when, doubtless, I should be fingering the pulse of today's beautiful letters. Well, I've spoken my piece about Hemingway and the animals, and it will lead naturally to one on Mr. Jeffers.[152] If I tried hard I couldn't be as lousy as Red Lewis is in the current *News-Week*. In at least three ways, it's pitiful. I suppose there is a year for all of us when the clock stops—never to go again, as one of my rediscovered poems has it—and for Red it was 1920.[153] That piece of his would have done nicely in *The Smart Set* seventeen years ago. It's archeological now. And poor Red thinks it's off tomorrow's book. . . . And I'm sorry but I can't take Dorothy. I went to this semester's cocktail party—Houghton Mifflin for Cloete—and there she was talking like God. She doesn't bother to reason any more, just asserts. She was asserting about F D R's speech to the naughty nations.[154] She asserted it was swell—wonderful—the dawn of a new day. When I asked her what it meant, and kept on asking her, she didn't bother to say she didn't know—she just said it didn't matter. . . . But it was a good week. This was the week when Broun forbade the President to bring pressure to bear on Black, for that would be executive interference with a judiciary that must be independent.[155] It was also the week when Max Lerner found out that one could join the Klan in order to serve the liberal idea.[156] In such matters we should never use the superlative, but I'll say those items are as choice as any I can remember having seen. . . . *U. S. Camera* is out and I still can't take gravure. It's getting, by God, so I can't take Steichen, either. At least in the mood of "comment." . . . There's a new gelatine plate process, though, that may land me far out on a precarious limb. One of my opponents flashed a proof on me the other day and only extra-sensory perception kept me from calling it half-tone. . . . Reading a swell job on pulp magazines in *Variety*, I summoned the author, figuring him as the man to do our long-desired article on the sex pulps. I expected to see a little Broadway smoosh with a velvet collar benny and cloth-top shoes or thereabouts. He appeared without a hat in flannel slacks & a gabardine jacket, with a Harvard brogue that meant Fox Club or higher.[157] ... For the first time since I came on the sheet we have sixteen articles actually in the works. And I've got exactly 32 others listed as in meditation. But no poetry.... The inevitable-disclosure-of-the-week: Vincent Sheehan has just emerged from a sanitarium—manic-depressive.[158] ... Line-from-Cambridge-of-the-week: H. Zinsser in Medical School faculty meeting: "Oh, for Christ's sake, Conant, forget you're a college president for a minute." ... Which brings up a weighty question: who will succeed Thos. Nelson Perkins on the Corporation? They'll need a man and a half to take his place. And another half to bring H. James up to par.[159]

Yours

Benny

NOTES

1. Williams (1889–1953), prolific writer of novels and short stories, *SEP*.
2. Correctly, "Deep Water," short story, *SEP* 204:26 (20 February 1932). Marquand began publishing short stories and serials in *SEP* and *Ladies' Home Journal* in 1922.
3. Union Boat Club, private club for oarsmen, 144 Chestnut Street, Boston. Myopia Hunt Club, private club and golf course, South Hamilton, Massachusetts, founded 1894.
4. Norfolk Hunt Club, Medfield, Massachusetts, founded ca. 1900.
5. In 1935.
6. Private residential apartments near Harvard Square in Cambridge, later acquired by Harvard University and incorporated into Adams House.
7. BDV's *SEP* stories about Harvard: "The Precarious Attitudes of Robeson Ballou," *SEP* 203 (26 July 1930); "Back Bay Nights," *SEP* 203 (15 November 1930); "The Frivial Wick," *SEP* 203 (28 March 1931).
8. In the 11 January issue of *Life*, Hergesheimer appeared with Mrs. Evalyn Walsh McLean (1886–1947) when her son "Jock" was presented to society at an elaborate party.
9. Boston law firm, founded 1895 by Arthur Hill; now Hill & Barlow.
10. Thomas Bailey Aldrich (1836–1907), author; *The Story of a Bad Boy*, 1870. Aldrich, a native of Portsmouth, New Hampshire, succeeded William Dean Howells as editor of the *Atlantic Monthly* in 1881, serving until 1890.
11. By Philip Guedalla (British, 1889–1944), 1936, about 1837–1937 in world history; reviewed by Garrett Mattingly, *SRL* 15/14 (30 January 1937).
12. *Catherine de' Medici and the Lost Revolution*, by Ralph Roeder (1890–1969), 1937.
13. Johnson, *Jordanstown*, 1937. Probably Fisher's *April: A Fable of Love*, 1937; or *Odyssey of a Hero*, 1937.
14. V. N., Virginia Nirdlinger Whitehill, published a review in *SRL*, 9 January. Lerner (1902–1992), journalist, economist, "Marxian liberal," editorial staff of *The Nation*; *America as a Civilization*, 1957.
15. (French) moderately sensual woman.
16. "Let *Saturday Review* readers protest to their Senators against Roosevelt's Supreme Court plan.—Democrat." *SRL* 15/18 (27 February 1937), page 22.
17. (1891–1939), playwright and screenwriter; *They Knew What They Wanted*, 1924; Pulitzer Prize in drama, 1925.

18. (Latin) Doctors of Letters.
19. See *Phrenology Applied to Marriage and to the Major Social Relations of Mankind*, by Lorenzo Niles Fowler (1811–1896), 1850?, a book that was in BDV's library.
20. Ogden High School.
21. Stationer and bookseller, longtime friend of BDV.
22. By John Ruskin, ca. 1886.
23. Sanskrit epic poem of ancient India, approximately 100,000 couplets, completed approximately 400 CE.
24. *Mabinogion*, medieval Welsh tales, collected by Lady Charlotte Guest, 1838–1839. Grimm's fairy tales, famous German collection, *Kinder- und Hausmärchen*, 1812 and 1815, collected by the brothers Jakob (1785–1863) and Wilhelm Grimm (1786–1859) and widely translated. Marie de France, French trouvère (fl. 1160–1190). Chrétien de Troyes, French poet (fl. 1170–1190), wrote romances in rhymed couplets; *Perceval: Le conte du Graal*; *Yvain*.
25. In Arthurian legend.
26. *Across the Plains, With Other Memories and Essays*, 1892. "Crabbed age and youth cannot live together./Youth is full of pleasure, age is full of care," from Shakespeare, *The Passionate Pilgrim*, 12.
27. 1865–1866. *cestus*: (Latin) girdle, waistband. Possibly this memory sparked the title of BDV's Easy Chair for July 1937, "The Cestus of Hygeia."
28. Thomas B. Percy (English writer, 1729–1811), *Reliques of Ancient English Poetry*, 1765 and later editions, 3 vols.
29. Henry Thomas Buckle (1821–1862), British writer; *History of Civilization in England*, 1857–1861, unfinished.
30. Joseph Butler (1692–1752), British theologian and moral philosopher; *The Analogy of Religion, Natural and Revealed, to the Constitution and Course of Nature*, 1736.
31. Leo Nikolayevich Tolstoy (1828–1910), great Russian novelist and essayist; *War and Peace*, 1865–1868; *Anna Karenina*, 1875–1878; *What Is Art?*, 1897–1898; *Resurrection*, 1900; *Ivan Ilyich*, 1886.
32. Lucretius (Titus Lucretius Carus, ca. 94–55 BCE), Roman poet and philosopher; *De rerum naturae* (On the Nature of Things), 7400 lines in Latin hexameters. *Anglo-Saxon Chronicle*, annals, calendars and narratives in seven manuscripts noting and describing events in England from the first through twelfth centuries. "Piers Plowman," described as "the greatest poem of the Middle English alliterative revival" (*OCEL*), ca. 1367–1370, attributed to William Langland (ca. 1330–ca. 1386). *Mirror of Perfection*, by St. Bonaventure (French, ca. 1217–1274). Which recension of the Koran BDV read is unknown; probably an edition based on the translation by George Sale (English, 1697?–1736).
33. Felix Fay, journalist in *The Briary Bush* by Floyd Dell, 1921.
34. "A Sagebrush Bookshelf," *Harper's* 175/5 (October 1937).
35. Haeckel (1834–1919), German zoologist and natural philosopher, specialist in morphology and an early promulgator of Darwinian evolution; originated the well-known assertion that "ontogeny recapitulates phylogeny." Andrew Carnegie (1835–1919), Scottish-born American steel manufacturer, philanthropist, and writer, in 1901 sold his entire Carnegie Steel Corporation to a consortium headed by J. P. Morgan, thereby launching the United States Steel Corporation. Thereafter, in an active retirement, Carnegie donated his personal fortune of some $350 million to a variety of charitable causes, including $60 million for the construction and support of more than 1,600 public libraries in the United States. Henri Bergson (1859–1941), French philosopher and humanist; Nobel Prize in literature, 1928. Spencer (1820–1903), British philosopher.
36. Eleanor Roosevelt, "This Is My Story," *Ladies' Home Journal* 54 (April 1937 through January 1938).

37. (b. 1911); *I'll Mourn You Later*, novel, 1936; *The Grown-Ups*, 1937, reviewed by Frances Woodward in *SRL* 15/16 (13 February 1937); spelled "Catherine" in the review and in reference works; "Catharine" on the book in an ad in *SRL*, 6 February.
38. *SRL* 16/2 (8 May 1937).
39. Husband of Allene Corliss.
40. Mrs. J. V. Emerson; occasional reviewer for *SRL*; daughter of Paul Moody (1879–1947), president of Middlebury College, 1921–1942.
41. Dwight L. Moody (1837–1899), revivalist preacher; founder of the Northfield Seminary, 1881. Paul Moody published *My Father: An Intimate Portrait of Dwight L. Moody* in 1938.
42. (French) choice morsels.
43. Norris (1880–1966), prolific writer of serials. Baldwin (1893–1978), prolific author of romances.
44. (Russian, singular *blin*, plural *blini* or *blinis*) pancakes.
45. Pitirim Aleksandrovich Sorokin (1889–1968), Russian sociologist, founding chairman of the Harvard sociology department; *Social and Cultural Dynamics*, vols. 1–3, 1937; vol. 4, 1941.
46. Haggard (1903–1995), literary agent with Curtis Brown.
47. The fashion district, near Macy's and Penn Station.
48. In Pennsylvania, site of the greatest and most decisive battle of the Civil War, 30 June–3 July 1863.
49. The Shenandoah Valley, strategically important to the Confederate Army.
50. Chancellorsville, battle in Virginia, 2–4 May 1863, Generals Hooker and Lee commanding, a Confederate victory, where, however, General Thomas J. "Stonewall" Jackson (Lee's "right arm") was killed.
51. James Longstreet (1821–1904), Confederate general, lieutenant to Lee. John Fulton Reynolds (1820–1863), Union general, killed at Gettysburg. George Gordon Meade (1815–1872), Union general, commander at Gettysburg. Union general Winfield Scott Hancock (1824–1886); later a candidate for U.S. president, 1880. Alexander Stewart Webb (1835–1911) "bore the brunt of Pickett's charge" at Gettysburg (*DAB*); later he was president of the City College of New York.
52. Island site of Acadia National Park, near Bar Harbor, Maine.
53. Battle sites at Gettysburg; "The advanced Union line arranged by General Sickles stretched from Devil's Den to this point" (Gettysburg National Military Park Virtual Tour, Day Two).
54. Roland, legendary hero of the medieval French epic, *The Song of Roland*, who died defending Charlemagne's outnumbered rearguard against the Saracens at the Battle of Roncesvals.
55. Little Round Top, a crucial nexus at Gettysburg, 2 July 1863, a small hill successfully but bloodily defended by the Union side.
56. Daniel Edgar Sickles (1819–1914), Union general; later a congressman and diplomat, known as the "Yankee King of Spain."
57. Confederate States of America.
58. New York, near the intersection of New York, New Jersey, and Pennsylvania.
59. Henry Holt, publishers. *A Diplomatic History of the United States*, 1936, by Samuel Flagg Bemis (1891–1973), historian, professor at Yale; Bemis had won the Pulitzer Prize in history in 1926 with *Pinckney's Treaty*.
60. "Proposal to a Pulitzer Committee," *SRL* 16/3 (15 May), supported Morison.
61. Mariya Bashkirtseva (1858–1884), Ukrainian painter, resident in France; her journal, in French, was published 1887. A biography based on the journal, *Fountains of Youth* by Dormer Creston, 1937, was reviewed in *SRL* 15/23 (3 April). Oscar Odd (O. O.) McIntyre (1884–1938), Broadway columnist and chatman, McNaught Syndicate. Herodotus (ca. 484–430/420 BCE), first of the great Greek historians; *Histories* (of the Persian wars).
62. "Art of the Night," *SRL* 16/2 (8 May).

63. Parker (1873–1940), police detective in Burlington County, New Jersey, who kidnapped a lawyer, Paul Wendel, and extorted a confession from him in the Lindbergh kidnapping case; Parker and his confederates were themselves subsequently convicted of kidnapping. Harold G. Hoffman (1896–1954), governor of New Jersey (1935–1937). As a member of the Board of Appeals, he rejected Bruno Hauptmann's appeal; Hauptmann was executed in 1936.
64. Lawrence Joseph (L. J.) Henderson (1878–1942), biochemist and sociologist, professor at Harvard, friend and mentor to BDV.
65. *SRL* 16/9 (26 June 1937).
66. "Senate Report, No. 711," by Burton J. Hendrick (1870–1949), about President Roosevelt's court-packing plan.
67. *White Mule*, 1937, part 1 of trilogy by William Carlos Williams (1883–1963), physician, poet, and novelist; sent to N. L. Rothman.
68. "Redheaded Reporter," by George Britt.
69. Sandoz (1896–1966), author and historian; *Old Jules*, memoir, 1935 (Atlantic Prize for nonfiction, 1935); *Slogum House*, 1937. BDV's laudatory review of *Old Jules*, "A Violent, Fighting Pioneer," appeared in *SRL* 13/1 (2 November 1935), reprinted in *Forays and Rebuttals*.
70. BDV's "English '37: The Novelist and the Reader" went through *SRL*'s editorial slot for eleven weeks, 26 June (16/9) through 4 September (16/19), after which Canby wrote the editorials for 11 and 18 September (Amy Loveman also contributed to 18 September); BDV resumed his editorials on 25 September (16/22) with "The WPA Guides."
71. Psalm 95:4 (*BCP*), inscribed on the Mead Memorial Chapel, highest point on the campus.
72. John Edgar Park (1879–1956), president of Wheaton College, 1925–1944. Wheaton, a college for women in Norton, Massachusetts, was founded 1835; coeducational since 1987.
73. (1808–1875), seventeenth president of the United States, succeeded to the presidency upon the assassination of Abraham Lincoln. His term was marked by intense strife with Congress and among his own Cabinet over post–Civil War Reconstruction, and culminated in 1868 in his impeachment before the Senate; conviction failed by only one vote.
74. Aleksandr Fyodorovich Kerensky (1881–1970), Russian leader of the February Revolution; prime minister, June–November 1917. Following the overthrow of the Menshevik government by Lenin and his followers, Kerensky fled to America, where BDV met him on at least one occasion.
75. (1876–1956), head of the Reconstruction Finance Corporation that helped to put banking on an even keel during the Depression.
76. Orval Webster Adams (1884–?), president, First National Bank of Salt Lake City; vice president, Utah State National Bank.
77. In Bennington, Vermont, 422 acres. Millard Fillmore (1800–1874), congressman from New York state and thirteenth U.S. president, came from a Bennington family.
78. Now the Carter Hotel, twenty-four stories, at 250 West 43rd Street and Times Square.
79. dido: "(U.S. Slang) a prank, a caper; a disturbance." (*OED*)
80. "A Reporter at Large: Mr. Grover Whalen and the Midway," by Joseph Mitchell, *The New Yorker*, 3 July 1937. Carpenter (1906–1992), British actress.
81. *My War with the United States*, 1937, was reviewed by "L.J.H., Jr." in *SRL* 16/11 (10 July 1937). Ludwig Bemelmans (1898–1962), Austrian-American artist, writer, and prolific illustrator, emigrated to the United States in 1914 and served in the American army. Among his works are the beloved *Madeline*, 1939, a book for children; and *My Life in Art*, 1958.
82. Raoul Dufy (1877–1953), French painter and designer.
83. Nelle's husband, Robert S. Forsythe.

84. Hatton William Sumners (1875–1962), congressman from Texas and chairman of the House Judiciary Committee which had held the court-packing bill without action since February, gave a speech on 13 July. Robinson (1872–1937), senator from Arkansas (1913–1937) and Majority Leader, died on 14 July. On 22 July, the bill was recommitted to the Senate Judiciary Committee.
85. What was called a "watered-down" bill was signed by President Roosevelt on 26 August; it included nothing about the Supreme Court but reorganized procedures in the lower courts.
86. (French) of our days.
87. Lloyd K. Garrison (1897–1991), Harvard '19 ('20), dean of the University of Wisconsin Law School; chair, National Labor Relations Board, 1934; Harvard Overseer, 1938–1944. He was the great-grandson of the abolitionist orator William Lloyd Garrison. Jefferson Davis (1808–1889), president of the Confederate States of America. Jackson is probably Robert Houghwout Jackson (1892–1954), Assistant Attorney General, 1936–1938; Solicitor General, 1938–1940; Attorney General, 1940–1941; Associate Justice of the Supreme Court, 1941–1954; after 1937, President Roosevelt made five more appointments to the Supreme Court before finally appointing Jackson. Jackson later served as chief counsel for the United States during the Nuremberg trials, 1945–1946. *The Struggle for Judicial Supremacy*, 1941.
88. The nominee was in fact Hugo Lafayette Black (1886–1971), senator from Alabama, who had supported the court-packing bill. The nomination was controversial.
89. (Latin) did it.
90. Oakes Ames (1874–1950), noted botanist and horticulturist, specialist in orchids; director of the Arnold Arboretum in Jamaica Plain, Massachusetts; *Economic Annuals and Human Cultures*, 1939.
91. In the most patrician neighborhood of Cambridge.
92. Lamont (1902–1995), socialist writer and activist; son of Thomas W. Lamont.
93. Frederick Norris Robinson (1871–1966), professor of English at Harvard, noted expert on Chaucer.
94. Apparently Martha B. Eliot, later a teacher at the Beaver Country Day School in Chestnut Hill, Massachusetts.
95. "Lord, I want to cross over into camp ground," from Harry T. Burleigh's arrangement of the Negro spiritual "Deep River."
96. ". . . so and no otherwise—hillmen desire their Hills," from "The Sea and the Hills," 1902.
97. Louis Florey, Sinclair Lewis's secretary and factotum.
98. The Austin Riggs Sanitarium, West Stockbridge, Massachusetts.
99. Book, 1935, and play, 1936 (with John C. Moffitt, 1901–1969, screenwriter).
100. Lewis and Thompson eventually divorced in 1942.
101. (1894–1991), greatest of American choreographers and teachers of modern dance.
102. Louis Horst (1884–1964), composer, Denishawn Company.
103. Robert Devore Leigh (1890–1961), founding president of Bennington College.
104. Garmisch-Partenkirchen, Bavaria, 1936. Donne (1572–1631), great British metaphysical poet, rediscovered in the twentieth century.
105. (1809–1891), senator from Maine, diplomat; vice president of the United States, 1861–1865.
106. Phillips Exeter Academy, outstanding private secondary school for boys in Exeter, New Hampshire, founded 1781; coeducational since 1970. The Chautauqua Institution, founded 1874 at Chautauqua in New York state; summer educational center for religion and the arts.
107. (1893–1976), author and engineer; professor at Bennington; *Hear Ye, Sons*, 1933.
108. William Heard Kilpatrick (1871–1965), educator, established the "project method" at Bennington; founder of the John Dewey Society.

109. See *Dedication of the Restored Old First Church of Bennington, as Vermont's Colonial Shrine, Sunday, August 15, 1937*, edited by Vincent Ravi Booth, 1937.
110. "I will go back to the great sweet mother,/Mother and lover of men, the sea." Swinburne, *The Triumph of Time*, 1866.
111. "Sleep that knits up the ravell'd sleave of care," *Macbeth*, II/2.
112. Bacon (1887–1954), poet, translator, reviewer in *SRL*.
113. ref. to William Halse Rivers Rivers, British anthropologist (1864–1922); *History of Melanesian Society*, 1914; *Instinct and the Unconscious*, 1922; *Psychology and Politics*, 1923.
114. Agar (1897–1980), historian and critic, married to BDV's Bread Loaf colleague, the novelist Eleanor Chilton (1898–1949); *The People's Choice*, 1933, Pulitzer Prize in history; *Who Owns America?*, 1936 (with Allen Tate).
115. (1872–1962), professor of English, Stanford University, close friend of BDV.
116. (1894–1981), playwright, novelist, professor at the University of North Carolina; *In Abraham's Bosom*, Pulitzer Prize in drama, 1927; *Plough and Furrow*, essays, 1963.
117. McKaye (1875–1956), playwright, poet, translator. "The Over-Soul," essay by Emerson, 1841: "...that Unity within which every man's particular being is contained and made one with all other."
118. "Speech to the Scholars," *SRL* 16/7 (12 June 1937), twenty quatrains in iambic tetrameter (Long Metre).
119. *The Fall of the City*, verse play, 1937.
120. Pratt's "The Pulp Magazines" was the leader in *SRL* 16/10 (3 July).
121. Inga Pratt, an artist, drew caricatures of Bread Loaf personalities; three of these, two of BDV and one of Fletcher Pratt, were printed in *The Uneasy Chair*. One of Pratt's hobbies was raising marmosets. Margaret Bourke-White (1904–1971), photographer for *Life*; *You Have Seen Their Faces*, 1937 (with Erskine Caldwell); *Portrait of Myself*, autobiography, 1963.
122. Pratt published one book in 1938 and two in 1939. Eugène François Vidocq (1775–1857), detective, founder of the French Sûreté, was the model for Inspector Javert in Hugo's *Les Misérables*. This book of Pratt's does not seem to have been written. Alexander the Great (356–323 BCE), king of Macedon and conqueror of the middle and near East. Pratt's book may have been what eventually emerged as *The Battles That Changed History*, 1956.
123. Hobart College, founded in 1822 in Geneva, New York; gradually merged, after holding classes jointly in the 1930s, with William Smith College for women.
124. Possibly Joseph P. McEvoy (1895–1958), author.
125. Kappa Gamma Chi, a literary fraternity.
126. "The Liberation of Spring City," *Harper's* 175/6 (November 1937), was one of BDV's most widely admired Easy Chairs and was reprinted several times, including in *Minority Report*, 1940.
127. (1904–1979), author, screenwriter, and humorist, published frequently in *The New Yorker*.
128. Gould (?–1957), author; "An Oral History of Our Times," said to be 9 million words; profiled by Joseph Mitchell in *The New Yorker*, 1942, as "Professor Sea Gull." Kreymborg (1883–1966), poet and editor; at various times edited *Glebe*; *Others*; *Broom*; and *American Caravan* (1927–1936).
129. Burke (1897–1993), poet and literary critic, Bennington College; *Attitudes Toward History*, 2 vols., 1937.
130. Newbro's Herpicide, a quack anti-dandruff formula, 1898.
131. "Who Exposed Black?" by Robert S. Allen, *Nation* 145/13 (25 September 1937).
132. A radio speech, 1 October, widely deplored in the press; Norman Thomas, on 3 October, pronounced Black "morally disqualified" to sit on the Supreme Court because of his prior membership in the Ku Klux Klan.

133. Sherman Minton (1890–1965), senator from Indiana, 1935–1941; Associate Justice, U.S. Supreme Court, 1949–1956, appointed by President Truman. Lloyd Kirkham Garrison (1897–1991).
134. Robert Maynard Hutchins (1899–1977), illustrious liberal educator and humanist; president of the University of Chicago, 1929–1951, earlier dean of the Yale Law School; active with Encyclopedia Britannica and Great Books of the Western World.
135. Pierce Butler (1866–1939), associate justice, U.S. Supreme Court, 1923–1939.
136. Black is today considered one of the all-time great justices of the U.S. Supreme Court.
137. Stone (1872–1946), U.S. attorney general, 1924–1925; associate justice, U.S. Supreme Court, 1925–1941; chief justice, 1941–1946.
138. Loveman reviewed *John Jay Chapman and His Letters* in *SRL* 16/24 (9 October).
139. *General von Steuben* by John McAuley Palmer, 1937; reviewed *SRL* 17/4 (20 November 1937). Friedrich Wilhelm L. G. Augustin Baron von Steuben (1730–1794), a native of Magdeburg in Saxony, emigrated to America and served with great distinction during the Revolutionary War in the Continental Army, in which he was commissioned a lieutenant general; he became a citizen in 1784.
140. "The First Anti-War Play," *SRL* 16/25 (16 October); *The Trojan Women*, play by Euripides, 416 BCE. Hamilton (1867–1963), British classical scholar; *The Greek Way*, 1930; *Three Greek Plays*, 1937. Zora Neale Hurston (1891–1960), noted writer of the Harlem Renaissance; *Their Eyes Were Watching God*, 1937; *Dust Tracks on a Road*, autobiography, 1985. Fannie Hurst (1889–1968), author; *Lummox*, 1923; *We Are Ten*, stories, 1937. Hurston's "Fannie Hurst: by her Ex-Amanuensis" appeared in *SRL* 16/24 (9 October 1937).
141. (1882–1942), actor.
142. *Hamlet*, II/2.
143. Barrymore's famous performances were in 1923.
144. Sir Johnston Forbes-Robertson (1853–1937), British actor.
145. "My name is Norval; on the Grampian hills/My father feeds his flocks. . ." from "Douglas" by John Home (1724–1808). ". . . It will keep the little life I have/'Til the coming of the morn," from a song (before 1868) by Amelia Blandford Edwards (1831–1892), British Egyptologist.
146. "Spartacus to the Roman Envoys in Etruria," "Envoys of Rome, the poor camp of Spartacus is too much honored by your presence." From *The Standard Speaker; Containing Exercises in Prose and Poetry for Declamation in Schools, Academies, Lyceums, Colleges . . .*, by Epes Sargent, 1861. "It was a dark stormy night/As the train rattled on . . . ," from "The Baggage Coach Ahead," song by Gussie L. Davis, 1896. "The Face on the Bar Room Floor," song by Hugh Antoine D'Arcy (1843–1925), 1887. "Beautiful Hands," by Ellen (or Emma) M. H. Gates. "The Blue and the Gray," song by Francis Miles Finch (1827–1907). "Marco Bozzaris: the Epaminondas of Modern Greece," by Fitz-Greene Halleck (1790–1867), 1827. "Banished from Rome! What's banished but set free?" from George Croly (1780–1860), Irish poet and journalist, Anglican cleric.
147. Reply to Hayne, from Daniel Webster's speeches in the U.S. Senate, January 20 and 26, 1830. Robert Green Ingersoll (1833–1899), writer and freethinker; he nominated James G. Blaine for president at the Republican national convention in 1876.
148. *One Hundred Choice Selections: A Repository of Readings, Recitations and Declamations, Comprising Brilliant Oratory, Thrilling Pathos, Sparkling Humor, Impassioned Eloquence, Laughable Burlesque, Temperance Effusions, &c.* [. . .], published irregularly by Phineas Garrett (1870–1914).
149. "Play all your changes, all your swells,/Play uppe 'The Brides of Enderby,'" tocsin in "High Tide on the Coast of Lincolnshire," by Jean Ingelow (1820–1897). "The Angels of Buena Vista," by John Greenleaf Whittier: "Speak and tell us, our Ximena, looking northward far away . . ." "Somebody's Darling," Civil War song by Marie Ravenal DeLacoste (d. 1936), music by John Hill

Hewitt. "A Child's Dream of a Star," by Dickens, originally in his periodical *Household Words*, 1850–1859.

150. "Five-Cent Christmas Card," *Harper's* 176/1 (December): "But idealism tells us that hatred and tragedies count for nothing so long as we are right." Hemans (1793–1835), British poet; her most famous poem was "Casablanca": "The boy stood on the burning deck/Whence all but he had fled."

151. *The Romance of Nick Van Stann*, by John Godfrey Saxe (1816–1887), Vermont attorney, poet and humorist, 1889: "I cannot vouch my tale is true,/Nor swear, indeed, 'tis wholly new." "The Frenchman & the Flea," apparently a song, "The Frenchman and the Flea Powder." "There's But One Pair of Stockings to Mend Tonight," traced to Savannah (Georgia) *Republican*, 16 January 1862.

152. "Tiger, Tiger!" *SRL* 16/25 (16 October 1937). "Rats, Lice, and Poetry," *SRL* 16/26 (23 October), editorial. Untermeyer had reviewed *Such Counsels You Gave to Me*, by Robinson Jeffers (1887–1962), California poet, in *SRL* 16/24 (9 October).

153. "But it stopped—short—never to go again," in "Grandfather's Clock," very popular sentimental song by Henry Clay Work (1832–1884), 1876.

154. On 5 October, in Chicago, President Roosevelt suggested a "quarantine" of the aggressor nations.

155. Heywood Broun was then president of the Newspaper Guild.

156. "Hugo Black: A Personal History," *Nation* 145/16 (9 October 1937).

157. Undergraduate final club at Harvard; 44 Boylston Street.

158. Correctly, Sheean (1899–1975), journalist and author, renowned for war reporting; autobiography, *On Personal History*, 1935.

159. Presumably a reference to Thomas Nelson Perkins's brother, James Handasyd Perkins (1876–1940), banker.

6

1938 LETTERS

The year 1938, when DeVoto left the editorship of *SRL* and moved his family back to Cambridge, was convulsed like 1936. He described the "seismology" of the magazine, which was struggling financially, in several letters. The normal time for professional meetings, just after Christmas 1936, took DeVoto again to the Modern Language Association in Chicago, where he enjoyed seeing old friends. But in March, as the management of *SRL* floundered, DeVoto hoped to return to the Harvard faculty and made a forceful case for it. By that time, the darkening political scene in Europe brought forth significant discussion in the letters: Sterne's anguish over the Eden resignation was answered by DeVoto's increasing concern about the likelihood of war, accelerated by the annexation of Austria; in September, the sellout at Munich followed but this tragedy was submerged, for the moment, by the hurricane that devastated New England.

The hurricane had followed hard on another crisis: Robert Frost's psychological breakdown that precipitated a painful scene at Bread Loaf. Despite these major upheavals, DeVoto could point to some favorable accomplishments in 1938, notably a trip to his wife's birthplace in northern Michigan and his successful entry into documentary Mark Twain studies. For Sterne he also wrote at length on the New York anti-rent riots and on recent scholarship on Emily Dickinson, and filled his letters with Harvard gossip, including a comedy in the form of a screenplay, about Paul Buck's successful Pulitzer Prize.

333 Ridgeway
White Plains, New York

[24 January 1938]

Dear Kate:
Harry Scherman has asked for and received another two weeks but the story has spread so far that you'll hear it from the City Press if I don't tell you soon. Nevertheless this is still under the hat until public announcement.

About Nov 15 Lamont had all of us to lunch and announced that, what with the new depression & what-not, he couldn't carry the SR any longer. If we could find any way of carrying on without him, he'd help out up to ⅓ for the first year; otherwise, he wanted to shut up shop by January 1st. I'd expected something of the sort ever since September, and had been certain of it for a month because Noble Cathcart carrying a secret looks like Mrs. Dionne eight months gone.[1] As for me, I saw little hope of getting either another angel or, without a new business office, anybody who could put the sheet on a paying basis. But the rest of them wanted to make the try, so I strung along. As far, that is, as I was allowed to. Sure enough, in the course of a week or so it developed that Harry Scherman had always believed that the SR could be made to pay its way—as it could—and had wanted now & then to try his hand at it. Only now he was becoming (a) an author & (b) a radio advertiser, & he didn't know whether he wanted to take up a new & difficult job. He set Dec 1 as the date when he'd say for sure. He's been moving it up from week to week ever since, & with a patience I can't understand, Lamont has played along with him.

That's all I know for sure. The staff at once broke into two groups, me & the rest of them, with the latter holding three or four secret conferences a day & several more by night. I don't understand just why. By November 15 everyone, even Henry, was saying that the *Review* was the best it had ever been, and they all supported me effectively and, I supposed, willingly. Nevertheless, they dropped me out of their calculations at once & have now got to a position where Lamont's action is all my fault—I failed them, I let them down, and I'm a damn bad editor. I don't know, I say, what's gone on in all these conferences. I do know that for some time now, Harry Scherman has been deterred from saying yes only by inability to find an editor who satisfies his specifications. I don't know who he has considered in the past. I do know that at the moment he's considering Elmer Davis, Fred Allen, and a third unnamed candidate. I should guess that the first two would say no. Elmer was offered the sheet after I turned it down in November 1935 & replied that he had neither the temperament nor the health for the job. On the other hand, he's had hard sledding this year and a regular salary might be more attractive than it was. Fred Allen is not a literary editor, and I should expect him to stay with *Harper's*—he will succeed Lee in due time & own stock in the firm. I suspect that the unnamed one is Fadiman. He's the natural choice, I'd say. Curiously, he's the only one it would really hurt to be succeeded by. For one thing he would give the public the impression my colleagues now have, that I was a bad bust as an editor, and besides I have a profound hunch he's just a smart aleck.

What Harry ought to do—and what I should have advised him to do if at any time he had consulted me, as he hasn't—is to make George Stevens editor and hire a couple of people of approximately my quality to write regularly for the magazine & give it a settled tone & pt of view. George is no writer but he has energy, enthusiasm, ideas, & the passionate drive that an editor ought to have. He's damn hard to get along with and at regular intervals has to be prevented by main force from letting his prejudices force him into a bad boner. He's neurotic as hell too, but if an editor isn't to begin with he's certain to be before long, so that doesn't matter.

Well, you can see the situation I've been in. Institutions, as I've remarked before, are damn queer. On Nov 15 I was a Savior; as of today, I'm the rat that ate the tallow up. Lots of ironies. To begin with, I was assured before I took the job that Lamont would consider three years the proper time to show results in. I don't blame Lamont for not taking the rap now, for every dollar he spends now would be worth two later on & he's poured 3/4 of a million into the sheet all told—and I doubt very much that he told anyone to give me that assurance. Nevertheless, the three who represented him did give it to me, severally & in concert, and now assert they did not. Of course, I would not have left Cambridge, even leaving Harvard, without it. So as of Feb 1st I'm stuck here without income & with an expensive lease. It was also part of the bargain, from the first approach, that I was to have summers off & need not do anything at all for the *Review*. Last summer I wrote for it every week, read ms, & kept up with what was going on in the office, but it now develops that part of my failure is the cynical negligence & selfishness that led me to take the summer off. And so on. Why go into detail? The cream of it all is this: I'm going to try to get back into Harvard—there's only a very slim chance but I intend to take it—and the person whom James B. Conant relies on for extra-curricular opinions of English profs is Henry Canby, who, it has shown quite plainly of late, has a powerful resentment of me for having displaced him in the first place.

Well, there we are. As for me, I'm going to try to write a serial. Also I'm probably going to spend my afternoons going through the unpublished Mark Twain material. That isn't sure yet, but I think it soon will be. I'm doing my damnedest to keep from being forced to run the *Harper's* literary section—I'd be a good buy for them, if a bad one for Harry.[2] I'll make my try for Harvard as soon as the *Review* is settled. I'll be offered other teaching jobs when the news gets out and, if I don't sell the serial & don't get into Harvard, I'll probably take one. If I sell the serial & don't make Harvard, I'll probably go to Cambridge & work in the library for a year, on the frontier book.... At any rate, by God, I'll be a writer again in a few weeks, and by God & all His holy saints, I'll be out of New York by June, & very possibly before. So this story has a happy ending.

And will have some further installments, no doubt. I've just given you the author's tonight. There's a lot of comic relief.

For the rest, Bunny is home again and too damn active. I've had some more migraines. No wonder. At that, I'm in better condition than anyone else at the office. George has no fingernails left & only fragmentary fingers. Poor Helen has had the weeping jitters for a month.

Yours

Benny

Bowne

[7 February 1938]

Dear Benny:

I have a better idea. Don't write a serial. Don't go back to Harvard. Run for President, instead.... Well, H.G. Wells nominates Conant in this week's *Collier's*....

I've not written sooner because we've been cast down over the sudden death of Eddie Soholka, a nice kid who has been a patient here for five or six years. One day he was around paying off on the Farr-Braddock fight.[3] The next day he had a haemorrhage. The next it was diagnosed as pneumonia. And three days later he was dead.... Williams told me it was probably a good thing as he was developing symptoms of meningitis. T.b. meningitis is 100% fatal, runs a three-week course & is the most exquisite torture known to man.

I've just finished the Lyons book (Leonidoff kept it for four months).[4] Quite a job.... Whaddaya say we stick to democracy?

Yours,

Kate

333 Ridgeway
White Plains, New York

[7 February 1938]

Dear Kate:

No by God. If Wells can get Conant into the White House I won't run—I'll turn over the Utah & Westchester delegations en bloc. Not out of any access of patriotism either but in the blinding vision of the greater problem solved, how to save Harvard College. Ken Murdock would succeed & the Committee of Nine could disband.[5]

But that makes clear who it is I've always vaguely confused with Dean Birkhoff. It's Leon Henderson, another man absolutely impermeable to stimuli from the exterior world.[6] One night in Florida he said that Iowa farm land has a "natural value" of $400 an acre. Frost and I spent six hours taking him through utility, exchange, and the theory of money & Iowa farm land still had a natural value of $400 an acre when we—or rather I—quit.... I haven't read that Wells article but I can tell you that it cost $3700 and originally consisted of nothing but the autumn feeling of America. Anything else that may now be in it came from the hand of Wm Chenery.... All over America Wells has been talking as if Conant was Rebecca West's first son.[7] The answer: he came over here to get Harvard to save the world by publishing a new encyclopedia. I don't know how long he figured on to write it.

This week I folded up with what is called influenza by the unprecise technicians who practise medicine. Somebody ought to take a running dive into my unconscious & find out why for the last year or two a couple of degrees of fever have been enough to knock me off my nut. I seem to go goofy at 101° now, whereas aforetime I could lecture & write stories at 103° with a clear & tranquil mind. This episode was probably just somatic protest. It seems that Harry Scherman asked for, & Lamont gave him, another period of grace while he tried to make up his mind, and I wonder just why I've been so sure that the business civilization was the intelligent part of America. Me, I'm OK—except for the flu—but poor Elmer Davis, who said yes and then found out there was nothing to say yes to is fit to be tied. And may have to be: I don't remember when I've seen a gentle guy so violent. All these negotiations have been conducted in the profoundest secrecy, so that I might be neither informed nor affronted. Except that Elmer has promptly reported to me every conversation immediately it was concluded. So now he's acquired my deepest fear: that the election may fall on Fadiman.

The reason I'm OK is that I've got this much in common with FDR: I'm fine as long as I've got a plan. My plans are made and I'm only waiting for the gun. My frame of mind is that of an ex-editor, if not yet, quite that of a writer. At that, for the first time in weeks, my editorial has some prose in it. My God, Kate, what a degeneration you've watched. I thought of it the other night, lying awake & slowly simmering with a low-grade infection. During the last 8 months my letters to you have attested the blunting of a pretty good intelligence & the deliquescence of a once decently crisp prose style. I could think, as of June 1936; I could even write. I probably did both when I was writing to you. God knows I've done neither, here or in print, for something more than a year. I've got to put myself through some damn hard calisthenics, once the gun is fired. I can probably get my mind in order without too much pain, but English prose is something else. I'm by no means sure that, once you've learned it, you can learn it again, once it's gone.

At that, Malcolm Cowley lets me come in fourth.[8] It's not too bad to finish behind Horace Gregory & Max Lerner.[9]

Aline Bernstein's "The Journey Down," which you heard about, is no damn good. I'm going to say so next week.[10] The girl is entitled to the awe & admiration of all people, for it appears that she out-talked Wolfe, but she talks the reader into coma. I can take just so much sensibility. Faulkner's *Post* stories make a queer book.[11] I'd like to give them 3000 words but can't. I've made my point before: that he should have gone on from *Sartoris* and should have let himself be a comedian.[12] But I'd like to show cause. That's all I've read except a bit of curiosa recalled from my adolescence with the aid of Vincent Starrett, called "Stringtown on the Pike."[13] It must have been pre-puberty, not adolescence, for I remember that it jellied my bowels & spine both & God knows it doesn't on re-reading. Starrett writes me that he has also found *Tales of the Telegraph*, which I recalled in that alcoholic evening at Chicago.[14]

Did I or didn't I send you a copy of Mattingly's blurb?[15]

Clerical limerick, from Paul D. Moody, D.D.:

There was a young girl from Madras
Who had a most beautiful ass
'Twas not round & pink
As you probably think
But brown & long-eared & ate grass

Nadir? Yes.

Yours

Benny

Bowne

[CA. 23 FEBRUARY 1938]

Dear Benny:

The whole hospital, like the world at large, is in a state of mild hysteria over the developments in Europe.[16] The sentiment, naturally enough, is 100% pro-Eden. (Did you hear Wickham Steed Monday night?)[17] This business starts one wondering again whether I detest Germans because I grew up during & immediately after the war, or because they really are as boorish, brutish, pig-headed, unrealistic, unimaginative, self-centred, sadist-masochist, servile, arrogant, cowardly-bullying, hysterical, dull & generally repellent as I think they are. It's idiotic to blame the whole thing on Hitler; he really is, as he says he is, Germany.

Thanks for Bill White's book. I was disappointed.... Started *Imperial City* but thirty pages was enough.[18]... Thanks so much for the dope about Casey & your activities in the *Post* '37 matter.... Oh, damn, the no-confidence motion was just defeated.... That Chamber-pot!

Yours,

Kate

333 Ridgeway

White Plains, New York

[17 March 1938]

Dear Kate:

Do you love art? I don't. Maybe I will later on & when I do I'll take the prescription. But L: get out *The French Revolution* & read it over.[19] ... Well, this item out of the chaos interests me more than most. Yesterday Ernest Jones flew to Vienna from London, & today the Princess Bonaparte from Paris, to see what could be done about protecting Freud.[20] Two Hollanders who are famous in psychoanalytical circles but unknown to me are offering sanctuary, and spending plenty of money to get him to The Hague. And tonight some NY analysts are leaving for Washington to put up credits & try to get visas for the little group of Vienna analysts who work with him.... A couple of weeks ago in New Haven Erik Homburger, who worked with him for eight years, said that no one would be able to persuade him to leave. He's lived in the same apartment since his marriage, feels that his work is done, & will not go.[21] I said then that perhaps, since he's 84, he could do most for the world by being killed by the Nazis, but in two weeks that has ceased to mean anything. It was a sentimental exhalation from the delusion that the world has shame or conscience.

It doesn't prove a damn thing that there have been some great men.

Another thing to read right now is the preface to *Heartbreak House*.[22] ... A curious thing, these days do vindicate literature. I fell to talking with a gent who knows me better than most & reads some way into the dilemma at the basis of my intelligence, or nearly any intelligence of the modern world: how to find something to do that I can respect. He accuses me of despising literature. But it's now possible to contradict him here & there. What, he says, what could you say in defense of literature at the Judgment Seat? Well, I said, when you read *Hamlet*, or see it, and get engaged with it, you do get into a dimension that, momentarily, for the duration, gives you reconciliation, and it may be that, when you have finished some trace of it, a speck or granule, is left clinging to you. Reconciliation with what? says he. Reconciliation with death always & primarily, but perhaps, sometimes, with the greatest literature, reconciliation with life. Great literature is of two modes only, mankind against the gods and, at the greatest, mankind accepting the gods. Well, it may be that the qualities of great literature exist in all honest literature for some people, for certain people sensitized in the rhythms of chance, though those qualities are watered down like a homeopath's medicines till the tenth part of a grain serves to make a million drams, and only a globule of that diluted tincture clings to the soul. But if books, & the writing of them, & the reading of them, are vanity & a striving after wind—can you, or the Adversary, name some activity of the race that is something else?[23] They bind up no wounds, but neither do they march in armies.

So Germany won the last war last week and kicked off on the next one, which also it will not win.[24] Today was twenty-one years ago. Today I was reading on the Harvard Club's ticker about the panic on the London exchange, the Polish ultimatum, & the many little releases from Austria.[25] Twenty-one years ago it was the Avery bar, the night I went to the *Tailor-Made Man* with Dave Snodgrass & Ed Stephenson, & it was those resonant periods of Woodrow Wilson about America giving all that she has & all that she is, without stint or measure, God helping her, she can do no other.[26] And the literary man's glance over his pen at Luther: *Gott hilf mir, ich kann nicht anders*.[27] Well, Wilson at least knew what would follow from Versailles, and it is to be assumed that Clemenceau in hell, Lloyd George unhappily still on earth, have now got a bellyful.[28]

As for us, we could save time by starting domestic organization right now. We are going to have hell organized out of us from now on—forever. We are going to & we'd be sensible to begin. The utmost that optimism is capable of is this: that by getting the cowpox we can avoid the smallpox. If we go 15% fascist maybe we won't have to go 100%.... It seems to me that John Haynes Holmes's sermon of yesterday had its theology on ass backward, as well as its history.[29] Ours will be Puritan in form, but if Puritan in content then it can be tolerable.... Manifest destiny, as of last week, ceases to be jingoism & becomes mere self-preservation. Chance has had me reading, these last two weeks, the preliminaries to the War of 1846–48, and it's all there. It always has been there & the European parallels are exact & ominous. My platform becomes that of James K. Polk.[30] And it can—and I think will—save the nation. If the republic dies during the operation, that was only to be expected.

My own little intrigue seems to have been blown wide open & scattered over eastern North America by a series of editorials in the *Harvard Crimson*.[31] I could have served myself better, it appears, by being not so popular among students. Another year would have seen the last of them out of college but the survivors' zeal has probably done for me.

I'd write your book if I had time—or money. That isn't a job for me unless I have 3 secretaries, each of them as good as Rosy. I can't carry the legislation & press releases & polemics of the New Deal in my mind, dear—I have to earn a living.

I haven't got either Dunne or Menninger. I'll see what I can do. I advise you to chuck the former &, if you really want to go psychic, to look up that old one about the two maiden ladies who just happened to see Marie Antoinette about twenty years ago.[32] Menninger is pretty good but would have nothing in it you don't know. However, I'll make a try for them. Though to get a Knopf book is about as easy as to avoid a Dutton one. All that Alfred gives away is food & he only does that because he can share the meal & return a neat profit on the advice he gets in exchange for it.

I wonder what we're going to do for England this time. It was probably not a roving soul or a love of winter crossings that took my late employer to London three weeks ago.

When we go into dictatorship, I hope they will measure the tails of women who want to wear uniforms. Fat bitches in Sam Brown belts are my deepest scar from the last one.[33]

Mem: watch the literary reds become spies & agents provocateurs for the Dept of Justice.

Yours

Benny

333 Ridgeway
White Plains, New York

[30 April 1938]

Dear Kate:

There are few authentic thrills in literature, & fewer by far in scholarship, and I have an abnormally high flashpoint anyway. But you may figure what it was like to come without warning, and in the midst of dreadfully dreary jokes and memoranda, upon some twenty pages of notes that, some years after they were written, became parts, or didn't become parts, of *Huckleberry Finn*.

I break an oath to do this, but you must taste one of them. This was one that didn't bear fruit:

> "Quilting. The world of gossips of 75 years ago, that lies silent but stitched into quilt by hands that long ago lost their taper & silkiness & eyes & face their beauty & all gone down to dust & silence & to indifference to all gossip."

Those 20 pages have been a glorious experience—I think the summit of my literary experience. Somewhere there may be more of them. And maybe I'll write a piece about them & the related stuff I've found about *Tom Sawyer*.

A great day.

Yrs

Benny

[picture postcard: Angel Moroni Monument,

Hill Cumorah, near Palmyra, New York][34]

[POSTMARKED HUDSON, NY, 27 JULY 1938]

Here were many mighty works & a great outpouring of the spirit so that I prophesied and entered into the Kingdom Celestial.

B

Walpole, New Hampshire.

[2(?) SEPTEMBER 1938]

Dear Kate:

Hell no. One manuscript more wouldn't even be perceptible in the heap I've read through in the last two weeks. I trust the comment is full enough. I'd expand it to three-quarters of an hour at Bread Loaf but I wouldn't say any more. The gospel according to DeVoto (Uncle Belly as the psychopathology of everyday life made the speaker of the evening call me on Tuesday night) is just this: a story is about one thing, a story is developed, a story is dramatized.

It was a good conference, the best yet by a Mormon block. Primarily because there were some writers there. Theodore Strauss, Harriet Hassell, Josephine Niggly, a gent named Ford, another one named Turtellot, all Bread Loaf Fellows, were pretty good, and Strauss is going to be better than that.[35] (He did "A Night at Hogwallow," which I didn't give a prize in the L-B novelette contest.)[36] But the nicest Fellow, and one who is going to go farther than the rest of them except Strauss, is Elizabeth Davis, a very pretty child from Michigan with one of those voices, like Josephine's in MT, whose teleology is to knock me for a row of nostalgic heartbreaks.[37] Someone wrote me about a long story of hers in *Good Housekeeping*, called "Fourteenth Summer," and it turned out to be damned good. I think I've done for her exactly what I did for Frances Prentice and Kitty Bowen four years back: pulled her out of words and vegetables and meteorology into action. (Frances, appearing with Charlie for a week-end, remarked that she was the complete Bread Loaf product: she went there and hasn't written a word since.) The Davis girl had never seen an author before and her introduction to the life literary ought to last for a while. Since JJ wasn't to appear for several days, I fastened on to her and took her, that first evening, to the Long Trail with Robert Frost. My headlights showed a porcupine waddling off through the shrubbery and Robert said, "I hate those bastards!" and got out and chased it, yelling for a club. The beast escaped for he was too intent on murder, I too weak with laughter, and Davis too bewildered to find a club. But that study in black and white of America's greatest poet running hellbent behind his shadow over the boulders and among the rock-maples of the main ridge of the Green Mountains, and yelling oaths at the porcupine and me should be in somebody's book. If I do an Easy Chair called "The Fretful Poet and the Porcupine" it will be because I know a literary memoir when I see one in the flesh.

The Green Mountains fairly crawled with wild life. Middlebury Gap is lousy with deer this year and the highway department ought to put up signs. Josephine and I saw eleven in one evening and, unless deer move faster than a Series 40 Buick, they were different deer. On the night of the wildest storm I ever saw in these parts Bob Bailey, driving down the gap to see how much road was left (also with Davis), saw a white rabbit in his headlights and chased it here and there through the remnants of a rainstorm, a cloudburst I mean, and a diminishing gale, till he finally cornered it. That was anyway a mile, also cross-country. Bob's intention seems to have been to restore it to its young after this cataclysm of nature, but life was just fantasy for the ensuing twenty-four hours. The storm had blacked out the entire gap and we all crawled to bed by flashlight and through puddles three feet deep, and so Bob had to wake me at three-thirty and take me out to pick grass for the rabbit. And all the next day whenever anyone got into an automobile, the rabbit was there first, and whenever anyone went anywhere there was the rabbit loping ahead of him or else Bailey loping after the rabbit. In the face of it, I don't wonder that Herschel Brickell delivered an entirely uncalled-for denunciation of Robert Nathan.[38]

Quite apart from its professional features, which had me delivering seven lectures, conducting eight round tables, and reading enough mss to produce an *American Caravan*, the conference was exhausting to the emotions.[39] I feel as though God had milled and bolted me, and that's Frost's fault.... Come a week or so, I think I'd better write you the story, for I'll have to get it phrased in order to understand it, and I don't know any other place to phrase it.[40] The point is simple enough. Frost's demon is loosed, and either a genius is breaking up or it isn't. I don't know. I still see reason to hope it isn't, but these are terrible days for people who reverence him. He breaks down into about equal parts willful child, demanding child, jealous woman, and mere devil. Elinor's death has not only accelerated a process that had already scared hell out of me but has also removed the only effective check to it. Well, it can come out two ways. It can find some new equilibrium and fusion that will produce a great work, probably in prose if I read the signs right, or it can just produce a grotesque downfall of a great man, the greatest person of our time, a mere dissolution, a distillation of envy and jealousy and quivering ego that will deliver him forever into the hands of his enemies and make his friends a defensive circle ringed round him in a hopeless effort to keep him covered with fig leaves and their cloaks.

And it's going to be hard in Cambridge, whither he's going to move, having been elected one of the Overseers. Hardest on Kay Morrison, who alone can manage him a little, and on me, who in the last couple of years have become his closest confidant and have undertaken to write the only book about his poetry that will ever be written by a man who knows him, understands the poetry, and has exhaustively studied the period of which he is a part. As early as last winter it was apparent that he couldn't take me on the only terms anyone will ever get a chance to take me on, or at least couldn't refrain from trying to make his terms. It's damned funny. I'm on record, over my signature, with the declaration, in complete sobriety, against the whole background of the age and my announced standards, that Frost is not only the one great poet of his period but also the finest poet in the whole sweep of American literature. He knows that my book will be merely a documentation and development of that judgment. And that isn't enough. He must try to woo me, cajole me, petition me, threaten me into absolute subjection. I must have no other poets beside him, living or dead, but especially living. I must flame with all his million grievances against the others. I must deliver over to his whim and control, his absolute control and his slightest momentary whim, my entire faculty of judgment. He knows I won't, and yet he is driven, practically every minute I spend with him, to make me, either by thunder or by pathetics, or by personal malice or by wild threats. So, of this recent chaos, which began for me at least when he came through New York with Elinor's ashes, the indiscriminate vengefulness and jealousy and compulsive bitterness, I get a specially poisoned share. I can take it. But by God what it's going to do to my basic ideas is something to worry about. For many years before I knew him and throughout all my relations with him till now he has been important to me primarily because his existence proved that there was such a thing as a sane genius.

Well, I'm going to remember a remark of Charlie Curtis's for a long time. Charlie and Frances got to Bread Loaf in time for the blowoff, last Saturday. Archie MacLeish came to talk and read his poetry. Robert had been specifically warned by Kay not to make a scene and I had prepared Archie for one. (Archie, the whitest man in the literary business, doesn't yet know exactly what happened and left muttering dazedly, "Robert has lost his pride—there can be no rivals of Robert Frost.") But Robert interpreted some allusion of Archie's to Spender as a slur at him.[41] So when some twenty of us, staff and fellows and Frances and Charlie, were gathered in the staff cottage afterward, in one of those evening bull sessions that alone take me back to Bread Loaf, Robert saw fit to make an attack of unearthly brilliance and pathetic envy and jealousy on Archie. It was ghastly, it was indecent, and Ted Morrison and Herschel Brickell (who worships Robert) and I tried repeatedly to interrupt it or head it off or put a stop to it, and none of us got anywhere. The less initiated were gaping, terribly uncomfortable but fascinated. Some of the more initiated were shuddering, some were on the verge of tears. I got mad at Robert for the only time in my experience and voiced a direct rebuke that wasn't intended to call him to his senses but only to put a stop to an intolerable situation—and got nothing, except some subsequent hours of denunciation. Ted was crushed, flouted, all but beside himself. He had to go out twice and walk around in the rain and hold on to himself—and come back to an atmosphere of people at each other's throats, a perfectly tangible atmosphere of the inconceivable and intolerable. That room was just so many knives. And just as Ted came in from his second walk, Charlie Curtis came up to him, Charlie a little tight, rosy, radiating good nature and affection for the place where his own love affair had taken its final pattern, the place which he was now visiting for the first time. I saw him go up to Ted, and I found time to think, this is the essential and immortal Charlie, this is the Charlie we all know, and this is going to be good. So I edged up too, in time to hear him say, from the bottom of his full heart, "Ted, what I like about Bread Loaf is, people have such a g-o-o-d time here."

Yours,
Benny

Walpole, New Hampshire.

[11 September 1938]

Dear Kate:
I'm in the backwash of a beautiful, a really soul-stirring, migraine. I've consulted the local faculty and find no extrinsic reason for it, so it must be the unresolved guilt carrying over from having got mad at Frost. God knows he's been my father image these last three years, and God knows I was plenty mad at him at Bread Loaf.... I spent Thursday and Friday night with him at St. Johnsbury and came away, if to migraine (which had opened up before I went), nevertheless considerably relieved about him. Thursday night, talking till I fell asleep and Avis had to carry the burden, he was as superb as I've ever seen him and no difficult moments. Maybe that *crise*[42] at Bread Loaf was his low tide.

He summoned me to Concord Corner, a few miles from St. Johnsbury, to look over a place he wants me to buy.[43] He's got interested in the Corner the last couple of years and is making over two houses there and threatens to buy some more. It's a spectacular place he showed me, a house on a hill at whose foot there's a big pond shaped, as Bunny promptly said, like South America, and beyond the pond a vista stretching away clear to the Franconia range, all seven of which show magnificently reflected in the pond. A hundred and twenty-odd acres, most of it in pasture and wood of course. Two springs, one above the house. An old orchard for decoration and firewood. The house would need about two thousand dollars put into it. The whole for sale at five thousand, which means four thousand or even thirty-seven-fifty. I don't want to put more than three thousand into a place that calls for two thousand more right off, but I could tackle this without too much strain. But I don't think I will.

For one thing, it's too damn far. If we're saying no to Peacham, which is the loveliest spot on the map of Vermont, because it's anyway a five hours' drive from Boston, what's the point of going to a place that's nearly six hours? And though it's a really spectacular view, it isn't as spectacular as the one from Peacham Hill nor as charming as the one at South Lincoln which I would have bought earlier this summer only I found it two days after it had been sold. (Didn't tell you about that; it was one of the Bread Loaf incidents, and South Lincoln is the Danvis of Rowland Robinson's stories, one of the places I somehow couldn't ever get to when I started for them, like Sharon, and so never saw till this year.[44] Mt. Abraham was fairly in your lap, at this house, and the whole valley of Lincoln and Bristol stretched out in front of you. A grand place.) But the payoff is really Concord Corner itself. I'd never been there, though Concord itself, two miles away, is perfectly familiar to me. It's a genuine specimen of the Vermont abandoned town. Frost paid seven hundred dollars for his two houses, and he can pick up the five or six others that make the village at the same rate. The farms are all like the one he showed me, unfarmable; lived on, that is, by French Canadians. And the villagers are just vestigial. Frost has a genuine liking for everyone, but I can't like relics. He also talks about its being unspoiled, meaning there aren't any college professors there. He hopes to get some of his friends there and establish what I called, to his face, a phalanstery.[45] But my God, I'd rather have college professors than Vermont poor whites. I don't want to live in Greensboro, where there are fourteen hundred pedagogues in the summer, but Peacham with twenty-odd would be about right.

After all I like my Vermonters unlicked. The whole point about Vermont is solvent independence. (I'm going to interview the Governor next week, I think, and maybe write about him from that text.) When they're neither solvent nor independent, hell, you might as well move into the TVA. Practically alone among the literary advertisers of the state, I recognize the existence of a poor white population, but that's no reason for moving in on a pre-emption.

Frost is closing the South Shaftesbury house and, I think, will sell it. He appears to be going to move Carroll [*sic*] off the stone house to sell that too.[46] He'll never go back to Shaftsbury—can't stand the idea. He's getting reckless with his money, too, which is both un-Frost and un-Yankee. He wanted to give me one of his Concord Corner houses, at one point. He'll try to give it to the Morrisons. He'll end by giving it to someone.

This was the summer I was going to buy a Vermont house. Why do you never do what you plan to do? We haven't even looked, and the only convenient alibi is the weather. We swept through Thetford Hill, Bradford, and Newbury the other day, and I've always thought it would come to that part of the state in the end. Logic says three hours from Boston, so weekends will be possible without pain, but that practically limits it to twenty-five miles west, northwest, or north of Brattleboro and, say what you will, that isn't even the third-best part of the state. Avis, with Lake Superior reawakened in her blood, has suddenly plumped for the Champlain valley. Well, Burlington is one of the most civilized towns in America and charming to boot, but the Champlain and Winooski country happens to be the most affluent part of the state and a decent place would cost from ten thousand upward. And it's so damned far. I could live all year in Burlington with great comfort, and in fact have been holding it in reserve in case a literary career breaks over me, but my God you can't weekend there. Me, I'll be satisfied with a house and woodlot and a southern exposure, but Avis wants a vista, and that cuts out the next most logical part, around Bethel, and the next, around Chester.

However, I have broken all precedents by actually reading one of the books I said I was going to this summer, the first volume of Proust.[47] Pretty damn hard going and, if you ask me, a resumé of nineteenth-century literary styles. I'm assured that, beginning with *The Guermantes Way* I'll begin to get it.[48] I hope so, but even so it's like getting round to liking a European trip six months after you get home. There has been too much anatomy of the heart for my taste and too much "registration." I hope it all comes home in the end, but I could stand three hundred fewer pages about Odette and Gilberte. Meanwhile the history of the Mexican War I have to read gets into my dreams and I haven't touched the armful of the Albert Bigelow Paine I brought up to give me a flying start on my job. Or any of the other stuff I simply had to read.... I have read the Halsey book that Kip Fadiman was so coy about, as if the wench hadn't been his secretary.[49] Any slap at our English cousins is so much gain, but this wench works pretty hard for some of her wisecracks. My ten years' old proposal was to send Jean Nathan or Thomas Beer to England with a commission to do this book. It's still a good idea.

No use, Kate. There are still too many peristaltic convulsions traveling through my frame to make for clear thought. I'll call this off and continue it when the mind has cleared. Gynergen begins to let me down. I'll have to take to the hypodermic form. The local faculty wants to give me thyroid but I won't take the affront. Giving me an energizer is, still, on a par with giving Hemingway an aphrodisiac.

Yours,

Benny

[*handwritten by BDV:*] Mailed about 3 PM Sunday. What day does it arrive?
[*handwritten by KS:*] Arrive Wed noon

32 Coolidge Hill Road
Cambridge, Massachusetts

SUNDAY [25 SEPTEMBER 1938]

Dear Kate:

Well.

It was quite a storm.[50] I didn't realize that it was till it was practically over, when, looking out of the kitchen window, I saw the hill road below us, which had been shut out with trees all summer long.... Everybody's got to tell his story (I listened to Ted Morrison's last night—they were on the Mountain and the road to Middlebury one way and Hancock the other just ceased to exist and they came out by tractor—and Kenneth Murdock has disappeared into the blue) so you've got to learn to take it.

I'd been alone with Bunny for eight days of rain and recurrent headaches while Avis moved the household up here. Tuesday looked bad and I telephoned her to come up to Walpole early instead of late as she'd planned. She did so and, Wednesday being dry for a change and looking better, we packed the car to the guards and started off with nothing on our minds except the probable collapse of the Buick. It has been collapsing at short intervals ever since we got back from Michigan and my moderate prayer now is that it may hold together till the 1939 models are out and I can see what they look like. We got down to the village and started to say goodbye to people but learned that the Keene road was out, the Brattleboro road was out, and only the shun pike over the hills open and that problematical. Considering all the rain, and the visible Connecticut, that made sense, so we went back to the house and unpacked the car and took it for granted that the roads would be open the next day. Then it began to rain some more.

Toward noon it cleared and I remembered that I was once a newspaperman and set out to take some pictures. They won't be very good for the clouds came back but I did a thorough job on the Connecticut at Bellows Falls, which was whooping through the gorge; the Green Mountain Power Co.'s dam, which was being cleared and stripped as rapidly as a big crew could do the job; and Cold River, which was inconceivably high and came over the lower road just after I did.[51] Back at Walpole, there were rumors that Greenfield was under water, that Shelburne Falls was in trouble, that the B & M or the B & A had had a wreck at North Adams, and that Keene and Marlborough were now isolated.[52] I still don't get any of this. The Connecticut was plenty high but as yet nowhere near flood level. At four o'clock, when it began to rain again, my one emotion was regret that I hadn't kept going that morning. I figured that Boston must have been attainable one way or another, and I guess it was but I'm just as glad we stayed in Walpole.

It was about twenty minutes past five when it started to rain like hell and blow like hell. That's all I figured it: just a bad storm. My concern was threefold, to keep Bunny from getting scared, to keep the doors and shutters on the house, and to keep the two fires in the cellar from causing trouble. There was no need to worry about the first. The kid was excited but not scared and when he got too excited I stretched out on a couch with him and told him Big Chief Tommy stories till he was sleepy. At one point I said, "Well, Bunny, this is something to remember—you've seen a sixty-mile gale." That was just fifty percent off. For the rest, I keep [*sic*] lashing things down and milling round after various odd bits up till eleven o'clock, when it was obvious that nothing more could be or needed to be done. But I knew at twilight that it was more than a gale. All summer long you couldn't see the village from our house, and now you could. None of the magnificent elms on our place were blown over but a couple of them were pretty well stripped.

After about a half-hour of it a tremendous run-off came down the hill above us and curved round the house, flowing down over the terrace. It was about forty feet wide and God knows how deep, missed the house by about thirty feet, and kept flowing for nearly an hour. The lawn is terraced and there's about a six-foot drop, over which this water cascaded with a roar loud enough to drown out the wind. Also for half an hour or so a creek flowed rapidly through the cellar. I was phoning the plumber to ask him what to do about the furnace when the telephone went out. The lights had gone long since, taking the stove and water-system with them. There were plenty of morals for the prospective country squire and that was the sharpest of them. Also: keep plenty of dry clothes on hand. Every time I went out I got soaked. But my God we had it easy. We weren't even alarmed.

I got the idea the next, Thursday, morning when I went out to take a look. The hill was denuded. Here and there a few trees were standing but in general the effect was as of a giant lawn-mower erratically used. The roads were blocked everywhere and there were no wires up. And you could see the whole stretch of the valley and the Connecticut looked like Long Island Sound. It was over the Central Vermont tracks, over Route 5, over all the lowlands that had ceased to be tobacco farms after the flood of 1936.[53] We climbed over trees to get down the hill and found barns blown down, houses unroofed, and the elms and pines simply flattened.... This is one storm that altered a countryside. Hundreds of thousands of elms are down and the New England landscape is changed forever.... The village had suffered plenty of damage but no loss of life. People were killed at Westminster, across the river, and Bellows Falls, five miles up. The cemetery, a dignified one beautifully forested, had hardly a dozen trees left standing and some of them had opened graves when they were uprooted. Most of the forestry projects, all of them that ran to pine, were absolutely levelled. The roads were blocked everywhere. No lights, no telephone at first, nothing coming through, and of course no radios except those that ran by battery.

I poked around all Thursday, taking pictures and listening to things. The town had the hill road cleared by noon and a half dozen others by night. We could drive a mile either way on #12 and could get across the bridge to Vermont, to fifty feet of Vermont, I mean. Then the Connecticut swept in with a tremendous current and all the lowlands to Westminster were under water. It was most interesting to follow, by radio, the extempore organization forming to deal with the disaster, and to hear the rumors that were sent out. We learned that the Vineyard had been wiped out, that the Agassiz Museum had been destroyed, that Boston was under martial law. The slow growth of the realization that a really tremendous disaster had occurred was quite an experience. We moved down to the Walpole Inn and hung round the telephone office trying to get either phone calls or telegrams through.[54] No chance.

Friday the best advice over the radio was that only one road to Boston was open, by way of Nashua, and that Nashua couldn't be reached by Keene, Franklin, or any other way from Walpole except possibly from Portland—and Portland couldn't be reached. But one car had got through from Fitchburg the night before and several came up from Keene while I was getting information. Avis thought we ought to wait another day but I wanted to get home and so we shoved off. It was easy. No difficulty at all and only about a dozen places where the going was hard, usually because of trees down for a couple of hundred yards at a stretch but occasionally from washouts. Normally I'd drive from Walpole to Cambridge in just under two and a half hours. It took us four and a quarter, including a brief stop in Nashua for lunch. The irritating thing was that the day looked threatening and, since even a brief rainstorm would close things indefinitely, I pushed on without stopping for any of a hundred photographs I wanted to take.

It's quite a sight, New England after the big storm. Keene got it really terribly. The Ashuelot always overflows after a heavy dew and this time it had a cloudburst. Also there are some miles without hills to break the wind. One of the most beautiful forests in New England was the memorial park north of town, forty or fifty acres of magnificent white pines some fifty years old. Not one of them is standing now. It looks precisely like the stretches of Florida forests that were flattened in November, 1935. But that's true of all the pine groves. Pines can't take it, apparently: too shallow rooted. The millionaires' estates round Dublin are the same way. Peterborough is always ugly at high water and this time it had a fire too: the whole west side of the business section north of the bridge is flat. There was apparently a break in the storm some twenty miles round Wilton; very few trees down and no barns. From there to Nashua we saw little damage but at Nashua we picked up the Merrimack, high over the B & M tracks, and wreckage everywhere. This part of Massachusetts isn't damaged much. Lots of magnificent elms down, all the way from Nashua, but little else. Brattle Street is practically treeless, and the Craigie House looks naked. Harvard Yard was pretty well blown down but the University has managed to get hold of the only crew of tree surgeons in these parts and has already saved a good many trees that otherwise would have had to go. I haven't been in to Boston yet but, apart from the waterfront, nothing much has been disturbed.

I want to get down to the shore, especially along Buzzards Bay but I'm being a citizen and obeying the authorities.[55] That, of course, is where the worst of it is. So far as I've been able to check up in thirty-six hours, nobody I know except Elmer Davis, who is reported by the *Herald-Tribune* to be missing, got into trouble. Today's papers say nothing about Elmer and I'm still hoping, but Mason's Island is just a strip of sand rising out of the water and his house is only one story high.[56] Frances Curtis was in Providence and Phoebe was in New Haven on their way to Stonington and are OK. Most of the Cambridge gang had returned in preparation for registration. Nobody has been able to learn how the summer places took it, except those who were on them. Kenneth and Perry Miller left for Hill on Thursday and haven't been heard from. The best guess is that all the M houses at Hill are flat, being built on a thin shelf above an underground river. Also that Hill can't be reached at all from either Danbury or Franklin. Ted reports that Rochester, Vt., which was practically wiped out in 1927 and again in 1936, has been practically wiped out for the third time and that our pals in the furniture factory, which survived the two earlier floods, have now given up and closed the village industry. There must be a lot of that in the interior Vermont valleys. I haven't seen anything about Bethel but all that country must have been chewed to pieces. The dams saved Barre again, though—twice in two years—and Montpelier is OK. The gaps and notches have probably been washed completely free of roads. Middlebury Gap, which contains Bread Loaf and Ripton, has been. God save us the swell curve in Smugglers' Notch.[57]

Well, this is just me checking in. I'll write you a letter before the week is out—provided no refugees or relief work get dumped on me. I'm up to my ears in arranging a library on shelves I didn't build myself and God has no more exasperating job. So it's back to noisy plumbing, unpainted houses, and the untraceable smell of leaking gas—to the place where my friends are—to, I'm almost ready to admit, Mountain Time. It would be a bird of ill omen to welcome me, Ernie Simmons, whom I'll probably choke, slowly, some day.[58] The Deknatels materialize out of thin air on the doorstep, it seems that the Hillyers have moved back to Cambridge slums to economize and live directly across the street, there's a Yale historian next door, and this morning Bunny dropped an r. Cambridge is the damndest place.

Yours,
Benny

[unsigned and possibly not sent; cf. next letter]
Bowne

[Probably early October 1938]

Dear Benny,
Well, this is one war we would surely have gotten into. Never, not even in 1917, have I seen American public opinion so thoroughly aroused. The entire hospital—from Dr. Williams to the orderly—is brushing up its vocabulary for Chamberlain's benefit. Every person I've spoken to or heard from—and this includes liberals of all shades, Republicans, Democrats (pro- & anti-New Deal), Socialists, Communist Party members & Communist sympathizers—seems to feel that the Berchtesgaden-Godesberg-Munich sell-out was one of the stupidest, as well as one of the most perfidious, episodes in the long & perfidious history of the British Empire.[59]

Of course there is the possibility that German expansion is inevitable, that if it doesn't happen now it will happen twenty years from now, that it might have been better if America had stayed out in 1917 & let Germany win then instead of now. I find this very difficult to swallow, not only because Čechoslovakia is such a splendid little state, not only because Naziism is so emetic, but because the German character as such is so emetic. In fact, as far as I'm concerned, Nazism is the essence of the German character. I realize that that is an emotional reason, but there it is.

Bowne

[before 7 October 1938]

Dear Benny,
Christ, how I hate linen writing-paper!

* * *

Well, we got off pretty easily although we didn't think so at the time. My first inkling came Wednesday afternoon when a broadcast of Maurice Hindus' from Prague was called off because the Columbia antenna on Long Island had been blown down.[60] ... About five o'clock I was sitting up in bed eating supper, a bridge-lamp shining on my tray-table, radio softly playing dance-music, a G.E. electric heater whirling away in the corner of the room—zip, everything stopped ... silence, semi-darkness, cold. Nothing but the grey light seeping through the French windows & the wind screaming outside. I saw a few branches sailing through the air, but I didn't hear until the next day that a half-dozen trees on the place had been uprooted. Several people were drowned in Po'keepsie & several others killed by falling trees. The roof was blown off the Henrys' house in Stamfordville, & the Warrens, whose house stands on a bluff overlooking Wappingers Creek, report that the creek was within two feet of the bluff-top.

The cessation of power, of course, completely paralyzed the hospital. No light. No water, no heat, no nurses' call-bells, no elevator, no dishwashing machine, no anything. Some of us telephoned down town for White Rock & flashlights, but roads were out & taxis couldn't get through.[61] About seven PM Bullard came around with candles. About nine o'clock the power came on. Finis.

* * *

The Germans are a race of subthyroid adrenocentrics.

The Germans are a race of anal-erotics.

The Germans are a race of bastards.

No matter where you start, that's where you end.

Never—not even in 1917—have I seen American opinion so unanimous & so aroused. The entire hospital, from superintendent to orderlies, is still brushing up its vocabulary on Hitler & Chamberlain. Everyone I've talked to or heard from is in a pother of righteous indignation. If France & Britain had fought I wouldn't have given us six months to keep out.

Among the bitterest of Chamberlain's critics has been Leonidoff. Much as he hates the Bolsheviks he hates the British still more: on the principle, I suppose, that it's easier to forgive an enemy than a double-crossing friend. Now he is hoping that Germany & Russia will get together & skin the lion.

In retrospect, I don't see how we could have thought the dirty business would turn out other than as it did. Your friend Fred Scherman blue-printed it & so, somewhat less specifically, did Geoffrey Garratt & Norman Angell in their books.[62] Everyone has known for a long time that Chamberlain & the Cliveden set are pro-Fascist. N. C. has certainly made no bones about wanting to play with Hitler & Mussolini, & as far back as April I remember *Time* remarking that the British press was busily building up a picture of Czechoslovakia as "a remote little country with a funny name" which could not possibly be any concern of Britain's. And do you remember NC's speech of Tuesday the 27th: "It is incredible, it is horrible, etc. that we in England should be getting ready to go to war on behalf of people whom we don't even know"—or however it went?

Certainly it seems to me that an anonymous writer in the *Trib* is closer to the truth than either Dorothy Thompson (who, in case you don't read the *Trib*, considers the Sept. 21 Runciman Report mere propaganda, tailored to justify the Berchtesgaden agreement) or Walter Lippmann (who takes the view that the Runciman report was the cause rather than the result of the Sudetenland cession).[63] This writer says that he had it from an authoritative source in Whitehall, as far back as the beginning of May, that England intended to see that Hitler got the Sudetenland on a platter.[64] He says that in England the Runciman Commission was never considered anything more than window-dressing, that Lord R. was sent to Prague simply to stall for time until

Chamberlain & Hitler could devise a way to transfer the territory without getting Russia & France on their necks. I dare say that all the *opéra bouffe*[65] of the past month was also necessary to prepare British public opinion, as opposed to Whitehall, for the shock.

. . . Your letter arrived Wednesday noon, & damned welcome!

Yours,

Kate

NOTES

1. Elzire (Mrs. Oliva) Dionne, mother of the Dionne quintuplets (born 28 May 1934 in Quebec, to worldwide amazement and acclaim).
2. Harry Hansen.
3. James J. Braddock, "The Cinderella Man" (1906–1974), heavyweight champion 1935–1937, defeated Tommy Farr (1914–1986) in a decision after ten rounds, 21 January 1938.
4. *Assignment in Utopia*, autobiography of journalist Eugene Lyons (1898–1985). His "Reporting Russia: Twenty Years of Books on the Soviet Regime" was published as the leader in *SRL* 17/9 (25 December 1937); rebutted in Letters, *SRL* 17/13 (22 January 1938).
5. Appointed by President Conant from among the senior Harvard faculty, in the wake of the Walsh-Sweezy affair, to study and make recommendations on faculty hiring and tenure policy. The members included Professors Murdock, Schlesinger, Frankfurter, and Perry, all supportive of BDV; their presence on the committee made it awkward for them to plead his case for rehiring.
6. Apparently the economist Henderson (1895–1986).
7. Rebecca West had a son, Anthony West (British author, 1914–1987), out of wedlock, by Wells.
8. In "Reviewers on Parade," *New Republic* 93/1209 (2 February 1938), about reviews of Dos Passos's *The Big Money*, 1936; BDV's review, "John Dos Passos: Anatomist of Our Time," appeared in *SRL* 14/15 (8 August 1936).
9. Gregory (1898–1982), poet, leftist writer, reviewer for the New York *Herald Tribune; Chorus For Survival*, 1935; *History of American Poetry, 1900–1940*, coauthor with his wife, the poet Marya Zaturenska, 1946.
10. "The Journey Down," 1938, reviewed in "Fiction Drowned in Talk," *SRL* 17/18 (26 February 1938).
11. "Faulkner's South," BDV's review of *The Unvanquished*, *SRL* 17/17 (19 February).
12. *Sartoris*, published 1929; published again in 1973, in an unabridged version, as *Flags in the Dust*.
13. Starrett, *Penny Wise and Book Foolish*, 1929; *The Private Life of Sherlock Holmes*, 1933; *Persons from Porlock*, 1938. "Stringtown on the Pike," by John Uri Lloyd (1849–1936), pharmacist and novelist, 1900. He also wrote *Etidorhpa, or the End of the Earth*, 1895; *Felix Moses, the Beloved Jew of Stringtown on the Pike*, 1930; "Fragments from an Autobiography," *Eclectic Medical Journal*, July 1927.
14. *Tales of the Telegraph: The Story of a Telegrapher's Life and Adventures in Railroad, Commercial, and Military Work*, by Jasper Ewing Brady, 1899.
15. *Bernard DeVoto: A Preliminary Appraisal*, by Garrett Mattingly, 1938, a short book about to be published by Little, Brown.
16. Anthony Eden (1897–1977) of Britain, appointed foreign secretary in 1935, after prolonged disagreement with Prime Minister Neville Chamberlain (1869–1940) over the government's policies of yielding to Hitler's and Mussolini's territorial demands in Europe, resigned on Sunday,

20 February 1938. A lengthy debate in the House of Commons on Eden's resignation began on 21 February. Churchill's *The Gathering Storm* (Vol. 1 of *The Second World War*) does not mention a no-confidence motion, but a Labour motion of censure was defeated, 330-168, after furious debate. Three weeks later, on 12 March 1938, Nazi troops marched unopposed into Vienna, and Hitler proclaimed the annexation (*Anschluss*) of Austria into the German Reich.

17. Henry Wickham Steed (1871–1956), editor of the London *Times*, 1919–1922; *The Hapsburg Monarchy*, 1919.
18. Novel by Elmer Rice, 1937.
19. By Thomas Carlyle (1795–1881), Scottish writer, 1837.
20. Princess Marie Bonaparte of Greece (1882?–1962, granddaughter of Napoleon's nephew), psychoanalyst, a disciple of Freud. William C. Bullitt, ambassador to France (and coauthor, with Freud, of a psychobiography of Woodrow Wilson that was not published until 1966), also joined the mission to rescue the great psychoanalyst, whose theories were anathematized by the Nazis on scientific as well as racial grounds. Jones tells the story in his *Life and Work of Sigmund Freud*, volume 3, chapter 6.
21. At Berggasse 19 in the Währing district of Vienna, near the Votivkirche; it is now a museum, complete with Freud's couch and collection of ancient statuary.
22. By Shaw, 1920.
23. Vanity and a striving after wind, from Ecclesiastes 4:4.
24. Germany's annexation (*Anschluss*) of Austria was proclaimed on 13 March.
25. The Polish ultimatum refers to a border dispute with Lithuania.
26. *A Tailor-Made Man*, comedy by Harry James Smith (1880–1918), 1917. David Snodgrass (1894–1963), Harvard '17, Ll.B '21; dean of the Hastings College of Law, San Francisco, 1940–1963. Ed Stephenson, probably Clarence Stephenson (1895–1977), who spent one year at Harvard Law School. From President Wilson's message to Congress, 2 April 1917, asking Congress to declare war on the Central Powers.
27. Martin Luther (1483–1546), German Protestant theologian: God help me, I cannot do otherwise.
28. David Lloyd George (1863–1945), Welsh statesman and orator, liberal prime minister 1916–1922. He and Clemenceau (the "Tiger of France") dominated the negotiations at the Paris Peace Conference in 1919, insisting on territorial concessions and a harsh indemnity to be imposed on Germany, as well as an acknowledgment by Germany, in the Versailles Treaty, of responsibility for starting the Great War (the so-called war-guilt clause).
29. Holmes (1879–1964), Harvard '02, Unitarian clergyman and social activist who helped found the American Civil Liberties Union and the National Association for the Advancement of Colored People.
30. James Knox Polk (1795–1849), eleventh president of the United States, 1845–1849.
31. Not an editorial but an article: "DeVoto rumored to be returning to College next autumn," 15 March 1938.
32. (1755–1793), Queen of Louis XVI of France, guillotined during the Revolution.
33. Sam Brown belts, usually made of wide heavy leather with a rectangular brass buckle; for police use, with holsters and accessories.
34. Where the Prophet Joseph Smith, in a revelation from the Angel Nephi (later Moroni), was directed to find the golden plates upon which was encoded the sacred text of the *Book of Mormon*, 1820.
35. Strauss (b.1912), screenwriter; *Isn't It Romantic?*, 1948; *Four Days in November*, 1964; *The Indomitable Teddy Roosevelt*, 1986; producer, *The Bridge at Remagen*, 1969; *Dark Hunger*, novel, 1946 (later retitled *Moonrise*). Hassell (1911–1970); *Rachel's Children*, 1938; in *The Art of Fiction in the*

Heart of Dixie: An Anthology of Alabama Writers, 1986. Josefina María Niggli (1910–1983), Mexican-American writer; *Sunday Cost Five Pesos*, play; short stories. Charles (later Charles-Henri) Ford (1908–2002), Mississippi-born avant-garde poet and surrealist photographer and publisher, active in Paris, 1931–1934; founding editor, *Blues* magazine, 1929–1930. Arthur Tourtellot (1913–1977), author, historian, television producer; CBS; *Be Loved No More: The Life and Environment of Fanny Burney*, 1938.

36. 1937.
37. Possibly Elizabeth Gould Davis (1910?–1974); *The First Sex*, 1971.
38. Nathan (1894–1985), Harvard '16, author and screenwriter; *Portrait of Jennie*, 1948.
39. *American Caravan: A Yearbook of American Literature*, edited by Van Wyck Brooks, Alfred Kreymborg, Lewis Mumford, and Paul Rosenfeld, with "seventy-two contributors," 1927.
40. Much of the crisis with Frost is recounted by Stegner, who was present, in *The Uneasy Chair*, Part IV, Chapter 6, "An Incident on Bread Loaf Mountain."
41. Stephen Spender (1909–1995), British poet.
42. (French) crisis.
43. Correctly, Concord Corners.
44. Sharon, Vermont, birthplace of Joseph Smith.
45. The Phalanstery was the main meeting house of the short-lived Brook Farm community. See BDV, *The Year of Decision: 1846*.
46. Robert Frost's son Carol; BDV probably is thinking of Carroll County in New Hampshire.
47. *Du côté de chez Swann* (Swann's Way).
48. Part III, *Le côté de Guermantes* (1920–1921).
49. *With Malice toward Some* by Margaret Halsey (1910–1977), 1938; reviewed by Clifton Fadiman in *The New Yorker*, 20 August 1938.
50. In loss of life and property, the hurricane of 1938 still stands as the most destructive storm ever to strike New England, which recorded 600 of the 700 deaths; 3,500 were injured and 63,000 were made homeless. Nearly 9,000 buildings were completely destroyed, and more than 75,000 were damaged; an estimated 2 billion trees were blown down. In the Connecticut River valley, where the most intense part of the hurricane passed, rainfall varied between 10 and 17 inches. Because the storm occurred during the unusually high tide of the new moon at the time of the autumnal equinox, the peak storm surge came to 17 feet above normal high tide at Providence, which was five feet under water downtown. A wind gust of 186 miles per hour was measured at the Blue Hill Observatory.
51. With headquarters in Montpelier, the Green Mountain Power Co. is the supplier for much of Vermont's electric power.
52. Boston & Maine Railroad, from 1841. Boston and Albany Railroad, chartered 1870, since 1900 part of the New York Central system.
53. Central Vermont Railway Company, reorganized 1870 from a conglomerate of many smaller companies.
54. 297 Main Street, Walpole, built 1760s, eight rooms.
55. Between Rhode Island and the western side of Cape Cod.
56. Mystic, Connecticut, near the Rhode Island border.
57. Near Mount Mansfield.
58. Ernest J. Simmons (1903–1972), professor of Slavic languages; Harvard, Cornell, Columbia.
59. The climax of Anglo-French appeasement of German territorial demands in the summer of 1938. Hitler insisted that the rights of the Sudeten Germans, in the German-speaking part of Czechoslovakia known as the Sudetenland, had to be satisfied by actual cession of Czech territory into the German Reich. The Czech government expected to defend this territory even

by going to war with Germany, and possessed the strongest army in central Europe next to Germany's. Czechoslovakia was also protected by a military guarantee from both France and the Soviet Union. Britain was pledged to support France, but not Czechoslovakia, and this weakness was exploited by Hitler. In two meetings in September 1938, at Berchtesgaden and at Bad Godesberg, Prime Minister Chamberlain and Foreign Secretary Lord Halifax, together with the French and Soviet ministers, failed to reach an agreement that would satisfy Hitler, and the British began mobilizing for what seemed like a certain outbreak of war with Germany; but at the last minute Chamberlain went to Munich for a third meeting with Hitler, the French ministers, and Mussolini of Italy, with the Soviet Union excluded. Under British pressure, and equally anxious to avoid war, France reneged on its promise to defend the Czechs. The Munich Pact, signed on 30 September, provided for immediate cession of the Sudetenland to Nazi Germany, which in turn pledged to respect the new borders; Czechoslovakia thereby lost her major fortifications and industrial centers. Germany occupied the rest of Czechoslovakia in March 1939. See J. W. Wheeler-Bennett, *Munich: Prologue to Tragedy*, 1948.

60. Hindus (1891–1969), Russian-born writer on Soviet affairs; New York *Herald Tribune* correspondent during World War II; *Green Worlds*, autobiography, 1938; *Mother Russia*, 1943. The Columbia antenna was probably CBS.
61. White Rock, mineral water and soft drinks, since 1871.
62. KS possibly means Harry Scherman, *The Promises Men Live By: A New Approach to Economics*, 1938. Garratt (1888–1942), author; *Mussolini's Roman Empire*, 1938; *The Shadow of the Swastika*, 1938. Sir Norman Angell (1872–1967), British economist and author; *The Great Illusion*, 1910; *The Great Illusion 1933*, 1933; *The Defence of the Empire*, 1937; *Peace With the Dictators?*, 1938; Nobel Peace Prize, 1933.
63. The so-called Runciman mission, under Walter Runciman (1870–1949), 1st Viscount Runciman of Doxford, arrived in Prague on 3 August, 1938, to discuss German claims to the Sudetenland. The Berchtesgaden agreement, from the conference on 15 September.
64. Whitehall Street in London is the location of many governmental offices.
65. (French) comic opera.

7

1939 LETTERS

With the serial publication of John August's *Troubled Star* in 1938, followed by its appearance in book form in 1939, DeVoto's financial stability seemed assured for the moment, following his departure from *SRL* and move back to Cambridge. (Another John August thriller, *Rain Before Seven*, would follow in 1940.) In 1939 DeVoto increased his involvement in Mark Twain documents and began to plan two important collections of unpublished writings, soon encountering exasperation, however, because of interference on the part of Twain's daughter, Clara Clemens Gabrilowitsch. At about the same time, DeVoto completed a major portion of a draft of a novel but was already dissatisfied with it and soon set it aside. DeVoto had time for some amusing Harvard gossip and for visiting the New York World's Fair with his son Gordon, as well as the recapitulation of a misunderstanding involving Granville Hicks and Allan Nevins. In early June he announced to Sterne that his daughter Elizabeth was to be born on his birthday, 11 January 1940 (the predicted birthday turned out to be correct but the child was his second son, Mark Bernard DeVoto).

The political situation in Europe became rapidly more threatening in March as Germany occupied the remainder of Bohemia and Moravia. War broke out in Europe with the Nazi invasion of Poland on 1 September. In October, with much of the war news quiescent, DeVoto wrote extensively about Havelock Ellis's works and about his own efforts as an amateur psychiatrist, but Sterne largely steered clear of response.

32 Coolidge Hill Road
Cambridge, Massachusetts

[11 January 1939]

Dear Kate:

Thanks for being an agent provocateur (-se?) and I've just remembered I didn't send you a *Coolidge Hill Gazette* and so do.[1] (By the way, Marshall Best for some reason gave me two copies of Van Doren's *Franklin*, a good book. I suppose you've read it, but could Bowne at large use the spare?) And while the Collectors' Book Shop was finding out for you, it bought eight copies from the publishers for $10 and is offering them to you at a pleasant advance. Stanley Hillyer got a wire yesterday that they couldn't use any more, but I think they will. I think they'll use some at $5 a copy. The plot is now off to a proper start.... It all originated from Stanley's notion that Mr. Frost would give them a poem if I asked him to, and I did. Meanwhile my son remembered that he'd written a poem two years ago and kindly contributed that—he has talked about little else since it was accepted, and says he's going to write another one as soon as he gets an idea. Stanley and his colleague, Peter Poore, then went on to the idea of a poetry page and got Hillyer's contribution. I suppose I appear by courtesy, for services rendered. But, realizing that a Frost first is a Frost first, I told the boys they could get a printing press out of this, and they probably will, though, well nurtured Shady Hill Children as they are, they contribute half their profit to hurricane relief.... But I seem to have started something for while I go on gently raising the price of the December issue, Charlie McLaughlin, assistant editor in charge of the January number, has snagged a poem from Archie MacLeish and another one from Ted Morrison—and Joe Dinneen, the hard-boiled novelist-reporter who got *Harper's* sued for half a million dollars, is hellbent to plaster the whole thing over the Boston *Globe*, Shady Hill so far holding off on the theory that publicity would go to the boys' heads.[2]... And I swear to sell some of them to the rare-book trade at $25 apiece.

No note on a case history this time. Frost was here for Christmas dinner—when the family were all out of bed together for the first time in ten days—and again on New Year's Eve, and he seemed nearer what he was three or four years ago than he has been at any time since then. I have a strong hunch that Kay Morrison pitched into him and gave him hell.... And, if she did, about time too.

It was an impromptu gathering on New Year's Eve. Nothing was intended except that Avis and I were going to play the harpsichord records Henry Reck gave us and feel snootily superior to the Times Square broadcast at midnight.[3] But it occurred to various people in various conditions of liquor that they ought to see the new year in with the DeVotos and at midnight there were eighteen of them in a Cambridge living room drawn to Cambridge scale. Henry Parkman had brought one bottle of champagne—try separating one bottle of champagne into twenty parts sometime.[4] And Frances Curtis was jingled, and I'd never seen that before, because Frances' nose gets red when she takes too much and she labors to prevent that at any cost. But it's a highly amusing experience and I wish this was a Boston novel gathering, not a Cambridge one, for she certainly has picked up some of the funniest scandals I've ever heard. Charlie had a wonderful time—my God, I wish I could have fun the way he does. All evening long he was having an abstruse debate with Ted Morrison, who thinks naturally in metaphysical terms and speaks them even more naturally, about "if you scale Shakespeare down to Noel Coward." At intervals I sat in and listened but I never found out what it was about. And Doris Parkman used to work for the *American Magazine* and learned that with writers it's best to use a trowel, so that by midnight you would have to scale Shakespeare up quite a bit to come out even with me.[5] ... I don't need to be told why I have this strong resentment of unmasked flattery.... But she moved on to Frost after a while. And I got scaled down OK for Sally Buck explained in detail why John August is so much better than I am.

Well, the literary are the literary and maybe Alfred McIntyre has lost a best seller, for Walter Edmonds cut me flagrantly yesterday on Mass. Avenue, and that was because Alfred asked me and not Walter to the Little-Brown directors' dinner, which has happened before. All Alfred's parties are drunken but the directors' dinner is Something. It begins at noon, though I refused to come in before seven. And how it takes you back, to see a gang of middle-aged and elderly men who have been drinking for seven hours. And my God how I hate to make after-dinner speeches. I don't know precisely why, for I don't hate to make any other kind of speeches. But they get me down. I took four cocktails to prepare myself for it, and so lost all the point of the various wines Alfred had provided and may have hurt him deeply by not recognizing the turtle soup. And laid up trouble for myself by promising him before witnesses that he'd have the manuscript of MT by January 1, 1940.... As time goes on I become convinced that I'm writing *War and Peace*. Or, as Alfred suggested, the encyclopedia that Gene Field wrote about. What the hell does one do, though? I only know how to write according to my own sense of the proper treatment of scenes. It's either that or throw the thing away, and I don't know whether I'd survive throwing it away again. And my sense of the proper treatment of scenes spins it on and on and on. If you know the answer you can serve Little-Brown by telling me what it is.

Did I write you from the Harvard Club? I intended to and then lost heart—and then, as defence against the MLA, kept pretty boiled. Kenneth Murdock and I wandered over to Wally Frank's and bought a lot of pipes. I told the inner shrine what I thought of them. Who should flag me at Columbia but Dicky Quintana, Professor at Madison (and, oh God, I think Alfred wants me to do some scouting there when I go

West next month) and great authority on Swift and Coleridge. I agreed to prepare a Tom Sawyer and a Huck Finn for the Limited Editions Club—did I tell you Tom Benton is going to do the illustrations for the first?[6] And there's something in the air at Columbia that gives me the willies. It appears not to be like Harvard College.

Oh, I managed to talk with George Whicher but didn't manage to get anywhere. People keep breaking in on us and we've postponed the discussion till the roads are agreeable in March or April. I'll let you know what comes out of it. But George isn't very deft in his Freud.

...This was cut short by the arrival of Hans Zinsser, who breaks my heart these days, and a lot of things have prevented my resuming—including the *Ibéria*, which arrived yesterday and which I have been playing most of the time since.[7] You shouldn't do such things but I'm glad you did, though it must have been a guess—how should you know that I like it best of all Debussy? It's glorious. And the best climax in modern music. Or it seems that way, playing it half a dozen times hand-running.... My take has been pretty big on records, this last month. I've splurged pretty heavy on my own account and apparently all my friends have gone out to celebrate my new machine. Have you heard "Shadrach"?[8] It's something—Rosy gave it to me.... Well, do you know anything better to do these days than listen to music? Play music, maybe. Charlie Taylor began about a year ago on—well, guess. The recorder. So now there's a chorus (choir?) of them and they're going to give a recital at the Fine Arts.[9] Thirty of them. The damn things seem to run from the size of a bazoo [*sic*][10] up to something that must be six feet long only it curls up like a tuba. All of which is news to me. I guess I could listen to two or three pieces by thirty recorders but I'm not going to spend the evening.... From time to time I play with the notion of getting a xylophone. It's the only instrument I feel competent to study.[11]

So Felix goes to Washington, apparently as a hint to Hitler.[12] He's the closest-mouthed man on earth and I've seen him only casually this year, but I feel fairly sure that this wasn't counted on as much as two months ago. Everyone understood he would get Brandeis's place but not Cardozo's. And you've got to hand Franklin something. It's no secret that Felix was dead set against the Supreme Court Bill, fought it every way he could, and made himself distinctly unpleasant in the White House. Well, he's a magnificent advocate but in the six years I've supposed this was coming I've never been able to think of him as a judge. Yet clearly the same thing was to be said about Brandeis when he was appointed. The local Bourbons are furious, but not as furious as they'd be if they hadn't long since passed the point of overload. I think it's excellent for Henderson, for instance, to take this kind of kick in the guts. I once heard him finally answer a bewildered and annoying ass who kept insisting that Mr. Frankfurter explain just what his program or platform might be, "I believe in the dignity of human life." He really does—and, the last time I saw him was envying the zest of Salvemini—and I think the dignity of American life is enhanced by his being on the bench.... Curiously, the one job he really wanted, the one job he would have selected for himself, was the Presidency of C.C.N.Y.[13] He has been active in the deposition and would have been glad to spend the rest of his life in the vacated chair, if there weren't graver things to do. I met him on the street a month ago and he said, if you really believe in education, that's the most important job in the American colleges.

I saw Jim Landis at the Shady Hill meeting last night and asked him how long before he'd follow Felix there.[14] He said he was out of the government. I said I thought we had made clear that the Supreme Court wasn't part of the Government. Jim's eyes flashed and he said, "By God, I did my damndest to make it part." ... Well, the man I'd like to see on the bench is Reed Powell. There'd be tang in the opinions.

Well, have you seen anything funnier than Walter Lippmann's discovery of religion as a social force, followed by Dorothy's acknowledgment that he had something there?[15] ... Henderson gave Lippmann a set of Pareto about a year ago, and this may have issued from the gift.

Bill White is coming to town to lecture on Conant's extra-curricular-history foundation.[16] Thank God. There's one of the swellest gents in America, and Cambridge can use him.

Yeah. Forty-two.[17]

Yours,

Benny

32 Coolidge Hill Road
Cambridge, Massachusetts

[14 May 39]

Dear Kate:

All the original MT is in the late lamented too—and is likely to remain there. No, the trouble is quite simple: Scale. The job I started in to do could only be done at greater length than I ever had the courage, or belief, to admit; so what I did was a progressive compromise that got progressively more unbearable. I'm not thinking highly of myself as a writer of fiction these days. Nor as John August who, unhappily, will soon have to warm up. I think John used the only useful part of the Three Twins in *Troubled Star*, the anonymous letters.[18] What was Chess in Back Bay? I don't remember my titles. If it was the lady of *Thaïs*, I doubt if the magazines could swallow it. Go on suggesting, God knows we need a buildup, John & I.

The latest to object to Mark's mild coarseness in "Letters From the Earth" are, God help us, after I have slowly won over the assent of Clara & the Spirit Land, Gene Saxton

& the House of Harper's. So there won't be any MT book next fall. I can't undertake to prepare another one in time. I'm off this evening to NY—to make a speech at the Fair tomorrow for Dorothy Thompson's sake—and I suppose I'll have to ask Gene what the constructive interpretation of Free Hand to Publish Anything is.

And also, probably, tell him that his fears were unjustified and I've just recommended Vardis Fisher's Mormon novel for Bk of the Month.[19] Dept. of Eaten Words: it's a good novel, Fisher can write a good novel, there can be a good Mormon novel. Postscript: one thousand pages.

But what does it do to the Houghton-Mifflin Fellowship novel about the Mormon hegira? Or, for that matter, to the faint notion of making that hegira the main hinge of *Empire*?[20]

It seems that here was when I got interrupted. I hope I don't again, for I'm off to NY again on Tuesday, and I wouldn't have gone this time if Dorothy's telegrams had said it was the P.E.N. Club that hung & was to hang on my words.[21] From the telegrams I understood it was Western Civilization. Though why we keep that obsolete noun I don't know.... My xenophobia was at its worst. I had a wench from New Zealand and a pastor-poet from Switzerland affixed to me for two mortal hours. It's a hard choice but I plump for Suisse. Any gathering of writers is the most futile thing. But writers making speeches add an unnecessary futility.[22] Of that endless program only Henry Canby and I know how to get our voices past our neckties to the first row of seats. And I think I don't need any more ancestor worship & childhood reminiscences of the young Manns.[23] Though Erika, who was also affixed to me for an hour, is moderately pleasing to the eye.

The World of Tomorrow hasn't got the eggshell off yet.[24] Practically the only cheesecake available is in the Aquacade, and it is so temperate—well, so frozen in dirty water & a bay breeze that you can only feel sorry for it.[25] A lousy show—preposterous & dull. The variations that can be wrung [*sic*] on the Australian crawl are pretty limited. And it's melancholy to see Johnny Weissmuller & Stubby Kruger doing the same sad clown act off a diving board that they were doing as undergraduates at NU in my time.[26] And the Holm person may stimulate Billy Rose but I doubt if many of his customers will understand why.[27] ... The General Motors trip through tomorrow broke down just as I reached the traveling chairs. Probably powered by Ford. The new trains, engines, & Pullman cars make agreeable seeing and, if I can go back, I'll watch GE make lightning.[28] Some excellent Dutch beer and a really good restaurant—the Swedish bldg., chairs cost $3 an hour. Buses take 25 minutes to go a distance I later walked in 9 minutes. No private cars on the grounds except Dorothy's—she entered like Flagstad, with retinue & escort and I don't think I can take any more Dorothy—God must have missed her badly, these 3 hours. . . . I did see an electric eel light some neon tubes and Bunny, if his feet held out, would probably be delighted with the whole show. But the electric wiring is definitely bad & Tomorrow needs a lot of syn chronizing [*sic*].

The New Yorkers are divided about the war. Bruening is committed to May 15 for the actual outbreak, which is already absurd.[29] Most of them see this year as a race between Hitler & the British govt., exclusive of Mr. C., to sign an alliance with Russia. Elmer Davis, however, goes whole hog as usual and thinks that the alliance England is playing for will turn out to be with Hitler. Eli Potter expects nothing so drastic. Eli is further committed to the reactionary, the primitive thesis that there really is such a thing as money and therefore there may prove to be such a thing as demobilization—for, he admits, the first time in history, Eli sits comfortably on the fulfillment of his printed prophecies about domestic politics—less comfortably on his apprehensions about manifest destiny. He took issue sharply with Elmer's thesis that the class line will be sharply drawn in 1940 but agreed with him that the apparent policy of the New Deal to abandon that year *pour mieux sauter*[30] in '44 is God damned folly for us all.

Cambridge the incredible has been Cambridge the cataleptic all spring. Foreign anxiety, domestic nerves, and the coldest season since 1816 have suspended all its customary activities, even, so far as my information extends, adultery.[31] There was a foretaste of comedy when it began to look as if Kay Born was starting in search of her adolescence but, in the east wind, it came to nothing. Even the radical wenches have ceased being funny—I can't call the League of Women Shoppers anything but grotesque.[32] Hell, even psycho-analysis is routine. I am now so familiar with Bill Barrett's masochists that I could probably substitute for while he takes another cram-course for the 8-hr. specialists exam he expected to flunk yesterday in Chicago but they bore even him, whom I've never before known to be bored. But there was a moment when he saw a patient whom he had dismissed a couple of years ago as cured—she was a pianist who suddenly wasn't able to play the piano—and asked her how her symptoms were. She said they were entirely cured, & added enthusiastically that she never played the piano any more, she was studying folk-lore. Bill's build must have turned many female phantasies in the direction of careers in analysis, but, a strong oral aggressive, he'll get fat pretty soon. . . . John Taylor's resistance was worn thin or else he's growing confident for he is now analyzing Victoria Lincoln, after years of refusing to on the incontrovertible ground that Vicky is just crazy. Also some hardy soul in NY is analyzing Johnny Farrar. . . . Oh, my favorite student, Gene Saxton's boy Mark, now works for John (so many young men do—for a while) and is publishing a [?]d[*illegible*]etist yarn this spring.[33]

A dull season. A dull letter—I apologize. How can blood be lively, these days?

I talk to the Henry Adams Club tomorrow and then put the instrument away till Fall. On Tuesday to Manhattan again and I'll stay there till this MT business is settled for good, one way or the other. Clara arrives from Detroit and the Great Beyond next week. If I could take Rosy with me, Clara would not live long after arrival.

Yours,

Benny

[BEFORE 6 JUNE 1939]

[newspaper clipping pasted at the top:][34]

[Deatherage] denied that he was an agent of Fritz Kuhn, leader of the German-American Bund, and said he had met the man only once.[35]

"I met him in New York," he said, "in the Harvard Club—a very opportune place for that sort of thing—and we talked for a half hour."

Considering your present habitation & its fame, maybe I oughtn't to mention it, but I can't help wondering whether the real purpose of the recent White Paper[36] is

I to appease the Arabs <u>or</u>

II a) to appease Hitler,

b) indirectly to stir up anti-semitism in Britain, & so make the long-wished-for alliance with Hitler more palatable, and

c) to alienate the US & USSR (both of whom C., of course, hates) & thus make the English-German alliance more inevitable.

If England signs up with Hitler, what will Canada do?

What an eerie feeling it is to see all the radio serials of the past six months materialize in the Dies Committee reports.[37]

What was Meriwether Lewis' Indian girl friend's name?

Believe it or not, S. J. Perelman is even unfunnier on the radio than he is in print.

Observation: the Trylon & Perisphere have replaced Chamberlain & his umbrella as the favourite subject of obscene jokes.... I suppose you've heard the suggestion that Grover Whalen be preserved as a public park when the Fair is over.[38]

I loved the *SRL* picture of you all but wrapped up in the American flag.[39]

Next time you have fifteen free minutes & are feeling amiable, I wonder if you'd look in the DAB or wherever for this Jacob Broom of Wilmington who seems to have been my great-great-grandfather.[40] All I know is that he had something to do with the Constitution.

The Century Association
7 West Forty-Third Street
New York

[?11 July 1939]

Dear Kate:

Well, there's a lot in that Nevins-Hicks episode that doesn't meet the eye at first glance. And the poignant part is that all this last year I've been estopped by it from taking the periodic pot-shots at Granville that have pleased me more than they ought, for some years, and have annoyed him more than is sensible. For, like Johnny Farrar in person, Granville is controversy, always leads with his chin when I'm around—just the way I do when Ernie Simmons is around, or the way Avis does when Vicky Lincoln is around.

Some background. When I took over the *SRL*, the literary left, which was still organized in those days, determined to do a job on me and nominated Hicks, its big critical gun. For weeks word went round that Granville was going to skin me and nail the hide on the L I D door.[41] He talked fierce—but he lost his nerve and backed out, I don't know why: either my adjectives still stuck in his gizzard or else he divined that I'd find occasion to tell in print the story Neilson told me about him at Smith (amusing but Another Story). So the job was transferred to Bunny Wilson, newly restored to good standing for this one episode, who had to get up his reading over a weekend and fizzled it—not even a boom.[42] . . . But Granville saw a chance to box me when I published Hillyer's "Letter to Bernard DeVoto," which was originally written to Ted Weeks but converted when Ted wouldn't buy it for the *Atlantic*. Hicks, assisted by half the literary left, wrote a long series of couplets, very scabrous, about Hillyer & more scabrous about me, and sent them to the *SRL*. The idea was I'd reject them, the *New Masses* would publish them, & I'd be an enemy of free expression with my pants down. So I wrote him that they were too bum poetry for me to run as a contribution but, if he'd scale them down to space, I'd run them on the Letters page as comment. So he put them away till the book came out, & then the *New Republic* ran the less offensive ones, suppressing the others because someone told Cowley I loved to bring suit & would invoke the law of libel for publicity's sake. And Granville was madder than ever at me. See files of the *New Masses*. . . .

Well, some years ago I was at Sam Morison's for dinner and it was a very alcoholic evening, as all evenings are at Sam's, and talk turned to John Reed, whom I had recently lectured about, and Sam said that Waldo Peirce had some letters from Reed written during the last few months of his life, in which Reed went very sour indeed on the Great Revolution, called it a betrayal of mankind, yearned to come back to the U S & spend his life writing poetry, etc. Sam said Waldo had shown them to Hicks but the betting was they wouldn't be mentioned in Hicks' book.[43]

three or four years pass

A few weeks before I left New York (in the happy delusion that I was leaving it for good) I was at Nevins's for dinner. Commager was there & a couple of lesser historians. Nevins had been trying for months to get me (a) to come out in favor of his proposed "popular" magazine of history[44] (cf. Nevins in the *SRL*, & DV in the Easy Chair), and (b) to agree to do the volume on Am lit since 1920 of the four supplementary volumes he is editing to bring the *Pageant of America* up to date.[45] Now Nevins is a pompous gent but I had no previous intimation that he is an ass as well. I know he wrote too many books and I found that night that he iced his claret. It was not an alcoholic evening—not on cold claret & a watery cocktail—I only called it one in the *New Republic* to give Nevins that much out.[46] In the course of the evening, talk getting round to Hicks, I told them Sam's story. Proper air of historians' honor but no comment beyond that.

I got out of New York and last fall I suddenly got a letter from Michigan from a man who presented himself as a scholar & said he was deeply interested in exposing Hicks, & I had been given him as the source of the story about Hicks in Nevins' new book, & would I come clean & give him all my dope. Investigating, I found to my horror that Nevins had a new book called *The Gateway to History* and there, not naming Hicks but referring to "a biographer of John Reed," of whom there are [*sic*] only one.[47] Clearly Hicks was smoking me out with the guy in Michigan and thought that at last he had me by the short hair. I wrote Nevins & asked him what the hell. The book is devoted to the rules of evidence & the nature & tests of evidence in history—& the bastard had never even phoned me to check his story. He wrote back, however, that he had never mentioned my name to Hicks, that he was denying he had Hicks in mind, & would I please hurry & prove the story. I had to hurry & apologize to Sam Morison. But I decided that I didn't love Hicks enough to come to his rescue as long as he kept trying to kid me with editorials in the U of Michigan *Daily*, written by loyal legionnaires. So I shut up—and grew thin & haggard whenever I had to pass up the rare, ripe opportunities to kid Granville that he kept offering at Harvard all year. Even when he forced Nevins to apologize in the N Y *Times* & Nevins said he had the story on the authority of a "leading literary critic" and a "leading historian," which was just a damn lie, I still shut up.[48] But when Hicks wrote to the New Republic quoting Nevins as saying that "I had first-hand evidence & repeatedly assured" him he could tell the story "in complete confidence of its accuracy" I said, oh, hell, I used to think historians were good but this one is on Granville. So I ate my crow. It didn't taste good.

So now I get to eat some more crow in public. I'm going to do a piece on Vardis Fisher's Mormon novel.[49] But, after that, maybe I can return to the offensive.

Yrs

Benny

Bowne

[August 1939]

Notes on the Traumdeutung:[50] (Department of Couture)—The other night I did New York in a lemon-yellow chiffon dinner-dress & a long, tight silver lamé coat, with a bell bottom & a small, stand-up sable collar. Hair on top of head with two California poppies stuck in it.... Last night, however, dancing with Josef Beck, I wore shell-pink mousseline de soie[51] with a square decolletage, ~~gathered~~ shirred from diaphragm to hip-bone.* Very ingenue.... Beck was nice, but extremely pale. I don't believe his health can be good.[52]

* * *

Bea is betting two bucks that Poland won't be Muniched. I'm betting it will.

* * *

I'm reading the Auden-MacNeice Letters from Iceland and—to my intense surprise—liking them.[53]

* * *

Our inventive young orderly wants to know why not typewriter rolls with occasional perforations to obviate continuously changing sheets, & an automatic revolving eraser attached to one of the keys. Well, why not?

* Also a long bob.

Yours,

Kate

32 Coolidge Hill Road
Cambridge, Massachusetts

[written 9 September 1939]
[11 September 1939]

Dear Kate:

Turning of the tide. The Kraft-Phenix Cheese Company has decided that I must have been eating its stuff when I talked about the pith of weeds and exudations from trees, so I've had to get out of bed and deal with that.[54] Jesus, I love viruses. Twice in one summer seems a little excessive. If I pick up one in the next twelvemonth I'll imitate Kraft-Phenix and sue the Harvard Medical School.

I can see that this is going to be pretty non-consecutive. I wobble from toe to intelligence. Raucous yell, you're telling me?

I haven't seen Alfred McIntyre yet and Ray Everitt remains incorruptible, but I think you can scratch Waln and Bridge. In alcohol, Alan Collins let slip the fact that Ethel Vance is a <u>new</u> account for Curtis Brown, and that rules both of them out. Helen Everitt had a sagacious guess when I saw her a couple of weeks ago but I've forgotten which English potboiler it was. Helen is about to be delivered of her fourth child and when I take the flowers round I'll get the name again. It didn't mean anything to me.

Helen was at Sam Everitt's place, way up on a mountain at Snowville, N.H. A big rain washed out the roads, isolated her there with three small children, and brought on false labor pains. So she told herself that they were false—and had the children boil up some water in case they weren't. A good girl.

She was certainly missed at Bread Loaf. Happily Hester Bailey came along this year and understudied her. It was a dull session. No explosions. No good looking fellows, hardly a good looking customer, only a couple of nuts, just routine. It was highlighted, of course, by the crisis abroad but godawfully tiresome apart from that. Alan Collins and Holmes Alexander put on a really heroic drunk which belonged in the best tradition but that was all.[55] Except that, preparing the way for my present reinfection, I played tennis steadily while an incredulous staff sat on the sidelines and made the most comical remarks. Oh, very comical indeed. So Bob Bailey and I beat Everitt-Morrison, Everitt-Agar, Agar-Morrison, and other combinations you wouldn't believe, a pleasant satisfaction to a man who is under no Everitt necessity to be either a conqueror or an athlete.

Why, I think you're wrong; I think the boys will go ahead and have themselves a war. Hitler has the considerable advantage of realizing that this isn't 1918, as everybody else seems to think it is. He has the disadvantage that it's probably nearer to 1918 than he believes. Now and for a considerable time to come strategy counts a hell of a lot more than tactics, and grand strategy a hell of a lot more than strategy. My guess is that it will be a diplomatic war for quite a while and may be a diplomatic war throughout. The Siegfried Line is probably impregnable—at any price the French are prepared to pay.[56] Just possibly it mayn't be; Gamelin's model of it may show a seam somewhere, though on a front of only 200 miles that's unlikely.[57] That's the first point of reference, however, the disproportionate cost of attack in the West. Strategically Poland counts a hell of a lot less than people are assuming at the moment, and Russia doesn't count a whole lot. Strategically, the three most important foci of attention are Rumania, the Turkish Army, and the Far Eastern Fleet. Grand strategy is repeating the pattern of 1914; Italy is the essence of it. Unquestionably the boys crossed up the war which the allied staffs had laid out, which was to begin by knocking off Italy. It's not so unquestionable that the 1914 pattern has been violated. I don't see that there's anything in Poland or anywhere else in Europe that Hitler can use as money for Mussolini, whereas Africa is full of hard cash. As a historian, I believe in the uniformities of history. There has never been a time when Italy had more than nuisance value and there has never been a time when you couldn't buy Italy for cash on the drumhead. Also, it appears to me, so far, that Hitler has made exactly the same mistake that the German Ministry made in the summer of 1914, that he has let himself be boxed, that he's licked before he starts, and that the outcome is not in doubt. There is no reason to suppose that Germany can do anything decisive before next spring, and by next spring she'll be unable to do anything decisive. My money says the war will be something less than a year long.

That's where I stand on September 9th, 1939. File for reference.

What can happen to the so-called American Republic in that year is what gives me the jitters. I think the housewives had better stifle this yell for price-regulation before it goes any farther, and at the moment I don't know whether Father Coughlin or Dorothy Thompson is the worse menace; after listening to both through a haze of fever I thought that Coughlin seemed the sweeter. The stock-market boom is also full of pleasant possibilities for the administration. And the growth of public emotion is the biggest out that the New Deal has had offered to it. Let's not talk about this. I'm still too jittery. When I can play tennis again I'll summarize it in an Easy Chair.[58] Also I'm looking into the possibilities of badminton.

Elmer Davis has fallen in a soft spot.[59] He needed one and I'm damned glad.

As for me, I've got to survey the magazine business. I was just going broke when the war came—and I don't remember the magazines of 1914–1918 well enough to know what to do. I've sent out some feelers.

Harvard begins to drift in—and looks a good deal like Warsaw. Everybody under the rank of President knows that it has been reduced to the status of a second-class power, and it seems unlikely that even Conant can shut his eyes to that realization much longer. There is bound to be something in the nature of reaction, repair, and reintegration sometime but as yet there is no sign that it's begun or even that the disintegration has been slowed up. I've never seen such rapid decline in any human institution. Well, certain marriages perhaps. But Harvard in 1939 looks less like Harvard in 1934 than the U.S. in 1939 looks like the U.S. of 1926. It still doesn't seem credible but there it is.

The Nazi elements aren't back yet so I can't satisfy that curiosity, but some of the Stalin cells are and they are too unhappy to be as funny as I'd hoped.[60] However funereal the times, there will be that relief, one's Stalinist friends.

I cleaned up my darkroom and developed the films on hand, which sufficed to demonstrate that I've taken two strips of Leica films and two film packs since last November. Like everything else about me, my photography suffered a seismic change this year, and I've done no writing, apart from the Easy Chair, since April. I suppose I had it coming to me. As literary coach and impromptu psychiatrist, I've told several hundred writers that there is such a thing as exhaustion, that there are periods when the batteries must be recharged, that it is essential to slow up and have a good time now and then. But it never occurred to me that I came under the principle. I was exempt, I was the inexhaustible energy. So I got sat on my can.... Well, in the course of a couple of months I at least raised the body physical to what is roughly called condition, and I can contemplate the continuance of the program with something like savoir-faire. I weigh two pounds less than I did when discharged from his majesty's forces in December, 1918, my waist has gone down two inches, and I've climbed a mountain for the first time since 1925. The idea convulses me as much as it shocks my friends. I now approach the resumption of literary activity. There is the usual rush of promises made. Those attended to, it will be advisable to make some money, if the magazine business is not taken over in the limited emergency. I could start writing my frontier book tomorrow but I'm keeping it in the unanswered mail basket for the time being.

Part of my virus reading was several issues of *Vogue*.[61] Is your sex really going to validate my extrapolations by putting on corsets? I wonder what that will do to modern love. And, casting round among the women I know, I can think of none who won't look grotesque with that kind of figure, even Rosy who has little or no tail. Two generations of emancipated womanhood have carried evolution a long way in the direction of steatopygy, and it's just obscene to emphasize the trend. Back to Crete, as it were. Someone quoted Elizabeth Hawes as saying that American women took out their neuroses in headgear, but that just shows that Elizabeth Hawes needs instruction in history. And this is quite true: a wench I know who had her breasts lifted in 1926 is now in Phillips House having them fatted up again.

As for my own sex, it's presenting me with a number of cases of senile love. I carried one all last year and now I've got another one in the consulting room and a third hesitating outside the office door. There would be one gratification from a Roosevelt dictatorship: the intellectuals would probably make mandatory the ligaturing of the vas at sixty. And if I were Conant I would establish a geisha house for the comfort of professors nearing retirement. The mournful thought strikes through, however, that among the areas of experience disregarded by or unknown to Mr. Conant is the one that Ellis used to call the phenomena of tumescence. And that's a thought I'll present to the Opposition: let the next committee of inquiry study the effects on Harvard administration of impotence and senility in the Dean's office. Maybe the geishas should begin operating in University Hall; maybe there would have been no Walsh-Sweezy case if George Birkhoff had been able to derive any personal reference from looking at a window weight.

Minor social irritation in a wartime world: the reappearance of the shaggy dog story. I heard it three times in forty-eight hours at Bread Loaf; on the third, day, John Marquand repeated it from the stand; since I got back to Cambridge I have heard it six times, and I've been bedridden most of the time.

So on to *The Web and the Rock*, which I've got to ingest for Ted Weeks' sake.[62]

Yours,

Benny

32 Coolidge Hill Road
Cambridge, Massachusetts

16 October 1939

Dear Kate:

You can have this war. I've been out in the wilderness trying to find out what I think about it, and the answer is, I don't. It's quite clear who's lost it and who's won it, but I'm damned if I can see where the Allies come out or for that matter go in. The only sensible conclusion is that the *SEP* is a good magazine.

As a textbook strategist I point out that the pattern of modern war, set in 1870, has been knocked all to hell, the Blitzkrieg along with the rest of it.[63] And maybe that's the answer: the general staffs haven't got any textbooks to draw on, they can't predict this year's eclipses from last year's almanacs. Or maybe it's the breakdown of military psychology: the practical engineering required to manipulate machines stymies them. More and more the pattern looks like a simple error in judgment.

I still hold by what I said some weeks back: I can't believe there'll be anything serious on the West front before spring—and not then by the German army.[64] My military consultants say that the German staff doesn't know anything about how a mass air attack works and may be holding back for just that reason. Maybe; what I wonder is if the offensive from the air isn't just as big a risk as the offensive against fortified lines. If it fails, that is, it's fatal. I can't [offer] any other explanation for its having been withheld so long—Dorothy Thompson's notion that Hitler is goofy is too simple. I can't believe that either side looks on war as just a matter of making faces, in the assurance that if it does anything more the government will fall. I can't accept the comforting supposition that A. Hitler asked in the Russian army on his flank just for the sake of scaring the Allies into a peace: presumably Russia wasn't the only party that profited from the bargain.[65]

How do you attack the Allies? Well, if you don't send the air fleet over Great Britain (be damn sure, for all the scareheads, you don't send it out for the British fleet), then it seems to me you attack either Palestine and Egypt or the British and Dutch East Indies and, possibly, Singapore.[66] You don't attack Egypt and Palestine unless you've got Turkey lined up and, on the showing now, you won't. So I still say, keep your eyes on the Far East.

How do you attack Germany? Obviously by sitting tight and letting the reserve stocks get depleted. And by, pretty soon, paying Italy the colonies you promised her twenty years ago.

And, hell, that's where I stood when the war broke out. It doesn't, in the light of Russia, make sense. But what the hell does make sense? It doesn't make sense that Hitler let the Allies mobilize unmolested, but he did. It doesn't make sense that the Allies took no steps in advance to prevent Russia handing over to Germany convenient ways of access to the open sea, but apparently that's what happened. It doesn't make sense that they haven't taken over the German air bases and fortifications opposite Gibraltar, but they haven't.... So maybe Russia's being in doesn't affect anybody but Russia—and victims—and I still came out where I went in, it ought to be over by Spring. And, whether it was the Allies or Russia that had him licked, Hitler was licked as soon as he started.

In short, I can't make anything out of it and why the hell should I? I made Fletcher Pratt a bet at Bread Loaf that we'd occupy Curaçao, one way or another, within six months, and I still think it's good. I shrink from telling you what I think

[*page missing?*]

struck a pretty good one. It was sent to me by John Murray, whom I've never so much as met, but he was just as sure as the others that I'd be glad to cooperate.[67] And I'd like to sit in his office and hear some of these phantasies elaborated in situ.... And I think it would be something, either critically or analytically, to have a real analysis of a good novel, from the time when it began to be laid out to the time when it was sent to the typist. I'd like to follow those projections and displacements. I wish to God that Kubie would do one—to my certain knowledge he has analyzed three pretty damn good novelists. If it weren't for his—quite inevitable—contempt for literary activity we'd get some good reading. Or is it that? He told me once that an analyst couldn't help being jealous of a novelist—they were both in the same business, both making men and women. That was nine and a half parts salad oil, but there's some vinegar in it too. Even better than Kubie, maybe, would have been Bill Herman who died, my God, it's nearly four years ago. He was a damned fine analyst but he was a better healer, and a good part of that was pure swami, pure intuition. Bill wouldn't do—his literary taste is bad. He talks a lot about the Mark Twain dream story I've been playing with for a year, and he's read all the dope and I'll probably do a paper with him on it, but hell, I can do that sort of thing myself. What I'd like, well, I suppose I'd like to see an analysis of a novel in process, but I'd rather analyze one in process. It would be something to follow ma and pa through all those dissolves, yes, and Mattie Guernsey, too, and the Brewer's Daughter, and Skinny Browning. And it would be fun to see what Bill would look like in a patient's novel—that's one reason why I've got to meet John Murray now. This isn't a bad looking novelist and I had to discuss some scenes with her that rioted even to me—Murray must have had some torrid hours.

Well, this has been on the machine twenty-four hours and I've played three more sets of tennis—it's a good fall, that way—only this time I won. Let us devoutly thank Silenus who led me wrong so many years, for this was George Kuehn, athlete, football player, and onetime student of mine.[68] My menopause is getting more like puberty from day to day. Two years ago three sets of tennis would have given me hysterical heart failure.

I wish some women's college would ask me over for a speech. John August is slowly settling into blueprints and I haven't an idea how the current adolescent talks, thinks, or dresses. Eighteen months ago I listened to Mary Murdock for a weekend but she's at college. Jack Page's sister is the only other one I know—she gets her hand held in this week's *Life*—and she wants to be an editor so bad she can only stutter and cook when I'm around.[69] There are five Shady Hill School teachers across the road but they put on their grammar in my presence.[70] And all the Radcliffe girls whom my friends teach composition write stories about college girls who become flaming leaders of revolt—that's what happens to literary fashions, they work out of the back door into the colleges. Probably I'll set the scene in 1846 and fake the dialogue.... I return under a bad omen, Collier's carries the lousiest tripe I ever wrote.[71] Littauer wired me for it, I did it in four days, and all that, but never again. God knows what the menopause has done to me, but if it's that bad I'll start teaching short-story writing by correspondence.

Meanwhile Dr. Dietrich has held his press conference.[72] I wonder if this isn't part of a curve that's rising toward continuity. I've been waiting for the Dumba - von Papen - Bernstorff series of egregious bulls in public psychology.[73] The boys were much better than the Allies all through the first four weeks, but wasn't the *Iroquois* warning a straw in the wind, and isn't this press interview a really bad one?[74]

Yours,
Benny

32 Coolidge Hill Road
Cambridge, Massachusetts

[26 November 1939]

Dear Kate:

Don't call in any outside talent on this but you can exercise your own talent for research and ratiocination. I ran into Alfred McIntyre at a cocktail party after the Yale game—I'd say there was no other pleasant event that day—and did oil his joints and pry at his crevices till this emerged: the letter Z, or just possibly the word Zee, or perhaps by a lateral pass the word or letter Zed, figures in the title of an earlier book by Ethel Vance.[75] That doesn't tell me anything. Also, Alec Woollcott guessed her name right. Alfred said "her."

The Ogden High School team I played substitute right half on could have run either of those teams past the Brighton abattoir. The worst Harvard team since those drear days when Arnold Horween used to coach them to throw laterals for the opponents to score touchdowns on—this one had a beautiful spot pass to the Yale roving back. And the first Yale-Harvard game I ever saw where both teams stank. Tramping back home—in duckhunter's drawers, mountain climber's stockings, ear muffs, and the sealskin cap that Kitty Bowen gave me—I decided that it probably sounded exciting over the radio and I probably had no great interest in football any more. Which adds more but by now superfluous evidence to the hypothesis that what happened to me last spring and summer was one of the climacterics.... It's eight years since I propelled Emmy Darrow to and through a dozen post-game parties, and Bill Sedgwick and I were speaking for the first and last time and he wanted to give me a set of Walter Savage Landor because Al Delacey hadn't been able to take Emmy away from me, and Don Born choked a Smith girl, and Ginny Deknatel was sitting in a lap never known to be indecorous before, Sam Morison's, and a woman named Eunice, unknown to everyone, walked into the Borns' party with a cop, looking for a husband equally unknown, and the next morning a friend of mine, feeling in his overcoat pocket for his gloves, found a female nipple there.[76] ... Dorothy Hillyer announced that she was going to have a cocktail party this year and, what's more, it was going to be a Prohibition party. There has never been a sounder idea. But it wasn't, and I guess it never will be again for any of us. Too many old students calling me "sir." Or what's as bad, asking if they could dedicate books to me. Too many assistant profs telling me that I was a bad guy on their Ph.D. exams. Too many world-wanderers making home port for a night and crying because the Eli's won. Worst of all, Alfred McIntyre has colitis.

But he's going to bring out a collection of Easy Chairs and SRL pieces. We had that out last week and he's only whimpering a bit now. So titles are now solicited.

If the James Ford house at Lincoln is the new Gropius number there, you can have it.[77] There are now three in a cluster, and I want to know the functionalism of an outside ramp and a main deck in the Massachusetts climate. And in that half-pastoral, half-sylvan and altogether early nineteenth-century landscape, they look as out of place as Mark's Presbyterian in Hell. But I bring myself to say anything against Gropius by sheer force of character only, for his wife is the most beautiful woman in Massachusetts, or for all I know anywhere else.[78] Not excepting the wife of the younger Sert who sometimes travels with her.[79]

Surely I must have told you about the de Cordova castle and art gallery. It has been bequeathed to the town of Lincoln, and it is the God-damndest most hideous building you ever saw, and you never did see such a collection of junk. He made his pile from a glass factory, and then the junk dealers of Europe and the Orient unloaded on him all the junk they hadn't been able to sell to Hoosier schoolteachers and San Francisco millionaires. It is godawful, though I remember with some tenderness a marble nymph on whose tail every visitor has longed to strike a match. You can get the general idea from the fact that Julian, when he retired from business, found himself possessed of three or four thousand surplus glass doorknobs, which he had constructed into a fountain in front of the castle. Colored lights play on and in it at night. And Julian is also a composer, and cannot be prevented from playing some of his compositions for you on his pipe organ, an instrument which should be forbidden millionaires and duffers.... It's fifty to one that, when he does die and the deed has to pass, town meeting will reject the bequest. But I hope not, for the residual legatee is Harvard.

Speaking of Harvard, a rumor ran round the Stadium that Conant has resigned. The absolutely inconceivable has become routine.

Why, we analysts treat dreams ad hoc, not generically. If you find out what a dream means, which you usually don't, you do so by patiently following down the associations. That's where the method of free association is at its purest. Some of the hardy souls who think that symbolism is not a complex thing would tell you that any kind of climb is just an immediate symbol of sexual intercourse. What isn't? Nothing I've ever heard a Freudian allude to. Others, and these would seem more sensible, would point out that this is a dream of frustration, of, apparently, increasing and even climactic frustration. Again, what isn't? And, so what? More to the point is the fact that you call it a "ghastly" dream. That proves that, whatever it symbolizes, it has a considerable emotional importance for you, and probably an anxious one. Anxiety states are, if the profession will excuse me, rather commoner than one wishes in dreams. Well, what anxiety? How do I know by U.S. mail? I sit there and you talk on about the dream and pretty soon you're telling me how the butcher's boy threw some horse dung at you when you were six and that brings up the time when you heard a mysterious noise in the dark and from there you go on to the little girl who thought babies were laid like eggs—and pretty soon we begin to get something about the real content of the dream. Then I have you tell it to me again, and it has changed from your first version. So we examine the difference, which is pretty important.... Tell the dream to yourself a few times, in odd moments, and see what you're thinking about a few minutes later. If you get a common pattern, or a common theme, or a common channel of association, that's what the dream is about.

But my God, girl, if you didn't read "Studies in the Psychology of Sex" when you were sixteen or eighteen, what did you do for erotic titillation?[80] You certainly don't need to read it now—which is the rockbottom proof that Ellis accomplished a hell of a lot—but even so you'd find some amusement in the case histories. The British army officer who took on everything animal, vegetable, and mineral is as fixed in my memory as anything in the literature. And there are literally hundreds of comic bits here and there. It has probably the best study of sadism-masochism ever written, and in fact three-fourths of it is the ultimate authority, and also is well within everyone's common knowledge now. The psychology is hooey and some of the sociology, which he prided himself on, is even worse. And for God's sake don't read *The Dance of Life*. Ellis was really a great man and so there are necessarily some occasional fine things in it, a sentence or two at a time, but you and I wrote the rest of it when we were freshmen and believed that Life was a Rhythmic Oneness. No, we didn't, it was the pair with the fat fannies and thick eyeglasses who grew up to discover that the Soul of Our Time aspires to Godhead by way of Picasso and clarinets.[81] I can only say that Lewis Mumford probably agrees with every word of it and thinks it damn fine.

The reason why the more excitable believers say that stinginess is sublimated anal eroticism is that there does seem to be an observable tendency of infants and small children to enjoy holding on to what they've got, and is sometimes prolonged past the age at which it is normally forgotten. I haven't read that there is any corresponding fixation on letting go. So what is abnormally strong generosity? Obviously not a single or pure thing and obviously not a simple one. Over-compensated stinginess sometimes, perhaps. Oftener, perhaps, a simple guilt direct from the Oedipus relation which is thus allayed by self-punishment. Oftener still, a complex guilt treated by prophylaxis. All that is reasonably simple, which means that it's reasonably absurd. The mind is the most economical of energy-transformers but produces the most complex products. I'd say that, wherever any of these channels out of the Oedipus can be detected, you can also detect, if you watch closely enough, at least one other channel from the same place, by way of the castration anxiety. Two drives that probably exist in every psyche are the drive to repudiate maturity and the drive to deny one's sex, and no psyche ever subdued either one of them one hundred percent. Compulsive generosity could be an armistice signed with both, especially the latter. And there's a far more primitive element too, the eternal it's me, O Lord, standin' in the need of prayer.[82] [*Next sentence handwritten in pencil:*] Also the still more primitive bribe for love.

None of which means a damned thing when abstracted from the sum total of the individual mind. We analysts are prone to forget that these energies are not in our mind but in the patient's. The simple truth is, we tend to forget there is a patient. So, with that, I guess, I've lost the appointment recently conferred on me.

Yours,

Benny

NOTES

1. Enclosed with the letter: *The Coolidge Hill Gazette*, January–February 1939, 3 pp. mimeographed, containing news, advertising, and poems by Archibald MacLeish, Howard Baker, Donald H. McLaughlin Jr., and Theodore Morrison. On the verso of p. 3, BDV's note in pencil: "I'm afraid a good newspaper has been corrupted by literary aspirations."
2. Joseph F. Dinneen (1897–1964), journalist; *Ward Eight*, 1936. See Dinneen, "The Story of Beano Breen: Portrait of a Prominent Bostonian," *Harper's* 177/6 (November 1938). James Michael

Curley's lawsuit followed publication in *Harper's* (September 1936) of Dinneen's "The Kingfish of Massachusetts." Dinneen's *The Purple Shamrock*, 1949, was about Curley.

3. Probably Wanda Landowska's recording of J. S. Bach's "Goldberg" Variations.
4. Parkman (1894–1958), Harvard '15, attorney and Boston city councilor; Massachusetts state representative and senator, 1929–1936.
5. *American Magazine*, a Crowell-Collier publication, founded 1906.
6. Founded 1929 by editor George Macy (1900–1956); BDV reviewed the Club's edition of Rabelais in *SRL*.
7. *Ibéria*: No. 2 of three *Images* for orchestra by Claude-Achille Debussy (1862–1918), great French composer, one of the founders of musical modernism.
8. "Shadrack" by Robert McGimsey, 1931.
9. Boston's outstanding Museum of Fine Arts, on Huntington Avenue in the Fenway, has a large collection of older musical instruments and a long tradition of support for performances of music before 1700.
10. Bassoon; perhaps BDV meant "kazoo."
11. According to Stegner, *The Uneasy Chair*, BDV played the mandolin in college.
12. Felix Frankfurter achieved an enduring reputation as a professor at the Harvard Law School, but left a less stellar legacy as a member of the U.S. Supreme Court, where, especially in later years, he was often a conservative dissenter. A native of Vienna whose family fled to America to escape anti-Semitic persecution, Frankfurter was much criticized during and after World War II for his failure to speak out in behalf of Jewish immigration and rescue efforts.
13. Frankfurter was a graduate of the City College of New York ('02).
14. James Landis (1899–1964), New Deal lawyer; dean of the Harvard Law School.
15. Walter Lippman (1899–1974), liberal editor, writer, and statesman.
16. The University Committee on the Extra-curricular Study of American History. William Allen White (1868–1944), journalist, commentator ("The Sage of Emporia"). White's lectures were 24 and 25 April and 1 May 1939.
17. 11 January was BDV's forty-second birthday.
18. In "The Bucolics of Decadence"; see Appendix A.
19. *Children of God*, 1939.
20. Much of *The Year of Decision: 1846* is concerned with the Mormons' move to Utah.
21. Thompson was president of the American Center of International P.E.N.
22. The New York World's Fair had opened on 30 April; writers scheduled to speak included Jules Romains, Erich Maria Remarque, Arnold Zweig, Pearl Buck, Ernst Toller, Scholem Asch, Hendrik Willem Van Loon, Thomas Mann, André Maurois, Lin Yutang, Joseph Priestley, Klaus Mann, Henry Seidel Canby, Erika Mann, BDV, Raymond Gram Swing, Vincent Sheean, Mary Colum, Raoul Roussy de Sales, Phyllis Bottome, and Katherine Ann Porter. The topic for 10 May was "The Ivory Tower or the Soap Box?" with Canby as chair; BDV, Colum, Erika Mann, and five others spoke at this session.
23. Klaus (1906–1949) and Erika (1905–1969), writers, were two of Thomas Mann's six children. Erika, the oldest, was in danger in Germany when the Nazis denounced her father, then in exile; she was able to escape by marrying the poet W. H. Auden in June 1935 and thereby acquiring British citizenship. She published two books about Thomas Mann, three volumes of his letters, 1961–1965, and a book about Nazi Germany, *School for Barbarians*, 1938.
24. The architectural highlights of the New York World's Fair were the Trylon and Perisphere, respectively a seven-hundred-foot-high triangular tower and a sphere two hundred feet in diameter, enclosing the City of Tomorrow.

25. The Aquacade was built by Billy Rose (1899–1966), songwriter, promoter, Broadway producer, and nightclub owner. The Aquacade pool was dyed purple.
26. Weissmuller (1904–1984), gold medal Olympic swimmer in 1924 and 1928; played Tarzan in twelve movies. Kruger (1897–1965), actor and stuntman.
27. Eleanor Holm (1913–2004), Olympic swimmer who married Billy Rose in November 1939.
28. The General Electric exhibit at the World's Fair featured some high-voltage displays.
29. Heinrich Bruening (1885–1970) was chancellor of Germany, 1930–1932; exiled by Hitler, he became a lecturer at Harvard and Columbia. The Soviet Union, after its exclusion at the Munich conference, remained deeply distrustful of British and French claims of willingness to oppose Hitler, despite the British guarantee (March 30) to Poland. On 23 August 1939 Russia and Germany signed a pact pledging mutual nonaggression. One week later, on 1 September, the German army invaded Poland. Britain declared war on Germany on 3 September. On 17 September, the Russian army occupied eastern Poland, by the terms of a secret agreement with Germany.
30. Short for (French) *reculer pour mieux sauter*, to retreat in order to jump better.
31. 1816 was known as "the year without a summer," when frost and snow in June in New England made for widespread agricultural disaster; see Henry and Elizabeth Stommel, *Volcano Weather*, 1983.
32. Founded 1935, folded 1945; supported workers' rights.
33. Mark Saxton (1914–1988), novelist and editor, Harvard '36, student of BDV, later editor at Farrar & Rinehart, Harvard University Press; *Danger Road*, 1939.
34. Probably from the New York *Herald Tribune*.
35. George Edward Deatherage, national commander of the Knights of the White Camellia, in testimony before the House Un-American Activities Committee (Dies Committee), 23 May 1939. The Knights, founded in New Orleans in 1867, were a white-supremacist organization similar to the Ku Klux Klan. Kuhn (1896–1951), a naturalized American. The Bund promoted the Nazi cause in America in widely publicized meetings until Mayor La Guardia of New York instituted an investigation of its finances; Kuhn, prosecuted by Attorney General Thomas E. Dewey, received a jail sentence for embezzlement.
36. The so-called MacDonald White Paper of 17 May 1939 effectively revoked British commitment, as expressed in the Balfour Declaration of 1917, to support a national homeland for Jews in Palestine. The White Paper announced a termination of the Palestine Mandate within ten years as well as severe limitations on Jewish immigration.
37. Martin Dies (1900–1972), congressman from Texas, established and chaired the House Committee on Un-American Activities (HUAC) in 1938. Following World War II, the HUAC broadened its investigative scope in a wave of anti-communist fervor, summoning hundreds of government workers, public personalities, and figures in the entertainment world to testify about their alleged communist affiliations. The HUAC was abolished in 1975.
38. Whalen (1886–1962), attorney; official greeter of New York City.
39. *SRL* 20/4 (20 May 1939), page 12.
40. Broom (1752–1810), delegate from Delaware to the Constitutional Convention of 1787 and a signer of the Constitution.
41. League for Industrial Democracy, socialist organization founded 1905; Jack London and Upton Sinclair were among the founding members.
42. Edmund Wilson (1895–1972), author, editor, critic.
43. *John Reed: The Making of a Revolutionary*, 1936. Hicks publicly renounced his membership in the Communist Party following the Nazi-Soviet pact of August 1939.
44. This ambition was realized in 1949 with the founding of *American Heritage* magazine, with Nevins one of its leaders.

45. No update has been identified of the *Pageant of America* series after 1926, nor any formal connection of Nevins with the series at any time.
46. "Aftermath of a Cocktail Party," *New Republic* 99/1282 (28 June 1939), referring to Granville Hicks's letter of three weeks earlier (7 June).
47. *The Gateway to History*, 1938.
48. New York *Times*, 12 February 1939; Nevins's apology said that the story would be withdrawn in the next printing of the book.
49. "Millennial Millions: The Story of the Mormons," *SRL* 20/18 (26 August 1939).
50. *Die Traumdeutung* (English edition, *The Interpretation of Dreams*), by Freud, 1900.
51. (French) silken muslin.
52. Josef Beck (1894–1944), foreign minister of Poland; signed a military alliance with England on 25 August 1939; died in internment in Nazi-occupied Romania.
53. Louis MacNeice (1907–1963), Irish poet; with W. H. Auden, *Letters from Iceland*, 1937.
54. Founded by James Kraft (1874–1953), inventor of process cheese and promoter of Philadelphia Cream Cheese, Kraft-Phenix was established by merger in 1928; now Kraft Foods International. BDV no doubt was eating the cheese. "Unrest in the Kitchen," Easy Chair, *Harper's* 179/3 (August 1939), decries process cheeses as resembling laundry soap and "unfit even to bait mice with." John H. Kraft, executive vice-president of Kraft-Phenix, wrote a polite rejoinder in a three-column letter in "Personal and Otherwise," *Harper's* 180/1 (December 1939). In "Number 241," Easy Chair, *Harper's* 211/5 (November 1955), BDV writes, "A cheesemaker tried hard to suppress me" but did not succeed.
55. Alexander (1906–1985), novelist, biographer, political columnist and journalist; *Aaron Burr: The Proud Pretender*, 1937.
56. The German fortifications in the Rhineland, opposite the French Maginot Line.
57. Maurice Gamelin (1872–1958), French general and commander of Anglo-French army forces, 1939, was dismissed in the French debacle of May 1940.
58. "The Oncoming," *Harper's* 180/1 (December 1939), reprinted in *Minority Report*, 1940.
59. Davis became a news analyst and commentator for CBS radio, continuing until 1942, when he was asked to direct the office of War Information; he returned to radio after the war.
60. The Nazi-Soviet nonaggression pact, ostensibly a friendly agreement between two antagonistic ideologies, caused an ideological rupture in the American communist movement and massive desertions by party members.
61. A glitzy Condé-Nast publication. BDV satirized it in "Ninety-Day Venus," Easy Chair, *Harper's* 201/3 (September 1950).
62. Novel assembled and edited by Edward Aswell from Thomas Wolfe's drafts and directions; published 1939, 695 pages.
63. In the Franco-Prussian War of 1870, the Prussian army with its rapid-fire repeating rifles and modern artillery soon overpowered the French. The term *Blitzkrieg*—(German, literally) lightning war—referred to Germany's use of swift-moving motorized divisions (especially tanks, which had played little part in the Great War), enabling the conquest of Poland in less than a month.
64. BDV's prediction was wrong; beginning on 10 May 1940, Hitler's armies overran Belgium, the Netherlands, and finally France in a little more than one month.
65. The Soviet army invaded Poland on 17 September, and eleven days later the partitioning of Poland between Germany and Russia was proclaimed, as specified in a secret protocol signed as part of the nonaggression pact of 23 August. At the same time, the Soviet Union occupied Lithuania, Latvia, and Estonia, eventually incorporating the Baltic republics into the greater USSR. The new territory thus acquired undoubtedly saved the Soviet Union when Germany attacked in 1941.

66. The Battle of Britain, in the summer of 1940, resulted in a narrow victory for the Royal Air Force; the German Air Force (*Luftwaffe*) then turned to night bombing of England's cities ("the Blitz"). British naval power in the Pacific was essentially eliminated by the Japanese in December 1941. For a combination of reasons, above all poor planning, the British fortress at Singapore fell to the Japanese in 1942. Germany did not take part in the Pacific war.
67. Also known as Jock Murray; psychoanalyst.
68. Silenus, one of several horse-eared "aged satyrs," companions of Dionysus: "so perpetually stupefied with drink that they were unable to distinguish truth from falsehood" (*CE*).
69. Katharine (Kaki) Page, *Life* 7/16 (16 October 1939), p. 52.
70. Gordon DeVoto identifies two of them as Barbara Bacorn and Libby Wilson.
71. Presumably "The Sound of Silk," *Collier's* 104 (21 October 1939).
72. Otto Dietrich, Hitler's press secretary, held a press conference on 13 October.
73. Constantin Theodor Dumba (1856–1915), ambassador of Austria-Hungary to the United States, 1913–1915. Franz von Papen (1879–1969), on Bernstorff's staff in 1917; later, in 1932, he was briefly German chancellor. Count Johann Heinrich Bernstorff (1862–1939), German ambassador to the United States during the Zimmermann affair of 1917, had to inform President Wilson of Germany's resumption of unrestricted submarine warfare (1 February 1917); this new policy was one of the precipitating factors of America's entry into the Great War. Bernstorff, who was favorable to the United States and opposed to the Nazis, retired from government service and lived in Geneva, whence he published his memoirs in 1936.
74. On 4 October 1939, the German Grand Admiral Raeder announced that the S. S. *Iroquois*, an American passenger ship carrying 776 passengers and crew, would be torpedoed near the American coast; President Roosevelt then announced that a convoy would be sent to escort the ship to safety. The ship was not attacked, and arrived 11 October in New York after passing through a three-day storm at sea.
75. Yale 20, Harvard 7, played on 25 November.
76. Walter Savage Landor (1775–1864), British poet and essayist.
77. The James Ford house, by Walter Gropius and Marcel Breuer (1902–1981), Hungarian-American architect.
78. Walter Gropius (1883–1969), German-American architect; cofounder of the Bauhaus School of architecture in Weimar. When the Bauhaus was suppressed by the Nazis, Gropius came to America and was professor of architecture at Harvard from 1937 to 1952. Ise Frank was his second wife.
79. Josep Lluís Sert (1902–1983), Catalan architect, collaborator of Le Corbusier, professor of architecture and dean of the Harvard Graduate School of Design, 1953–1969; he came to the United States in 1939 after the Spanish Civil War. His uncle was the Catalan painter and designer José Maria Sert (1874–1945).
80. Ellis's book was published in 7 vols., first appearing 1893 in collaboration with J. A. Symonds. The short version, *The Psychology of Sex: A Manual for Students*, was published in 1933.
81. Pablo Ruiz Picasso (1881–1973), great Spanish artist, amazingly prolific in all media and genres but especially painting; his huge canvas, *Guernica*, painted in 1937 as an anguished protest against the bombing of the town in northern Spain, was an outstanding feature of the Spanish pavilion at the New York World's Fair.
82. From a Negro spiritual.

8

1940 LETTERS

DeVoto's second son, Mark Bernard DeVoto, was born uneventfully on 11 January 1940, which was also DeVoto's forty-third birthday. A long letter to Sterne describes the medical aspects of Avis DeVoto's pregnancy, which appealed to the frustrated physician in DeVoto. Another John August novel, *Rain before Seven*, was published in *Collier's* beginning in May. Well paid for this and its predecessor, *Troubled Star*, DeVoto moved rapidly to the planning stage of a major historical work, which, he told Sterne, would be dedicated to her. On 9 May, accompanied by his former student, the historian Arthur Schlesinger Jr., DeVoto set out on a motor trip to the mountain West, informing Sterne by several daily postcards, as the war in Europe exploded in mounting catastrophes. Avis DeVoto and Gordon took a train to Utah to meet up with DeVoto in June; Mark, six months old, was left in the care of nursemaids in Cambridge. Sterne, in the meantime, moved from the Bowne Hospital to a succession of other facilities, returning to Bowne only in November. DeVoto's next letter from the West reached Sterne on 26 June; though depressed by the war, he was rhapsodic about the country that he had not seen for sixteen years. In Europe, France surrendered to the Nazi onslaught after barely a month of battle, and Britain faced the likelihood of imminent invasion across the English Channel.

On 14 July DeVoto wrote at length, with abundant geographical details about his western trip. In the heat of August, he sent Sterne a letter with the handwritten first-page draft of the long-planned book about the year 1846 along with a dedication page: "To Katharine Grant Sterne." Further progress on the book is noted, and meanwhile DeVoto's second collection of essays, *Minority Report*, was published. In the November Easy Chair DeVoto observed disdainfully that Americans everywhere were refusing to face the inevitability of war with Germany; he was unprepared for the uproar that followed. By the end of the year DeVoto expressed his hopes of buying a house in Cambridge.

⁂

32 Coolidge Hill Road
Cambridge, Massachusetts

[22 January 1940]

Dear Kate:
There are innumerable duties and exhaustions in my current state of multiparent, housekeep, and guardian of an older brother's psyche. Add the activities of John August and the reaction from several months' anxiety about Avis, and no wonder I get tired.

When Elizabeth's sex turned out otherwise I gave up all rights in nomenclature, and Avis has named the arrival Mark Bernard, of which I will say only that the first half is at least better than the second. But the truth is, there are no masculine names but Bill, so why protest?...It was, in the end, an easy confinement. Avis undertook to do the job on January 10th but when she got to the delivery room, took thought of herself, went back to her room, and pulled it off the next day in something like two hours, handily, without damage, and practically without inconvenience.

The moral shapes up so that I am on the brink of writing another treatise on the Yankee character. On Eddie Harding.[1] Over a period of ten or twelve years I have come to have a considerable liking for him, a perpetual joy in the way he ticks, and, gradually, a strong respect for his intelligence and an almost unlimited one for the character aforesaid. As for the intelligence, I originally thought so little of it that I rejoiced when Bunny knocked on the door two weeks prematurely, with Eddie on his vacation in Maine, and put the job up to Bristol. But I've come to see that it's a characteristic Yankee intelligence—absolutely incapable of speculation, meditation, or in any real sense of the word scientific thought, it holds hard what it knows, thinks things through, relies on itself, and will not be stampeded....As this pregnancy and confinement have demonstrated.

Seven or eight years ago George Reynolds diagnosed a mild secondary anemia in Avis. It responded promptly to treatment but it gradually proved to have peculiarities of its own. Reynolds was one of Minot's lesser associates and he got to love that anemia like a firstborn child. What was peculiar about it was the fact that the treatment wouldn't stick—he could never get it to the point where Avis could give up her diet and her Lextron.[2] He sometimes got her period of grace up to between two and three months, but always in the end, bang, the count would drop and back she would have to go onto a strict diet and to Lextron again. Going back, she'd run up her count to four and a half million in about a week, which also was rare in the Minot records. So was the fact that, even with the count way down, the hemoglobin would be high. It was, from

George's point of view, a beautiful case, and he and Minot too used to study it in a kind of holy rapture. As for Avis, it never bothered her. Lextron is easy to take and she is a strong oral erotic—who was sentenced to eat large quantities of the very best food and could do so in the serene confidence that she would not thicken anywhere or add an ounce to her trett.[3]

Mark-Elizabeth was arranged for before we went to New York and was actually conceived no great time after we got there. Beforehand we had it all out with George Reynolds. There was nothing exactly like this case in the Minot records, but his judgement was that pregnancy was absolutely safe. Go ahead. Besides, Avis's demonstrated ability to respond to treatment was an anchor to windward. So we went ahead. But, something short of two months gone, Avis miscarried. That promptly brought down on her a two-year prohibition. The preliminaries having been attended to long before, she did no more, last spring, than tell George she was pregnant when she went round for her routine blood count. He rested on his former opinion and that was that.

A couple of weeks later he died—he was a time-expired man, had been for years, and his leaky heart was even more famous in local medicine than his cyanosis following the squash he insisted on playing regularly. Avis felt fine—pregnancy has always been complete euphoria for her. With George dead she was under no urge to keep close watch on her blood. There was his measured and twice-repeated judgment to rely on, and what the hell. And I was in New York so much that neither my hypochondria nor my frustrated leanings toward medicine got round to being concerned about her. But when I got back in July, I finally thought about it, suggested that maybe Lextron and laziness were not enough, and packed her off to Minot's office. She was assigned to a chap named King, younger than Reynolds, very keen, very scientific, very eager and on the ball. And the next thing I knew King was phoning me and telling me that he didn't think she had to lose the child, this thing had been found just in time, another two weeks would have been too late. Her count was below three million and King and, apparently, the whole force there—something like twenty of them—were in an uproar. They've continued in an uproar ever since. They began to feed her iron and other things besides Lextron, to inject liver in her tail every five days, etc. They also began to talk in vague and unpleasant ways about transfusions—to her. And—to me and Eddie, about a Caesarian.

But they got her blood up to two and three-quarter million, which they regarded as the last verge of minimum safety. It hung there and they suspended overt threats—to me. Apparently they kept working on Eddie, who kept standing them off. Eddie didn't know anything about anemia. He knew that there were pregnancy anemias; he'd seen quite a few; they didn't bother him. He wouldn't be bothered. Then shortly after the first of November, her blood dipped and kept dipping till it was down to two and a quarter. They got it headed up again temporarily, by redoubling their various treatments, then it dipped again. So they descended on Eddie, about the first of December, and commanded him either to produce labor in her then or to perform a Caesarian. Eddie came round to see me.

Eddie wanted her to round out her term. He didn't know anything about anemia, but he knew the facts of his experience. He had his knowledge of the patient. He had his experience-dictated theorem that the less you interfere with the orderly workings of nature, the better chance you've got of coming out on top, no matter what. He had also the independence to go round and study the records at Boston City Hospital, which delivers more babies than any other four in Boston, and to consult with the docs who practice most in the slums. He got an assurance from both of them that plenty of successful labors and recoveries were on tap with a count of a million and a half or even less. In his judgment, it was better to go ahead on the present basis, no matter how ominous, than to produce labor or to take the child by Caesarian. King and his buddies wanted to relieve her of the drain on her blood. Eddie wanted to maintain her physiological equilibrium. But, Eddie said to me, don't forget I'm being opposed by the man who knows most about blood in the whole damned world. So what do you say?

Well, as I've remarked, I've gradually come to have a considerable respect for him.... He looks like James B. Conant, like John Taylor, like some five hundred other spare, stripped, broke-up feldspar faces. All those boys looked forty at twenty and will look forty at eighty. It's a type—you see it in the portraits of Harvard divines running back to 1650. He has an inexhaustible and inexhaustibly entertaining store of prejudices. Most of his ideas are out of the eighteenth century—except his political ideas, which are B.C., and his social ideas, which are antediluvian. He makes L. J. Henderson look like a radical and A. Lawrence Lowell look like a democrat. He's a Grotonian and a Porcellian. I've always gotten along with him most amiably, for so far as he's concerned, since I'm a writer, it follows that I'm incurably eccentric if not in fact mad, but there has never been any point whatever on which our minds could meet as my mind meets, say, Kenneth Murdock's. Not even the fact that we were both Conant's purgees gave us anything in common—Eddie was cleaned out of the hygiene department when Arlie Bock came in. And that, I think, is his abiding sorrow. Like me he has this irrational love of Harvard, and like me he was well placed there. Unlike me he doesn't have to work for a living. The Hardings were in the China trade for some generations, and Eddie's practice has always been selective.

Well, I think I know the qualities of that particular kind of intelligence. I was, let me say, on a spot. King and his buddies had given Avis a bad scare, but not as bad as they were giving me. And a Nobel Prize winner in science is something to buck but I finally said, it's your case, Eddie. And Eddie said, by God if it's my case I'll stand 'em off.

He stood 'em off. They put on a really shocking drumfire, a good part of which hit Avis, though it wasn't intended to, till toward the end her psychology was pretty damn bad—and would have been worse if Eddie hadn't practiced the ancient, Hippocratic art of bluff. Birds like that can apply pressure—I promise you that, of my own experience. But Eddie, though he couldn't phrase the idea, held fast to the notion that artificially disturbing an equilibrium was worse than letting a dangerous one work itself out. At one point they told him they wouldn't be responsible for the consequences if he didn't do a Caesarian there and then. He told them he'd be damned if he would, and he didn't. Finally, he compromised. He sent her to the hospital and gave her two small transfusions. And they stood by with a young battalion of donors, practically in relays, and they cross-typed enough people to restore all the wounded in Finland. They arranged to have a representative and a donor on hand in the delivery room. Etc. As a psychiatrist, I'll say it was shocking bad technique.

Eddie gave her the two transfusions to shut King up, not because he had any idea they'd help out on her problem or his. But actually, I think, they took her over the hump, so that the various treatments King was using were able to take hold, as they hadn't been before. At any rate, her blood was back to two million, six hundred thousand when she went into the hospital for delivery.

Eddie brought her through that without losing a drop of blood, without a single laceration, with exactly four and a half grains of that yellow barbital salt,[4] a little gas, and about ten minutes of cyclopropane. He sent the donor home unused—that was pure swank on his part, and he did give her 500 cc two days later, just to mollify King. Four hours after the kid was born, she was telephoning various interested friends, a bit groggily but quite effectively. Six days afterward, her count was three and a half million. Two days after that it was four million, six hundred thousand. The kid weighed seven pounds, ten ounces at birth. He lost just under an ounce in the loss period and now weighs eleven pounds. She is giving him between twenty-eight and thirty ounces of milk a day. Eddie, with the vainglory of the episode still on him, telephoned to Joe Garland, our pediatrician, and said, "What happens to a week-old baby that gets twenty-eight ounces of mother's milk a day?"[5] Joe said, "He chucks up six ounces of it." Eddie said, "DeVoto baby don't," and hung up. God knows what he's said to King. If King belongs to the right clubs, he's said plenty.

So, as of today, I'll say once more, there's a hell of a lot to be said for the Yankee mind.

... Well, we're all in and out of hospitals. Frost, after a series of colds, suspected bladder stones, and God knows what else, as well as his habitual hypochondria, went to Phillips House for piles. He issued a press bulletin saying that Mr. Frost was resting on his laurels after a legal operation by Dr. Faxon. I wired asking if he could prove it was his laurels he was resting on.... Don Born finally going into pneumonia, the woman whose novel I'm reading crashed through with a remark I should have made a thousand times in these ten years. Out of the arms of her psychoanalysis, she said "Don is really trying to commit suicide." And, of course, he is, has been ever since I've known him, to avoid growing up—and so has Kay. God knows why I never saw it before.... And I'm going to call on John Abbott, as the only local psychiatrist whose social standing is sufficiently exalted to give him weight, and direct him to get Frances Curtis out of bed damned quick, or she'll stay there for twenty years. Fran has always had a strong belief that she'd make a fascinating invalid. Two days in bed with a cold have always given her a regal pleasure and I've suspected a good many of the colds. Ever since Phoebe got married last fall, she's been visibly declining—which is most interesting in itself—and she's been in bed ten days with a mild sprain in her back, of about one-quarter the awkwardness of either George Stout's sacroiliac or mine after any game of badminton.... And at midafternoon of January 11, Bunny reported a fiendish headache and an all but immeasurable urge to vomit. I'd been expecting just that—or diarrhoea. I took him to the Square, bought him three comics and two small trucks, and the headache disappeared and there was no vomiting. Exactly on schedule and according to the texts, he got constipated three days later. That over, he is apparently adjusted. God knows what goes on underneath. Tonight he sighed to be living in Lincoln, and a few minutes later he said he was only a wreck of his former self, he wanted to be living on Mason Street. It was at Mason Street that he spent the first two years of his life.... Which is like his violent complaint, when we moved to White Plains, that the furniture in that house was so close together that he couldn't live there. Actually, the rooms of that house were bigger than those at Lincoln, the only house he knew. But at Lincoln Avis and I had had separate rooms, whereas at White Plains we had what the Westchester culture calls a master bedroom, and two articles of furniture were certainly closer together than he'd ever seen them before.... How is the amateur psychiatrist treating his only son who has become the older brother? Well, all discipline has been relaxed, there have been sermons on helpfulness that would sicken an evangelist, I have admired his strength and size and power practically continuously, I've turned over my bedroom to him for the duration, I've described his own infancy in great detail and demonstrated how clearly superior in all ways he is to the child he was nine years ago, I've enlarged on Avis's pangs at separation, and how she's phoned him every day, and, playing for the deeper levels, I have explained how an infant has absolutely no control over its bowels and bladder. That, the Ice Follies, and an air of rough male comradeship ought to do the trick.[6]

John August closes this. I've got to attack Installment VI tomorrow.... Paternity shuts off the war, the famine, and the election, but not serials, dear.

Yours,

Benny

32 Coolidge Hill Road
Cambridge, Massachusetts

[2 MAY 1940]

Dear Kate:

Jesus, I don't know how you summarize political parties in the Republic, short of a million words....

Well, there are continuities... of a kind. Don't ask too much of them. In general, there has always been a simple dichotomy (a more fundamental one, I mean than the ins and the outs), and for the most part it has always taken about the same expression it has now. There has usually been a party which stood for debtor class and another one which stood for the propertied class—in the rough. Each has always been badly confused and impeded by the discordant elements which, the American equilibrium being so unstable, it has had to incorporate or form alliances with in order to get, or retain, power. It is, however, a fundamental mistake to think of the dichotomy as analogous to the English one, since not even the Southern Democracy had any function as a <u>landholding</u> class. (You will be much nearer the truth if you will think about them as, in the typical American way, exploiters of new land—by means, as it importantly happened, of human machines.) Nor is there any division similar to the beautifully neat (and altogether unrealistic) one that French analysts believe in, the *rentiers*[7] vs. the *spéculateurs*. Neither landholders nor *rentiers* as such or per function have ever had any but the mildest importance. What we have had from the beginning is a party which stood for the inflation of currency and one that stood for the contraction of currency. A party for the relief of debtors and a party for the sanctity of mortgages. A party for the support of agrarian and laboring interests, and a party for the assistance of trade, manufacture, and banking. Less consistently but in the main, a party which aimed to develop the home market by assisting the producers, and a party which aimed to develop it by assisting the manufacturers. Even less consistently but in the main till recently, a party which stood for less national and centralized authority, and a party which stood for more of it. The confusion introduced by this last consideration is paralleled in all the others to a lesser degree, but by and large all the parties named first in the above oppositions have been one and the same party, and all those named second have been the other party.

There is also a kind of continuity in pattern—at least in growth and senescence. Take Jefferson's Republicans, who torturously and tenuously survive in Franklin's New Deal.[8] The party began to coalesce round him during Washington's first term, in part because of the activity of Jefferson, the intellectuals he was allied with, and groups and interests that had been most crimped by the compromises that went into the Constitution, but in greater part because of the plain bearing of Hamilton's fiscal policies and the groups and interest they plainly served.[9]

Everything in this period is so fluid that all lines are blurred and no statements hold absolutely. But in general it is true that the Republicans were what Jefferson's ideas held them to be, small landowners, small merchants, mechanics, free laborers. Sure, but also they were the Southern planters (in the main, not always) and they were the western pioneers. The link between the last two classes is obvious. Until the new lands in Georgia, Alabama, and Mississippi were opened up, there was no such thing as a solvent planter. They had been in debt to English factors from the beginning, and as that debt receded after the Revolution it merely found its way increasingly northward. (In fact, it is arguable that there never was, in all American history, a solvent Southern planter. DeBow said as much for twenty years before the Civil War and Helper proved it, or nearly proved it, just on the eve of hostilities.[10] But during the last quarter century before the war there was in the Deep South such an illusion of solvency as we can remember from H. Hoover's time.) The planters were, in actual fact, a debtor class, albeit a garnished one. And the rockbottom fact of American history is that all frontier communities are debtor communities. These were the interests principally served by the Jeffersonian party.... Let us be clear: by and large men belong to parties because they think their interests are served by those parties, and by and large parties think they are serving the interests they actually do serve.... But also there were other elements, whose relationships to these others could be indicated only by long parentheses. Notably there were the immigrants and the internationalists. Tammany began on the immigrant vote.[11] And there rallied to the Republican party all those whom the blatant Anglomania of Hamilton's Federalists had annoyed, angered, or cost money.[12] And all those who felt that the torch lighted in America must be handed on to Europe, by way of France. And finally, the reformers. In a sense, down to Jackson, reform was properly only clarification and extension in areas where nothing had been shaped or provided for.[13] But the battle cry and the effect was the same.... This has been the make-up of the Democratic party, fairly steadily, ever since.

Jefferson's Republicans did not completely establish or fill out the pattern—there are gaps in it. This was due not only to the fluidity of everything but also to the fact that they had no real Opposition. The Federalists were a genuine party but they could not survive an Adams, a foreign war, and the death of Hamilton. They are one of the two major parties in American history that have been blown up in toto. It is interesting that the death blow was an act of usurpation that happened to run counter to a sentiment. For what killed the Federalists was primarily the Alien and Sedition Acts—and the ammunition they gave the Jeffersonians.[14] (There were, of course, many intricately related things but let them go.) Without those Acts, the undeclared war with France would certainly have lost them 1800 anyway, and might very well have destroyed them—because things <u>were</u> so fluid. Finally, nobody could fill Hamilton's shoes and the organization was not yet rigorous enough to go on without someone who could. (Note that the Republicans did not perish because of Jefferson's Embargo Acts, which did far more damage than the A and S but did not offend a sentiment.)[15] By 1800 it was clear that the Federalists were done for, nationally. They declined into a sectional party, dwindled, and committed suicide with the Hartford Convention.[16]

Now as outlined above, there are obvious contradictions in the Republicans, of the kind that always make any party course a zigzag and produce the continual frictions and cleavages that impair American party government—and, I think, not only establish the movement of our history but provide the necessary freedom of movement that permits our economic and social system to function. And there is implicit in them a major paradox. It is the major paradox not only of the Jeffersonians but of our entire political structure, and in one form or another it has raised hell with every party in our history. It is this: that whereas the interests of the debtor classes, and especially of the frontier, require the central government to be as limited and diffuse as possible (emphasizing "states' rights" or the federal republic), those same interests also necessitate a centralizing tendency which must constantly invade the rights of the federated states and accrete power. Jefferson had been in office just two years when he faced this rockbottom fact. (His was, genuinely, a "reform" administration to begin with, though Gallatin's reforms look a hell of a lot like Hamiltonianism.)[17] If the Mississippi were closed, then trans-Allegheny America would simply fall off from the seaboard. He had to get at least lower Louisiana. He got Louisiana. He had no power to do so and it violated all his principles and beliefs—except self-preservation, Anglophobia, and the voice of the people. In effect, he set the whole mould of the future.... The strongest nationalizing, which is to say centralizing, force in our history is the expanding frontier. In its own interest the debtor class has always been forced to forge the instruments which exploited it. The party in power has always accelerated the tendency, no matter how vehemently it has denied doing so. Louisiana was one form. "Internal improvements" was another. So was "the American system." So was "free land." So was the tariff.

Yet the outline was neither clear nor complete down to what the texts still call the Jacksonian revolution, by which time everything we know today was established. The Whig party had grown up to inherit, roughly, the interests served by Federalism and to add to them the interests of the expanding mercantile class and the embryo manufacturing class together with the rudimentary financial system growing out of both. Yet nothing is ever so simple as the textbooks make out. Notably, the strong Whig interest in the South is a paradox and the stronger one on the frontier is a greater paradox. Furthermore, though the central onslaught of the Jacksonian Democracy, which was Jefferson's Republicans in modern dress, was directly at the financial system which had now learned to use its teeth in protection of its interests, still it is astonishing how much support the Democrats drew from financial interests either excluded from or at war with the system. Many financial interests are always served by inflation and many others have exactly the same interests as the debtors they have mortgages on. It is right here, with the rise of the Jacksonian party, that the modern complexities of our politics begin.

The national lands were the biggest single determining force, together with the speculation in them by financial interests, the need for debtor relief, and the development of wildcat banking which, effectively if not by design, provided it. There was also growing up the manufacturing system that was to become dominant after the Civil War. The financial system that was implementing that system was, effectively, what the Democrats were aiming to destroy. Yet (a) it was essential to much of their own functioning, so that (b) they could not muster enough strength to overthrow it, and (c) though they compromised, they sufficiently damaged it to weaken their own organization internally.

It was a hell of a lot less simple a party than Jefferson's. And it was a hell of a lot like Franklin D.'s. It had to swallow the alliance that has always since then partly paralyzed it, the marriage between the agrarians of the first part and the mechanics and city proletariat of the second part. This, the second great paradox of our political history, proves something or other about America, for what God hath put asunder the Democracy has, on the whole, kept together. When the Democracy has been out of power, it has been because this shotgun marriage has been broken. The fundamental interests of the two groups are both relatively and absolutely at odds, and the party has looked a hell of a lot less looney whenever the farmers have been detached.... Jacksonism did not come to power by a mass uprising of the common man, especially the frontiersman, as the texts usually say. It was, besides that marriage, pretty exactly the New Deal. It had an energetic nucleus of intellectuals who worked well with the first full crew of professional politicians, as distinct from paid politicians, ever developed here. It had also the best organized press up to that time. Jackson was really a front for the politicians and especially the intellectuals. They have been curiously underestimated and even ignored by the historians and my pupil (who may go West with me, by the way), Arthur Schlesinger Jr., is going to make a reputation very easily because of them.[18] We hear about Jackson's Kitchen Cabinet: what we do not hear is that its effectives were the intellectuals of whom Amos Kendall was the bright star.[19] Blatantly during both of Jackson's administrations and less openly for another twenty years, Kendall was both the Charlie Michelson and the Tommy Corcoran of the time. Beyond and behind Kendall were a good many others, notably the young George Bancroft and the older Orestes Brownson (the first real advocate of the class struggle in America if not in the world, a pre-Marxian, and the author of more platforms and presidential messages than has been acknowledged).[20] To these were added the discouraged but not disenchanted reformers (as time went on), like George Ripley.[21] And to these, the lunatic fringe—for a while, till the rising Republican party drained them off.

(I wonder if Kendall shows the future of Corcoran. He declined into a kind of lobbyist—for many years the Man To See in Washington. I suspect—no one has proved, few have ever studied him—that he got a large cut in a good many projects he put across. Yet he remained, also, as much a giant as there was in those parts. The *Diary of a Public Man* which Sandburg quotes so extensively and so effectively was almost certainly written by Kendall.)[22]

It was the intellectuals, really, who grappled with the one firm reality that Jacksonism ever came to grips with, the developing corporation. It was the corporation, a good deal more than the factory itself, that implemented the industrial revolution and, in doing so, changed the financial system forever. The boys had a pretty good idea of what it was and was becoming, and what they wrote about it might just as well have been written by A. A. Berle.[23] They never had a clear idea what they wanted to do about it, and of what they wanted to do they were able to do only a part, which on the whole was worse than nothing at all.

They were always impeded, sometimes nullified, and frequently made idiotic by the discordances within, which as time went on produced the strains that culminated in the schism of 1860, though by that time senescence was so far advanced that the same break-up could have occurred from half a dozen other tensions. With two interregnums they governed the country for thirty years, and fairly well, considering, during the first twenty of them. Like all government, theirs was a resultant of partially tangential forces, not a program, not a party government. What threw them when they tried to control the developing corporations was what threw them throughout, the conflicts between the divergent interests of their own components. You cannot incorporate in a party the frontier, the plantation system, the mechanics and proletariat, and the metropolitan machines—without considerable friction. Thus the protective tariff, which the Democracy always swore they were opposed to, was a subsidy to manufacture paid for by the farmers, yet the West had to have internal improvements, which only the tariff could pay for. Furthermore, manufacturing was thus subsidized at the expense of the planters, yet the planters had to take it because the Democracy would lose the city machines if they didn't—and had to keep the city machines in line if they want to go on governing. So, in actual fact, the tariff was never seriously lowered (except once) during the Democratic administrations and was sometimes increased. Polk, who was honest, blind, and a promise-keeper did, as I shall show in my book, raise hell by forcing a tariff for revenue only through Congress—and, since he had elected to fight a foreign war simultaneously brought the national treasury the closest it had yet been to bankruptcy. Only the famines in Europe saved him—and won the war.... The tariff was only one of several dilemmas but it would take a lot of space to specify the others. The point is, government is always by guess and by God, issues seldom correspond to interests, and the young John Chamberlain has finally got it through his head that there are a multiplicity of functioning systems in America, several of which combine in precarious equilibrium to produce a party—and partially hamstring it.

What happened to the Democrats during the Fifties was a result of the inconceivable stupidity of the Southern planters and the accelerating energies of the industrial revolution. Beyond question, the planters were the biggest fools in our history, which is a weighty superlative. They never learned how to farm land, they never had intelligence enough to analyze their interests, and they never learned any skill either in politics or in economics. They are most readily understood not as agrarians but as exploiters of natural resources—who used up land (by means of expendable human machines) precisely as lumbermen used up forests or the miners used up lodes and veins—and as exploiters who, nevertheless, committed themselves to an agrarian economy, and a one-crop agrarian economy at that. The spread of cotton culture southwest created the illusion of prosperity, the flush times. With incredible folly, they thought they could perpetuate the phantom by political means—and for political control of Congress they paid the price of economic subjection. Which is exactly half of the Civil War. It was, furthermore, a subjection by anarchy. The manufacturing system and the financial system developed on strict Darwinian principles, without effective control of any kind. Which is half of the remaining half of the Civil War.... For political control of Congress, conceived as protection of slave property in protection of cotton, they delivered themselves up hogtied into the keeping of the financiers. The intelligent thing to do would have been to make an alliance with the developing system, rather than fight it head-on, taking what they could get, keeping a share in what they had to give up. But sublime ignorance of economics ("Cotton is king" was gospel at a time when, as Helper pointed out, the hay crop of the North alone was worth more than the entire cotton crop), plus the delusion of secession, which was really a delusion that southern cotton was necessary to French and British economy, made them mad.

Defence of the status quo invariably and inevitably becomes petrifaction. During the Fifties the Democracy hardened into an intense reaction, concerned about only one thing, the constitutional defence of slavery, and armed with only one weapon and that terroristic, the threat of secession. They yowled about the tariff, but they voted for it, buying votes for the protection of slavery thereby. They became a mere orthodoxy, with their heels dug in. Efficiency departed from their bureaucracy, not courage only but intelligence departed from their leadership—the descent from, say, Calhoun, to, say, Jeff Davis or Rhett or Yancey (from the tidewater aristocracy to the Deep South parvenus) is approximately the descent of Niagara.[24] Planless, leaderless, unintelligent, ignorant, opposed to the main currents of political and economic development, they contracted arterio-sclerosis as a party and were dead before they were defeated. They kept power during the Fifties by place and momentum—the accident of history that gave them a respite because the Whigs were annihilated and the Republicans merely being born.

They unconsciously developed the major public policy which the Republicans were to apply consciously: that of, as I have said somewhere, buying the farmer in order to sell him out. They did it inadvertently, but they did it and it has been the major domestic policy of American politics for something like ninety years.

The Civil War destroyed the Democracy. It came back after the war to rest one-half of its paradox on the Solid South, to slowly regain the city machines, and to slowly come into national power again by the time-honored process by which the minority party incorporates all the parties of dissent, protest, agitations, and political and economic lunacy. From the Greenbackers of 1870 down to the LaFollette twins of today, by way of the Granger movement, Populism, Free Silverites, Mugwumps, and anti-imperialists, they have all been gathered to Democracy's bosom.[25] (It is to be said of third-party movements that, though their program is usually adopted, as Wilson put into effect practically everything Bryan campaigned for in 1896, their energy usually comes to little in the end and they make the interior stresses and contradictions so great that they hasten the ultimate break-up and defeat.) But there was one outstanding and overwhelming difference—they had lost their historic alliance with the Middle West. And this is the third great paradox of our political history and one of the basic facts about America—and it also says something or other, I don't know what, about the power of sentiments. So far as there has been an American agrarian party, actually and historically, it has been the Democracy. The strongest southern interest is and always has been agrarian. The Midwest and Western agrarian interest is its natural ally against the exploitation of the East—which is to say, of industry and finance. The Republicans, because they had the leadership and because the Democrats were blind and crazy, succeeded in detaching the Midwest from this alliance during the Fifties. They did so by realistically serving the Midwest interests, at a time when (as a minority party) they could afford to and when the Democracy didn't have brains enough to serve any interest, even its own. The Civil War, converting the Republicans to the party of power, industry, and finance, also handed them the Midwest in apparent perpetuity. And this was mere sentiment—the Union forever, down with the traitors, vote the way you shot. Iowa, Ohio, Wisconsin, Illinois, the rest of them might start to stampede off in favor of the Grange, the Populists, or anyone else who seemed likely to readjust, even a little bit, the terrible economic inequalities created by the protective system, the Republican financial system, and the concentration of economic power. But all the GOP had to do for thirty years was to wave the bloody shirt and all it had to do for nearly twenty more was to draw on its war chest. This is a stupefying fact. It enabled the system to change the economic set-up of the world. It delivered the Midwest into the pockets of Wall Street and it made the whole story of the West that of what I have called a plundered province.[26] And this in defiance of plain interest. The spectacle of an Ohio wool-grower, in 1870–80 or –90 voting for a tariff on wool because there was a picture of Honest Abe in the postoffice is not only stupefying, it's inconceivable. But there you have it, and that was American history 1865–1912, and for a hell of a lot longer than that. The one overwhelming service of the New Deal was to readjust that tremendous dislocation—for how long? Those whom the GOP had put asunder were joined together in 1932 and 1936 but they probably won't stay joined next November.

[*marginal note:* The next great paradox—disregarding the War—is already aborning, the Southern industrialists turning Republican]

The Whigs were, by a hair, a more contradictory collection than the Democrats. Always far stronger locally than nationally, it was an effective Opposition by fits and starts but too greatly strained within to elect more than two Presidents, both War Heroes, or to hold power once it got it.[27] It had an extraordinary number of able leaders but had too many for its own good—their personal rivalries, quite as much as the divergent interests they served, weakened the party. It grew by the process of incorporation through the Thirties and Forties, and the incorporated material was so indigestible that it died. But Clay and Webster were tremendous powers, though they were never able to fuse an effective organization. They stood for the emergent mercantilism, manufacture, and finance, but it grew too fast for them, was too little aware of what its own interests were, and, in short, they never caught up with it. But they did save the nation at the most critical crisis before the War, 1850, and by saving it then, saved it in 1860.... They are my favorite party and I could go on at length, but there's no point.

The Republican party made the most astonishing growth in our history. It was approximately six years old when it won in 1860.[28] It was even more a union of warring antitheses than the Whigs. Abolitionists and Cotton Whigs voted for Lincoln, which is to say, Communists and Liberty Leaguers voting for Franklin D.[29] Its Free Soil inheritance, by which it first began to drain off the prairies, was at violent war with its New England, New York and Pennsylvania high-tariff, pro-factory inheritance from Whiggery. It attracted all the reformers, suffragists and labor reformers as well as abolitionists, and in its earlier phases is an index to all the crank notions of the time. Yet the nucleus round which all these elements coalesced was the Free Soil and "smart business man" coalition. In any given small town the local banker stayed Whig as long as he could, then turned Republican in the hope that mortgages would stay sound. The fires of war really are the fires of war and the party of A. Lincoln, which kept its Free Soil promise by passing the Homestead Act (which was either an irreparable damage to the nation or the most powerful assistance ever given the poor man, or both, and you can take your choice for I don't know) came out of the war the perfected instrument of entrenched financial interests—interests which it had entrenched.[30] Another war measure, the Pacific Railway Act, was the beginning of a long line.[31] So was the National Bank Act.[32] From both the interknit effects ray out till they blind you.... But as a matter of fact, all subsequent history of the U. S. is the history of the Civil War and you had best not get me started on that. And there is no need to characterize the post-1890 Republican Party down to, shall we say, 1940.

This should be glossed by a treatise on issues. But that would merely show that each party has in its turn used both sides of every prominent issue—and I've got to go to bed.... If this isn't the sort of thing you want, put in another call card. But make it fast, for I think I'm leaving for the West in about ten days.

Yours,
Benny

32 Coolidge Hill Road
Cambridge, Massachusetts

[9 May 1940][33]

Dear Kate:

It occurred to me as soon as I had fired off my hasty sketch of the art of government not only that I had said Barnwell Rhett where I meant Howell Cobb but also that my habitual approach to political history is by no means the clearest one and that the clearest one is simply to look at maps of national election votes.[34] You can have a hell of an amusing afternoon and get closer to the bedrock realities if you'll have Vassar send over Paullin's *Atlas of the Historical Geography of the U. S.* and apply yourself to that section.[35] Watch the colors change and understand politics. But you'll have to rig a tackle for Paullin, for it weighs at least six pounds.

I've had a month of research now, the first month I've had since the summer of 1936, and it's been swell. And it's a good thing that this Western trip is cutting it short for otherwise I'd probably never get out of the Mexican War and my book would be as heavily overbalanced on that end as I've been afraid it would be on the Mormons. I thought I was through with the Mexican War. I proposed just to glance through ~~all~~ the Civil War memoirs to check up on the functions of their respective authors in the earlier war, and to look through a few newspapers for rumors and correspondence—I had done the editorial long before. It was something under a week's job, as I saw it. So one thing has kept leading to a dozen other things every day till I've got spellbound and greedy and am barely past Taylor's first campaign.[36] It's rich, ripe, and rewarding. I'll probably never use a ten thousandth of the stuff, but I don't give a damn, it's of its ownself gorgeous.... One thing would be to exhibit our own Trojan Horse tactics and our own Fifth Column not only in Mexico but in Texas too.[37] Another nice thing would be to study the rhetoric of American generals. I always thought that the correspondence between Hood and Sherman both before and after Atlanta was unrivalled but it wasn't.[38] It is restrained compared to Ampudia and Arista on the one hand and Taylor (whose letters Bliss wrote for him) on the other.[39] ... There were some pretty remarkable men in the old army and the most remarkable of them was only a name for me till last week, Ethan Allen Hitchcock.[40] He must have been one of the most remarkable military men ever. He was not only a universal genius—Halleck and Cox were too—he was a natural phenomenon.[41] Did ever a Brigadier write treatises on the Vedas, on the mystical meaning of Shakespeare's sonnets, on Spinoza and Swedenborg?[42] Ethan Allen's grandson did, and on a dozen other even more abstruse metaphysical subjects besides. As colonel of an infantry regt. and commanding Corpus Christi[43] in Taylor's absence, he wrote out a six hundred page translation of Swedenborg and corresponded with, for God's sake, Henry Wadsworth Longfellow, on Rosetti's ideas about the mystics.[44] A little later, as Scott's inspector-general, which is to say as chief of staff of the army of invasion, he read Hieronomus on Lobos Island, the most barren stretch of sand in North America, and corresponded with Theodore Parker on the Oversoul and the hideous injustice of the war he was engaged in.[45] He was as capable as his grandfather of telling people to go to hell, too, and told a lot of them in turn, including half a dozen Presidents. I get a historian's hunch about him, too: I'll bet that the Civil War research that Sandburg's book has begotten among the cloth will show that he created a good many of both Stanton's and Lincoln's ideas on strategy, which have always seemed to me too good to be amateur ideas. Yes, and I've had some fun finding out about Mayne Reid, too.[46] ... The job I started to do, the Civil War generals in the Mex War, would work out best in fiction. But there is a curiously dramatic effect in seeing them in the pupal stage—McClellan quite as big an ass as he ever was, Meade fuming and fretting like a schoolmarm, Semmes swashbuckling, Lee the same God-damned Christer.[47] Their letters give them away, they could hoke the reminiscences but they couldn't hoke a letter to the folks back home. As for the memoirs, I have verified my recollection that Grant's is the best of them by three lengths, and Dick Taylor's the next best.[48] Try them some time, there is worse reading.

Also I had forgotten the single humanizing moment of Halleck's. You get to thinking of him as bloodless, bleak, and intriguing, and as nothing else. But he did write to Sherman, when Ben Butler set out to blow Fort Fisher down by exploding a shipload of gunpowder, that Butler could do as well or better by farting at it.[49]

Well, young Schlesinger has decided to go with me, and we're off as soon as he finishes a paper, Thursday or Friday of next week probably. To Kansas City by the shortest route, which appears to be Buffalo-Cleveland-Indianapolis, and then to the serious business of the Santa Fe trail. I'm leaving as much as may be to the inspiration of the moment and the logic of geography, but I hope I can go in over Raton Pass—I hope, that is, that I can bring myself to forgo history and the Cimarron for scenery and the Breasts of the World.[50] If I can it will be a victory for aesthetics over realism and the romantic has taken few rounds in my career. The general plan, as of now, is to strike north from Santa Fe east of the mountains, pick up the Oregon Trail in western Nebraska, and see whatever is accessible till Shady Hill is out, Schlesinger comes home, Avis and Bunny join me, and the trip degenerates into a tour of national parks. Information is that South Pass is all but impassible but I'm going through with it if I have to walk.[51]

Somewhere along the route I'll have to read proof on "Minority Report." You named a book, it appears. Which required me to change the title of the title piece, so as not to exaggerate it beyond its importance. I have a horrible suspicion that someone else used "Monte Cristo in Modern Dress" but I can't help.[52] Rosy has to read proof on the Mark Twain book and nobody reads proof on John August's book. Alfred McIntyre decided he wanted that last and promptly found himself alleviating my traveling expenses by five hundred dollars, to his great surprise and sharp pain, for that's more than its predecessor reduced my debt to him. Somebody seems to be advertising it somewhere already, for I got a hot wire from Random House. *Collier's* starts running it on the 25th, and I hope you'll have the decency not to take advantage of my absence—if I hear you've read so much as an announcement of it I'll force the next Malcolm Cowley on you.... I still don't believe in the ease with which the Mark Twain book has gone through. Harpers contented themselves with objecting to a paragraph in my introduction in which I made remarks about Paine; I'd just as soon omit it, now I can blow it up to full length and run it in a scholarly sheet. Lark is protesting in this morning's mail that both Theodore Roosevelt and the late Senator Clark are libelled, but I can handle that by wire.[53] Of course Clara Clemens may yet get a message from Beyond, but by that time Harpers will have it set up, and no Clemens ever argued against an expenditure.

Three-quarters of my predictions about the war having been vitiated, I withdraw all the remaining ones except the guess that it will be finished in 1940. The last bunch, anyway, were based on the hallucination that the British would fight. It is all but impossible to think of a world that is not erected on the British Empire, but Hitler appears to have been right in his judgement of it and the English, so the sooner we begin to try to think of it, the better. The local historians are now busy telling me that the English have been in worse situations often enough before, which is true but irrelevant. Crane Brinton argued at the bootblack's this morning that they were in far worse shape after Corunna and added that this time the U. S. wasn't going to go in on the side of the dictator.[54] Crane, with all the others, holds out that the European pattern is fixed for all time, that eventually all the others gang up on whoever seems to be establishing mastery of the continent. Sure. Historians, like general staffs, always think of the last war, not the current one. Alec Robey, my current knothole on big business, says that Bethlehem Steel and others are planning for an eight years' war.[55] Sure, mathematics makes it clear that the Allies must win in the end—if there is time enough before the end. Hell. I see the problem of aerial warfare every few minutes in the reading I'm doing. Zachary Taylor was as near an imbecile as ever held a high command. In the first engagement of the Mex War, Palo Alto, he arranged his artillery in the pattern sanctified by the great Napoleon, who had established for all time that you can use cannon for other things than salutes. Taylor, that is, posted his guns in from his flanks, so that they could be protected by infantry squares—against cavalry and infantry. They included two eighteen pounders, heavy guns for the time, and a couple of artillery officers who could shoot them. So Palo Alto was, properly speaking, only a cannonade—the Mex duly charged the flanks with both infantry and cavalry and got mowed down at three-quarters of a mile. The pattern of the future was set in the first half-hour of Palo Alto and the pattern worked out though nobody, not even Scott, got the idea.[56] By the middle of 1862 Buford and perhaps a couple of other Union officers began to understand that a rifle kills farther away than a saber does, and a cannon kills at an even greater distance.[57] Tactically, Gettysburg and the entire campaign in the East was [*sic*] won when that realization broke over the military mind. Lee lost Gettysburg because the great Stuart—who had read his books and, besides, knew that the Southerner is a cavalier—performed marvelous feats of horsemanship with banners waving and Buford using [*sic*] a horse as a means of getting some rifles to a desirable place. Cavalry charges were as obsolete as duelling pistols, and it is one of history's benevolences that at last Stuart blundered into some modern cavalry on its way to a firm position and perished like an antique hero in a charge. Victory in battle follows concentration of fire power and an airplane is just one of Buford's horses, a way of getting it there faster than an infantryman can carry it—or, for that matter, a tractor drag it.... But I can't make out what arrangements we'll make with Canada. It presents a pretty problem in sentiments. If there is anything in history, we could acquire our Fifth Column with no trouble at all. Whole provinces have done their damndest to be incorporated in the past, though whole other provinces have risen against the threat. I don't know how you salve the wound. Statehood is out of the question from our point of view, territorial status from theirs. A league of Western Hemisphere nations would shove South and Central

America off the other end, a customs union would not protect us, a protective occupation under any name would involve civil war, and you can work out the answer if you know how. If you get it, tell me what it is. But I still think we'll take Curaçao first of all, though it is now certain that we'll have to take the British and French West Indies too.

Didn't the Easy Chair once predict the resurgence of Manifest Destiny?

Yes, and how will we feel when someone remembers that the fleet is in danger off Hawaii, and brings it home?

Yours,
Benny

[postcard, Bird's-eye view of Morrisville, N.Y.]
Morrisville, N.Y.

May 20, 1940 [postmark]

Saturday. One day out. I seem to have got started
Benny

[postcard, Cleveland Public Auditorium, Cleveland, Ohio]
Medina, Ohio

May 20, 9 AM [postmark]

Medina [sic] Ohio apparently has no glories of its own to celebrate, but Medina County advertises itself as "The Home of the Garbage-fed Hog"
Benny

[postcard, Thomas Hart Benton murals in Jefferson City]
Jefferson City, Mo.

May 23, 1940, 6:30 PM [postmark]

You know, these things are pretty good. The longer you look at them, the better they get.... And St. Louis is a very alcoholic town, which is why I'm 24 hours behind schedule
Benny

[postcard, Madonna of the Trail, Council Grove, Kans.]
Council Grove, Kans.

May 25, 1940, 5:30 PM [postmark]

Just to keep you professionally informed.

Also Kansas beer is very bad beer
Benny

[postcard, Toothless Nell, Boot Hill Cemetery, Dodge City, Kans.]
Dodge City, Kans.

May 28, 1940 PM [postmark]

This town is a phony. Maybe Hollywood ruined it. Anyway, I'm getting out of it fast. Where the West Broke Down

Benny

[postcard, Taos Indian Pueblo, New Mexico]
Santa Fe, N. Mex.

May [?]29, 1940, 11:30 AM [postmark]

In the SW, apparently, the art of the post card breaks down. Pause in Santa Fe while I write an Easy Chair. This has been a strange trip, motoring through a peaceful countryside while the world dies.[58]

Benny

Jenny Lake, Teton Natl Park

June 15
[forwarding postmark: June 25, 1940;
note on envelope: "Rec'd Wed. June 26th"
(at St. Francis Hospital)

Dear Kate:

I haven't had the heart to write. Even my postcards fell away. Yesterday's paper—a *Salt Lake Tribune* which I got in Idaho Falls—told of the fall of Paris.[59] Elmer, tuned into late today, was saying something about a new statement of Roosevelt's that I appear to have missed.[60] That I have come so far is a triumph of self-control. Or of Avis—who urged me on by telephone every few days and joined me at Ogden, with Bunny, a week ago today. Granted equal fortitude, I'll be going on for two or three weeks more.... I sent in my name to what seemed the likeliest person in the likeliest place, a week before I left Cambridge, and I'm more or less on call. And you do have the damndest, or the best, luck with the books I dedicate to you, don't you? Or maybe I can write it evenings, after retreat.

It has been, this trip, an intense experience. I'll send you a copy of my notes when I get home. I'll maybe be writing about it, too.

This was always the loveliest place in a beautiful country. The Matterhorn of the Grand Teton is above my left shoulder, and the evening cold has come down from its snows.[61] Cottonwood Creek clatters outside my door, and the hills, all day long, have been masses of lupine, larkspur, Indian paintbrush & wild roses. Teton Pass is far more magnificent, even, than I remembered it.[62] I took Bunny up a hillside there to play in snow—2800 feet above the top of Mt. Washington or exactly level with what they're now calling Mt. Ogden, at my birthplace.[63] From the Pass down to Jackson's [*sic*] Hole must be the most spectacular vista in America—far more so than New Mexico from Raton Pass. I had forgotten this country, Kate, and now I won't.

My God, the evening is all gold and gray. And the river smell. What poem is in my mind, & who wrote it? "The unforgettable river smell."[64]

We drove over Teton Pass in something under an hour. I think it took me two days the last time I came this way. There was no Teton Park then—and the Park Service has enormously improved things. The road, the Tetons—with a lot of other things too—the West is a better country than it was in my time. Better, even, than when I saw it last fifteen years ago. Civilization has moved fast here.... I'll be writing about that too, given a typewriter.

But I must say I get fed up with its self-conscious aspects. The cowboy songs you hear when trying to tune in on some news. The Coronado Cuarto[65] that was exploiting New Mexico down to the lousiest Indian. The "community whisker-drive" in Walsenberg.... And, considering what Jackson's Hole evokes in my iconography, it was a shock today to see something called "The Cowboy Bar: the Finest Rustic Bar in the World."[66] Jesus.

I thought I had something to say to you. Maybe I did and it's just that 7000 feet still drug me, come sunset.... An economical drinking-country too. One ounce does the work of three at sea level, and I have an enormous respect for what seemed to me, when it ~~occurred~~ exerted, just an ordinary alcoholic capacity twenty years back. I noticed it first at La Fonda in Santa Fe, where one Martini apiece sent A S & me reeling into the dining room as from a bachelor dinner.... Maybe all I had to say was, there's a hell of a lot of America, and most of it is damned good to look upon, and it's gone forward, not back, these last ten years.

We stopped, ten days ago, at Muddy Gap, Wyoming, to see if there was word of the road through South Pass. Muddy Gap is three shacks, all filling stations, where two roads cross in the desert between Sweetwater & the badlands. A woman came out to man the pump, said she hadn't heard any news for three days, and "Has Roosevelt declared war on them yet?" A week before that, outside of Trinidad, we stopped in the dark to listen to Roosevelt's "fireside chat"—was there ever an unlikelier name for a war message?[67] Some Mexicans leaned up against the car to listen too. When it was over and I started up the engine, one of them said, "I guess maybe America declare war pretty soon now." But I put that into the Easy Chair I wrote in Santa Fe.[68]... The rancher I talked to in Teton Basin this morning—that's Pierre's Hole, if you know your West—to check my battlegrounds, said "I was in the last one & I'm ready to get into this one too." That seems to be the sentiment everywhere, though I must say the young are not ebullient. Archie MacLeish says that he & the rest betrayed the young.[69] I'm glad he's found the grace to deal himself in, but if he remembers that I've been kicked about the cellar for 20 years for saying just that, I'll be better off than I'm likely to be.... "smell the unforgettable, unforgotten river-smell..." Rupert Brooke, by God, "Grantchester," and that was both another war and another past.[70]... The West begins where the dead animals on the road are not chickens or skunks but jack rabbits. Or when the State Highway Commission orders you to slow down to 50 at curves. Or where menus dwindle to chicken & steak, both fried.... The Middle West, however, as I may have observed before, for your education, begins where the salad is the first course.

You can have the Southwest. I concede the grandeur, but it's a dead land. The inhabitants, furthermore, are all seeking the Navajo's last communion with the Religions of the Orient. I came home at Taos Pass, when the timber began to march up the mountains.[71]... Maybe I did wrong to implore you not to come West. The beauty of this country is not to be told—though in a decent world, I was ready to begin to try telling. I had forgotten too much—something of the distance, something of the emptiness, more still of the light. I should have, in that book, quite a bit to say about the light. It diminishes you—saps your individuality, reduces you to a point. I understand a good deal about this culture & this history that I didn't have brains enough to understand twenty years back. But the loneliness is not to be told in words—only felt, with remembrance, a hell of a lot deeper than the breath or the pulse. But I'm not of this country now, if I ever was. I'll be quite content never to see Utah, at least, again.[72] My farewell image of it is the most beautiful of all, Bear Lake[73] from the top of the ridge, with rose mountains on the far side—but, moving on into Idaho, toward the pink mountains, I was not as much leaving home as going home.... Yeah, there was a lot I could have said about the West, and it's been a fine trip, while the world died.... You might send me a word c/o the Postmaster, Houghton, Michigan, where I'll pick it up in ten days or two weeks, if my self-control holds. After a day or so here, on to Yellowstone.

Yrs
Benny

7 North Randolph Ave.
Po'keepsie
St. Swithin's Day[74]

(GOD, LET IT NOT RAIN!)[75]

Dear Benny,
This is something like sending radio signals to Mars, but here goes another....

As you see by the dateline, I've moved again. This is a good nursing home—clean, well-run, with excellent food. As a matter of fact, I think my hyperthyroid appetite has rather set Mrs. Hover back on her heels. She seems to be used to patients who feel sated after a poached egg.

I'm fighting like hell to keep from going back to Bowne, which has gradually become a den of horrors in my thinking. I think I'm going to lose, though.... For a while there was a harebrained plan for four of us to take a little farm within commuting distance of Po'k., but the difficulties of finding a farm, a housekeeper, a jalopy & the cash are pretty baffling. This idea is still kicking around, however, & something may conceivably come of it.

I've considerably increased my reputation as a screwball by telling all enquirers that the British are going to win. Don't ask me why, they just are.... Not that that'll be an unmixed blessing either. There was a tall, blond, languid Canuck interne at St. Francis' who kept telling me in Oxford accents what a tragedy it would be if the cultured Canadians ever joined up with us Houhounyms [*sic*].[76]

Note of Progress:—Cornelia Kinkead reports that Rosie has gotten Herman to take the picture of Hitler off his radio.

Note of Progress:—The Germania Society has refused the use of its hall to the local Bund.

* * * * *

I've been catching up on John August.[77] A damned good job, if you don't mind my saying so.

Yours

Kate

32 Coolidge Hill Road
Cambridge, Massachusetts

[14 July 1940]

[forwarded to Hover Nursing Home from St. Francis Hospital]

Dear Kate:

9,255 miles. 624 gallons of gasoline. 42 quarts of oil. And General Motors makes good cars—no engine trouble, no trouble of any kind. A new set of spark plugs at Ogden, a carburetor adjustment at Las Vegas, a new battery at Idaho Falls—the last because I didn't have sense enough to realize that all this driving was keeping the generator in action at the same rate it was set to in the fifty miles a week of Cambridge. But U. S. Rubber does not make particularly good tires. I bought a new set before I left. One let go altogether at 6500 miles—in the middle of a newly oiled stretch which beautifully ruined one pair of trousers, one shirt, two shoes, two socks, two garters, and a lovely pair of blue shorts with a red stripe down the leg. Three punctures, one per remaining tire, in the succeeding thousand miles. U. S. Royal Cords, their first-line tire, and I may say it's the second time a set of them has gone sour on me. They are just not built for fast speeds and long drives. Next time I buy rayon.

Avis extracted a husband's promise that I would not drive more than 50 miles an hour, which is pretty good sense in New England and, besides, represents about the possible maximum anywhere north of the Worcester Turnpike or east of U. S. 7. So I said nothing till about the third day after she and I got started, and then casually remarked that 65 was about the optimum for a two-lane road with a high crown. After ten thousand cars have passed you doing 80 or 85 you begin to get the idea, and she didn't realize she was doing 75. Driving in the West has nothing in common with driving in the metropolitan east. You may drive for two hours at a stretch without seeing a town, a curve, or another car. Montana slows you down to 55 after dark, by statute. Wyoming suggests 50 for sharp curves. In Colorado and Nebraska the statutory limit is 60. At Rock Springs we saw a tourist camp advertised; it was in Winnemucca, just 650 miles away, and that represents a Westerner's day, if he makes a late start.[78] I met a salesman in Ogden who drives from Denver once a week, 52 times a year, makes five calls on the way, and does the drive in one day. My beloved Beatrice spoke of the terrible Ocean Drive, south from Oregon, so narrow, so full of curves, so treacherous that it took them more than two full days to drive it, 1200 miles.[79] Your sense of distance is already haywire because of the scale of the country; your sense of speed, of relative speeds, gets altogether cockeyed. But your reflexes take it in their stride, and you just adjust to the new conditions, never passing a car if the one coming toward you is less than a mile away. This makes a pretty problem, analytically; I'll see what can be done about it.... I suppose the Westerners can take it, but I found that 450 miles was about all I cared to do unless the next tourist camp looked lousy. There comes a point where, quite suddenly, you feel tired. Tired all over. From there on it's a drag, and if you're driving straight west, into the sun, it gets to be something on the edge of torture. I wonder, too, if solitary drivers, in the treeless country and at such speeds, don't get into a semi-hypnotic state; I know that I was frequently damned glad, for safety's sake, that I had someone to talk to.

As I remarked to you from Jenny's Lake, it's a beautiful country. A half-dozen pictures crowd into my mind, the moment I write that: Bear Lake three-quarters of a mile straight below you from the divide, with the canyon opening out and rose-pink mountains on the far side of that morning-glory blue; the great Red Butte near Independence Rock[80] that all the emigrants wrote about, the most vivid red; another Red Butte, a canyon that we tortuously followed on the worst stretch of the trip, making for South Pass, full of flowers, odorous with water, occasionally opening to give a glimpse of the Wind River Mountains, which are among the best mountains there are; Jackson Hole from the top of the divide in Teton Pass; the three Tetons, the most glorious of all peaks, and never more glorious than through the altar window of the Chapel of the Transfiguration at Moose; the Canyon of the Yellowstone; Dunraven Pass—hell, eight out of nine thousand miles was beautiful, for let's not ignore the shoreline of Lake Superior, Lake Bemidji, or the pastoral sweetness of the long drive down the St. Lawrence, and I wish to God I'd get round, sometime, to doing that last on the American side.[81] I found least like what I expected it to be the Montana country east of the mountains. I had thought of it in terms of the Wyoming deserts to the south of it, whereas I should have been thinking of it in terms of the buffalo country, immensely big and immensely green. Even the Wyoming country has something, if not for me. It fascinated young Arthur and it entranced Avis, what she saw of it. I've never liked it and revisiting it did not change my taste. I can take it up the Platte Valley to Casper, where there is green stuff and flowers, a pepper of cedars on the buttes and badlands, and a feeling that life is supportable here, at whatever cost. I left the Platte where the trail did, however, at the mouth of Sweetwater, and from there on to the Wind River Mountains I was under a kind of oppression that has, with the corresponding if more intense feeling I got in New Mexico, clarified much I've read in the journals of emigrants. You see too far, in too bright light, and you see too little. The writhing buttes are all very splendid, and the colors are beyond conception, but there is no shade, no refuge, and no life. As one diarist put it, there is no place to <u>hide</u>. Nothing grows, for God knows greasewood is not an organic thing. The sun, the emptiness, the glare, and the everlasting wind etch away first your individuality, then your personality itself. You are diminished to a mere dot in your own consciousness, and you become a kind of sentient lifelessness—if I'm not talking like Mary Austin God forbid. I emphasize the sun, and yet there is as much sun, as much emptiness and lack of shade for that matter, in the high Montana plains, which exhilarated me. It must be the lack of vegetation.... I'll see what Bill Barrett and Kubie have to say about it, particularly the latter, who seems able to coordinate my unconscious with my objective observation and analysis, if any. But if I'm right, then I understand the migration better than I ever did before, and a hell of a lot of its sequelae.

Yet Wyoming is not the deadest land I saw, nor was the oppressiveness greatest there. And I can check by Arthur. We had lunch at Dodge City—a damned trumpery, phony town, clumsily trying to exploit its past and being very stupid about it, plastered over with signs that are both untruthful and unbearably jocose, counterfeit even its central pride, Boot Hill, which is not Boot Hill—and an hour later were already in the Dust Bowl. An hour of it had reduced both to a kind of phantasy of doom. By the second hour, I was practically pathological, and welcomed a telephone sign, got out and called up Avis, to assure myself that people still lived on this earth. Wyoming is inanimate, but that part of Kansas has been killed. I don't know which is more appalling, the crops sticking up through the dust and petrifying just as they stood five years ago, or the occasional Dept. of Agriculture attempts to bring the land back, very brave and hopeful doubtless but patently unavailing. That was a ghastly afternoon, out of Doré's Dante.[82] We were no sooner across the Colorado line than the country began to pick up—irrigation, most of it from the Arkansas. We hurried on to Bent's Fort, near La Junta, and by the time I was surveying that I felt human again.

And I would not forget the rivers, having mentioned the Arkansas. That one isn't much, but there are those that are. I wonder how, having visited it a hundred times before, I was ignorant that the Snake is a noble and beautiful stream. The Yellowstone too, and I have sworn that, if the world ever straightens out, I'll go back and follow the Yellowstone all the way. I got a sense I never had before of the fundamental watershed—the Red, the Arkansas, the Rio Grande, the Missouri, the Green, the Snake, the Yellowstone, the Big Horn, Maria's, the Milk. (A good line in one of the Montana historical markers, easily the best ones we saw, written with a sense of style and an excellent grasp of history, referred to the chance that the wayfarer might, in certain seasons, think of the Milk as "trivial or even dusty.") I did not touch the Madison, the Gallatin, or the Jefferson in their best stretches and the Madison was, with the Bear and the Gunnison, the romance of my boyhood. Incredibly, in the recurrent war mood of what-the-hell, I hurried past the Three Forks and did not visit them, though I was within five miles. (That's part of the psychology of panic, I may do a piece on it. The same thing kept me from detouring to Fort Union and made me slight one of the objectives of my whole trip, Soda Springs, where I spent less than an hour.) But the Snake is, finally, the best, and it must be something in Hell's Canyon. I kept going down to it whenever I could—and sometimes, as the journals will inform you, that's not too easy. Most of all, I think, I'll remember how it flows through the clean and enormously socialistic little town of Idaho Falls—whose socialism it creates, the town having had the sense to grab the falls and make electricity there. That's a gorgeous tumble, a quarter of a mile wide and maybe forty feet from top to bottom, spray everywhere, prismatic in the sun, kids, young men, and old maids catching five pound trout at the foot of the falls fifty yards from the main highway, a gorgeous rumble of falling water, a vast whiteness in the rapids above and below the falls, and an immense blue from there on. It's magnificent higher up, too, where it comes out of Jackson Hole. And the branch of it named after Meriwether Lewis flows through a canyon that we'd hear about if the Yellowstone wasn't so close to it.

And speaking of Meriwether Lewis, I find that a boyhood in the mountains plus Uncle Sam's careful training of an intelligence officer have soundly supported historical research. All my recreation of the country from the journals was right, in the parts that counted; all of it, in fact, except the Montana plains, which I didn't need, anyway. I was at home at all the key places, and hardly needed the compass, protractor, and other aids that I took with me. And I found the research at hand when needed, no matter how thoroughly I had forgotten it. The Lewis and Clark country, for instance, was right at my finger tips when I got there—and except for a hurried review when I wrote an SRL piece, that's the farthest away of all, the first systematic reading I ever did.[83] We struck a small, unidentified stream, for instance. I couldn't find it on the oil company map and saw no reason for getting out a good map. Pretty soon a marker said that this was the farthest north Lewis had come on his return trip. I said, then that's Maria's River. It was. I hadn't traced his course for nigh onto twenty years, and I felt as cocky as if I'd forecast a pennant winner on July 4. At Fort Laramie I was able to strut—call off various dispositions and then open Parkman and verify them in detail. In Pocatello, I looked up a local authority and soon found that her dope on where the trail came over into Soda Springs didn't agree with my sense of geography. I've looked it up since I got back, and I was right. So maybe I'll offer my enlistment to the topographical branches. But it's very reassuring to a man contemplating a book.

I'll make a copy of my notes and send it to you—you needn't read it but on the other hand maybe it will amuse you. I've got to do it myself for Rosy refuses to try. Most of them were written with the car in motion, and A.S. never held himself down to any mere 65 on curves.

But then again, if you read me in print you'll be reading them for quite a while.

The excruciation—is that a word?—lapsed after the fall of Paris. There's no need to describe or analyze what it was up to then. Thereafter, like you, I began to see possible tolerations, if not ways out. And, though Arthur suggests that this may have resulted from the substitution of a wife for a historian as traveling companion, I don't think that's it. I have always been able to resolve my doubts about this country by taking a motor trip, and God knows I took a big one this time. But it isn't the cheap mysticism of seeing so much bigness, so much security, and so much natural loveliness. And God knows it doesn't come from talking to Westerners or in fact and citizenry west of Buffalo. We were prophets of disaster everywhere we went, in fact it was Arthur and I, calling on Irving Dilliard, who produced the *Post-Dispatch's* celebrated "Roosevelt is driving us to war" editorial.[84] The most enlightened opinion was like Dilliard's—we've got enough mess of our own to clear up. There's not too much of that. Mostly it's we're safe enough, nobody is going to pick a fight with us. Though, of course, the wave we were in advance of may have followed behind us, and a man should really make the trip again now and see how the boys are feeling two months later.... But there is a considerable reassurance in making such a trip, and it isn't intangible. You get an irrefutable testimony of national health and vigor that you don't get sitting on your tail in Cambridge. You see how well things are working. Specifically, you see a vast bulk of evidence that the system has kept going better than you had thought, that it had made advances during the last ten years and is still making them, that American civilization has widened and deepened. And I'm afraid you get a pretty genuine respect for New Deal accomplishments out there. I came an alarming distance back toward the road I publicly forsook. I'm going to do a piece about that so I won't excite your emotions here.

I'm by no means sure I'm going to vote for Wilkie [*sic*].[85] I'm going to listen to the campaign—and with a queasy realization that not only are no issues going to be joined and no action taken while it goes on but that the fundamental paradox can't be resolved. In spite of Elmer Davis's explosion in the Century Club a year ago, which I probably narrated to you, it seemed likely that Wilkie is an administrator. The greatest weakness of the New Deal—excuse me—is administrative. But when you vote for Wilkie you're voting not for him but only for the Republican Party, which completely failed to administer the United States through twelve years.[86] And has not changed either its structure or its skin. There is no administrative salvation in the G.O.P., which will elect him if he's elected, nor, so far as I can see, apart from a lively critical sense in the candidate himself, any realistic thinking anywhere among its intellectuals or mouthpieces.[87] I don't see that we'll be any better off with Joe Martin than with Tom Corcoran.[88] Mr. Hoover is at some pains to describe the sweet unreality of the logical daydreams of the Brain Trust, and God knows that rouses a sympathetic vibration in me, but phantasy is no worse an endowment for government than memory of A. T. & T. at 305.[89] Wilkie's principal qualifications, so far as his public utterances show, are a kind of general or, better, unspecified courage and a gift for making phrases. Those are exactly Mr. Roosevelt's principal public qualifications also. They redeem the public ineptness of his party just so far as they go and they may cleanse a spot here and there but the leopard's skeleton is just what it was, and I can't love it. As yet there has been no sign that he is going to localize the courage by talking straight to the electorate—which, again, is just like F. D. R. I heard his Kansas City speech.[90] From time to time you have alleged a prissy quality in what Franklin says. I grant it. But I found a folksiness in Wendell's manner that was just as hard to bear, and just as insulated against the realities. Unquestionably he is a better man than either of the pair he licked. Whether he is as good a man as his running mate is questionable. McNary, in fact, is of the type that would be most useful now—the type of mind, I mean, not of policy.[91] But McNary too is a nominee, not of a great popular uprising as our prettily cooperative myth-makers are telling us, but of a Republican Party that is something over ninety-eight percent of just what it was from 1920 to 1932. God help the Republic.

There remains the constricted area of fiscal sense, and in that small area one had better make up his mind how to vote. It is not enough to denounce the Democracy. Whether we shall get any more than denunciation, the campaign will show. Unhappily it will not show whether, if we do get more than that, we can expect anything from then on. . . . Certainly neither administration is likely to be much different from what the other would have had to be, in matter of armament and foreign relations. That a man who has run a big utilities company is going to have a more efficient administrative set-up than the present one is pure phantasy, which is denied a fortiori by the make-up of his party. That "business" will cooperate with him is just folklore. Business is already "cooperating" with Roosevelt to the best of its ability, which is not phenomenal. If that notion is stripped of its protective phraseology, we end up with Doheny and Sinclair, the only kind of "business" that the event is not certain to put in command, whoever is elected.[92] And those boys do not make a satisfactory basis for armament.

As for me, I'm waiting on events. My name is in—in a couple of places. I hear also on pretty sound authority that the junior service is thinking of commandeering my pen. That seems odd of the junior service but I suppose I can publicize aircraft carriers as well as I could tanks or the home front. But nothing will be done anywhere till after the election anyway, and on that assumption I'm going ahead with my book, meanwhile walking curiously around the local Harvard group of preparers. The academic mind is wonderful, almost as wonderful as the literary mind, but out of these formal ballets I may get some practice for more important things.

Yours,
Benny

32 Coolidge Hill Road
Cambridge, Massachusetts

[5 August 1940]

Dear Kate:

There was a curse on the earlier venture. There may be one on this. God knows the omens in the sky are plentiful enough. I say only: Well, I've started.

Yrs
Benny

[*enclosure, handwritten:*]

August 5, 1940

I

January, 1846: Background for War.[93]

John T. Hughes, a bachelor of arts, had seen much during the year of decision, and had been part of ~~it.~~ what he saw.[94] When he sat down to write his history he remembered a story which, he said, was doubtless more beautiful than true. Early in that Spring of '46, a prairie thunderstorm struck a party of traders who were returning to Independence from Santa Fe. It passed over and the red sun dipped to the prairie's edge, and the traders ~~shouted~~ cried out with one voice. For the image of an eagle was spread across the sun. They knew then that "in less than twelve months the eagle of liberty would spread his broad pinions over the plains of the West, and that the flag of our country would wave over the cities of New Mexico and Chihuahua."

Fire in the Roman sky when Caesar was assassinated was in Hughes's mind—and Manifest Destiny.[95] But he missed a sterner omen.... When Biela's comet came back in 1832 people had been terrified because it was calculated to pass within twenty thousand miles of the earth's orbit.[96] The dread eased, and in 1839 when the visitor returned it was too close to the sun to be seen. Santini calculated its next perihelion passage at February 11, 1846.[97] True to its assignment, it traveled earthward toward the end of '45. In Rome Di Vico ~~saw~~ identified it on November 28, and Galle in Berlin ~~identi~~ saw it two days later.[98] By mid-November all watchers of the skies had reported it. But on January 13 of the year of decision, the omen came out of Washington.

Matthew Maury was a universal genius, but his passion was ~~oceanography~~ the movement of waters.[99] In that January he was laboring, as he had labored for years, to perfect the basis for scientific study of winds and currents. There was to come out of his labor the science of oceanography, and methods of reporting the tides not only of the sea but of the air also that have been permanent, and a revision of the art of navigation. But he was also Superintendent of the Naval Observatory, and so ~~night~~ he ~~also~~ turned his telescope nightly on Biela's comet. It was on the night of January 13 that he beheld the ominous and ~~unspeakable~~ incredible. On its way toward perihelion, the comet had split in two.

There was a new department in Niles' Register for January 3. It was called "Are We to Have War or Peace?" The war [*breaks off*]

[*dedication page:*]

To

Katharine Grant Sterne

[before 17 August 1940]

Benny, I'm so damned honored! This is going to be a great book. And I think maybe the omens seem worse than they are. It's easy to see how an intelligent book on that particular phase of our history could be extremely valuable in our present vicissitudes, and probably Elmer is right again that "What you and I are doing in the course of our days work is probably the most useful thing we could do."... Oh, & may I repeat, if, between now & publication, you should come to regret that exceedingly generous dedication, please don't hesitate to change it.

Yours,

Kate

32 Coolidge Hill Road
Cambridge, Massachusetts

[17 AUGUST 1940]

Dear Kate:

But yes, dear. Also the South maintains a white-black wage differential. Also, the negro health problem has been solved, in so far as it has been solved, which is a quarter of a millimeter, exclusively by funds from the national treasury and private, northern foundations. Also, negroes are kept from voting, organizing, asking for higher wages, collecting what is owed them, suing for damages, or protesting when beaten up.... Furthermore, someone should tell you that there is a national mortgage system which keeps farmers in debt to Republicans. Moreover, the La Follette Bill did not put an end to the exploitation of sailors.[100] Yes, and it is true that the Ford Company, the Associated Farmers, and seven thousand other organizations combine against working men, who are also members of what we are calling our democracy.[101] Shall I send you a book about tenant farmers? Did you know that the lumbering and mining industries have wrecked areas of our society and moved on, leaving those areas to rot away? Have you heard that the people who shell pecans in Texas get from ten to forty cents a day, and that that represents about the average net wage of the migratory fruit pickers Mr. Steinbeck was writing about?[102] Whereas those who follow the wheat harvest can always count on a dollar a day, or twenty cents an hour, or even more.... So now we invite these people to get out and fight for America, and you get three guesses who makes good material for Adolph's agents to work on. Maybe you better vote for Roosevelt as a war measure. The New Deal knew about these things and has, a little, acted on them.

I'll send you Apley before I leave for Bread Loaf—I'm going up for a couple of days to see Edith Mirrielees—but I won't be able to get to Widener before I go, and since Rosy is vacationing in Maine I can't look up your ancestor's ancestors till I get back.... Have you seen "A Man Named Grant"? Houghton-Mifflin Fellowship product, not bad.... I dunno that I'll try the new Brooks. What I've read in the papers seems to me sweet, empty, and feminine. He was better when he wrote about books without bothering to read them. His mind always was soft, but now it's sugary as well. So why did Kip Fadiman make a classic of the new book?[103]

And, yes, John Charles Frémont was—primarily—Old Bullion's son-in-law, and if his memory still stinks in Arizona, that's probably because he wouldn't take Old Bill Williams's advice about crossing the Sangre de Cristo in the winter time and, what with one thing and another, some of his men ended by eating some of the others.[104] In the sixty-three manuscript pages to which Ch. I has now extended, and the real point of the chapter still to be introduced, I've got him, in two passages, from St. Louis to Sutter's Fort by way of Great Salt Lake and Donner Pass, handsomely to Don José Castro, the general of California, and is marking time, waiting for something or other, no one has ever known what.[105] I explain that he was a literary man, and maybe that covers it. He was quite a guy—my God, how prolific America once was with personalities. Nature marred this one with an ironical snicker. He was always on the verge of greatness and always played it wrong, with the highest ideals and in the most rhetorical manner. Benton's daughter was a sweetheart, though, a beauty, passionate as hell I judge, a bluestocking, and on the word of A. Lincoln, a virago.... Oh, my God, I've just realized I've got to get Lincoln into Ch. I, and I've passed the place where he fits. Well, in January, he was trying some cases and preparing to fight it out with Gen. Shields for the Whig nomination, against, of all people a ribald God could have selected, Peter Cartwright.[106]... One of the most serious gaps in American historiography is that no one has written a modern or even an acceptable biography of Benton. The profession lets me down badly through most of my chosen field, and very seriously right there. The job done on him nearly fifty years ago by that other literary gent, Theodore Roosevelt, is one of the curiosities of our literature.[107] If found in a time capsule and identified as the work of one who became President, it would confound students of our political and social system forevermore.

I am appalled to realize that the opening chapter of this book will run anyway seventy ms. pages, forty-five in typing. At the very least, ten of them must come out. Furthermore, they are all but impenetrable. Presumably, any one who should contrive to come through them to Ch. II would thereafter find some interesting reading, but anyone who got that far wouldn't need anything soft like interest. And I see no way out of the embarrassment. If I'm going to write this book, it is first of all necessary to explain some things. Yes, and the writing so far is ~~all~~ doughy. That does not bother me too much. I'll get the grit and water out of it when I put it through the machine. Nor does it bother me too much that, looking back over it, I have so far found six whopping mis-statements. After all, Rosy will type the final version—I think—and read the proofs. And suppose I get through with an average of six mistakes per chapter? Well, on the basis of the stuff I read collaterally as I write, I will hang up a record for accuracy in the field. I'm afraid I'm losing some of the awe of historians that has attended my days. Nevins's *Frémont*, which is his second book on the same subject and may therefore be called a revision, doesn't even get the geography right more than sixty percent of the time, and my God, there are maps, there are even surveyors' plots, there are even aerial photographs.[108] And this afternoon, consulting a monograph merely to assure myself that I'd covered the available literature, I found Joseph Smith's death misdated by a year,[109] the Mormons arriving in Salt Lake Valley thirteen months before they left the Missouri River, and in two paragraphs four mistakes about Francis Parkman that, I should think, no one who has read *The Oregon Trail* could possibly make. And I've just read the critique of the Fred Shannon–Walter Webb controversy by three specialists in Western history, including, for God's sake, Harrison Dale, whose *Ashley-Smith Explorations* I have always innocently considered the finest job in Western history.[110] They say all sorts of things about the controversy but not once does any of them appeal to the facts. Perceiving some flaws in Shannon's argument I wrote a private memorandum for Arthur Schlesinger, early last winter. (No, it didn't convince him—he said Shannon must obviously know more about the field than I, and that was that.) When I wrote it, I combed out the facts and asserted that Shannon ignored them. Maybe I did so because I'm a literary critic; anyway, the historians either didn't know the facts or weren't interested in them. Or maybe history is just like literary criticism.

Or maybe this is DeVoto on the defensive. I haven't read that piece on Sikorsky, so I won't diagnose. But a symbolic volcano, even in eruption, could be different. The profession usefully dwells on the alliances between lust or desire and rage, and if a volcano turned up in my dreams I should first scrutinize it as a probable allusion to my father, who bellowed at me through most of my childhood. The Primal Scene that is the profession's preoccupation at the moment is usually interpreted by the child to mean an angry attack on mother, not a sexual assault.... Interesting confession by Bunny on the way back from camp, though his assumption was fallacious. Shortly after he and Avis joined me at Ogden, young Arthur Schlesinger, who had not yet left for Cody, took him out for a walk to ease some of the tension of the train-trip. I had forgotten that fact but when he told me this story I inquired when it took place and he said it was on that walk. Seems that he and Arthur saw two Mallet locomotives meet head-on in a tremendous collision which shattered the locomotives to pieces and scattered mangled corpses over the landscape.[111] What does a father do? Well, I congratulated him on having composed a perfectly swell *Collier's* story and suggested that he write it down, so presently he was grinning and suggesting that maybe I'd better not tell Ma about it.... I stopped off for a night with Kubie at Cotuit before picking Bunny up. I fell to talking about the mood I sometimes felt on the plains, the immense emptiness with no place to hide in and the terrific sun reducing one's personality to a dot—I think it explains a lot about the psychology of pioneering. I characterized it as incipient agoraphobia. Not at all, says Kubie, it's really claustrophobia. He explained for half an hour but I haven't got it yet. I get only that Kubie sees both phobias as an expression of the same anxiety but that isn't enough to explain the pioneers to me, or the plains either, and literature is going to suffer.

Bunny, getting home again, promptly spent some hours casting his cakes. I abruptly realized that he usually does this on changing his environment and the thought struck home that he is probably a DeVoto, he probably has migraines. A happy thought. Well, since the last one I had lasted six days and could not be budged by enough ergotamine tartrate to abort half the sinners of this diocese, I called up Eddie Harding, told him I was fed up, and ordered him to find out something about migraines or find someone who knew something about them. He turned up a gent named Van Stork at Boston City who is spending Rockefeller money on the research and I was all prepared to go see him, but maybe it would be better judgement to send Bunny.[112] ... It's very agreeable to have the kid home again, and these are the blissful days when there's still a hangover from camp, when he straightens his room and makes his bed (and mine too), hangs up his clothes, leaps to get things for you, and reproves you for untidiness. He is skinny and muscular and brown and has been growing. But I must insist, for all your soft words, that the baby is no prize-winner for looks; he looks, in fact, quite a bit like Jim Farley and enough like Bill Barrett to raise eyebrows on Coolidge Hill, and neither of them is my idea of beauty. He has my potato lip and wispy blond hair that's not mine nor anyone's, and Bunny was a cherub from the Florentine Renaissance. I can't send you a picture to prove it for they're all bound in a book. But Mark has not yet bawled out loud and has whimpered only when a nurse got soap in his eyes, and he spends most of his waking hours softly chuckling to himself, with occasional loud peals of laughter. It's a damned funny world to him, and maybe that's the way out. But also this is a Cambridge house, not the summer hotel we lived in at Lincoln, and loud peals of laughter at seven A.M. make me a little less than paternal when it was just 4:21 when the Chittenden fell out of my hand and I began to see Buffalo.[113]

[*handwritten addendum*]

If you've still got it, send me that last letter from Elmer—people keep wanting to read it.

Do you want to read Ch. 1 if I get it into type, say a month from now? Or two months.

Or should we wait for the first 1000 pages?

Yrs

Benny

S & N Bowne
Po'keepsie

[BEFORE 26 NOVEMBER 1940]

Dear Benny,
Well, I didn't get to vote, of course. But if I had, it would have been for FDR for, like you, approximately Dorothy's reasons. Of the two guys, I like Willkie better. I think he's more honest &, in any absolute sense, more intelligent, but I think I detect in him a naiveté that's too dangerous to play with in these times. And, like FDR, I think the coalition of extreme Left and extreme Right was pretty sinister.

SGS on the recent election: "I am DISGUSTED. All I want to do is forget it."[114]

The only other diversion around these parts is Betsy McLean, WKIP's gal-announcer.[115] She lost her job at the radio-station a month or so ago, but landed on her feet as Sterholm's lieutenant for the campaign.[116] Coincidentally she seems to have been sleeping with half the unmarried men in Po'keepsie (I have yet to hear of her sleeping with any married ones) each of whom thought he was the only etc. etc. Of course, the inevitable happened & is happening.... She's an attractive wench, in her thirties, but with dove-grey hair, & the most insinuating voice since Marlene Dietrich.[117]

How is the great migration going?

Kate

I'm sending back F. Pratt & M. Arnold with much thanks, when I can get someone to wrap them.... Is Havelock Ellis's autobiography a big (physically) book?

Bowne

[BEFORE 28 NOVEMBER 1940]

Dear Benny,

I guess you're right: the best poem.

I seem to have missed that warmongering in Michigan piece. Was it the November Easy Chair? That issue of *Harper's* got away from me when I moved on Oct 24th, & I've been trying to get East 33rd to send me another ever since.

Did I tell you that Gladys came up to Po'keepsie to vote?[118] As recently as last Spring she was following this Party line, urging that we forget about Europe & address ourselves to our domestic problems. So you can understand that I damn' near fell out of bed when she blandly announced that she was going to vote for FDR because he had such good relations with England and, after all, that was the important thing.

Later

Harper's finally came through with a November number that looks as though it had spent the last two weeks in Roumania. By God, Benny, I'm proud to know you!

Conversely, if you'd like to read twelve pages of unmitigated eyewash, I recommend the condensation of Anne Lindbergh's "The Wave of the Future" in the November *Reader's Digest*.[119] It made me physically ill. I'd rather have the overnight diabolism of Goebbels than that kind of rot; and you don't need to be a semanticist or a logician to make it look like Swiss cheese.[120]

I've mentioned Hiram Johnson to my trigger-men.... But what will the Senate be like without Henry Ashurst & Key Pittman?[121]

Yours

Kate

NOTES

1. (1888–1965), Harvard '11.
2. A vitamin supplement that Avis DeVoto took for more than ten years after Mark's birth.
3. Correctly, tret, "an allowance of 4 lb. in 104 lb. (= 1/26) on goods sold by weight after the deduction for tare" (*OED*).
4. Nembutal, a barbiturate hypnotic.
5. Joseph E. Garland (1893–1973) pediatrician and author; *An Experiment in Medicine: The First Twenty Years of the Pratt Clinic and the New England Center Hospital in Boston*, 1960; *The Choice of a Medical Career: Essays on the Fields of Medicine*, 1961.
6. The Ice Follies at the Boston Garden.
7. (French) stockholders, investors; persons of private means.
8. Thomas Jefferson (1743–1826), third president of the United States, headed the party freely called Democratic Republican by historians; its main political opposition was the Whig Party, which collapsed in the 1840s and was reborn in the 1854 as the Republican Party.
9. George Washington (1732–1799), first president of the United States, served his first term from 1789 to 1793.
10. James D. B. De Bow (1820–1867), author and editor, professor of political economy, founded *Commercial Review of the South and Southwest*, 1846–1847. Hinton Rowan Helper (1829–1909), author, attorney, and diplomat; *The Impending Crisis*, 1857.
11. The Tammany Society, or Tammany Hall, founded 1789, became in the nineteenth century a principal instrument of New York City politics and remained powerful well into the 1960s, but hardly exists today.
12. Alexander Hamilton (1757–1804), the first secretary of the treasury, was coauthor (with James Madison and possibly others) of *The Federalist*; Washington and John Adams, second U.S. president, were the only presidents from the short-lived Federalist Party.
13. Andrew Jackson (1767–1845, known as "Old Hickory"), attorney, trader, general of the Tennessee militia; seventh president of the United States (1829–1837).
14. Enacted in reaction to the French Revolution then engulfing Europe and enforced between 1798 and 1801, these gave the president power to deport aliens, and to prosecute critics of the national government. The acts were clearly contrary to the First Amendment to the Constitution which guaranteed freedom of speech and of the press and were soon repealed; persons convicted under the acts were pardoned by President Jefferson.
15. Jefferson was president from 1801 to 1809. The Non-Importation Act of 1806, the Embargo Act of 1807, and the Non-Intercourse Act of 1809 severely restricted foreign trade and effectively ruined the shipping industry for several years, but failed to keep the United States from being drawn into war with England in 1812–1814.
16. Federalist representatives from the New England states met secretly at Hartford, December 1814 to January 1815, to consider formal opposition to "Mr. Madison's War," with some extremists recommending secession from the United States. The convention approved several more moderate resolutions but these were mooted after the Treaty of Ghent was signed on 24 December 1814, ending the war.
17. Albert Gallatin (1761–1849), Swiss-born secretary of the treasury after Hamilton; diplomat at Ghent; later president of the City College of New York.
18. Schlesinger (1917–2007), Harvard '38, professor of history at Harvard, later professor of humanities at CUNY; *The Age of Jackson*, 1946, Pulitzer Prize in history; *The Age of Roosevelt*, 3 vols., 1957–1960; *A Thousand Days: John F. Kennedy in the White House*, 1966, Pulitzer Prize in biography; memoir, *A Life in the 20th Century: Innocent Beginnings, 1917–1950*, 2000. He wrote his undergraduate thesis on Orestes Brownson.
19. (1789–1869), attorney and journalist; postmaster general of the United States, 1837–1840.

20. Bancroft (1800–1891), author and historian, known as the "Father of American History"; minister to England, 1846–1849; *History of the United States*, 10 vols., 1834–1874. Brownson (1803–1876), "educator and philosopher" (*ANB*); Arthur M. Schlesinger Jr., *Orestes Brownson: A Pilgrim's Progress*, 1939.
21. (1802–1880), clergyman, writer, critic, cofounder of the Brook Farm Community.
22. This was published anonymously in *North American Review*, 1879.
23. Adolf A. Berle (1895–1971), Harvard '13; author, attorney, braintruster in the Roosevelt administration; assistant secretary of state for Latin American Affairs, 1938; *The Modern Corporation and Private Property*, 1932.
24. John C. Calhoun (1782–1850), congressman, secretary of war, 1817–1825, vice president of the United States, 1825–1832, resigned in 1832 to become senator from South Carolina; secretary of state, 1843–1845. Robert Barnwell Rhett (1800–1876), southern statesman, architect of secession; see the next letter. William Lowndes Yancey (1814–1863), southern politician, Confederate commissioner and senator.
25. The Greenback Party of 1874–1876 sought to erase farm debts by inflating the currency; nominated Peter Cooper for president in 1876. The National Grange of the Order of Patrons of Husbandry, founded 1867 to represent the interests of farmers; the oldest agricultural organization in the United States. The People's Party or the Populist Party, founded 1891 when the Knights of Labor joined with the Farmers' Alliance. The party elected two senators and carried four states for president in 1892; in the 1896 election the Populist alliance with the Democrat William Jennings Bryan split the party, which faded rapidly thereafter. After the panic of 1873, the Free Silver movement supported fluctuation of the price of silver; eventually arrived at a ratio of 16 to 1 in valuation of silver versus gold (Bland-Allison Act, 1878). Mugwumps, epithet for Republicans who supported the Democrat Grover Cleveland for president over the Republican James G. Blaine in the election of 1884.
26. "The West: A Plundered Province," *Harper's* 179/3 (August 1934), reprinted in *Forays and Rebuttals*, 1936.
27. William Henry Harrison (1773–1841), ninth president, known as "Tippecanoe" for his victory in an Indian battle (7 November 1810), died only a month after his inauguration; Zachary Taylor (1784–1850, known as "Old Rough and Ready"), twelfth president, 1849–1850.
28. Abraham Lincoln, sixteenth president, was the first Republican president.
29. The Liberty League was a short-lived organization of anti-Roosevelt conservatives, 1934–1940.
30. The Free Soil party of 1847 opposed the institution of slavery in former Mexican territory; in 1848 it supported Martin Van Buren for president. The Homestead Act of 1862 granted 160 acres, a quarter section, of national land to homesteaders.
31. The Pacific Railroads Act of 1862 chartered the Union Pacific Railroad the same year.
32. 1864; superseded by the Federal Reserve Act, 1913.
33. The postmark on BDV's envelope is dated 9 May 1940, the day before the German army launched a massive attack on Belgium and the Netherlands, with the invasion of northern France soon to follow.
34. Cobb (1815–1868), attorney, governor of Georgia, 1851–1853; congressman; major general, Confederate army.
35. By Charles Oscar Paullin (1868/9–1944), 1932.
36. Zachary Taylor (1784–1850), general during the Mexican War; twelfth president of the United States (1849–1850), died in office.
37. Fifth Column, "a group of secret sympathizers or supporters of an enemy that engage in espionage, sabotage, and other subversive activities within the defense lines or borders of a nation" (*W3*), a term originating with the Spanish Civil War.
38. John Bell Hood (1831–1879), Confederate general. The battle for Atlanta was in July 1864.

39. Pedro de Ampudia (1803–1868), Mexican general, commander of the Army of the North, 1846. Mariano Arista (1802–1885), Mexican general; president of Mexico, 1851–1853. William W. S. Bliss (1815–1853), colonel; private secretary and son-in-law to Zachary Taylor; Fort Bliss in El Paso, Texas, is named after him.
40. (1798–1870), grandson of Ethan Allen, commandant at West Point, 1829; lieutenant colonel in the Mexican War, author, philosopher, and Rosicrucian; *The Doctrines of Spinoza and Swedenborg Identified*, 1846; *Remarks Upon Alchemy and the Alchemists*, 1857; *Remarks on the* [Shakespeare] *Sonnets*, 1865, 1867; *Fifty Years in Camp and Field*, memoir, 1909.
41. Henry W. Halleck (1815–1872), Union general-in-chief, 1862–1864. Jacob Dolson Cox (1828–1900), Union general; governor of Ohio and congressman.
42. Vedas, the oldest Hindu sacred texts, from 1500–500 BCE. Baruch (Benedict) Spinoza (1632–1677), great Dutch-Jewish philosopher. Emanuel Swedenborg (1688–1772), Swedish philosopher and mystic.
43. In 1845.
44. Possibly Dante Gabriel Rossetti (1828–1882), British poet and painter, one of the founders of the Pre-Raphaelite Brotherhood.
45. Possibly Hieronomus Cardanus (Geronimo Cardano, 1501–1576), Italian mathematician, physician and astrologer, a pioneer in probability theory. Parker (1810–1860), clergyman; *A Discourse of Matters Pertaining to Religion*, 1842.
46. Thomas Mayne Reid (1818–1883), Irish-born author, playwright, and Army captain, wrote some sixty books, including novels, short stories, and plays.
47. George B. McClellan (1826–1885), Union general, commander of the Army of the Potomac, known to be hesitant and excessively cautious of his forces; Democratic candidate for president, 1864. Raphael Semmes (1809–1877), Confederate naval commander of the *Alabama*; attorney.
48. Richard Taylor (1826–1879), Confederate general, son of Zachary Taylor; *Deconstruction and Reconstruction: Personal Experiences of the Late War*, 1879.
49. Benjamin Franklin Butler (1818–1893), Union general, governor of Massachusetts, congressman 1883–1884.
50. Raton Pass, between Colorado and New Mexico, south of Trinidad, Colorado. The Breasts of the World refers to the Spanish Peaks (Las Cumbres Españolas), twin mountains in the Sangre de Cristo range of south central Colorado, near the New Mexico border; the name is roughly a translation of the Native American Wahatoya.
51. In southwestern Wyoming at the Continental Divide, south of the Wind River Range, about sixty miles north of Rock Springs.
52. The new title of BDV's *SRL* article (21 November 1936) criticizing the award to Eugene O'Neill of the Nobel Prize.
53. Probably William A. Clark (1839–1925) of Montana, senator 1901–1907, an outstanding art collector; his collection went eventually to the Corcoran Gallery of Art.
54. Bootblack's, probably Felix's, a newspaper shop on Massachusetts Avenue opposite Harvard Yard. Corunna, battle in Spain against Napoleon's Peninsular forces, 16 January 1809, won by England at great cost.
55. A. Alexander Robey (1898–1975), Harvard '20, manufacturer.
56. Winfield Scott (1786–1866), general; Whig candidate for president, 1852.
57. John Buford (1826–1863), Union general.
58. On May 24 the British army, under overwhelming German infantry and air assault, began a massive evacuation of its forces across the English Channel from the French port of Dunkirk, assisted by a flotilla of more than a thousand naval and merchant ships and small boats; by

June 4, some 330,000 men, including 100,000 French and Belgian troops, were successfully rescued in what came to be called the "miracle of Dunkirk." The small covering British force at the Pas-de-Calais was ordered to fight to the death. All of the British Expeditionary Force equipment was abandoned or destroyed.

59. The German army entered Paris on 14 June, after Paris was declared an open city.
60. Upon Mussolini's announcement that Italy had declared war on France and England, President Roosevelt, in a speech at Charlottesville, Virginia, said, "On this tenth day of June, 1940, the hand that held the dagger has struck it into the back of its neighbor."
61. The Matterhorn, on the Swiss-Italian border, 14,692 feet high. Grand Teton, 13,772 feet high, the tallest mountain in the Teton Range.
62. 8,431 feet.
63. Mount Washington, in New Hampshire, 6,288 feet, the highest mountain in the United States east of the Rockies. Mount Ogden, in the Wasatch Mountains, 9,572 feet.
64. Rupert Brooke.
65. The Coronado Cuarto Centennial Commission, 1935–1940, celebrated the tetracentennial of the southwestern explorations of Francisco Vázquez de Coronado (1510–1554) in numerous publications (University of New Mexico Press).
66. In Jackson Hole, Wyoming.
67. Trinidad, Colorado.
68. "Letter From Santa Fe," *Harper's* 181/3 (August 1940).
69. Presumably in *The Irresponsibles*, 1940.
70. Brooke (1887–1915), British poet, killed in the Great War; "The Old Vicarage, Grantchester," 1912: "To smell the thrilling-sweet and rotten/Unforgettable, unforgotten/River-smell, and hear the breeze/Sobbing in the little trees."
71. New Mexico.
72. BDV visited again in 1950, 1953, and 1954.
73. Idaho and Utah.
74. 15 July.
75. According to an ancient English saying, if it rains on St. Swithin's Day it will continue to rain for forty days.
76. The Houyhnhnms in Part IV of Jonathan Swift's *Gulliver's Travels* were a race of intelligent horses.
77. BDV's *Rain Before Seven* was published under John August's name in *Collier's* 105 (25 May–27 July 1940). The title comes from an old rhyme, "Rain before seven/Clear before eleven," which also exists in many other versions.
78. Rock Springs, Wyoming. Winnemucca, Nevada, is actually closer to 540 miles from there.
79. BDV's cousin Beatrice, daughter of Samuel Dye Jr.
80. Wyoming, along the Oregon-California Trail.
81. Lake Bemidji, North of Duluth, Minnesota.
82. Gustave Doré (1832–1883), French painter and illustrator, published Dante's *Divine Comedy* in 1861 and 1868.
83. "Passage to India," *SRL* 15/6 (5 December 1936), reprinted in *Minority Report*, 1940.
84. Dilliard (1904–2002), journalist, editor of the St. Louis *Post-Dispatch*; later university professor, Princeton. During the 1950s Dilliard regularly sent clippings of *Post-Dispatch* editorial pages to BDV.
85. Wendell Willkie (1892–1944), lawyer, Republican candidate for president, 1940; *One World*, 1943.
86. 1920–1932.
87. G.O.P., Grand Old Party, epithet of the Republican Party.

88. Joseph Martin (1884–1968), congressman from Massachusetts; Speaker of the House of Representatives, 1947–1949, 1953–1955; campaign manager for Wendell Willkie, 1940.
89. American Telephone and Telegraph Company.
90. On 24 May.
91. Charles L. McNary (1874–1944), senator from Oregon and minority leader, supported the New Deal, including appropriations for forestry, parity prices for agriculture, etc.
92. Edward L. Doheny (1856–1935), petroleum executive (Richfield Oil); in the Teapot Dome scandal of 1922 and later, it was revealed that he lent money to Secretary of the Interior Albert B. Fall (1861–1944). Doheny was acquitted of bribery in 1930, but Fall, in the first criminal case ever involving a sitting cabinet officer, was convicted and served nine months in prison, 1931–1932. Harry F. Sinclair (1876–1956), oil magnate, was acquitted of conspiracy in 1928 but convicted of contempt the next year; he outlasted the scandal and eventually recovered much of his high standing in the oil business.
93. This initial draft of the beginning of *The Year of Decision: 1846* differs in many details from the published version.
94. John Taylor Hughes (1817–1862); *Doniphan's Expedition; Containing an Account of the Conquest of New Mexico;* [. . .], 1847.
95. Gaius Julius Caesar (102–44 BCE), Roman general, dictator and historian.
96. Wilhelm von Biela (1782–1856), German astronomer.
97. Giovanni Santini (1787–1877), Italian astronomer, professor at the University of Padua.
98. Francesco de Vico (1805–1848) director of the observatory at Rome. Johann Gottfried Galle (1812–1910), assistant director of the Berlin Observatory. On 23 September 1846, following precise coordinates calculated by the French astronomer Leverrier, Galle made the first visual identification of the planet Neptune, whose existence, in a triumph of theoretical physics, had been predicted from analysis of perturbations in the orbit of Uranus.
99. Maury (1806–1873), astronomer and oceanographer; *The Physical Geography of the Sea*, 1855.
100. "An act to promote the welfare of American seamen," known as the La Follette Seamen's Act, 1915.
101. See "Who Are the Associated Farmers?" by Richard L. Neuberger, *Survey Graphic* 28/9 (September 1939).
102. *The Grapes of Wrath*, 1939.
103. In *The New Yorker*, 17 August 1940.
104. Old Bullion, sobriquet of Senator Thomas Hart Benton (1782–1858) of Missouri, who supported the hard-money policy of the Jackson administration. Old Bill Williams (d. 1849), born William Sherley Williams, trapper, guide, mountain man; a mountain and a river in Arizona are named for him.
105. Castro (1810–1860), military governor of California, 1835–1836.
106. James S. Shields (1806–1879), Irish-American attorney, Union general, senator. Cartwright (1785–1872), Methodist preacher.
107. *Thomas Hart Benton*, 1887; *Thomas H. Benton*, 1899; *Thomas Hart Benton: The Story of His Life and Work*, 1903.
108. *Frémont, the West's Greatest Adventurer*, 1928; *Frémont: Pathmarker of the West*, 1939.
109. The Mormon prophet was martyred on 27 June 1844.
110. Harrison Clifford Dale (1885–1969), Wyoming historian; *The Ashley-Smith Expedition and the Discovery of a Central Route to the Pacific, 1822–1829*, 1918.
111. After Anatole Mallet (1837–1919), French designer.
112. Theodore J. C. von Storch (1905–1965), neurologist at Harvard Medical School and Boston City Hospital, a research specialist in migraine headache. See C. J. Boes and D. J. Capobianco,

Cephalalgia 25/5 (May 2005), "Chronic migraine and medication-overuse headache through the ages."

113. Hiram Martin Chittenden (1858–1917), military engineer and historian; *The Yellowstone National Park: Historical and Descriptive*, 1895; *The American Fur Trade of the Far West*, 1902; *History of Early Steamboat Navigation on the Missouri River*, 1903.
114. SGS: Samuel Grant Sterne, KS's father.
115. Poughkeepsie's first radio station began broadcasting in June 1940; first affiliated with NBC, later switched to ABC.
116. Hardy Steeholm.
117. (1901–1992), German-American movie actress and singer; *The Blue Angel*, 1931; *Destry Rides Again*, 1939.
118. Gladys Myer.
119. Anne Morrow Lindbergh (1907–2001), writer, wife of Col. Charles Lindbergh; *The Wave of the Future*, a tract that echoed her husband's isolationist position, was widely perceived as endorsing the inevitability of Nazi rule in Europe.
120. Joseph Goebbels (1897–1945), Nazi minister of propaganda.
121. Pittman (1872–1940), senator from Nevada.

9

1941 LETTERS

Sterne's father, Samuel Grant Sterne, died on 8 January. DeVoto, in between analyses of the home front and extensive prognostication about the war, began writing a John August serial, which became *Advance Agent*, published during the summer in *Collier's*. DeVoto commented further on the naval war. In May, he located a large house at 8 Berkeley Street in Cambridge that would meet all the family needs, including the large, two-room study; as a new resident of "old Cambridge" he found he had much to learn and more to say. He found ongoing dissatisfaction with Shady Hill School, where Gordon DeVoto attended. The personal problems of DeVoto's friends evoked extensive commentary, especially the Murdock-McLaughlin divorces and remarriage and the deterioration of Robert Frost's psyche, and Sterne herself suffered an emotional crisis in November. Following the attack on Pearl Harbor, DeVoto's war analyses resumed with renewed vigor.

Bowne

[AFTER 9 JANUARY 1941]

Dear Benny—Maybe you ought to know that my father died on Wednesday.[1] He was an extraordinary man, especially extraordinary for these times—kind, decent, honorable & a gentleman—& I loved him very much.

Yours,
Kate

32 Coolidge Hill Road
Cambridge, Massachusetts

[AFTER 9 JANUARY 1941]

Dear Kate:

There is no cure for loneliness and loss. I'm sorry. Remember that you have friends. Make use of them. Make use of me—if, in a senseless world, there's a chance I can be of any use to you.

Yours,
Benny

Bowne

[JANUARY 1941]

Dear Benny,

Thanks & thanks for your letter.... You're doing a hell of a lot to save the day by just being...

Yrs,
Kate

Bowne

SUNDAY [19 JANUARY 1941]

Dear Benny,

Did you hear Maynor this afternoon?[2] Quite a voice.... Damn ASCAP![3] This is a time of my life when I could do without hearing Stephen Foster every fifteen minutes.

Everyone is being awfully kind, as you predicted. I've had letters from men who went to school with Dad, who went to college with him, who rowed with him in four-oared shells in 1902 or 1908 or 1915, who worked for him for two years or thirty years. They say all the usual things, & I have the damned-fool conviction that they are all true.... Maybe the words of the man who was his friend from the time they both wore rompers will do as well as any: "He was a most unusual man, honest, able, thoughtful. And I am sure that he never deliberately hurt anyone in his entire life."

My cousin's kid who is a freshman at Tallahassee is keeping a puppy in her room, unknown to the authorities.[4] A feat, I call it.

You haven't a couple of damned absorbing books you'd like to lend me, have you?

Yours,
Kate

32 Coolidge Hill Road
Cambridge, Massachusetts

[8 February 1941]

Dear Kate:
Dodd book coming up—I'd lent it to Dave Owen.[5] . . . Two odd things about it. Howard Mumford Jones (see index) has never been in Berlin and doesn't know anyone of the name alleged. Some months before he died Dodd remarked thoughtfully to Arthur Schlesinger that it had been a mistake not keeping a diary while he was in Germany, he regretted it now.

Why shouldn't you dream of your father? You knew it hurt to have him go away when you were four. You're recapturing the knowledge you had then that he could come back. And a good thing, too; one way or another, one dress or another, we try to heal our hurts.

I think that by the time you've finished it, or sometime in the succeeding six months, you'll decide that Grierson's book goes pretty damn deep. It's very strange and strangely moving—and it's the only explanation in print of the feeling those people had (and they're the ones, the Middle Westerners, who are hardest to explain while the United States was heading into Civil War, during the months and years very much like those we've lived through[)]. It has taught me, I think, a good deal about that war. . . . Everything about it is strange, even the copy which I sent you, which I picked up on a stand some months ago for a dollar and learned, what appears not to be recorded in any of the brief articles about Grierson, that there was an illustrated edition. I sent you that one because it's lighter than the other English edition, which I had stolen for me from a library—it's that rare. There is said to be an American edition too but I've never seen it. Only one historian of the Civil War that I know of mentions the book and he just mentions it, dismissing it as an interesting reminiscence by a nephew of General Grierson. That's the level of Allan Nevins's understanding; for him the only part of the book that exists is the trivial chapters at the end, which bring in Frémont's headquarters. Apparently nobody but me realizes that it is important. . . . Grierson himself was passing strange and dope about him is extremely hard to get. He came back to New York as an old man, about the time he wrote this book, and lived there a while with a curious character who was his nurse and valet and had very probably been his lover. He, the valet, appears to have disappeared, may be alive still, may have died in a flophouse, and when I once thought of reprinting the book I couldn't because he was Grierson's heir and, if still alive, still owned the copyright.[6] Grierson is not, probably, the Francis Grierson whose poetry you know [*handwritten in margin*: a "Georgian"—].[7] He wrote poetry but no one except me knows it. Grierson was his mother's name, his father's was Shepard—Irish aristocrats, as you get from the book. He was put in a boys' choir in a St. Louis cathedral, where it transpired that he had a really remarkable voice. He went to France and had a career, quite a remarkable one, as a singer.[8] He found that he had a gift, which with the mysticism that was growing on him he thought inspired, of improvisation at the piano. He played in this way for his friends, sometimes gave recitals (which he wouldn't take pay for) for musicians, and some command performances for the late Queen and others. Half-way through his life he decided that he had a religious message, changed his name to Grierson, and began to write religious essays. They're in French and for my part they're mystical and that's that. He wrote, in English, a mystical life of Lincoln which is intense as all hell and, again this is me speaking, it's nonsense. But he had decided that his real mission was to write *The Valley of Shadows* and he dedicated himself to the job, of remembering just what he had seen and felt in his boyhood in the Sangamon country. It appears to have fallen into the void. I've read pretty widely in the Civil War and I never ran into it. Shaemas O'Sheel alluded to it in a letter to me about ten years ago, and that's one of the deepest of my literary debts.[9] I think you'll remember the book. You'll probably even find out—I persuade myself that I did—that dialect is merely an awkward phonetic rendering of the real thing. I know damned well you'll remember the Load Bearer and the flight of the slaves.

Did I tell you that someone, possibly the author, sent me a book by Charles Honce?[10] Just about the books he's liked and some amusing things he's run into as a newspaperman. And newspapermen write that kind of book very well. There's a strange little guy up in Montpelier who looks like a half-drowned cat—or, more precisely, a quarter-drowned Fletcher Pratt—and does the publicity and advertising for the Green Mountain Life Insurance Co. Named Crane—maybe you saw, or I told you about, the book he did, me editing violently, for Alfred Knopf, called *Let Me Show You Vermont*.[11] Well, that little runt wrote some sketches about how he used to be an AP editor and they're simply swell, although they also have probably never traveled ten miles all told from the Stephen Daye Press, which published them.[12] Honce's book has done me the service of recalling Melville Davisson Post and Frederick Irving Anderson to me, and deciding to spend a couple of days in bed with the cold I'm still swimming under, a one-man epidemic, I had Rosy bring me all that Widener had of both.[13] Post is an in and outer, I find, and the ones I remembered, the Uncle Abner stories, are his best by a Mormon block. But everything of Anderson's is pure gold, and I've started the library hunting for the two books it hasn't got. Honce says he's still alive and, by God, living in Vermont. Next summer I seek him out.

I'd like to write a piece about Honce's book. I like people who like to read books because they like to read books, and there are damned few of them. I take time out to think of how many of them I know and find that I know you and Avis and nobody else. Me, I was long ago corrupted—I began to read books for Knowledge and I have a sense of guilt when I enjoy anything. Except that I do enjoy technique, which is the payoff why I'll never be a critic.... By the way, do you ever listen to Ted Weeks on the radio? I suppose not, it's at ten-thirty and I hope to God you're asleep by then. But if you ever do, what do you think of his performance? I have become increasingly, over a period of a year, his source-in-ordinary and it slowly begins to dawn on me that I ought to charge a fee, propose a sister act, or set up on my own. My parish priest voice is better than his and I seem to know a hell of a lot more than he does about the things he puts into programs.

I'd write a piece about Honce's book if it were possible to write about anything but the war. God Almighty, what a time! I suppose, really, no more hangs in the balance than hung there when the English reared their brushpiles along the Channel, waiting for Boney.[14] Or when the summer dragged out in Washington, nothing was heard from Sherman, a hundred thousand wounded came up from the Wilderness, the Irish hung Union soldiers and negroes from lamp posts in New York, Indiana seemed likely to cross over to the Confederacy, and some one with a rifle shot from under a tree and drilled a hole in A. Lincoln's top hat.[15] I don't like the subterfuges and unwillingness to see the facts—and yet I know that is the way this country ticks. In February of 1861 Charles Francis Adams was writing a friend that it seemed best to let the erring sisters depart without a struggle, and his sons were saying the same thing a little more elegantly.[16] In February of 1917 I myself believed that the individual was everything and it mattered more that George Moore could write a pretty sentence than that the poor should starve, whatever that line is I'm fumbling for. The young, as I encounter them at least, have shifted to the line of the-army-shall-not-leave-these-shores, which is fairly rapid progress, more rapid than the general feel of things. I took comfort in telling one of them last night, William Carlos Williams's son, that he seemed to be for a twenty-five-year rather than a three-year war. But we get twenty-five years, I imagine, in any case. I should imagine that the war will complete what Roosevelt started, the disappearance of my class. The rich will probably be able to ride whatever tide finally sets in, the poor and the unorganized have been organized and will occupy the position of the middle class as we are forced out. Unless, of course, the rich truly become what my current parallels are designating them for purposes of propaganda, the southern planters, in which case they'll go too. But the real forgotten man is neither Sumner's nor Roosevelt's, he's Jules Romains'.[17] I don't like it. I don't like the war, either. The final ingenuity is that we are forced to cooperate cheerfully with our own destruction. I hate to think what, for instance, education is becoming. It would have been ever so handsome of God to charge a full chromosome with intelligence.

Jim McLaughlin is an adult infant and, for my money, a highly dangerous man. He is half of the reason, Carl Joachim Friederich [*sic*] being the other half, why I got out of the local defense committee. A professor at the Law School, where he is called Tallyho—you know the yarn about the American at the hunt who yelled "Here comes the son of a bitch" instead. Loud, assertive, a natural bully. His conversation is mainly how he played 72 holes of golf yesterday, how at 50 he can still go four rounds with a semi-pro pug half his age, how you weaklings fell out when we were climbing Mt. Washington but I went on and passed scores of boys on the trail, how I could go in and pitch five innings better than anyone they've got and nine innings fully as well as any, how at Michigan I carried the ball on seven straight plays and pulled the game out of the fire. He plays catch with his kids, Bunny's age or a little older, and calls them yellow because they won't stand up to his speed. He called the Harvard boys yellow bastards at a war mass-meeting last fall. He's the only man I know who uses that adjective regularly in his casual talk. Everybody is yellow. Very much like the late Theodore Roosevelt, probably inspired by the same inner dread, and with not a bit more intelligence. In fact, he sometimes tries to take a swing at people who make him mad, and everyone makes him mad. There was some thought that he'd put the slug on me, after a defense meeting at which I'd had to denounce and help vote down one of his idiotic letters, and Ted Spencer and others formed a cordon round me when we went out, but by that time he was being sore at his natural ally, Friederich.[18] Guys like him, like them, are going to rise to the top like a scum, now. Friederich is a German mystic, McL is our native thug and vigilante, and it doesn't make any difference which side such people are on, the net effect is invariably the same. Add in William Yandell Elliott, the Southern fool, and Bruce Hopper, the plain ass, and figure how much sense, hope, reason, or stimulus to action or admiration there is in the defense set-up at Harvard.[19]

Makes a nice note to end on, doesn't it? Well, Mark has his first cold—in fact, I got mine from him—, Bunny is awaiting the mumps, and I have not yet got a serial.

Yours,

Benny

32 Coolidge Hill Road
Cambridge, Massachusetts

[16 May 1941]

Dear Kate:

Things widen out and maybe there'll be a phonograph record in your mail some morning. I told Don Born I had sent you some specimens and he was a little wounded. It seems the spirit is what counts—the act is personal and it's almost a faux pas to appear by the hand of a third party. If I know him, he'll make amends to you. He is also troubled lest you should not understand that the Easy Chair one was done in liquor. I don't quite know how you could fail to.

The shocks you felt were me finally wondering why I subscribe to *Financial World*.[20] And also making an offer for a Cambridge house—at half the assessed valuation. If I don't get it at that price maybe I won't try for another but clear out for Northampton or Vermont, as I should have done years since if I had any character, guts, or common sense. But I ought to get this one, if only for poetry's sake. It belonged to William Roscoe Thayer, who was the first editor of the *Graduates' Magazine* and a historian who spent his life wanting to be a Harvard prof, against the desires of the President.[21] As I remember his stuff about Woodrow Wilson, though, I edge him a bit on common decency, and moreover I have never greatly admired John Hay.[22] But a happy parallel has me talking about Cambridge plumbing in a forthcoming *Harper's* piece on touring New England. God may know why the Cantabrigians like to mortify the flesh and why they especially regard a usable toilet as indecent, but I've never known. The tradition of bad food, hideous clothes, and submarginal physical comfort goes back as far as the first President of Harvard and doubtless beyond. Of my Harvard friends only the house-masters and those who live in apartments have cans I wouldn't be ashamed to send a guest to, and not all of those have as many as two chairs a man can sit in for ten minutes without paralyzing himself from the hips on down. The late Mr. Thayer was not niggardly in the matter of cans. His house has seven of them, three of which are placed in nooks and niches which suggest that he or his relict had some impairment of function, but, even fifty years ago, he must have bought them all at demolition sales.[23] The house is also lighted by gas. It was built for the centuries and every beam is sound and every wall plumb. But the minimum—the minimum initial—expenditure to bring it up to the standard of comfort of a Mormon who is not by nature sybaritic is, by the estimates, forty-five hundred dollars.

The house on that street I'd really like to have is Richard Henry Dana's.[24] It's a honey, it's pure ecstasy. But it's also far beyond my means.

Collier's have not only scheduled John August's screamer before it's finished, which is without precedent, they have also scheduled it so that the first number and maybe the second will be in type before it's finished. Which has Kenneth Littauer calling me up every day or so to implore me for God's sake don't drive an automobile or visit any sick friends. Oh, God, that stuff is fearful tripe, and if you respect the ruins of a magazine writer once fairly intelligent, don't read it.... The consolatory phantasy had come to be a notion that, just for the luxury of it, some day I ought to write an intelligent mystery. That has led to some thinking about the field (did you read a New York prof's article on whodunits in a recent *Harper's*?[25] I couldn't even make out what he thought he thought about them, and I looked up the one he's written and it's unspeakably bad), and some speculation, and a rather astonishing observation.[26] The last is: in the whole area of mystery and crime stories, sexual motivation is so sparse and infrequent that you can practically say it's non-existent. I don't mean sex is out. There's a whole school of gay, presumably gay, bits about the blonde taking off her clothes. Sometimes we get a blonde who sleeps round to complicate the plot. Occasionally, in the hardboiled school, the sleuth sleeps with a blonde on his way to the solution, sometimes even as a step in the solution. Very occasionally the corpse is there because somebody had been jealous of it. The not-lamented Van Dine once suggested that a suspect was a pervert, though she turned out not to be.[27] Chandler, who's one of the best, hurled a whole hive of homos into *The Big Sleep*, and a number of others go just about that far.[28] But neither lust nor perversion nor any of the cognate motives have ever had a really good play, so far as my reading goes, and I bet you that something pretty nice could be done. Yet half the crimes you read about in the papers issue from sex in one way or another, practically all those you have ever taken a genuine interest in, either in the papers or in the behavior of your friends, hinge on some distortion of sex, and at a guess most of the unsolved mysteries that fascinate the connoisseur would be solvable if we had an analyst's notes on the participants. I've acquired a notion that a humdinger could be done altogether in that area. Frustration, distortion, symbolism, expiation—you could work out a honey of a crime and a set of clues and a method of solution that ought to stand the aficionado on his ear. I've been so taken with the notion that I've written to Kubie, asking him if it's as good as I think it is.... It does not appear when I'd get time to turn out this model for the world.

Speaking of sex crimes. My anticipation about Bill Barrett's kids are beginning to be gloomily borne out. Poor Binks, who is basically the most amiable and easy-going eight year old I've ever seen, is higher than a kite, has been ordered out of Shady Hill for the preservation of the class, bullies every kid not big enough to set him on his tail, is on the verge of a half-dozen tics, and practically cannot sit still. I took him and his sister—with Bunny and another kid—to the circus on Saturday, and I had to ignore the other three, a circus not being a desirable place to ignore any kid in, and all but lie down on him to keep him within bounds. In six weeks the poor kid's personality has entirely changed, and I don't see how a psycho-analyst is going to take comfort in the fact.

An English instructor, one of Ted Morrison's stable, named Schorer has done a pretty damn good novel.[29] I'll send it to you when the neighborhood has finished passing it around. There's a run of pretty good Western books, reminiscences mostly. L-B's latest Doctor is not too hot. The Pulitzer awards establish a new low.[30] The Jonathan Edwards is nothing at all: spit at a biography counter and you'd hit six better.[31] The Sherwood play has been inflated out of all conscience by the nobility of its sentiments—and what Sherwood play hasn't been?[32] Leonard Bacon is an amusing and half-witty rich snob who writes pleasant verse.[33] So what about it? As for the history award, I probably predicted it to you. I predicted it, at least, to Paul Buck months ago and

Paul he said the same, and maybe it's just as well I don't run a literary page any more for somebody ought to say the obvious. The meek and mild Arthur Schlesinger has a tremendous drive for power and he dominates every committee he gets on. He's been on the history committee for four years now. Score: Van Wyck Brooks, two pupils of Arthur's, and a book by a friend and supporter of Arthur's which he edited after the author died.[34]... One of the most annoying of my pupils, however, has run into Parkman's Oregon Trail notebook, and I'm in a box.[35] Probably I'll have to collaborate with him in an article but maybe there's a way out.

****

Signifying lapse of four days. Rosy got a cramp, it turned into flu, and my present guess is it's a nervous breakdown. I guess I'll have to get rid of her guy: I once got rid of a husband for her. So the girl we had doing some special typing sprained an ankle. So the serial hit a snag—above remarks even more urgent therefore. So this was the week LaFarge's committee would want a hurry-up job of propaganda. So now I've got a cramp. And meanwhile it looks as if I'm buying a house though the heirs are still stunned by the undersized offer.... But, I mean to say, this is one of those weeks.

I haven't got any ideas about the Hess business.[36] Except that those who think Hitler wasn't in on it can't play on my strategy board. I note Walter Lippmann's great thoughts.[37] Was I slipping, through February and March, when I agreed with him most of the time, or just what?

And I don't know what Washington is going to do. My Navy leak has been so elephantinely secretive for exactly two weeks that I suspect Washington may be going to do something. The wise guys have been saying the Azores—which ought to have been on the agenda for many months—but, if anything in that direction, why isn't the present Vichy *crise* the proper time for Dakar?[38] And, if so, how? Even, who? Probably the British, by a switchover, the Atlantic Fleet taking over some of their run. But you can't hold Dakar short of a full, and fully mechanized, division on the spot. Where's it coming from? Not ours, certainly. In the present state of the press, you couldn't embark anything larger than a company of marines without having it in the headlines before the ramps were up. Not in that direction, at least. It is true that nothing has been carried in the papers about the reinforcement of Alaska, which has been going on for weeks, or about the calling up of the naval reserves, which occurred something over two weeks ago. Every paper in the country knows both facts and hasn't said anything. But an AEF would be different.... You could, of course, take the Azores with just the fleet. But that would bring in the Portuguese question, and you'd have to take Dakar almost at once anyway.

Kiplinger says that the anti-war sentiment in the Middle West is what is holding Roosevelt up.[39] Herbert Agar's gang says the same, and it's a good guess.[40] When

Gauleiter Lindbergh made his Minneapolis speech, nobody whom the local committee would even consider could be found to answer him.[41] . . . *PM*, on the other hand, had it all doped out that Roosevelt's Wednesday speech was to propose Union Now. Which gives you, if you need it, the measure of *PM*.[42] If you want me to guess about the speech of the 27th, here goes.[43] Provided it isn't another of Archie MacLeish's trochaics-and-hydrogen blats, provided it really says something, it will be preceded by consultation with the Sister Republics and a protectorate over Martinique, and it will declare a state of total emergency. There goes DV over the dam. Well, if anything is ever going to be done, now's the time. If anything is to be done, that probably is the most discreet way of doing it. And, as a man who voted for Frank three times, I can remember how often before this I've worked something out to that effect before this, and it turned out to be just another passage in belles lettres.

And I still say, now if at all, and if not at all, then the hell with him, and if not now God help us all.

Yours,
Benny

32 Coolidge Hill Road
Cambridge, Massachusetts

[28 May 1941]

Dear Kate:

Do you need any further material for a possible homily on the particularly cockeyed course and sequence of my personal relations to a cockeyed world? Then reflect on the fact that I would achieve ownership of the dilapidated real estate known as a Cambridge house at this particular stage of the inflationary cycle, income tax, and specialty taxes.

For, by contract, title to pass on July 1, I am, with the Cambridge Trust Company as by no means silent but willing partner, owner of 8 Berkeley Street, together with the fixtures, rights of way, easements, and privileges thereunto appertaining—among the privileges being title in fee simple to an alley way among which St. John's Seminary owns an easement so limited that the City of Cambridge will notify me once a year to block it off and placard it as a private way for twenty-four hours with witnesses.[44] The peculiarly appropriate accident I've already mentioned, its being the William Roscoe Thayer house, appears to be not so accidental after all. For Kenneth Murdock, who once courted a daughter, reared back and said, "My God, you even begin to look like him," and I see what he means. . . . I got it for $750 less than half the assessed valuation, and the bank is giving me a mortgage for all except $500 of the purchase price, and I'm putting $3500 into immediate renovations. (Yeah. I know what comes after that.) So for

$4000 I'm getting quite a bit of a bargain, and I don't care what money is or is called in the next year or so. Berkeley Street runs parallel with Brattle, about half-way to Garden. St. John's is back of me, the Craigie House next to St. John's—there will be no apartments and no traffic so long as present ideas last in Cambridge, which ought to be for another century at least. On one side of me is a Miss Bumstead, a rock of the Episcopal Church, and on the other an amiable loony, Franklin [*sic*] McVeagh, who is the surviving half of identical twins whose better identity died in an automobile accident, he was a tutor at Harvard when I was.[45] I am not as far from Walter Edmonds, on Berkeley Place, as preference would dictate.[46] . . . Time is not so long as we might think. I think of Thayer as a modern, albeit an elder; but it develops that the reason why there are so few electrical connections in the house, and those mainly in the kitchen and the enormous double library which my books will not more than two-thirds fill, is that Mrs. Thayer was afraid of electricity. By any calculation she could have been no more than twenty-five when there would have been electric lights all around her, but there you are. But her timidity took at least two thousand dollars off the estate for her heirs. And also I have to put in a whole new furnace—with even *Time* forecasting an oil shortage.[47]

Well, I won't inflict the concerns of a householder on you. You may assume that Avis has begun crusading. And also, the complicated ceremonials of Harvard College are at work and I am requested to attend Commencement and to sit among what two separate letters of protocol refer to as the dignitaries.

Rosy came to work this afternoon for the first time since I took her home in a state of solution two weeks ago, and I took her home again an hour later. I am not going to practice on Rosy, and the fact that she wouldn't let me while life was left in her is only one, and much the weaker, of two reasons. Somebody ought to practice on her and no one will. She thinks she is just sick. She is sick as hell and has been ever since I've known her, but neither pills nor diet will restore her. She could not bring herself, possibly, to consult the mildest psychiatrist but nothing short of the deepest analysis would do her any good. So, I gather, she is in for no sweet time. Indefinitely. I know nothing whatever about it and she won't ever say anything, but I don't need explicit information. And I gather that I was both belated and superfluous when I remarked to you that I'd probably have to separate her from her guy. I gather—through the pores only—that the trauma, the precipitating cause, is that he removed himself. . . . She has the most turbulent unconscious I've ever scrutinized, and I make no exceptions whatever. The only peace for her is in being somebody's daughter. She succeeds with Perry; I'm eight or ten years too young for her to succeed with me—which is the prime cause of all the hell she has always raised. Meanwhile, the still less perfectly suppressed part of her urge tries to make peace for her as somebody's mother—and never succeeds. Furthermore, she has to mother some unqualified son of a bitch. Compared to her one-time husband, the present guy is a white man, but outside that comparison he is a teetotal son of a bitch to any eye. And eight years younger than Rosy. It makes a pretty problem, why she can sleep only with a son and only with a son who is an ass, a weakling, a rotter, and a bastard. Meanwhile I have the far from happy knowledge that she is certainly in for a hell of a lot worse time than she has ever had before—and thinks that she is on the mend and it was just a stomach upset with some odd psychological accompaniments, which only meant that she was over-tired and probably a little unhappy.

Also a guy on the outskirts of my circle blew his cylinder head last week with a report that could have been heard as far as Poughkeepsie if you had been listening. He's at McLean, and I guess he'll stay there. Unless Gauleiter Lindbergh has it in mind to legalize incest.

Schizophrenic story. The theatrical booking agent who is waked from slumber by a telephone call from the Great Alonzo, who wants a contract and, as the conversation develops, does nothing but talk. Agent's mounting exasperation and hauteur, since he books the finest talent in the vaudeville business, is finally cut off by the Great Alonzo's explaining, "But you don't get the situation—I'm a dog."

****

Hiatus. Meanwhile your letter has come and the President has spoken. I see I wasn't clear about Berkeley Street. No, not Brattle. A good half the houses on it could be bought for what I'm paying or even less, but no thanks. The trucks have ruined it, the assessments are what they were twenty years ago, moths and rust and rats have corrupted,[48] and though one or two of them might have seven privies you can be damned sure that none of them has seven toilets. I've got high enough plumber's bills to pay—I can't run a line to the sewer. A Brattle Street address would delight the soul of an Ogden Goth who was once offered the head editorial writer's berth on the *Boston Evening Transcript*, but I'll look down on their back yards and thank God I don't have to carry water from a well.

Roosevelt only by half, or less than half, cut off the limb I got out on.[49] The only sensible interpretation of what he said is that the Atlantic Fleet has already taken station off the Azores, and in fact I decided several days since that that, or a patrol past Dakar, must be what all the heavy secrecy of my Navy outlets meant. I hope it does.... I hope—and God help us all, this shows how far it has become possible to doubt the administration at such a time—that there is action in that speech, that it isn't just some more oratory. I persuaded myself last night that it wasn't. On the surface, such a speech cannot be backed down from, and, with no returns from Charley Lindbergh or the Middle West, I'd say that any sign of letting down from it would produce a social disaster. So it's go ahead from here. It's got to be. It's got to be fast. And there was at least this much comfort, I could detect not a single trochaic passage in the speech, which would indicate that Archie was not in on the writing. Archie is as swell a guy as it has ever been my fortune to know, and I consider that a mind like his in a high place, in any place where it can influence public policy, is one of the gravest dangers we face. I'm sorry as hell, but I'm going to fall on him from chin to chin at Phi Beta Kappa.[50] I conceive that active war began last night. I think the outcome of it is not in doubt. But I'm also deeply afraid not only that we're going to make some dreadfully costly mistakes but even that we've got to make them and come close to disaster before we can be effective. I've been telling Mollie Brazier that she could go home by midsummer 1943.[51] I think not, now I actually feel the cold water. Say 1945.

Well, as we used to say in '17, see you in Berlin.

The Harvard style goes on and on, and I value my two years on the *Graduates' Magazine* for I couldn't translate the letters without them. The University Marshal writes me this morning—I'm fairly sure—that, as a dignitary, I wear neither the academic dress of the graduates nor the morning clothes of the President and Fellows but a quiet business suit of dark blue, which he advises me to have as light in weight as possible. I have no blue suit.

Yours,
Benny

32 Coolidge Hill Road
Cambridge, Massachusetts

[12 JUNE 1941]

Dear Kate:

I'm no internist. I'm not even one of the psychosomatologists who are busy cutting the assumptions out from under the feet of honest men. Nor can I weakly pander to your egoism in supposing that, even accepting your unconscious as the battlefield of everything from the Wars of the Roses on up to the ultimate visitation from Mars, your most involved moment is faintly comparable to Rosy in her moments of most extreme serenity.[52] You just don't know what you're talking about. God has sheltered you from the unlovelier aspects of unconscious motivation.... Nevertheless I will say that you describe a constellation which all the boys are reporting these days and most of us are periodically experiencing. Typically, you should now develop a conviction that you've got appendicitis, or a stomach ulcer, or cancer of the ~~bowles~~ bowels. (I dunno why I never can spell that word the first time.) I repeat, I'm no internist but I do know that some part, from 1 percent to 99.44 percent, of that constellation is what the boys are calling war anxiety. That you have not got a stomach ulcer would seem to exclude you from the psychosomatologist's rough classification of those who actually get them, mamma's boys and papa's girls who set out to be homo and never made the grade. That the 99.44 percent symptoms haven't localized in that area of you goes a long way to prove that you haven't got a really serious case of war anxiety.[53] So, at least, the faculty tells me. Any war anxiety that doesn't show itself in the abdominal cavity is, they say, about as important as a sneeze.

Unless, of course, you wake up some morning with a conviction that Somebody put cow-itch in your pajamas, or told the nurse to sprinkle something deadly in your food, or stuck a pin in a wax image with your name on it.[54] That also seems to be happening in quantity these days. Let me know and I'll survey the situation again.

As it is, nation-wide statistics under study have already revealed (a) an increase in hospital admissions for appendicitis, stomach ulcer, and ulcer of the gate of the pylorus every time the Reich embarks on some new campaign or wins some new victory, and (b) exactly correlating with it, an enormous rise in the graph of every physician's patients who think they've got the above or cancer of the same region, or gall stones, or something similar. Nobody has yet been willing to philosophize it into a conclusion. But, taking it into account and adding the further fact that actual fluoroscopy shows definite "nervous stomachs" at such times, and the additional fact that I myself have had three stomach ulcers since May, 1940, I'm willing to say that America has bowel trouble.[55] And what else have I been saying for the past year and a half?

Your consultant adds this for your guidance. "War anxiety" is an adequate characterization of these things but only a surface description. Old man Proteus.[56] Just your general and your specific anxieties reactivated by military depression. Besides all the normal burden of fears, dreads, lusts, desires, contempts, and idiocies with which a considerate Providence endowed us all, you have to handle a number of individually specific ones. Notable among them, on the basis of nine years in bed, is a magnification of everybody's resentment of his body. How many times has Herb Waite examined an intolerable eyestrain of mine which didn't exist? Just Papa's vocation utilizing everybody's contempt of the body. It's part of the game, and it's very, very clever in selecting the right areas and organs for symbols. What the hell are the facts behind every intellectual's conception of The Puritan?

There is a Dana House on Brattle Street, two doors north of Craigie House. Craigie House itself is a Dana House, if you want to argue. But the Richard Henry Dana House stands with its long side on Berkeley Street at the point where Berkeley Street makes a right angle east to come out on Garden Street beside the Commander Hotel, and faces the end of Phillips Place (coming from Mason Street and the Radcliffe Library) where it makes a right angle east to join on the angle of Berkeley Street. It's a sweetheart. If the Philistine American public rewarded its artists as Waldo Frank used to ask it to, that would be my house now. Anybody who wants it can have it, for twenty thousand dollars and ten thousand more fixing it up.

I took L. J. Henderson to dinner last night (to a roadhouse in Lunenberg where I achieved the triumph of getting an admission from him that a breast of duck supreme was almost as good as any cheese sandwich he'd eaten in France) and he confirmed the idea that I am a Goth kicking busted statues about the Capitol. I've brought home to him the fact that the Damndest Place isn't what it used to be. What there is left of the old Cambridge is beginning to be reconciled to these things but will still get a deep shock from seeing the Thayer House pass into the hands of a hack (though Basil King lived kitty-corner from it and the author of *Pollyanna* and other emetics just across the street) and, for God's sake, a hack who not only admits he was born in Utah but admits it at every opportunity.[57] I asked Henderson, whose wife was some distant connection, probably through the Richardses, with Mrs. Thayer, who was a Waterhouse, why Thayer never got to be a Harvard professor.[58] He suddenly opened a new continent, a new universe, of speculation by saying, reflectively, Well, he was a good deal of a Tory. So from now on, when I can't sleep, and don't want to take a nembutal, I've got something to do nights, I can wonder what kind of mind would seem Tory to L. J. But, I said, it must have been more than that, during the Eliot regime, and still more during the Lowell regime, it took something between TNT and an act of God to deny the faculty to someone named Thayer. L. J. scratched his head and pondered and finally brought forth the suggestion. Well, he was pretty difficult to get along with. And there's another continent opening up. At that time the faculty included, among a good many, Kittredge, Toy, Whipple, Lyman, Lanman, Kuno Francke, Bierstadt, any one of whom would have been willing, even glad, to give Satan the first three bites.[59] I get the idea, though, for Sprague told me that Thayer spent years lambasting the classics dept with a discovery of his that Helen of Troy was 120 years old.[60]

Paul Buck is more comforting. Paul says, "You'll be bringing the street back. Used to be the most distinguished street in Cambridge. Time was when everybody who lived on it was in *Who's Who*." And I get another slant on the sack of Rome. The house was built as a wedding present for Mrs. Thayer's parents. She was born in it, was married in it, lived out her life in it, and died in it. It is roughly the size of the Commander Hotel and was filled from mansard roof to the farthest corner of the basement with possessions, all of which descended six weeks ago into the reluctant lap of two surviving daughters, only one of whom is resident hereabout.[61] They wanted to get out from under fast.... I know that feeling, it's one of the sickest, most Oh God, is anything worth living for emotions in the world.... When my poor Dad came East to live with me, he stored all the pitiful stuff he and my mother had accumulated. And when he died I simply wrote my aunts, take anything you want and have the rest hauled to the dump.... Some of the stuff was lovely and priceless, like a presentation set of china from Jenner to Dr. Waterhouse, some fine furniture, some correspondence with the great, including, surprisingly, Whitman, a couple of imposing portraits, some good etchings, a couple of Ingres, etc.[62] The daughters took the best of it, and then there remained seven freight car loads of just stuff. They got in dealers and appraisers and prepared to have an auction, intending to give the rest to Morgan Memorial.[63] But there won't be any auction. Mrs. Thayer was survived by a sister, Mrs. Sampson, long a widow, childless, who lives on Brattle Street and is the proprietor of the only electric automobile left in these parts. Besides the Brattle Street house, which is the size of an armory, she has two country houses which, the daughter tells me, she has already filled from earlier estates. And day by day Mrs. Sampson kept adding to the list of things which she refused to let her nieces auction off. Day by day, they kept turning up gone—Mrs. Sampson had sent the chauffeur over to get them. Avis bought a couple of sofas, a pier glass, some chairs, etc. They were duly tagged with her name. One day the tags were gone. The daughter put some more on. Next day, when the daughter got there, the articles themselves were gone. So for several weeks, till now there is hardly anything to be moved. The most footless stuff—old fire irons, a carpenter's chest, a Franklin stove that was falling apart, that sort of thing, tons of it. Most of this was, of course, just the pitiful need of an old woman to hang onto things she knew, things that were part of her identity seventy-odd years ago. But, I think not all of it. Just that there is an irremediable acquisitiveness in the New England soul. I took a carpenter over the other evening for some estimates, and there, in the twilight, down on her knees, was Mrs. Sampson digging up a white lilac.

But the old boy certainly did handsomely by me. He added a library of two huge rooms, with bookshelves to within a couple of feet of the ceiling on eight walls. They will hold so many more books than I've got or expect ever to have that I'm ripping the shelves off one whole wall and having cabinets built along half of another one. For the first time in my life I'll have enough space to work in—I can even keep my jobs separated.

Yeah, and day by day the margin between the assessed valuation and what I'm paying for remodeling grows smaller.

You saw that Alsop and Kintner printed our sub story.[64] . . . Rosy gets no better from what she insists on describing as nervous fatigue. I'll give her one month more and then I'll step in and make her go to a psychiatrist. That's the kind of a God damned brainless fool I am. Yes, and set it down in your commonplace book that a person can live a long time without witnessing any act that calls for as much sheer courage. In the distribution of my estate, perhaps you'd like my Vachel Lindsay drawing. . . . Josephine is legally separated and will be divorced in August. So that's that, and I wonder what the next step in her zeal for self-destruction will turn out to be. There's an unconscious that could get as far as the quarter-finals with Rosy's. . . . Bill Barrett goes to Reno at the end of the month, not, as he contemplated at one time, to honeymoon with his pretty while they get divorces. I don't think Bill has any unconscious. Every time I see him I expect him to whistle on his thumbs and invite me to play some marbles.... Add cash value of dignity. The heating company that has contracted to put in a furnace and system for $1912, cash, wanted a down payment. Being momentarily fed up with this seller's market I said, sorry, not till you start work. They said, contract's off. I said, OK, I know some other heating companies. They said, wait a minute, and went out and phoned my bank and asked who is this DeVoto. They got that far and the bank said, He's Phi Beta Kappa Orator at Harvard this year, and in two minutes it was agreed that I needn't pay a cent till the job was completed.[65] That's as close as I've ever got to the old myth that you could cash a check anywhere if you showed your key.... Having persuaded myself that Harvard and I won't create a mutual embarrassment by going after Brooks and Jeffers on Friday after bestowing degrees on them Thursday, I have now realized that much the better bet is A. MacLeish, the black center of my target.... Isn't all hell due to break loose in Libya?... Bunny has won his first athletic triumph, placing first, as Pythagoras of Samos, in the javelin throw, at Shady Hill College's Olympic Games.[66] Clad in a chiton, which the breeze twitched to show a pair of blue swimming trunks which he had thoughtfully put on so that his white drawers wouldn't show, he stood and was crowned with a wreath of what I take to be catalpa leaves, and damn near bust with pride. I snapped that moment, and I hope to God I got it.

Yours,
Benny

8 Berkeley Street
Cambridge, Massachusetts

[8 September 1941]

Dear Kate:

Neither Wilson nor Howe has come in yet and the former isn't likely to, publishers being what they are, but if either does, you get it. Though I read a couple of chapters of Wilson in the *Atlantic* and thought it was winning of him, but not quite precocious, to have learned about Freud.[67]... As for your dream, I think I see some religious symbols in it, though just what is a [*handwritten in margin:* British] slang term for trunk, dear? And though, as I must have told the class, they aren't symbols till you find out what associations they produce. Associate to that dream for three minutes and tell me fully if not honestly what you produce and I'll take off. But if you must have a psychosis, by all means go paranoid, it's the only one that can amuse the bystanders and I think the only one that can be much fun.... They're pulverizing the fore-brains of the schizos at the Massachusetts General now and I think it's a worse stink than anything in Bedlam, I think it's an outrage and cries to God, and I'm also thinking about raising hell about it in the public prints.[68] In short, it gets me. I recently saw one poor old hag awaiting the operation with her arms bound, and is it supposed that the terror of maniacs doesn't matter? There's an exact and neat classification for your Mrs. A but, the *American Illustrated Medical Dictionary* being in that seventh still-unpacked crate, I can't tell you what it is.[69] Maybe she was going into a premature menopause? Or maybe she couldn't bear the thought of going home? John Murray has a gal in McLean right now who did just that.

Meteorologically, this was immensely the coldest session of Bread Loaf ever. Tennis was out of the question except for a couple of days, there were four frosts, Helen Everitt appeared in a ski suit, and John Gassner's wife brought up a coryza bug at the beginning of the second week which flattened at least fifty and even got past my B Complex.[70] As system, it was better and more equitably managed than ever before, in so much that I got nicked only seven dollars for liquor, whereas I have never before got out of it for less than twenty-five. (One year when I was banking for the club bar, I came out sixty-five in the hole.) That was the doing of Claude Simpson, an accession and a demon pianist.[71] I had a better time than I've had since the early days. We turned up one novelist, a newspaperman named Richards from Memphis, and two poets, one and a half of them being a Pennsylvania Dutchman named Roethke, whom you'll hear from some time, the remaining fraction called, so help me, Cedric Whitman.[72] Constance Rourke, the s—well, try that on your Freud.[73] Constance Robertson, the stirpicult from Oneida who was there as a student some years back, turned up again as a Fellow, with a new novel and a healthy fight with Johnny Farrar, which it was a lot of fun to handle for her, and was much the best looking woman on the mountain.[74] Frances Curtis did a beautiful job. So did Helen Everitt—and it is clear that in the curiously interknit gangs I travel with Helen has succeeded to the place vacated by Kay Morrison, all us males are from twenty percent upwards in love with her. Precedent went all to hell and Dick Brown did not twine a vine leaf in his hair till the last night and then, the bastard, locked himself in his room.[75] And I entered on my glory, gathered the harvest of a pious life, and got the Garter at last, for Chester Kerr, up there to talk to an author, remarked quietly and with complete conviction, "Benny, you are the scourge of publishers."[76] Johnny Farrar, he says the same.

But it is the screwiest place, and this year was no exception, and I think maybe somebody ought to tell Ted how babies come. The children's librarian from Detroit who was making a big play for Raymond Everitt last year when I went up for a lecture, but amiably paused in it long enough to prospect me, was this year, or I don't know euchre, wrapped in the arms of a hard-visaged and very rugged middle-aged woman also from Detroit. I told Ted this winter she meant trouble, and I was right, but Ted has explained the trouble on other grounds quite satisfactorily—to him. He never sees a sexual motive till it's confessed in court and then tends to scout it as probably misunderstood. When the poet Cedric Whitman went off to Montreal, drunk, for three days, with a long-suspected who is some six times as burly as he, Ted thought of it as an undergraduate prank. I dunno what he'll do if he goes walking by the brook some night. Meanwhile he looks grayer and more harassed and more beaten, and has no suspicion at all that there is such a thing as psychical adultery, though he should have read the gospel. I am sorry—the hell I am, I rejoice with a bitter zest—to say that Frost has gone a hell of a lot farther down the path I have frequently described in these notes—and predicted to the last comma three years ago. I'm damned if I can look on him any longer as tragic or damned, or even paranoid. He has just become what I didn't believe in when I was younger, an evil man, a man of great evil. When I see him making a holy show of himself—and giving the whole show away to anyone sensitive enough to see it, and there must be more than the four I know about—I no longer wince on his behalf, or mourn for my own beliefs, or sadden on behalf of literature. I think of the lives he has ruined completely, a sizable sum by now, and the greater sum of those he has warped and twisted, and the almost innumerable wounds he has inflicted—and, by God, I gloat.... At Bread Loaf Louis Untermeyer—a white man, as white a man as there is and by far the best friend and stoutest champion Frost has ever had—told me he could take no more of it and didn't intend to. Over a period of some seven years or more, now, I've seen Frost practicing destruction on Louis, and I don't blame him. I didn't tell him the red-fuming nitric acid Frost has poured over him in my private hours with Frost, but he told me some part of the same about me in his privacies with Frost, and it was no news nor novelty, though I confess I hadn't figured on his jealousy of Mark Twain. Louis boiled over to me in a moment of intolerable bone-bruise which extended to several hours of taking our back-hair down, I greatly pleased to be confirmed and he grateful to find that he wasn't having hallucinations. I suppose we have both suffered impairment in that long before I knew Frost I had predicated much of my warfare against intellectuals on the assumption that art need not be neurotic, as demonstrated by Frost, whereas Louis has fought the battle of poetry all over the United States on much the same belief. But, in the final assay, we both win since neither of us has been devoured. What most disgusts me is that Frost now flagrantly uses the anti-Semitic weapon against Louis, and what most disgusts Louis is that, like Unser Charlie, he can feel no emotion against the Nazis. His Phi Beta Kappa poem ends up with a striking but rather coy line, "I have had a lover's quarrel with the world." The truth is that in his entire lifetime no one's pain except his own has ever had any reality for him, and the personal pains that have most distressed him have been the unlovely ones, all of them rooted in envy and resentment. The death of a world has never meant anything to him but the chance that someone might use it to diminish his public reputation. At B L my evening entertainment consisted of a lecture on Manifest Destiny based on my book. Frost saw a chance to take a crack at me and by his familiar in-seven-turns-oblique technique began to show that he, I, and the Nazis all had the same notion about world domination and how right we were, since the future belonged to the U.S. Three years ago I would have submitted and held my peace; as little as two years ago, I would probably have tried to turn it aside so that he need not expose his nakedness to the world. This time I wasn't having any, so I came out in front to meet him and in the end had him loosing his once-gnomic perceptions to this effect: we must first let Russia be beaten, for we don't hold with Russia, then we must let the British be beaten, for they have always stood across our path and despised us, and when those two are done for then we can step in and be the world. He felt masterful and male till he saw what had been done to him, the audience was bewildered as hell but worshipful of greatness, but at least Louis and I felt content.

Meanwhile one shattered soul in the center of all this, Kay Morrison, was pleasanter to me than she has been for some years but is strained, empty, and forever changed. What most fascinates me in the whole set-up is a question I probably will never get answered in full: how much does she consciously understand what has been happening? And the least pleasant prospect of the years ahead is the knowledge that I'll see her get the point bit by bit. She has saved a great man for the world—or for some additional years of querulousness, envy, fear, and destructiveness. She has helped a once great talent keep within the legal bounds of sanity, so that its own evil has not had to submit to any restraint and may now dissipate through aimless malice and spite into the early stages of senility. She has become the last symbol of the unconscious phantasy of the greatest American literary man of the generation. She has eased—a little—some of the innumerable guilts of the family he destroyed and the wife he killed. She has, moreover, stood symbol of an impotent desire, animating the ashes of a great man in psychic intercourse. She has slipped into fulfillment by means of that fictitious desire—out of wifehood with a small literary man who, of course, could never have been great or even large. She has also found again the image of the Dean of Washington Cathedral who was too much her father.[77] She is the psychic mistress of the greatest man she ever knew or ever will know, and doubtless that's very fine, if cold and, to the exterior view, obscene. And, quite without being aware of it, I'm sure, she has poisoned one of the decentest guys that ever lived, and poisoned herself also, with a bane that may be precious but will kill slowly, over a long time. Who the hell is she, now? Only the virgin mistress of an envious and impotent old man—who once was sweet and kind and warm and labored decently with the hard conditions of her life. She is not sweet nor kind now, and she's cold as hell, and if she doesn't feel the self-accusation in that coldness, your commentator does. The bastard will be dead eventually, and what then? At best, she'll have the best to make she can of a once-loved husband who never will understand the kind of castration she's inflicted on him, and of a family already too heavily stamped with that image. At worst, she'll go on venerating the dead image of the great. And maybe that isn't the worst for the rest of us, who, at last, will be able to think it's funny.

In 1935 his flagellae reached for Avis and me. Avis is too tough and I know too much. So he moved on to the Morrisons and there it has stuck.

Well, the hell with it. Helen and Frances, Fletcher Pratt and Louis—that's a good enough gang for anyone. This year there was a distinct addition, one Phil Cohen, radio gent extraordinary from the Library of Congress.[78] A good guy. I hope to hear more of him.

I should have said, back some space, that the manic seizure of your Mrs. A, whose exact name I continue to forget, has probably had fore-runners, if you dig in deep enough. Probably also she'll snap out of it. Unless, that is, my second diagnosis is right and home is worse than transitory mania.

My favorite British gal, Mollie Brazier, who has been working with Bob Schwab on brain waves, has now taken an additional job with that wintriest and most punctilious of Beacon Hill bachelors, Henry Viets, a research on one of the rarest diseases, something called myasthenia gravis pseudoparalytica.[79] Exclamation point. Viets has the only clinic on it in the world and has now run a series of about eighty cases. Two ways into it have so far suggested themselves: there is a drug which will take the patient (if used early enough) over the danger period, which ends at about the age of forty-five, and females who lose it entirely within forty-eight hours of becoming pregnant and get it again within forty-eight hours after delivery. The last, obviously, is a flagrant sign post. Which is where Holy Church enters. Lately a woman came back to the clinic in a very bad way, so far gone that the drug was useless. Viets had her record and twice, during pregnancy, she had recovered completely. He said, What ho, she'll have to get pregnant, after which we can give her the drug. She was too far gone to get pregnant in God's way, so he proposed artificial insemination. Her husband thought he could collaborate but, at the last moment, balked and insisted on asking the priest. Father O'Toole said sure, go ahead, but had a night to think it over, called up just before the operation (process?) was to be performed, and said, no, the Church forbade.[80] The gal died promptly. I still think it would have been OK if they had phoned the Bishop. But I'm trying to figure out what the bastard's grounds were. It is certainly not the sin of Onan, nor can I see that it is any closer to a sin against nature than a good many practices permitted in the hog latin of the manual for confessors that I once sweated out.[81] If you know the doctrine he thought he was applying, clear up my confusion.

I go broke about three hundred dollars short of completing the desirable renovations at 8 Berkeley Street, and the living room rugs and downstairs curtains must await dividends or unscheduled lectures, but I'm damned glad I'm in this place. My soul shakes its claustrophobia and comes out of its hoops. I'll walk enough from room to room to keep in condition. I have by no means finished with the big double room I'll have to get accustomed to calling a library, but already the vista is soothing to the eye. All my reference books will be in reach of this desk, there are places for my maps, the good Mr. Thayer's vast mahogany writing table holds my jobs and keeps them separate—I've got a place to work in at last, and maybe I'll work in it. Transferring Mark has proved no problem; we conditioned him by bringing him over a good many afternoons and letting him play in the room he was to sleep in. Bunny has the kind of set-up I've always wanted him to have. I have only a little impeded the defence program, with zinc, copper, aluminum, and chromium. God knows how the heating system will work, or what it will run on, but it's in and would have been only a little cheaper if done in gold plate. Burn a candle for me: I'm back on the frontier again and would like to stay there for a while. By the way, did you say you wanted to read it in takes, as finished, or not?

Grapevine says that leases for Natal, Pará, and the Galapagos are signed. Says that flatly and intimates, if I know the code, that bases in Ireland are being occupied; perhaps Africa also, though I can't imagine where, unless Liberia, which, my maps show, has no harbor big enough for the Navy to make much use of. My colleagues have decided that Roosevelt is a non-interventionist and prophesy that he will not take us in as long as he thinks the British will hold out. This represents a complete about-face on the part of said colleagues, and as for me, I still think that the tempo is accelerating and he's taking us toward a foreseen end as fast as the country, complicated by the problem of his charm which you mention, will permit.... Fletcher Pratt was with the gang who went to Iceland, in fact his pal the Admiral sent him back on a mail destroyer so he could keep his Bread Loaf engagement, and the destroyer ran spang into the Churchill-Roosevelt meeting, having been tuned on a different wave-length when all shipping was warned away.[82] On appearance, it was ordered to stay put till 12 hours after the assembled navy had left, and there was Fletcher, the only newspaperman in the world who knew what and where, unable to send out a story. Anyway, that convoy consisted of five ships, transport and supply, and it was protected by a battle wagon, two first class cruisers, an air-plane carrier with the correspondents (the *Wasp*, which I watched growing at Quincy), and a squadron of destroyers. It seemed sufficient. Fletcher says they had a submarine in their sonic ear all of one day and were aching to drop eggs on it, would have done so if it had come within reasonable range.... The darkest word he has is that the Navy thinks His Majesty's navy is falling off. Don't keep the ships up, were badly outshot by the *Bismarck*, have lost a good deal of their effectiveness. He says the *Illustrious* was able to get only four planes in the air, after a warning that allowed twice as much time as an American carrier needs to shoot its full complement aloft.... The local transients from the British Navy have just had hell bawled out of them, officers, ratings, and seamen, for spilling so much information, and no wonder. With two drinks every British officer I've met becomes just as reticent as any Yankee storekeeper. Finally, after more trouble with the police, they took over a CCC camp in Townsend, where they have a countryside full of ex-maidens by now—and have recently been joined by Free French uniforms from the biggest submarine in the world, which recently made Portsmouth.[83] ... With Perry Miller, Kenneth Murdock was here the other night, drinking deep, and I'll return to that matter later.

Yours,
Benny

8 Berkeley Street
Cambridge, Massachusetts

[30 September 1941]

Dear Kate:

There is no escape from God's ellipse, and if, as the chaplain of Herman Baker Post, No. 9 of Utah, I got a low, uproarious pleasure from conducting funerals of dead buddies, I paid for it conducting Lee Hartman's funeral.

... If you had any notion that Cambridge is the one place in the New England culture that dissents from the New England fiat that property is gentility, dismiss it. I am now genteel, and no one doubts that, in succeeding to the possession of 8 Berkeley Street, I have become one of the elect. I have been bidden to represent the arts at a Good Neighbor dinner of my good neighbor Sarah Wambaugh—with the result that I now ache to get her and Dorothy Thompson into a sixteen-foot ring and see who will get the first word, and the last.[84] I have had the sharp pleasure of catching Jim Munn in, as it were, *flagrante delicto*,[85] pumping Bunny. I have been called on by an amateur cartographer and consulted about the errors in local bench marks. I have been called on by a series (and one which obviously projects into the future as far as thought can reach) of female fragilities, tottering on two canes, oozing reminiscences of John Fiske, soliciting my thoughts on the decay of the clergy, and, most of them, bearing manuscript essays on The Dread Utility of Toothache which I will please get into *Harper's*.[86] I have been called on by a retired physician who once drove to Mexico in, by my clock, four hours and forty-five minutes. I have been called on by a woman who wants me to devote my leisure hours to making Braille books for the blind poor, by one who converses with the dead, by one who wants me to extinguish the impudence of modern young women, by one who invites me to take up morris dancing in a Berkeley Street group, by one who is cognizant of a Popish plot in the White House. I have received a copy of the history of Berkeley Street, by a Miss Allyn dead these forty-five years, whose dear papa wrote the Latin grammar—a history which I will send to you if you will promise to live purely for a week, eschewing dreams of phallic objects in the waters or elsewhere.[87] (Box is a British term for trunk, dear.) I have been asked to take each side of the dispute over the right of way of St. John's which I think I've already hinted to you. It is assumed, God knows why, that this baptized member of the Holy Roman Catholic Church of Jesus Christ of Latter Day Saints belongs to the Church of England. That may be a snoot at my ancestors, as not possibly of the *Arbella*, or it may be a great tribute to me as obviously of Tory Row.[88] I have been invited to join a Shop Club, contribute money to a fund for the alleviation of the hardships of dogs in England, to end forever the immorality of modern literature, and to devote one-fifth of the estate I am assumed to have somewhere to Bundles for Britain.

And I can't take it. It would not become one of my years to exhibit gerontophobia, but I'm going nuts. Between men now in their forties and men now in their seventies there exists a greater gap and cleavage than between any two other generations in recorded history. And, in the Cambridge culture, that gap is doubled and redoubled and doubled again. It has always been possible to be amused by Cambridge gentility, at a distance. It isn't going to be, close up. I sit talking to them, or rather listening, and my manners are as courtly as any ever taught in Mormonry, and any habit or action of my mind, if exhibited to them, male or female, would pain, distress, and horrify them. Or terrify them. You should hear one Mrs. Holbrook explaining, with the greatest sincerity, that worry over the possibility of pregnancy gave her generation character, but there is no character in today's young wives. What can you make of it? How can you enter in? It is assumed that the owner of some square feet of over-assessed Cambridge earth breathes that air. It is assumed that I have no coarsenesses, no convictions, no ideas later than 1870, no beliefs not sanctioned by Piggy Elliott, no mind outside the cobweb of amenities that were stale when the first Peabody got out of here to seek the more robust, more virile London of the young Queen. They never had anything that I value in life and there is gone from them everything but a sweet awareness of a sweet, intangible propriety which somehow compensates for the lack of all sap, juice, tang, color, and strength. I can learn from them to remember that the literary I have made a career of ridiculing were, after all, rebelling against something, though, on the showing, God knows why.... The mould has been here always, I think; certainly it was here when Francis Parkman and James Russell Lowell were young. They hated it or derided it: Howells adored it with, he actually tells us, an actually palpitating heart. But in those days, as now, Harvard was the living thing round which the paper lace of Cambridge gentility was stitched to fit if not to decorate. In those days, Harvard renewed itself from Boston; now, from the provinces.... But the Cambridge I exist in is Harvard and I can't take the other Cambridge. I have always suffered from a phobia of giving unnecessary offence but I'm afraid I've got to make myself unequivocal. Or I'll be tapped for the Society for the Preservation of New England Antiquities.[89] Or preserved by it.

Probably the association is inevitable.... Did you ever read a novel of not much fame even in its day and its day [was] when you were in diapers, called "Nuptial Flight"?[90] I couldn't for the life of me tell you anything about it except that it was amusing and that it dealt with the fact that sometimes, in the season called youth by the literary, people do amusing things just for the hell of it and enjoy doing so. There recently appeared in Cambridge, bringing her son to settle him in Harvard, a pleasantly dressed matron of forty-five who, I am happy to say for my own taste over the years, still possesses as neatly sculptured a pair of legs as this year's Miss America can possibly have. So she phoned me, and I took her and the boy to a select bar and had a drink with them and we talked amiably for an hour and the boy will bring me any knotty problems that may arise. I may have alluded to her in the period of this correspondence when I was writing my autobiography as a Legionnaire. In those days she was a contralto and could tear your heart out by the roots, or I thought she could, which did quite as well. And for a while we enjoyed ourselves and she moved on to more promising fields and I fell hard for Skinny Browning and what not. So it became known that she wasn't going to study singing any more but was going to get married, as in fact she did, with what issue I have now seen. But it occurred to me that it would be fun to see if I could get her to postpone the wedding long enough for me to spend the night set for it with her. So I could and did, and somehow that was a hell of a lot of fun then and seems so now, though all I can remember about it is the fact... Good Christ, Kate, I get senile.

Frost has also bought a house in Cambridge. He has always been spacious in the possession of dirt and gets more so year by year, but in Vermont he walks his boundaries when he buys. And in Cambridge, as I have the best reasons to know, the property lines bend, dip, swoop, and turn back upon themselves; one needs a lawyer and a surveyor as well as a conveyancer. He ordered his cellar filled with coal. It began to be delivered and the truck had difficulty getting the right angle for its chute. So Robert, ever helpful, went out and chopped down some of his hedge and had the truck drive down between the hedge and his neighbor's line. So a virago was on his doorstep next day, one of the fragilities I complain about, and a lawyer wrote to him forbidding trespass and pointing out the law. When he beefed to me I could only tell him that, in my experience, good fences make good neighbors.[91]

I don't know who succeeds to *Harper's*. I suppose Fred Allen and, on that supposition, I put in his hands my resignation from the Easy Chair, to reject or accept as he may see fit.[92] No editor should be bound by the commitments of his predecessor and it's known to me and a good many others that Fred thinks my stuff is lousy. On the other hand there must be some who feel as I do, that unless Lee's shoes are filled more adequately than Fred can fill them, there'll be another name, presently, on a list honorably headed by *Scribner's* and the Century. Yes, and the *Mercury*. Fred has all the right thoughts, but so solemnly. God help us all.

Yours,
Benny

Bowne

[EARLY OCTOBER 1941]

Dear Benny,
Well, it was quite a Series. And I wonder what future generations will make of the fact that the start of Hitler's Grand Offensive went almost unnoticed in the furor over Mickey Owen's ninth-inning fumble.[93] . . .

Alec Cummins, the huntin', shootin' rector of Christ Episcopal Church (he used to be president of the Pleasant Valley Rod & Gun which came to be known as the God & Run Club) has been talking for two years about the impending (Oct 26th) 175th Anniversary of Christ Episcopal Church, "the oldest church in the mid-Hudson Valley." So, last week, Joe Jones of the Dutch Reformed Church announced that his church would celebrate its 225th anniversary on October 22nd. Alec furiously alleges that the D.R.C. was formed by the union of two earlier churches, both of which lost their charters in the merger. Joe calmly alleges, with some reason, that Alec is splitting hairs. What fun for the spectators!

A letter from Jimmie (Jacqueline) reports that, after two months at the shore, she's so burned that, instead of saying, "Hello," people now greet her with "How!"

From the July *Punch*:[94] a) Tommy writing home, with palms & pyramids in middle distance: ". . . I can't tell you where I am, but there are Pharaohs in the bottom of my garden . . ."[95] b) RAF captain drops a pawn behind the enemy's lines on a chessboard, by means of a tiny parachute.

Yours,
Kate

8 Berkeley Street
Cambridge, Massachusetts

[7 December 1941]
Sunday—6 PM

Dear Kate:
This is the evening when I was going to write to you. I gather you won't wonder that I'm not. You'll be listening to the same bulletins.

I took Bunny to see a movie—Sunday afternoons are supposed to belong to him. This Rita Hayworth–Fred Astaire thing, with a March of Time about the New Order in America.[96] A Harvard boy next to me whispered that a radio flash had announced attacks on Hawaii & the Phippines [*sic*]. I thought he was pulling my leg. So he wasn't.

First guess: the attack on Pearl Harbor must be too big to keep the fleet covering the Hawaiian I's—and won't. I can't believe the *West Virginia* is sunk, as they're still reporting her.[97] Second guess: they couldn't have done better by us. Of all ways for it to begin this is incomparably the best for us. I wonder how much Nye-Wheeler & Unser Charlie would sell out for tomorrow?[98]

First time I ever wished I didn't have a family. I'd like to take my leaky & jittery chassis into this somehow. Probably I will, at that.

Don't get ideas, darling. I'll be writing you pretty soon.

Yours

Benny

8 Berkeley Street
Cambridge, Massachusetts

[14 December 1941]

Dear Kate:
Well, Cambridge has had its first evacuation—from the village of Coolidge Hill. Taisybelle[99] Hale (and you will please not challenge that name, for it's authentic) has convinced her husband Rufus, withdrawn her three kids from Shady Hill University, and packed the family off to Marlborough, New Hampshire, for the duration. No bombs, she believes, will fall on Marlborough, but I have sent her a postcard pointing out that the town is on the Ossipee fault line. She has long been a favorite character of mine. A daughter of the House of Harper, she was immensely interested one night when it came out in the course of my conversation that Mark Twain was a pseudonym, that the great man's name was Clemens. Rufus is also something of a pet and I number the collapse of his dreams, now, among the fragments of a world blown to hell. He has lived for only one great day, the day when he should see his son Houston run out on Soldier's Field, a member of the Harvard football team at last. The old world was full of rue, though, and

it wouldn't have happened. We used to see Houston practising his future from dawn to dusk all year round, with Rufus coming out to help as soon as he got home from State Street, but Houston would never have made the grade. He had whatever the right name is for the brittle-bone condition you sometimes read about. Week by week, he snapped knuckles, cracked femurs, and broke tibias in three. Put him in a neighborhood softball game and you could hear bones crackling like popcorn.

The Army has erected a listening post with range-finder and searchlight right next to Shady Hill, but, alas, on the playing field of its neighbor, Browne & Nichols.[100] The B & N kids have been taken for jeep rides and SHU abides in humiliation. There are similar posts and a good many AA guns all the way down the Charles, presumably for the defence of the Watertown Arsenal and MIT. In fact—and I violate no military secrets—there are nineteen AA on the Tech athletic field. One is not permitted to approach closely but from a distance they look to be of a calibre hardly great enough to embarrass a kite.

We are full of air raids and, though I'm signing up to be a warden (nobody seems interested in making anything else of me), it appears that we are making all kinds of mistakes and false assumptions. It will be a long time before we'll have to defend London here. It does not appear where mass attacks by bombers are to come from for quite a while yet, and meanwhile a blackout is already proved to be only less damaging than a large-scale raid. What I fear most is the pattern of panic-derision-apathy that is all too American and, in its first stage, extremely New England. Last Tuesday's scare appears to have been an honest false alarm, the Navy at Portsmouth spotting either some of its own planes or some of the Army's (my information fails here) as hostile.[101] It scared a hell of a lot of people; it enraged even more. Both are bad. I do not see why the formula requires us to be hysterical while making intelligent preparations. The boys who are talking about a "token raid" are OK. I don't doubt that there'll be something of the sort somewhere along this coast, and before long, at that. The last time I saw Fletcher Pratt, who is supposed to know about such things, he said that Germany is known to have one carrier completed and at least one more on the way.[102] Possibly the loss of half your carriers is a cheap price for the results of a good U.S. scare, but if I were Herr Raeder, I think I'd try to do something besides scare Boston or New York.[103] Well, there's Pratt & Whitney at Hartford and its equivalent in a good many other places.[104]

Twenty thousand people were supposed to attend the "Unity" meeting in Cambridge, Thursday. By my estimate, four hundred showed up. The difference did not appall me, as it did my companions. After twenty-four years, I think, we have learned to distinguish between morale and hysteria and a good many million Americans know that oratory will not win the war. Apathy toward Four Minute Speakers would be a valuable apathy and I hope we get it by the long ton. Otherwise it was an experience for the analyst of public character. And it was topped off by a band from the Cambridge Fire Department that was beyond belief. When they started to play "The Caissons Go Rolling Along," the audience stood up in the belief that it was the National Anthem, and no wonder.[105] When they finally played the N A the cornets and the trombones were in different keys. I lasted through five out of six speeches and then came home, probably mortally affronting Holcombe, who was the sixth.[106]

Well, let's expert. You have to begin by guessing. I guess that the brown brother will not get either Singapore or the Philippines.[107] We should know about that pretty soon, for if they don't get them in a month at the outside, they won't get them at all. If they fail to, the Pacific war, I judge, will then assume the form long designed for it, a war against communications, and the brown brother will have to go back to his defensive positions. That is the overall expectation, and I do not honestly see, on the present basis of public knowledge, how anything else can happen. The affair at Pearl Harbor, I judge, has added to the plan, but I don't think it has fundamentally altered it. The headlines which tell us that the Jap fleet "turned tail" off Hawaii (and just why are the announcers calling it Havaii?) only told us that the Jap command knew its oil, both literally and figuratively. The most authoritative of my group of those authoritative sources that the President warned us against says that eighteen ships were sunk or put out of commission at Pearl Harbor. No way of knowing, but at worst I don't think that adds anything except time. What may alter the basic war there is what nobody has seen fit to talk about: how much shipping have the Japs picked up or sunk? If it's a sizeable total, then the time added is considerable, and it's quite possible that it's considerable enough to change everything. If so, then the war against communications, which is the whole thing, gets changed into a sporadic, not a steady, war. Which would be just too damn bad.

Unquestionably the allied war is proceeding. The submarines are out. So are the destroyer squadrons. I can't imagine where the bombing squadrons are massing but they're certainly massing somewhere. A convoy must be under way for Hawaii and the skies westward from San Diego must be full of planes. We should presently begin to hear of Jap ships knocked off in the North China Sea and westward of there. Just where Alaska fits into this God knows, but a development far greater than anyone realizes has been going on there for well over a year.[108] But we won't hear of any major offensive for a hell of a long while yet, which is clearly the point of Pearl Harbor. Meanwhile, if we do hear of successful reinforcement of the Philippines, we're all right.

The *Grossgeneralstab*[109] has certainly got something in process of hatching. Something in addition to the Spain–North Africa stuff that my fellow experts have been talking about for weeks. I dare say something will blow loose in South America, but just what I don't dare guess. I will guess, though, that we'll take, possibly have taken, the

Caribbean positions I've been doggedly prophesying about all these years.[110] Curaçao is still the best bet, and Martinique only a little way behind. And, for a wild one, I wonder if the mail address of the First and First [*sic*] Marine Divisions will not presently be Cape Verde, by invitation of Brazil?[111]

Will Hitler get the French fleet?[112] Wouldn't you?

I have no idea what my relation to all this will be. My job is obviously to support my family, if possible—and God knows what will happen to the serial business—till some obvious use for me shows up. I'm shoveling all the coal I can, currently, on the book. I don't know just why, but again I don't know why not. If I get to finish that, it will at least be finished, though that doesn't mean anything, either, beyond an impalpable psychological vindication. I'll join the various activities round Cambridge, patrolling Berkeley Street, doubtless from eleven to three with a blue flashlight and a pair of rubber gloves, and otherwise fanning the home fires. Archie will have none of me in Washington and I won't be in Washington, clearly, unless he passes on to still more resplendent uses. Just as well, no doubt, for I'm no expert, though more an expert than Archie by a Mormon block. I've sent in enlistments to Jim Landis, who heads OCD in Massachusetts, and will get one off this week to the Governor.[113] Dunno if either one can use a pen.

Please don't send me a Christmas present. Buy a stamp or give the equivalent to some service or relief organization. I had planned to send you the new Huck Finn, which won't cost me anything, but George Macy has let me down entirely this time and it won't be ready till at least February. Just for the hell of it I'll send you a carbon of my lectures. They're hastily done but you ought to have some amusement from some of them.

Yours,
Benny

NOTES

1. On 8 January 1941. An obituary appeared in the New York *Times* on 9 January: "Samuel G. Sterne, president of the S. G. Sterne Sign Company, 609 West Forty-third Street, died early yesterday at his home, 1085 Dearborn Road, Palisade, N.J., after a long illness. He was in his seventy-first year. Mr. Sterne was well known in the New York area as an oarsman for many years and was a founder and past president of the Lone Star Boat Club of New York. He leaves a widow, Mrs. Stella Kisch Sterne, and a daughter, Katharine." The death notice on the same day: "STERNE, Samuel G., beloved husband of Stella Kisch and devoted father of Katharine G. Funeral from his late residence, 1085 Dearborn Road, Palisade, New Jersey, Friday at 10 A.M." In the *Times* of 10 January: "The Board of Directors, officers and members of the Lone Star Boat Club announce with deep sorrow the untimely passing of its founder, honorary member and former president, Samuel G. Sterne, and extend their profound sympathy to the

members of his family. Jack Levin, President." The Lone Star Boat Club of 240 West 54th Street was organized in 1887 as "America's first Jewish rowing group." (*EJ*)

2. Dorothy Maynor (1910–1996), black American soprano. The broadcast on WABC featured the Chicago Women's Symphony.
3. American Society of Composers, Authors and Publishers, founded 1914, supervises radio broadcasts and collects and distributes royalties and performance fees for live performances and broadcasts.
4. Barbara McCann.
5. (1898–1968), professor of history at Harvard, 1927–1968.
6. A new edition by Theodore Spencer of Grierson's *The Valley of Shadows* was published in 1948 by Houghton Mifflin for the History Book Club, with an editor's note by BDV.
7. Possibly Francis D. Grierson (1888–1972), British crime novelist.
8. Under the name Jesse Shepherd.
9. O'Sheel (1886–1954), poet and writer.
10. (1895–1975), journalist; possibly *Ballade for a Bibliomaniac's Birthday*, 1940; or *Authors in False-face*, 1939; or *Mark Twain's Associated Press Speech and Other News Stories on Murder, Modes, Mysteries, Music and Makers of Books*, 1940.
11. Charles Crane. *Let Me Show You Vermont* was published in 1937.
12. *Pen-drift, Amenities of Column Conducting, by the Pendrifter*, 1931. The New York publisher was named after Stephen Daye (ca. 1594–1668), the first printer in colonial America.
13. Post (1871–1930), lawyer, mystery writer. Anderson (1877–1947), journalist, short story writer, *SEP*, *Everybody's Magazine*.
14. The brushpiles were intended to be ignited as signal flares on the first sign that Napoleon's invasion flotilla, assembling at Boulogne in the spring of 1803, was under way. The naval threat to England was decisively removed on October 21, 1805, when the combined French and Spanish fleets under Admiral Villeneuve were obliterated by the Royal Navy under Viscount Nelson off Cape Trafalgar in Spain.
15. The bloody Battle of the Wilderness, 5–7 May 1864, near Chancellorsville, Virginia, with one hundred thousand Union troops under Grant against sixty thousand under Lee. After heavy casualties on both sides, Grant was able to resume the offensive. The violence in New York City occurred during the draft riots there in July 1863.
16. The most famous version of this occurs in a letter, 1861, from Winfield Scott to William H. Seward: "Say to the seceded states, 'Wayward sisters, depart in peace.'"
17. William Graham Sumner (1840–1910), professor of sociology at Yale; "The Forgotten Man," essay, 1916.
18. Carl Joachim Friedrich (1901–1984), distinguished political theorist, professor of government at Harvard, 1926–1971.
19. Elliott (1896–1979), professor of history and political science.
20. New York monthly, later biweekly, 1902–1997.
21. Thayer (1859–1923), journalist, editor, historian, biographer; Harvard Overseer; president of the American Historical Association; editor of the *Harvard Graduates' Magazine*, 1892–1915; *The Dawn of Italian Independence*, 2 vols., 1893; *The Life and Times of Cavour*, 2 vols., 1911; *The Life and Letters of John Hay*, 2 vols., 1915; *Theodore Roosevelt: An Intimate Biography*, 1919.
22. Poet, diplomat, historian; ambassador to Great Britain, 1897–1898; secretary of state, 1898–1905; *Pike County Ballads and Other Pieces*, 1871; *Poems*, 1890; *Abraham Lincoln: A History*, with John Nicolay, 10 vols., 1890.
23. The house actually had only five toilets.

24. (1815–1882), author and lawyer; U.S. attorney for the Massachusetts district, 1861–1866; *Two Years Before the Mast*, 1840.
25. "A Sober Word on the Detective Story," by Harrison R. Steeves (1881–1981), professor of English at Columbia College.
26. *Good Night Sheriff*, 1941.
27. S. S. Van Dine, pseudonym of Willard Huntington Wright (1888–1939), art critic and novelist; author of the Philo Vance mysteries.
28. *The Big Sleep* by Raymond Chandler (1888–1959), 1939; *Farewell, My Lovely*, 1940.
29. *The Hermit Place*, 1941, by Mark Schorer (1908–1977), author, taught at Harvard, 1940–1945, and at the University of California at Berkeley, 1945–1977; *William Blake: The Politics of Vision*, 1946; *Sinclair Lewis: An American Life*, 1961.
30. There was no award in fiction.
31. *Jonathan Edwards, 1703–1758*, by Ola Elizabeth Winslow (1885? –1977), 1940.
32. *There Shall Be No Night*, 1940.
33. (1887–1954), poet; *Sunderland Capture and Other Poems*, 1940.
34. The Pulitzer Prize in history for 1941 was awarded to *The Atlantic Migration, 1607–1860*, by Marcus Lee Hansen (1892–1938), who also had won the Pulitzer Prize in drama in 1924.
35. Mason Wade (1913–1986); *Francis Parkman, Heroic Historian*, 1942. See *LBDV*, pp. 112–14.
36. Without telling anyone, Rudolf Hess (1894–1987), deputy Reichsführer of Nazi Germany and well known as one of Hitler's top assistants, flew solo to England on 10 May 1941 and parachuted out of his plane, on what he said was a private diplomatic mission to persuade England to accept Hitler's peace terms; Hess was apparently convinced that England could not win the war, and in all sincerity expected to negotiate an agreement between the two nations. Informed of Hess's flight, a stunned Hitler announced that Hess had gone crazy. Hess was promptly jailed at Churchill's order for the rest of the war; convicted of war crimes at the Nuremberg trials in 1946, he was given a life sentence and committed suicide in Spandau Prison in Berlin forty-one years later.
37. Probably in *NYHT*, or in editorials in the New York *World*.
38. On relations between the United States and the Vichy government of France; American shipments of food to unoccupied France depended on the temperature of Vichy's relationship with Berlin. Germany demanded Vichy's consent to send forces to France's colonies in Africa, especially Dakar on the west coast, to forestall a potential American invasion, and in Syria as a base of attack against the British in Iraq. On 11 May, Vichy issued a warning against an attempt by the United States to seize Dakar.
39. Willard Monroe Kiplinger (1891–1967), journalist; *The Kiplinger Washington Letter*, weekly since 1923.
40. Agar was then the London correspondent for the Louisville (Kentucky) *Courier-Journal*.
41. Charles Lindbergh, still a national hero fourteen years after his historic flight across the Atlantic Ocean, was a leader in the America First movement; he had been impressed by the accomplishments of the Nazis in the rebuilding of their own nation, and, entirely willing to overlook German atrocities, he expressed his certainty that all of Europe, and eventually America, would need to come to terms with worldwide German dominance. His wife's pamphlet, *The Wave of the Future*, expressed and supported his view but was widely condemned. "Gauleiter," a Nazi function, means "district director."
42. A New York tabloid newspaper, 1940–1948, daily except Saturdays and Sundays, when it appeared as a weekend magazine; founded and published by Ralph Ingersoll.
43. President Roosevelt's speech on 27 May indeed did declare a state of unlimited national emergency.

44. Cambridge Trust Company, 1336 Massachusetts Avenue in Harvard Square; a small, conservative bank still administering BDV's estate. The Episcopal Theological School (now Episcopal Theological Seminary), on St. John's Road, adjacent to Berkeley Street.
45. Josephine Bumstead (d. 1950), at 12 Berkeley Street. Francis Wayne MacVeagh, Harvard '21, 6 Berkeley Street.
46. Walter Edmonds lived at 5 Berkeley Place, around the corner.
47. BDV retained coal-burning equipment for this furnace, as a precaution against oil shortages, for years after the war.
48. Matthew 6:19: "Lay not up for yourselves treasures upon the earth, where moth and rust doth corrupt, and where thieves break through and steal."
49. At a press conference of 16 May, President Roosevelt spoke of the danger of a possible German attempt to occupy the Cape Verde Islands, the Azores, and French bases in Africa. On 27 May, with the proclamation of unlimited national emergency, he confirmed that Germany would not be allowed to gain these bases, nor in Iceland and Greenland, and that the United States would continue to supply England.
50. BDV was slated to give the Phi Beta Kappa address at Harvard on 20 June 1941.
51. Mary A. B. Brazier (1904–1994), British-born neurophysiologist, authority on brain waves.
52. Wars of the Roses: "Intermittent struggle, 1455–1485, for the throne of England between the noble houses of York (whose badge was a white rose) and Lancaster (later associated with the red rose)." (*CE*)
53. Ivory Snow soap powder was advertised as "99.44/100% pure."
54. Cow-itch, also spelled cowage: "a tropical woody vine...having crooked pods covered with barbed brittle hairs that cause severe itching." (*W3*)
55. This seems to be pure hyperbole; BDV was never known to have had a stomach ulcer.
56. In classical mythology, a sea-god who can change shape to avoid capture.
57. Regarding old Cambridge, see BDV, "The Third Floor," Easy Chair, *Harper's* 204/3 (March 1952). William Benjamin Basil King (1859–1928), "clergyman, novelist and spiritualist" (*DAB*), lived at 1 Berkeley Street; rector of Christ Church (Episcopal) in Cambridge, 1892–1900; *The Abolishing of Death*, 1919; *The Conquest of Fear*, 1921. Eleanor Porter (1868–1920), author of *Pollyanna*, lived in Cambridge but not, as far as is known, on Berkeley Street.
58. L. J. Henderson's wife, Edith Lawrence Thayer Henderson, was the sister of Miriam Stuart Thayer, who married Theodore William Richards. Richards (1868–1928), Harvard '86, Erving Professor of Chemistry, did outstanding work in precise measurements of atomic weights, for which he was awarded the Nobel Prize in 1914. He was the doctoral advisor of James Bryant Conant, who married his daughter, Grace Thayer Richards. William Roscoe Thayer married Elizabeth Hastings Ware, granddaughter either of Henry Ware (1794–1843), Unitarian clergyman and professor at the Harvard Divinity School, or of his brother William Ware (1797–1852), Unitarian clergyman. Both brothers married daughters of Benjamin Waterhouse (1754–1846), physician, noted for introducing the practice of vaccination to America. Waterhouse Street, off Garden Street adjoining the Cambridge Common, is named for him.
59. Crawford Howell Toy (1836–1919), professor of classics, Hancock Professor of Hebrew and other Oriental languages. Whipple, probably George Chandler Whipple (1866–1924), Gordon McKay Professor of Sanitary Engineering. Theodore Lyman '97 (1874–1954), physicist and spectroscopist, Hollis Professor of Mathematics and Natural Philosophy. Charles Rockwell Lanman (1850–1941), Wales Professor of Sanskrit. Francke (1855–1930), German-born literary historian and founder of the Germanic Museum at Harvard. No professor named Bierstadt is known at Harvard; BDV may have confused Heinrich Conrad Bierwirth (1853–1940), '84,

professor of German, with Albert Bierstadt (1830–1902), eminent German-American painter of western landscapes.

60. Oliver M. W. Sprague (1873–1953), '94, professor of economics.
61. Commander Hotel, on the corner of Berkeley Street and Garden Street, facing Waterhouse Street and the Cambridge Common; now the Sheraton Commander.
62. Edward Jenner (1749–1823), British physician, discoverer of vaccination; *Inquiry into the Cause and Effects of the Variolae Vaccinae*, 1798. Walt Whitman ("the Good Gray Poet," 1819–1892), outstanding American poet and journalist; *Leaves of Grass*, 1855. Jean-Auguste-Dominique Ingres (1780–1867), great French classical painter.
63. Established 1895; founding organization of Goodwill Industries.
64. Robert E. Kintner (1909–1980), journalist and radio and television executive (ABC, NBC), and Joseph Alsop jointly wrote a column in *NYHT* between 1937 and 1941.
65. BDV's speech, on 20 June, was titled "The Waste Land and the Irresponsibles." Frost read a poem on the occasion as well.
66. Pythagoras (fl. ca. 530 B.C.E.), Greek mathematician and mystic, discoverer of incommensurable quantities.
67. Probably "Ernest Hemingway: Bourdon Gauge of Morale," *Atlantic* 164/1 (July 1939); "Dickens and the Marshalsea Prison," 165/4 and 165/5 (April and May, 1940); "The Kipling that Nobody Read," 167/2 and 167/3 (February and March, 1941).
68. This refers apparently to the new neurosurgical technique called prefrontal lobotomy, fashionable in the 1940s but subsequently discredited as a treatment for mental illness. Bedlam, Bethlem Royal Hospital, London, from ca. 1400.
69. By W. A. Newman Dorland (1864–1956), many editions; BDV's was probably the eighteenth.
70. Gassner (1903–1967), theater critic; his wife was Mollie.
71. Claude Simpson Jr. (1910–1976), professor of English at Ohio State University and Stanford; *The British Broadside Ballad and its Music*, 1966. An excellent pianist, Simpson was known for his ability to improvise with melodies using his friends' telephone numbers as scale degrees.
72. Robert Richards, probably identical with the author of *I Can Lick Seven*, 1942. Theodore Roethke (1908–1963), outstanding poet and teacher; taught at Michigan State, Penn State, Bennington College, and (1947–1963) the University of Washington; *Open House*, 1941; Pulitzer Prize in poetry, 1954. He was of Prussian ancestry, not Pennsylvania Dutch. Whitman (1916–1979), poet and classical scholar, professor of Greek at Harvard; *Orpheus and the Moon Craters*, poems, 1941.
73. Rourke died in March 1941.
74. Robertson's new novel was probably *Salute to the Hero*, published by Farrar & Rinehart in 1942.
75. Brown, administrator; professor of English at Middlebury College, 1932–1955.
76. Kerr (1913–1999), publisher, director of Atlantic Monthly Press, 1940–1941; later director, Yale University Press.
77. This information seems to be incorrect.
78. (1911–1992), Harvard '32, radio producer and adman; director (with MacLeish) of the Radio Research Project at the Library of Congress.
79. Robert Schwab (1903–1972), physician and neurophysiologist.
80. Human artificial insemination has been forbidden to Catholics since 1897.
81. Sin of Onan, see Genesis 38:8–10.
82. At a secret rendezvous aboard the cruiser *Augusta* and the battleship *Prince of Wales* in Argentia Bay, Newfoundland, Prime Minister Churchill and President Roosevelt met for what became known as the Atlantic Conference, 9–12 August 1941; the Atlantic Charter, pledging

mutual efforts against Nazi Germany and for an association of world nations after the war, was signed on 14 August.

83. The CCC, Civilian Conservation Corps, organized in March 1933 and disbanded in 1942, was one of the most successful and popular of the New Deal measures; it enrolled half a million men in 2,600 camps throughout the country by 1935, and among many other accomplishments planted three billion trees on the public lands. The biggest submarine at the time was the *Surcouf*, 4300 tons displacement; launched 1931, lost in February 1942. The Portsmouth Naval Shipyard in Kittery, Maine, is directly across the Piscataqua River from Portsmouth, New Hampshire.
84. Wambaugh (1882–1955), Radcliffe '02, authority on international law; *Monograph on Plebiscites, With a Collection of Official Documents*, 1920.
85. (medieval Latin), "while the crime is blazing," in the very act (*AHD*).
86. Fiske (1842–1901), prolific author, historian, and philosopher; assistant librarian at Harvard; *The Discovery of America*, 2 vols., 1892.
87. Alice C. Allyn probably lived into the 1930s. Her brother was a founder of Allyn & Bacon, publishers of textbooks. BDV apparently confuses her family with Joseph Henry Allen (1820–1898), who first published the well-known *Latin Grammar for Schools and Colleges* in 1888.
88. *Arbella*, Flagship of John Winthrop (1588–1649), colonial governor of Massachusetts, who organized a fleet of 11 ships to bring emigrants from England to America in 1630. Tory Row is now Brattle Street.
89. Founded 1910; 141 Cambridge Street, Boston; now called Historic New England.
90. By Edgar Lee Masters, 1923.
91. From "Mending Wall," by Frost, *North of Boston*, 1915.
92. Allen was in fact appointed editor of *Harper's*, serving until 1953.
93. The Grand Offensive in Russia. The German invasion, which had been very successful following the surprise attack on 22 June, was beginning to falter in early October with the onset of the mud season and early winter. The Germans got almost within sight of Moscow on 5 December, but were forced back by an unexpected Russian counterattack. On 5 October 1941, in the fourth game of the World Series, with two out in the ninth inning, Mickey Owen (1916–2005), catcher for the Brooklyn Dodgers, dropped a third strike; the New York Yankees went on to win the game 7-4, and won the Series the next day.
94. British humor magazine, 1841–2002, famous for cartoons and satire.
95. Tommy Atkins, sobriquet of a British soldier. The punning reference is to "There are Fairies at the Bottom of My Garden," song by Rose Fyleman (1877–1957), British singer and writer.
96. Hayworth (1918–1987), movie actress, born Margarita Carmen Cansino. The movie was *You'll Never Get Rich*, 1941. The New Order was a small but noisy coterie of Nazi sympathizers which had been active in the United States.
97. The USS *West Virginia* and seven other battleships, and as well as eleven smaller ships, were sunk at their moorings in Pearl Harbor; because these were in shallow water, most of them were later salvaged, but the *Arizona* exploded when a bomb struck her magazines; 1,177 men were killed on the *Arizona* alone. The navy's aircraft carriers were at sea and escaped the attack. In all, 2,280 personnel were killed at Pearl Harbor, as well as 68 civilians, and 188 aircraft were destroyed on the ground.
98. Gerald Nye (1892–1971), senator from North Dakota, had chaired the "merchants of death" investigation into worldwide arms sales in 1934. He had opposed Lend-Lease and supported America First, but voted to declare war; so did Senator Burton Wheeler of Montana. The next day, Monday, President Roosevelt asked Congress for a declaration of war against Japan, which passed the Senate unanimously and the House with only a single dissenting vote.

99. Correctly, Taciebelle.
100. Private school in Cambridge for boys, founded 1883; coeducational K-12 since 1974 following merger with the Buckingham School; now Buckingham Browne & Nichols. Mark DeVoto graduated from the twelfth grade in 1957.
101. A false air raid alarm on 9 December, in response to enemy airplanes supposedly approaching the Atlantic coast, was corrected during the afternoon by an announcement that it was a "dress rehearsal." The Fore River shipyard in Quincy and the Boston Army Base sent all their civilian workers home; Mayor Tobin ordered all Boston schools closed, but the all-clear notice came before the order could be sent out. Which enemy airplanes might have been detected was never made clear; war was not declared by Germany and Italy until the morning of 11 December.
102. In fact the German navy never had aircraft carriers.
103. Erich Raeder (1876–1960), German Grand Admiral, 1939–1943.
104. Of East Hartford, Connecticut, manufacturer of aircraft engines.
105. "Caisson Song," British, from the Great War: "Over hill, over dale/As we hit the dusty trail..."
106. Arthur Norman Holcombe (1884–1977), Harvard '06, professor of government; *The New Party Politics*, 1933. He lived three houses away on Berkeley Street.
107. Singapore was surrendered by the British on 15 February 1942; the last United States forces in the Philippines surrendered 9 May 1942, and some 90,000 troops, mostly Filipino, were taken prisoner by the Japanese.
108. In June 1942 the Japanese attacked Dutch Harbor in the Aleutian Islands, as a diversionary move prior to the Battle of Midway.
109. (German) great general staff; BDV probably means something else.
110. From England, under the terms of Lend-Lease, the United States acquired Caribbean bases in Jamaica, Antigua, St. Lucia, Trinidad, and British Guiana; also in Bermuda and on Ascension Island in the South Atlantic. In possessions of the Netherlands, the United States constructed bases in Aruba, Curaçao, and Surinam; also a base at Patos Island, a Venezuelan possession. A U.S. naval base had already existed at Guantánamo in Cuba since 1903.
111. The Cape Verde Islands, off the west coast of Africa, were a Portuguese possession.
112. Much of the French fleet, based at Toulon on the Mediterranean coast, was scuttled in November 1942 when American and British forces landed in North Africa.
113. Landis, dean of the Harvard Law School, 1937–1947; he had just been appointed national director of the Office of Civilian Defense (OCD). Leverett Saltonstall was governor of Massachusetts, 1939–1945.

10

1942 LETTERS

Reflecting on what his own role might be, DeVoto nevertheless repeatedly showed his fascination for news of the war and exercised his fondness for predicting grand strategy. By February he was able to declare the new book finished. He also delivered himself of a long appraisal of his friend Archibald MacLeish, director of the Office of Facts and Figures, soon to become the Office of War Information; suppression of war news became one of DeVoto's most persistent complaints in the ensuing years. Sterne in turn sent DeVoto some extensive information about her family and about the inadequacies of the nursing staff at Bowne Hospital. In May DeVoto went to Kenyon College in Ohio to receive an honorary degree. Soon after he began writing another John August serial and was able to announce to Sterne that *The Year of Decision: 1846* would be adopted by the Book of the Month Club, assuring abundant sales. Hoping to avoid further contretemps with Frost at Bread Loaf, DeVoto attempted to omit a visit in 1942 but was ultimately cajoled into coming for a few days; shortly afterward, with relief, he abandoned the John August serial. In October DeVoto wrote about the personal crisis of his friend Robert Hillyer, and later about further problems in the Mark Twain Estate. In a long, ruminative letter, written shortly after the Allied landings in North Africa in November, DeVoto balanced the flaws of Roosevelt's New Deal with those of prior wartime administrations, ending with a facetiously expressed hope that Sterne might find some 22-caliber ammunition for Gordon's rifle practice; when Sterne sent a thousand rounds, DeVoto's amazement was total. As preparation for his forthcoming Patten lectures for Indiana University, DeVoto sharply criticized Van Wyck Brooks's latest, and guardedly praised the young scholar Alfred Kazin.

Bowne

[BEFORE 30 JANUARY 1942]

Dear Benny,

Jesus Christ, what a month! Well, let's skip it.

Getting back to *1846*, or *The Year of Decision*, or (stubbornly) *Westward I Go Free*, the Lowell Lectures have given me an immensely helpful all-over view, & it seems to me that readers of The Book might well be given a similar panorama right at the outset. It's (what I've read of it) an immensely engrossing & thrilling job (and a timely patriotic service in that it gives perceptive Americans a hell of a good idea of what they're fighting for), but even perceptive Americans are ignorant as hell of their own past, & I think you ought to be explicit—even at the risk of being obvious.

Horrors of War Dept: Of Bea's two kid cousins who were drafted into the Army, one is working in the bacteriological lab on Church St. & living at home, the other is teaching mathematics at Fort Monmouth.[1] ... Tough.... Clarence Le Clair, who has been at Bowne for twelve years, five of them as chef, has enlisted in the Navy.... At the first try, they turned him down for tachycardia, but told him to quit drinking & come back in eight days (yesterday). This morning there was a message pencilled on my breakfast egg:

I'M IN THE NAVY NOW!
(A BAKER)
CLARENCE

Clarence is one of the twelve Le Clair brothers (two sisters) from Rusticoville, P.E.I.[2] Three of the boys are in the Canadian Navy, two with the Canadian forces in Great Britain. Reuben, who is a Bowne orderly, has recently been reclassified as 1-A. That'll make seven Le Clairs fighting the Axis. A great people, the Canucks.

Oh, God damn it, this paper is all gone!

Kate

8 Berkeley Street
Cambridge, Massachusetts

[30 JANUARY 1942]

Dear Kate:

Editorial opinion has to move faster these days. A flurry of activity by the Massachusetts ARP organization has kept a letter to you half-finished on my desk for about five days, and a lot of its wisdom has been deflated in that time.[3] Except that the remarks about Churchill look pretty good, now that he has talked without saying anything, and I don't like the turn the government is taking *chez* our ally. I wonder if Churchill can survive a defeat in Libya plus one in Singapore.[4] It isn't as clear that he's going to get the first as it was when I started to write to you, but there's no reason to suppose that what the academic world has strangely decided to call the brown dastard is kidding anyone when he names February 10 for the Stronghold of the East. Whether Churchill can survive it, at a guess the British Empire can't. I'm a bit hazy about the details but I think that only Alaska and Hawaii have full territorial status now, and I dunno if even the war powers would enable Roosevelt to confer full territorial status on Australia by Executive Order. Limited status, hell yes, and maybe the brethren down under would take that.

Let us, however, take what comfort we can in such places as it may be offered to us, and it seems evident that the affair in the Macassar Strait has been a very pretty job of work.[5] I make it at least sixteen ships officially sunk to date and at least twenty-five damaged—damaged, what's more, a hell of a long way from home. If the dastard has nevertheless landed some troops, still that's a hell of a sick convoy. Do we pin the rose on Hart, on Wavell, or, more likely, the Dutch?[6]

Still, the biggest news by far is Roosevelt's prompt release of the Pearl Harbor report.[7] Not the report itself, though that's big stuff, but his prompt release of it. It is by far the most statesmanlike act that has issued from the White House in seven years come Michaelmas. It goes a long way toward proving that we aren't just using words when we talk about democratic government. Churchill has never shown a comparable frankness, and nothing remotely comparable in the last year. The truth about Narvik, Crete, Greece, or even Wavell's Libya offensive, for instance, is still bottled up somewhere.[8] The effect abroad ought to be enormous, and enormously good. We are at least permitted to hope that Roosevelt's example may infect the departments of Navy and Army press relations.

But good God, what a report! It's incredible. Nearly every paragraph is incredible but the crowning incredibility is that submarine.[9] Lt., s.g., Doe comes overside and says, oh, by the way, I just sank a hostile sub. Oh? says the flag officer on duty, big one? Good going. So they all go in to breakfast.... That there hasn't been a nation-wide groundswell of indignation is another ominous sign that this nation is too God-damned smug for words. It will take an air raid, it will probably take a big one. And you're probably right about April. Bad weather ought to stop any transatlantic effort till then. Though, as I keep humbly pointing out to my superiors here, it doesn't have to be transatlantic. The Nordic dastard has one carrier that's known, and probably several that aren't known.[10] If he should decide to pay one for [*sic*] a half million tons of steel diverted to bomb shelters and I dunno how much rubber to gas masks, there are going to be some official faces among the East Coast military quite as red as any at Pearl Harbor. The Army, in collaboration with the CD boys, has organized a really bang-up system, and any plane that flies into [it] is going run into trouble.[11] But it's organized on the serene assumption that the aforesaid plane is going to be flying the great circle course and will be picked up somewhere the other side of the northern boundary of Maine. Any dastard who comes in past the Nantucket lightship is going to embarrass the system acutely.

I've had only one story lately—my pals are getting detailed fast, most of them to submarine duty. This one concerns the Ferry Command.[12] Which, by the way, is an extremely effective organization and one that can't be bothered with red tape, channels, procedure, ceremonies, or due form. First looeys give orders to brigadier generals; gents who were piloting for Eastern Airlines a month ago draw up flight schedules for men twice their age. Etc. Well, the Ferry Command transported Harriman to Moscow—was it in November?—in a Consolidated Bomber.[13] The big Boat the British like so much. (Not that I urge that strongly. Papa is getting fed up with the British notion that if it hasn't got a clutch like we put in an Austin then the hell with it. And Papa has talked more than he's been interested in talking with the British Purchasing Commission underlings hereabout.)[14] Four or five man crew and the pilot in charge was just a few weeks out of Pan Am. Come the end of the mission, the pilot hadn't had any orders from HQ. So he radioed, "How do you want me to take Harriman home?" The guy on duty at HQ was fed up with sappy questions and, in a moment of exasperation, radioed back, "Take him round the world." The pilot had a couple of charts in his control room so he, by God, did so.

Right on the *Duke of York*. You probably heard that the British Navy gummed its orders, the destroyer escort didn't show up at the appointed station, and she made the crossing by her lone. The *Queen Mary* is in drydock here; for an overhaul, not damaged.[15] She's from Australia but that's all I know.

As for the Irish, up to and including Eamon De Valera, you may remember that I gave them to you long ago.[16]... There was a hell of a good letter about them in the *Herald* this morning, signed "Edward Callahan." But it was probably written by a Ginsburg.

As for *Etudes littéraires*,[17] the advice of one who knows nothing is to scrap them for the *Causeries du lundi*.[18] Or have I got that title wrong too? Anyway, it's better stuff, under any name. But I remember Murray's *Trojan Women* as one of the best jobs ever.[19]

The trouble with Westward I Go Free is that it just doesn't sound like history, which after all I persuade myself I'm writing, and my inadequacy-feeling wants the boys to make sure that they share the belief.[20] Arthur Schlesinger, Jr., would accept that kind of title as legitimate, but it would give his father a fit of pure sacrilege. Not that Arthur Sr.'s official approval counts—this is certainly Sam Morison's year to get the Pulitzer award, and quite right at that.[21] But my seat among the brethren is at best precarious, and it would be lost forever, as my seat among the academic literary was lost long ago, if I showed any irreverence, poetry, or, for that matter, originality. (Just this morning

I began my last assault on John Charles Frémont, and there strayed into my mind the reflection that both Donald Adams and Irita Van Doren, yes, and Amy Loveman too, will invite Allen Nevins to review me.)[22] . . . I don't make out what kind of panoramic statement you desire. I have already inserted in the first chapter, immediately following Biela's Comet, a straight-faced statement that this book deals with a turning point, that it treats the western frontier experience as a national experience, and that it covers a lot of stories which are bound together by more than the fact that they all start in the same year. Will that do? The Lowell Lectures added up to about 48,000 words. I sadly grant you that a preliminary statement of that length would not be disproportionate to the book that follows.[23] . . . Well, I've got the Saints to Zion, and I promise you it's a relief to know that I don't have to write another damn word about the Mormons or read another damn journal by one of them. (I read Hosea Stout's journal, though, sneaked out to me from the Church library by a spy.)[24] If it's possible to be fed up with a million people, I'm fed up with Mormons. For a couple of days I was stopped short by the sudden, cold realization that I must now go into my act. I got going again, though. And I've had another realization. In a way, a very feeble, minute, diluted way, the brethren are very much like the literary. I mean, in spite of hell, this book will do one thing, even for the profession. It will make up their minds about Stephen Watts Kearny.[25] For the next period of years whenever they have to refer to him—one footnote or one textual allusion per book—they'll refer to him in my terms. In so far I'll have contributed to historical opinion. It isn't very far but there's a certain satisfaction in saying a good word for a good man who has been dead for ninety-five years and has taken a beating of one footnote or textual allusion per book through most of that time, just because a first class son of a bitch happened to be the son-in-law of Thomas Hart Benton. If ever there was an assassination in history it was Benton's job on Kearny, and I'm glad, this late, to do my five cents' worth toward repairing it. I don't know much about Kearny as a man. I only know what he did, his reports, his image in some journals and letters, and Benton's howls. But he sticks out as a man and a brother, an intelligence, an effective man, a man of honor, a man of achievement, in that ruck of prima donnas, adventurers, Hamlets, and incompetents. He did his job. I don't know a better epitaph.

Well, John August's book has had a third printing and Raymond Everitt is beginning to get interested in it.[26] That sort of thing does not happen to DeVoto books, you will have observed. What's pleasanter, it's being treated with the utmost seriousness in the reviews. I dunno why John's feeblest effort catches on, but it seems likely to. And if I ever issue a public admission, it will be because I want to share the *New Republic* with others. Mr. August has always been a fine writer in those columns.

While you're making up titles, you could make one up for the DeVoto that Dumas Malone will be bringing out this spring. I've made a little book of the Tom Sawyer and

Huck Finn introductions, called for this book only "The Phantasy of Boyhood" and "Noon and the Dark," and the lecture I delivered at the U of Chicago a couple of years back, called "The Symbols of Despair." If you know something snappy to call an ill assorted treatise on Mark Twain's artisanship and the way his mind works, shoot. Having made a book out of it, I decided I might as well dedicate it. I might as well dedicate it to Rosy, who did all the hard work that it represents. When she put the mss. together and found the dedication, she bawled. And I just don't get Rosy. I was prepared to have her laugh, say nothing, or forbid the dedication; I was not prepared for tears. I used to think I knew something about your sex. That was a hell of a long while ago. I used to think I knew something about Rosy. I'll concede that one. Or maybe it just means that Henry Gerlach's successor is in the offing.

Measles has hit Shady Hill University. It's just a question of time.

Yours,

Benny

8 Berkeley Street
Cambridge, Massachusetts

[13 FEBRUARY 1942]

Dear Kate:

Though the passage will have to be rewritten, because my tail was dragging, nevertheless be it set down that at 1:48 P.M. on Thursday, February 12, the last word but one of my book was written. The last one will be added tomorrow in the I trust awed presence of whatever portions of my gang drop in to drink a cocktail in celebration thereof. A rough count makes it 190,200 words. That's quite a few words. I haven't the foggiest idea whether the book is any good, and I can't really call it ended since there'll be another six weeks of revising, but I'm willing to sit back in chair and concede that finishing means something to me. I may say to you, whose name goes on it, that the betting has been against it a good many times, that I have dodged writing it with God knows how many perfectly valid delays and inhibitions, that there have been times, spread over a good many years before I started it, when the concept haunted me, and a good many times since I actually got to work on it when nightmares and vampires and hippogriffs and anthropophagi swarmed up out of the Id and scared me pretty damn close to quitting it. God didn't want me to write that book. In a sense God never wanted me to write any book, and I don't forget that at Lincoln, a few days after I finished SG, I got boiled and was seen stuffing the ms. into a fireplace and preparing to touch a match to it. This book may never mean anything to anyone, and I don't know if it's going to mean anything to me, but having finished it does mean something. I have, by God, written that book.

Little-Brown, especially Raymond, will now go into their act. As Alfred McIntyre increasingly coddles his hypochondria, as Raymond increasingly runs the firm and the firm settles down to specializing in best sellers, I make little sense there. They're going down to Portland and take another beating on a prestige book and God how they dread it. Just to insure that they'll dread it fairly realistically, I drew fifteen hundred dollars more on it last week. Their pain is a little eased, and their emotions confused, by John August, who has just gone into his sixth printing, with more apparently to come. This week's prize letter was from Raymond, saying that, since J A was developing into a successful writer, I'd better consult with my publishers as well as my editor before beginning another one. I don't know what about, but be sure I'll get informed.... Some oaf in the Boston *Globe* has challenged me to deny that I'm J A and it gets me down, for I don't want it working into the literary sheets. I've forgotten why I don't, but I'm stubborn.

The Civilian War Effort is getting me down. Red Cross takes two evenings a week. ARP takes another one, plus too many afternoons, and will presently take more, now that we approach the stage of tests and blackouts. Fifty Minutes With Ten For Questions Speaking takes at least one evening a week, sometimes more, and is about to enlarge disastrously, for Perry Miller is sending me on a tour of the military camps. It would be a hell of a lot simpler to enlist.

The best slant I get on the military these days comes from reflecting on the damage to my own ideas. For my ideas are derived from the best ideas the military have been having in the last ten years. I have read a couple of the Army journals regularly and others occasionally, I've read the Naval Institute stuff and some of the service publications, and I have always seen and talked with a number of the supposedly bright boys of both services. My expectations and calculations were theirs; so I know how the boys have been upset. And I have a pretty good idea that it's going to be a long time before brains fit to fight a modern war get high enough in either service to do much good.

What scares me worst is the apparently total failure of G2.[27] For years the boys have been telling me, Army and Navy both, have been bragging to me about the incomparable intelligence service they had, the best in the world. That seems to mean, ultimately, better than the French and British—and to depend there chiefly on the French and British intelligence, which ignored them, some months before the storm broke. But their story has been that they had the cold dope on everything. And it works out that they didn't have the slightest bit of dope about Japan at all. Not only fleet and troop dispositions, but even the size of the preparation. The simple, wholesome fact is that they have been caught flatfooted. And that scares the hell out of me. I cling to the apparent demonstration that they were able to take the fleet to the Marshall Islands at the right moment.[28] But the clinging is not comfortable.

About a week after Pearl Harbor, while I was still holding on to Singapore and even the Philippines, in accord with Plan B, developed on the assumption of the British alliance, there wandered into my house and drank my liquor like an honest sailorman a senior lieutenant who threw away both Singapore and the Philippines and a good deal else.[29] His story was that if we could concentrate on Java and hold it, and if we started that within sixty minutes from date, maybe we'd have a chance in the Pacific. Java, he said, is the key to everything, and it's the one thing we can hold, and we can hold it if we move fast. I handsomely presented him with practically everything the Japs have since taken, and bade him remember all the charts and graphs in the *Proceedings*.[30] He said, yeah, you talk like Newport, and wandered out and has been shipped somewhere. I didn't know what he meant then, but I begin to.

But, on yesterday's action in the Strait of Dover, we don't look as bad yet as the King's Navee.[31] A melancholy thought, but one that has been forecasted in my hearing by a number of our own.

Still, the military look better than the civilians as of today. Apart from a few of my fellow wardens and the fortnightly group who convene at Harvard to talk about the Larger Issues—and talk about them as if they [were] Ec A[32]—I don't know anybody who even reads the papers. Simeon Strunsky says the people are not complacent, they have done everything the administration asked them to and are trusting the experts to win the war. Even so, that would be hellish bad stuff, considering the experts, but I say Simeon is wrong, the people are complacent as hell, and the United States war spirit so far is alarming. The country is full of people sufficiently skeptical not to put down a bet in April on any sports-writer's forecast of pennant winners, but we need to produce a hell of a lot of people practically instantaneously who know that you don't win war with statistics of potential production. The historian in me is aware that we're farther along and in better mood than we've ever been at this stage of any other war, but this isn't any other war. I've just done an Easy Chair called "Toward Chancellorsville."[33] I don't think we can afford Chancellorsville this time. I don't think we can afford Fredericksburg, and possibly we can't afford Second Bull Run.[34]

That being said, I add that I'm more melancholy than scared. I wonder how good the Japs or Heinies look to my opposite numbers. L. J. Henderson died on Tuesday, after having apparently recovered from a successful operation for a slight cancer of the bladder. An embolism hit him. So goes another of my fathers,[35] and I have always felt toward him the various loves and hates one is supposed to feel for fathers. I remember chiefly what Hans Zinsser once said, that you had to love L. J. because his damned foolishness brought out your protectiveness. He was damned good to me, from 1919 on. And when I came back to this town in a condition of shakes and phobias, he was the only one besides Hurlbut who told me he didn't give a damn how many tremors

I exhibited, come on over and talk. Furious conflicts, lusts, and fears which he never had the faintest awareness of made his Id seismic and produced an exterior that made a good many laugh and scared hell out [of] far more. For some, I think, he has been very bad. For many more years he has been the most powerful intellectual influence they have had or will have. Nobody I've known could be more idiotic, but he was idiotic on an inspiring scale. And within its proper limits, and within very wide margins on both sides of its proper limits, his was the strongest mind I've ever known. Part of the curdled portions of me were curdled by him. He was a great man. Great men are wayward things. Maybe sometime I'll write a book about that.

But I get reminders about the stage I've reached. Hans, Lee, L. J. They come fast now.

This is a tolerably woeful script, isn't it? . . . Well, the dope from Macy is that the Yale Press blew hell out of the printing job and *Huck Finn* has to be done over. That postpones your copy some more and also postpones the little Mark Twain book that Dumas Malone is preparing. I've seen the illustrations and like them better than the ones Benton did for *Tom*. . . . A neighbor of mine has developed the delusion that he's a cat. I'm told that there were forewarnings, that each time a child was born to his wife he confidently expected it to be a kitten. . . . My favorite New Hampshire neurotic, whom I take to dinner every six months, is an intellectual and there has occurred to her a dilemma of the species. Taking to raising stallions, for the clearest reasons, she lately took a Negro stableman. Being an intellectual, she has no race prejudices, quite the contrary. But when the stableman has now made his fifth pass at her she has begun to realize that race purity must be preserved. . . . On the other hand, producing a book twice as long as Madariaga's seems to have cleansed Sam Morison completely of the anti-Semitism that broke out in him like galloping rabies when Madariaga found that the Admiral of the Ocean was a converted Jew. We had just got used to steering Sam away from such subjects when he began to denounce us a proto-fascists. We are dull to the great danger sweeping America but Sam, he assures us, will wake us up. . . . Did Bunny have the measles when I wrote? He sailed through them but Cambridge has practically no schools just now. And over in Somerville a wave of scarlet fever gathers. . . . Mark having been shot in the tail by Joe Garland to avert or diminish the measles has now confirmed an opinion of doctors that already had him screeching whenever he caught sight of Joe. I don't blame him: the customary inoculations, an impromptu operation on the knee, a session with the stomach pump, and now a shot on the tail about the size of those they gave last war for tetanus.

Among my friends this appears to be not the neurotic year I anticipated but the year when people get arthritis. What are your friends having?

Yours,
Benny

[*handwritten enclosure:*]

when he started in to build that mill, on shares, he had some notion of ~~taking~~ rafting lumber down those canyons. But, on Bidwell's word, he was a good millwright and ~~the de~~ built a good mill.[36] Six of the Mormon Battalion were working on it under his direction, besides three ~~other~~ Gentiles and a number of Sutter's Indians. But they got the wheel set too low and so the tail race had to be deepened. They would dig during the day, then turn the water in at night to clean it out.

Trist and the Mexicans had not yet signed their treaty at Guadaloupe-Hidalgo [*sic*].[37] Brigham Young was at Winter Quarters again, where he had at last had himself "sustained" as President of the Church of Jesus Christ of Latter Day Saints, and was preparing the emigration of '48. At Washington, the court-martial told Lt. Col. Fremont that he might submit a written defense, and Mr. Polk wrote in his diary, in a crazy fear of an inconceivable rebellion, "The conduct of Mr. Trist and Gen'l Scott, who seem to have entered into a conspiracy to embarrass the government, gives me great anxiety. They have both proved themselves [the man who won the war and the man who saved the peace] to be wholly unworthy of the positions which they hold, and I most heartily wish they were both out of Mexico." Many soldiers, scattered in detachments in many places, heartily wished themselves out of Mexico that January day. In Congress they were ~~bitterly~~ quarreling about the bitterly felt but not yet understood. The Comanche were licking the wounds that a campaign by William Gilpin had cost them, and preparing this year's slaughter. ~~In many places~~ Scattered about America new Bill Bowens, not so many this year, were dreaming of spring, when they too could take to the Trail.

On that Monday, January 24, 1848, Marshall turned the water out of the tail race as usual, and toward midafternoon got down into it to see how much progress had been made.[38] Not much, for they were down to bedrock. A few inches of water covered that granite shelf. Marshall saw something shiny under that water. He stooped to pick it up.

That was what Henry Bigler and his homing fellow saints ~~could~~ told Jim Clyman beside the Truckee, in August '48.[39] A month later, the news was spreading through the East.

~~So when, in~~

The continental nation was not going to be balkanized; [Feb 12, 1942 / 1:48 PM] it was going to become an

empire

6:06 PM

February 14, 1942

[*witnessing signatures:*]

Rosamond Chapman

Martha N. B. Smith
John Dos Passos

Bowne

[BEFORE 24 FEBRUARY 1942]

Dear Benny,
I was touched & excited beyond measure to get the *consummatum est.*[40] Only a transient bellyache prevented my toasting "empire" with what remains of the Christmas Scotch.... Very many thanks!... "Become an empire," yes: but right now I'm scared chartreuse that it ain't gonna stay one. I have the Japs in Pocatello by Whitsun.

Who, by the way, is Martha N. B. Smith?

You know, I take it, how sorry I am to hear of L. J.'s death. I feel, now, as though Gage Ewing had died twice.[41]

Not arthritis. This is the year my friends are having babies, of assorted sexes. Bill Wilson became a grandfather (a daughter of a daughter by his first wife) on the same day he had to register for the draft. (He'll be forty-five in May).... Jimmy, our cute little Scotch kitchen-boy, went on a two-days' brannigan to celebrate the occasion (registration, not childbirth) but most of my 36–45 age friends are, I think, quietly hoping that they'll be called up. I don't like being a female zombie, right this minute.

I can't illustrate my state of mind better than by telling you the kind of thing I laugh at these days: Feller on the radio says as how he was drivin' through town the other evenin', & he seen Amnesia Paddock, the local receiver of stolen goods, settin' on Mayor Hardcastle's lap. Shore did give him a turn, seein' a fence settin' on a politician like thaat....

Yours,
Kate

Bowne

[BEGUN 22 FEBRUARY, FINISHED
SOMETIME BEFORE 9 MARCH 1942]

Dear Benny,
The flag is flying, as on all legal holidays. There is a high wind out of the North. But the really ominous fact is that the sturdy silk has been splitting, longitudinally, all morning, & has, not more than four minutes ago, lost a stripe. Howard, the orderly who just removed my dinner tray, informed me that that means we are going to lose a state, probably California. It was all I could do, not to kick him in the face.

I'm beginning to feel that the only qualities that have any survival value in this screwy world are cowardice & an inferiority feeling.

Victorian Vignette: I lived with my maternal aunts only up to age 7, & I never saw them again until I was 21 but I remember from my childhood certain hushed references to "Aunt Mary" who, even to my infant perceptions, lived, or had lived, under a cloud. Recently I asked Aunt Genie about Aunt Mary. Here is her reply:

> Your maternal Grandma, Cornelia Duval Grant, has several sisters. Mary, the eldest, was cut off from family relations because she was divorced. (In those days, no one mentioned that word!)
>
> Well, the desertion did not help poor Aunt Mary any. Your Uncle Lou used to visit them without saying anything. He became very fond of Mary McKenna McCook, the only daughter of the first marriage. She married General Ed McCook, a retired Army Officer; has two daughters, Roberta Victoria & Katharine.[42]
>
> After their mother died, reacquaintance occurred. I remember when I returned from a three years' sojourn in Europe, that I met Mary McCook & her two babies at the Grants'. Everybody remarked what a sensible, good mother she was.
>
> The Summer my son Dick was born, I stayed with Grandma Grant, & became well acquainted with Mary McKenna McCook, who also had a cottage at Riverside, Conn. Her brother Harold, & her sister, Frankie, lived with her & the General, & I learned much of how to take care of a baby.

(lapse of one week)

> Grandma Cornelia Duval Grant's sisters were—Mary, of whom I have written, & of whom Addie Mack said to Lou, "Mary was the handsomest & most beautifully educated of us all, but she didn't have one grain of common sense."
>
> Kate (& *sic*—K), mother of Bernard Hughes, her only child, an artist. Addie Mack was fond of Bernie, who was our (self-invited) guest several times while he apparently was looking for a job as illustrator on N. Y. newspapers. Bernie was a generous ne'er-do-well. . . .
>
> Adeline Duval Mack married (was married, in those days the parents made the matches) a rich man, then Thomas Mack. Her mother & younger sister came to live with her. Addie, who longed for a family, had no children. Tom (John was his very rich brother) lost his money when the Civil War broke out, & her mother, Adeline Peacock Duval, with daughter Julia, were going then to live with the Aunt Montgomery, when Mrs. Duval died of cholera morbus. Julia went to live with her mother's sister, Mrs. Isabel

> Montgomery, a rich widow, who died of cancer, & whom Julia nursed. She left her money to Julia & Cornelia's relatives contested the will, & when the suit was won & everybody paid, there was left $1,600 for each of them.
>
> Julia was living then with Grandma Grant. She was lovable, & trouble made her nervous, but not bitter. Joseph Rianhart [*sic*], a distant relative, came to visit, & Julia married him. They had two children: Joseph, who died in infancy, & Julia, who is in California, married to her first cousin, Harold McKenna. Aunt Addie Mack used to go & stay with them sometimes, & she said the children were all very bright....

The letter from which the foregoing is an excerpt arrived a couple of weeks ago. Yesterday came this postscript:

> Did I mention in my last that Lou was named for Aunt Isabel Montgomery? She wanted Grandma Grant's "next" named for her husband, Austin (a form of Augustin). Lou was christened "Louis" after Grandma's father, Louis Duval, and "Montgomery"—which did <u>not</u> please her aunt. However, she did <u>not</u> withdraw the promise of the Christening Cup, and, after her death Aunt Julia (Duval Rianhard [*sic*]) came to live with Grandma Grant, bringing the cup for Lou. Nellie Grant, not having a cup, grabbed Lou's cup and, in spite of the opposition of the family, she had her initials engraved on the cup when she was going to "Sharon" to boarding school. Lou had already received a cup from his godmother. His godfather was Joe Rianhard [*sic*], who gave Lou a silver napkin ring, still extant at 456.
>
> ...Addie Mack was a remarkable woman. After her husband's business was destroyed by the Civil War, she did all sorts of things to help him. She <u>should</u> have been a writer*, instead of running boarding-houses, and teaching Elocution, and little schools (she used to bring home the Arithmetic work, & make one of her boarders do the sums etc., for Aunt Addie 'hated figgers')....[43]

* * * *

Quite a few things have happened since I started this letter on Washington's birthday.... Po'keepsie has had its first trial black-out (Feb. 27th)—a great success.... Roosevelt was in residence at Hyde Park over the week-end of March 1st. The entire mid-Hudson Valley knows the moment he arrives, from those two pursuits, trimming the tree-tops at ten-minute intervals....

The Missing Miniatures have turned up.... Reuben, our senior orderly, has been turned down by the Army because of an upper plate, and Howard, our junior orderly—aetatis 19—has enlisted. Everyone at Bowne, as elsewhere, has been wrestling feverishly with income-tax blanks, and Aunt Addie's grand-niece has developed advanced catalepsy trying to add 2 + 2 + 1, with the aid of all the fingers of her left hand & a child's abacus.... Last, & by far worst, is a letter from Johnny which begins: "Dear Kate: I hope this isn't going to be too much of a shock, but I suppose I'd better tell you & get it over with. Dave was killed down at Ft. Bliss.[44]" ... A swell guy, a fine flier, & one of the best marriages I know anything about. Johnny's letter was heartbreaking—very quiet, factual, reticent, and utterly without hope. Mrs. Hatcher wants JCC to come to her in Florida, but JCC is going to Washington to work in the War Department.

Yours,

Kate

* She was, in a sense. According to Dad, who admired her exceedingly, she was one of the first movie scenarists.

Harvard Club
27 West 44th Street

[22 March 1942]

Dear Kate:

From Fletcher Pratt:

(1) The battered and rebuilt *Illustrious* was finally ready to put to sea. She did so. About 200 miles out from Norfolk a U 5 bomber came through the clouds & saw her. What ho, says the bomber pilot, this is no American ship, & he lets go. The *Illustrious* is now back in Norfolk under repair & the Army has a letter from Mountbatten congratulating it on its marksmanship.[45]

(2) The *Sims*—that general receptacle of the peculiar—was proceeding on her lawful occasions when the same thing happened, only this bomber missed.[46] So its pilot was grounded for 60 days for bombing an American ship & 60 days more for missing it.

From Herbert Agar:

The smart money in Washington says that the *New Yorker* program is going to be adopted—that a big reorganization will happen soon & Elmer Davis will be sitting on top of information & propaganda.[47]

Rumors originating in excellent places:

(1) The *Langley* is sunk but not all the next of kin have been notified yet & so no announcement.[48]

(2) A raid on the Bonin Islands like the one on the Marshalls has been completed & will be announced as soon as the fleet has left Pearl Harbor again.[49]

Nasty rumor believed in less well informed quarters: the Navy mistakenly depth bombed the *Surcouf* & sank her.[50]

Personal observation: Freedom House, at least to the exterior view, resembles a collaboration between Peter Arno & Helen Hokinson.[51]

Other publishing news: Macmillan are going to circus a novel by G. Hicks.[52]

K. Littauer ceased to be fiction editor of *Collier's* Friday midnight & became Major Littauer, U.S.A., Air Corps.[53]

Better chew & swallow this—it appears to violate D O R A throughout.[54]

Yrs

Benny

8 Berkeley Street
Cambridge, Massachusetts

[26 April 1942]

Dear Kate:

I'm in a state of moral energy and intellectual deliquescence and can't remember what I've reported on. Well, by default it's going to be "The Year of Decision: 1846." Little Brown insist on heaving in the number, on the ground that everybody will suppose I'm writing about now—as I am—and if the thing ever gets into a reprinting I'll quietly drop it. That will leave a title of sufficient dignity, though a complete misnomer. However.

Annual refrain: why does anyone ever suppose that April is a spring month? An April snowstorm in Boston was an April blizzard in Portland and I felt as guilty as the night I condemned half the Pennsylvania Historical Society to pneumonia.[55] The lady chairman kept on being jittier, or whatever the comparative is. She had previously written asking me if I spoke broken English and again asking if I could make myself heard. So she worried about everything from six-thirty when she took me to dinner, till eleven-thirty when I said good-night to the Universalist minister who had a party for me. When I asked for a cocktail at dinner she implored me not to get drunk and just before we opened up she begged me not to say anything off color. I never liked Maine. I hope the Women Voters will be more urbane.[56]

I am now practically a pre-medic. You may have noted that I completed two Red Cross courses. In the course of them there shook down a kind of group, some twenty of us, Shady Hill teachers, the State of Maine guide who chauffeurs across the street and is my one dependable vice-warden, a Harvard boy, a couple of printers, a pediatrician, a Cambridge councilman, some miscellaneous housewives, etc.—a gang who got to be a kind of cheering section or fraternity. We decided that we ought at least to practise what we knew and ought to learn something, if possible, most of us refused to take the Red Cross instructors' course when invited to, and we shopped round. One of the gals got in touch with a Dr. Aldrich, who has been teaching the WDC gals and he agreed to take us over.[57] I haven't had so damn much fun since the intellectuals decided that Van Wyck Brooks was not an intellectual. Aldrich is a honey. He appears to be a leading authority on burns, and he is plenty hard. He threw out all the Red Cross stuff: splints, pressure points, dogma, everything. Even the triangular bandage—"I only know how to put them on babies." He visualizes what conditions will be like if there ever is an air raid or anything like it, which is a hell of a lot more than anyone else I've listened to has done. When he says first aid, he means first aid, and he uses the word "emergency" to mean emergency. We now splint broken arms to the chest and broken legs to the other leg. "There is no first aid for burns." We shove a finger, hand, or knee into something that's bleeding. We are to be given the theory of emergency obstetrics—"about a hundred babies born in Boston every night." (But he doesn't know the average age of Berkeley Street.) He talks about falling bricks rupturing spleens—that sort of thing. He intends to take us in to an amphitheater, so we can get over the fainting stage. I watch some of the younger Shady Hill schoolmarms turn green when he talks, and I am, by God, going to lure Rosy into attending once. I wish I had a movie camera.

While he was talking about shock, he let fall a honey. Said that when the *Hindenburg* burned at Lakehurst, eight people died of burns who would have certainly lived if the photographers had let them alone.[58] The guy whose photograph in nothing but a pair of air-brushed drawers was everywhere—that guy was made to stand up twenty-seven times to have his picture taken. When I tried to pump him he shut up like a clam—said too many people were involved—but it's a pretty thing.

I've been so engrossed in first the triangular bandage and lately the double spica that my entire psychiatric practise seems to have been taken over by the profession, and I don't see the profession any more.[59] Or maybe the war has engrossed the neurotes. When I was in New York I asked Kubie if it had turned up in his patients' phantasies, and he said practically not at all. His one war case is a high-up Britisher whose term in the U.S. is drawing to a close and who will soon be ordered home, which will be just too bad, for he has developed an absolute phobia of airplanes and of the sea. The guild is meeting here at the middle of May but all my speaking dates come then and I won't be able to attend much.[60]

And no war stories. Everybody is ordered away and I don't see any uniforms except the ensigns that Henry Reck drags in. My mine expert has been ordered to anti-submarine duty and scooped the Navy by having lifeboats painted yellow on the interior—they kept hearing survivors' stories about planes not spotting them but had not thought of visibility. Henry Florey is back in Montreal, so I'll get something from that front in due time.[61] If I could conceive a serial in decent time, I could look forward to touring some of the Army by late summer, but I'm not conceiving. My closest touch with the military is by short wave from Berlin and Rome—I have learned to play my instrument well enough to get Tokio but not well enough to get clearly enough to understand what's said. I have no respect for German propaganda if there is any idea that it is to be received by the Americans. It isn't, of course. The idea is that the party line is announced by the broadcasts, then the local chapters, including the Chicago *Tribune*, take it up. I hear Fred Kaltenbach, Paul Revere, E. D. Ward, Jane Anderson, OK, and the rest, including one with a definitely Yiddish accent and another whose voice is a caricature of all the caricatures of low-comedy Germans.[62] If you are not equipped for short wave, you aren't missing anything, not even a laugh.

Just goes to show and maybe there is the evil eye. Forty-eight hour hiatus, here, and you will find above a statement that my practice has lapsed. That was where Rosy called me up and said "Come over and give Elaine a drink—she's crying." So I treated an obstinate case of hysterics but I guess there won't be any follow-up. Elaine Breed, the perfect typist, who has been working for me and the Mark Twain Estate for nearly a year now. She just bawled and bawled and I got no leads. I know she's married to what we are now obliged to call a Pulham and has two kids that she'd a hell of a lot rather be away from than with, which is why she works for me, and I know further that she used to write advertising copy for the Ritz in New York and thinks that town is the kingdom of heaven, but I know no more.[63] I have been regarding her as an excellent stabilizer of Rosy's unconscious and a kind of sphere of influence that allows me to visit my Widener study in a reasonable expectation of peace. I'm going to resent it like hell if this is just a first attack.

So last night, at my new medical course, some of the gang were off in a corner playing with a patent stretcher when one of the gals fainted. What did that gang of graduate first aiders do? They bawled "Doctor!"

Voice from upstairs: "Pa! What does 'seduce' mean?" Bunny, I instantly interpret, is reading *Life*. I escape by saying "What's the context?" and then explaining what "context" means, by which time he wants to turn the page.... He's in a hell of a rebellious and extremely interesting and engaging stage. His reading appalls me: right now he has to be pried away from the *World Almanac*. He derives an intense pleasure, a pleasure which is not in the least mathematical, from statistics. Just statistics as statistics. Shady Hill University sadly reports that he can not be induced to take an interest in bird walks. It does not grieve me. He has suddenly interested himself in baseball, and one of the few satisfactions of these days is playing catch with one's son. His ingenuity at dawdling and losing time quadruples, in so much that his brother has interpreted the phrase "I am!" as an expression of anger and so uses it. Words, in fact, have the same pleasure and about the same meaning for Mark that statistics have for Bunny. He speaks with great clarity and no coherence whatever. He has now learned his alphabet, as Bunny did at exactly the same age, and we will see whether the University will keep him from reading till he is seven.

[*handwritten addendum:*] Oh God, life is just interruption. Two more days out & I'm off to Chicago in two hours. But the perfect SEP story seems to have occurred somewhere on the North Shore. I hope, I desperately hope, at Manchester. Vouched for by the Navy. Apologetic guy calls up the local police station. A young lady and I are out for a walk—I know we're crazy, I know this is absolutely absurd, but we see something out on the water & we really think it is a periscope—will you please tell us not to be silly. Cops call up the Interceptor Command. I C sends out some crates. Score: one sub at—I pray—Manchester.

Yrs

Benny

8 Berkeley Street
Cambridge, Massachusetts

[17 May 1942][64]

Dear Kate:

Gordon Chalmers does not produce as stately prose as Paul Moody when it comes to justifying the degree, but his ritual is a hell of a lot more high church.[65] It's all in Latin and the candidate kneels to be lassoed with the hood and holds it till bidden "Surgē, Doctor."[66] . . . It's a high church college, strictly limited enrollment, high standards, and, I gather, a comfortable endowment. A very pretty place, too with one of the richest lawns I've looked on in years and some mellowed old buildings, including one alleged to be from Bulfinch plans, though when Bulfinch went in for early American collegiate gothic I wouldn't know offhand.[67] It's an hour's drive from a railroad, far enough south of the lake for Ohio to be breaking up into pleasant hills and valleys, the farms as rich as anything north of Lancaster County, and one roadsign I passed saying nostalgically, "Marion."[68] Contrary to my expectation, I enjoyed the trip, with its pleasantly cloistered folk and the leisurely air of any small college. Unquestionably a large part of me hankers for the life of a scholar. John Crowe Ransom seemed sleek and contented, but I gather the boys do not vigorously air their opinions there, for what seemed to me an amiable literary discussion with John seemed to some of them just short of a fight.[69]

Train service gets worse and worse. Old cars, badly repaired. All trains late. All trains overcrowded. A vast roar of freight going by all the time and a lot of rolling stock in view that hasn't been in view for a quarter of a century. The rationing of travel which we read about is going to be perfectly all right with me.... All northern Ohio blazes all night long and if a car-window glimpse means anything, the industrial U.S. is humming. Two weeks ago the last twenty miles into Chicago really struck awe into me. Toledo forcibly reminded me of Toledo. Maybe I've narrated some of the adventures of an infantry officer there last time.... I hanker to get out and see some of this first-hand. If I can ever get the accursed serial done, I'm going to take a running dive into it somewhere.

My gloom about the Coral Sea seems, for once, not to have been justified. And isn't it pleasant to, for once, be gloomier than the news? I persuade myself that the evidence indicates a comfortable number of planes on hand, and Bill Barrett, just in from California, claims to know that enormous quantities of them have been going out. Henry Flory is in again but I have not yet seen him long enough to glean more than the fact that they fly them to Australia in six days, flying by night only when there's a moon—some kind of Pacific cloud formation that's dangerous when you can't see it. That indicates a properly arranged ladder of bases. He says the formations scatter in a few minutes and don't see one another all day long, and then all land within two minutes of the appointed time. Henry came back by boat, going well to the south of New Zealand, and then took a plane to England a half-hour behind the First Lord of the Admiralty, to check up on him.[70] He came back from England by boat, and two boat voyages are all he wants for the duration. There is nothing like the leisurely, calm security of a bomber crossing the Atlantic in six or eight hours.

Bill Barrett is going to be a major. Charlie Taylor has fulfilled all the bitter day-dreams of one born just too late for the last war and is now a Captain, charged, I gather, with the awful duty of turning ordnance reports into English. Perry Miller departs in great secrecy on what is obviously the same assignment. In fact, the secrecy around Cambridge is getting to be something of a DeMille effect. A Nieman fellow, on leave from PM, told me wistfully the other day that if he were assigned to cover the war he wouldn't feel any obligation to get out of Cambridge.[71] When I asked him why he didn't cover it, then, he simply said "I can't, they won't talk." It may [be] easily guessed what goes on in the Cruft Laboratory, but just what the high tension lab is doing that requires sentries and automatic rifles is beyond guessing.[72] Suddenly there were no more artillery officers round the Square, and suddenly the town was full of Signal Corps officers. All of Henderson's old Fatigue Lab staff are in uniform—and don't wear the regimentals gracefully. And some of the God-damndest uniforms are coming to pass; I met a chap the other day whom it took two minutes to identify as an elderly physician of the neighborhood and he was wearing a costume hitherto unknown to man. I asked him what it was but that was forbidden information—as most conversation seems to be getting to be. "I think it is not military information," Ralph Perry said when I asked him about one of his assistants he hasn't seen recently, "that Jack has had his appendix removed."[73]

The analysts are convening here for nearly a week. Phone call from Kubie and I'll get together with him this evening. Probably going to be a secession, a bunch of New York enthusiasts, and maybe an expulsion, the Horney group.[74] Horney herself has scandalized the fraternity by proposing self-analysis. No stories from those who have so far arrived, except that Bill Barrett had that old one about the air raid warden and the girl he was riding on his bike, only it was a woman's bike. Somebody is going to have a dart into the Army Air Corps for psychiatric stupidity, and there will be some amusing papers and fights, but the newspaper editors, convened by the Nieman gang, are stealing the show and I'll listen to them mostly.

My own medical career progresses. This guy Aldrich—Robert Henry Aldrich—is a jewel. I locate him now. He is the guy who first demonstrated that people who survive the shock of a burn die of infection. He also developed the gentian violet treatment. When he lectured to us on burns it was the most stirring description of the investigating mind I've heard since Zinsser. Well, we had obstetrics, which he is convinced is going to be the principal problem in our local raids, and I now know how to deliver babies in the street. Simplest department of medical practise, says Aldrich. The class blew its instruction pretty badly—also a couple blew their lunch when he showed a color movie of a Caesarian section. We got it well in mind that our first step when the lady started screaming was to find out if this was her first baby, that we learned her husband's name, if possible, and whether she was a Catholic. Then, with the victim stretched out in the street and pains increasing rapidly from one a minute, "What's the first thing you do?" says Aldrich. Various suggestions, variously sapient, from the fathers, mothers, and virgins of the class. Aldrich shook his head. "First take off her pants," he said. After he got the baby born through various emergencies, he returned to the subject and said that if the job ever fell to any of the men present, they'd better, if possible, provide themselves with a chaperon. A couple of the audience didn't get him. Why, they demanded. For the same reason a doctor has a nurse in his office when he first examines a woman, Aldrich says. One bird still didn't get it, so Aldrich says, for self-protection. Still didn't register, so, "Well, suppose we go out of this building and find you out on the playfield taking off a woman's pants," he says, "conceivably it might be open to misinterpretation." So then he posed a question. You see a woman coming out of a bombed house, a woman you know is about ready to give birth. A bomb falls and she gets her head cut off by a section of flying glass. Remembering that you have got eight or ten minutes when you could save the baby, do you do a Caesarian? "We wouldn't have any equipment," one guy suggests. "Well," says Aldrich, "probably you'd have a pocket knife." Quite a guy, all around. Marian Schlesinger's obstetrician has been called up—I don't know why the Army is taking so many baby snatchers—so I've given her my phone number.

Rosy grows more inscrutable. It is quite true that she has ditched the prize son of a bitch she was beginning to anchor to, but apparently for no more profound reason than that there has showed up a friend of hers in the uniform of a captain of the Black Watch[75]. The idea of Rosy doing anything for a simple feminine reason is more than I can understand.

My simple job for the newspaper editors is going to be to review and evaluate American intellectual history during the last quarter century.[76] The night before that I kid my betters at the annual Henry Adams dinner, and those two speeches seem to be absolutely the last of my spring season.[77] I can barely conceive the next three weeks, with only one job to think about. That's John August. I have got a scheme all doped out and on Tuesday Max Wilkinson,[78] *vice*[79] Major Littauer, comes up to talk it over. Even in the tripe business the war raises hell. It's a lovely scheme, but it may be vetoed. By whom? By the State Department.

Meanwhile, I'm beginning to get proofs on the book. It was originally my intention to withhold the inclosure from you until the book should be ready. But I think I'd better submit it to you, praying you, however, to issue no objections. I don't know precisely what the production schedule is going to be, but I may be able to send you a set of folded sheets, which would enable you to read a twelve pound book in comfort, in about a month. OK?

Yours,
Benny

[enclosure: galley proof page from *The Year of Decision: 1846*:]

DEDICATION

Dear Kate:

While I was writing this book you sometimes asked me what it was about. Reading it now, you will see that, though it is about a good many things, one theme that recurs is the basic courage and honor in the face of adversity which we call gallantry. It is always good to remember human gallantry, and it is especially good in times like the present. So I want to dedicate a book about the American past written in a time of national danger to a very gallant woman,

TO

KATHARINE GRANT STERNE

Yours,
Benny

Bowne

[BEFORE 20 MAY 1942]

Dear Benny,

You shouldn't have sprung that dedication on me in my, er, weakened condition. I bawled for an hour. God knows I don't deserve it, but I am very honored & very, very proud. I do thank you, Benny, from the bottom of my heart.

It's humiliating to have to admit how over-generous you are in your judgment. I'm not especially scared of mice or snakes or thunderstorms or (prospective) air-raids, but, by God, I am craven in the presence of spiders, cymbals, bad dreams & the tubercle bacillus.

May I hope to see those pages about the middle of June? I'll braid asterisks in my hair & celebrate Midsummer's Eve properly, for once.[80]

Let me assure you that that pool-table mentioned in *Time's* review of Ilka Chase's autobiography is absolutely authentic.[81] The house (in Suffern, N.Y.) was given to the Order by the first Mrs. T. F. Ryan and, as *Time* reported, the table came with the house.[82] It's adjustable for either pool or billiards. Mollie was stationed there in '30-32, and again (after stretches at Rosemont & St. Walburga's) in '40-41. She and Mother Mary Campion used to drive from Suffern to Po'keepsie, in the world's trimmest station-wagon, in nothing flat. They always brought huge quantities of fruit, flowers, magazines & toiletries, & panicked the hospital with their breezy entrance.

I've noticed the Army's tendency to take baby-snatchers & baby-doctors, too, and, frankly, it's puzzled me. Surely the Women's Auxiliary isn't going to be <u>that</u> big.... But the prize story of the week concerns a local lawyer, a guy built somewhat on the lines of the earlier Joe Alsop. With the aid of fasting, prayer & innumerable Turkish baths, he finally made the Army weight-limit & was shipped off to North Carolina. He writes his sister that, so far, he has only been killed once: seems he was disguised as a tree & the umpire ruled that there were no trees of that size in North Carolina. Now he's hoping for a transfer to the Pacific Northwest.

Thanks again, Benny! I wish I could really tell you how damned set-up I am.

Yours,

Kate

****

[enclosure, letterhead]

JOSEPH F. STEEGMULLER • MORTGAGE BROKER • GREENWICH, CONNECTICUT

May 2, 1942

Dear Katie: —

I'm giving you the first opportunity to get in on the ground floor. As you see, I am a successful inventor and have the world by the tail or the victim by the arm or leg, whichever is first presented or the more seriously injured.

The idea is this: —A careful survey by Babson[83] indicated a possible outlet for the Steegmuller Splint of 6,759,843,723, which at a net profit each of 304 provides an annual income of $9,854,000. Do you wish to purchase a half-interest in my patent for $7.89? I'll hold the option open until 1:10 PM, May 3rd.

I've taken a first-aid course so that is how the splint came about. I am therefore capable of splintering anyone and all I can say is: —The Lord help you if I once get a traction hitch on your ankle. In the advanced class I was the only man in the group of thirty five so what with four females putting a splint on an arm and five splintering a leg at the same time I got a case of the jitters that nearly put me back in Bowne again. I've really put this splint on the market and if Dr. Williams wishes to order a thousand or two for Bowne they may be obtained from Bloomingdales.

Bertha says she thinks of you every day and wonders if you receive the thought-telegrams sent by short wave? Francis, by the way, is writing a new mystery story having to do with short-wave about which you may expect to hear before long. Both Francis and Laurence are still undrafted but with the new classification it would not surprise me if they were called. Sherman said it long ago.

We would love to hear from you. Give my love to Florence and all the Sweeties I left behind.[84]

Joe S.

[*with newspaper clipping from Greenwich Time, Greenwich, Connecticut, Saturday, 2 May 1942, with front-page photograph of Joseph Steegmuller and his splint*]

8 Berkeley Street
Cambridge, Massachusetts

[19 June 1942]

Dear Kate:

Note on the bilious temperament. Half an hour ago Ted Spencer strolled in and said, "The radio just announced that Churchill is in this country."[85] In one breath young Arthur Schlesinger said, "That means the second front," and I said, "There goes the

Near East, Egypt, and probably Russia too." But haven't the last few weeks seen the experts in damndest delirium yet? They've guessed wrong so consistently that Fletcher, who never guesses right, has looked better than he ever did. I guess the real strength of Elmer Davis was that he never did any experting.

He walked into the worst job in the world.[86] If he makes any order at all of it, he'll be accomplishing a miracle. The mess could not possibly be worse: the simple fact is that the services of information are, as he takes office, in a state of total breakdown. All the worst qualities of the New Deal got focussed in those branches and I doubt if Elmer—or Roosevelt or God—has power enough to bring them back to anything resembling even efficiency, still less the sort of intelligent service and leadership we need. Within a week I have seen a grown and hardboiled man actually crying over the failure.... The worst is that, even if Roosevelt now means to back him up, which is at least open to doubt, he can't possibly mean to very long. There will now be centered on Elmer all the pressures, leverages, and attacks of the people he is now displacing, and it seems inevitable that Roosevelt will begin taking back everything he has given away, bit by bit but nevertheless paralyzingly. Our best hope [is] that the honeymoon will endure long enough for Elmer to do so good a job that mere public opinion will neutralize the pressures. He's a better man than George Creel ever was.[87] Unfortunately Roosevelt has not got Wilson's willingness to back a subordinate to the hilt and there was grown up since Creel's time not only a bureaucracy of information but also a kind of idealist in office, like Archie, who has a more persuasive title for mere lust of power.

Well, the appointment held up the August *Harper's* while I killed a column and a half and had to readjust the rest.[88]

There's more war at Ipswich than anywhere else hereabouts. A lot of my gang live there and I've been summoned out several times lately for lectures and the like, and it's exactly like moving into the zone of operations or an Angela Thirkell novel, or what I take one to be for God forbid that I should read one.[89] The basis appears to be no more than any other shore town has: a dimout regulation on all roads near the water and a couple of company of soldiers guarding the beach from something or other. But Ipswich sinks a sub a night, sometimes two, and never sinks one till a rubber boat has landed John August characters from it. Every plane that goes by—and what with the various patrols and replacements, a lot go by—is making out to sea to sink another one. Every time a minesweeper takes its daily sighting shot within sound of Ipswich, it's still another submarine, and the blimp that came by when I was last there was spotting the secret radio station which is communicating with them. I got no support for my statement that it's easier to triangulate on land, and when I proposed an easy test for the stories of depth charges which everyone is telling, namely that you could find dead fish shortly thereafter if the story was true, I was practically accused of subversive ideas.

Moreover, Ipswich is where the Germans are to land in force, which is why all the John August characters come to spy out the land. Also, if the anti-aircraft defenses of Boston prove adequate, Ipswich is where the thwarted bombers are going to dump their loads, coming back. And all this with the most elaborate secrecy and a conviction that us outsiders had damn well better wake up quick, for there's a war going on.

Mollie Brazier, the sedentary Englishwoman who somehow contrives to get around more than anyone else I know, was lately in Atlantic City for the AMA—where she exhibited brain-wave machinery—and at a lunch turned up a melancholy Lieutenant Thompson, who eventually proved to be Larry Thompson, but yesterday curator of rare books at Princeton and my successor in the criticism and probably the biography of R. Frost.[90] As dinner went on he proceeded to unfold to her a reasonably complete, if not particularly perceptive, outline of the Morrison triangle. So if Larry is talking the whole world will presently know, and I think that Robert's friends ought to be a little more discreet than Robert is. Also, if Larry understands what has happened, then anyone can understand, for he's a reasonably intelligent young man but not gifted at what we call psychology. Well, I've encountered none of that triangle very often this year, though I have seen Frost occasionally by design. The last time I saw Ted he looked as if even he had begun to catch on, and the last time I saw Kay she looked and acted like a common scold. In fact, she bawled me out and I did what I could not have conceived of doing a few years back, I told her she was making a fool of herself and be so good as to stop it. I have never seen the like. Once she was sweet and warm and somehow clad in her own charm. Now she's cold and stiff and envious and sharp and obviously helldriven by her own lacks. Moreover, as an expert in the poetry of Robert Frost, as unquestionably the most expert expert now living, I perceive that Robert has had all he wants of her in the role of mistress and has now nominated her to be the north pole of his penitence, and I can think of no more painful role for an ex-mistress, even if her mistressing has only been psychic. I suppose I should see grandeur in his possessiveness, his destructiveness, but I don't. He is unquestionably a great man and a great bastard.

Well, I'm a damned fool. I have no objection to voicing my opinions, but I would choose the house of Dave Little to ask, under the pressure of several cocktails, when Mr. Conant was going to develop some ideas about education.[91]

One of his purgees, Avis's obstetrician and my favorite Bostonian, Eddie Harding, has lately been made chief of surgery at the Boston City Hospital. Eddie does not even try to conceal his satisfaction, for, raised to the belief of many generations that Harvard College formulates the judgments of heaven, he took his purging uncommon hard. Otherwise the appointment would hardly penetrate his gloom at being rejected by the Army on the ground that fifty-three is a little old. This, you understand, proceeds exclusively from Roosevelt's knowledge that Eddie opposes him.

That's quite a place, the Boston City, and maybe it's just as well to have one hospital in Boston that Harvard does not run. It keeps on trying to grab it, and Eddie's appointment is in part a Tufts and B. U. stand against the grab, Harvard having tried seismically to get its own candidate in for nearly a year. I sometimes drop in there to see a pal, and the acres and acres of floor space, hundreds and hundreds of nurses and internes, and thousands and thousands of out-patients waiting their turn can depress you or inspire you. The little cluster of research hospitals vibrate with tremendous investigations and equally tremendous antipathy to MGH.... Well, my own medical course goes on. I can now treat blindfolded a victim who is casually suffering from a crushed foot, a compound fracture of the femur on the same leg, evisceration, and a broken neck. Moreover, the great Aldrich assures me I am a born midwife, and it was I who solved the dilemma of the five-months-old infant suffering from a fractured skull. We now meet only once a week but it is unquestionably the week's high moment for everyone in the class—rather the fraternity, for we now have picnic suppers, gang up on visitors and inspectors, coach each other surreptitiously, and write letters to the papers. I find that Boston, medically and socially, is split into two warring camps on the merits of Aldrich. I have seldom known a man to be so liked and hated by his colleagues. I gather that the dislike originates in the fact that he was very brash when very young and the further fact that he can handle liquor better than the profession is willing to trust itself. No one could slander him any to our fraternity, and I could rest my whole case on the fact that here is an outlander, in no degree whatever a Grottie, a Porky, or even a Harvard, whom Eddie Harding likes and respects. I trace his slight stammer to the fact which recently transpired, that he was married for some years to a literary lady. It comes out that we must have met each other back in the days of Theodore Hill, Boston's jazz age, which would imply no recognition of each other when sober. He assures us that our regular study of colored movies has hardened us to blood—which I venture to doubt. Avis has subsequently held on to her lunch and only Pappy Fallon, a printer who comes all the way from Milton to attend, has acted on her precedent, but I still think that the first duty of first aiders will be to treat themselves for panic. Aldrich is taking all those who will attend to operating sessions, which come in my working hours, and assigning us by twos to evening duty in the receiving rooms of various hospitals. I will presently go forth on that last assignment: bear yourself patiently until I report. I wonder how they treat intoxication now? In my Harvard days I sometimes spent evenings with intern friends in dispensaries, and in that vanished age the treatment was a tumbler full of Epsom salts and instructions to take a walk in the open air.

Bunny goes to camp in a week. I'm writing as John August, though as yet with no guess as to whether this is the stuff of just a trial heat. The Harvard faculty begins to come back, resentful of summer duty. Parts of it drift by in uniform, a costume not particularly becoming. Schoolmarms will mingle with freshmen. All my post wardens are in Maine and the raid—Mr. Hoadley sets it for the 26th—will find me rescuing the elderly unassisted.[92] Cars have come back to the streets, for the A ration has been doubled until new cards appear. The Charles is full of the power boats that can't go to sea. The new Coca Cola plant is storing books for Harvard.[93] The Square has been desecrated by a ladies' footwear, shoe, and underwear store.[94] Shoppers push garden carts. Paul Robson [*sic*] is going to play Othello at Brattle Hall.[95] And the bushes of Berkeley Street are full of strollers, who used to be parkers on the abandoned sections of the Concord Turnpike. Summer.

Also, to do some experting of my own, I think the clutch is here.

Yours,

Benny

8 Berkeley Street
Cambridge, Massachusetts

[16 August 1942]

Dear Kate:

Excuse. I begin to get your point about the weather. It moved on to these parts about six days ago. Well, all I can say is that up to that unhappy date, this was the best summer we ever had here.

The DeVoto War Analysis Service seems to be maintaining its brilliant one thousand. Altogether wrong on everything so far, and the Germans are too making for the Caucasus. However, the Service is stubbornly insisting that some kind of SECOND FRONT is preparing and that the date, originally set here for August 15, is not more than two weeks off at this moment. If something big has not come to the support of this stubbornness by September 1, the Service will convert its plant to the icing and packaging of books about the war. There are too goddamn many converging currents. Something has to be up. I can't believe, either, that yesterday's Berlin story about an AEF in Iraq or today's *Times* story about Egypt indicates the direction.[96] I am still playing the coast of France, though conceding more smoke to the Norway notion than I did at the last forecast.

Note, moreover, that our Service has approximately the correct dope on coastwise convoy losses and on the movement of American tanks to Egypt.

Best yarn of the last couple of weeks. The Navy finds unavoidable certain deficiencies of its inland aviation training fields. Moved up a gang from Iowa to patrol duty out of New York, recently. One corn-fed pilot came in from a flight and announced that there was a yacht anchored a little way out, a big red yacht with the owner's name painted on its side: Ambrose.

The Bread Loavians, this year denied the mellow exasperation of their Uncle Benny, are passing through on their way to the cote. Fletcher Pratt has been here for a couple of days, full of his customary inside stories, phantasies, and attractive guesses. I always scale Fletcher down fifty percent and then deduct another one-third to allow for mathematical error. What remains this time is fenced off with pledges of secrecy of different degree, and I hardly know what can be passed on. Well, the PBY, the Catalina of our British friends' reluctant admiration, has always been a swell job for its purpose but so slow that it has been extremely vulnerable to attack by pursuits.[97] A system has now been worked out whereby it can tow a Spitfire or the new Grumman Thunderbolt (which Fletcher insists is the best fighter in the skies) behind it.[98] Come the Focke-Wulfs, the tow plane casts off, goes into action, and returns to a home field up to seven hundred miles away.[99] Some of them along our Atlantic coast have been ringed round with 140-foot circles of steel and go out and set off magnetic mine fields, wherever located.[100] Fletcher says that the planes which the *Wasp* took to Malta were Spitfires equipped with a highly secret device which enabled them to take off from the flight deck.[101] The *Wasp* was taken slowly through Gibraltar just before nightfall, with the result that a couple of hundred German planes of mixed species came down on her as she neared Malta.[102] Whereupon the 85 Spitfires took the air and shot down two thirds of them. He adds that Shangri-La was the carrier *Ranger* and Doolittle's planes which took off from her were equipped with this same device, apparently one of the hottest of all our developments.[103]

There is some talk that Fletcher and I may work our respective avenues, he the Army and I Elmer Davis, to see if we can't get some kind of assignment writing military history. I think we'd make a pretty good team. I would reduce his phantasies, temper his spleen, and leaven his GOP Republicanism, and the two of us could probably provide more background in American military history than any other pair of news-trained professional writers.

As the Bread Loavians stop off to report, I rejoice more than ever that I finally found the bowels to say no. I have enormously enjoyed Bread Loaf and, looking back, I wonder that its State of Mind has not blown itself to pieces long since. It is an annual two weeks of concentrated psychosis. I think that in any event this will be the last conference, and my skin tells me that it has a large chance of blowing up with a great bang. Heretofore there have always been automobiles. When the internal pressure got too great one could, and those of us who were veterans did, get off the Mountain for an hour, an afternoon, or a weekend. An expert reader of pressure gauges, I long since formed the habit of disappearing well in advance and so spared myself some of the worst moments. This year there will be no gas. One will stay on the Mountain, take the pressure as long as possible, then pitch in. Furthermore Ted, who has never appreciated the plain fact that the bar in the staff's clubhouse (for the establishment of which I fought a bloody battle and which I defended against every kind of pressure and attack) has actually been the stabilizing element.[104] It has been. You cannot get fifteen writers, some of them good writers and some of them literary temperaments, together for two weeks of such horrible exhibitionism, attack by frantic literary ladies, envy of minor and small-town geniuses, and mere human cussedness focussed by seventy-five panting customers—you cannot assemble such staff and expect them to behave themselves through such an ordeal unless they have a Room of Their Own, a stated time when they can shut the yammerers out, and plenty of liquor for the restoration of their natural self-respect. I perceived that in my first year. I fought a terrific battle in my second year. I forced the issue in my third year and ever since have succeeded in holding the position.

Ted has always been uneasy about shutting the customers out—he has always yearned to find some way of making Brook Farm grow on the Mountain for two weeks.[105] He has always been apprehensive as hell about the staff's liquor, the customers' gossip about it, and the possibility that something really undesirable might happen. (Apart from a few heroic drunks, nearly all of them put on by visiting geniuses or young Fellows, nothing ever has.) He has had a dozen apprehensions of his own, and has had the pressure of Middlebury College, excepting always Paul Moody, which thinks that liquor is evil. And, of course, he has had his annual batch of complaints from furiously activated women in their middle years who want to crash the barrier, probably disrobe the staff, and in any event find out what Goes On. So this year he has notified the staff that they won't be able to get ice, that the conference can't afford to pay for a steward of the club room (which it only has a couple of times, anyway), and that there can't be any liquor in the clubhouse—Treman Cottage, the staff's sanctuary. Ted is too God damned innocent for this world. Even Bunny, who has yet to taste wickedness, could predict what is already happening. The Everitts, already aware that you can't drive down to the liquor store at Brandon whenever you need to, had bought two cases of gin and a case of Scotch. They got Ted's note on the eve of departure and at once doubled the order. Fletcher filled the back of his car with liquor on the same reasoning, began to feel the natural qualms, and while he was here stocked up with such additional explosives as brandy and Pernod.[106] Instead of occurring well offstage, the drinking will now be spread all over the reservation, in all the cottages, which contain customers as well as staff. It will be in smaller groups, so there will be more of it. It will be in smaller groups instead of in a big, general one, and so cliques will form. The staff will unite only to murder customers, who have never been murdered before, and will spend the rest of its time murdering one another, which has never been possible before.

And that is far from all, and Ted, let us repeat, is too God damned innocent for this world. I have said damned little to Fletcher about the central situation at any time, but he is no fool. He said, What's the low-down, why aren't you coming to Bread Loaf? I stuck to my story. He said, nuts, is it Kay you can't take or is it the triangle? Helen Everitt, who has no nerves, was already jittery before she left. Frances Curtis, who isn't going and for approximately the same reasons, called me up and offered to bet me three to one—and no takers, I add—that the great man would bring the conference to an end before Friday of the first week. I have not seen him since May but the stories that drift in exhibit him as still more unbuttoned and still more demanding, and Kay as querulous to the point of breakdown. By God, I'll bet something happens.... Ted spent an evening here ten days ago—he was down for some Harvard duty and, being alone, felt free to come. He breaks my heart and the fog of his bewilderment is thick and impenetrable. Did I send you *The Witness Tree*?[107] I meant to. Well, while Ted was here I permitted myself a couple of remarks about Frost—I'm still sore about a wholly unmotivated, highly malicious lie he took occasion to tell about me in public several times last spring—and Ted simply would not permit them. He talked on and on about Frost, in a tone of worship tempered only by amazement. So he hit on the theme of how Frost was all men and how, to Ted's amazement, some of the ugliest emotions man could feel turned up in the poetry of this genius. He offered in evidence a poem from the new book, "The Subverted Flower." It's one of the cryptic ones in the latter-day doggerel which no one has the guts to tell Frost he ought to suppress. It tells how the man turns to a beast, a coward, "base and fetid" and so on. A chunk straight out of the riot, and I don't see how anyone could fail to see it for what it is. Ted sees it for what it is—by formula. But there must be a couple of dozen of us at least by now who knew it for what it was at first glance. My first glance at it was in the fall of '38. But I knew what it was some months before—at the exact moment of that famous blowup of that famous August.

> She was standing to the waist
> In goldenrod and brake
> Her shining hair displaced.

I wandered all unwarned into that August blowup thus. The last time I had seen Frost, nothing. (It was some weeks before.) The first things he said to me when I met him again was, "I want you to take a picture of Kay for me." Well, I'd taken many pictures of Kay. Yes, but this was a special one. All right. So we went and got Kay. And he posed her for me in some goldenrod.

I don't know which is more wonderful, genius or innocence.

Yeah, and look what the very thought of Bread Loaf does to me. Better forget this page.

Yours,

Benny

Century Club
7 West Forty-third Street
New York

[16 September 1942]

Dear Kate:

How to be young again, in one lesson. Throw a serial into the ash can. After months of agony, I finally realized why I was suffering so. The cool, keen, tireless DeVoto mind clicked. I got there in the end, darling, I got there. Why was I suffering so? Because this piece of tripe was a piece of tripe. It was a piece of tripe of such odor as in all my years I have never encountered elsewhere. That realization filtered into my mind at exactly 11:07 A.M. Sunday. At 11:08 I said in ringing tones: "The Hell with it."

So the hell with it.

Pausing only long enough to write a piece to finance the trip, I thereupon—or yesterday—set sail for N.Y. Figuratively speaking.—The 5 hour trains now make it in 6 hours & 10 minutes.[108] And if you want to go to the can, wait till the train stops—that's how I got that contusion over my right eye. It has got enormously worse since I came to Westport in August & unbelievably worse than it was in March.

Anyway, I'm a changed & improved man. I feel like a patent medicine ad. My eyes shine, there's a lift in the hips, & God help all editors who accost me. Who is John August going to be next? Well, either B. DeVoto or John Buchan.[109] I'm of two minds whether to write a novel or whether to fulfill an ancient phantasy of mine, to write a thriller for the deckle-edge trade.[110]

I've spent most of my time so far trying to get a seat to *Star & Garter*, so far unsuccessfully, so I haven't heard much.[111] I'll report in a couple of days (at this moment the FBI is going through its DeVoto file, for I've pulled a wire to get a look at the *Iowa*).[112] Well, this: from July 15 to September 15, exactly no (zero) sinkings off the Atlantic coast anywhere. In that time 2 subs ventured into the area. Score, Navy 2. One off Cape May, one northward, I didn't get where but presumably off Newfoundland.

But the point I'm making is, the fool may have lost 5 or 6 months, but for the moment he feels swell.

I'll pick this up again presently.

Yrs

Benny

Bowne

NOV 8TH [1942]

Dear Benny

Well, here it is.[113] And may God guide their tanks!

We're learning. How we are learning! Like about a hundred million other people, I've spent a good part of to-day eating the hard words I've said about U.S. recognition of Vichy.[114] And maybe there's something to be said for strict censorship after all.

May I say, too, that I think it was pretty big of FDR to take what he has taken—including Willkie's tirades, including abuse in the press, including, especially, his shellacking at the polls—with a grin, when he had this magnificent ace up his sleeve all the time.[115] I'll think thrice before I again call him a cheap politician.

I've asked a few likely people about .22 L.R.'s, but all I've got so far is guffaws.... I have a plan in mind which may rate me a visit from the FBI & may also ~~rate~~ net me some cartridges—I hope!

Yours,

Kate

Maybe I should explain that stony silence since Oct 4th has been due to a little heart attack on that date. All these years, Leonidoff has been telling me that the trouble with my heart is functional, not organic. Now Leonidoff has gone to the wars (Camp Shelby, Miss., to be exact) & Williams has taken over some of his chores. "Nonsense," says Williams, "a combination of myocarditis and endocarditis." Maxie, as a good little assistant should, agrees. Deyo, Poughkeepsie's one remaining cardiologist, whom they called in consultation, thinks that the heart is damaged, all right, but that the proximate cause of all the fireworks is an obstreperous thyroid. I've swallowed enough Lugol's to the multitudinous seas muddy considerable.[116] Seems to help, too.

Deyo is quite a guy. I never was more surprised than the first time I saw him. People keep talking about "old Dr. Deyo." Old Dr. Deyo, hell!

Had a quaint little night special during the Late Unpleasantness, Hilda Hjertberg, of Göteberg [*sic*], University Heights & Po'keepsie. She is competent, conscientious, kind (pardon the Luce-talk), but a shade slow on the uptake. For instance, I rang for her one morning about five o'clock. When she came in the room, I was sitting up in bed, retching violently. She looked at me in complete silence for about thirty seconds, then said gently: "Do you feel nauseated?"

And how is <u>your</u> bug?

Look, dear, daytime radio has <u>nothing</u> but fillers & overset.

What is the Dill Pickle Club?

About the songs, I certainly can't love the current crop, especially not "Praise" etc., but "This Is the Army" isn't bad, "Don't Set Under the Apple Tree" was gay while it lasted, and there's a wacky number called "Little Bo Peep Has Lost Her Jeep" that gets me, especially the immortal couplet:

"She goes chug-chuggy
In her old Blitz-buggy"[117]

Seems to me that the best story of the war to date is the one about the U.S. ship that zipped into Oran harbor full-speed-ahead, never slackening until she banged into the jetty. Seems the bridge-to-engine-room telegraph had been bombed out (unknown to all), but the French took the whole performance as simply another instance of American dash, & cheered to the hilltops.

I could take my onetime colleague H. Baldwin's cries about A Separate War and The Most Important War more seriously, if I didn't keep remembering, irrationally, perhaps, that a) he was a pre-Pearl Harbour Isolationist & b) his middle name is Wasch.[118]

Sure, I'd admire to read Gene Rhodes—I never have.[119] But if it's judgment you're looking for, better try some other counter.

Yours,
Kate

Nov 16th
[23 November 1942]

Dear Kate:
Uncle is lying down, with the remnants of the God damndest migraine in the history of literature smouldering in his left ear. Since the good & eccentric von Storch went to occupy a chair at the Albany Medical College I've let the program go more or less as he left it.[120] The trouble is that migraines, like female adolescents, change their shape. I've come to accepting the new shape as part of original sin & the imbecility of the medical profession. Part of the War Puritanism I'm diagnosing so profusely on all sides. So it wasn't until the 3rd day of this one that I phoned Harry Aldrich. (My instructor in obstetrics & for some time the Family Doctor—Eddie Harding, at the age of 53 and with a hernia only lately repaired, having gone off to chase the glories of that other war he was in.) Aldrich called it a migraine & poured enough ergotamine into my veins to float the *Normandie*. The point about ergotamine, however, is that if you don't take it early in the attack you might as well take essence of Sen-Sen or even prayer.[121] So—and this seems to be the pt—he then produced a pill which must be made of TNT & hellfire, fifty-fifty. Codeine never does anything to me except lower the threshold of my

profanity & the only time I was ever jabbed with morphine it just stimulated my endocrines. But this pill blew me from here to there in 30 seconds flat and I've been walking back for 18 hours. God knows what it is—Harry won't tell—but it can be described as active. I think it would enormously reduce the smelting process if used at the Mesabi & it certainly ought to be considered very seriously for filling the blockbusters we'll be dropping on Tokio.[122] If I know my post-Freud therapy—which holds that the insulin shock treatment gets its results psychically—this one has scared migraine out of me. I'm going to wear one on my scapular from now on.

Yes, Mr. Roosevelt has looked pretty damn good under the stress of secrecy, political asininity, and the pontificating of everyone from Willkie down to the [?] Kernan Plan (which looks pretty good right now) and on to DeVoto, Sterne, & Dorothy.... It could be that he will rise to the war; it has happened twice in our history, even if you think that Wilson didn't. The James Madison who let the Federalist secession plot play itself out without Presidential interference or retaliation was a hell of a lot bigger man & wiser statesman than the Jeffersonian—or Lockeian—ideologue who had first suspended & then restored the Embargo Acts.[123] From 1812 to 1816 there were a good many things that would have wrecked the US forever if the abstract intellectual had not somehow found in himself new qualities of steadiness, steadfastness, foresight, courage, and sheer will that certainly had not been visible in the man who up to that time had been merely a disciple & a writer of editorials.[124] And certainly the United States has existed as a continuity since 1860 primarily because Lincoln could grow to meet the emergency. The whole truth about Lincoln—and the magnificent truth about the American system—is that emergency piled on emergency just drew out of him a more flexible ability, which finally got exalted & even noble, to meet emergency.

It could happen with F.D.R. Leaving his personal characteristics out of the equation for the moment, there is a striking & even deadly parallel between what he has to do & what Lincoln had to do—I mean in regard to the components of his administration. Then, the effective brains & the effective energies of Management (in <u>that</u> case management of domestic, middle class sentiment) were such Republicans as Seward, the Blairs, etc.—with their equivalents in the States such as Morton.[125] Whatever they had been in the preceding 5 or 10 years (and Seward, for instance, had been so radical that Lincoln got the nomination as a safer man), they were, for purposes of fighting the war, conservatives. Unquestionably they were both the strongest force toward victory and the representatives of the largest body of private sentiments—in sum. Fight the War to Save the Union. I take it that the McNutts, Byrnes, Barkleys, Douglases, etc. of today correspond to them exactly—and, under post-war stress, incapable, some of them, of reverting to Republicanism, as the Blairs reverted to Democracy when the radicals took control.[126]

There was also a large & powerful body headed by Sumner, Stanton, Stevens, Andrews & the like, & using Chase as their figurehead—as their analogues of today are using Wallace (but, at a guess, won't be able to use him much longer)—who consciously & deliberately used the war as a means of effecting political & social changes which would have taken 50 years of peace to effect.[127] The Hendersons, Arnolds, Cohens, etc.[128] Then & now properly called the Radicals.

There were also the War Democrats—Willkie, Saltonstall, Stassen, today's "good" Republicans.

Lincoln's problem was to harmonize these energies & control them. He did so, but by a hair. With the prestige of victory he could certainly have held the radicals in check after the war. He was killed. The Radicals became openly what they were, and are, semi-secretly, they became totalitarians. That did it. The totalitarian liberalism & humanitarianism of Sumner, Wade, Stanton, Stevens, Andrews & the rest became the greatest social & political obscenity in our history.[129] And can easily duplicate that achievement now & surpass it.

There are two questions, I think: how far Roosevelt understands the ratio between ordered & explosive social change in war conditions, & how able he will be to keep his own best friends under his own control. We are already hearing about the Global Democracy and other hooey that corresponds to the atrocious idealism of 1918 that took the League of Nations entirely out of the world of fact & so made it impotent. We hear it especially from Wallace, with, I suspect, Archie MacLeish, writing the speeches as the true totalitarians like Hopkins, Henderson & other social workers draw up the plans.[130] Global Democracy means TVA & Tugwell's Resettlement & NRA & the Greenbelt spread over the world at the muzzles of American guns, paid for by American taxes, & made economically possible here only by a totalitarian domestic organization—a transformation of the one created by the war & accepted as a war necessity.[131]

The US after the war is going to be either a totalitarian New Deal state, or else it is going to be a compromise worked out between federal & federated forms of group democracies. Wallace & his gang vote for the all-out totality, with the US doing good to everyone by force if necessary. And this means, over the long curve, the absorption of South America & finally war with China or Russia or both.

Now the interesting thing is that, much as we have heard about all this from Wallace et al, we have not heard a single solitary word about it from Roosevelt.

At the end of this war various economies & social systems besides ours will be flourishing & likewise facing the necessity of adjustment and transformation. Various others will be facing the necessity of repair & recuperation. God help us all if we, the U.S., lack the realism to meet them in terms of economic & social—well, parliamentarianism. The dream of the social-worker statesman, in the Henry Wallace mind, seems to be to dot the world with an infinitely reproduced blend of Montgomery Ward and Hull House.[132] It seems to me the maniac vision of a Madame Blavatsky turned loose in a powder mill.[133] It is possible only backed by total force, and we can get that force only by total means at home. I hate—and fear—this aroused revivalism worse than anything else in the world. I have some confidence that a man like Henderson can appreciate facts & even change his sentiments about them, but I think that Wallace & his gang—including my one-time pal Jim Landis—can destroy civilization, the remaining vestiges, out of sheer vision. But Roosevelt, I think, will drop him. Has dropped most of them & is dropping the rest.

It is a blatant fact that the miracles which permitted us to invade Africa 11 months after Pearl Harbor have been performed not by the uplift minds of the administration but by military men, technological engineers, & industrial administrators. The last two will be altogether without function in the Wallace world—and certainly the world in which they were trained is dead forever. On the other hand, the particular kind of intelligence they have has been absolutely lacking from the New Deal since the beginning. The government must learn how their jobs are done & they must learn why the New Deal is necessary. This kind of compromise must be achieved & the whole future of the US pivots on 2 questions, whether it can be achieved in time, & whether it can be achieved outside the bureaucracy.

Have you ever retired to your oratory & meditated on a pressure group composed of 10,000,000 veterans?

Well, did you see the issue of the *New Republic* that hit the stands just as the news of North Africa came out? It was very soothing to my type of mind.[134] But the revived DeVoto Forecasting & Vote-sampling Service did very well, I think.... It now sends you without comment a "feel" which its Washington representative has (the same who took it out on that limb & forecast a Second Front in France by August 15, & claimed to be inside the White House when it did so): that something is preparing in—

well, you'd never guess —

in

Kamchatka

Locally there was a quickly smothered submarine scare two weeks ago. So quickly smothered & with such swarms of official smotherers that there probably was something in it. I was working another lead at the time & this one was shut off so fast that I never got details. I'd guess it had to do with saboteurs or perhaps even sabotage.... Also a wildly idiotic tightening of dimout regulations and a positive decimation of doctors. I question the good sense of blackout & dimout altogether. There has ceased to be any possibility whatever of any widespread air-raid against this coast, and, if there should be, it is quite impossible to blackout either Boston or New York. The dimout is even more futile and has long since ceased to have any realistic object whatever. Everybody knows this, including the Army & the OCD. Why do they keep it up, then? Well, this is one of the fruits of our army system. The fuddy-duddies & incompetents who are weeded out to prevent disaster in the field are given jobs in the Service Commands with nothing to do but impair the efficiency of their juniors & to assert the Army insecurity-feelings on the civilian population. The same principle makes the First Naval District a boneyard of numskulls interested primarily in maintaining protocol. Washington lately had to intervene to save from court-martial the captain of a cruiser in for refitting after months at sea. He had jeopardized the service by over-riding Navy Yard rules that would have kept some of his crew without shore leave. The Chief of Staff is principally interested in improving the grammar of ship reports.

I doubt if you'll get any 22's, though I'll call your name blessed if you do. They are my only venture into black market—if unrationed goods are a black market—and if other stuff is as scarce as they are, we're OK. I dunno what would be a peace time price, [?] maybe 3.50 to 4.50 a thousand. Well, I've bought 3 pkg of 500 each, on leads supplied by friends, and I've paid 5, 6, and 8 dollars respectively. The last was sheer robbery, but I submitted lest I find no more and that's the whole economics of black markets. Meanwhile I obstinately & tiresomely solicit everyone I know to comb every small town hardware store—the principal hope—and once a week or so some friend brings me in a box of 50. I urge you to risk Leavenworth or eternal damnation if you see a chance. If it's just the FBI you're afraid of, leave them to me.[135] Practically all of them were students of mine at Harvard and the others have become close friends, interviewing me about James B. Conant, Leverett Saltonstall, and Cornelia Otis Skinner. You understand further that my lust for .22 long rifles is unselfish parenthood & patriotic citizenship looking toward the future safety of the republic. I don't use them—I teach Bunny to.

It's damned nonsense, too, the Army's using them. Nobody in the Army gets subcaliber practise except people in training as musketry instructors. If they're capable of being musketry instructors, they should spend their time firing .90 caliber rifles. If they're capable of profiting from sub-caliber practise, they aren't good enough to be learning for musketry instructors.

40% reduction on fuel oil. Probably more to come. Got any books you want stored in the east room of my library?

Maybe I identify with you—as the brethren put it—when I get laid up. Maybe I just have time then. But have you noticed how faithfully—I've noticed how illegibly—I write to you when I get laid up? I realize every now and then that we've been writing to each other a hell of a long time. I've certainly written more letters to you than any five—or ten—people, choose them any time in my life. I wonder what the brethren would make of the relationship & the emotions that have come to cement it. It's a very deep & warm & tender feeling, my dear, however complex & whatever the faculty might make of it. The obvious thing is that I certainly never would have written to a man as I have to you, that you have represented some blend of wife-daughter-mother to this odd soul, & that you have got yourself seriously tangled in its oddities.

Don't—by a natural enough progression—don't send me a Christmas present. I think there should be Christmas for children. For the rest, it should go to those who have earned it.

There is a perfectly swell Army song but it seems to be confined to one division—at Ft. Meade.[136] Don Born brought it hence a week ago but I was too lazy & alcoholized to take it down. Don, who believes devoutly that the war can be won by pep talks, lectures on American history, & singing—and may be right—did his damndest to get [it] out of camp & on the networks but the phobias of radio & the US Army prevented. The chorus alludes to the infantry's drinking another beer, so it won't reach you over the air.

Don wrote the handbook telling the Army how to behave in Morocco. After the Army got there. Some of his statistics interest me: highest venereal rate (76%) in the Caribbean; highest suicide rate, the Alaska highway.

My impulse to analyze the grand strategy of the next six months seems to have evaporated.

Yrs
Benny

8 Berkeley Street
Cambridge, Massachusetts

[14 December 1942]

Dear Kate:

I've been excessively occupied as an internist, epidemiologist, and practical nurse. At least four separate epidemics have hit Cambridge in the last month and this is the year, you may have heard, when the neighbors take care of one another. Two different variants of the flu bug, the one ambitiously designated by *Time* "pneumotitis" (which is scaring the pants off the local medicos, what's left of them), and lastly a sweetheart for which the faculty have found no better name than "virus pneumonia." The flu interests me most, in that the boys have finally come round to observing what everybody who has ever had what is gaily called influenza more than once has known all along, that from year to year it varies in the symptoms it exhibits and the organs it affects, and they have now moved on to a really soul-stirring feat of critical and creative intelligence, they have decided that that phenomenon may be worth studying, may provide a clue to the nature of the virus. Actually, MGH, which has never authorized any research in anything not clearly defined and classified by the first Dr. Bigelow's *System of Medicine*, has now voted a study of variants in the symptomatology of influenza.[137] This is as great a personal triumph for me as the decision, nearly a year old now, of the polio boys that, just possibly, a climatic factor might be at work.

Well, the two flu bugs working side by side are very interesting, and one does not confer immunity against the other. Or, if it does, then it's an immunity of not more than a week. But the "pneumotitis" is a genuine bottled in bond sweetheart. The boys have now discovered, to their holy horror, that there are a good many walking cases of it, perhaps thousands. Victims may not feel bad at all, or may feel just a trifle depressed or in a mood to quarrel with their spouses, but if someone thinks to stick a thermometer in their mouths they've got about one degree of fever, and they are exuding the virus at every pore in great clouds. That appears to clear up the mystery of its prevalence. It's a versatile baby, too, developing more damned kinds of symptoms than a Peruna ad, and it's long-lived.[138] The boys think it is gradually getting more severe as the months pass, and expect that another twelvemonth may sharpen its teeth.

From Boston's current disaster medical science appears to have learned one thing, that you've got to go easy on plasma.[139] They've killed a number of people with edema of the lungs who had a clear right to live. It's a finding of considerable importance, if sound.... But that night will go down in the history of horrors. I've had an earful but am in no mood to repeat them. It's a wonder if anyone has learned anything, for the hospitals were not only swamped, they were practically paralyzed. MGH did bethink itself of a lately instituted research in burns and so thoughtfully wrapped some of the victims in pressure bandages, as the schedule called for. It duly reports that these people averaged a degree less fever when the infection set in. But they'll be skin-grafted, as otherwise they needn't have been.... An obscenity has been the rush of drug houses and various clinics to get their projects and methods, ointments, tradenames, and whatnot into the papers. Stuff has been pouring in from all over the country, and the hospitals have had to beat salesmen out of the wards with ball bats. Huck Finn was not the only one who could feel ashamed of the human race. And trust us Catholics. It now appears that God saved the Boston College football team from a fiery death by having them lose the game with Holy Cross that afternoon.[140]

And at Chelsea Naval Hospital—to clear up this subject—one beholds the evanescence of heroism and the obsolescence of personal histories. The Midway boys had it all their own way till cases began coming in from Guadalcanal.[141] Those boys ruled everything for a happy time but now they're just boys, for wounded are coming in from North Africa.... Thoughtful note, in Alabama there's a new military hospital a-building. 70,000 beds.[142]

The mobility of veterans is a pleasant improvement over the last war. There's a constant stream of them arriving from all over the war, some in the line of duty, some seemingly just a new policy of giving the boys a rest. At the moment the town is flooded with navy. Some of the ships seem to have got shot up a bit. Also, three of them crossed the Atlantic westward without a shell in their ammunition rooms, having fired every last one during the engagement. This reveals something or other about the Navy, but let us not try to determine what, except that we seem to be confident of commanding the seas.

Inclosures exhibit all of the literary life I have had time for lately, and please return. In the same mail with Dorothy's letter arrives one commending my piece from—Faith Baldwin.[143] It gave me pause. But I'm afraid it also raised my critical judgment of her, for she asked me why I didn't write fiction any more and said she'd been missing it. The literary life is going to cost me another friend. The American Library Association decided not to put *Studs Lonigan* on its hundred books for English readers, and Jim and his publisher have seen Fascism stalking our streets. After due thought and research I'm constrained to bring in a finding that the Association is silly but is not forbidding thought to exist in the United States, and there goes a beautiful relationship. Jim has to be told from time to time that it isn't necessarily fascistic to dislike his books but this is the first time I've had to tell him so in a semi-official way, and he won't take it.

I wish either you or I had character. The future needs a war diary badly and is going to get a million of them, all vile. I tell myself that it's too late to start one now, but it really isn't, so I beg you to start one. On behalf of posterity. A whole million and not one of them good, not one of them by either of us. It's clearly God's bidding, but I simply have not got character enough. If you don't, there won't be one.

The boy Kazin has come close to writing a good book about the incredible lit of our time, closer than any one yet, though still full of the vices of his kind.[144] You'd shudder to see what he says of Beer. I've been reading a barrel of such books—this is the season when we repent our springtime promises and I'm sore as hell I ever agreed to go to Indiana—and why is it that literary criticism is the dullest, dreariest, most sodden of all reading? Unless for the reasons I've been alleging all my life. I plowed through Brooks from beginning to end, I took as much Mumford as I could, I did some Lewisohn and I tried some Frank, but the Frank was beyond me, as always. I tackled Eliot again and all the others, even the bright, dead thinking of the Stalin Invasion. God, it's depressing, and, worse still as I grow older I can't so firmly hang onto my conviction that all the brethren except me must be insane. I hope your guardian angel will fend off all impulses to look into that sort of stuff. I turn now to better things and have got back much strength by simply leafing through reports of the Geological Survey and Bureau of Ethnology, wondering much why that kind of thing is an unworthy labor at contemptible jobs whereas Ernest Hemingway is culture.[145] Under Aldrich's guidance I'm going into the history of the treatment of burns, which hardly advanced over Hippocrates, hell, over the Chinese of the 6th century B.C., until the loathsome 1920's. As part of this I've reread *Arrowsmith*, unread since I was getting ready to lecture about contemporary literature at Harvard, and whereas it still seemed pretty good to me last time, a decline from the rapture I felt when it was first published, this time it just stinks.[146] I can't feel that what Lewis Gannett called the hurt boy in Lewis or what Kazin calls the creation of a myth atones for sentimentality, inferior imagination, and a vast quantity of what it grows simpler to call plain ignorance and plain lying.[147] When I once mentioned the book to Zinsser he said that it made him puke. I think I fully understand why, making all allowances for Hans' own romanticism about his profession. The book and such a man as Hans are mutually exclusive; one conception forbids the other, and Lewis was withheld from appreciating either that kind of man or that understanding of a job. Nor is any other scientist in that report commensurable with any I've ever known, and I've known my share.

I was amused to see Brooks's several references to Zinsser, as little frank, as instinctively evasive of reality, as all the rest of his stuff. It was through Brooks that I met Hans. By the time I got back to these parts in 1927 I was already far enough along with my Mark Twain book to know that I was going to have to upset Brooks altogether. I presently learned what I hadn't known before, that Brooks had had a violent manic-depressive crash. It worried me and I wondered if I ought to leave out the attack on him or perhaps put it on other grounds and aim it at some other exemplar of the same ideas. I remarked to L. J. Henderson that I'd like to talk to some friend of Brooks and he said "Zinsser knows him." So I asked leave to call and went to that study in the Medical School which I was to know by heart before much longer, and had tea there in a winter twilight, and put the case to him. He said, no, obviously I had to hew to my line, no matter what effect it might have, and it might, in fact, even have a good effect, since Brooks was soft-minded at best and could profit from some stern opposition. Later I heard a good deal about Brooks's troubles, including some really dreadful scenes, and I've done my wondering. How good was Hans for a man who leaned on him at such a time? Hans never had any conception of nervous disease, never believed there was anything that exercise and hard labor—and perhaps a girl—couldn't straighten out. There were those half-sidesplitting, half-tragic passages with Hart Crane. I don't know if he was good or bad for Brooks. And I'll never know whether my book had any effect one way or the other. Brooks has referred to me by name only once, in an interview, when he said that, in spite of my complaints, my book really proved that he had been right. A half dozen *obiter dicta*[148] in *Oliver Allston*[149] are probably slanted in my direction but they don't come close enough for me to be sure. Well, it looks as if he'll get another chance, for I won't be able to keep these lectures from frequently pivoting on him. *Allston*, which I've lately read for the first time, seems to me to be one of the most complete dead giveaways in literature. It fascinated me, it was hypnotic, I felt like one of Noah's sons. A couple of times, in that long-dead controversy, I had had to say: clearly no man, no matter how wrong-minded, could say such things as this if he had read the books he is talking about. Nothing pained Mumford more in the long reply he wrote—why, I was actually accusing the Master of reporting on things he hadn't read, and even Mumford knew that that would be, if true, a species of dishonesty. So in *Allston* (Oliver from Santayana's threnody to loveliness, Allston, the great artist whom Cambridgeport's anesthesias to beauty castrated and destroyed) Brooks says out and out, not once but a dozen times, that his impetuous love of truth led him to slay books and authors whom he had never read. He nowhere suggests he had any feeling, then or later, that it was not quite the thing to do, it's a mere functioning of the literary intuition. He also remarks in detail that all his life he had been unable to read history. Mumford was also grieved when I remarked on it.... Jesus, Jesus, how the literary stink, and how one Zinsser is worth the lot of them. I have been chewing over and banking in the reservoir of things to do sometime a kind of portrait of him. Also one of L. J. Maybe, sometime. They were good men.

I guess I shouldn't write letters on a snowy Sunday afternoon. The hell with snow.... How goes the battle?

Yours,

Benny

NOTES

1. In New Jersey.
2. Prince Edward Island.
3. ARP, probably Air Raid Patrol.
4. On 27 January 1942 Churchill survived a vote of confidence, 464-1. Singapore, long considered impregnable against an attack from seaward, surrendered to the Japanese on 15 February, following an invasion from the mainland across the Johore Strait. On 2 July, following the fall of Tobruk in Tunisia to the Germans, a motion to censure Churchill lost.
5. Macassar Strait, between Borneo and the Celebes Islands, in the Netherlands Indies. The *New York Times* reported 3 large ships sunk by combined British, American, and Dutch naval forces in a battle on 24 January.
6. Admiral Thomas C. Hart (1877–1971), commander in chief, Asiatic Fleet, 1939–1942. Archibald Percival Wavell, 1st Earl Wavell (1883–1950), commander in the Middle East; Viceroy of India, 1941–1947; *The Palestine Campaigns*, 1928; *Generals and Generalship*, 1941.
7. Report of a presidential commission headed by Associate Supreme Court Justice Owen J. Roberts, dated 23 January 1942 and released the next day, when a complete text appeared in the *New York Times*.

8. Narvik, in Norway, was the site of a serious defeat for British forces in April 1940; this precipitated the fall of the Chamberlain government. Outnumbered British forces in Crete were defeated by the Germans in the spring of 1941 in a massive airborne invasion by paratroops.
9. At 6:33 AM on 7 December 1941, an hour and a half before the air attack on Pearl Harbor began, a small Japanese submarine was sunk just outside the harbor by the destroyer *Ward*.
10. In fact the German navy had no aircraft carriers.
11. CD, Civil Defense.
12. Formed to transport airplanes and pilots to England.
13. W. Averell Harriman (1891–1986), politician, industrialist, and statesman; chairman, Union Pacific Railroad; ambassador to the Soviet Union; governor of New York, 1954–1958.
14. The British Purchasing Commission negotiated for purchase of aircraft.
15. RMS *Queen Mary*, passenger liner, built 1936, now at Long Beach, California. At 80,774 tons, this was the second-largest ship ever built.
16. De Valera (1882–1975), American-born mathematics teacher, writer, and Irish statesman; prime minister of the Irish Free State, 1932–1949; president of the Irish Republic, 1959–1973.
17. *Literary Studies*, by André Maurois (1885–1967), prolific French writer and philosopher, published in 2 volumes, 1941 and 1944.
18. Monday Chats, newspaper columns by Sainte-Beuve, 1851–1862.
19. Drama by Euripides (fl. ca. 485–406 BCE), Greek tragedian; condemns wars of aggression. Murray's translation was published in 1915.
20. From Thoreau, "Walking," 1862. BDV did not use this as a title but included it in a page of Invocation at the beginning of *The Year of Decision*.
21. Not this year but in 1943 Morison won the Pulitzer Prize in biography for *Admiral of the Ocean Sea: A Life of Christopher Columbus*.
22. J. Donald Adams (1891–1968), editor of the *New York Times Book Review*.
23. BDV did include a three-page chronology of events.
24. (1810–1889), Mormon pioneer; LDS missionary to China, 1852. His journal, composed in the thirty-eight-letter Mormon alphabet, was discovered by BDV's spy, Madeline McQuown, librarian in Ogden.
25. (1794–1848), general in the Mexican War.
26. *Advance Agent*.
27. Army Intelligence.
28. On January 31, 1942, a Navy carrier raid attacked the Marshall Islands; the USS *Enterprise* was damaged by air attack. It was not until two years later that the Marshall Islands would be recaptured from the Japanese.
29. The British garrison at Singapore surrendered to the Japanese on 15 February; Corregidor, the last U.S. holdout in the Philippines, surrendered on 6 May.
30. Magazine published by the U.S. Naval Institute, since 1874.
31. On 11–12 February, in a well-planned "Operation Cerberus," the German battle cruisers *Scharnhorst* and *Gneisenau* and the cruiser *Prinz Eugen* exited the harbor at occupied Brest, and in daylight, under cover of fog, passed through the English Channel while British radar was jammed. All three ships were damaged by mines, but despite heavy attack from the air and from shore batteries, they reached home port safely. The successful escape of the ships was a major embarrassment to the British government. King's Navee, reference to Gilbert & Sullivan's *H.M.S. Pinafore*, "I polished up the handle so carefullee/That now I am the ruler of the Queen's Navee."
32. Harvard freshman course in economics.

33. *Harper's* 184/5 (April 1942). The Battle of Chancellorsville (Virginia), on 1–3 May 1863, was a Confederate victory, but General Thomas Jonathan "Stonewall" Jackson (b. 1824), an outstanding leader, was killed.
34. The Battle of Fredericksburg (Virginia), on 13 December 1862, Generals Burnside and Lee, was a Confederate victory with great losses. Second Bull Run, 28–30 August 1862, Generals Pope and Lee, a Confederate victory.
35. Stegner used this phrase as a chapter title in *The Uneasy Chair*.
36. John Bidwell (1819–1900), politician and farmer; Prohibitionist Party candidate for president, 1892.
37. Nicholas Trist (1800–1874), negotiator; Polk's emissary to Mexico.
38. James Wilson Marshall (1810–1885), prospector.
39. Bigler built the mill at Sutter's Fort; see M. Guy Bishop, *Henry William Bigler: Soldier, Gold Miner, Missionary, Chronicler, 1815–1900*, 1998. Clyman (1792–1881), pioneer, trapper, rancher; see Charles L. Camp, *James Clyman, American Frontiersman . . .*, 1928. Chapter 2 of *The Year of Decision*, "The Mountain Man," is principally concerned with Clyman.
40. (Latin) it is finished; John 19:30 (Vulgate).
41. Bacteriologist in BDV's *We Accept with Pleasure*.
42. General McCook was possibly with the Fifth Kentucky Cavalry.
43. About elocution, see "Adeline Duval Mack's School of Elocution and Dramatic Art," Georgetown University Library Special Collections, Varia, Box 16, folder 1863.
44. New Mexico, adjacent to El Paso, Texas.
45. HMS *Illustrious*, British aircraft carrier, 23,000 tons, repaired May–December 1941. Louis F.A.V.N. Mountbatten, Lord Louis Mountbatten, Prince Louis of Battenberg (1900–1979), vice-admiral, Supreme Allied Commander for Southeast Asia, Viceroy of India.
46. *Sims*, destroyer, 1,570 tons, launched 1939; sunk 7 May 1942 in the Battle of the Coral Sea.
47. See *The New Yorker*, 14 March 1942, "Talk of the Town."
48. The USS *Langley*, AV-3, originally a collier launched in 1911, was converted in 1920 to the Navy's first aircraft carrier, 11,500 tons; she was then converted to a seaplane tender in 1937. Disabled under air attack in the Netherlands East Indies on 27 February 1942, she was subsequently scuttled.
49. Bonin Islands, north of the Marianas, east of Okinawa.
50. This rumor persists. According to the official report, the French *Surcouf*, at that time the largest submarine yet built, was rammed by an American freighter while submerged near the Panama Canal, on 18 or 19 February 1942. See Churchill, *The Second World War:* vol. 2, *Their Finest Hour*, 1949.
51. Freedom House, a nonprofit and nonpartisan organization founded by Eleanor Roosevelt and Wendell Willkie, supported democracy, human rights, and freedom throughout the world. Peter Arno (1904–1968), composer and *New Yorker* cartoonist. Helen Hokinson (1893–1949), *New Yorker* cartoonist.
52. *Only One Storm*, 1942.
53. Army and Navy aviation were merged with the establishment of the Air Force as a separate service after World War II.
54. Defense of the Realm Act.
55. Historical Society of Pennsylvania, founded 1824, Philadelphia.
56. BDV gave an address, "Responsible Citizenship Makes Responsible Government," to the Biennial Convention of the National League of Women Voters on 28 April; see *FPOS*, p. 198.
57. Robert H. Aldrich (1903?–1967) later became the DeVoto family physician.

58. The *Hindenburg*, a German airship filled with hydrogen, caught fire and exploded as it was docking at the Naval Air Station at Lakehurst, New Jersey, on 6 May 1937 after crossing the Atlantic Ocean from Germany; thirty-six lives were lost.
59. Double spica, a bandage wound around in a herringbone pattern.
60. The Newspaper Guild, union of professional journalists.
61. Henry Cecil Flory (1910–2001), horseman and investment counselor, vice president of Keystone Custodian Funds, Inc.; pilot during World War II with Royal Air Force Ferry Command; cofounder, Boston Rugby Club.
62. Frederick William Kaltenbach (1895–1945?), known as "Lord Hee Haw," American broadcaster for the Nazis; died in a Soviet prison camp. Paul Revere, sobriquet of Douglas Chandler (1889–after 1968); tried for treason, 1948, and sentenced to life imprisonment. E. D. Ward, pseudonym of Edward Leopold Delaney (1886?–1972); ultra-right-wing lecturer, broadcast from Germany 1939–1945. Jane Anderson, ex-wife (divorced 1918) of composer Deems Taylor; broadcast for Radio Zeesen under the name "The Georgia Peach." She was indicted for treason in 1943, but the indictment was dismissed in 1947; her whereabouts since then are unknown. "Mr. O.K.," sobriquet of Dr. Max Otto Koischwitz, also known as "Doktor Anders" (= Doctor Otherwise); professor at Hunter College until 1939, when he fled to Germany; died of tuberculosis in Berlin, 1944.
63. Pulham, reference to *H. M. Pulham, Esquire*, novel by Marquand, 1941. Ritz-Carlton Hotel, 50 Central Park South, thirty-three stories, seven hundred rooms.
64. BDV wrote this letter following his visit to Kenyon College, where he was awarded an honorary degree.
65. Chalmers (1904–1956), president of Kenyon College since 1937. Kenyon, college for men founded in Gambier, Ohio, in 1824, was and is renowned as a strong liberal arts institution and as the host of the *Kenyon Review*; women were admitted from 1969. The founding president of Kenyon was Philander Chase, Episcopal bishop of Ohio.
66. (Latin), rise, Doctor (lit., teacher).
67. Charles Bulfinch (1763–1844), outstanding American architect. Old Kenyon Hall was designed by Norman Nash; Bulfinch designed only the steeple.
68. Warren G. Harding (1865–1923), twenty-eighth president of the United States and a native of Marion, was editor of the Marion *Star* before he was senator.
69. Ransom (1888–1974), Carnegie professor of poetry and founder of the *Kenyon Review*.
70. Admiral Sir Dudley Pound (1877–1943).
71. The Nieman Fellowships at Harvard, established in 1938, are awarded annually to practicing journalists for a year of unrestricted study and research.
72. Physics laboratory at Harvard.
73. Ralph Barton Perry (1876–1957), professor of philosophy at Harvard; *General Theory of Value*, 1926; *Thought and Character of William James*, 1935, Pulitzer Prize in biography, 1936.
74. Karen Danielssen Horney (1885–1952), controversial German-American psychoanalyst; *The Neurotic Personality of Our Time*, 1937; *New Ways of Psychoanalysis*, 1939; *Self-Analysis*, 1942.
75. The Royal Highland Regiment; now the Third Battalion, Royal Regiment of Scotland.
76. Presumably an address to the Nieman Fellows at Harvard; see Easy Chair "Number 241," *Harper's* 211/5 (1955), reprinted in *The Easy Chair*, 1955.
77. Probably for the Henry Adams Club, for graduate students in history at Harvard.
78. Associate editor of *Good Housekeeping*; Littauer & Wilkinson, agents.
79. (Latin) replacing.
80. 20 June.

81. (1905–1978), actress, author, playwright, columnist; *Past Imperfect*, autobiography, 1942, reviewed in *Time* 39/20 (18 May 1942).
82. The house was given to the Society of the Holy Child Jesus by Ida M. Barry, first wife of financier Thomas Fortune Ryan (1851–1928).
83. Roger W. Babson (1875–1967), business forecaster and author; founder of the Babson Institute (now Babson College) in Wellesley, Massachusetts, 1919.
84. Florence was a nurse at Bowne Hospital.
85. Churchill visited Washington, D.C., on 19–25 June.
86. By executive order, President Roosevelt established the Office of War Information, subsuming the Office of Facts and Figures and four other agencies, and appointed Elmer Davis as its chief.
87. Creel was head of the Committee on Public Information in the Great War.
88. BDV's Easy Chair, "Give It to Us Straight!" *Harper's* 185/3, predicts that Davis's power to disseminate news will be contested and weakened by the military, by agency directors, etc. See also Easy Chair, *Harper's* 211/5 (November 1955), "Number 241," also in *The Easy Chair*, 1955: "My luck has been good."
89. Thirkell (1890–1961), British novelist in the Trollope tradition; *Cheerfulness Breaks In*, 1940; *Marling Hall* (fall 1942). Avis DeVoto owned most of Thirkell's work.
90. AMA, American Medical Association, founded 1847, the largest and for many decades the most conservative of the professional organizations for American physicians. Lawrance Thompson (1906–1973), professor at Princeton and biographer of Robert Frost; *Robert Frost*, 3 vols., 1966–1977. Vol. 2 of this series, *Years of Triumph: 1915–1938*, 1970, won the Pulitzer Prize in biography in 1971.
91. David M. Little (1896–1954), tutor in English at Harvard and assistant dean; master of Adams House; secretary to the university.
92. Probably Leigh Hoadley (1895–1975), professor of zoology and master of Leverett House.
93. On Soldiers Field Road at River Street, near the Business School.
94. Probably Touraine, on Brattle Square.
95. Paul Robeson (1898–1976), outstanding Negro bass-baritone and actor. Brattle Hall is the Brattle Theater on Brattle Street.
96. AEF, Allied Expeditionary Force. The *Times* story was about the German threat to British forces in Egypt after the fall of Tobruk.
97. The PBY *Catalina*, twin-engine patrol-bomber flying boat, made by Consolidated Aircraft, 1936–1945; it was extremely slow at 179 mph.
98. Spitfire, British fighter airplane, from 1938. The Thunderbolt (P-47) was made by Republic, not Grumman, from 1941.
99. The Focke-Wulf FW-190, German fighter plane, from 1939.
100. This description appears to apply to degaussing equipment for ships—not aircraft—that was successfully adopted by the Royal Navy as a defense against magnetic mines.
101. Probably the JATO (jet-assisted takeoff), introduced 1941.
102. On 20 April 1942, about 30 British Spitfires were destroyed by a combined German-Italian air attack; those that survived turned out to be crucial to British defense of Egypt.
103. Shangri-La was the fictional paradise of James Hilton's novel *Lost Horizon*. General James Doolittle (1896–1993) commanded a group of sixteen bombers that raided Tokyo and Yokohama on 18 April 1942, causing little damage but great astonishment that the Japanese homeland could actually be attacked. Doolittle's planes took off not from the *Ranger* but from the new carrier *Hornet*, which daringly approached within 750 miles of Japan. President Roosevelt

announced to the press that the planes had come "from Shangri-La." The carrier *Ranger*, CV4, launched 1933, was part of the Atlantic Fleet.

104. The clubhouse at Treman Cottage. For several summers after BDV's death, Avis DeVoto presided over the bar at Treman.
105. Short-lived experimental farm and utopian community in West Roxbury, MA, 1841–1847.
106. Sweet French liqueur, from 1805, made from star anise, with a high alcohol content.
107. By Robert Frost, 1942.
108. In 2004 the ordinary trip between South Station in Boston and Penn Station in New York still requires nearly five hours; the Metroliner and Acela express trains, when functioning properly, make the trip in about four hours.
109. John Buchan, 1st Baron Tweedsmuir (1875–1940), Scottish novelist and politician, very prolific; *Greenmantle*, 1916; *Prester John*, 1910; *The Thirty-Nine Steps*, 1919; *Nelson's History of the Great War*, 24 vols., 1915–1919.
110. Probably Knopf.
111. Revue starring Gypsy Rose Lee and Bobby Clark, opened 24 June 1942, ran for 605 performances.
112. Battleship, BB61, 45,000 tons, launched August 1942, decommissioned 1990.
113. In Operation "Torch," the first large-scale Allied offensive of the war, on 7–8 November 1942, American and British forces landed in Morocco and Algeria.
114. The United States, after entering the war against Germany in December 1941, purposefully did not declare war against occupied France but maintained a cautious course of recognition of the Vichy regime in expectation of eventual liberation. During the "Torch" landings, some resistance was encountered from French forces in North Africa, but it soon faded after a cease-fire was wrung from Admiral Jean-François Darlan, the French Naval Minister and the highest-ranking French commander then loyal to Vichy. See William L. Langer, *Our Vichy Gamble*, 1947.
115. Following the national elections on 3 November, the Republican Party gained forty-three seats in the House of Representatives and nine in the Senate, but without dislodging the Democratic majority in either.
116. Lugol's solution, containing potassium iodide and free iodine. The multitudinous seas, from *Macbeth*, Act II scene 2, "... this my hand will rather/The multitudinous seas incarnadine/Making the green one red."
117. "Praise the Lord and Pass the Ammunition," song by Frank Loesser (1910–1969), 1942; the title line was first uttered by Lieutenant (j.g.) Howell Forgy, Navy chaplain, during the attack on Pearl Harbor. "This Is the Army," title song from the revue by Irving Berlin (1888–1989), 1942. "Don't Set Under the Apple Tree," by Charles Tobias, Lew Brown, and Sam H. Stept, from the musical *Yokel Boy*, 1939. "Little Bo Peep Has Lost Her Jeep," by Jerry Bowne and Frank De Vol, 1942; recorded by Spike Jones.
118. Hanson W. Baldwin (1903–1991), journalist and writer on defense, *New York Times*, 1929–1968: wrote almost every day about the war. His middle name was Weightman.
119. Eugene Manlove Rhodes (1869–1934), western writer much admired by BDV.
120. Private college, founded 1839.
121. Sen-Sen, licorice-based breath-purifying candy, made by Adams Chicle Company.
122. Mesabi, region in Minnesota famous for rich sedimentary deposits of iron ore.
123. The Federalist Party opposed the War of 1812. Lockeian, reference to John Locke (1632–1704), British philosopher; *Two Treatises on Government*, 1690; *Essay Concerning Human Understanding*, 1691. The Embargo Act, 1807, and Non-Intercourse Act, 1809, were the result of Jefferson's efforts to sustain American commerce with European nations while avoiding involvement in

the Napoleonic wars. The Non-Intercourse Act was repealed in 1810 but was reimposed in the same year by Madison's presidential proclamation; its enforcement was seriously injurious to the American economy.

124. James Madison, who succeeded Jefferson as president of the United States in 1809, had been one of the principal authors of *The Federalist* essays defending the new Constitution, 1787–1788.

125. Francis Preston Blair (1791–1876), adviser to President Lincoln; Francis Preston Blair Jr. (1821–1875), his son, Democratic candidate for vice president, 1868; congressman from Missouri, opposed drastic measures during Reconstruction. Morton is probably Oliver P. Morton (1823–1877), governor of Indiana, later senator, an ardent Reconstructionist; possibly BDV means Levi P. Morton (1824–1920), banker, congressman from New York, ambassador to France; vice president, 1889–1893.

126. Alben W. Barkley (1877–1956), senator from Kentucky; vice president, 1949–1953. Douglas is probably Paul Douglas, New Deal economist and author of the Douglas Credit Plan; senator from Illinois, 1949–1967. The Blairs supported President Andrew Johnson in the fight over Reconstruction.

127. Salmon P. Chase (1808–1873), Chief Justice of the United States Supreme Court, 1864–1873.

128. Leon Henderson (1895–1986), New Deal economist, head of the Office of Prime Administration. Arnold is presumably Thurman Arnold, while Cohen is probably Benjamin Victor Cohen (1894–1983), New Deal lawyer and advisor.

129. Charles Sumner (1811–1874), congressman, later senator from Massachusetts; Radical leader. Benjamin Franklin Wade (1800–1878), senator from Ohio and president pro tempore; Radical leader. Thaddeus Stevens (1792–1868), congressman from Pennsylvania; Radical leader. Andrews, possibly Sidney Andrews (1835–1880), journalist.

130. Harry L. Hopkins (1890–1946), advisor and assistant to President Roosevelt; secretary of commerce, 1938–1940. See Robert E. Sherwood, *Roosevelt and Hopkins: An Intimate History*, 1948, 1950.

131. The Resettlement Administration, 1935–1936. NRA, the National Recovery Administration. The Greenbelt Towns program was founded by Tugwell and others; Greenbelt, Maryland, was the first of three planned communities.

132. Montgomery Ward, mail-order merchandising corporation founded in Chicago, 1872; closed 2000. The Hull House, founded in 1889 in Chicago by Jane Addams and Ellen Starr, provided a social center, day care, kindergarten, and an employment bureau. Addams (1860–1935) won the Nobel Peace Prize in 1931.

133. Helena Petrovna Blavatsky (1831–1891), Russian mystic, occultist, and writer, founder of Theosophy; Theosophical Society, 1875.

134. Probably "The Structure of Power" by Robert S. Lynd, *New Republic* 107/19 (9 November 1942).

135. See BDV's Easy Chair, "Due Notice to the FBI," *Harper's* 199/4 (October 1949), reprinted in *The Easy Chair*, 1955.

136. Maryland.

137. MGH, Massachusetts General Hospital. The three famous Doctors Bigelow in Boston were Jacob Bigelow (1786–1879), his son Henry Jacob Bigelow (1818–1890), and grandson William Sturgis Bigelow (1850–1926). No "System of Medicine" is known by any of these. Henry Bigelow, surgeon, published a *Manual of Orthopedic Surgery* in 1845, and attended the first public demonstration of ether anesthesia at Massachusetts General Hospital the following year; see *The Year of Decision*, "Interlude: Friday, October 16." The famous *System of Medicine*, edited by Sir John Russell Reynolds, 5 vols., 1866–1879, went through several editions.

138. Peruna, cure-all patent medicine, approximately 25 percent alcohol.

139. On 28 November 1942, at the Cocoanut Grove night club on Piedmont Street in Boston, with over one thousand people present (25 percent over legal capacity), a fire suddenly spread through flammable decorations; fire exits had been locked and the revolving door at the main entrance jammed under a stampede; 492 people died in fifteen minutes. See Jack Thomas, "The Cocoanut Grove Inferno," Boston *Globe*, 22 November 1992.
140. Boston College cancelled a victory party planned for that evening at the Cocoanut Grove.
141. In the Solomon Islands; the battle for control of the island lasted from August 1942 to February 1943.
142. This seems unlikely.
143. Dorothy Thompson's response to BDV's December Easy Chair, "Wait a Minute, Dorothy," *Harper's* 186/1; see *LBDV*, pp. 114–119.
144. Alfred Kazin (1915–1998), critic, writer at *Fortune* magazine; Distinguished Professor, Hunter College and City University of New York; *On Native Grounds*, 1942; *A Walker in the City*, 1951; *New York Jew*, 1978; *Writing Was Everything*, 1995.
145. United States Bureau of Ethnology; after 1894, Bureau of American Ethnology, under the Smithsonian Institution. John Wesley Powell was its first director, from 1879.
146. *Arrowsmith*, novel by Sinclair Lewis, 1925, about a physician.
147. Gannett (1891–1966), author, reporter, literary editor of the New York *Herald Tribune*.
148. (Latin) casual remarks.
149. Oliver Alden, protagonist of Santayana's *The Last Puritan*; Washington Allston (1779–1843), Harvard '00, Romantic painter, poet, and novelist, died in Cambridgeport (area between Central Square and the Charles River).

11

1943 LETTERS

The 1942–1943 winter was a hard one, and DeVoto complained about the firewood shortage and health problems but also offered further guesses about the future course of the war. The main events of 1943 began with the long-awaited publication of *The Year of Decision: 1846* and DeVoto's trip to give the Patten lectures at Indiana University. DeVoto liked the university but found Hoosier society in general stiflingly provincial and all but totally unconcerned about the war. Home again in Cambridge, he evaluated Harvard's reception of the new book. In exasperation over Shady Hill School's treatment of his son, DeVoto withdrew Gordon to place him in another school. The turbulent relationship with Frost, whose visit to Indiana overlapped with DeVoto's, came to a crisis point that DeVoto probably considered a permanent rupture. During the summer, after ongoing difficulties, DeVoto discharged Rosamond Chapman; took note of the fall of the Fascist regime in Italy; and moved his family to Cape Ann on the Massachusetts North Shore for the summer, where he enjoyed the company of several literary-minded psychiatrists. Sterne, who liked hot weather, complained about deteriorating conditions at the Bowne Hospital and wrote a long letter about her family history. In the fall, DeVoto noted several possibilities for travel abroad as an official historian for the U.S. armed forces, following the example of his friend Sam Morison; after much negotiation, extending into 1944, all such overtures fell through. During his entire life DeVoto never left the American continent.

Bowne
Tuesday, +62° F

[AFTER 21 FEBRUARY 1943]

Dear Benny,
Agony is the word for Cerf.[1] A really painful inferiority-feeling came through the loudspeaker; & it was no doubt that which drove him to such *bêtises*[2] as that Kipling preferred Cockneys to Colonials, & that *Kim* is a dead-ringer for an Eric Ambler thriller.[3] I thought LG & HAO showed remarkable patience in the face of such persistent japery.[4]

I'm still trying to figure out what Lester Markel used to call "the news peg" for *Time's* piece on Toulouse-Lautrec.[5] Surely such a letter written in 1937 doesn't qualify as spot news. The first piece I ever did for the *Times* was on T-L—a show of drawings at the Knoedler Gallery.[6] Incidentally, that piece brought me one of the most unstudied (and valued) compliments of my brief & trivial career. I met Alfred Barr on Fifth Avenue near Fifty-sixth Street (the Museum of Modern Art was then in the Heckscher Building):

AHB: I see you're working on the *Times*.

KGS: Yes.

AHB: Why didn't you tell me?

KGS: Well, it was rather sudden…

AHB: Ummm…I was reading the *Times* Tuesday & I said to myself, "For God's sake, what's happened to Jewell?[7] He's writing criticism!" And then I came to the end of the Lautrec piece & there were your initials….

What did you think of the Strawinsky C Symphony?[8] Only so-so, I thought…. But, by God, it is good to hear Koussevitzky again on Saturdays.[9] It almost restores my youth…. And speaking of youth, did I mention that I was thirty-five on New Year's Eve?[10] The formal entry into what D. Sayers calls "that halcyon period between the self-tormenting exuberance of youth & the fretful *carpe diem*[11] of approaching senility."[12] Wish I were in better shape—literally and, er, figuratively—to enjoy it.

Every time I relax & say a kind word for Roosevelt I regret it almost at once. I hadn't forgotten Hague, or Kelly-Nash, or Guffey, or Crump, or Chavez, or "Chip" Robert, or the Earle & Flynn appointments, or the Supreme Court Packing Bill, or the "second Louisiana Purchase," or the Senate "purge," or the 1940 Democratic Convention, or the New York mayoralty elections, or the torpedoeing (sp?) of the London Economic Conference, or *l'affaire* Black, or that double-talk with the Constitution, or gold-note repudiation, or opposition to the Hatch Act, (not to mention his shady reputation in local politics, as a landlord, or as an employer), but I <u>hoped</u> that <u>maybe</u> he had come to believe some of his own fine phrases, that the leopard had, in fact, shed his spots.[13] Sheer fat-headed optimism.

Maybe it <u>does</u> require a shyster like FDR to deal with the things now dominating the international scene, & certainly you are not the first to observe that the children of this world are wiser in their generation than the children of light. But, by God, if we don't get the shebang on a basis of decency & honesty & integrity & fair-dealing pretty damn' soon, I don't see that we are ever going to do it. *Realpolitik*[14] has had a thousand chances & has failed a thousand times. As Mary Pickford might nauseatingly put it, "Why not try good-will?"

I'd admire to have heard that special vespers (for Brotherhood Week) at St. George's, Stuyvesant Square, on Sunday.[15] Harry Burleigh sang, of course, & the Negro troops quartered in that section.[16] They say it was something.

One of the great features of the camp season at Cotuit was Harry Burleigh's annual visit. He would come for dinner, sit at Miss Emma's right, and, later in the afternoon, conduct informal vespers. He is a great artist & a great gentleman and I think the point (secondary, of course, to the pleasure of the occasion) was not altogether lost on all the little Spence & Beard & Bennett chicks.[17]

Aunt Genie spent January in St. Luke's with *herpes zoster*,[18] but is now at home with a nurse and, says Barbara, a terrifying disposition. Well, who can blame her, herpes must be hell.... For a slight horror note I enclose Barbara's artless vignette of Harold Neuhof who operated on me in 1933 and 1935 (a circumstance which Barbara has obviously forgotten if she even knew it). For a laugh I enclose John Clark on Labour vs. the Learned Societies.

Do you detect a sinister, even eerie, note in the current crop of popular songs (e.g., "It Seems to Me I've Heard That Song Before," "Black Magic," "Weep No More My Lady")?[19] I suppose it's just a matter of a minor key, a few chromatics & a judicious use of the diminished seventh, but they give me the creeps.

Monday, & still plenty hot.

Well (diffidently) I <u>would</u> like to have a trade copy—to lend. I'm marking up my sheets for my own convenience, & I once loaned my leather-bound copy of *We Accept* to Kronid Melenko, a mistake I'll never repeat. He returned it to me with two pages turned down, which so enraged me that I ran a temperature of 105° & didn't speak to him for three years.

I hope you won't mind my remarking that you seem to be living off the lean of the land. Bowne hasn't seen a steak for months. We have roast beef once every two or three weeks, but it's practically inedible: tougher than Himmler & tastes like desiccated caribou.[20] ... Of course, I haven't had a real steak for ten years. Hospital steak is just <u>called</u> that.... My father was a great aficionado of red (Christ!) meat—I cut my teeth on a T-bone & learned my alphabet at Jack's—& I know stewed rump when I taste it.[21]

I hope you are not going to expect me to say something intelligent about *1846*. I'd as soon write a critique of the Book of Genesis. I do feel qualified, though, to toss a bouquet at Matt's graceful & skillful profile; & I'd like to remark that Avis' review of the Hough book handed me some of the best laughs of the season.[22] (That was a nice jacket on *Snow Above Town*—no?)

Thanks for the loan of AKYPD.[23] Shall I return it to Cambridge or Bloomington? There are good things in it, of course, but on the whole, I found it dull, prolix, fatuous & wrong-headed. I heard her say she wrote the book in a few weeks and, by God, it sounds it. Personally, I think the payoff on Miss Mead occurs on pp. 115 & 162 where, spang in the middle of a book on American life, habits, character & customs, she twice misquotes "The Star-Spangled Banner."

[*? pages missing; no closing or signature; enclosures not found*]

[envelope: Hotel Graham, Bloomington, Indiana]

[March (?) 4, 1943]

Dear Kate:

This machine was not guaranteed to me and I offer you no guarantee. If you want some good, clean fun, good, clean rage, try to rent a typewriter. Better still, try to buy one, as I did a few weeks ago. I count it as something of a triumph to have turned this one up at all, and I haven't seen anything like it since I worked for the Ogden *Standard-Examiner*.

After three days it looks like an interesting university and a hell of a dull town. I shall be taking Red Lewis apart in a couple of weeks, but I never get into a college town in the Middle West without feeling that he had a point. Bloomington looks like Logan, Utah, except that it has no backdrop, or even like Escanaba, where I entered into the holy state of matrimony in the [*crossed out*], no the sight of God and according to the laws of the State of Michigan, and worse I can say for no town. But the university appears to be first-rate. Everyone I have met is intelligent, the buildings have every decade of the nineteenth and twentieth centuries stamped on them, as the buildings of a university should, the Lincoln collection in the library is damned fine, and my first audience, this afternoon, got what I was saying and I gave it no favors. The Hoosier dialect on all sides is pure American poetry, and I hope I can learn to differentiate its shadings and locales—I've always wanted to. It should, however, be heard in sultry afternoons, of which there is no immediate prospect, for I blew in with a blizzard and the thermometer was down to zero last night. Hoosier hospitality has not yet shown itself. I have been left most carefully alone—and I am no lover of hotel rooms. The Graham is at least a hotel, though I can hear everyone on the fourth floor going to the can, and it sets an excellent table. Or maybe the sight of butter and sugar has gone to my head. The town appears to do its drinking in pure dives—pure as hell but still dives. The roads are still blocked with snow, but the town is sufficiently far south to begin to be hilly and I imagine there are places to walk. I expect to spend such time as

I have in the Lincoln collection, but the university has lined up a lot of clinics, classes, discussion groups, and faculty clubs for me to meet and today the Army caught up with me in a passionate telegram. I imagine I'll have to go to Chicago while I'm here and take to the road for a long tour as soon as I can thereafter, meanwhile trying to teach English instructors by mail how to teach history. If, meanwhile, spring should come on I wouldn't like it at all.

I'll tell Raymond to send you a trade copy. Well, I certainly don't expect you to go over the book in the way I'm all too scared Fred Merk will, but you can moderately contribute to the decorum of American letters by (a) specifying such larger sections as you think the best and any small effects that may have seemed to you achieved, and (b) saying briefly whether you think the method and structure effective. So far as I know the job is orchestrated in a way which nobody has bothered to work out for historical narrative before; the job I now propose, the last four years before the Civil War, could be done in just that way, if that is a good way. I think it is—at the moment. I have my periods of thinking it stinks. So what about it? Shall I work through from the Dred Scott Decision to Lincoln's First Inaugural in that way, or shall I play it straight, as though I were Arthur Schlesinger or Charles Beard?[24] And, in terms of the method itself, do I, by the end of the book, get dividends on the intolerable weight, slowness, and multiplicity of the first 150 pages? In short, dear, I'm not asking you to be a historiographer, but is history art or isn't it?

The New York Central is by no means as crowded as the New Haven. In general, I'm coming to understand, the north-south roads and the southern east-west ones are the atrocities. I traveled the celebrated Southwestern Limited and it was no more than half full. It had shed its club car, which is vexatious, and greatly simplified its dining car service, which is all to the good. Serving a tenth-rate meal with all the panoply of the Ritz has always been screwy. Now you don't get a butter-knife, they don't pack your tomato juice in ice, there are no more than four items to choose from, there are only half as many waiters and they get you out of there in half the time. I favor making things permanent. It will be pleasant, however, when the engineers come back to work. I haven't been on a train in more than a year that started or stopped in any Christian way. It will also be pleasant when WAVES, WAACs, and the like stop traveling.[25] In fact, it will be pleasant when they cease upon the midnight with no pain.[26] They now march down the streets of Cambridge (and Bloomington) and they neither beautify the streets nor soothe my jaded soul. It has been irresistibly borne in on me that when gals march their stomachs sag, and I wonder what the top kick or his equivalent says. "Suck in the guts" is the established admonition, but it hardly seems appropriate here, and I wonder if it's anatomically possible. They didn't march in my war, and my memory of women in uniform is what the Sam Browne belt did to the fanny, which was plenty, but these gals stick out before and it's not pretty. But I will treasure your girdle manufacturer, and for God's sake ship me any others you may hear, for stories remain scarcer than porterhouses.

Send Mead back to Cambridge—I'm going to read Lincoln here. And maybe I'm not going to read Mead, for you confirm my prepossessions. I ought to read her for Frances Phillips is a nice person and the young anthropologist who belongs to the Morale Committee and speaks the only English thereon I can understand—a chap named Kluckhohn, if that's the way you spell it—assures me that she will remodel my ideas and perfume my soul.[27] But I have read her on Melanesians and other clucks and she was screwy and I don't know that a screwball is reformed by deciding to do something about our thinking here at home. She is said, however, to have a spectacular love life. Melanesian, probably.

I brought along with me a couple of William Gilpin's books for a closer study than I've ever given them before. Probably the Lincoln collection has postponed that, but I think the time is ripe for a piece on Gilpin. Mark him in '46—he's with Doniphan.[28] There was no occasion to say so in the book but he is a kind of homegrown geopolitician, if that's the right word. I think that the geopolitics thing has gone far enough now so that enough people would know what you were doing if you took it for a ride. Have you any memory of a piece I once wrote about Etzler, the pre-Technocrat?[29] Gilpin had a lot more brains than Etzler, and some of the things he did look like inspiration now—his Iso-Thermal Axis is precisely the line of the Axis today, for instance—but I think there'd be some fun in presenting geopolitics as something born in Kansas City in 1850, and born out of speculation about the Pacific Railway. In fact, the Pacific Railway was only one link in the great railroad system which, in his vision, circumscribed the heartland and sent feeders to all the lush and lovely lands outside. And it wouldn't be too bad to have that Alaska line, right now.

Well, it seems proper to devote the rest of this evening to wiring the Army. I have now established really straight-line communication. It runs to Cambridge or at the moment Bloomington, to Chicago, to Gambier, to Washington, to Gambier, to Chicago, to Cambridge and Bloomington. Letters get answered in less than three weeks and telegrams in no more than ten days, which is practically instantaneous. So how would you teach an English A instructor to teach American history?

Yours,
Benny

[envelope: Hotel Graham, Bloomington, Indiana]

[5 March 1943]

English A: One Page Theme
Title: Incident, or America Was Promises

In the Midwest culture they dine at twelve noon and they dine heavily. I dined exceedingly heavily today, being bidden to sit at the right hand of Leland Stowe, who was playing a one-day stand here.[30] Soup, ham, sweet potatoes, corn pudding, asparagus tip (canned) salad, lemon meringue pie. I staggered over to the Lincoln collection, got out some Herndon stuff, read as much as five pages, collapsed on a sofa, and was dead to the world for a full two hours.[31] Then at four o'clock I went and did my stuff, holding forth to some selected literary undergraduates at what is called a prose clinic until about six-fifteen. I came back to the hotel and, about seven o'clock, decided that I wanted a drink. There are no drinks at the hotel, so I thought I would go out somewhere and get me a sandwich. Pure ritual—I wasn't hungry.

Yesterday Helen Everitt's sister showed up at my lecture, coming fifty miles by bus from Indianapolis, so I took her to the hotel for dinner, but stopped off at a dive for a cocktail on the way. Just a dive. Small bar, enormous juke box, really and dreadfully enormous juke box in nine intermittent colors, loud laughter of college youth, marine in the corner getting lugubriously drunk, that sort of thing. However, it was clean and I thought it likely to be better than the half-dozen others on the town square and probably capable of providing a sandwich.

The half-chorus-girl, half-deaconess waitress handed me a menu. It listed half a dozen hamburgers, cheeseburgers, chickenburgers, and the like. Then it listed: small sirloin steak, large sirloin steak, T-bone steak, porterhouse steak, minute steak, filet mignon, chopped steak. I asked the waitress if it meant what it said. She thought for a moment this was some city-slicker attempt on her flagrant virtue but finally said, for gosh sake, yes. I said, could the cook make up a nice little raw salad (that's what you ask for in the Midwest, dear). She said she guessed so.... Well, I had forgotten that the Midwest calls a porterhouse a T-bone and vice versa, and ordering a porterhouse got what I wasn't looking for. BUT, by God, though I'll probably collapse as soon as I finish this report, I have just come back from one of the best God-damned meals, one of the half dozen best God-damned steaks I ever ate. That steak was an inch and a half thick, it was some sixteen inches each way, it had been hung for about three times as long as steaks get hung anywhere these days, it had been cooked by an artist, it yielded to the touch, and the salad was an honest job. Price, including an old-fashioned and a dab of sherbet, one dollar, sixty cents. I want to repeat, that was one hell of a fine steak even if I wasn't hungry. If I remember the vocabulary right next time and really get a porterhouse to scale and *ad valorem*,[32] well, this is a discovery, and I thought that you might like to know about it while chewing at your weekly piece of broiled bathmat *au jus*.[33] Just think of Bloomington.

[*some pages missing; unsigned*]

Bowne

[AFTER 5 MARCH 1943]
TUESDAY, -4° F.

Dear Benny,

Damn it! I knew I shouldn't have mentioned that February thaw. No sooner was that letter in transit than the thermometer dropped 60°, & we're still chipping ourselves out of a first-line blizzard. (The hospital has a rakish roof which gives off sound-effects as of Alpine avalanches at half-hour intervals.)

I don't agree with you at all about the first 150 pages. They contain some of the very best things in the book and, while they are certainly multiple, I did not find them either heavy or slow. In fact, it seems to me that these pages are a microcosm of your whole method, and if they fail, your method fails. But, by God, they do not fail! (Clip & send to Dept. of Understatement.) Incidentally, I wish you'd tell me why the spellings "Tamaulipas" & "Santa Anna" look odd to me? What've I got them mixed up with? and, teacher, what do you know about the Hadji Ali and the Texas Camel Corps?[34]

Liked your Easy Chair.[35] Yeah, to bring it down to the Roosevelt-Hilton—or Hollywood—level, even Shangri-la is just a place where some bombers took off.... My candidate for a post-war Nepenthe* is West Virginia.[36]... And don't you think Sgt. Kahn writes pretty?[37]

I don't often get an attack of the-world-is-too-much-with-us, but when I think of millions of men & women all over the country spending precious days of their brief span figuring things like "Net loss in Column 5, lines 1 and 2. (The amount to be entered as Item 8(a), page 1, is (1) this item or (2) net income, computed without regard to capital gains or losses, or (3) $1000, whichever is smallest.)" It seems to me we've let the thing get out of hand. In the sweat of our brow let us earn our bread (*si possumus*)[38]; but can't we, somehow, simplify the bookkeeping?

Sure I remember Etzler. And this Gilpin sounds like pay dirt. Speaking of Alaska, and, in your character as a topographer of the Rocky Mountains, is it true that the Alcan Highway follows the worst of all possible routes?[39] And why in hell didn't FDR use a little of that Dutch stubbornness on the Fla. Ship Canal?[40]

What do you make of the Standley storm-in-samovar?[41]

And was that porterhouse <u>alias</u> T-bone up to the standard of the T-bone <u>alias</u> porterhouse? Ah, Benny, there may be beef in Gilead,[42] but on the Eastern Seaboard we will soon be eating whale-steak. Better seize the day!

* Or is that something you drink?

Yours,

Kate

Friday. +50° F.

[envelope: Hotel Graham, Bloomington, Indiana]

[17 March 1943]

Dear Kate:

End of the day of profit taking.... You're thinking of Santa Ana, galloping ponies, and a stretch of sand ridge. Whether you're also thinking of tamales or M. Petipas, I wouldn't know.[43] ... There is no dictionary or other reference work nearer than the University, but to my best belief Nepenthe is the forgetfulness-cocktail much recommended by E. A. Poe.[44] ... I don't think it was the Texas Camel Corps. It was part of the QM Corps of the U. S. Army. There are a couple of monographs about it, a couple of highly imaginative books, and a vast amount of official documentation, of which, years ago, I read more than is good for any man's soul.[45] There are some legends in the West and a good many yarns about the imported Bedouins who took care of the camels. What do you want to know? I'll send you any dope when I get back. Or we can always wire Rosy, though I think that at the moment she's in New Haven disdainfully pawing over the newly opened Morse Collection.[46] (To the Yale Librarian's generous permission to print any of his Mark Twain letters when Professor Stanley Williams had published whatever he wanted to of the collection, I snootily replied that if Dr. Williams would get in touch with me I'd take up his request for permission to publish them without prejudice.)[47] The camel experiment was made when Jefferson Davis was Secretary of War. It was recommended, I believe, by and certainly carried out under the direction of Edward F. Beale.[48] What kept it from succeeding was the inability of camels to speak English and the distrust of them by American soldiers. If it had been kept up a few years longer it probably would have succeeded, pre-automobile transport in the desert would have been enormously facilitated, and zoos would not display camels. It was a good idea bungled.... What I hear about the Alcan Highway is twofold, and take your choice: that it's the biggest scandal in the war and that only heroic obstinacy of far-sighted men saved America by getting it located in the present route, safely out of range of carrier-based Jap planes.... As for the flare-up in Moscow, I'm constrained to believe that it's a bit of that magnificent duplicity aforesaid, and if so, so much the better. I greatly admire Joe's army, Uncle Joe, and Uncle Joe's plain speaking, and the more plain speaking Uncle Joe hears and the more ice water he gets spilled down his spine by ambassadors and others who happen to trip while carrying a tray, the better for him, us, and everyone.[49] If the admiral would now write an Ostend Manifesto or offer Finland to the Poles or something similar, the air would be wholesomely cleared.[50] The sooner he understands that he's got to trade for his horses—and trade close—the sooner we'll get down to fighting the war cooperatively. His public utterances, and those of his ambassadors, have been too God-damn truculent and Adolph-plus-Ribbentrop to be borne.[51] I hope to God somebody detours a convoy and tells him he can have it when he talks pretty and not before.

But also if Mr. Wallace wants an answer to his recent question, I can give him one.[52] Are we going to repeat the mistake? Are we going to double-cross Russia? Are we going to pull out of the international set-up? Mr. Vice-President, we are.

You have frequently had it on my authority that the Middle West is America. You will presently have it on the authority of William Gilpin that the civilization of the Mississippi Valley is destined to dominate the world. All that being so, you've got to take it as it is, and nothing whatever will change it. Thus grows the tree. Since September 1939, I have touched some part of the Middle West about every six months—perhaps oftener, on the average. And I have now been resident in this community for two weeks.... The head of the government department convened seven or eight of his colleagues last night. He once held an exchange appointment at Harvard and is determined first that I shall understand the Hoosier culture and second that I shall not suffer the illusion that Harvard is important to it. Half-way through the evening he asked, apropos of nothing whatever, "DeVoto, are the people in the East more internationally minded than we are?" So I let go.... For at least six hours of every day I have been here, and usually for twelve hours, I have been consorting with students and faculty. I have talked to hotel clerks, traveling men, waitresses, loafers in bars, grocery clerks, newsdealers, newspapermen, everybody I could get hold of. I have eavesdropped on every conversation in my vicinity. And up to and including last night, up to and including this moment, I have yet to hear any discussion of the war whatsoever. No one has said a word about it, no one has talked about a battle or a campaign, no one has permitted any word of mine introducing the subject to go farther than the next sentence, usually a Hoosier-dialect joke. There is one solitary exception to this, the curator of the Lincoln collection, a young chap about to go into the Navy—and his ideas have been concerned exclusively with the coming Russian imperialism—but they have at least been ideas about the war. There is not even that much exception to the second observation: I have heard no discussion whatever of the end of the war, the terms of peace, and the possible part of the United States in what is to come hereafter.

Sixteen names of Indiana alumni killed or dead in the war are posted in the administration building—no, in the Student Union. The local papers and the Indianapolis papers carry many stories about the local boys in the service, local heroes dedicated, local people going into service, etc. Indiana leads the states in Navy enlistments. It is well toward the top in war bonds. Leland Stowe was here and blasted hell out of indifference both publicly and in the duty-lunch that followed, where a number of people did ask him questions about the Russian army (and maybe that should also be listed as an exception to the above)—and I have not heard a single word about him or his speech since. The town—and all the towns I drove through en route to New Harmony and Vincennes—is plentifully bespangled with service flags.[53] And the simple, flat, immitigable fact is that the war is not an element in anyone's thinking.

Let's say it this way, and let's further grant that I have talked to no one who has lost a relative of the first degree in the war, though I have talked to several who have lost friends. The war exists exclusively as one further item of New Deal spending and New Deal mismanagement, one further step in the New Deal effort to bankrupt the thrifty and destroy capitalism and the primary virtues. And the end of the war exists exclusively as an opportunity to put the Republican Party back in power, which alone is fit to govern the United States. There are no problems of winning the war, there is in fact no day by day course of the war. There are no problems to come out of the war except that of repairing the damage done by the New Deal. There are no international problems.... Stet. Stet, OK. Thirty.

Of war news as such, the Indiana newspapers do not average three columns an edition. In addition, of course, they carry the columnists, especially the Scripps-Howard columnists and most especially Pegler.[54] The editorials do not discuss the war as such. They talk plentifully about war legislation and occasionally they make faces at Hitler, but I have yet to read a local editorial discussion of any military or in fact any international aspect of the war. We are in the Chicago area and the *Tribune* and the *Sun* circulate thoroughly. You know what the *Tribune* is. Well, in a curious way, the *Sun* is damned near as unrealistic. It carries pages of war news, some of it, though not enough, by its own war correspondents, and yet the effect is again of a local political dispute. Its contention with the *Tribune* and its daily assaults on the Republican state machine are certainly all to the good, but I can't help feeling for the *Sun* too the war is just an episode in the New Deal, if seen from the other side.

The campus has been stripped of male undergraduates, up to about seventy-five percent. Innumerable faculty men have gone into the services or the auxiliaries. The Navy has a school for yeomen and one for Waves on the campus and in the dormitories. The Army has a small school and will have an enormous one by the middle of April. A big ROTC drills every day.[55] And there is no war.

Last Thursday the alumni secretary (named Dixie Highway) and a professor and an assistant professor of American history and a visiting Elk from Wabash drove me to New Harmony and back by way of Vincennes.[56] We were in that automobile for fourteen hours. There was no mention of the war. Well, there was one Hoosier story.... You don't know what a Hoosier story is. I knew, I even liked them, I don't now. A Hoosier story is what you have to hear before you can buy a pack of Chesterfields, get off the bus or out of the elevator, begin your lecture, bring the President to tell you what he said to the Legislature, or get the chambermaid out of the room so you can change your pants. There were one thousand Hoosier stories in that car and, in order to show you what a Hoosier story is, I'm going to tell you the one that involved the sole mention of the war. You won't know what a Hoosier story is, even so, for a Hoosier story is dialect and deadpan yokel face, but here goes.

The draft board caught up with one of the brushrunners, twenty mile up the crick beyond Gnaw Bones. (All this, you understand, is drama, not narrative.) They told him he had to go to war. What war? They tried to tell him but couldn't make it plain, so they sat down, went back to the beginning, and told him about Hitler. Lots of exclamations, here, all about the dirty son of a bitch, but in the Hoosier dialect and full of the rich vernacular of rural America of 1935. Finally, in tremendously excited indignation, the cottonmouth says, Why'n't they kill the son of a bitch? They explain that that's pretty hard. But you got rifles, ain't you? Yes, but it's pretty hard to locate him. Well, says cottonmouth, that's easy, all you got to do is wait around, sooner or later he's got to come out on the front porch to piss.

That's the war in Indiana. It lacks the virulent Roosevelt-baiting I always encounter in Chicago, but it will suffice. You can tell Mr. Wallace.

...This has lain here two days. No mention of the war in Bloomington but the Indianapolis *News* has carried an editorial about Giraud.[57]

I would eventually have got John if Lee Hartman had lived.[58] There's no chance under Fred. Fred keenly feels his own lamentable insufficiencies, he's not a thinker and John is. Further, John is protected, served, and adored by Kay Jackson.[59] Do you know her? She is a pretty, soulful, and energetic, even intelligent gal—who should have married a Drunkard in 1870. I know nothing about her husband except that he seems to be a pleasant guy.[60] It may be that his defect is that he's In Business but I think there must be something far worse. For Kay lives in the most orgasmic adoration of and slavery to not only John, for whom she systematizes his jobs and gives him such ideas as he has, God help us, but also Herbert Agar, for whom she runs Freedom House singlehanded.[61] I said orgasmic and I mean orgasmic. No nun of the perpetual adoration ever worshiped Jesus as she worships that pair. In their presence, at the mention of their names, in mere recollection of them, her eyes are of love's moment. Her vision is hot, panting, sweaty, and her breasts drip milk. They are the great men of the world, civilization depends on them, she shivers and shudders to the nobility of their ideas, she is in constant heat for both. It is about the saddest spectacle I know.... And what John says about my book, whether in fact he says anything, will depend on her moist palms and quivering lips.

I now eat two steaks daily. But I am not recognized by the English department. And why did I bring a dinner jacket?

Yrs

Benny

****

[envelope: Hotel Graham, Bloomington, Indiana]

[23 March 1943]
[postmarked 10:00 AM]

Dear Kate:

Jesus! When you put in a good word for a book, you do a thorough job of it. It isn't that good a book, daughter. But it's a good book and I'm damned glad you think so. When I bust that novel, I told you I'd put your name on a good book some day and here it is.

I've heard a number of those Boraxo programs that came within my knowledge and they were all OK, absolutely sound as to history.[62] One about the Cement Mine exactly followed the facts, and you seem to have the dope about the camels. If you don't mind, we'll wait till I get back to Cambridge before looking up the bibliography. At the moment Rosy appears to be in one of those to hell with the male sex moods that frankly scare me. As soon as I get back I'll clip her one on the jaw and cut her down to size but it can't be done by U. S. Mail. If I tried, she'd only enter the ring an odds-on favorite. I should think that Bonsal's *Beale* would be in the Poughkeepsie Library.[63] It's a good book—at least I remember it as one, I haven't looked at it for ten years or more and told the Kit Carson crawl through the cactus from memory.[64] My copy was stolen by a Chicago newspaperman who knew a lot about the fur trade and was building up his library.... Beale became a magnifico in California, practically a caliph, in the large and far-off times that followed the Gold Rush. It is quite true that the camels scared hell out of the Army horses, but the thing ought to have been pushed through regardless. It was a perfectly sound idea and could have done a lot for the desert country. For many years after the experiment was abandoned, there were wild and gorgeous yarns about solitary prospectors supposing that they had got alkalied at last because they saw camels. Many of those yarns were certainly true. How long the strays lasted no one knows, but a camel is a long-lived beast. Out in the Raft River country in the summer of 1922 I met an old desert rat who claimed to have seen a camel in Utah's Dixie in some unspecified year. He had been alkalied for at least forty years but it's quite possible that that particular story was true.

You will be pleased to know that the war hysteria in the East is due to the high percentage of foreign-born in the population. This was explained to me by a full professor of sociology last night at supper given by the President following a concert by the Indianapolis Symphony which called on my dinner jacket for the first time since I've been here.

I said loudly, "Jesus Christ, the United States is in the war too," and chalked up another gaucherie, for we do not swear in mixed company here. I was a mite roused and when the good professor and his wife challenged me to explain the facts that seemed to annoy me, the alleged indifference to the war, I supplied an explanation. I said that, with the possible and solitary exception of a Mormon village beyond the Kaibab, this was the most provincial society I had ever encountered. I said a lot of things that will go down on the list—it's a large list already and has made the DeVoto occupancy of the Patten Foundation a spectacular bust.[65] But by God that stands. This is the most indurated smugness I've ever seen outside the Mormon Church—it's more profoundly smug than the New England States Mission which currently practices on Brattle Street.[66] It is shot through with Ku Klux, Silver Shirts, Liberty League, and all the way back to APA, to the Know-Nothings, to the Knights of the Golden Circle.[67] God really designed me to be a college teacher and it is not often that I rejoice in having left the profession, but I'm glad the lines never fell to me at I U. Ames, Iowa is Paris compared to Bloomington and all the Iowans I know are cosmopolitans compared to any Hoosier I've met—save possibly the President, I haven't made up my mind about him yet.[68] I'm supposed to be Early American, I'm supposed to love the native reality, I'm supposed to luxuriate in the autochthonous. But the Hoosier has got me down. The conscious cultivation of the bucolic gripes me—and not of the bucolic merely but of the backwoodsy folksy, the yokel pose cultivated so assiduously that it's no longer proper to call it a pose. I get fed up with fifty-year-old college professors educated at Columbia, Harvard, Oxford, and the Sorbonne, acquainted with the whole reach of their subjects, resident for some years in foreign countries, exposed to the full reach of the intellectual life of their time—I get fed up with such men when they take care to speak bad grammar, drawl in the vaudeville manner locally approved, look slyly deadpan, and pretend an ignorance of and indifference to any intellectual or artistic matter whatsoever. I get fed up with the society that would have their heads in ten minutes if they didn't do just that. If Indiana is native American, I'll take the ghetto. Or South Boston. Or what has the same rating here, Harvard.

I suppose I can take Hoosier stories for the rest of my stay, but the only thing that is going to permit me to is my forthcoming interlude in Chicago—and, for Christ's sweet sake, who ever thought I'd be glad to be going to Chicago? (If you want to hear my liturgical voice, tune in on John Frederick's "Men and Books," Saturday, 3 P.M. Poughkeepsie time.) . . . What's your picture of Margaret Weymouth Jackson?[69] Mine was of a young gal recently out of college working for a country weekly, shy, timid, sweet, retiring, uncertain of herself. She turns out to be a couple of months short of grandmotherhood, a hundred and eighty pounds, a voice like the switch engine whistle that wakes me at four A.M., a laugh like artillery fire—loud, vociferous, assertive, and as she says loudly, "common as dirt." She is common as dirt at the top of her voice persistently—and girly-girly, folksy, coy, pettish, and altogether intolerable. Hoosier.

Elmer Davis asked me to report observations. I have done so once. And when I get home and get the time, I'll report plenty. I get no time here and my sociology pal last night was distinctly snooty about the fact that I'm clearing out for three days during this week, when no lectures are scheduled for me since Charles Merriam is occupying another Foundation here.[70] The first three days of the week and Sunday are full to the brim with appointments, but I ought not to cheat the University out of three days in between. I didn't tell him but I'd be glad to fill those days if anything I said made any impact whatever on anyone. Well, let's say anyone but the three historians who have palled around with me and who do really take apart what I say. The rest evaporates like desert run-off. The Hoosiers turn out in vast crowds, for Indiana supports culture and the Patten Foundation is culture and highly paid culture at that. But I talk into a feather bed. No one agrees, no one disagrees, no one argues, no one disputes, no one says a God-damned word. By the grace of God, I'm going to be here the night when first there is no reaction whatever to Frost, and by the same grace I am going to be gone when a couple of repetitions of the experience drive him berserk.

But if you've still got the letter I wrote you about Indiana and Mr. Wallace, hang onto it, for I'll want that impression when I come to write a piece about the Middle West and the War.

Yours,
Benny

****

8 Berkeley Street
Cambridge, Massachusetts

[20 April 1943]

Dear Kate:
Please take me out in the sacristy and admonish me. Tell me I'm too God-damn amiable, innocent, and compliant. Tell me I've got to say no.

This is one of my frantic periods. Or have I any other kind? With two fixed points, the second half of John August and a tour of the provinces for the Army, I have got myself involved as of now with: trip to New York to lecture to Polish Institute and go on the air for Freedom House (that insatiable and soft-eyed Jackson wench), book review for SRL, book review for Irita, manuscript-reading and soul-lifting operation for Kitty Bowen, annual battle with Shady Hill University, depositions and representations to Dies Committee and Kerr Committee saying they are wet as hell about one of their victims, Rosy's psyche, diplomatic ceremonies for delegation of visiting British publishers, and what may turn out to be an assault on the Massachusetts Historical Society.[71] I think I'll just stay in New York.

Rosy starts off with her tinkerer today. That may take her off my hands for a while. Again, it may eat into such sleep as my other commitments have left room for. I have been on call ever since I got home, and I've been called frequent. I'll report when I hear what the tinkerer has been saying to her. John Taylor assures me he's pretty good. In a way I envy him, if she really sticks with him. I wish to God I had time and opportunity to make a chart of that psyche. There is nothing faintly like it in case history, magic, folklore, or religion. It is new to science.

Letters from Bloomington fairly outline the job that Frost has done on me since my departure, and I must admit it is a masterly job. No one in my experience has faintly approached his skill and sureness at the indirect sneer and the character-annihilating joke. Whatever image I created for myself at the University has now been displaced by the image of a half-sinister, half-foolish, wholly third-rate, wholly inept literary amateur who has delusions of grandeur, a swollen ego, and a revengeful disposition. That, of course, is only the picture he has been painting of me everywhere since August, 1938, but this is the first time he has ever followed directly on my heels. It makes me kind of mad.

I never said a word against him at Bloomington. Quite the contrary, I did what I could to smooth the way before him. I called him, in private, about lying about me, indirectly, at Brigham Young University. I had careful notes by a pal and a supporter of mine. The old bastard couldn't take it. He lied some, he explained some, and most of all he complained like a baby.... It's astonishing how many people are using that word "baby" about him, nowadays.... Then he made an all-out effort to re-inclose my loyalties, re-establish the situation of five years ago, and, I suppose, insure the book I once intended to write. Larry Thompson's book is not only a thoroughly bad one, which wouldn't bother Robert in the least, if it were bad in the right way, but it has been denounced as such from practically every literary rostrum in the land, and I take that to be the reason behind his three-day attempt on me.[72] After all, I'm the only member of my generation who knows him well, understands his poetry and thinks it great, and can write pleasingly: that combination of facts never leaves his awareness for a moment, much as he hates my guts.

Well, I held out against him for twenty-four hours. I told him that I wasn't interested in and didn't want to hear his explanations. Moral cowardice—I'd been through enough turmoil over the situation, I didn't want any more. The reflex of good sense was finally activated, however, and I let him go. So he launched such a series of narratives, lyric poses, and marginal glosses as I could not put on paper in less than a month. Avis says I've got to put them on paper, that, in fact, I've got to write down my memory of the whole damned episode from 1938 up to now. That's just fine, but when do I get the time.... The net result of the forty-eight-hour soliloquy is that I don't know what I think or believe about the whole damned triangle now. The trouble with the lies of a man of genius is that they are lies of genius, the explanations of a man who knows more than any other writer of our time about the workings of the human mind tend to explain even when you are convinced that they are probably altogether falsehood. A good deal of what he said I could accept on the basis of what I know about him, Kay, and Ted. It fits. Also, he said it, and I therefore tend to reject it altogether. In sum he said two things: that he was not living with Kay, which I assured him I did not in the least doubt (I did not say, physiologically), and that he and she were bound together in the world's greatest love since Adam's time. That last is where I do not know what to think. He also said that when he appeared on the scene, the marriage between Ted and Kay was already ended, and that, gents, is a God-damned lie. In and round these statements he said millions of other things, every one of them pure inspiration but I don't know how many of them damned lies, and that's my trouble.

I took care to say one thing and took greater care to say no more. I said that I held him responsible for destroying my friendship with the Morrisons. So that is now on record before Kay's eyes, probably was within thirty-six hours.

I notified him that he was being extremely indiscreet. Not that it mattered, for he has said to at least a dozen others to my knowledge, and scores of others in my guess, the substance of what he said to me. So now he's said it, of his own volition, I feel curiously emancipated. The triangle no longer involves my emotions; I am fascinated by it, I want to watch it develop and see what comes of it, but I don't give a damn any more. But I'm fed up with his compulsions. So far as they've involved me I've never made a protest or a reply. I think I will now. Certainly, the pressure in him has quadrupled since he talked to me in Bloomington. He'll curse me and go out to get me for his own damned compulsive loquacity, precisely as he did in August of '38 and the succeeding four months. I think that this time I'll pick me a spot, just one. I'll pick it sagaciously and I'll use it. I'll let him have one broadside, private or public as sagacity may indicate, and I'll remind him that the life insurance tables give me the probability that I'll outlive him—and let it go at that.

I'm also toying with the idea of meeting Kay somewhere on neutral ground and summarizing what he had to say in Bloomington. I can see a lot of virtues in that, but I'll probably think of Ted and forbear. It would clear my ideas but I'll bet I never do it.

But I have finally found the guts to tell Ted out and out that I ~~didn't~~ don't want to come back to Bread Loaf. I can't say I like working with him for the Army, with all this bulk of garbage and the unsaid between us.

I keep turning the irony in my hands: the hottest hellfires I've ever seen in a human soul, the ghastliest welter of human destructiveness, the most dynamic evil—and this in the author of the poetry on which for many years I based my bedrock belief that art is not necessarily neurotic. He is a whirlpool of feculent matter.

The hell with him.... Purely, dear, a nester is a homesteader. The term is an anachronism in my book, for it was first used by cowmen and used contemptuously. The nester came in and fenced off the range, made birdsnests in it. I can send you Wade's *Parkman, Wah-To-Yah* when Elliott Perkins returns it (it's a hell of a heavy book, for I gave my copy of Grabhorn's beautiful edition to Edith Mirrielees), *Down the Santa Fe Trail*, *Ordeal by Hunger*, Elliott's *Scott*, and/or *The Great Plains* (but not till I've done a piece on the Intermountain West for the new venture in propaganda, *Transatlantic*—oh, yes, that's promised for May 15 too, and an Easy Chair comes in between).[73] Also Bryant, Thornton, Ruxton (getting up to verify this, I perceive that God or some mortal son of a bitch has made off with the better of his two books), several Doniphan journals, several fairly no good Mormon journals, a vast quantity of fur trade material, a vaster quantity of Mormon material—and so on. When you're applying to libraries, why not think of mine? *Clyman* is unobtainable. It was published in an exceedingly small edition by the Calif. Hist. Soc. and vanished into college libraries. The last available copy of that edition was sent to me by the Society itself some five or six years ago, by American Railway Express. It disappeared somewhere en route. I sequestered Widener's copy for over two years but have returned it to the usages of scholarship.

Here comes Shady Hill University. I'll come back when there's opportunity. Some people went overland to California in '41, but the emigration is generally supposed to have begun in '42. I dunno about Doaks and have no *Pioneer Register* but I'll look him up.[74] I remember an Englishman named Doaks, not an American. Wally's book is *Darkling*, not *Clash*, whatever Eddie Balmer called it.[75] He has just decided to write a life of John Wesley Powell, but my lecture will beat him to print.[76] But you may loose your romance freely, for no one can prove that the camels did not breed.

Yours,

Benny

Bowne

[BEFORE 9 MAY 1943]

Dear Benny,

Correction: Heraus mit dem coccus.[77] I should not essay German.

How are you? I understand that strep throat can be a very nasty piece of business indeed and that, as you suggest, the cure is a Charybdis.[78] ... I've not been too fit myself; the usual spring flare-up, probably. My next-door-neighbor (a really incredibly dumb grade-school teacher from Flatbush, whose Brooklynese bears about the same relation to English that Roumanian does to Latin) had a haemorrhage about 1:30 a.m. last Tuesday. She rang & rang but our night-nurse, Lizzie Sullivan Albertson, makes a point of not answering bells in less than an hour. Finally Guinan (the patient) jumped out of bed, rushed out into the hall, haemorrhaging all the way, & bellowed:

"Mrs. Albertson! Mrs. Albertson! Come quick! Come quick!"

"Who wants me?"

"I want you! I want you! Hurry! Hurry! Hurry! Hurry!"

"All right, I'm comin' as fast as I can! Whyn't you put on your bell & wait?"

That clipping you sent me was what the kids call transcendent. Where did it come from, the *Denver Post*? Reminds me of a story of Georgie Clark's: couple of gaffers were discussing their married lives. Jones had no children: "Well, it was this way. A week or so before our wedding, we were looking for an apartment. We were in the bedroom of one—the one we lived in for ten years, as a matter of fact—when the superintendent was called away. Well, I just couldn't stand it any longer. I grabbed her & threw her on the bed etc. etc. She raised merry hell—bit & scratched & yelled. I let her go, of course. We were married the next week, & I never brought the subject up again."

Do you ever listen to Bessie Beatty (WOR—11:15 a.m.)? You should—for the laughs. (LAUGHS.) The other day she related how she introduced her husband, Bill, to Malvina Hoffman:[79] "And ever since then all I've had of my husband is a piece. A little piece. A little piece. A little tiny piece. About an inch & a half..."

There's plenty scarcity of censorable foods here too. Severest local shortages seem to be poultry, potatoes & eggs, but the severest Bowne shortage seems to be, simply, food.

I don't care for that lush, Bricker, do you?[80] And it would be an exaggeration to say that I am suffering from an unrequited yen for John L. Lewis.[81] As for Fred Libbey, if he isn't getting berries from Berlin I'll eat a gross of John-Frederic's jardinieres. And would it be indiscreet to request the key to ¶s 1 and 2 of your May Easy Chair?

It's more than kind of you—it's really damned wonderful!—to offer to lend me books. But I'm going to decline. You see, being tied in bed, I have to depend on nurses & maids to hand me books & to look after them when I'm not reading them. Dust accumulates, occasionally they get dropped, once in a while something gets spilled (as you will observe from the envelope of one of those Bloomington letters on which Lizzie Albertson spilled Library Paste—she spilled water on another batch & I damn' near pasted her). Well, if a library book gets dog-eared, or thumb-marked or otherwise marred, it is very, very unfortunate. But I take it that a certain amount of wear & tear is the common lot of library books. Whereas yours...

My favorite female, Edith Hamilton, read part of *The Trojan Women* on Columbia's Invitation to Learning program a couple of weeks ago.[82] ...Did you hear A. MacLeish vs. G. Boas (L. Untermeyer referee)?[83] I begin to see what you mean about Archie's type of mind.

Of course, R. Frost has never seemed to me quite so great a poet as he does to you (poetry is a field in which I have absolutely no competence), so, on the face of it, his behavior classifies him less as a genius than as a bastard & a lunatic.

I began to suspect the imminence of something big well over a month ago when practically all the soldiers of my acquaintance turned up on leave (in many cases quite unexpectedly) at almost the same time. I wouldn't attempt to predict what it's going to be. Would you?

I suppose you saw that definition of a wolf: a goon who takes out a sweater girl & tries to pull the wool over her eyes. And then there's the one about the two British soldiers who took out an American girl. She was wearing, among other things, a V-necked sweater.

Sailor: "I say, is that V for Victory?"

Girl: "No, it's for Virtue." (then, thoughtfully:) "But it's an old sweater."

Yours,

Kate

Bowne

[BEFORE 18 MAY 1943]

Dear Benny,

I doubt if I could explain it to a Carnegie jury, but each Founder's Day Edition seems more handsome than the last. I suppose I need not say that this one is, by immeasurable odds, my most valued possession.

What's the matter with Harvard? Are they crazy? Or just jealous? At that, since Baldwin & "Dragon's Teeth," I'm beginning to feel that Fadiman's nomination was an intolerable slur.[84] I might consider the Nobel. Pulitzer, no.

Yours,

Kate

8 Berkeley Street
Cambridge, Massachusetts

[18 MAY 1943]

Dear Kate:

Paragraph 1, Conant. Paragraph 2, Hutchins. Sorry, I threw the damned essays away, but they were lovelies.

Four years and nine months ago, and at any time since, I would have diagnosed Frost as suffering from senile dementia complicated by paranoia, except for one awkward fact: that Merrill Moore had made the same diagnosis.[85] With Merrill Moore in New Zealand, where doubtless he is becoming an authority on wombats and exhausting the paper supply in sonnets, it may eventually become possible for distance to perform the miracle of convincing me that it's possible for him to be right once.... I submit two typical specimens from a good many duly conveyed to me from Bloomington by a man on the spot and with a first-rate capacity for reporting.

"You know, Benny has been under the care of a psychiatrist, who has told him that I am not good for him, that if he is ever to succeed he must not cultivate my company: I am too strong for him and have a bad effect upon him. You know, though I've been around all these years, Benny just discovered me. It's amusing."

"Benny has always been a difficult man, but I notice that since he's been here and since his book's been accepted by the Book of the Month, and so many people have been saying nice things to him, he seems a much happier person."

He has pulled that psychiatrist and I'm bad for him, I'm the stronger personality and he's jealous line all over the United States. I have thriftily kept a number of letters from people who were variously aghast, indignant, and amused on hearing it. I've never said anything about it. I wouldn't now except that a particularly vicious job he did on me at Bloomington has been followed by some truly stinking stuff here in Cambridge but [*sic*] now I'm going to. A couple of days ago I found myself suddenly realizing that I was going to hunt him up and tell him to shut up, with details. I hunted him up but he's at Ripton, getting the farm opened up and, probably, another poem written saying how dangerous he is to husbands. (Cf., for example, "The Discovery of the Madeiras" in *A Witness Tree*.[86] Also, from the notes I made at Bloomington: "Let men let their wives around me at their risk.") He'll be back in a few days. I will carry out the program.

That clipping was from Tom Ferril's *Rocky Mountain Herald* and, now I think of it, I'll have him put you on the free list for it's by all odds the most amusing reading matter that comes my way.[87] It's a little weekly which Tom's father founded many years ago and which exists only to carry legal notices. His father died a year or so ago and Tom's wife has been carrying it on, because Tom hasn't got time to and the graft is too pleasant to be given up.[88] Tom, with the help of various hands from time to time, writes the front page, though he gets almost as much fun from a page of boiler plate which he buys God knows where. He's one of the best poets and one of the best minds in the United States. I wonder I never thought to sign you up long ago.

Really, there isn't any opposition to '46 at Harvard except in the English Department, which opposes everything I do, and a couple of members only of the History Department. When I wrote, I was smarting from Arthur Schlesinger's attitude. There's another historian who scratches my ticket in public and private every time he gets a chance, but I really thought Arthur would like the book. I realize now that there never was a chance he would. Years ago, many years in fact, I got to thinking of him as a radical historian, but it was only that he fought like hell to get the kind of history he was doing legitimatized—in those days the elders in the American Historical Association snooted the social historians as superficial and actually had Arthur kicked off his first committee. Once he'd won that battle he became a complete Tory but had a psychic scar, the need to justify himself by marching to the presidency of the Association, and that made him not only a Tory but an orthodox historian who had to play politics with one hand and, so to speak, walk the strait and narrow with the other, if you permit. Now that he's President, he's also Pope, which is to say far more royalist than the king, far more orthodox a historian than ever Channing was.[89] I'll be saying some of this in Easy Chair presently, but for one thing, professional historians do not pass judgments, they uncover and dissect facts.[90] Judgment is unscientific and always unwarranted. I said to the head of the history dept at Indiana, Still, you'd commit yourself, wouldn't you, to a statement that on the whole, it's a good thing that the sequence from, say, the Declaration of Independence to the adoption of the Constitution, happened and happened about as it did. No, that would be unhistorical: a thousand years from now, or even sooner, it may easily be evident that the dismemberment of the British Empire was, on the whole, bad for civilization. Pros are scientific, they don't offer judgments, and Arthur goes around Cambridge complaining that Benny is too positive, too controversial, he passes judgments. Again, an orthodox historian insists on any historian's having professional training, of which I have not the slightest item. He knows nothing about the field, he tells everyone, but Benny is not a historian, how do I know that he knows what he's talking about, there's nothing on the record to give me confidence in his ability to use sources or to weigh evidence. Again, as a pro—as a pro who is neither Beard nor Sam Morison—he has a soul-weary conviction that it can't be history if people read it. In all simplicity he said to me, "I can't understand how it sells so well. Why do people read it? What is there in it that makes people take it so seriously?" Again, he has found a couple of mistakes—in maps, not in the text—and he has labored them all about Cambridge. [*handwritten in margin:* I have marked scores myself in Arthur's books.] Actually, no historian who ever lived has been able to avoid small mistakes in a book that length. I recognized a dozen as soon as I saw it in print, and a dozen others have been called to my attention by others. And finally, as Paul Buck says, I lost Arthur's vote for the Pulitzer Prize—he's on the committee—when I tossed in that note about the Shannon-Webb controversy. I knew I would. Arthur has a politician's loyalty to his faction and a father's loyalty to his pupils, and Shannon is both.

I must have written you about the controversy, which was sidesplitting a few years back, and which damn near split the Social Science Research Council down the middle. Paul Buck and others tried to dissuade him from publishing the report, once it was seen to be silly, but he insisted—and so even the historians have been split ever since. Shannon is the trigger man of the AHA, a bilious gent who quarrels with everyone and once actually denounced me for having praised him in print. Actually, he knows no more about Webb's subject than he learned in a summer spent in Widener Library, being paid to do a critique of Webb's book. He knows far less about Webb's field, oh, a great deal less, than I do. Webb's book is brilliant and revolutionary, it breaks new ground, it adds a new instrument and a new hypothesis to history. It makes plenty of mistakes, small mistakes, but, as I've said above, what book doesn't? Arthur thought it was wonderful when it came out—Webb belonged to his faction—and actually helped, as a member of the committee, to give it a Loubat Prize, which is the highest award a historian can get.[91] And he recommended it to the Soc Sci Council to be studied and reported on as an inspiration for young historians. Then, thriftily using the same stone, he got Shannon appointed to make the study. Shannon is a trigger man and all books are bad, unless he wrote them. So, with one summer's work in Widener, he brought in this farcical report. Arthur showed it to me in manuscript, since I had become a Webb booster. It makes three main points against Webb. I am not qualified to criticize one of them, but the second, the cattle business, I know a good deal about, and the third, the technology of firearms and the techniques of Indian warfare, I know a hell of a lot about, in so far that no professional historian in the country, and only a half dozen amateurs, knows as much, or half as much. I speedily saw that Shannon's report was full of holes. I went round and told Arthur so and solemnly advised him not to let the report go any farther. He said he must assume that Shannon knew more about it than I did. So I took time out of a crowded season and wrote a small monograph on the single point of the Colt's Revolver. It was short and far from complete but there was enough of it, point by point, with specific documentation, to blow what Shannon had said about Webb higher than a kite. Arthur said, would I submit it to the Council? I said no, it was for his private information, it was incomplete and hastily done, at some later time I'd do the job thoroughly (and I will). Apparently that refusal clinched the matter, if there was ever any chance Arthur would tolerate the evidence. There wasn't much chance, for Shannon was a historian, a pro, and a student of Arthur's, and I'm none of those. He said again that he knew nothing about the subject, which I was pointing out to him, but must assume that Shannon knew more than I. So I blew round to Paul Buck and showed him the little monograph. Paul, who already had his doubts about the report, said in effect, Jesus Christ, and hurried off and told Arthur he'd make himself a public laughing stock if he let the report be published. No, by God, truth must prevail, and, after a cosmic meeting of all the Council, committee, and contracting parties, at which Webb invoked the departed spirit of Robert E. Lee and formally took Texas out of the Union for the second time, it was published. With the result that people have been holding their sides ever since—and others have been undergoing acute heartburn.

Actually, there were only three historians whose approval I truly wanted, Camp, who is an amateur, Paul Buck, who is the most intelligent historian I know, and Fred Merk, who is the final and forever authority on Oregon and one of the great historians of the West in general.[92] I have clean bills of health from all three. Fred is as distressed as possible about the judgments and generalizations that scare Arthur, but he has signed his name to a detailed statement that the history is unimpeachable. Camp has apparently elevated me to the judiciary, and Paul says quite honestly and sincerely that I am a leading historian and must go on from here.

The English dept boys, especially Matthiessen and his protégé Levinne [*sic*], are foaming at the mouth.[93] But hell, they always do. I'm sorry I said anything about it.

Jesus, this began as one page before picking up after lunch. I've got to finish a review, type a piece there isn't time to have Elaine type, and explain to Shady Hill University that I can't help it if my son writes well, it isn't plagiarism, it's just heredity—before dinner.

Yours,
Benny

8 Berkeley Street
Cambridge, Massachusetts

[18 May 1943]

Dear Kate:
I guess I shouldn't lie about taxes. I have a hell of a hunch that I sent you a sophisticated set of answers to an inquiry & sent the Commonwealth of Massachusetts a chummy letter about Arthur Schlesinger & a ms. about the West.[94] Did I?

The ms. contains two emended emendations originally by Kip Fadiman.

I have had, this afternoon, a touching & flattering compliment, one that has me positively fluorescent. A rancher at Goleta, California, which is hellish hot & hellish dry country, writes that he has just finished '46 & wishes that I would write a history of the US so that his son could have the kind of story of his country that he never had & always wanted.[95] I call that nice.

I haven't kept you abreast of this year's installment of my five years' battle with Shady Hill—it's been too violent. It would be funny if the school had not done vast damage to Bunny, in so much that he couldn't possibly go anywhere else. I think I made myself clear today. I explained that a child who has written a long theme in better English than they are accustomed to, even if he be a child who has emphatically not responded to the school's evangelical demand that he come to Jesus, has not therefore necessarily had that theme written, even in part, by his father. Bunny, for some reason to me unknown, wrote thirteen pages on "The Military Career of Ulysses S. Grant." (Possibly it stemmed from his visit to the Tomb.) It was pretty damn good. So the hysterical virgins who line that sawdust trail informed him that, of course, I had written it. Progressive-evangelical education is a sweetheart. In a low way, I rejoice over this one: it is never too early for a boy to learn cynicism.

I had a nice curtain line. I had, for $2, bought a Grant autograph, which he pasted on his title page. Departing with a handful of apologies, I said, "I hope you won't detach that signature for the library—it's genuine."

Yrs
Benny

8 Berkeley Street
Cambridge, Massachusetts

[28 July 1943; postmarked from Lanesville/Gloucester, Mass.]

Dear Kate:

Our favorite sheet assures me you spent the Fourth in Poughkeepsie.[96] Also your recentest failed to take account of the subsequent weather, which, if I'm a judge, has been even more hellish. God knows it's easy enough to keep cool here. One has only to walk into the North Shore water. God knows this is a wonderful place. God knows this is an especially wonderful vacation place. And God knows, maybe, why every time I go anywhere near any place called a vacation place I stop sleeping altogether. My normal sleep is such a small, underweight, unrationed quantity, it seems a bit ridiculous of my unconscious to deprive me of that nominal or token amount on the wholly unjustified suspicion that I might, otherwise, enjoy myself.

Bunny, however, though he (and Mark too for that matter) is clearly going to be a DeVoto insomniac, is enjoying himself. By God, without sleep, clinging fearfully to a few hours of working in the morning just so I'll know the world is with us, crabbed, windbroken, approaching senility, a lousy tennis player, a swimmer from the Ogden & Weber rivers, by God, I say, I run a better summer camp than any Old Wonalancet I've ever seen.[97] The kid is completely relaxed, burned black, putting on weight, gunning perpetually, and having a good time. Thanks to your miracle he has qualified as Sharpshooter, & Sharpshooter first-bar since he got here & is well along toward his second bar. (The NRA adds nine bars to its Sharpshooter medal before going on to Expert, which is canny.) He's brought his average up 13 points in less than a month and shoots a damn sight better than I do. He has suddenly broken through his phobia of tutelage in swimming, consented to learn how to breathe, and now swims better than I ever did. That means, I trust, that in another six weeks he'll be a swimmer. As it is, he scares the pants off me, poking his faulty strokes through that glaciated water a quarter of a mile off shore at high tide. And his conversation & acquired information continue to stagger me.... What the hell difference does it make that I don't sleep?

Remember way back when I thought I was a photographer? I decided to take some snaps of Mark & got out the Graflex. And by God! There'll be trees growing out of his head & his face will be frozen like a statue's.... He is busily imitating Bunny. A violent case of brother worship. And it drives Bunny nuts. Also, as Bunny did at this age, he's reading all the road signs, cartons, labels, etc. (much puzzled to find his name in so many places), and this time I will not be cowed out of my good sense by advanced pedagogy. If he wants to read, he can read.

Vast dearth of conversation. There's a desert botanist from California in one of the houses at the Point, a colleague of Oakes Ames's I gather, but he's being a father even more heavily than I and besides has a wife who is offended by liquor. Manley Hudson & Janet are a quarter of a mile away, but they both bore the hell out of me.[98] Rumor says that Molly Putnam, Mrs. Rank, & another lady analyst will be hereabouts for a week or so.[99] Maybe I'll get a story or two out of that. We're being driven to import our talk—I've asked the Kubies up for a week, Ted Spencer will be by to see his dog, & Mollie Brazier has reserved a weekend. Pretty soon I'd be just making signs.

Marquand didn't do a Bread Loaf scene, God damn it. The new book is probably the best Marquand, for he's doing it deliberately now whereas *Apley* was at least half-inadvertent.[100] Mighty easy reading, first-rate slick stuff, mighty empty book. A couple of set pieces, one on a literary cocktail party, one on a little place in Connecticut. The hats will be in the air. But I am now ready to say out loud that he ought to stop being ashamed of Newburyport High School, that, in a word, he's a stinking snob and a damned thin mind. The tragedy of life for J. Marquand is that the well-born are not always the filthy rich. And that's that. Anybody can go to Harvard but a Grottie is something else. In short, dear, I'll send you the novel if you want to read it, but it's a book I can truthfully say I don't regret not having written.

Whereas Miller's book on the American Revolution is damned good.[101]

****

Somewhere I spoke of a ten-cent emperor and I can't remember where.... I think the Musso business is part of a prepared plan, I have a dreadful hunch that part of the preparation involves the Archbishop, and the resignation of Mussolini, the assumption of power by the King, and the appointment of Badoglio were all clearly forecast to me by Salvemini well over a year ago and a number of times since.[102] Salvemini said that there would be that effort to play with the State Department when the going got rough and he said it had a pretty good chance of succeeding. I thought of that yesterday when, walking up the hill from the beach, I saw Henry (lt. j. g.) Reck waving his arms

& managed to make out that Mussolini was out. I presently called to mind that Badoglio once pacified Libya, that he is the Duke of Addis Ababa, that he has stooged for Mussolini innumerable times, and that his alleged opposition to his Master is just talk. I also experienced a most unpleasant flash of realizing that I have come to depend more on Churchill than on Roosevelt, that I don't believe Winston will ever be lured into doing something flashy because it's flashy. Finally, I rejoiced that both of them are out on the unconditional surrender limb so far that it probably can't be sawed off.... Yes, and for all that, the news that Henry shouted to me, that kept being repeated from all programs with a desperate lack of detail, that all the whoopers-up were rendering idiotic with this talk of the Collapse of Fascism—the news, I say, was something to remember while there is breath to me. It's the First Marines at Belleau Wood, who not only stopped the bastards but counterattacked.[103] It's the changed color in the water which won't be a flood for some hours yet but means that the dam has burst. It's Step One of a plan, no doubt, and for all that something has come to an end. Twenty-one, twenty-two years? That's a fair slice of my life & a larger one of yours, but it isn't a hell of a long time, come to think of it, to demonstrate what has now been demonstrated for—well, how long? Hitler said for a thousand years, when he bawled over the ether as the tanks went into Holland. I don't think it's been demonstrated for a thousand years. Let's say for a sizeable hunk of time. That particular variant of the illusion has spun its cycle in twenty-one years. I'll give Nazism eighteen months more than half as long.[104] Let us now hang Cardinal O'Connell and take Crete.[105]

Yrs
Benny

Bowne

[BEFORE 10 SEPTEMBER 1943]

Dear Benny,

If anyone had told me last spring that I could have lived through a summer like this past Summer & survived, even in the attenuated & shattered shape in which I now survive, I should have called him an addled optimist. Since March—really since last October—I have not had more than two or three hours sleep any night—& that in the merest fragments. I've had <u>no</u> sleep at all Rest Hours. And the remainders of the days have been spent with ears stuffed with cotton, fingers stuck in ears, waiting, cringing, for the next barrage.

The author of this torture is a creature named Guinan. How shall I describe Guinan to you? She is 5' 1" and weighs 187 lbs. She's not exactly fat, though—stocky, solid, chunky are better words. She has a short, thick head. She is indescribably clumsy—continually stumbling, dropping things, knocking things off tables. All her movements are loutish & imprecise, as though she did not have complete control of her muscles. And she is somewhere between an idiot & a low-grade moron. Nearer the idiot, I should say. (It is irrelevant that she comes from Brooklyn & talks in a high, penetrating, nasal voice & with an accent that is barely understandable.)

All this, of course, would be of no moment to me were it not for her cough. There never was another such cough—the doctors & nurses will bear me out on that. It is loud—about 6,000 decibels, at a guess. It is hard—each of those 187 lbs. is behind it. It is sudden—"like an exploding cannon" was Deyo's phrase. It is—in the euphemistic phrase—extremely productive. It rasps, it wheezes, it shatters, it gurgles, it howls, it snarls. It starts in fortissimo, goes into a slight diminuendo, then works up to another crashing crescendo. Then a series of short, sharp barks. Then a long, bubbling hawking. Then an explosion like a four-ton block-buster. Then, just as you think the attack is subsiding, it starts in all over again, louder & juicier than ever. It literally never stops, except for the hour or two at a time that she sleeps at night. And then she snores. (I don't sleep, though. I lie awake waiting for the next. I have to eat with my fingers in my ears, snatching a hand away to grab a bite of food, to keep from retching.)

The doctors have tried to show Guinan how to catch her cough—a simple matter—but apparently she's too stupid to comprehend. She just opens her mouth & lets go with everything she has—which is considerable. The nurses hate to go into her room (which is next to mine), & there isn't one that doesn't say she'd go nuts if she had to listen to it 24 hours a day.

Well, don't say I didn't warn you.

Oh, yes, Guinan supplements the cough with several other sound effects: burps that must surely cause considerable alarm around the Fordham, Weston & St. Louis seismographs; nose-blowings that are answered by hounds in Columbia & Putnam counties; farts that contravene every convention of decent & humane warfare. Jesus, Benny, what am I going to do?

Yours,
Kate

[10 September 1943]
[postmarked Lanesville/Gloucester]

Dear Kate:
By the grace of God, I shall be going back to Cambridge and occasional natural sleep on the 14th. It has been a sensationally successful summer for the kids. It has been something less than that for me. I can't remember so long a period of boredom. Boredom is how I finally diagnose my state of mind, boredom composed chiefly of sea, abstinence from gasoline, errand running, a conviction of Avis's that the best way to give Benny

a rest is to let him superintend a dozen four year olds, lack of readily available conversation, lack of people willing to walk, and inability to get time to do an occasional bit of work. I may add that the state of mind has had other diagnoses, a good many other ones. This being the habitat of Harriet Robey, the place has been infested with psycho-analysts, and I added to the infestation by inviting the Kubies up for a week.[106] My lightest yawn and my briefest silence have been plentifully and generously interpreted for me. Kubie contented himself with the simple and not too inaccurate remark that I was undergoing a mild depression because I had treated Frost rudely, but half a dozen others have enthusiastically analyzed me down to the worn buttonhole on my fly. Mrs. Rank, whom I eventually came to like considerably, conquering my xenophobia and swimming through her accent by main force, expended the whole content of her ex-husband's book about artists on me. I don't know whether I succeeded in informing her that I'm no artist, but I tried. An Amazon named Pavenstadt—I do not guarantee the spelling—plunged into depths too dark for me as yet to follow her and summed up by inviting me to read an essay of Freud's called approximately "On First Seeing the Acropolis."[107] I'll look it up when I get back to Cambridge, but my guess is I've just been bored as hell.

But, speaking of Frost, another impatience to get back to Cambridge is to find out the how and why of the Dartmouth appointment.[108] I hesitate to differ from Kubie, but I have a lively phantasy that DeVoto got his man.

And speaking of phantasies, I think I may have been used in the late battle between Elmer and the armed services. A disinfected version of two letters I wrote to him as reports will be out as the next Easy Chair.[109] They were considerably hotter in the original, they were composed at the proper time, and I think they may have been used.

Avis professes to have had a superb summer. I am, of course, no analyst but only a husband. As such I refrain from observing that, whereas in Cambridge she will go for weeks without a drink and will frequently turn a derisive eye on the old fashioned with which I customarily prepare for dinner, she has daily taken on enough cocktails, immediately on putting Mark away for the evening, to bring her rapidly to a condition of satisfaction with practically everything, including the Atlantic Ocean.

And as a final phantasy, an ancient one of mine has been fulfilled within the past twenty-four hours. I have actually been asked to write a book which will be centered on Abraham Lincoln. Not, I may say, by my own publishers, who never think of me as a possible author but only as an unpaid editorial advisor. It's a heady and ego-soothing invitation and for a few hours I've actually considered accepting it.

Let us occasionally remind ourselves that there are writers who are also white men. I even have an instinct for them. Early in my acquaintance with Lee Hartman, he used occasionally to offer to introduce me to some writer instead of spending the evening in a speakeasy. I took him up just once and told him there was a man I wanted to meet. That was how I first met Elmer. For years I have wanted to meet James Boyd and I finally did a couple of weeks ago, and he's as swell a gent as I've ever known. His son is in the Coast Guard and located in these parts, and he says he intends to forsake the South occasionally and visit him, so it may go beyond this meeting. I've seldom seen anyone I clicked with so instantly. A white man, but the sad news is that he says he's not going to write any more novels, he's going to write poetry. Christ, with poets a dime a dozen in Rockport.... I met him at Kitty Bowen's. Kitty has been staying in the Eastern Point palace of her late aunt, Cecilia Beaux, and it may be that you would have been interested in the dozens of canvases that seemed to me academic and too formal to be borne.[110] She has finally begun to subside after upheavals over the Holmes book violent even for her.[111] I have never understood why she needs an accoucheur but she does and, Frances Curtis withdrawing a couple of years ago, I've had to be it. I spent some months trying to transfer the duty to stronger shoulders than mine, to Helen Everitt, but Helen, usually without fear, would have none of it, so I guess I'm in for it. Kitty now wants to write a book about an American woman and has developed no ideas beyond that. I'll suffer. But it will be worth it. The Holmes book is a sweetheart. Various hands, especially the lawyers, will treat it roughly when it comes out, though I'm the only person alive who will know the parts which are pure Kitty fake, but it's a damned good book and the best judgment on the *Autocrat* ever written.[112]

Some day I ought to send you some pages from a Kitty manuscript. "Two hours before breakfast, Wendell strolled down the lane at Beverly. Behind him ______ was moving busily in the kitchen. He could smell the sweet aroma of coffee, coffee brought in the ______ perhaps, round the ______, by his own ______ ________. Last night's talk was in his mind as the scent of the _______ mingled with that of coffee. The Dred Scott decision. ______ had said, "_____________." No. Life was more than that. The phrase casually uttered by _______ after midnight. Passion. Passion and danger...." Marginalia: "Ask Hill who was the maid that summer.[113] Find out when the Dred Scott decision was written—Benny will know. See if any of his relatives had ever been in the China trade. Could he have been talking with Cabot Lodge? Find out what shrubs bloom in July at Beverly...."

She had Ernesta staying with her, Mrs. Sam Barlow, the ex Mrs. Bill Bullitt. Have I ever said forthrightly that Ernesta, that faded international beauty, is the most objectionable woman I have ever known, more objectionable than any other woman I could imagine in malice or despair? She is, and that's understated. I don't run into her once in three years but I wouldn't want a stomach ulcer any oftener than that, though I choose the ulcer over Ernesta. She has the mind, the personality, the ethics, and the habits of a tapeworm—no, of some parasite considerably less complex and less clean than a tapeworm. And her sweet condescension to Kitty, who is a person, a mind, and a talent, has sometimes driven me to rudenesses that this hanger-on of the truly rich would never tolerate provided she had mind enough to understand them. I horrify Kitty and doubtless give her sleepless nights, for she thinks Ernesta is wonderful beyond words, but some day I hope to make it crude enough for Ernesta to get.

We ate lunch on Cecilia's terrace, overlooking the formal landscaping of the Eastern Point. I was wearing ragged jeans and half of a shirt, Boyd some shorts that had served some years as a feed bag in his stable, Kitty something which for want of more accurate knowledge I will call a Mother Hubbard,[114] Avis a pair of slacks that had been ripped on Ben Butler's rocks, Kitty's daughter a couple of small handkerchiefs. So Ernesta lacquered her face and varnished her hair, put on a formal afternoon dress, added a hat out of *Vogue*, and sat there looking pained because Boyd ate ship's biscuits with his hands.[115] I wondered who paid for the dress and hat.

****

Here, yesterday, your latest letter and the news about Italy arrived together at high noon. And, my God, you appall me. Are you sure you have taken a stern enough stand with the authorities? Or are you suffering from the timidity that bids us not complain against invalids? It seems to me that you are paying Bowne for, among other things, a decent amount of quiet and privacy, and that, paying for it, you should insist on getting it, no matter whose feelings are hurt. My advice is necessarily limited to two items, which are not necessarily alternatives: (a) get tough with the authorities and stay tough, and (b) get Guinan poisoned. The trouble with all institutions is that they hate any alteration of any established procedure worse than anything else. You may be ridden down several times, or seven times seventy times, but if you stay tough, my guess is, you'll get there. For it is also true of institutions that they yield to determinedly unpleasant people. That last is one of the great, basic secrets of society.... Is this person related to Texas?[116] If so, then, several generations back, I knew a relative of hers who was a priest in Salt Lake City. A nice guy.

My mood is to discourse learnedly about the armistice with Italy, but the mood of my family is to get me the hell down to the beach, so that must go for a time. You will not, eventually, be spared.

There has also arrived a letter from Fletcher Pratt, a report in due form on this year's Bread Loaf session. In view of Page 1 herein, you may be interested to know that, following one exhibition, Kay Morrison threw a glass, which Fletcher carefully estimates to have been five-eighths full of highball, at R. Frost. I was exceedingly interested.

Yours,

Benny

8 Berkeley Street
Cambridge, Massachusetts

[3 December 1943]

Dear Kate:
I hope to get the service restored presently. This is just ad interim. Phrase: vestige of Washington.

Since I got back to Cambridge I've mainly been running a hospital and occasionally occupying it. I hope to God that the curse put on this house last January expires at the end of the month. Both kids, the student I've imported to watch over them, & the maid were out for two weeks.[117] Avis turned up first a blazing arthritis & then, so help me God, trench mouth. My contribution was a mild & comparatively pleasant coryza. But then the day came round when I had to have my third typhoid, paratyphoid, & typhus shots unless I wanted to repeat the whole series on my next venture in Washington—what the hell, I may go anywhere according to the War Dept. So I took them & it proved injudicious to take them during an infection. I wrote an Easy Chair about the Lindberghs at a temperature of 104° and it must be something for it has drawn no response from Fred, who has written me at least two pages about every other one since he took office.[118]

I seem to remember that I wrote you from Washington twice, or once from Washington & once from the Century on my way back. That would cover the payoff: [?] it's out on North Africa & various subsequent proposals ending in a really hot one, to do the job on Guadalcanal. Previously the Navy had tried to survey me under the Army's nose & offered me the Marines on Guadalcanal. McCloy & Surles offered me the whole job. Navy, Marines, & Army, & Elmer backed it up enthusiastically.

That was what we had fixed on when I left. Nothing has turned up since, except another raid by the Navy—they seem to want me & their stuff is in excellent shape. But they're such bastards & probably it wouldn't get past King anyway.[119]

I've written to Surles & McCloy, suggesting a little haste.[120] But the latter is in Cairo—probably where he was heading when he told me London—and nothing will happen till he gets back. I've also written to Elmer, & considerably more directly. The simple truth is that those three are the only people I ran into who want anything to come out. The Historical Section gave me every possible runaround. So did every other branch of the Dept I touched on. I saw a good deal more stuff than I was intended to, but only because I remembered some of the moves in the Army game and because I quickly found out how to play one jealousy and one intradepartmental interest against another. What I told Elmer was that any attempt to write genuinely informative stuff is absolutely certain to be sabotaged unless really heavy pressure is brought to bear from above. I think McCloy is probably a big enough shot—for

Army stuff—but he has got to be told about what his project is up against, by Elmer, not me, & I or whoever tries to write his jobs for him has got to be able to appeal straight to him. I doubt if McCloy carries enough weight to get a combined-operations job done. To drive three services in harness probably can't be done short of the C in C.[121]

Anything you may have heard about Army-Navy friction was understated. And by God the Navy is the worse of the two. The boys have decided that they can win anyway the Pacific war unassisted and they're by God going to do it at whatever cost. At a guess the cost will be damn high.... I have, quite seriously, laid out two steps toward a permanent military policy for the U. S. (1) Temporarily suspend the Army-Navy football game & all other athletic contests; (2) Break up Annapolis & West Point & scatter them through the state universities. I am damn well not kidding. The Nazis are a formal opponent & the Japs are even something of an enemy but the real grudge fight in this war is between the Army & the Navy.

As for censorship & Military Security—Jesus! I could tell you stories but isn't the Patton story typical?[122] Well, I sat in the Temporary L of the Navy building & read combat reports on Pacific operations. I said, "Did Fletcher Pratt see these?" (They are printed but restricted to personnel.) My mentor said no and complained bitterly about inaccuracies in Fletcher's Midway piece.[123] I said, "It went through this office for okay. Do you want mistakes published or don't you?" Blank incomprehension. Or:... Gen. Marshall in person talks to some wounded boys at Walter Reed, back from Africa.[124] He found out they didn't understand a damn thing, just knew they'd been sent out to a hill & got shot there. So he ordered the Hist. Section to write a pamphlet—restricted—on the Bizerte campaign so these boys could find out what the point of going to that hill was.[125] Hist. Section did so, got it by all the mines up to Security & there got told by Gen. Strong that organizations smaller than a division could not be identified.[126] Bizerte was last May.

Well. The hell with it. Here I sit immune to everything but cholera & await orders.

Yrs

Benny

NOTES

1. Bennett Cerf (1898–1971), publisher and author; founder of Random House.
2. (French) stupidities.
3. *Kim*, by Kipling, 1901. Ambler (1909–1998), British writer of mysteries and spy novels; *A Coffin for Demetrios*, 1939; *Journey into Fear*, 1940.
4. Lewis Gannett and Harry Overstreet.

5. Markel (1894–1977), writer, newspaper editor; edited the Sunday *New York Times* from 1923 to 1965. "The Dancer and the Dwarf," *Time* 41/8, 22 February 1943. Henri de Toulouse-Lautrec (1864–1901), French painter and illustrator.
6. 1 December 1931.
7. Edward Alden Jewell (1888–1947), author, editor, and art critic; KS's boss at the *New York Times*; *The Charmed Circle: A Comedy*, 1921; *Americans*, 1930; *Paul Cézanne*, 1944; *Georges Rouault*, 1945.
8. Stravinsky's *Symphony in C*, composed 1938–1940 for the Chicago Symphony Orchestra, one of the major works of his neoclassical period.
9. Serge Koussevitzky (1874–1951), Russian double-bass player and outstanding conductor, director of the Boston Symphony Orchestra.
10. This is the first precise mention of KS's birthday.
11. (Latin, literally) grasp the day; seize the opportunity.
12. Dorothy Sayers (1893–1957), British medievalist, poet, essayist, editor, and author of much-admired mystery novels featuring Lord Peter Wimsey.
13. Patrick Kelly and Edward Nash, Chicago machine politicians. Joseph Guffey, senator from Pennsylvania. Edward Hull Crump (1874–1954), machine politician, congressman from Tennessee, mayor of Memphis. Dennis Chavez (1888–1962), senator from New Mexico (1935–1962). His appointment to succeed Senator Bronson Cutting, who was killed in an airplane crash, was widely regarded as a political payoff; nevertheless Chavez was elected and regularly re-elected, achieving a distinguished liberal record in the Senate. Lawrence Wood Robert, Jr. (1889–1976), Atlanta businessman, assistant secretary of the Treasury, resigned February 1936. Earle, presumably George Howard Earle III (1890–1974), governor of Pennsylvania, 1935–1939; United States minister to Bulgaria, 1940. Flynn, probably Edward Flynn (1891–1953), Tammany Hall official and machine politician; national chairman of the Democratic Party, 1940–1943, campaign manager for President Roosevelt's third term; memoir, *You're the Boss*, 1947. The "second Louisiana Purchase" refers to Westbrook Pegler's comment on the dismissal of indictments against the Huey Long machine, 1936. The Senate "purge": at the end of May 1938, during the primary election season, anti–New Deal senators denounced the administration's attempts to support pro–New Deal candidates over incumbents. The London Economic Conference was held in 1933. The so-called Hatch Act of 1939 prohibited use of public funds in political campaigns, as well as promises of favors from federal officials in exchange for contributions.
14. (German), sometimes translated "politics of reality": "A usually expansionist national policy having as its sole principle advancement of the national interest" (*AHD*).
15. Episcopal church. The concert was on 21 February.
16. Harry T. Burleigh (1866–1949), outstanding Negro singer and composer.
17. The Spence School for girls, 22 East 91st Street; K–12, founded 1892. Miss Beard's School for girls, 6–12, founded 1891, Morristown, New Jersey; merged in 1971 as Morristown-Beard School. Bennett School, Millbrook, New York, near Poughkeepsie, later a college; founded 1890s, closed 1977.
18. More commonly called shingles, a painful viral inflammation of the peripheral nerves of the skin.
19. "It Seems to Me I've Heard That Song Before," by Sammy Cahn and Jule Styne, 1942; no. 1 on the Hit Parade for thirteen weeks. "Black Magic," by Harold Arlen and Johnny Mercer, 1942, from the movie *Star-Spangled Rhythm*. "Weep No More My Lady," by L. Wolfe Gilbert.
20. Heinrich Himmler (1900–1945), Nazi chief of the SS and Gestapo.
21. Probably Uncle Jack's Steakhouse, 440 Ninth Avenue.

22. *Snow above Town: A Story of Wyoming*, by Donald Hough (1895–1965), 1943.
23. *And Keep Your Powder Dry*, by Margaret Mead, 1942.
24. Epochal decision of the U.S. Supreme Court, in *Dred Scott vs. Sanford*, 1857. Dred Scott (ca. 1800–1858), a Negro slave, had been brought by his owner to live in a northern free state; Scott's claim, that his residence in free U.S. territory had liberated him from his slave status, was denied on the grounds that as a slave he was a property, not a citizen, and therefore had no standing to bring suit. The majority opinion, written by Chief Justice Roger B. Taney, held that the federal courts had no jurisdiction over property rights in the slave states. The Missouri Compromise of 1820, which admitted new states to the union in pairs, one slave and one free, was thus held to be unconstitutional. The decision was widely considered one of the decisive events that led inexorably to the Civil War. Charles A. Beard (1874–1948), historian, professor of political science at Columbia, later cofounder of the New School for Social Research in New York; *The Rise of American Civilization*, with his wife, Mary Ritter Beard (1876–1958); revised edition, 1956.
25. WAVES, Women Accepted for Volunteer Emergency Service (later the U.S. Navy Women's Reserve). WAAC, Women's Auxiliary Air Corps.
26. From Keats, "Ode to a Nightingale."
27. Phillips (1896–1986), editor. Clyde K. M. Kluckhohn (1905–1960), professor of anthropology at Harvard, an expert on the Navaho.
28. Alexander William Doniphan (1808–1887), attorney, colonel of Missouri Mounted Volunteers.
29. "What the Next Hour Holds," *Harper's* 173/1 (June 1936), reprinted in *Forays and Rebuttals* as "What the Next Hour May Bring Forth," 1936.
30. (1899–1994), journalist; Pulitzer Prize, 1929; *No Other Road to Freedom*, 1941; *They Shall Not Sleep*, 1943.
31. William Henry Herndon (1818–1891), Abraham Lincoln's law partner in Springfield, Illinois; *Herndon's Lincoln: The True Story of a Great Life*, 3 vols., 1889.
32. (Latin) according to value.
33. (French, freely) in its own juice.
34. Jefferson Davis, Secretary of War during the Franklin Pierce administration, 1853–1857 (later president of the Confederate States of America), after experiences in the Mexican War, undertook to bring camels from the Middle East for possible use as pack animals in desert warfare. The camels' master was Hadji Ali (1828–1902), a Syrian known as "Hi Jolly." The project was soon abandoned, but by 1855 the corps numbered more than one hundred camels, which prospered in the desert Southwest for at least several decades. The Texas Camel Corps was privately reconstituted in 1995.
35. *Harper's* 186/5 (April 1943), about writers on the fighting front, and literature emerging from the war experience.
36. Nepenthe: "A drug or drink, or the plant yielding it, mentioned by ancient writers as having the power to bring forgetfulness of sorrow or trouble" (*RH2*).
37. E. J. Kahn Jr. (1916–1994), staff writer, *The New Yorker*, from 1937; prolific writer of essays; his personal reports describing his army service were a regular feature during the war years; *The Army Life*, 1942; *G. I. Jungle*, 1943; *The Stragglers*, 1962.
38. (Latin) if we are able.
39. The Alaska-Canada Highway, now called the Alaska Highway, 1,522 miles long between Dawson Creek, British Columbia, and Fairbanks, Alaska, was built in only eight months, March–October 1942, connecting several military airfields. Many Negro soldiers were used in the project, which was then the only land route to Alaska.
40. The sea-level Florida Ship Canal, a WPA project in 1935, was excavated by the Army Corps of Engineers for six miles from Dunellon, Florida, to the Withlacoochie River, at a cost of $5.4

million. Congress refused further financing of the canal in 1936. The project was renewed in 1964, halted in 1971, and deauthorized in 1990.

41. Admiral William H. Standley (1872–1963), Chief of Naval Operations, 1933–1937, was called out of retirement to serve as ambassador to the Soviet Union, 1942–1943. On 9 March 1943, while renewal of Lend-Lease was being debated in Congress, Standley, in a press conference in Moscow, complained that Lend-Lease materials were being offered to the Soviet people as originating in Russia, without credit to the United States. The Lend-Lease bill authorizing a one-year extension nevertheless passed the Senate on 11 March, 82-0. Standley resigned on 1 October and was succeeded by W. Averell Harriman. See Herman Wouk, *War and Remembrance*, 1976.
42. Cf. the Negro spiritual, "There is a balm in Gilead"; Jeremiah 46:11: "Go up to Gilead and take balm."
43. BDV is probably thinking of Marius Petipa (1818–1910), great French dancer and choreographer, active in Russia, called the "father of classical ballet." *Petit pas* in French would mean "little step" or "little dance."
44. From Poe, "The Raven" (1845): "'...respite and nepenthe from thy memories of yore!/Quaff, oh quaff this kind nepenthe, and forget this lost Lenore!'/Quoth the raven, 'Nevermore.'"
45. *The Uses of the Camel: considered with a view to his introduction into our western states and territories...*, monograph by Joseph Warren Fabens, 1865.
46. Willard S. Morse, mining executive, collected more than two thousand items relating to Mark Twain; the Yale University Library acquired the collection in 1942.
47. Probably Stanley T. Williams (1888–1956), professor at Yale, authority on Washington Irving.
48. (1822–1893), naval officer, explorer, and diplomat.
49. Uncle Joe was Churchill's sobriquet for Joseph Stalin.
50. Signed in October 1854 in Ostend, Belgium, by the three American ministers to Great Britain, France, and Spain, as part of a Manifest Destiny plan to purchase the island of Cuba from Spain. Because of anti-slavery opposition in the United States when it became known, the Manifesto was repudiated and withdrawn by William L. Marcy, secretary of state in the Pierce administration.
51. Joachim von Ribbentrop (1893–1946), Nazi foreign minister.
52. On 8 March 1943, three days before the Senate approved the Lend-Lease extension, Vice-President Wallace spoke at Ohio Wesleyan University about the need for better Soviet-American relations: "Without a close and trusting understanding between Russia and the United States, there is grave possibility of Russia and Germany later making common cause."
53. New Harmony, site of the former Harmonie on the Wabash (1814–1824), utopian community which was sold to the Owenites (1825–1826).
54. E. W. Scripps (1854–1926), newspaper publisher chiefly on the West Coast and in Detroit, Cincinnati, and Cleveland, partnered with Roy W. Howard (1883–1964) to form the Scripps-Howard newspaper chain in 1922.
55. Reserve Officers' Training Corps, mandated by law for every Morrill Act (land-grant) university.
56. Wabash College, men's college in Crawfordsville, Indiana, founded 1832.
57. Henri Giraud (1879–1949), French general, commander of French armed forces in North Africa.
58. John Chamberlain.
59. Katherine Gauss Jackson (1904–1975), daughter of Dean Christian Gauss of Princeton; editor at *Harper's*, 1938–1969.
60. Andrew Jackson (died 1955), attorney.
61. See letter 22 March 1942.

62. "Death Valley Days," radio program sponsored by 20 Mule Team Borax, in the 1940s on NBC; later on television, and in 1965–1966 hosted by Ronald Reagan.
63. Stephen Bonsal (1865–1951), historian; *Edward Fitzgerald Beale, a Pioneer in the Path of Empire, 1822–1903*, 1912.
64. *The Year of Decision*, Chapter 13. Christopher (Kit) Carson (1809–1868), pioneer and soldier.
65. The William T. Patten Foundation Lectures were established in 1937.
66. A Mormon church was built on Brattle Street in Cambridge in 1954, adjoining Longfellow Park.
67. The Silver Shirts of the Silver Legion of America, founded by William Dudley Pelley (1890–1965), occultist and fascist agitator. The anti-Catholic American Protective Association, APA, was active between 1891 and 1897 in Iowa, Omaha, and Kansas City. The Know-Nothing sobriquet was applied to the nativist and anti-Catholic Order of United Americans and Order of the Star-Spangled Banner during the 1850s. Their pro-slavery factions split the Whig Party, whose northern elements regrouped and formed the Republican Party. The Knights of the Golden Circle, also known as the Copperheads, a pro-slavery group founded in the Midwest in 1854; ten years later it became the Order of the Sons of Liberty, opposing the war.
68. Herman B. Wells (1902–2000), a bank executive, was president of Indiana University from 1938 to 1962.
69. (1895–1974), short story writer, *SEP*, *LHJ*; lecturer at Indiana University.
70. Merriam (1874–1953), political scientist, professor at the University of Chicago.
71. "Mr. Freeman's Continuing Study," *SRL* 26/22 (29 May 1943), review of Douglas Southall Freeman, *Lee's Lieutenants: A Study in Command*, vol. 2, 1943. The book review is probably "A Natural History of Politics," *NYHT Book Review* (17 October 1943), review of Wilfred E. Binkley, *American Political Parties*, 1943. Dies Committee, the House Committee on Un-American Activities, chaired by Martin Dies, congressman from Texas; deposition unidentified. Kerr Committee, a subcommittee of the House Committee on Appropriations, chaired by John H. Kerr (1873–1958) of North Carolina.
72. *Fire and Ice: The Art and Thought of Robert Frost*, 1942. Frost chose Thompson as his official biographer in 1939. Thompson eventually published three volumes of biography (1966, 1970, and [with R. H. Winnick] 1976) and a volume of selected letters. Thompson's coverage of the BDV-Frost quarrel is detailed and evenhanded.
73. *Francis Parkman, Heroic Historian* by Mason Wade (1913–1986), 1942. *Wah-to-Yah and the Taos Trail...* by Lewis Hector Garrard (1829–1887), 1850. Perkins (1901–1985), lecturer and professor of history at Harvard, 1937–1969; master of Lowell House, 1940–1963. From 1959 to 1963 Avis DeVoto was his personal secretary at Lowell House. Grabhorn Press, San Francisco. *Down the Santa Fe Trail and Into Mexico: The Diary of Susan Shelby Magoffin, 1846–1847*, edited by Stella M. Drumm, 1926. *Ordeal by Hunger: The Story of the Donner Party*, by George R. Stewart, 1936. Charles Winslow Elliott, *Winfield Scott*, 1937. *The Great Plains*, by Walter Prescott Webb, 1931. *Transatlantic*, published in London from 1943 to 1948.
74. *California Pioneer Register and Index, 1542–1848, Including Inhabitants of California, 1769–1800, and List of Pioneers*, by Hubert Howe Bancroft (1832–1918), modern edition, 1964.
75. Wallace Stegner (1909–1993), writer, professor of English at Stanford University, Harvard, and the University of Wisconsin; close friend of BDV, whose biography, *The Uneasy Chair*, he published in 1974, followed by *The Letters of Bernard DeVoto*, 1975. *On a Darkling Plain* is the correct title of Stegner's book. *Clash by Night* is a play by Clifford Odets, 1942; cf. Matthew Arnold, "Dover Beach" (1867); "And we are here as on a darkling plain/Swept with confused alarms of struggle and flight/Where ignorant armies clash by night."
76. *Beyond the Hundredth Meridian: John Wesley Powell and the Second Opening of the West*, 1954; BDV wrote the Introduction. See *LBDV*, pp. 319–26.

77. (German) out with the.
78. "In Greek mythology, a female monster. Because she stole Hercules' cattle, Zeus hurled her into the sea. There she lay under rocks across from Scylla and sucked in and spewed out huge amounts of water, creating a whirlpool." (*CE* 6th ed.)
79. (1887–1966), sculptor, worked in Rodin's studio in Paris; *Heads and Tails*, 1936.
80. John W. Bricker (1893–1986), governor of Ohio, anti-labor, anti–New Deal; Republican candidate for vice-president, 1944.
81. (1880–1969), president of the United Mine Workers of America.
82. Hamilton (1867–1963), British classical scholar. The program ran for fifteen years, from 1941, on CBS.
83. George Boas (1891–1980); *Philosophy and Poetry*, 1932.
84. Clifton Fadiman in *The New Yorker* 19/6 (27 March 1943), reviewing *The Year of Decision*: "This department timidly commends Mr. DeVoto to the attention of the Pulitzer Prize judges." Esther Forbes's Paul Revere biography won the Pulitzer Prize in history in 1943; *The Year of Decision* possibly was published too close to the Pulitzer deadline to be considered for 1943. Hanson Baldwin, daily reporter on the war for the *New York Times*, won the Pulitzer Prize in journalism, 1943. *Dragon's Teeth*, by Upton Sinclair, 1942, a Lanny Budd thriller (no. 3) about the Nazis, Pulitzer Prize in fiction, 1943. The Pulitzer Prizes were announced on 3 May.
85. (1903–1957), Boston psychiatrist; *M: One Thousand Autobiographical Sonnets*, 1938. By the time of his death the number had grown to over one hundred thousand.
86. Frost's *A Witness Tree* is dedicated "To K. M./for her part in it."
87. Thomas Hornsby Ferril (1896–1988), journalist and poet; editor of the *Rocky Mountain Herald*; poet laureate of Colorado; *Westering*, 1934.
88. Helen Ferril, author and editor; *The Indoor Bird Watcher's Manual*, 1950; *The Second Indoor Bird Watcher's Manual*, 1951.
89. Edward Channing (1856–1931), professor at Harvard; *History of the United States*, 8 volumes projected, 7 completed, Pulitzer Prize, 1926.
90. The column appeared in *Harper's* 187/2 (July 1943).
91. In 1931.
92. Charles Lewis Camp, paleontologist and amateur historian, was a recognized author of several works on fossils.
93. F. O. Matthiessen (1902–1950), professor of English at Harvard, specialist in American literature. Harry Tuchman Levin (1912–1994), Harvard '33, Irving Babbitt professor of comparative literature, taught at Harvard 1939–1983; *James Joyce: A Critical Introduction*, 1941; *The Gates of Horn*, 1963; *Why Literary Criticism Is Not an Exact Science*, 1968. During the 1950s Levin and BDV became good friends.
94. Apparently *The Intermountain West*, otherwise unidentified under this title.
95. Goleta is near Santa Barbara, on the coast; rancher unidentified.
96. Probably the *New York Times*.
97. New Hampshire.
98. Hudson (1886–1960), professor of international law, Harvard Law School; judge, Court of International Justice.
99. Marian (Molly) Cabot Putnam (1893–1971), Boston psychiatrist. Beata Rank (1896–1967), psychiatrist, widow of Freud's disciple Otto Rank (1884–1939). Her nickname was "Tola." BDV developed a fast friendship with her, and dedicated *The World of Fiction* to her in 1950.
100. Marquand, *So Little Time*, 1943.
101. *Origins of the American Revolution*, by John Chester Miller (1907–1991), 1943.

102. On 24–25 July King Vittorio Emmanuele III (1869–1947, reigned 1900–1946) dismissed Benito Mussolini and appointed General Pietro Badoglio (1871–1956) head of the Italian government. Badoglio had commanded the Italian army that invaded Ethiopia in 1935; on 23 September 1943 he surrendered all Italian forces to General Eisenhower.
103. Battle of the Great War, 6–25 June 1918. Particularly heavy casualties were encountered on 6 June by the marines of the Second Division; during the battle, the site changed hands six times.
104. BDV's estimate was good; the Third Reich lasted twelve years, three months, and eight days.
105. William Henry O'Connell (1859–1944), archbishop since 1907 of the Boston diocese, the third largest Catholic diocese in the United States. On 22 July, O'Connell publicly deplored the Allied bombardment of Rome, which in fact was not captured until June 1944. Crete was taken by the Germans on 20 May 1941.
106. Robey (1900–1993), social worker and writer; see her affectionate memoir, *Bay View: A Summer Portrait*, 1979.
107. Eleanor Pavenstedt (1903–1993), of the American Psychoanalytic Association. Freud, "A Disturbance of Memory on the Acropolis," open letter to Romain Rolland on his seventieth birthday, 1936, *New Introductory Lectures on Psychoanalysis*, Freud Standard Edition, vol. 22.
108. Frost had been named as George Ticknor Fellow in the Humanities at Dartmouth College.
109. *Harper's* 187/5 (October 1943).
110. Cecilia Beaux (1855–1942), portraitist, whose home in Gloucester was called "Green Alley."
111. *Yankee from Olympus: Justice Holmes and His Family*, 1944.
112. *The Autocrat of the Breakfast Table*, by Oliver Wendell Holmes, Sr. (1809–1894), 1858.
113. Probably Arthur D. Hill.
114. "a woman's loose usually shapeless dress." (*W3*)
115. See BDV, "Ninety-Day Venus," Easy Chair, *Harper's* 201/3 (September 1950).
116. Texas Guinan (1889?–1933), nightclub actress, famous for "Hello, sucker!"
117. The student was probably Ernest Haggard, graduate student in psychology, Harvard Ed.M. '44, Ph.D. '46.
118. *Harper's* 188/2 (January 1944).
119. Ernest Joseph King (1878–1956), admiral and commander in chief, United States fleet, 1941; chief of naval operations, 1942–44. A hard-boiled personality, he was an excellent leader and administrator.
120. Alexander D. Surles (1886–1947), major general, director, War Department Bureau of Public Relations, from 1941. John J. McCloy (1895–1989), attorney, banker, assistant secretary of war; *The Challenge to American Foreign Policy*, 1948.
121. Commander in Chief.
122. George S. Patton (1885–1945), major general, outstanding tank corps commander, known as "Old Blood and Guts." On 10 August 1943, visiting a field hospital during the invasion of Sicily, Patton slapped a soldier suffering from battle fatigue, calling him a coward; the story was first publicized on 22 November. Patton was severely reprimanded by General Eisenhower and made a public apology.
123. "The Mysteries of Midway: Americans in Battle, no. 5" and "The Knockout at Midway: Americans in Battle, no. 6," *Harper's* 187/1–2 (June and July 1943).
124. George Catlett Marshall Jr. (1880–1959), general, Army Chief of Staff; secretary of state, 1947–1949; secretary of defense, 1950–1951; Nobel Peace Prize, 1953; author of European Recovery Program (so-called "Marshall Plan"), 1947. Walter Reed Army Medical Center, Washington, D.C.; from 1909; named after Major Walter Reed (1851–1902), outstanding military physician.
125. Bizerte, strategic seaport in Tunisia.
126. George V. Strong (1880–1946), major general, G-2; assistant Army Chief of Staff.

12

1944 LETTERS

Bernard DeVoto's fifth and last John August novel, *The Woman in the Picture*, was published in *Collier's* in January. Still hopeful, but increasingly doubtful, that he might serve a historian's mission for the navy, he spent time in Washington negotiating with the War Department; not until April did he give up the idea entirely, although there seems to have been one further overture from the army. DeVoto confided to Sterne that he had started to take up work again on the frustrated *Mountain Time*, but it would not be published until 1947, his last completed novel. In early March, DeVoto casually discussed a proposal that eventually grew into one of his finest efforts, *Across the Wide Missouri*, published in 1948; in May he also mentioned plans for a project on Lewis and Clark. April began to reveal a furiously busy springtime, as DeVoto's Patten lectures were published as *The Literary Fallacy*, provoking a storm in the critical press and a rabid personal attack by Sinclair Lewis about which DeVoto wrote little to Sterne; simultaneously the Boston censorship case of *Strange Fruit*, quarterbacked by DeVoto and the Civil Liberties Union of Massachusetts, made news when he and a bookseller were arrested. This was also the season of political primaries, and DeVoto, distressed over the Roosevelt administration's suppression of war news, offered his personal support to Wendell Willkie's foreign policy platform, but this became moot when Willkie withdrew from the Republican race after being trounced in the Wisconsin primary.

For her part, Sterne sounded an increasingly desperate note about conditions in Bowne Hospital; in June, DeVoto offered to try to intervene. Two months later, on 31 August 1944, Katharine Sterne suddenly died of heart failure after twelve years of hospitalization.

8 Berkeley Street
Cambridge, Massachusetts

[AFTER 26 FEBRUARY 1944]

Dear Kate:

All the resources of an obstinate nature as well as those of a fine versatility in avoiding boredom have not availed me to stop Bunny telling me the movie he's home from, which is why this begins some three hours later than it otherwise would have. Cambridge School is amazed by his literary capacity but his narrative gift lacks compression and finesse. Moreover, he has acquired a tag, "you know," heaved in wherever us more practised narrators turn from the action to the scene, and it pensively reminds me that the nearest this family has ever come to divorce—on, I should say, my initiative—was a period when Avis was saying "and so on and so forth."

Yeah, wire on my birthday, but I was too privy-bound to acknowledge it. But no, as yet nothing whatever from the Metro$_{pol}$itan Museum (I have abandoned my egregious optimism about getting a new typewriter) and never mind, my dear, it would be nice to have some Homer prints but the hell with it, time, as they used to say when that basso emetico[1] was on one program only, marches on and is full of more useful deeds.

...Oh God. Here Bunny rushes in to protest the illogicality of the English tongue and especially its orthography. It is not a new protest. This time the word is "acreage," which, understand, is not spelled the way you would, at first sight, pronounce it if you didn't know the rules.

Worse still. I said, "Will you please hold your trap?" He said, "You mean, close it, don't you?" Jesus. Parenthood or words to that effect.

Well, I have been impinging on your jurisdiction and it may take me back for a moment or so to the history of the Great West. Do you read *Fortune*? I don't any more, having let my subscription lapse at last after many years, in belated recognition of an ennui always marked and for some years acute. Well, in the current issue of *Fortune* you have seen, or could see, some color reproductions of some water colors, date 1837, by one A. J. Miller, featuring the butchering of a buffalo, the only known views of Fort Laramie, a buffalo herd, etc.[2] *Fortune* has some eight or ten. There are about two hundred all told, and newly found. I had Fred Deknatel over to tell me whether they were any good or just stunk. I don't know about the critical mind. Me, I don't pretend to have one and so, when called on, I can tell in clear—and few—words what the book in question is trying to do, how well, on the whole it does it, and whether, comparatively, it is worth doing. In the course of an hour or so Fred allowed that these were technically quite good, that the man had been well trained and, if an academician and somewhat tinged by the residual romanticism of the time, might nevertheless be called a competent workman with a good sense of composition and some eye for detail. That being attended to, I can and could say that, for my part, they are unique. They are spot news pictures, photographic journalism of an altogether remarkable kind, absolutely invaluable as *Life* going to town on the Indians, fur trade, and scenery and technology of the mountain era.

It's this way. Didn't I send you Ruxton's "Adventures in the Rocky Mountains"?[3] Sir William Drummond Stewart appears in it briefly as a character and modeled a good deal more.[4] He was a Scottish baronet and, I find, there is a Gainsborough of him, in black velvet shorts, on his mother's knees, with two brothers decoratively draped round them.[5] He was at Waterloo as a youngster and, growing up, became a wanderer in far places as befitted one of his station. In due time he came to the Great West and became enamored of it. He abode there in great content for the better part of ten years.

That [?] condemned Cambridge School has given its aspirants a week's vacation, with another week to follow in April. Consequently there is no home work and no set bedtime for the Young. Bunny has wandered in here and explained that his heart is full of loving kindness, he feels we spend too much time alone and apart from each other, he doesn't want me to be lonely, and so he will sit here and read while I write. So he is in my big chair with his back against one arm and his feet over its back, reading *Guadalcanal Diary* for about the thirtieth time and only partially aloud, and whistling intermittent bursts that are probably raising hell with the evening labors of the devoted slaves in the supersonics lab.[6] Presently he will begin giving me choice plums from the book....

Like a good many other British sportsmen, Stewart found that the West was his meat. He loved to shoot buffalo and the lesser fauna, he loved to fight Indians, he loved to associate with the casehardened mountain men and compete with them at their own crafts—and he was no slouch as a competitor. However, he liked his comforts, and he traveled the wild with what amounted to a safari. Fifty or sixty assorted drovers, herders, voyageurs, hunters, cooks, and handy men; hundreds of horses; silk tents; a stock of liquors, wines, cigars and whatnot; a stock of hunting equipment and trade goods comparable to that of any fort in those parts. Ruxton has him outfitting a couple of forlorn trappers who had been robbed and stripped by Indians, outfitting them as they had never been before, and that is quite in character and probably historically true not once but a good many times. The Britisher on safari is likely to do himself well, but the desert had never seen such luxury as Stewart abode in. You see him dining off exquisite china in the company of, say, Jim Bridger, whom he heartily admired, and bringing out the flavor of buffalo hump with a bottle of his best claret - Jim would infinitely have preferred raw alcohol - and interrupting the meal to go out and repel a raid by Blackfeet.[7] After he went back to Scotland he wrote a couple of novels about the West, mixtures of authentic portraiture and observation and some of the most fantastic nonsense that was ever lifted from gothic romance. And yet one must go a little easy. The heroine of one of them, *Altowan*, is a mysterious Indian priestess who is not quite an Indian but nevertheless exercises over the tribes a power and command hardly human.[8] She is as beautiful as all hell and there happens to her such a succession of adventures, natural and supernatural, as you can't imagine. I had always supposed she was cribbed from some minor successor of Mrs. Radcliffe.[9] But it turns out in Miller's notes that there was a halfbreed wench, half Spanish (Mexican, I suppose), who was beautiful as all hell, who did wander about with part of a tribe at her disposal, and with whom, Miller broadly hints, Stewart conducted a romantic affair that was not without a fleshly element.

In 1837 Stewart picked up an artist and hired him to go West and paint the country, the Indians, the trappers, and the fauna, and later to go to Scotland and paint murals in one of his three castles—alas, it has burned down. Two hundred of these [paintings] are the present haul. A character named Emery Reves who runs the refugee Cooperation Publishing Company and is allied with the refugee Hyperion Press, which you will know, proposes to make a book of about 140 of them, forty-odd in color.[10] He desires me to provide him with thirty thousand words of text, and I may at that.[11]

I have already revisited these glimpses. It appears that that no-account Wade whom I managed to keep in Harvard for three and a half years but could not quite save from expulsion, cannot be saved outside of Harvard either. He has caused me a hell of a lot of inconvenience in my time. Well, I browbeat Harpers into agreeing to publish the Parkman notebooks and shamed the Massachusetts Historical Society into consenting, and Wade's edition of them is dumped on my desk, and he has done it intolerably badly. He has provided the text but beyond that he has merely written a four-page introduction, which contains twenty-odd errors but no understanding of western history, and some notes which may have taken him a day to do and have taken me a week to correct. About one-third as many notes as he should have provided and practically none of them right. He has not made a pass at the two important jobs, the comparison of the notebooks with *The Oregon Trail* and the determination of Parkman's routes. I simply have not got time to do either. I am moved to tell Harpers not to publish the book until he does, but I know damned well that Wade, having had two large advances and being of that morality, would simply let things slide for good, and at least the text of the notebooks will be available.

I don't remember when the historical conscience awoke in me but it was before I began to publish my stuff. It horrifies me to see a responsible writer setting in his chair and guessing. I had to save Wade, in his life of Parkman, from such gaffes as identifying Stephen W. Kearny as Phil Kearny, dozens of such gaffes, in fact.[12] Now I must inform him that Antoine Robidou, practically as celebrated as Kit Carson, was not a blacksmith at Fort Laramie, that Parkman was wrong in supposing the Sioux gashed their muscles as a penance, that the Delaware did not wear warbonnets, that a fort which was on Cherry Creek, Colorado, was not on Laramie Creek, Wyoming, and so on and on and on.[13] I wish I knew what the use is.

As for fiction, I have finished the first block, the section which I set out to finish, and the decision appears to be to go on. It doesn't say how far. However, someone outside the book has read part of what I have done, Helen Everitt, my coach and custodian, and she delivers herself of the opinion that it is by far the best thing I have ever done. That is not excessive praise and, such as it is, I discount it. But there is one odd observation to make. I have not been in the least engaged with it, passionate about it, absorbed in it, I have merely felt impelled to get to work on it every morning at 8:45—that celestial hour when both kids have got off to school and it begins to seem possible to survive for another day—and keep writing till noon.[14] Nothing has stopped me, nothing has even flowed thin. I imagine it's objective, anyway. I don't promise to finish the book—as I conceive it, and on the proportionate basis of this part, the finished book would probably have to be published in sets—but I do propose to keep going as long as the impulse lasts.

As for my hospital practise, 1944 has so far been healthier than 1943 but not by a hell of a lot. Mark spends more time in bed than out of it, and the last week was marked by an epidemic of one-day grippe which laid low every member of this household except me. This is the year, apparently, when adults get children's diseases. Anne Barrett has chicken pox, Louise—no, let's get this right. Anne Barrett has German measles, Louise Hanson chicken pox, Ruth Schorer mumps, Eleanor Murdock impetigo, and one who shall be nameless a descended, a newly descended, testicle. Moreover, there is going on in Cambridge a strange and tiresome effort to bring back the jazz age. There are not many parties but at such parties as there are too many gents are found with their hands down ladies' waists, and ladies of forty or beyond at that, too many lunches are spilled in the hall, too many creaking elders fall through windows, and there has begun to be talk of such an artiness as I haven't heard for a quarter of a century. But, as the war goes on, no jokes.

However, my medical and psychiatric circles are now intent on a very choice case. MGH has a pseudo-hermaphrodite who wants to be converted one way or another. Consciously she, if that is the pronoun, wants to be female but the unconscious indications are that she wants to be male, and my God, you should hear the discussions.

I trust the enclosure is the one you wanted. You could have identified it by the beginning of the Lincoln collection.

Yours,
Benny

[enclosure, a photograph, not found]

[25 April 1944]

Dear Kate:

My God, there's a lot to catch up, so much that this may have to be done in takes—with me coming up for judgment Saturday. Yeah, that's my state of mind. I should say, Wednesday.

Well, Willkie. All of a sudden there was a mimeographed speech in my mail, with letter. It was the Concord, New Hampshire, speech on why we are maybe getting to be afraid of peace, out of Easy Chair, with explanation by W. W. that New Deal inroads on our Constitution and ways of thought are responsible.[15] So I wrote him, after he'd delivered the speech, that I agreed in great part and went on and supplied further qualms, together with the epithet that seemed to catch his eye (and that of every damned paper in the United States, at seven and a half cents a clip, Luce Agency), the Tired New Dealer line.[16] So presently Irita was on the phone from New York making talk about coming to Boston presently and could I be induced to take Gannett's column for a month come summer, with Lewis off to the wars. Presently, but that's not what I'm calling you up about, Benny, I want to introduce someone, and this is W. W. speaking. He took over and allowed that he'd been considerably impressed by my letter and was off to Wisconsin and could he quote from same if he fixed it up so that nothing could be traced to me. Says I, indignant like, use anything you want and I don't give a damn if it's traced to me or not. So he did so, at seven and a half cents a clip, and for a brief but dizzy period I was on the wire to Wisconsin, heaving in U. S. history by the scoopful at nearly any hour of the day or night. I wish to God I had his secretary, for she never missed a word.... There was that wistful moment in Milwaukee. Willkie was off holding court with bigwigs somewhere and she was taking down a batch of round shot to be heated up and fired. When I finished, she said most winsomely, "Got any ideas about labor, Mr. DeVoto?" I said I didn't think I had any that he didn't have or couldn't get from the papers. She said, "He's got to make a big labor speech tomorrow and he's so damn tired." I also wish I had a secretary that could say that last word the way she did.... It's a damn shame he called off in Nebraska, for there was hotting up a speech about how much more us plain people knew about every other war we were ever mixed up in than we're allowed to know about this one. It would have been a honey and I gave it barbs enough in my own share of it to know that it would have hurt plenty. Now I'm scared to death that in a rush of party loyalty he'll turn all his stuff over to Dewey, including my really gorgeous stuff out of the past. I'll be eternally good God-damned if I want to contribute anything to Dewey except a noose. I'm doing what I can in the June Easy Chair.[17] But the May *Harper's* has a lovely, lovely job before me, something called "The Man in the Blue Serge Suit."[18] It indignantly denies that Dewey ever took a stand against the man-eating shark.

Well, that's my political career. All my auspices and conjunctions are unfavorable, just now. The political career would get me all over the front page as a Republican at a time when I'm mixed up with the Boston cops. It's not going to help, either, that the May Easy Chair has a line, though it's quoted from elsewhere, about "the cops run straight to the Cardinal."[19] Why couldn't the old devil live another month?[20]

Washington. I had my bags packed, a hotel room reserved, and a set of assistants lined up. I may be on the payroll for all I know, and considering how long I wasn't, that wouldn't hurt a bit. About four hours before train time I said to Avis, "I don't think I'd better go," and she bawled and said, "I don't think you'd better," so I phoned I wasn't coming and I didn't. The truth is, Avis pooped out and the household went all to hell at about the same time. All year long she's had infections that have drained her strength, none too great anyway, as an anemic. It has also been Mark's winter to grow up and grow loose. Finally our maid quit—an Irish gal who saw ghosts and whatnot and shuddered away from the thought of another summer by that lonesome sea at Annisquam. For six weeks I was doing as much nursemaid and second maid work as I was literature, and we had a half dozen in for a day or two at a time. You know what it is to try to get servants at this dot of time. Avis was going quietly nuts at the prospect of my walking out, so I didn't.... Situation temporarily—at least—eased. We have, for the moment, not only one maid but another one as well, Avis is sleeping nights, and Mark has the first cold his parents have ever welcomed.

Not going to Washington left me free for the *Strange Fruit* episode, which was beginning to head up. I'd been doing what I could, which was nothing at all except write things here and there. [*handwritten:* and threaten the Coop.] I'd been pretty damn disgusted and for that matter still am by the gutlessness of Boston's best and the absolute indifference of New England writers. Disgust had been relieved by only a couple of moments. I had had the satisfaction not only of calling Dick Fuller a son of a bitch to his face and in the presence of a witness but of, thereby, getting him so mad that he went indiscreet.[21] Esther Hamill came down from the sticks for her spring visit and I took her to dinner. Boston's best restaurant having been lately put on my blacklist—when I took a Negro there and there was a lot of suave insolence—I couldn't take her to the Parker House but went instead to Joseph's, or maybe Josef's, anyway, that place off the Museum of Modern Art where the bohemian gather.[22] And up comes Dick with his hand out. I said, "I'm not happy to see you," and we went from there. It was quite an interview and it delighted Esther to the bottom of her romantico-literary soul. Dick got so mad that he said a lot of things he now regrets to beat hell—as always when any test or even any question or discussion of the booksellers' committee or the anti-obscenity statutes seems likely, he's put himself out of the way in a hospital. At one point he yelled that nobody was as eager as he was to make a test of the law, but why should the booksellers run all the risk, and if ever any damn publisher would risk an inch of his skin, there would be Dick, in there fighting.[23] I said, that's just fine, Dick, I'm authorized to say that Reynal-Hitchcock will fight this thing through if they can get a book sold in Boston, and I'll be in your store tomorrow at nine o'clock and you can sell me one. He crawled a thousand yards apiece in nine different directions in nine and three-fifths seconds, and actually, when we came to it, no reputable book store in Boston was willing to sell a book—unquestionably under orders from Dick. So the next morning, just to see if I couldn't get some more indiscretions I phoned him, with a witness on my extension. He said, I wonder if you realize you insulted me last night. I said, I worked hard to, let's just let it ride. So before I finished I got him to give me the names of some people alleged to be on his committee. He was probably lying, they are merely stooges if he wasn't, but there they are, in my notes, if the need comes. No newspaper was able to get a single name. He is a teetotal son of a bitch, and for my money he's nine times worse than the law itself. I'm quoting him, by office though not by name, in the Easy Chair and he'll head back to the hospital, if he's out of it by then.

All this time *Strange Fruit* had been making strange bedfellows. The sole other agitator was, guess who, F. O. Matthiessen, who hates my guts and always has. At the moment he loves me like a twin and long lost brother miraculously returned by the sea, but he makes it quite clear that the passion is for this date and train only. Incidentally, he's done a damned fine job. In fact, I'll take a bow and say we both have. We forced Reynal and Hitchcock, or rather shamed them, into signing up with us.[24] They didn't want any part of it and their lawyer, incidentally the best trial lawyer in Boston and now convinced we can't lose, advised them not to make a test since they were sure to lose. Publishers are not as gutless as writers or Bostonians and Curtice Hitchcock, a nice guy, is not so gutless as some of his colleagues, but all told he and his firm together didn't have two inches of bowel on view until Matty and I said, Well, boys, we'd like your support, we'd like your publicity, and we'd like your cash, but the issue transcends your interest and we're not going to call it off on your request, we're not going to delay in [*sic*: it?] for your sake, we're going to go ahead. They made one more play for postponement or what have you and then kicked in one lawyer and five hundred dollars, the same being absolutely all the money contributed to this case by anyone except the Boston committee of the Civil Liberties Union, headed by Matty, and B. DeVoto.[25]

I've had more damn fun watching a series of violent internal disturbances as Matty, thrown into intimate contact with me for the first time, has discovered that I'm not actually biting Jews and subsidizing fascists in my off hours. He hated me all through Harvard, he's hated me ever since, and he goes into pale rages and spits cotton at mention of my name, as a regular thing—he actually makes scenes. Now he's had to find out that I've got a hell of a lot of habits and ideas that come within the rigid limits of his approval. I have made just one malicious remark and that one was the honey of this world, so inspired that I have waked up many nights and wallowed in it. Not the remark, please, but the context. Some of the violent shocks have come from off-hours talk in which it has transpired that I am, really, quite decent about Russia, Matty's spiritual home. Well, when the lawyers were fixing up the case they—and I—took it for granted that the cops would lie. They said so, I said so, and various listeners, including Matty, rebuked us for cynicism. Well, at the hearing, the cops lied and how. Matty, like Avis, was genuinely shocked. That evening, he said, You said they would lie, Benny, how did you know? I said, Hell, I've covered the police desk as a reporter, I know cops, they have to lie and they always do. Thereupon I grew meditative and presently I said, I really didn't understand Russia, I really didn't feel at home with Russia, until the Moscow trials.[26] It was, I grant you, no heaven-parting stroke of wit, but nevertheless it was perfect and I want a summary of the incident carved on my tomb.

I should also record that Matty, who had written the *New Republic* that he wanted to review the LF when it came out, wrote cancelling the request as soon as the *Strange Fruit* business developed, feeling that this was no time to drive a wedge between allies.[27]

Well, we finally found a bookseller who was willing to take a chance. Not in Boston, and not the Coop—which I memorialized with such a letter to the directors. So we notified the cops and I bought the book and the cops got up and swore that I'd told them I'd heard a lot of Harvard students wanted to buy it and I was buying it so that I could distribute it among them and satisfy their desire. (Under the statute it is not a crime to buy but only to buy with intent to circulate.) So after I'd given them the lie on the stand (and made them so mad thereby that they perpetrated a bad indiscretion that same afternoon) and had qualified myself as an expert, the judge allowed that expert testimony was not admissible, that plain people must determined the morality of the book, and continued the case in order to read the book, and continued the case in order to read the book as a plain person, saying from the bench, "The issue of this case will depend on my opinion of the book."[28]

Well, we'll find out on Wednesday. There is, I'm afraid, considerable danger that the charges will be dismissed. For one thing, the judge is cantankerous and a complete bastard. He is not a bigot or a Christer but heavy damages were assessed against him for misfeasance of a trust and he came within one vote, probably bought, of being impeached therefor, and for thirty years he has raised holy hell with Harvard boys, qua Harvard boys, whenever some innocent drunk has been brought before him. Conceivably he is cantankerous enough to upset our applecart by finding the book not obscene. Again, the cops have made a number of atrocious mistakes and I think that the district attorney, who does not have to prosecute in the lower court but will have to as soon as we go upstairs, may be rejoicing because of them and may even have suggested them. He is running for the Republican nomination for lieutenant-general [*sic*][29] and the Republicans are supposed to contain the local literates, if any, and in any event he doesn't want this kind of notoriety at this time. It was a mistake of the first magnitude to charge me as well as the bookseller with a crime, for, notwithstanding Red Lewis, Commonwealth vs. DeVoto would make a hell of a swell title, in the current circumstances, to carry as a test case to the Supreme Judicial Court of Massachusetts and an even better one if we could go on to Washington. It was a bad mistake to lie on the stand about my declaration. It was a worse mistake to lie in the subsidiary proceedings against the irrefutable evidence of entries on the record of the clerk of the court. All told, there's about a one in three chance that we may be found not guilty.

If we are, of course, nothing whatever will have been established except that this one book is not obscene in Cambridge. There can be no ruling on the statute and no trial, even, in the lower court. There will be both if we get one step higher, to the Superior Court, but that isn't high enough. Our lawyers—Charlie Curtis is mine—have made every motion and taken every exception and written the right kind of brief to carry this thing all the way up, under the Fourteenth Amendment. I do not believe that the statute infringes that Amendment—I don't think we'll ever get to Washington. Charlie agrees with me but everyone else, including Morris Ernst who is sitting offstage waiting to take over, thinks that it does.[30] I think the best we can hope for—and it would do the job—is to establish in the Supreme Judicial Court of Massachusetts a precedent of requiring an entire book, and not an excerpt, to be judged obscene. That would put Massachusetts roughly on the level of Georgia or Arkansas, though not of New York.

Of course, His Honor might be cantankerous enough to slap the maximum on us, a thousand dollars and two years on me, twice that on my fellow criminal who has two charges against him, selling and possessing with intent to sell. In that event I'll collapse on the bosom of the national Civil Liberties Union, Baldwin's sentimental but useful crowd, which awaits summons.[31] I've agreed to pay my lawyer's fee and any reasonable fine.

If we aren't guilty then the whole damn thing will have to be done over again in Boston—by now a couple of bookstores have offered to cooperate. (Not the least amusing aspect of the affair is that Jordan Marsh have been selling the book all along, under the counter—and don't think I'm not going to make use of that fact, once I get out from under so that what I write is not in contempt of court.)[32] In that event, I may have to bow out. It might be bad tactics for me to appear again with all the outside uproar about my book going on, and it might be bad tactics for the same man to buy the same book twice for the same purpose. If I do cease to be a principal, I will be an expert, for the Superior Court will admit expert testimony, and you can be damn sure I'll continue to make myself offensive in print. I'm sorry, but I'm going to be disagreeable about this. I'm going to stick with it, for it appears to me that someone must, and if only Matty and I will, well, I will. And I am, by God, going to raise hell with the booksellers' committee, which is much worse than the law. Grapevine reached me today that I have succeeded in prying the Coop loose from it. If so, then I have rung one bell.

It seems to be bedtime. I haven't got round to the New York episode or the uproar over *LF*. More to come. As for the latter, I think I've rolled a stone into the garden that will take some leverage to get out.

Yours,
Benny

8 Berkeley Street
Cambridge, Massachusetts

[14 May 1944]

Dear Kate:
Oh, Jesus, I keep lapping myself backwards. The first time Harry Aldrich showed the Shady Hill Medical School a childbirth film, he switched it to rewind half a minute after the brat was fully delivered, and if I keep on losing time against my jobs that's the way I'm going to be. God, once I was young, once I was versatile, once I could keep twelve jobs going at once and come out ahead of the game. Now half that many get me down and eat into my evenings. And I'm so far behind on this serial report that, the congregation consenting, I think I'm going to skip the New York business entirely.[33] And if there's anything you want to know about me and Red Lewis and the Book Reviewers International, suppose you just ask the specific questions and we'll skip the rest of that too.

Well, let's add one observation: by the just and far-seeing providence of God, we are witnessing in the literary pages of America a laboratory example of what my book is about, the creation of a literary eidolon which has no reference to or control by what it is supposed to represent, to wit my book.

Clearing up a miscellany. I'll send you Wally's book, which I'd like back sometime or other, and Constance Robertson's (if Mollie Brazier has not walked off with it) on the same basis.[34] Also a copy of *Strange Fruit* with the compliments not of the author but of the agitator. This when a moment comes between telephone calls. I'm getting constipated for the first time in my life for the sole but sufficient reason that it's a damned short time between rings.... It wasn't your correspondent who gave that little dinner at the Parker House which had to be sat out so doggedly and unruffledly—if it had been I'd have made an even louder howl than I did—it was Roger Butterfield, who wanted to talk matters over with me and a small *Life* team he had brought to town, on which was Earl Brown, Harvard man, newspaperman, and good writer but a touch dark for the Parker House's taste.[35] A nice guy. He is now in jail in Chicago because a Congressman socked him, and I hope I can get that fact in print somehow.... As for the 150 pages. I never had them typed—too damn much else to do and to get typed. They are a unique copy and though I urgently want you to read them I have not so far been able to persuade myself that the American Railway Express can be trusted with them. Solution of that problem in due time. Patience, dear, patience—that's what people keep telling me.

It's a little hard for me to tell you about Matthiessen. My treacherous tongue, my ribaldry, my antic humor, my boisterousness, my malice, my jealousy—whatever it is—has always led me to turn away wrath with soft words in regard to him and sometimes the results have been unhappy. The truth is that I've always liked Matty in a mild way but he also stirs a kind of, well, let's say coarse amusement in me and I make wisecracks. Most Freudian, no doubt. Whereas Matty has always violently and openly and most repetitiously hated my guts. For years the Cambridge and suburban scene has been periodically enlivened, or saddened, by Matty's going into pale but far from voiceless rages about me. He hates my guts, and my ideas, and my beliefs if any, and my journalistic mind and all the nouns and adjectives now in everyday use. He had some part in my original firing from Harvard, I've never bothered to try to find out what. He put on a to hell with the signals, give me the ball act when there was talk of bringing me back. He interrupts his courses to denounce me. He holds seminars, specially summoned, in which his graduate students take DeVoto apart bone by bone, tie the guts in bowknots, and stamp on the remains. I come close to being his great crusade, and until the last few weeks saddened my hopeful soul I truly thought that he was the only person in the world who thought of himself as an enemy of mine.

Matty is a damned fine teacher and a damned poor writer. He is an academic, an idealist, an ideologue, a zealot, a fanatic. He is also a man who believes everything and a man visibly perishing of an inner conflict inconceivably violent. He is that monstrous thing, a Yale man, a Skull and Bones man, gone intellectual and radical. He is without sex—overt sex, I mean. I am quite sure that he has never had any sexual experience of any kind. Obviously stamped by hatred of his father, obviously scared pantsless by women, he has lived these fifteen years or more with, and taken care of, and subjected, and fought a long and murderous war with, a dipsomaniac pansy and painter possibly known to you, Russell Cheney—who now looks like an Oscar Wilde roué and is heading straight, and repulsively, toward the booby hatch.[36] Possibly he spells his name Cheyney?... Matty, I say, is without sex, sexual impulse, sexual motivation, sexual understanding. He is pathetically searching for an orthodoxy, any orthodoxy, and has tried a good many, notably Russia and the related lines. Like many of that species, he hungers for Catholicism and doubtless will eventually embrace it—even after the laboratory tests he's now getting over *Strange Fruit*. The worst I know of him is his insistence on dominating his disciples, to the point of slavery. Can you reach back into the abysm and come up against my outrage when one of my colleagues kept Joe Alsop from getting honors? That was Matty, and the ruction I raised then was repeated every so often while I was on the faculty, though he and I invariably voted the same way in department meetings. They may a little explain his phobia of me, though only a little. Much more is due to what he calls my cynical irresponsibility, though, drawing myself up, I prefer to speak of it as the decently skeptical intelligence of a man who has been about a little. But add all the known factors up, and I still don't know why the stimulus gets the result it does. I swear to God, he hates my guts, and he has made it quite plain that our current, and I may say very effective, alliance is limited to this single barricade.

I am, you probably saw, not guilty and Isenstadt is guilty. That's what we wanted, though it would have been pleasant, perhaps amounting to an extra ace, if I'd been guilty too. The magistrate, a complete son of a bitch whose biography I think I gave you, put on a gratuitous act, rebuked for summoning the press, as I did not, said that the author had put the dirt in to make the book sell, added an additional obscenity beyond those complained of in the summons (in that the author had a couple of guys get out of the car and take a leak behind some bushes), and reversed his interpretation of the law in the course of giving it.... We go to the Superior Court at the end of this month or the first of June and actually try the case there. I suppose you ought to get your client off if you can, but it would have been awkward to win there. We can't accomplish a damned thing short of the Supreme Judicial Court of Massachusetts. The trial in the Superior Court is likely to turn on the admissibility of expert testimony. Stone ruled that there couldn't be any such—he and the man in the street had to rule on immorality, obscenity, impurity, and a tendency to corrupt the morals of youth. If the upper court lets us, we'll haul them in by the train load. If it doesn't, we'll make offer of proof. And in my legal judgment, refusal to accept either will permit us to go on upstairs. Matty and I have persuaded the lawyer who mainly runs things, the Civil Liberties Union counsel, that he must not plead under an accepted legal axiom that a classic cannot be immoral. It was his idea that we could call this book a classic and go from there. Which shows that even one's own lawyer may miss the point of one's case. The farther I go in this world the more I like Charlie Curtis, and I wish he had the case in charge. The current urge to bring Ernst in would lose us everything all along the line.

It was our luck to have the Cardinal die just when he did. We'd have been in a hell of a lot better situation if he'd held off two months longer. And he buried, among other things, the Easy Chair—which raised not a peep here. A few peeps from down South, as I expected.

I seem to be in politics still. I have begun to write speeches for the Democratic National Committee—there appears to be no way out. And meanwhile Willkie and I remain like that. I'd admire to tell you his remarks at a small and secret dinner for him here a couple of weeks back, and still more the burden of a couple of letters I've had from him since, but he specifically placed everything off the record. It is reasonably hot stuff and I'm free to say that the Easy Chair's forthcoming analysis, written a week before he came up, sees pretty much eye to eye with Mr. W. I think more will yet come of this.[37]

Change signals. Investigating, I find that there's an extra copy of Wally, so that's yours to make such disposition of as you please, and so is Miss Smith. Mollie has indeed taken *Fire Bell in the Night*, which means a tolerably long wait for Mollie is not the returning kind. About every six months I go over to her place and lug back half a ton of my books. If you really want to read Connie, I'll put the screws on. I doubt if it's hellish good. She has a superb feeling for history and not a hell of a lot of capacity for fiction. She's constantly spoiling a fine biographer or outright historian by trying to make novels and I'd expect her to have done the same with this one. Did I ever tell you about her? She's the daughter of one of John Humphrey Noyes's stirpicults and prove [*sic*] positive that the old boy was right. She has a mind like a sword blade and a body like nobody's business. She is exactly my age and looks all of twenty-six in noonday or subtract eight years in any other lighting. When you were a child Community Plate[38] used to be advertised by drawings of Cole Phillips' very daring for that age in that they showed the gal to the knee, and damned fine legs too.[39] Those were Connie's legs and when I last saw her, a couple of years back, they were still the same.

I'll include a couple of ephemerae for the Bowne lending library. What do you want? A lot of stuff drifts in and out of this place from publishers. Not much of it is what anybody wants to read but one never knows. Try me out. One drifted in a while back that I hope to read sometime for it looks like what I've always yearned for, *Freedom's Ferment*, apparently a sound account of the reforms and radicalism of the early decades of the nineteenth century.[40] Looks good and it's yours for months for the asking, if you're interested.

I dunno whether I communicated my decision or have come to it since I last circularized you. In part it's a feeling I haven't got the guts to get to work on the Civil War, in part a feeling that what the hell, why should I even attempt fiction, in part the result of the intensive review of the fur trade I've been putting on for this Stewart-Miller job, and in part, no doubt, the result of all the barrage being levelled at me. At any rate, I've decided to do Lewis and Clark. And, he said slowly, do them for a long time to come.

If you are willing to except Donald Peattie's thick slice of ham and bad poetry of a couple of years back, there is no narrative history of the expedition whatsoever.[41] I'm quite willing to except Peattie. There is no considered appraisal of the considerable scholarship that has been expended on the Louisiana Purchase, and there is no effort to focus Louisiana on the expedition or vice versa. There is, in short, no adequate treatment. So I think I'll do one. It differs from the Civil War project in that I already have a solid foundation—and also in that it can be done in a couple of years. In the entire field I can see only one possible controversy, and all the literary critics I may have to discuss are dead. It can be worked on sporadically without loss—a prime necessity in my present circumstances. And just possibly I'll be able to do what no one, so far as I can see, has ever tried to do so far—work out the growth of Louisiana on the American imagination. But, Jesus, darling, the project calls for just those very qualities of discipline I most lack.... Also, I begin to muse, it may get me four tires and 2500 gallons of gasoline in the summer of '45.

Mark is learning to read—further revolt of a once progressive parent—and Bunny was launched into an interest in foreign languages by our New York trip. Apparently a Yiddish newspaper started it.[42]

Yours,

Benny

Bowne

(June 5th) [Monday]

Dear Benny,

That was pretty swell! You must be sick & tired of hearing this, but you really should have a program of your own.... By the way, Mary Norworth, who is something of a connoisseur of voices, raves about yours.... Pudden (Evelyn Dunne) was here last week on a flying visit, the day before she returned to Texas. She came up on the train in all that heat, as did my heroic cousin, Jack.

Note: Apparently mail to the CBI theatre goes by way of N.Y.[43] Iggie indicated his whereabouts by saying that he was "comfortably settled in with Kronid's old friend, Kitay." Kronid says that "Kitay" is Russian for "China." As simple as that.

Don't talk to me about the gutless. Would that we had a local DeVoto to tackle the whole filthy, callous, unspeakably corrupt administration of the Bowne hospitals.... I seem to remember having given you a hint—a very faint hint—of Williams' activities as a mass-murderer. Well, these facts, & countless more like them, are well known to the physicians of Dutchess County. They know, for instance, that "t.b.'s" & "non-t.b.'s," "positive" & "negative" cases are mixed with utter abandon in both buildings. In the other building, right now, there is a girl with a lung abscess (& no t.b.) sharing a 9' x 10' room with an old, irrational woman with a Gaffky 10.[44] Another girl left last week after 18 months' "observation." Final verdict: no t.b. During that 18 months, 3 of her roommates had died horribly, noisily & most contagiously. Melenko told her a year ago that there was no need for her to stay here any longer, but Williams kept her.

Marion Milton came here in July 1942. She continued to cough, run a temperature & haemorrhage occasionally, but every time she went to the examination room, Williams would say: "See! That cavity is all closed!" And Maxie would say: "Ja, bitte, das ist schön, nicht wahr?"[45] (Or whatever is German for "YES, Dr. Williams!") Melenko, on the other hand, told her, privately, that, far from being closed, her cavity was increasing its size. Acting on this knowledge, Marion asked repeatedly to be sent to Oneonta for thoracoplasty. Williams just ignored her. Finally Peg Fenlon, a friend of Marion's & a "graduate" of Oneonta, arranged for Marion to go up there for examination. The doctors there said, "For Heaven's sake, why didn't you come to us a year ago, or even six months ago? We might have helped you then. Now it's a 100-to-1 shot that it's too late. And in any event, we can't operate while you have that throat abscess." They did send her to Albany for treatment of the throat abscess, however. The Albany doctor (Stephens) wrote Williams a furious letter, laying him out for letting the infection reach such an advanced stage without treatment. But letters like that are a commonplace in Williams' life.... When Marion came back from Albany, she had something to say to Williams: "If you have no regard for my life, you might at least have thought of my four small children! etc. etc." Williams just shrugged.

Betty Van Wagener, a patient in this building, came to Williams for examination a year ago. He said: "Go home & forget about it for a year."... Now she's here in bed, a cavity in each lung. She has two small children.

Williams consistently allows patients who are "streaking" to go home for weekends. One of them is, even as I write, lying in a dark room, with dark glasses, his head splitting, his neck contorted, dying agonizingly of t.b. meningitis. Williams insists on giving pneumothorax to patients who have developed fluid, in spite of their protests; not infrequently with fatal results. He puts patients to work in accord with the needs of the hospital, rather than their physical capabilities. There is, at this moment, a man working in the kitchen, preparing food, who has a Gaffky 8. A haemorrhage case is working in the laundry. On the other hand, "arrested" cases, who are working in the other building, are kept there indefinitely under a kind of peonage system, while critically ill persons wait six months to a year for an empty bed. In the former category is Emma Wawalsky who, for the past two years, has worked all day in the kitchen down there, gone home every night (where she cooks, cleans, washes, irons etc. & cares for her husband & two children) & returned to work every morning at 6:30. But she's not "well enough" to go home, says Williams. In the meantime, her kids, 8 & 10, run wild all day on the streets. You may ask why she damned well doesn't go home anyway. Well, (a) she is an ignorant Pole, & greatly in awe of authority, in the person of Williams, (b) if she should ever "get sick again," she would have to come back here, (c) she fears that if she goes home without being discharged, the authorities will take her two children away from her & clap her in an institution.

Williams is a very smooth operator: glib, slick, extremely plausible. I don't believe that he is especially malicious (unless crossed, in which case he can be completely ruthless), just irresponsible, indifferent, callous & self-seeking. As long as he & his numerous relatives draw their salaries & other perquisites, & he isn't bothered by any troublesome problems—the hell with it! As I said before, there is enough plain, objective evidence floating around Dutchess County to hang him a thousand times, & there isn't a doctor in the county who has guts enough to do it. If you should ever feel like doing something for me after I'm dead, you might try exposing that bastard, it would be a distinguished public service.

Yours,
Kate

I'm enclosing a clipping from last Friday's Po'keepsie New Yorker. Williams, of course, knows very well that only bona fide Dutchess residents are included in the t.b. death-rate statistics. The fact that he would make a public statement to the contrary, is so characteristic as to need no comment.—K [*clipping not found*]

8 Berkeley Street
Cambridge, Massachusetts

[18 June 1944]

Dear Kate:
You touch on a vanity and on a phantasy. The old man believes that he has learned to speak in public naturally, to the pitch of the room, and in such a way that customers hear the words. Nobody but me agrees with you about a program, however, and that is my phantasy. I'd rather run an intelligent program than be John August, but I won't. A CBS man and a guy from the advertising agency spent two hours with me that Sunday, soliciting me to write some American Scriptures to be heaved into the intermission of the Philharmonic hour, and maybe I'll try, for God knows the price they pay is fantastic—it came out that Carl Van Doren gets $350 for just being interlocutor.[46] But writing is not what I have phantasies about, and it may be a belated flowering of my aunt's notion that I was designed to be a priest, which shows that you must be careful what you say in front of children.

Yeah, you must be. Mollie Brazier slipped me the restricted report on combat neuroses in North Africa—*Time* had a short, badly bungled piece about it—and I fell to discussing it with her, especially pentothal and why it wouldn't shorten the first or exploratory phase of psychoanalysis.[47] So she got round to tell about a case at MGH, a Pearl Harbor wife who got her husband sent back to this country by developing an ear-splitting, doglike bark. Next night Bunny began to bark. I cured him in one of the speediest analyses on record but it was genuine, all right, and it just goes to show that the war makes inroads on kids.... But the school year is over and I can see that it accomplished far more than at my most optimistic I thought one year could. The school, which has not once summoned me in extremis, in anger or despair or panic or anything else, has never set out a problem before me, has never reported itself alarmed or disgusted, the school agrees. They expected far worse than they got, and far harder. They have no term exams but do have those bastardly achievement tests, in which I have no belief whatever, except that, empirically, Bunny has taken them three times this year and come out higher each time, and the report they make on his mind roughly agrees with mine. They divide both "literature" and "mathematics" into various parts, and rank all tests according to grade, eleventh being highest and Bunny's normal grade being seventh. They scored him 6 on knowledge of literature, which is to say he couldn't identify any of the characters in the novels he is supposed to have read, never having read any novels, 7 on "mathematical computation," 9 on "mathematical reasoning," 11 on all scientific, historical, and informational gadgets, and 11-plus on spelling, what they call word sense, and all other aspects of "literature." Considering that he scored a bare 4 on the math last fall and didn't finish any of the others—having begun in the state of mind hanging over from Shady Hill—I'm disposed to believe that they indicate a little, and that most of what they indicate is that the school has sense and is used to it. They report no disciplinary troubles whatever and a developing sense that when he gets disciplined he has deserved it—both wild and heretical, from the Shady Hill point of view. They are going to keep him on the same basis for a month next year, to start him off, then require him to join the seventh grade, hold him to that as a minimum and encourage him to go as far beyond it as he will, and shoot him into the ninth, the following year. So the school estimates that, probably, he will have lost no time, in the end. Considering that I should have looked on a loss of three years as a small price for self-confidence and self-respect, or any part thereof, that comes close to a miracle. Jesus, Kate, the casual and high-hearted murder that an elderly virgin can commit out of a capacity for self-delusion and an evangelical bitterness of betrayed narcism.

You know, I'm sorry I didn't postcard you. Several days before I went down for the broadcast there was an impromptu gathering here at cocktail time and speculation turned to D-Day.[48] I said, Wait a minute, I'll tell you when it's going to be, got down an almanac, and reported: June 6. Ptolemaic system.[49] Harry Aldrich, who has sailed small boats in the Channel, had figured it all out: have to be in June, for the July winds are wrong, and it will be far enough ahead of the full moon in June, the 8th, to allow them to get there before dawn, say three days. Allowing for errors, it was just as good as the Copernican, or ONI, system and I carefully didn't mention Harry and am now confirmed in my local status as prophet.[50] That Monday night I left Larry Kubie's with a couple we'd been drinking with. She said, I figure the 22d but Pa here figures the 11th, what do you figure? I said, I've already lost, I figured tonight, and went down to the Grand Central and climbed aboard the Owl and went to sleep.

What I get from the horse's mouth, the horse being returned from GHQ by air to the local radar lab since things started, is that boys expected to take Cherbourg in 48 hours.

I'm sending a couple pkg of books. Sometime or other send me back Connie Robertson's. Turn over the rest to Bowne or the Boy Scouts, at your pleasure. Dunno how many you've read, dunno how many will interest you, but take more than a glance at *The Great Image*.[51]

We're off to the Goddam shore on Tuesday: Ames Estate, Bay View, Gloucester. Up till lately it looked to be a reasonably slow summer, but my God how the work has piled up. I've damn well got to do a brief John August—everything pivots on that. I've got to get into the clear by October 1, when I'm going orating for the Air Corps. But Irita is damn hard to shake off—she wants me to run Gannett's column for a month.[52] There's that CBS business to scrutinize, and the Writers' War Board orders me to write an entire hour of broadcast on let's not lose the peace this time.[53] Canby has got to have a piece for his memorial issue, and Fred Allen has handed me a hellish special assignment. I guess it won't be insomnia this summer.... I'm taking four boxes of reading matter on the fur trade, some of it dovetailing nicely into the Lewis & Clark stuff. The farther I go with Mrs. Porter's scholarship on Stewart and Miller, the more it's certain I've got to do her job as well as mine, and I've written Reves that he needn't expect a book before winter.[54] Jesus, the rich collector mind. And I've got to check not only her history but her art. I've already demonstrated that some of the watercolors painted on the spot in 1837 were not painted on the spot or till ten years later. Now I'm endeavoring to suggest to her that you don't take an entire atelier with furnishings to the Rocky Mountains and so it's unlikely that the enormous oil was done at the time and place aforesaid. Suggestion won't take. I have been unable to convince her that the scenes in a novel differ from historical events and it's in her mind that I'm just a nasty critic. She read it in the papers, what's more.

But I think I'm going to establish American History, Inc., and go into the market. How long has this been going on? While I was in N.Y. I talked to Max Wilkinson, now at *Good Housekeeping* and much happier, and he said, write us no more than 1200 words on what dozen books I ought to read if I don't know American history.... So yesterday, with the almost licentious generosity that characterizes me, I delivered one quart of medium rye apiece to Arthur Schlesinger, Paul Buck, and Fred Merk, all of whom were touched and grateful. I spent ten minutes on the phone with them, ten minutes merging their lists with mine, and two hours writing Max's piece. $750, less the price of three quarts.

Paul has even blocked out a series of things for me to do. I may take him as assistant.

Another improbable Cambridge divorce rumor has proved true.[55] Sam Cross, who has figured in the correspondence under his own name and other names and none, at the age of 52, divorcing Connie, who is pretty and witty and at a guess a live gall, in order to marry Kate Benedict, 38, who is walleyed, dumber than hell, practically inarticulate, a hell-driving male manqué and at a guess coldly virginal still though the mother of three. And by God. Kate owns a string of cotton mills but I'd say Sam must be the only man in the world who'd take her and them over Connie. The poor fool and the poor bastard. I wouldn't trust Sam half way from here to there, but he's an amusing gent, he's a nice guy, and he has got guts, guts of a quality and in quantity seldom seen on the Harvard faculty of these days. I'm on Sam's side, but Jesus, when I think of his being married to that little half-pint of fatuousness, my heart bleeds. But this is DeVoto standing by to watch the fun when Kate finds out that this is a model of the human male that won't be ordered around, subdued, or put in its place. Flashes from the ringside in due time.

Sex solidarity grows on me with the years. I like a man to be the man of his house. I wouldn't quite do it myself but I'm seeking round to find someone to separate Harriet Robey, the daughter of my Gloucester land-lady, from Alec, the poor bastard, and marry her, and show her that the male cannot be run. Great Grampa Beast Butler was a notable manager and it all comes out in Harriet. But it turns out she can't manage psychoanalysts, even shes, and I'll tell you that story later on.[56]

I am taking your letter about Dr. Williams to heart. Maybe before the summer is out I can get a leverage on somebody in the Dewey organization. I think I can. I expect to be a Willkie brain-truster for a few days before and after the convention.

Yours,

Benny

Ames Estate, Bay View
Gloucester, Massachusetts

[22 July 1944]

Dear Kate:
This is probably going to be episodic still but more regular. If it's hard going, well, I've got a thumb the size of a wrist & a wrist the size of ham. I was lately called a senile old man in print & judging by the way I fall that's right.

Well, oh, God, let's begin with a *Gloucester Bugle*.

George Leighton's leaving *Harper's* was, I judge, in part at least related to the Fur Lined article in this issue.[57] The adoring mind of Kay Jackson, I judge, never approved of him, & Kay at least in part got her man. At that, his conception of journalistic integrity always differed from mine.

Summer saddened more than there's any reason to be by a wire saying my fellow Legionnaire, Jess Holther, is dead. I've seen & heard nothing of him in more than 20 years and certainly the loss is in my ego, not my affections. But I can remember a hell of a lot of things, including sending him off to marry a girl that probably did nothing in 20 years to make life pleasant for him. I wonder what he got out of life and by God senile old man was right.

Follow with a note on nature's fecundity. For five days and nights our bay boiled with shiners. Dunno the species—little fish a few inches long. Billions of them. Sometimes so thick you waded in them like a bog. And chased in by millions of ~~herring~~ hake. All the kids on the Point threw the hake in by the hundred, and we ate roe by the barrel. All night long there was a hissing of [*illegible*] minnows and a constant splash of leaping hake and the screaming of millions of gulls. Made as much sense as the war, at that. Or my life.

Still sustained by your prodigality, Bunny goes on improving his marksmanship. The going is tougher as the upper brackets he has entered but he goes right ahead. He now shoots a .22 fully as well as I did at twice his age, doubtless as well as I like to think I once could. He's a first-rate shot, & you're duly thanked again. I don't know if he's having too good a time, otherwise. Adolescence begins to be hell.

Me, I don't and won't like the sea. It's excellent for Mark, it's too damn damp for me. I try to plow ahead with John August & with the Scottish baronet.[58] It comes out that I'm learning a hell of a lot about Indians. And about historians. The prospect of a Lewis & Clark book has brought me into correspondence again, after a lapse of years, with the Maine sourball, Kenneth Roberts, and I'm afraid he's right about the historians.[59] I've been going over a job by one of them who reported in the *Miss. Valley Hist. Review* that obviously '46 couldn't be sound for it contained no bibliography.[60] [*illegible*] can't even copy titles correctly in his bibliography and day by day I see scores of his statements which I know to be stupidly inaccurate at sight & other scores which upon investigation turn out to be as bad.

One unpleasantness is the working against time - the Army is still promising to send me out in October, though God knows to what end, and I have to finish a hell of a lot of jobs by then. A worse one is, for the first time in my life, neighbor trouble. I have lately asserted myself. George Copeland, the pianist and as repulsive a pansy as I've ever glimpsed, lives a hundred yards away with two sweeties, a Nazi and a Wop.[61] They do not like kids—under a certain age, that is. I can't forever keep mine from cutting across their lot to save a quarter of a mile to the Point and don't mind their chasing them off. When chasing them off became vindictive, however, I got annoyed and when the Nazi threatened to set his Boxer on Bunny I went over. I was quite ridiculous and extremely offensive, both in such quantity that the Wandervogel's belligerence turned soft. I remain offensive, have written Copeland a suavely haughty letter directing him to keep his servants in better behavior, and await the next move. I've always supposed that if I got nasty I could be a son of a bitch and that goes. As a matter of fact, I like the role—whatever that may reveal. There will certainly be a next move and I propose to return it from the net.

Elmer Davis promised me a year ago that the European war would end by November of this year. Maybe he was a little conservative. For, although I relished Vansittart's warning that this could all be a phony, I still can't help thinking how much this last month has been like August, 1914.[62] But I cannot bring myself to hope for a decision now. Quite the contrary. This is the period when I plump for a hard peace. I don't know what international lessons are, but if we have not been taught the dismemberment of Germany & some form of internationalization of its finance & basic industry, then I see no point in either Welles or Lippmann or anyone else now setting up a world for us to gaze into.[63] As for that world, I like this much about Lippmann, that it's as much as we can get, if we can get that much. It's the optimum of reasonable expectation. Curious how he turned realistic.

How does the product of my thumb read? The typing it does is even worse but I think I'll expose you to it next time.

Yrs

Benny

[1 August 1944]

[no salutation: DeVoto to Sterne]

I hope to write before the week is out. But meanwhile as a lover of our sweet Yankee tongue you certainly ought to know that it's All Snarled and Fucked Up and he's a Sad Sack of a Four Letter Obscenity meaning Fecal Matter

All quiet with the fairies at the bottom of our garden[64]
[*no signature*]

Ames Estate, Bay View
Gloucester, Massachusetts

[7 August 1944, postmarked Cambridge]

Dear Kate:
And is this a honey of a machine. Just watch.... Seems my mind was even more erratic than usual and I blended an idiom out of the other war with the one you wanted. Sad Sack goes as stated but Snafu is Situation Normal, All Fucked Up.[65] Like my various jobs.

Lately there has been such a run of weather as even I wouldn't believe of even Massachusetts, of even the Massachusetts shore. And you wouldn't believe that even I would be fool enough to get on a tennis court in it but, my wrist subsiding, that's exactly what I've been doing. There is no physiological surprise in waking up and finding my legs tied in knots—the asininities of senility familiarized me with that one long ago. But I have begun to wonder about all those efficiencies in foundries.[66] For one day I took some salt tablets before undertaking tennis at a hundred degrees plus and humidity as aforesaid. My tennis form is not by the book but there was nothing wrong, three minutes later, with my spewing and I want to know about the foundries. Well, my last year's partner was six months pregnant when the summer ended and this year she carries me even more successfully, being a navy wife and unpregnant, and so we're still winning and if you think that tennis at my age is obscene, you're right.

My fiction moves a little. Maybe I'll get it finished in time to attack the various things lined up for me and, that being possible, I haven't yet said no to Irita. I don't believe I ever said no to anyone and it seems a little late to try. I'm reconciled to never being even with any job from here on out. I could have the Mercury again, for about the fifth time I think, but I'll probably find sense enough to say that no.

I think I told you about the fecundity of our mother the sea as regards hake and shiners. There was a repeat performance with squid. They struggle less, smell worse, and are admired by the local gourmets. Everyone was frying them in batter or mixing them with the local shellfish in something alleged to be Spanish, but for my money they taste no better than tripe or any other rubber substitute. The Point is being experimental this summer. The fairies next door go down at low tide and gather in lobster shorts which they prepare in ways they chatter about. One gal makes stews of the mussels, undeterred by a long history of poisonings down at Beverly, just a few miles away, where one of the deadliest parasites known to science has been found in the mussels.[67] Various adolescents have reverted to a dish I also fathered at that age, roast robin. But the highest reach was the gal who was constructing canapes and a salad out of the local yarbs—urged on, no doubt, by a real herbery, or whatever the name is, down the line a little. When I casually passed by she was industriously digging in a patch of poison ivy. On the whole the drinking experiments have been sounder, and there would be real value in the discovery, if someone should make it, of how to render rum potable. There is damned little else. Except, as everyone hereabout has now learned, in the cellar of that foresighted gent Benny.

Here your note arrives. Maybe that was a cryptic allusion, and God knows I don't know what goes on at *Harper's* any more. But somebody had a piece in it about the Museum of Modern Art. I dunno how much truth there was in it. But, with all the fervor of her nature, and by God that is fervor, Kay Jackson knows it wasn't true at all, and didn't she know someone there, wasn't in fact someone there a friend of hers and so entitled to her loyalty? And it is some loyalty. Kay has a hundred breasts and they all give milk. She is the sweetest woman in the world and a good many have died of her sweetness and I gather that George Leighton was, in part, one of them. Anyway, it seems George took a stand, a stand of a kind he has taken rather steadily for a good many years, of a kind that has always made me distrust him. Stand: maybe it isn't so but it makes a good article. Well, the friction between George and Fred Allen, which has been constant, here came to a head and George got out. I gather it wouldn't have happened over that piece except for Kay's sweetness. Jesus, I walk round and round that gal and am scared beyond belief. She's pretty as can be and very bright, her soul is intense and pellucid, and she thinks writing and writers are the goal of life, evolution, love, and effort—and wonderful beyond words. Andy Jackson, her husband, is a good guy but he don't write. And Kay lives in an adoration at a thousand atmospheres, a continuous orgasm—yes, and I mean orgasm—of reverence and worship and ah-God for…first Herbert Agar, about whom I needn't tell you a word, and second and failing Herbert, John Chamberlain, about whom I need tell you even less. She is so God-damned sweet that she kills at a hundred yards. I suppose she's a tragic case—Helen Everitt says so, and Helen has never been wrong about anything—but I lose the tragedy in the spiritual glucose. I think Leighton's leaving will be very bad for *Harper's*. It will not only allow Kay, unopposed, to infuse the sheet with mother's milk, it will remove the last brake from Fred's earnestness. He has done better with the magazine since Lee's death than I thought possible—and than half the house of Harper thought possible when they wanted to hand me Lee's job on the day of Lee's funeral. But he could use Leighton's eight-minute-egg mind and he could use a touch of irreverence and lightness that nobody is prepared to supply. I think we'll continue to grow more like the New School for Social Research with increasing moments of the Town Hall of the Air.[68] Kouwenhoven—and I don't guarantee that spelling—is a nice boy and has the lightness Fred needs, but not in sufficient quantities and not backed by an intelligence of sufficient caliber.[69] God left him on our doorstep after delivering him from a teaching job at Bennington College—of which Fred is a trustee. He did a book of illustrations from the bygone *Harper's Weekly* some years ago, if you happened to see it.

In all the years I wrote for Lee I got maybe six notes from him—about my stuff, I mean—and none went more than three lines, saying, maybe, "Christ Almighty, have I got to teach you how to spell Shays' Rebellion" or, once in every five-year period, "That Easy Chair isn't as bad as usual." I always get at least one page from Fred and it usually runs into or through the second page, and meanwhile little notes keep coming in, all full of suggestions and praise (he raised me fifty dollars a couple of months back—and I must admit Lee wouldn't have done that, either). I detect an omen this month. I wrote a piece about Senator Taft, the Army, and our boys mustn't read Kitty Bowen's book.[70] Because it was written on this machine—Avis's portable, I explain—I overshot.[71] Nineteen lines long. So first I get a note from Mary Burnet, the nice young thing who has taken the place of Miss Watson, who read proof on *Harper's* for a hundred and four years. Mary says, cut nineteen lines when you get proof. Okay, I cut nineteen lines. Then I get a note—a letter—from Fred, saying it's a swell piece, repeat six times, but it was 18 magazines, not 21 (and that depends on which release you go by—DV), and you've run over 19 lines and I've taken the unwarranted liberty of cutting them for you. And then I get a note from Kouwenhoven, Fred is on vacation, you're 19 lines long and I've cut it for you, I don't think you'll miss anything vital.... The payoff will come when I see it in print. It's practically certain to be 57 lines shorter than it was.

Glad you like the current Easy Chair. I wrote it because Helen Everitt said I had to say something about why we went to church—she was cut down on her way to a train—and what Helen says to do, I do. But it has had one alarming result. I hadn't heard a word from Dorothy Thompson since she gave herself the satisfaction, a year or so back, of writing me that, though I was always awfully unjust to her, she had just been able to express her admiration of me, which was maximum and constant, by voting for my election to the National ~~Academy~~ Institute, to which, in her opinion, I ought of course to have been elected long ago. Walking round that, I concluded that Dorothy was telling me I'd been nominated and voted down, which I should not otherwise have known. Well, all is forgiven now, and I'm summoned first to Barnard and then to the sawdust trail. "The time, my friend, is late. We are about to be sold down the river—in victory—to the Nazis.... There is an international conspiracy to break the heart of Mankind." And so on. But the current Easy Chair proves that I am one of those who can stand at her right hand and keep the bridge with her.[72] I've got to answer that one, as soon as I can get time from John August.[73]... To which, immensely frustrated, I now return.

Yours,
Benny

[*handwritten on verso:*]Loom of Language:[74]
If you've got any use for or interest in it, no. If not, send it back sometime—Bunny is getting interested in languages. In my opinion, it's lousy

1360 Peabody St. N. W.
Washington, D. C.
September 4, 1944
Mr. Bernard De Voto
8 Berkeley Street

CAMBRIDGE, MASSACHUSETTS

Dear Mr. De Voto:

I was a close friend of the late Katharine Sterne of whose death on August 31 you may have read. Her death was, mercifully, as sudden as it can be considered sudden for one who was ill twelve years. Her heart failed on Wednesday evening, and she died early Thursday morning.

Katharine had frequently instructed me that, at her death, I was to send to you the letters which she had received from you. I have therefore arranged to have sent to you all your letters which I found among her possessions. I am also sending back the books which you recently sent her.

All Katharine's possessions, consisting almost exclusively of books, were left to me. She had, however, suggested to me orally some time ago that you might be interested in some of them since she knew that my small apartment could not lodge her collection. I have had no opportunity to examine the books and probably will not be able to do so for some months to come. I am certain however that the collection is as varied as Katharine's many interests. If you will let me know the kind of books you would be interested in receiving, I shall be happy to send them to you.

Since, unfortunately, there is no one closer than I to say this, I feel that I must thank you for your interest in Katharine. I know that the stimulation of your letters helped keep alive her intellectual awareness, her sense of participation in the world which amazed everyone who knew her during her illness.

Sincerely yours,
Beatrice Rosenberg

NOTES

1. Westbrook van Voorhis (1904?–1968), announcer.
2. Alfred Jacob Miller (1810–1874), painter.
3. George F. A. Ruxton (1820–1848), author.

4. (1795–1871), trader, captain in the King's Hussars, came to New York in 1832, and traveled to the Rocky Mountains with Miller in 1837.
5. Thomas Gainsborough (1727–1788), outstanding British landscape painter and portraitist.
6. Memoir by Richard Tregaskis, published in 1943 and later made into a film.
7. Bridger (1804–1881), "fur trapper, trader, explorer, and scout." (*ANB*)
8. *Altowan, or, Incidents of Life and Adventure in the Rocky Mountains, by an Amateur Traveler*, 1846.
9. Ann Radcliffe (1764–1823), British author of Gothic novels; *The Mysteries of Udolpho*, 4 vols., 1794; *The Italian*, 3 vols., 1797.
10. Emery Reves (1904–1981), Hungarian publisher and news syndicator. Hyperion Press was located in England.
11. This project grew into BDV's *Across the Wide Missouri*, illustrated with paintings and drawings by Alfred Jacob Miller, Charles (or Karl) Bodmer, and George Catlin. Published in 1947, it won the Pulitzer Prize in history, 1948.
12. Philip Kearny (1814–1862), major general, nephew of Stephen Watts Kearny; served in the Mexican War and the Civil War.
13. Robidou (1794–1860), fur trader and frontiersman.
14. This was one of BDV's fixed habits of working. Following lunch he would sometimes take a short nap, and then continue working on various tasks until about 6 p.m., the cocktail hour.
15. *Harper's* 188/4 (March 1944).
16. BDV was later a client of the Romeike clipping service, at 9 cents a clipping.
17. 189/1.
18. "Dewey: The Man in the Blue Serge Suit," by Richard Rovere, *Harper's* 188/6.
19. The May Easy Chair about the *Strange Fruit* case.
20. Cardinal O'Connell, archbishop of the Boston diocese since 1911, died on 22 April 1944 at age eighty-four; he was succeeded by Archbishop Richard Cushing.
21. Richard F. Fuller, president of the Old Corner Book Store in Boston and chairman of the Board of Retail Book Merchants.
22. For BDV, Boston's best restaurant was the Parker House, on Tremont Street. The Negro was the writer Earl Brown. Avis DeVoto remembered that one of the Negro waiters brought Brown a martini with two burned matches floating in the glass. Joseph's was located at 1010 Atlantic Avenue. BDV may mean the Institute of Contemporary Art at 955 Boylston Street in Boston (since 1936).
23. According to the Boston *Evening Globe*, 4 April 1944, the American Center for P.E.N. wrote a letter to the booksellers' committee protesting their action; it was signed by Carl Carmer, Dorothy Thompson, Will Irwin, Clifton Fadiman, Fannie Hurst, Manuel Komroff, and William Sloane.
24. The publishers of *Strange Fruit*.
25. The lawyer was Anthony Brayton, provisional counsel for the publisher. When the case came to trial on 12 April, the publisher's attorney, from the Boston firm of Hale and Dorr, was probably Joseph N. Welch (1890–1960), who became nationally famous in the McCarthy-Army hearings in 1954.
26. The Moscow trials of 1937, when Josef Stalin consolidated his absolute power by purging the Soviet military and intelligentsia of all suspected supporters of Trotsky.
27. LF, BDV's *The Literary Fallacy*.
28. Judge Arthur Parker Stone (1870–1961), Harvard '93, judge, Massachusetts Superior Court for the Third District. The case was continued until Wednesday, 26 April.
29. BDV probably means lieutenant governor.
30. Morris L. Ernst (1888–1976), attorney, counsel for the ACLU; *The First Freedom*, 1946.

31. Roger N. Baldwin (1884–1981) was a founder of the American Civil Liberties Union.
32. The Boston *Globe* reported 2,500 copies of the book sold up to 17 March 1944, presumably from many bookstores before the ban was announced. Dorothy Hillyer reviewed *Strange Fruit* in the *Globe* on 1 March.
33. The brouhaha in the *Saturday Review of Literature* between BDV and Sinclair Lewis. See the letters to Norman Cousins, editor of *SRL*, of 8 May and 19 May 1944 in *LBDV*; see also Cousins's review of Stegner's *The Uneasy Chair* in "The Controversial Mr. DeVoto," *Saturday Review/World*, 6 April 1974, in which Cousins discusses his own painful position as the twenty-seven-year-old editor of *SRL* in 1944. Myrick Land (1922–1998), in *The Fine Art of Literary Mayhem: Famous Writers and Their Feuds*, 1963, in a chapter on the affair, states that when BDV was nominated for membership in the National Institute of Arts and Letters in November 1944, "to the surprise of almost everyone—probably including Bernard DeVoto—Lewis made an enthusiastic speech seconding the nomination...and a little later when Lewis and DeVoto met in a New York Street which was crowded with Christmas shoppers, they chatted pleasantly a few moments and then went their separate ways." Avis DeVoto denied that this amiable encounter occurred, and was sure that BDV never forgave Lewis.
34. Wallace Stegner, *The Big Rock Candy Mountain*, 1943.
35. Butterfield (1907–1981), historian and journalist; *Life* magazine. Brown (1903–1980), Harvard '24, baseball player and newspaper journalist; *Life* magazine; New York City Council, 1949–1961.
36. Cheney (1881–1945) landscape painter, Colorado and Maine.
37. Easy Chair, *Harper's* 189/3 (July 1944).
38. Oneida silverware.
39. Phillips (1880–1927), illustrator.
40. *Freedom's Ferment: Phases of American Social History to 1860*, by Alice Felt Tyler, 1944.
41. *Journey into America*, 1943.
42. The famous one is *Forvertz* (the Jewish Daily Forward), published in New York from 1897; in 1990 it became a weekly but is still publishing today, and in 1995 a Russian edition also appeared.
43. CBI, China-Burma-India.
44. The now obsolete Gaffky scale ran from 1 to 9; named for Georg T. A. Gaffky, German bacteriologist (1850–1918).
45. "Yes, please, that is beautiful, isn't it?"
46. Carl Van Doren (1884–1950), critic, editor, biographer of Benjamin Franklin, author of *Swift* (1930); older brother of Mark Van Doren (1894–1972), poet and critic.
47. Probably *Time* 43/23 (5 June 1944).
48. Tuesday, 6 June 1944, the beginning of the Allied landings of some 176,000 troops on the occupied coast of Normandy.
49. After Claudius Ptolemy (Ptolemaeus, 2nd century CE), Alexandrian astronomer, who proposed a geocentric universe in a *Geographical Treatise*.
50. Nikolaus Copernicus (1473–1543), Polish astronomer, proposed and largely proved the heliocentric model of the solar system; *De revolutionibus orbium coelestium*, 1543. ONI, Office of Naval Information.
51. Possibly *The Land of the Great Image: Being the Experiences of Friar Manrique in Arakan*, by Maurice Collis, 1943.
52. Apparently BDV did not do so.
53. Established in January 1942, this nongovernmental propaganda office was headed by Rex Stout; its second annual report appeared in January 1944.

54. Mae Reed Porter was the owner of some two hundred paintings and drawings by Alfred Jacob Miller, but had no standing as a historian. See *LBDV*, pp. 294–301.
55. Samuel Hazard Cross (1891–1946), professor of Slavic languages, had married Constance Curtis in 1918.
56. Several of the psychiatrists at Bay View were women: Beata Rank, Lucie Jessner (1896–1979), and Eveoleen Rexford (1911–?).
57. George Leighton: (1902–1966) associate editor of *Harper's*. "The Fur-lined Museum," by Emily Genauer, Harper's 189/2 (July 1944), about the fifteenth anniversary of the Museum of Modern Art and the 1936 exhibition on surrealism. The title refers to Meret Oppenheim's famous fur-lined teacup and spoon.
58. Sir William Drummond Stewart.
59. Kenneth Roberts (1885–1957), Maine humorist and author of historical novels; *Arundel*, 1930; *The Lively Lady*, 1931; *Rabble in Arms*, 1933.
60. *The Year of Decision* was reviewed briefly in 30/2 (September 1943) by Colin B. Goodykoontz of the University of Colorado. The review does not mention a lack of bibliography; BDV was probably thinking of a different periodical.
61. George Copeland (1882–1971), outstanding concert pianist, a specialist in modern French and Spanish music. Wop: (pejorative and insulting) Italian.
62. Robert G. Vansittart (1881–1957), baron, British writer, head of the Win the Peace movement; warning not identified.
63. Sumner Welles (1892–1961), undersecretary of state, resigned 1943; *A Time for Decision*, 1946; *Where Are We Heading?*, 1948.
64. Reference to the song "There are Fairies at the Bottom of My Garden" by Rose Fyleman (1887–1957).
65. See also *Mrs. Byrne's Dictionary of Unusual, Obscure, and Preposterous Words: Gathered from Numerous and Diverse Authoritative Sources*, by Josefa Heifetz Byrne, edited with an introduction by Mr. Byrne, 1974.
66. Workers in steel foundries and other high-temperature occupations were required to take salt tablets to replace the salt lost by sweating. The Cape Ann Tool Works, with a foundry on Route 127 in Rockport, three miles north of Bay View, did defense manufacturing during the war; motorists and pedestrians who stopped to watch the forges were chased away by the local police.
67. Saxitoxin, produced by dinoflagellate algae (*Gonyaulax* spp.) and absorbed by clams and mussels, causes paralytic shellfish poisoning when the algae proliferate (so-called "red tide") and the mollusks are consumed. Since the 1970s a laboratory test for the toxin has made it a simple matter to determine safety for consumption of shellfish.
68. The New School of Social Research, now called New School University, was founded in Greenwich Village in 1919 by a distinguished group of scholars that included John Dewey, Thorstein Veblen, and Charles A. Beard. Correctly, America's Town Meeting of the Air.
69. John A. Kouwenhoven (1909–1990), author, taught at Bennington College 1938–1941; associate editor at *Harper's*, 1941–1954; *Made in America: The Arts in Modern Civilization*, 1948; *The Beer Can By the Highway*, 1961. BDV dedicated *The Easy Chair*, 1955, to Kouwenhoven, Kay Jackson, and six others.
70. BDV's September Easy Chair, *Harper's* 189/4, was about Title V of the Hatch-Connally Act, forbidding distribution in the armed services of any books that might be construed as politically activist.
71. All BDV typewriters, Royal office models and Smith-Corona portables, had elite type.
72. *Harper's* 189/3 (August).

73. BDV was working on what became *Mountain Time*, published in book form in 1947; in 1944 he decided that the book would be a John August novel, but after KS's death he changed his mind, and the book appeared serially in *Collier's* 117/5–9 (2 February–2 March 1946) under his own name. *Mountain Time* had been suggested as a title by Sterne several years earlier; a working title that BDV abandoned was *Everybody Got to Walk*.
74. *The Loom of Language* by Frederick S. Bodmer, 1944.

APPENDIX A

THE BUCOLICS OF DECADENCE

or Frank Merriwell among the Common People

In 1934, in response to Sterne's eager suggestions, DeVoto began writing this long memoir about his years in Ogden after the Great War, rather as though he were writing and assembling installments of an actual but sometimes fanciful autobiography. He kept at it into 1935.

Only one copy of this book has been printed, of which this is the first. The type is Remington Elite; the impression is on Goldenrod Bond.

Press of the [*illegible*], Lincoln, Massachusetts, from time to time.

PREFACE

My dear Forsythe—that is to say, dear Kate:[1]

Henry Reck brought some vodka down from Dartmouth, though just what the association of vodka and Dartmouth could turn out to be is one of the problems whose solution is essentially metaphysical and so beyond my aspiration. Well, vodka and I have an acquaintance of some standing and, musing over its involuted beginning, I found myself realizing that I got my dates scrambled a fortnight ago. The road-building and the Bakersfield episodes were of 1919, whereas the Raft River Valley and the ranch at which I acquired a permanent and insuperable phobia for mutton was of the summer of 1922.[2] Art was affronted by that confusion and, vodka being what it is, I felt very sad. Sad but determined to iron out the crimp. (For a variety of reasons, I think I should explain that, at this moment, I am ponderably considering what I had hitherto left of the vodka.) So I found myself putting together the pieces of Those Two

Years.[3] A curious time. Franklin Roosevelt had not yet met up with polio[4], Apostle Smoot[5] whom I once worked for was appointing Warren Gamaliel Harding to the Presidency of Utopia and Normalcy was as yet uncoined, and I was younger, there was a dance called the Maxixe and F. Scott Fitzgerald was considered a philosopher, Hoke Smith's name was still recognizable, the renaissance of American poetry was beginning to fade a little, I had not yet met Skinny Browning, dropping in at Spargo's Book Store I bought the only known first edition of Main Street, the papers were talking of a buyers' strike, and the House of Morgan, having gone off a war basis, was sending emissaries to ask German municipalities to borrow money. So I went into politics.

That ought to do for preface. I cannot, at the moment, foresee the time-lapse of these pages. They begin in June 1920, and at the utmost they cannot extend past May 1922, if they manage to get that far. Youth, you will remember, was in revolt, being lost, and though you had done with dolls you could not yet be nubile, and there are resplendent truths, historical and spiritual, which no doubt will be displayed in this interlude from the history of the Grand Army of the Republic.[6]

[*handwritten*]

If the narrative strays over areas hitherto covered in whole or in part, bear with it for continuity's dia[*illegible*]

CAST

(Blanks to be filled in later, as a capricious but eventually dependable memory may supply them.)

Principals

Louis Jesse Holther, attorney, newly fledged from the University of Michigan Law School; later, Judge of the Juvenile Court; later still, member of the lower house, Utah State Legislature.

Ensign Herrick, optician; later, Commander Herman Baker Post #9 of Utah, the American Legion.

Robert Major, Principal of the Riverdale School, Weber County; producer of amateur dramatics; later, goat.

Wendell Thomas Fitzgerald, first year man, law school aforesaid; sidekick.

Jack Littlefield, adjutant Herman Baker Post; adjutant Ogden Police Department.

Mary ________ Littlefield, his wife and slavedriver, believed to be wife in name only, proprietor of a shoe store.

__________ Nelson, ex-aviator; secretary to the Governor.

Frank Merriwell, Harvard '20 (as of '18), radical agitator; later, patriot and head of Americanization work in Utah.

Supernumerary actors:

Andrew Kasius, henchman; younger brother of Pete Kasius, friend to Merriwell.

Wade Johnson, City Attorney, Ogden.

Karl Hopkins, Superintendent, Ogden City Schools.

__________ __________, ex-member First Division, AEF; sgt. of Ogden Police.

Ted Littlefield, malcontent, hardboiled brother of Jack, above.

Godfrey Matthews, successor to Merriwell on Ogden *Standard-Examiner*; also, minister, First Congregational Church.

Archibald Moyes, Vice-Commander, Herman Baker Post (1920); brother to Mabel, Merriwell's first love.

Katharine, otherwise Katie, the Brewer's Daughter.

Irene, most genteel, from Sangamon County, teacher of English, Ogden High School.

Jessie, an alternate.

Charles J. Torongo, manufacturing optician, who claimed his name used to be Torongeau.

J. Ray Ward, politician; later United States Marshal in Utah; later still, Commissioner of Public Safety, Ogden.

Many lawyers, several bankers, assorted business men, a good many cops, several socialists and union officials, a few I.W.W., a number of so to speak doctors, two chiropractors, one Christian Science practitioner, school teachers, committeemen, Governor Mabey,[7] Mayor Francis, assorted women of various strata, several flappers, a blonde who knew how to shoot, Captain of Battery B Field Artillery, a broker's clerk, John Spargo and Fred Scriven of Spargo's Book Store, prohibition enforcement agents, a flying squadron from the Dept of Justice, and several hundred heroes.

⁜⁜

Between December 1918, when I ceased to be Lt. Inf., U.S.A., and September 1919, when I returned to Harvard, I learned one principle quite thoroughly: it's nice to know where your next plate of beans is coming from. The principle mastered, I have never departed from it.

In June 1920, I was offered a fellowship of $1000 good for any university in Belgium. I was too broke and too much in debt, having borrowed money for that last year, to take the offer. Harvard conferred the A.B. cum laude on me, in absentia since I was in New York, and elected me to Phi Beta Kappa. Several friends at once sent me interlinear Old Testaments, and I mailed in, from Ogden by then, my last ten dollars for a key, thinking it would make a nice decoration for the supernormal breast of the Brewer's Daughter. Too bad not to have gone to Louvain before the restoration.[8]... I went to New York, bearing letters from Byron Hurlbut. Awe comes over me and I recall that (a) Fabian Franklin, of a reactionary sheet then in existence, (b) Oswald Garrison Villard, and (c) Gay, then of the *Post*, offered me, or gave signs of offering me, jobs.[9] We can say this much for Katie, she kept me from being a liberal journalist. My career on *The Nation* was conducted from the Rocky Mts and consisted of some anonymous about Reed Smoot and some oh most ruthless book reviews, you know the kind, whatever changes the reviews in *The Nation* are the same per omnia saeculorum.[10] But New York could not buy me for I was experiencing a certain congestion and Katy had left for home, after a year at one of those schools that undertake to sandpaper the edges from the most vulgar but most wealthy.

An ignominious note at the very beginning: the truth is that Katie remained virgin of me.... I had met her during some few weeks in Ogden the year before, when I came home to sweat some malaria out of me and eat occasionally. I helped found the Ogden University Club, took part in an amateur show, and met Katy. She was tall and overblown; she was seventeen, then, claimed to be twenty, and had the build of a woman of thirty. But my God, how good-looking she was—for a while. In a year or two she got fat, very fat. It was a characteristic of her family to mature early; Fitz (see Cast) once spent an evening heavily necking (it was the necking era) her sister and nearly committed hara-kiri when I told him the child's age, which was thirteen. Katie's family were German, brewers and sugar-manufacturers, the most inconceivable of nouveaux riches, and they lived in an inconceivable house, called a mansion in our folkways, and ran about a dozen cars, and gave parties, and Katy was later married with a high-church Episcopalian ceremony... on the tennis court. She was pretty, more or less the way a brood mare is, and she had Gifts. She played the piano, and she Read Aloud. Most poignantly, I can remember her reading a war poem called "The Rouge Bouquet"—and don't correct the French, dear. "Trees" was another one.[11]

So, in June, 1920, I was in Ogden again and broke, oh, completely broke, a Harvard Phi Bete and a bright young man.... That's probably why my most deep-seated phobia is bright young men.... Also, I was sick. I didn't know it but I was: I was slowly acquiring an ailment which, just a year later, knocked the props out from under me, one from which, to judge by occasional comments in the press, I have not yet recovered. I thought I was going to write a novel. I began it, and presently I saw I didn't have anything to say and so, with the best literary judgement I have ever displayed, I tore it up. And, let me repeat, I was broke. I had been, at various times in my past, a machinist's helper, a reporter, a city editor, a cowboy, a baggage smasher, a deputy county clerk, a roadmaker, a car-icer, a timekeeper, a dishwasher, a hop-gatherer, a rimmer at a canning factory, a truck-gardener, a sprinkler-driver, a pole-erector, a trouble-shooter for a gas company, and at least a dozen other forms of migratory laborer. The Reed Hotel offered me a place as night-clerk, but I was still conscious of the Phi Bete key and turned it down; a week later, when I reconsidered, the place had been filled.[12] I couldn't go back to the *Standard-Examiner*, having had unpleasantnesses, and though I could have gone back to the Salt Lake *Tribune* or the *Rocky Mt News,* both of which I had once adorned, I seemed to be staying in Ogden, at least until the matter of Katy was settled.[13] When that was settled, I didn't have the price of fare out of town. Then Hopkins, the Superintendent of Schools, offered me a job teaching American history at the high school, come September. In those days I had an intense loathing of pedagogy and had sworn never to embrace it, but I embraced it with almost obscene relief. From September on I could eat. See first paragraph above.

Well, in July I made my play and lost it, for reasons never quite clear to my ego, and thenceforth the Brewer's Daughter lapsed. She was just older than the flapper, the new product of post-war America, and I began to investigate the flapper. I liked the results of the investigation. I used to gather in three or four of them at a time and just sit and listen to them. It was a good product, I'm sorry the flapper has gone, and I'm glad that I did a portrait of one of them—Jane, in The Crooked Mile, though God forbid that I should turn back to it and see how it reads in 1934. They were nice girls, young as hell and active—I used to watch them turn cartwheels with my chin dropping. And they chattered, and I liked chatter, and they danced marvelously, and I liked dancing, and they had figures like fourteen year old boys, nature being on the very verge of F. Scott Fitzgerald, and one of them was named Florence and another Afton and another Myra,* and I can't remember them or anything about them except that they were the monstrous paradox of gayety in that God-awful town.... My generation, the pre-war girl, was as dead already as the Gibson girl, as the Godey girl.[14] In the class of 1914, O.H.S., there had been three girls who each had a pair of silk stockings.

In July also I got a job as secretary to the Weber County Democratic Committee at $150 a month and any takings. It being obviously a Republican year, there were few takings. I could not speak in public (here the horns sound a theme), but I didn't need to, except occasionally as extempore introducer. I organized, I publicized, I made deals, I kept records. When Our Candidate, Jimmy Cox, came to Utah, I traveled across the state with him, he was (honoris causa)[15] a Phi Bete brother and we got stinkingly drunk, some fifty of us on that special train three times a day for nearly a week. It

* [*handwritten:*] So was Phyllis McGinley, now given to remembering her flapperhood in *New Yorker* verse. Phyllis nearly cost me a big toe once. Maybe the toe will get into this saga.

was discovered, four hours before legal time-limit, that a certain precinct down among the tules and the alkali had returned no organization but had some campaign funds allotted to it. A friend and I drove frantically out into the tules, woke up one Sorenson whose name was on our list as a precinct leader, organized the district and split the allotment three ways. Later we found that we had the wrong Sorenson, that our man was the Mormon Bishop and so a Republican, but he made no protest and neither did my committee. Then Jess Holther wanted the Republican nomination as county attorney, on his war record, and I went into that campaign too, and it was locally supposed that young DeVoto, being good enough to deal with two parties, would probably make a politician sometime. But Jess was a renegade Mormon and the church would have none of him. He wanted to get married, too, and had to put it off for a year. We wired to Marie, in Michigan, "Busted by Bishops" with a poetic quotation, and got drunk at Republican headquarters and then went over to my headquarters and made socialistic remarks at a speaker who was also drunk. And so on. In November, I was a Democratic judge of election and voted for Parley P. Christiansen, the Farmer-Labor candidate, and the Democrats were snowed under and Chas. Mabey, war veteran, was Governor of Utah, vice Simon Bamberger, and I was out of a job again.[16]

In July also I made a mistake.... Now the moral I didn't learn then was that politics is one thing but sociology is something else. Politics gave a good God damn what I did, but politics was over for Democrats on Election Day.... The mistake was quite easy. The University Club held its first Annual Banquet and asked its charter member, the Phi Bete from Harvard, to make a speech, and I made a speech. I couldn't make speeches and it was a lousy one at that. All I can remember is that I quoted Jefferson's Second Inaugural and said that we ought to let Debs and the political prisoners out of jail and repeal the ~~Lusk laws~~ Espionage Act and let the N Y socialists take their seats—a lot of platitudes that would have been laughed at as primer stuff anywhere but on Main Street.[17] But, quite innocently, I was a Bolshevik.... The Bolsheviks, dear, were what the pro-Germans of a few years before had turned into, what the Communists are now, or, if you prefer, the Nazis.... Old Simon Bamberger stood up and denounced me and Congressman Howell made a campaign speech and my brethren of the press agreed for my sake not to mention it, and the next day word went out to the mothers of Ogden and Hopkins came round to me and said there'd been a meeting of the Board of Education and he had to cancel my job at the high school.[18] Except at Democratic headquarters I was blacklisted, and it stuck. I was a radical, an agitator, a Bolshevik, and the purity of the American home and home industries had to be protected, and there was no place in the state where I could have got a job, except the one I had till Election Day. Quite literally, I was a dangerous person in Ogden from that night on. I was sap enough to enjoy the *enfant terrible* reputation but, the oboe carries the melody, I was in debt and would be broke again when Election Day came.

By September party funds were so low that my salary was cut to fifty a month, and part of that promised. In October my best friend died in France—though that doesn't belong to this narrative.[19] In October also I was getting more than apprehensive about that plate of beans. One night I was sipping white mule in Jess Holther's law office, where he had a shiny new desk, a set of that cumulative *Reporter* that young lawyers buy, and a lot of correspondence from the American Legion.[20] Jess had been Commander for the Herman Baker Post #9 of Utah until he resigned to enter the primaries for county attorney. For the Preamble of the American Legion Constitution forever separates the Legion from politics. Jess's connection with the Legion had caused me much ribald amusement, for I had been offered, remember, a job on *The Nation*, and was well outfitted with the best ideas, the very best ones. He had often suggested that I join the Post. I'd let him know why not with the greatest detail.

Jess was a short, curly-haired, blondish chap who had got out of law school just in time to join the Army. One of the half-dozen intelligent people in Ogden and by no means overburdened with that intelligence—shrewd and certain to be a good lawyer (later on, he made big money as the unofficial defender of all liquor-law violators in Weber County), with political aspirations, and a great yen to marry Marie. He did that, as the narrative will show, and it was even a worse mistake than my University Club speech. Jess was an authentic hero. At least, he had ridden a motorcycle within range of German howitzers once and had got a piece of shrapnel through his puttee. He jumped off, yanked his puttee off, found a slight scratch, deepened it with his pocket knife, rubbed dirt into it, and demanded a wound stripe, but the bastards turned him down.... Not exactly a simple mind, but not a complex one, sunny and jovial, a good pianist, energetic, full of amusing anecdotes, and possessed of that American college-boy attribute, the Sense of Loyalty.... Some day I intend to make a study of the University of Michigan, as a contribution to American sociology.

I should put it on the record, too, that Fitz was taking a year out from law school to make some money, so he could finish up. He was teaching eighth-grade English at a Junior High School.

Over a glass of white mule, Jess said, "Come on, Benny, join the Legion." I had a vision. I saw a way to get back enough respectability to hold a job in Ogden. I said, "OK, Jess, I will."

The next day I was a member of Herman Baker Post #9 of Utah, American Legion. [*handwritten: (More)*]

II

"Jess," our hero said, ""we've got to get some fun out of this Legion set-up, Or Else."

The study of Pareto has taught me the mechanics of dependent variables and has permanently shot the time-sense out of all my narratives. Please do not expect a coherent, progressive chronology in these memoirs. To impose one would obscure the beautifully chaste order of events and make it seem chaotic, which it wasn't in the least. Some generalizations, and then we must take up the variables independently.... It is well to say, too, that the thing was possible only because this was October, 1920. A year later, perhaps even six months later, the public could not have been made to cooperate so successfully; but ideas and emotions were in a state of very loose flux, especially ideas about the soldier vote and the homogeneity of the ex-soldiers. Again, one portion of me has always been a historian and less than six months before I had written a thesis for Edward Channing on the G.O.P. and the Bloody Shirt.[21] Furthermore, although I had been one of the Harvard Liberals, God bless them, I may say that, following a considerable experience as an infantry officer, I had few illusions about the great democracy.

In October, 1920, the Herman Baker Post had declined from the hearty, buddy-like enthusiasm of its founding and gave every evidence of imminent decease. It met weekly and did nothing but look sheepish, the buddies being self-conscious about parliamentary procedure and a little hesitant to drink white mule and shoot craps in the swell club rooms they rented, first from the University Club, later from the International Order of Odd Fellows. Twenty was about the average attendance, there weren't as many as fifty there till election night, and the entire effect was sleazy, blowsy, indeterminate and most, most dull. Let's not linger on the personnel. They were two-fifths Mormons, four-fifths drafted men, and five-fifths boobs. There was a sprinkling of AEF-ers and even a few heroes—or at least Military Cross and Croix de Guerre men. The average I.Q. must have been about oh-point-oh-four, but that of course is axiomatic. Any gathering, Lord Chesterfield says, is mob and may, nay must be treated as mob.[22] The Post had an enrolled membership of about two hundred. Weber County contained several hundred other heroes who hadn't enrolled. All the bum lawyers, bum doctors, bum insurance salesmen, bum dentists, etc., had ipso facto or per se joined. It was a silly, useless, bewildered and inert organization. It had never done anything and it showed no capability and no intention of doing anything.

But, suddenly realized, it was a potential instrument. I should point out that my motives were absolutely pure, they were those of the Artist. All I could get in the way of respectability I had already got by joining. It was then and remained for some months just exactly nothing, since no one yet dared to give me a job. So that all I expected or could get was just amusement. Jess, of course, was less of an artist. He wanted political jobs. Let me say right now, he got them. He was juvenile Judge within four months and he was a member of the Legislature later on, as a direct result of our efforts but after I had passed from the picture.... I don't know which of us first saw that we had something in the Herman Baker Post; probably it was a gradual and mutual fantasy, but unquestionably it began to clothe itself with reality because I knew about the Bloody Shirt. We were going to get hold of the Post. We were going to have a hell of a lot of fun with it. And we were going to make use of it. We were, in short, going to be bosses and have a machine.

We worked well together. Jess made an excellent executive and was fine for organization and detail. My forte was, at once, the hand that works the wires, and almost at once, the resplendent demagogue, the swayer of crowds, the waver of the Bloody Shirt. As for plans, strategy and divertissements, we were both good. First, however, I had to learn to be a demagogue. Jess and I began to attend meetings and to make speeches. I had to learn that art—and I want to tell you, I applied myself to it with a diligence that I wish I could summon up for the lesser occupations of these days. I omit the process—which was only to work on Arch Moyes, who had succeeded Jess as Commander, to create a Bureau of Legion Speakers, & make me the Bureau, and then get out and soap-box wherever a Legionnaire was wanted or could be shoe-horned in. I soon learned the art: I soon learned that the only trouble with me had been that I was trying to make intelligent speeches. Once I understood that I climbed far and fast. In six weeks I was known as an orator, and I'm not one to say that the reputation was undeserved. This is a leit-motif.

I commanded Andy Kasius and Fitz to join the Post and told them they were part of a machine. That was all right with them and we made them very useful indeed. Our first step was to announce that we had a machine. That's the basic principle of politics anyway.... And has been proved by the American Legion on a national scale. There was no soldier vote. There was no demand for a bonus. There was no chance that a bonus could be put over. Until some wise guys announced the contrary of those propositions. Then his propositions at once became self-demonstrating.... We said we had a machine and at once we had a machine. Word got out that the Holther-DeVoto machine was going to do things with the Post. Attendance perked up. I began to crowd the *Standard-Examiner*. My difficulties had been with Frank Francis, the editor and now Mayor of Ogden, not with the staff, who were friends of mine and mostly heroes. I signed up those who did not already belong to the Post, and the paper began to carry stories and editorials about the renewed activity of the heroes, what they promised for the fair city of Ogden, and what a force in social betterment and control they should be. The old hooey, already plenty familiar elsewhere but new in Ogden, that the heroes had saved the nation and should now take charge of it.

Our ultimate objective was, of course, the annual election of officers at the end of December, but we had several others on the way to it. We very much needed to get some official arrangements through at once. This was no job. Arch Moyes was the brother of my first love, a dumb, hot-tempered windbag who enormously valued the minute spotlight that fell on him as Commander. He wanted to succeed himself. I told him that the machine would put him through, and from that time on I controlled appointments. It was essential to get the glory of an activity I had proposed and had adopted, a big Post show which would soon go into rehearsal. Arch appointed Ensign Herrick, the man we had selected as our candidate, as business manager of the show and me as something else, I've forgotten what, publicity manager no doubt. The show was to be one of our main instruments of advance. We had to take Bob Major as director, since he was the only person in the Post who pretended to be in that profession. Bob was destined to provide most of our amusement and most of our trouble during the next year, but we didn't know that.

Next we staged a highly important act. In weekly orations I was now thundering the importance of increasing our membership. The Herman Baker Post was the herald of the new day and easily the most important feature of life in Ogden—it ought therefore to go out and gather in all the available heroes. I demanded a membership drive, the Post hurrahed, and Arch named Jess and me to conduct it. We put on a honey. The *Standard-Examiner* gave us thousands of inches, we held mass meetings night after night, I addressed lodges, benevolent societies, the commercial clubs, churches, young people's associations. And, this early, I did something that remains in my memory one of the greatest solaces of the whole episode. It was already supposed that the Legion was a creature of the capitalist exploitation, that it necessarily had a feud with the laboring man, and that it would scab and do special police work in all labor disturbances. Ogden, be it known, has always been a radical labor town. It was a focus of disturbance several times in the Nineties, some of my earliest memories of gore relate to the Switchmen's Strike of 1907, and there are a good many yarns still to be told of the I.W.W. there. So I buttered the A.F. of L. council, told them that the Legion was forbidden to engage in politics and represented the common man with almost maudlin sympathy for labor, and began to make speeches to labor unions. Finally, one noon-hour, I went down to the S.P. shops and sang my song to a mass meeting of over a thousand extremely hard-boiled machinists, switchmen, firemen, etc. Extremely hard-boiled: I still dampen my hat-band when I remember that meeting. But I pulled it off and even got a few converts from that crowd.... Meanwhile our committee had worked up a membership organization. We divided the county off into districts and elected members of the Post to canvass each district. We came into the actual week of our drive with all blow-holes open and a nigger on the safety valve, the press whooping it up, a dazzled national headquarters sending out a flying squadron from, I think, Kansas City, and all the leading apostles of business and all the pulpits in Ogden tying their whistles open for us.[23] In that week we got about four hundred new members and got dues from most of our lapsed membership. It was now known at national headquarters that the Herman Baker Post #9 of Utah was the livest in the West and that Buddies Holther and DeVoto were gents of polish and persuasion. I found myself appointed to the Legion's National Speakers' Bureau and to a resoundingly named committee which some of the Leaders, I think chiefly Hanford MacNider and T. Roosevelt, Jr., were quietly converting into a propaganda machine.[24] . . . No one noticed that our committee's organization was thoughtfully worked out. For purposes of the membership drive we had districted Weber County according to the voting precincts. In each precinct we now had a permanent committee. And every committee was bound to the Holther-DeVoto machine by conviction, performance and expectation.

We had selected Ensign Herrick to head our slate at the elections. Ensign was an optician. He had been in the AEF, he was dumb and loyal and officially honest but certain to be malleable, most of all he had worked hard for the Post. In fact he was the only person in the Post who had done anything for it till we took up the job. It was quite certain that he would be elected Commander in the natural course of events. In the art of politics you choose the candidate certain to win, if there is one, and then gloriously put him over at the last minute, in spite of all the bloody devils of corruption, decay, opposition and the kept press. We called him in one night and told him that we'd like to see him Commander, that we thought he had a chance to win if we threw our support to him, that we'd go to bat for him and give him our all. He loved it, and whatever else we might have to deal with, from that moment on we could count on Ensign. We did and we were always right.

One of my publicity devices might be mentioned here. Jack Littlefield, of whom more in a moment, didn't like a forthcoming visit of some traitorous and unspeakable Huns, who were coming to collect funds for the German orphans. We hadn't yet incorporated Jack into the machine, but by now we could have smothered him. I made an appraisal. Could we get more by raising hell over the Huns or by somehow associating ourselves with them? I finally decided on the latter, and the press backed me up. In an interview I, who as yet held no office in the Post, told Ogden that the Post had decided to let the Germans speak. The Legion, I said, had no quarrel with the German babies. We didn't care to deny milk to the most culpable child of the most culpable late enemy that existed. It was our decision that the Huns could speak in Ogden. . . . Observe that phraseology. I had already found it not only possible but extremely desirable and effective to talk that way. The most blatant moral of these memoirs is just that: if you talk that way, people will accept it as OK. I was letting it be known that there were some things that the Post could dictate in Ogden. Ogden agreed. That was quite right and proper.... But, I said, in order to make sure that the Huns didn't secrete any poison, in order to prevent propaganda and to keep the menace of righteousness over their heads the Post would send an official committee to the meeting. We did. We dressed up some twenty-five heroes in their uniforms, put Jack in charge of them, and sent them to the meeting, where they sat in the first row, scaring hell out of the poor damn speakers and making exactly the right impression on the audience at large. It was thus made clear that the Post had the right of review.

The incident made clear that we'd better take Jack Littlefield along with us, since he was the only hero who had made any opposition to our conduct or who had tried to do anything on his own. Jack was adjutant of the Ogden police, a short, red-headed Irishman, a fire-eater, ignorant, fanatical, shrewd, and, fortunately, corruptible. Take that last adjective away, present the fierce and honest dumb-bell, and you have what is the worst obstacle to smooth politics. An honest man without brains is what gums up the works every so often—this is the unanimous teaching of all machine politics, and when, years later, my studies revealed that by analysis, I understood it. Jack had a brother, Ted, who answered the description. When a wave of reform threw us out, it was Ted who rode the wave to control of Herman Baker Post.... Well, we could use Jack. We offered him the adjutant's job—the adjutant is secretary-treasurer. He liked the glory it promised, but glory in itself wasn't enough. So we told him that when we got into control the adjutant would draw a salary. As yet there was nothing in the treasury to pay it from, but we promised to take care of that. We did. So we had an invaluable accession to the machine. We now had the inside track with the police department. We had a fire-eater who was too dumb to know what he was being used for and whom we could always turn loose on a job we didn't care to do ourselves, we had police sanction, we had first claim on all confiscated liquor, we had the privilege of illegality, and, it soon proved, we had a man greatly gifted in getting action on back-pay, travel pay, compensation, and all the other privileges that Congress was giving to the heroes.

I was learning my stuff. Ogden has some kind of folk festival, I forget what. A street carnival came to town. A street carnival, dear, is a front of concessions and performances to cover the activity of gambling games, nice careful games in which all the numbers are 00. The first night the Ogden police raided it and shut it up. Fifteen minutes later the managers had been referred to me by Jack Littlefield. Jack, Jess, and I got fifty dollars apiece and, for five hundred dollars paid into the treasury, the Post signed an alliance with the carnival. Receipts, it was understood, would go into the benevolent and development fund of the heroes. Word went out in the carnival business.

At this moment, very sub rosa, we were having a ticklish time with the Legion show, but that had better be told separately—enough to say here that for a time I thought we were going to enter on our administration by presenting the Post with an $8000 debt. But we didn't.... The campaign was now in full swing. We had selected our list of officers and we had dropped Arch Moyes. I told him simply that we found he wouldn't do. He was a dimwit, he didn't even object, he simply hated me like hell, as quite a few were beginning to do. But I moved the purchase of a teakwood gavel mounted in silver and properly inscribed and had it presented to him, in fact had myself named to present it to him, on the night his term ended.

Election night was most amusing. About five hundred heroes showed up, all with their coats curried and their hair slicked back, ready to become a social force. Jack had got us some fairly presentable liquor—not as presentable as later on when we made terms with the federal officers—and we doled it out in the best places. Arch was black and lugubrious in the chair, still hoping that common decency would strike us down and a great wave of virtuous appreciation would sweep him back into office. There were a lot of minor and sporadic candidacies to which we intended to pay no attention whatever. We had at least seventy-five sworn upholders, and that was as good as five hundred. Another principle of politics: make the organization as small as possible, and let who will believe that he is part of it. At no time did we have to consider more than a dozen people—the rest simply added themselves to us of their own will.... Most of all, we were going to use oratory—my oratory. Our policy was to keep Jess, who was to reap the political reward, completely in the background, to keep me under the spotlight always so that I could constantly be in a position to take charge, and scrupulously avoid offices and responsibilities in the Post. We worked from behind. Well, Arch declared the meeting open for nominations for Commander.... Chesterfield is gospel: all gatherings are mob. The heroes became acutely self-conscious. Various of them stumbled to their feet and mumbled various nominations, with painful pauses in between and five hundred heroes staring at the floor. This went on until someone moved that the nominations be closed, then I got up, said not yet, please, and launched into an effort. Not for nothing had I played round the conventions and then gone out and learned my stuff. In thirty seconds five hundred heroes were hanging on my utterance. I strode about yelling and waving my fists. I fought the Marne and St. Mihiel and the Argonne.[25] I crushed the Hun, I challenged the Bolsheviks, I read the dawn of hope for the American hero in the sky and the national treasury. For about fifteen minutes.... The principle is simple. Pareto calls it argument by accord of sentiments. You say that the Hun must be crushed or the Democracy was saved. Then you name your candidate. At once he becomes the man who saved democracy and will crush the Hun.... In a full-organ burst I alluded to the enormous earlier services of My Candidate, begged that he be given a chance to serve more fully, and named him—that faithful servant of Herman Baker Post, that staunch member of the AEF, that plumed knight of democracy and the Legion, Buddy

Ensign Herrick.[26] We had thoughtfully distributed people about the hall to provide applause. They weren't needed. Five hundred heroes stood up and yelled. For about five minutes, our orator standing with arms folded on the rostrum and looking military and important. The cheering died out, I bowed and sat down. From the middle of the hall Fitz demanded the floor. He got it, he moved that the election of Buddy Herrick be carried by acclamation. There was one roar and it was so carried.

At once we had an object lesson: never expend more effort than the situation requires or you'll get into trouble. There was really no need of that purple burst. I should have reserved it for another time—concentrating right now on the important thing, the election, and getting that done very simply, as it could have been. Ensign was no sooner elected by acclamation than some long-ear from the sticks who had been moved to ecstasy by my shirt-waving got up and nominated me for vice-commander. That was immediately carried by acclamation too. And it simply wouldn't do. We had a Mormon bishop slated for vice-commander, very thoughtfully, and our policy was to stay out of office. I had to rush back to the platform and throw myself on the mercy of the audience. I did not aspire to lead, I said, but only to serve. Some less important office, perhaps, or this office at some later time, but, please, let me be one of the rank and file, let me serve as a private, let me stay on the sidelines and work in dungarees for the greater glory of the Post. Jess moved the reconsideration of the election, Andy Kasius hastily got up and nominated our bishop, Fitz made the set speech he had been appointed to, and the machine resumed operations.

We carried our slate, of course, with one exception. As soon as Herrick was in, our boys let more liquor loose. Fitz got very jingled almost at once. Someone had buttonholed Jess and me and taken us into the anteroom, the first application for favors. When we came back Fitz, on the platform, was drunkenly leading three cheers for DeVoto. It had occurred to him that poetry would be served by having me made chaplain, and he had done it. It was obviously impossible to decline a second election. I made my third speech of the evening.

We had a column on the front page of every paper in the state next day and a lot of columns in the back of the S-E. In an ecstasy of gratitude for the triumph of her husband, our new Commander's wife made proffer to me of her person. I declined and when the offer was extended to Jess, I pointed out that politics and sex were a damn poor mixture. That was a great truth, and we had plenty of demonstration of it later on. Meanwhile the Holther-DeVoto machine had taken over the Post, the police department delivered a case of Canadian Club to me by motorcycle, and I was chaplain.

[*handwritten:*] more

[*handwritten:*] Next issue: the unpredictable career of a Man of God

III

Historians invariably like to speculate about if's. It is amusing to try to dope out what would have happened to me if I had stuck to a single-minded utilization of the Legion. It is a fair assumption that I should have got as far in it as I have in the alternative careers of pedagogy and beautiful letters; that is, I probably could have made a comfortable living in it. Certainly I have shown more talent for politics than I have shown for either of its substitutes. The Holther-DeVoto machine could have controlled the State Legion within two years and the Intermountain Department within three—that is amply shown by the facts. That would have meant a minor national office for me by 1924 at the latest. By now I might easily have been National Commander—but probably wouldn't have chosen to be. The plain teaching of our experience was that the perquisites of office are much better than office. Unquestionably by now one or the other major party would have been taking care of me. I know a good many people who lacked my opportunities and are being taken care of. Presumably, if I had chosen honors, I could be beginning to get them by now. Hanford MacNider has been minister to Canada, and of his original group a good many have had territorial governorships, under-secretaryships, etc. Coming up with the next younger wave, I should probably be in that class now.

There was never any question of that. Without quite phrasing our objectives, we understood that we would make a single and sustained play in the Post and let it go at that. What we wanted was a seat in the Legislature for Jess and as much amusement for both of us as possible. It became clear that amusement would be best secured by absolute dictatorship of the Post. If we played State politics we should have to let others in, make deals, unquestionably do things we didn't want to do, and in general dilute the leadership and so the pleasure. We knew that we could absolutely control the Post for one year and we thought we could extend that control for one more year but not, if we kept it absolute, beyond that. The reform wave must always be counted on, and the only way to control it is to make a deal with it. Within the Post we didn't care to make deals. We would play it down the middle of the board as hard and as long as we could, then we would quit.

We had, of course, to engage in State and Department Legion activities. We needed support from outside and we needed the channels and privileges of the organization. We had learned one lesson quite well, and so we told the State and Department that we were a power to be taken into account and we were taken into account. When the State convention occurred at Provo in June, the Post sent as its official delegation Herrick, Jack Littlefield, Jess, Fitz, Andy Kasius, and me. At the convention I orated and Jess and I played politics behind the scenes. The Salt Lake delegation had the most votes, representing the largest membership, and so we told them that our machine would let them elect any candidates they pleased, on terms agreeable to us. That, dear, is politics and you must memorize the principle: always tell the boys that what is bound to happen is the program you have decided to put through. We disdained State offices but we demanded two places on the Executive Committee, appointed by the State Commander, and we would have it understood that our voice counted when the officers wanted to do anything. Two places on the Executive Committee was twice as many as any post was entitled to. We got them. You are permitted to guess who they were. So I nominated the commander of the Salt Lake Post for State Commander and he was elected, with a secure belief that I had mightily contributed to that end. We were sitting pretty in the State. We played the same hand next month in the Department.

Before we go back to January, the personal note. I was, without knowing what was up, getting sicker. The onset of the psychoneuroses is very much like that which you once described for tuberculosis. Especially in relation to alcohol. Herrick was a tank and I was becoming one. I had at my disposal everything that the police confiscated and presently, when I had Jack put through a spurious claim for travel pay, everything that the federal boys got. As for instance. Two chains of flour mills had been battling. One finally won, swooped down and merged all the flour mills in Ogden and put up some enormous elevators and then, to celebrate the occasion, had a lot of dignitaries from all the West in to a big party. They brought in an enormous assortment of wonderful liquor from California in a box car. Because of the dignitaries, a lot of them governors and senators, they supposed they wouldn't have to have protection. The federal boys held otherwise and, the afternoon of the party, took over the box car. They sold it back at a good price but they took out some of the finest for themselves and telephoned me. I asked for half a case of champagne for social purposes and two cases of whisky for Jess and me. They said OK and I sent the sergeant of police whose name I haven't yet remembered over to make delivery, which he promptly made. Again, it was always possible to drop in on any dive on lower 25th Street and ask for what I wanted—the privilege of the police had been extended to the manipulators of the Post. So, subject to queer states of mind that I didn't understand, losing weight, harassed by quite uninterpretable developments in myself, I was doing a lot of drinking. On the first of December I went to work at John Spargo's book and stationery store for a hundred dollars a month. In March, the Christmas rush and inventory over, I was let out and thereafter had no job for quite a while. Some days after our triumphant 4th of July, the ailment rose up and knocked me out. I was completely incapacitated till September, and effectively crippled for two years. But I had a job again in November, going back to the book store, and in December the triumphant solution of the Blackmail Plot gave me a better job, as the narrative will show.[27] Finally, in May 1922, as a proud gesture of the defeated boss, I forced my appointment as director of Americanization work in Utah. It was largely a sinecure but not quite, and since I was sick again, I resigned almost at once.

The resurgence of the G.O.P. had swept into office one Chas. W. Mabey as Governor of Utah and one Ray Ward as Commissioner of Public Safety in Ogden. Both were heroes and Ward had been captain of a National Guard battery that had contained a number of our boys. Mabey was a good politician but Ward was just a hack, so destitute that he had to wangle a two months' appointment as U. S. Marshal to keep him between election and Jan. 1st. He was just a boob and when we told him that we controlled the ex-service vote in Ogden and had swung it to him on his war record and would take it away from him if he didn't play ball, he played ball. Although Jack had supported another candidate, we made Ward keep him as police adjutant; and from then on we had any service we wanted from the city govt. Mabey was no fool but he wanted to keep on terms of fellowship with the ex-service votes and the State Legion made a deal with him, of which our part was the right to name his secretary. We named a wise guy named Nelson, an ex-aviator and pretty bright, as part of a complicated deal with the State organization. Nelson was very useful to us from that moment on. With Ward working for us and Mabey impressed, we then got to work on the Weber County Republican Committee. Jess had been beaten for the nomination for county attorney, but he had made campaign speeches and variously helped out. We told the Committee that we represented the ex-service vote, etc.—the old line. All things seemed to back us up and it was public knowledge that the Herman Baker Post was a power in politics. With Nelson giving us the inside dope from the Governor's office, with the county committee impressed, with Mabey favorable and Ward an open partisan, we soon got Jess appointed Juvenile Judge of Weber County. He was about 25 and his morals were nothing much and he wasn't married yet. It was, in the social interests, a lousy appointment. But it was good, and for us triumphant politics. In October neither of us was worth a cent in politics; in January we were sitting pretty.

It was both good politics and the kind of amusement we were looking for to make a show of power, and we did so at every opportunity. In orations and the public prints I was putting up a constant howl for the preferential treatment of heroes in public jobs. I soon found that we could actually dictate that policy in Ogden. We outfitted all the departments of the city with buddies and we took measurable strides toward enforcing the policy in private employment. For the public jobs and for mere straight work. Jack became a Post employment bureau. Where guile or force was required, I officiated. I couldn't have asked for anything for myself or the racket would have been shown up, but I could appear on behalf of someone else and represent the impersonal beauty of the heroes' cause. As a matter of plain fact, I was able to run a complete bluff many times. In business as in politics anytime anyone cared to say to hell with you we should have been quite helpless—shown up. But bluff, Zeitgeist, and the great principle of assertion combined—no one ever said to hell with you. I got a good many jobs for the buddies by simply telling the employer that he'd lose the Legion patronage if he didn't act white.

As for instance. The largest Gentile bank (non-Mormon) fired a hero who had been a kind of clerk. The hero went to Jack and Jack sent him to me. I had him find out how many members of the Post had accounts in the bank. Learning that it was something over a hundred, I forget how many, I went round to the cashier. I told him that he'd made a mistake in firing the hero. He said he hadn't. I said oh, yes, he had, for it was going to cost him something over a hundred accounts. He saw the light. The hero went back to work.... Good old hero. He's state inspector of banking now, and I suspect the lousiest inspector in the known world. As such, he lately sent me a check for seven percent of the $1200 I had on deposit there for my father when the bank failed four years ago.

Again, there was a brief flurry of alarm among the business men. Maybe the Post was getting too brash. This was the next autumn. They decided to announce independence of us and at the same time cash in on our efforts. We had invested a lot of money in plans for a big clean-up on Armistice Day—football game, dances, shows, carnivals, concessions, parades, advertising, etc. The Chamber of Commerce decided that Armistice Day wouldn't be a holiday—the merchants would keep open and rake in the coin we had prepared to corner for ourselves. I was now but a shadow of my oratorical self, but this was a challenge and it came at a bad time, for there was incipient revolt within the Post. DeVoto stormed to the hustings again, and the silver voice was good for one more cavalry charge. I invaded the Rotary, the Kiwanis, the Lions, the Optimists, the Engineers, half a dozen churches, and finally the C of C itself.[28] I turned the newspapers against their own bread and butter. I got declarations of astonishment and sorrow from the Governor and all other officials I could reach. I put on a ten days' heat and Armistice Day was declared a legal holiday and the Post made good on its investment and once more its power was vindicated.

As soon as our slate was inaugurated we equipped it with machinery to our complete satisfaction. Nothing whatever could happen, officially or even unofficially, that lacked our sanction. We did a beautiful job there, so beautiful that it saved our hides long after they should have been lost. And we went forward on our grandiose program of publicity, noise, and entertainment. Especially entertainment. I conceived that the lodges knew the common man—if they had rituals, then rituals were the right thing. That idea hadn't yet broken over the national organization—I probably led the country. So I wrote a ritual and drilled our officers, myself included, in it. It was a lovely thing. I know now that nothing is too thick for a mob and I frosted this ritual with some of the most gorgeous sentiments that have ever been expressed in bastard blank verse masquerading as prose.... Great gobs of it are now part of the official ritual, for the national organization heard of it, wrote in for a sample, and incorporated a good deal of my stuff.... We rehearsed it in secret until even Herrick, who was almost tongue-tied in public, knew his stuff. Then we unveiled it at a regular meeting. Just as we were ready to go, I discovered that the chap whom I had commissioned to get an urn hadn't got one. We had to have an urn. The climax of the service occurred when all the lights were switched off and a single beam was directed on a glistening urn on a black-cheesecloth-covered table at one side of the platform and the chaplain's sepulchral voice, rose out of the darkness in memory of the departed heroes. Liberally copied from the Book of Common Prayer and such parts of the Elks' eleven o'clock mystery as I could get my buddies to reveal to me. So here we were ready to begin our initial service and no urn. I was not appalled. I snatched up one of the Odd Fellows' beautiful, decorative, glistening and enormous brass gobboons, set it on the cheesecloth altar, and told the boys to shoot. We shot.

I had at first been furious at Fitz for conferring the chaplaincy on me, but it soon proved to be an excellent thing. In the first place it allowed me to sit on the rostrum and mutter directions to Herrick, who was an excellent wheel horse but had to be managed every minute. Also it allowed Herrick to give up the chair to me whenever the going got rough and we needed parliamentary devices and quick thinking. Also, it gave us a voice in the official circle, which he hadn't thought necessary but which became invaluable for putting over quick jobs between meetings. But most of all, it became the inexhaustible source of amusement. My official duties as chaplain of the Post are probably the richest memory I shall ever have.

I acquired a quasi-sacerdotal position in the town at large. A demand for my services set up among the churches and their subsidiary organizations. I was called upon to explain the spiritual side of the Legion movement to organizations like the Epworth League. Quite often I was asked to occupy a pulpit. At one time or another I spoke from every pulpit in Ogden except St. Joseph's and the Christian Science church. I was named to all the honorary boards of charity drives and similar activities.... Since I was never completely sober any more and seldom approximately sober, we had some amusing results.

And there was apparent a great spiritual growth in me. Already an expert flag- and shirt-waver, I now learned to wallop God for the sake of the mob. Probably my highest reach was Memorial Day, 1921. At ten o'clock I addressed a large congregation in Godfrey Matthews' (First Congregational) church, speaking most movingly about self-sacrifice and sweet and decorous is it pro patria mori. I cried a little myself from moment to moment. At noon I was to ride with the Mayor in an automobile in the parade. The heroes were marching together with the G.A.R., the Spanish War vets, the high school cadets, the Boy Scouts, the various auxiliary corps, and assorted organizations, including the Masons, the W.O.W., the switchmen's union, and the employees of the Pierce Canning Co.[29] Ensign and Jack and the other officers were with the heroes, but the chaplain rated the Mayor's automobile. About a quarter to twelve Fitz, on his way to the Post rendezvous, saw me striding down Washington Avenue. He took one look, saw the elongated, squirrel-hunter, 37-inch-stride that is still characteristic of my infrequent alcoholic moments, and decided that he couldn't parade that day. He grabbed hold of me and said, "For God's sake, Devote (that is the oldest of my nicknames), where did you get it this early?" (Fitz, I should have said long since, has a fanatical pride in doing things right. He loves to have all the details correct, no matter what they are, and he had a vision of my not being able to orate.) It was quite simple: after my church service I had gone looking for Herrick. Herrick had already left for the parade but his wife was home and to his wife I had long since meant one thing above all others: give the man a drink at once. She gave me several and now I was well primed. Fitz held me fast by the arm and led me to the Mayor's automobile. He got in beside me and held me erect all through the parade and kept jabbing me whenever my head started to fall. The parade ended at a Memorial Avenue of trees along one side of the Ogden Cemetery. This had been another of my ideas. The Post didn't pay for those trees—that was the city's privilege—but we had charge. We had named each box elder after one of the departed buddies, and we had secured a German cannon from the War Department, and now we were going to dedicate both trees and cannon. There was a platform, newly erected and covered with flags, and from that platform various ministers and the Mayor and the Post chaplain were going to address whoever cared to listen. And by estimate not less than fifteen thousand people crowded up to listen to us. Fitz was in despair when I went to sleep the moment the Presbyterian minister started his invocation. He couldn't rouse me at all during that prayer and though he did wake me while the Mayor was speaking I kept drifting off again. Poor Fitz had a bad hour, but he should have trusted his Leader. When the Mayor finished and the Mormon Apostle who had been allowed to act as toastmaster announced the chaplain of the Post, I strode forward, breaking out of Fitz's grasp, and began to orate. I hooked one arm over the Old Glory on the railing and though my feet kept sliding from under me I was anchored, and as long as I was anchored, I could talk. I want to tell you, I talked. It was simply beautiful. My mind was full of pinwheels and I couldn't see even the audience but I had one principle by heart, you can't lay it on too thick. That is the simple recipe of emotional oratory. It has to be damned thick before it can be good at all, and it can't, ever, in any circumstance, be too thick. I made it thick and I ran the scales soaring to height after height. I bellowed there in the sun for over an hour and it's quite true that women were fainting and strong men giving way to tears all through the fifteen thousand. It was a severe hour on Fitz. He was witnessing something very like a miracle, at least the perfections of an art with whose growth he was personally acquainted, but of all that crowd he alone knew the orator's condition and he was expecting me to pass out at any moment. I didn't. I brought that oration to a glorious close in a prolonged climax that exploded in skyrockets and immediately went off into a crying jag. Nothing could have been better. The fifteen thousand saw at once that the orator had been overcome by beautiful sentiments.

That speech remade me in Ogden. The reputation of red radicalism dissolved away and from that moment I was a patriot.... This reached me from Ogden a few months ago: "Bernard DeVoto," the Presbyterian minister remarked one day, "is a genius: he gets fifteen hundred dollars for a story." (Though how that information reached him I don't know.) "And, you know, I was probably the first to realize it. I was on a Memorial Day program with him once. The moment he began to speak I said to myself, 'DeVoto is a genius.'"... But, though the radical taboo was lifted from me, a social taboo was already taking its place. Prolonged alcoholism and eccentric personal behavior were closing Ogden's homes to me. I thought I was going to tell the story of Irene, and in a way I ought to, for you have probably never been informed about the gentility of the Midwest, of which she was probably the highest exponent, but that yarn was not intimately related to the political history and I've used up a hell of a lot of space more than I meant to, so let it go.

That Memorial Day was my highest flight, but I get more awe from remembering my biggest funeral.... Shortly after I assumed the chaplaincy, one of the buddies died and his family demanded that the Post bury him and that I officiate. There was no way out and after some demur I agreed, and did a neat, workmanlike job, ad-libbing as I found it necessary. Thereafter it seemed to be assumed that the Post was responsible for the laying away of all heroes. I usually got some parson to do the planting, but on request I was always willing to serve—it was best to keep the graft going, and there were undertaker's—excuse me, mortician's—and florist's and similar grafts. Then suddenly the morticians' trust pulled its wires in Washington and the War Dept began shipping the departed heroes home from France, each one to be laid away in his own Spoon River. This was one of the largest-scale experiments in emotion ever tried in America. Now, of course, none of the slain had ever been members of the Legion, but there was publicity and graft in taking charge of them, and by now very few families would have permitted us to back out. We threw a military funeral for every corp received in Ogden. The three leading morticians in town were all members of the Post, buddies Lindquist, Larkin and Kirkendall.[30] The last was the flossiest, patronized by the best set, and he was also Exalted Ruler of B.P.O.E. We divided the custom among them all, and the Post treasury got a rake-off for each job. Well, I'd thrown about eight successful funerals on the prepaid buddies when the War Dept shipped home a genuine hero.... When Beatrice Gale remembered a friend's brother who had been shot about 7 A.M. on November eleventh while building a bridge across the Marne, she was thinking of this case. He had volunteered to take a line across when two previous attempts had failed. He took it and they got him. All our other corps had been those of buddies who'd fallen in front of ice wagons or something similar, but this was a real guy. Furthermore, though I can't remember his name, I'd known him and he'd been a nice guy.... When I heard that he'd been marked for shipment I couldn't face the prospect. I had no morals and no qualms—this Legion business was politics and there is only one moral law in politics: when you finally make an agreement, stick to it. It didn't bother me to crib or extemporize prayers for the departed and to howl the tearful rhetoric at funerals, not in the least. But somehow this was different and I tried to get out of it. No chance. The family intended to have this boy planted in style and they intended to have Herman Baker Post do it and they intended to have a proved orator shoot the works. They had plenty, too, and were willing to spend it. They retained Kirkendall and by now Kirk, a sensitive artist at his trade, was convinced that I threw the nicest funeral to be had in Ogden. When he saw my reluctance he interpreted it as a levy and promptly offered the treasury a bigger cut. Well, I gave in. And I promise you, this was a funeral. The largest hall in Ogden is the Mormon Tabernacle, which seats about seven thousand. We held that funeral there. We mounted guard on the coffin for twenty-four hours, establishing a guard-house in one of the smaller rooms, where Jack kept a plentiful supply of liquor and where Fitz won $350 at craps from noon to noon. We got a caisson from Camp Douglas, in Salt Lake, and demanded that my old railroad, the S. L. & O., bring it up free of charge, which they did. Gov. Mabey found out what was going on and wired that he'd make a personal appearance. Which he did, with his full staff, in these Grand Inner Shrine dress uniforms that run about twelve pounds of gold lace each. I didn't like this any, but I had to go through with it. So I filled up right to the Plimsoll mark with liquor, put on my uniform, and appeared in the last guard-relief at the coffin and then, as the tabernacle began to fill, climbed up on the platform among the notables, shook hands with the Governor, learned that he intended to speak, went behind the organ console for a last shot of whisky, and came forward to conduct the services.[31] I'd enlarged on the ritual a good deal for the big show. We had hired help for the prayers, which delivered me from the post poignant embarrassment. There were seven thousand people in the hall and a good many more outside. I was plenty lit but by now I loved a mob. I suddenly decided that the occasion warranted an Episcopalian, that is a Harvard, accent. When I stood up to announce a violin solo by Mary Fisher, town prodigy, or part of an oratorio by the Methodist Choral Society, or whatnot, it was A. Lawrence Lowell reading prayers in Appleton Chapel. I got steadily more high-church and Oxford. I gave the Governor a good hand, with some neat bits about his dedication to public service, and the Governor orated for about twenty minutes. When it came my turn, I got the idea that the ceremony so far had lacked pathos and that pathos was what the family was most clearly entitled to. So, talking now in a manner indistinguishable from Hugh Walpole's, I turned on the pathos. The family was bellering inside of three minutes, and before I was done I had the Herman Baker Post almost unanimously in tears. There was [one] slight mishap, fortunately unnoticed; when I finished I made the sign of the cross. Well, I turned out pathos for half an hour and then declared that we were ready for the planting. I leaped down to where the guard of honor was standing at a statuesque parade rest round the flag-covered coffin and was transformed from conductor of the services to pall-bearer. We carried that coffin out to the waiting caisson in the street, between two massed rows of the great public.

The sergeant of police was also a pall-bearer, being a First Division man as the corp had been. I wish I could remember the sergeant's name. He was one hardboiled baby. He was tough, and I mean tough. He was very loyal and admiring to me, and he personally saw to it that I had a police guard whenever I got lit in public or attended a wild party, and night after night he had driven me home in a police car. But he was a First Division man, and a private. And I was a softie: I had white stripes instead of gold, and there were gold bars on my shoulder, I was a shavetail. He'd got terrifically liquored while mounting guard on the coffin, and all his resentments came to the service when I stepped down ahead of him and helped to pick up the coffin. That progress down that endless aisle was conducted to a steady mutter behind me. DeVoto, you bastard; DeVoto, you damn shavetail; shavetail the ———ing post of the Army; I'm going to get you; look out, DeVoto. And so on. He'd swoop forward and try to grab my heels. He'd run his hands out on the coffin handle and try to pull me backward. With my feeling for social correctness, it was ghastly. Just as we got through the door, he fired his final expedient. He said, I'm going to get you, and spat a tremendous quid of eating tobacco at me. I dodged and it hit Old Glory on the coffin. Unperturbed, always master of the situation, I put my cap over it and we marched out and hoisted the coffin up on the caisson.

It was a very hot day. Burial was to be in the Mountain View Cemetery, clear across town and some miles out in the country. We formed a long procession, led by the band that was originally founded by the father of John Held, Jr., then Kirk's squad car, the caisson, then about a mile of Post, mourners and common people.[32] The pallbearers marched on either side the caisson; I was just aft of the left front wheel. It was, I say, a hot day, and I wasn't held up any longer by the necessity of the sermon, and there was a full cargo of rye inside me. The sidewalks of Washington Avenue were black with the public, the Held band was tootling the Chopin number and Siegfried's Burial and similar nifties, Kirk had us throttled down till we were just moving, the damn caisson was groaning and grunting and squeaking and squealing the way they always do, the liquor was coming to a boil inside of me, and there I was looking straight ahead in the most military fashion for I was of an enormous dignity that day, and seeing that damn tire turn like the mills of the gods and a bit of Old Glory fluttering on the corner of the coffin where the delivered hero was sliding toward his eternal home.[33] Eighteen Mormon blocks, two and a half miles, we marched at less than half-time to the southern city limits. God knows how long, it seemed eternity, and my feet would start me off at a right or left oblique and I'd realize that I was lapsing from the approved military style and I'd jerk myself back like a marionette that's been kicked in the tail. I was forever sliding down a black incline toward unconsciousness, and forever remembering the honor of the Herman Baker Post and its chaplain and pulling myself back by one thin hair. The squeaks of the caisson got into the gas of the liquor and I was writing poetry while I marched, bright purple Kiplingesque lines about how hell would roar with laughter when we slid this bastard home but ho for the shined puttee brother—and we'll omit the phallic symbolism. And the sergeant of police, much drunker than I was, was three paces behind me and still hostile. His face too was sternly to the front and his mouth was closed, but between his teeth flowed a steady stream of obscenities, obscenities most personal. At Twenty-fourth Street, he described me in detail as homosexually inclined. At Twenty-fifth mere homosexuality seemed sweet and old-fashioned for he had remembered the cavalry. At Twenty-sixth, his fantasies had regressed to childhood. The DeVotos are hard to anger, especially when in liquor, but I began to get the idea that Bill, if his name was Bill, was going too far. The procession halted for a moment. I made a military about-face. Look-here, you bastard, I said, you batten down that G.I. can in your face or I'll damn well fill it for you. Yah, softie, what would you do? Boy, we'll have another trip with this caisson if I get started. Yah, you pansy, you goddamn shavetail—and some choice metaphors from the seamier side of life. We started up again and I had to about-face and march. Bill got really inventive now, and I began to use some of my own language, back over my shoulder. Voice from the other side of the caisson: for Chrissake, ain't you sons of bitches got any reverence? We're plantin' this guy, ain't we? Shut up and march. We drew even with a place where, patently and recently, a horse had been. A moment of terrible temptation. My better nature triumphed; the honor of Herman Baker Post was saved. Bill, intuitively understanding: Yah, you fairy, you didn't have the guts. DeV, over the shoulder: I'm going to get you, you bastard, I'm going to get you plenty. Bill: Yah.

My liquor was mostly bile now. I had an Army grouch, old style, at Bill. Gorgeous fantasies of destruction mingled with the poetry and the swaying and the blackness. But we reached the city limits. Kirk called the pall-bearers into his car, and from there on the processions moved rapidly. I sat by Kirk and Kirk's soul was champagne uncorked. This was his great day. Kirk had pulled a lot of noble funerals in his time but nothing that, for elegance and finish and éclat, could compare with this one. He went into a sort of croon. It was a rhapsody on the soul-satisfying perfection of art, the art of the mortician. How much care and forethought it took to get all the details right and bring them all together at the right time. The esthetics of make-up for the corpse, excuse me, it was from Kirk that I learned the word corp. The amenities of coffin lining, the intricate techniques of embalming, the more spiritual techniques of unobtrusive, sympathetic service to the departed's family, the discount for cash. And always and persistently, the art of the service. And, Ben, you got a gift, you got a vocabulary, it's downright pretty to hear you talk. Presently admiration overcame him. Benny, he said, why don't you quit horsin' around. You're old enough to take a real job now and settle down to your rightful place in the community. Say the word, Benny, and I'll pay you two hundred and fifty a month, and I bet in five years you're a partner.

The rye rose higher and higher toward the small focus that was left of my consciousness. We reached Mountain View. The pall-bearers got out of the car and reverently lifted the coffin to the—I think the technical term is elevator. The mourners took up their position. The Post formed. The Governor and the lesser notables massed at one end. We pall-bearers made a file on each side of the grave. The minister read his service. I stepped forward just about blind, and emitted the touching words I had given to the chaplain for such occasions, and then stepped back again and bent my head. The firing party let off three volleys. The trumpeter raised his bugle for Taps. He was halfway through it when all of my rancor flamed up again and I knew what I was going to do. With my head bent, I hissed at Bill, I'm going to bury you, you bastard, I'm going to bury you in this damn grave. Two more triplets, then the last, liquid, melancholy, descending notes. They ended. I turned to Bill and I was going to bury him. But I didn't get a chance. Quietly, gracefully, with a little sigh of contentment and fulfillment, Bill passed out and toppled on top of the coffin, in the grave.

[*handwritten:* Fourth (of five) installment: History of The Three Twins and how Blackmail came to Ogden.]

IV

One highly important fact in the life of the intellect, and one that incidentally makes detective fiction preposterous, is this: the deduction is never made. You may tie to that—I know no man of brains or of much experience who has not verified it to his own discomfiture. For at least seven years Hans Zinsser has been familiar with facts about typhus which, in retrospect, necessitate a glaringly obvious deduction about the relationship of the Asiatic and the Mexican forms; for at least three years, every bacteriologist who touches upon typhus has been as familiar with those facts as Zinsser can make them. No one ever made the deduction—Zinsser backed into the obvious discovery by accident, not by deductive logic. Or take Henderson. In the course of his work on the chemical equilibrium of the blood—it will probably get him a Nobel Prize some day—he finally established the fact, for all the world to note, that the carbonic acid in the blood is a function of the oxygen in the blood. Now the most obvious, the most glaring, the most stentorian principle of deductive logic is, if A is a function of B then B is a function of A. It shouts itself aloud from all the logic texts, nay from the very cram-books of sophomore calculus, and I suppose that no chemist, no scientist of any kind, can work three months without using that principle, in the abstract, at least fifty times. Did Henderson, having established carbonic acid as a function of oxygen, perform a simple, practically instantaneous act of deductive logic and conclude that oxygen must be a function of carbonic acid? He did not. After six or seven years more of exquisite investigation, of experiments the most minute and complex, of triply-intricate devices and verifications, he experimentally proved, much to his naive surprise, that oxygen was a function of carbonic acid.... The deduction is never made.

If I summon the lords of thought to this chronicle of my chaplaincy, bear with me. It is necessary to salve the *Minderwertigkeit*. The solution of a seven or eight months' mystery was well within my grasp a number of months before the mystery began. I was a bright young man, too, you will remember. But the deduction is never made.... I could have solved it without deduction if I had then had more than a Harvard Freudian's knowledge of the variant personality. But I had read Freud, I hadn't seen any in the flesh.

We go back now to about November, 1920. (The time-sense may be depended upon, the actual dates grow a little vague.) We were furiously establishing our machine and making ready to take over the Post, but we were not yet in power. This narrative has told how I suggested that the Post advertise itself with a show and had had Herrick made business manager and myself made some kind of officer, publicity manager I think. (Brigham Young loved the theater—and built what was probably the best playhouse in America for many years. As a result of Brigham's taste, Utah has always spawned amateur theatricals wholesale, and they are always events of much local importance. Even I. It was, you may remember, while playing in *The Gods of the Mountains* that I met the Brewer's Daughter.[34] And a theatrical chapter of my memoirs would contain some twenty other productions.) One Robert Major, a buddy, offered himself as Director. He was practically unknown to me, but he had directed a number of productions in the Mormon wards and seemed competent enough, and there was no one else in the Post who was capable of the job. (I had been unable to persuade Moroni Olsen, the John Knox of last year's Mary of Scotland, to join us, though Moroni was a veteran, of a kind.[35] Incidentally, when Moroni came east to storm Broadway, he thought that the name of the greatest Mormon angel would ring no bells and wanted to change it. I had great difficulty dissuading him from dropping the i.) Major wanted the job for though we wouldn't pay a buddy for working for the Post, he would gather reputation from a good production. I rather liked his grandiose ideas. He wanted to do a big job, for his reputation, and a big job would greatly benefit the Post. Also, it would cast lustre on Herrick, who was Our Candidate. I decided the bigger the better, so we went ahead. It got quite big.

How much is it desirable to tell about Major here? I got to know quite a lot about him before long. For one thing, I may not be as good a newspaper man as Red Lewis, but I have a faculty for acquiring information—it just seeps in, and when I want more I usually get it economically. Also, within a couple of weeks it became all too clear that Major was the Unforeseen Obstacle. He was what we hadn't counted on. He could wreck the whole damn program of the Holther-DeVoto machine, largely without knowing it, certainly without intending it. I had to be in instant readiness to annihilate the bastard—and pretty soon I was, though we were able to pull all our threads together and get by without moving upon him. Anyway, I acquired information.... He was a paranoid personality, with occasional forays into acute paranoia. He was a fairly handsome gent with palely sandy hair that had a tinge of pink in it and the most magnificent wave ever beheld on any stage. When the bills for The Three Twins came in, we learned that that wave had to be set twice a week during rehearsals and every day during the production. He was faintly Mormon, enough to summon the group-fealty of the Saints to his assistance when he needed it. He was a little vague about his service as a hero, claiming, as the need arose, to have suffered with the doughboys in the trenches, where many bayonet attacks had been either led or repulsed by him in person, and to have been a staff-editor of *The Stars and Stripes*.[36] That, however, was easy—we had Jack follow him up through channels and learned that he had been a company clerk at some debarkation point in France. He was, at the moment, principal of a little county school just outside the city limits. A greatly gifted person, he also Wrote. It was his idea, once *The Three Twins* had been decided on, that we would do well to interpolate some of his sketches—I read some later, when a friend of mine got sucked into the Major School of Histrionic Art that was run out of Hollywood, and no possible apprenticeship in ham could fit you to understand how awful they were. I vetoed that notion before I quit *The Three Twins*, vetoed it so forcibly that Herrick was able to make the veto stand. He also had temperament, like a movie tart in one of the fan magazines, and grandiose ideas. Grandiose ideas are diagnostic of the paranoid. He also had a quaintness which, as I proved up on it, I greeted with passionate thanksgiving, for it is became desirable to annihilate him that was the most available mechanism. The quaintness: he was fond of the newly nubile. With some despatch I uncovered several sub rosa stories in Ogden about Major and fourteen-year-old girls. At the time, he was courting another child. Discovering this fact, did I warn the child's parents? I was in politics, dear, I didn't warn the parents. To anticipate: when Major left Ogden, there was a wedding just before train-time. The bride was fourteen and a sensitive nose could have detected a thin odor of DuPont Smokeless #6.

The Three Twins decided upon, and denied remuneration for his efforts, he promptly applied what seemed to me a perfectly legitimate graft. He had founded some titanic organization of the Gopher Prairie sort.[37] It was called, I believe, The Ogden Panharmonic Tri-Art Terpsichorean and Polyhymnian Society. Its purpose was to produce shows for his aggrandizement—it had produced one already, alluded to in the clipping I recently sent you. It was composed of a lot of girls and a lot of women who hadn't been girls for some time—Ogden, you must understand, fairly sweats admiration of the arts. Major promptly hired the orchestra for *The Three Twins* from that society and also selected his chorus from it. It was an enormous chorus—it filled the Orpheum when the show finally went on. That was okay with me. If he could get either kudos or cash as a sideline, I saw no reason why he shouldn't; and the probable expense of so big a production didn't alarm me, we didn't want money for the Post, we only wanted advertising and further demonstration that the machine was livening things up.

The show got off to an ominous and tempestuous start. At the first meeting of the gigantic cast Major threw a fit of temperament and wounded purity—wounded purity was going to be his leitmotif for months to come—and broke down and cried and refused to go on. Someone had sent him an anonymous letter telling him that some of the cuties and some of the principals didn't love him and had resolved to gum the works by subtly interfering with his direction. He had to be soothed and stroked and kissed before he would reluctantly go on. He made clear that it was only his patriotism that prevailed over the insult, he was activated by the same flaming love of country that had kept him baring his breast to German steel week after weary week in the Haute Champagne. Or the Argonne. Well, we let him be kissed back into complaisance.

I unloaded after about a week. He countermanded some direction I had made—I forget what it was—and I decided I didn't care to parade with him. But also I had a good hunch already that I was going to be a hell of a lot more useful to *The Three Twins*–Herman Baker Post setup on the outside than I could possibly be on the inside. We solemnly charged Herrick with the whole responsibility and started leaving it alone wholesale. Major at once told the world that he had fired me for insubordination. He has made a lot of mistakes but that was the worst one he made in Ogden. In the mood that then dominated me, that of the political boss, that was the shortest way to annoy me. I marked him down. The show itself isn't important, let's make it as brief as possible. Jess and I concentrated on our political strategy, which took a lot of time, and forgot about *The Three Twins*. We were abruptly hauled back from forgetfulness by an appalled and shuddering Herrick. The show was ready to go on, five performances were scheduled, just before Christmas, with the Post election only two or three weeks away—the event at which all our plans and preparations were aimed. And, figuring the greatest possible return he could, Herrick couldn't possibly see a deficit a cent under $8000.

Herrick was a good business man, as business men go, and a good business manager for the show, but he was up against a wild man. I mean quite literally a wild man. I still grin when I remember that production. That enormous chorus had literally dozens of changes of costume, and the Herman Baker Post was paying for them (it was intended that the Etc Tri-Art Society should inherit them for stock) and they were of the finest. The scenery was being painted in Denver. There were items of, say, $65 for waving the Director's hair. There was an unexplained nightgown-pantie-slip set of $35, which never figured in the show and couldn't possibly have fitted any of the Director's loves. Three or four hundred dollars here, that much more elsewhere, special lighting effects, portable electric props for phosphorescent effects of the Director's own invention, wigs, gauzes, hospital supplies (John Culley, Ogden's best-loved druggist, sent in a bill for Kotex), Christ only knows what didn't get into that production.[38] Herrick had done his damndest. He'd tried to curry the paranoid down, but if he saved ten dollars here, he found five hundred spent elsewhere that he hadn't been consulted about. It was the most ambitious, and the wildest, performance ever staged by Ogden talent.

You are invited to guess how good news that was to a couple of politicians who had to get hold of the Post. We were the boys who were going to fill the treasury. We were going to tap the rock and let the oil gush forth for Herman Baker Post. And here we were, coming up to elections with a deficit of $8000. We had started out to be heroes and we were rapidly getting hung up as buffoons.... Furthermore, besides the deficit, there was another poignant danger. Certainly up to election time and most probably for some months thereafter, we could afford no hint whatever of inefficiency, disagreement, failure of the machine to function or to suppress insubordination. Major didn't realize it but he had us, for the time being, at his mercy. Much as we longed to get the bastard, we couldn't. We couldn't even, at the moment, stop him—everything would have got out if we had made any overt attempt to. We had to take it. We took it, and we smiled.

Obviously, however, the situation had to be met, and had to be met effectively. Well, we met it. It was a place for politics. We decided that the first step was to hold off any financial report until we were in control of the Post. After we got control we could hold it off indefinitely by sheer strongarm refusal to report. But how hold it off for the vital period between the end of the show and the election? I perceived the loophole:

keep the show going till after election. It was a desperate remedy, considering the overhead, and might well increase the deficit, but it was the only possible way to keep things dark until we took over the Post. So by God we took *The Three Twins* on the road. Herrick practically closed up his business. He put on a publicity campaign among the Legion posts in fair-sized towns in Utah, Idaho and Wyoming that would have done credit to a professional. Herrick was fighting for his commandership. We turned on the heat at home. We informed every creditor we dared to that all or part of his bill was his contribution to patriotism, to helping the boys out. We contracted to re-sell the scenery and the costumes—it was this bit, which Major attributed to Herrick, that begot the first unpleasantness later on. We salvaged every cent we could in every direction. Capacity houses in Ogden and a surprisingly good road tour, together with these inspirations of retrenchment, enabled us to come into office with a deficit of something over two thousand instead of eight.

I'll say this for him: it wasn't a bad production. It wasn't a good one by a couple of Mormon blocks, but the big orchestra and the expensive sets and costumes gave it an impressive finish. Major, as one of the twins, was grotesque. He had to sing and that was a mistake, he had to dance and that was even a worse mistake. But a couple of the buddies were pretty good and some of the home-town girls were better than that. I've seen worse.

The deficit had the indirect effect of insuring official honesty for some time. We had to fill the treasury—that was absolutely indispensable to our plans. So Herrick, Jess and I unobtrusively turned into the treasury all the pickings of our office. Jack saw no reason why he should and so he didn't—but his book-keeping more than made up for his selfishness. When we were at last ready to show the Post's books to all comers they read like a poem by E. E. Cummings. The best CPA in the Rocky Mountain area couldn't have made out where we stood or why. Jack is now a collector of internal revenue.

We squeezed by. But we were sore. Especially me. I had the same emotion I had a couple of years back when a student at Harvard decided I was a sucker, played me for a sucker, and made good on the play. I didn't like that pink-haired bastard. Furthermore, I had a political theory that it's bad stuff to let anyone in politics know that you've been outsmarted. It appeared to my plain sense that the curl had to be taken out of that hair.

[*handwritten:*] Sorry—this isn't a good serial stop. Well, maybe we can go on before I embark for B L[39]

V

Dear Kate:

By the grace of God nobody is coming tonight and no one has sent me a manuscript to criticize. I'm in a mood to finish the Detective Story, if one installment will do it, and somehow I yearn to get on to The Stews of Holden Green.[40] Not to mention Cambridge and the Sacred Dove—if that proves possible.

Well, let's see. We had, you say, the Three Twins Company on tour in the sticks. Let's go on from there.

Remember, please, that I had been annoyed. Also that Major's plan to grab off costumes and scenery for the Tri-Art Society had been thriftily frustrated. He was annoyed too. Especially at Herrick.... Well, the machine took hold of the Post and made a big show of activity and carefully doctored the books. *The Three Twins* disbanded. Major began to project grandiose productions, musical and dramatic, with his own society. Jess's appointment as Juvenile Judge came through from the new Governor's office. I grew more irritable and alcoholic and inexplicable, my weight fell off thirty pounds, I developed a vicious amusement—disconcerting the genteel of Ogden, and oh God, how genteel they were. I took Irene to The Charity Ball.... You can't know about The Charity Ball and I couldn't convey it to you, I couldn't convey to you the other side of the moon, the emotions of a proton, motherhood among the amoebae. But if I do that Ogden novel I'll have to convey it. White ties, dear. Also Prince Alberts.[41] In a ballroom maintained by a couple of beet-sugar millionaires—and named Berthana, after their wives.... Irene, as I've probably mentioned, was the most genteel of all, and she taught English at the high school. In the course of the dance I saw a youngster named Afton, I forget what else. She was all of seventeen, she was a pupil of Irene's, I recognized her as somehow related to the Brewer's Daughter. That was the moment that made me aware of the Flapper. And one of Irene's friends got married about this time and Irene decorously told me that she didn't think it was quite nice of Helen to talk so freely about being happy. And about this time, calling for Irene, to take her to one of those godawful dinners, I, as usual, primed myself with half a pint of Legion liquor so that I could endure the meal. Irene said tremulously, "You haven't really had something to drink?" She was the only person I ever heard of who read Stephen Phillips.[42]

Then for a moment it appeared that my late wooing of the Labor Vote hadn't done the Post much good. People began calling Herrick on the telephone—or, indifferently, Herrick's wife—and telling him that they were officials of the Switchmen's Union or high in the councils of the Steel Car Repairers' Union, and that the Legion, with Herrick as Commander, wasn't so hot. We were quite a little concerned about this. Almost at once, Herrick received a couple of unsigned letters which announced that Mr. Ensign Herrick didn't rate worth a damn among the tough babies in the railroad shops. They were going to get him. They were going to boycott his optical business and also the jewelry shop that shared the same building with him—the official watch inspector of the S.P.[43] Also, for reasons not clearly stated, they were going to beat up Herrick. We naturally coupled the letters with the telephone calls. No conceivable explanation sounded really good; we ended by concluding that somebody we had to tramp down in the Post had connections in the local trades-union council. We prepared to face some unpleasant publicity. A row with Labor wasn't at all what the Legion as a whole wanted, still less our Post with its finances still very bad. But, said the Chaplain, if they mean to have a fight let it begin now.[44] I considered that I could make just as hot speeches against Red Bolshevism as I had made in favor of the Flag and the Buddy Unity, and I knew by now that the best orations were the best bet. Then Herrick got another unsigned letter. It repeated the same threats—legally blackmail and punishable under federal statute, as who would know better than the Juvenile Judge—but also it alleged one specific grievance. Herrick, it seemed, have [*sic*] grievously cheated the little brothers of two who were high in the Ogden labor movement. He had bullied them and, in his capacity as business manager of the Legion show, he had done them out of their proper hire. So now we had a clue to the mutterings of labor. Without much effort we canvassed the child labor in the production and found that the only likely incident was that of a couple of boy scouts whom Herrick had hired to distribute posters and window cards through Cache Valley. Here I experienced the prelude of my career as Mastermind. I took the names of these boys, went to Scout headquarters and found out that they were pupils of Major's school, at Riverdale, just outside the city limits to the south. It was then easy to have a truant officer bring them into the Juvenile Court. They denied all knowledge of the letters, but we had only to separate them and question them apart, Jess looking as stern as a chap five feet six with curly hair and an incredibly juvenile face can look. Major had had them write the letters. He had even prepared drafts of each one for them to copy, and they had saved the drafts. We got them and I felt very happy.

It was best, I decided, to save them for a while. Better not give Major the spanking I intended to give him until the finances of the Post were straightened out and until some more attractive opening offered. But it was pleasant to have Jess, embodying the Law's majesty in Weber County, call in the county Superintendent of Schools and quietly lay the story before him. So, without giving Major any notion that this particular set of goods was on him, the superintendent told him that he was unfit to be a principal and would not have his contract renewed next year. I filed the various documents and waited my time. The revolt of labor was over.

Major now got himself engaged by the University Club to put on a show—the Club's third. I had appeared in both previous ones, had even had the lead in the last one, but this time I wasn't sitting in. When I received the customary five tickets to buy or sell, I returned them with a lordly note to the effect that, really, I couldn't afford to lend my support to a production in any way associated with Mr. Major. This gratified the queer mood I was in but was very silly and, quite needlessly, let Major know that I wasn't the bland admirer I still affected to be. He began to circulate the most amazing and amusing stories about me. He really believed them—I hadn't diagnosed him then and couldn't know that, but he did. Delusions of persecution and the paranoid frenzy. I thought I'd have to run him out of town or something, then I finally saw how funny it was. It wasn't quite so funny when, in September, being by that time hopelessly gone on Skinny, I had to explain to Mrs. Browning that, really, I wasn't a felon and really I didn't have a wife in a sanitarium for the insane or out of it. Happily Mrs. Browning, who was one of the saints of this world, either didn't hear or didn't understand the genuinely provocative yarns that he had circulated.

Major got into some sort of scrape at the University Club, as usual over money, and the Club felt irritated and Major discovered another set of conspirators. And Godfrey Matthews, the Congregational minister and one of the few intelligences in Ogden, said sadly to me that it was a shame the enemies Bob made, and he so innocent of all intent to harm, too. Why, the cast had hardly begun to rehearse when someone in it wrote an anonymous letter to Bob, telling him that some members of it were resolved to impede the production as much as possible, in order to make Bob look bad. And that, Godfrey complained, didn't tend to promote unity in the cast, either, they didn't tend to develop much brotherly love. I said yes, it was too bad, something of the same sort had happened with *The Three Twins*, and I went on thinking about the Elks' Show.

This amused me quite a bit. It was a big fee, the biggest in Ogden, and Major was trying to get it. The Chaplain decided otherwise—the Chaplain was now determined to embarrass the career of Robert Major in every way a skilled politician could. Neither Jess nor I belonged to the Benevolent and Protective Order of Elks, but Herrick of course did. Working through Herrick, and my friend John Culley, a Sinclair Lewis character who operated the town's largest drug store and largest fund of snappy stories, I soon put an end to that idea. Herrick got the blame: Major couldn't love him in the slightest. But now the Tri-Art Society brought a traveling symphony orchestra to town, with a brisk ticket-selling campaign by all the newly nubile, and there was a hell of an uproar over finances. The Society couldn't meet the—quite modest—guarantee and the manager of the orchestra called things off at five minutes to eight the night of the performance, and Major nobly gave his personal check for the guarantee. The next day the check wasn't worth anything. And so on. I don't know what happened or how it was settled. I do know that Jack Littlefield's wife, a termagant and the proprietor of a big shoe store, was mixed up with the Society and had something to do with the affair. So pretty soon Ogden began to bubble with stories about Mary Littlefield, much like the ones that were the cocktail at most dinner tables, the ones Major was circulating about me.

Jack Littlefield was an Irishman. He didn't beat hell out of Major, but the reason he didn't was that, when he started to, Jess and I threw him and sat on him till

Major, attacked at a University Club dance, got away. Thereafter there were sulphurous reports that he was going to shoot Jack. He was going to shoot me too, but on just what grounds I never knew. Anyway—this was now April or May—Jack said by God this had gone far enough and let's do something about the bastard. So I consented to make use of the Boy Scout material. We would disgrace Major before the Post. That would have a kind of poetry, it would satisfy my modest requirements, and it would enormously relieve Jack. We called a special meeting of the Post—a warning that something big was up—and notified Major, very formally, to be present at it.

I think he was actually entering a violent phase then. He was certainly in an exaggerated excitement, a typical paranoid seizure, had been for a couple of months, and remained so as long as I followed him thereafter. He didn't know what was up but he came to the meeting with a lawyer. Gene Pratt, of the same vintage as Jess, one of our members, and a genial phlegmatic fathead. I hadn't supposed that any preparation was necessary. We would just pull our stuff, get him to acknowledge it or else get him fired from the Post—either one was satisfactory for my purposes—and end up with a nice drinking bout on the liquor I had delivered from the Police Department. I had Herrick vacate the chair and put Squaw Douglass, one of our boys, in his place. And quite unexpectedly I confronted a dogfight. I had been underestimating, even I, the power of hokum. Herrick told his story. Jess made a grave, shocked speech explaining the treason of attacking an office of the Post and the heinousness of corrupting innocent youth in order to vent petty spite on a loyal servant of the Post. I sat back and listened, I didn't even expect to make a speech. So Douglass asked Major what he had to say—and we damn near lost control of the Post right there. Major stood up and began to orate. I don't know where he got the inspiration but he was magnificent. There had always been some depths of absurdity I had refused to plunge into. Major lived right there, and he had the buddies right where they lived too. He fought the war and the Crucifixion, tears streaming down his face, and the Chaplain, an expert in audiences, could feel that audience slipping away bit by bit. He didn't bother to deny the allegation—he was just noble. He was a wounded soul, he was a patriot, he was a veteran, he was Christ's image. On and on. I looked at two or three hundred buddies weeping in concert with him and snarling when he mentioned the Huns, and I thought, Benny, the Holther-DeVoto machine will be a gone sucker in about six minutes flat, in about ten minutes you'd better dive through a window to anticipate a lynching, for otherwise you'll go out of here astride a rail. Me a demagogue? Hell, I was just an amateur, a damn dilettante, here was the perfect art and me without a comeback. Jess's face looked as if he would have sold his seat in the legislature for a punched beer check. He looked absolutely sick. I looked at Fitz: I've seen the same expression on hypnotized men who'd been told they had taken a dose of salts. On and on, floods of oratory, avalanches of nobility. Douglass finally choked him out and in a still, frightened voice, asked me if I had anything to say. Instinct of the frightened servitor. I didn't, I even knew better than to say anything, but I stood up, thinking fast. This will show you how paralyzed, as an orator, I was: the first remark I pulled on that audience was a nifty to the effect that it was too bad Jesus had died so soon and so unnecessarily! I may have been the boss of the Herman Baker Post but I had a vivid hunch I wasn't going to be more than two minutes longer. But it was not for nothing that I had mastered the theory of politics and disciplined myself to public composure. Even as I made up aimless remarks I was casting about for the solution and I found it. I stopped my speech. I said yes, I did have something to say that bore directly on the subject. Would Mr. Douglass please call Andy Kasius. He called and Andy took a chair on the platform and my soul was at peace, for Andy had also been on the Three Twins committee and I remembered a conversation with him and I had my unanswerable argument. I said, "Brother Kasius, do you remember a certain conversation about Mr. Major that you had with me last December?" Andy said, "You mean when I told you about Mr. Major referring to the American Legion as a bunch of slackers and bums?"

Well, we were saved. But the business had been so close that, when Andy had finished his story and the Post was in an uproar, I was only too glad to adjourn the meeting after having Douglass appoint a committee to file charges, investigate them, and bring in a verdict. The next day I went to Gene Pratt. I was done with even the appearance of democratic government. I said, in effect, this bastard is a client of yours—now, here are the records of the Juvenile Court with the stories of the boy scouts, and here are the original drafts in your client's handwriting—either your client signs a complete confession of guilt in full detail for me to spread on the minutes of the Post or else I hand them to the Federal district attorney. Within twelve hours we had a signed confession in full. At the next meeting of the Post we spread it on the minutes with great fanfare. Jack was satisfied, we were more than ever proved to be the power in the government, Major was out, and things looked quite pleasant. But I had seen the direction that the wind would some day take, when the wind rose to blow us out. I knew more about politics.

For some reason Major didn't hold that episode against us. Not that he loved me any more than before, but he attributed this primarily to Jess—probably also to the committee of dim shapes that give off crimson smoke in the mind of the paranoid, the convention of malign gods that work evil on the innocent and pure.

Summer came on. And one day I folded up. For two months thereafter I was as effectually insulated from the objective world as I would have been in a tomb. I crawled back to some fragmentary participation in exterior reality. The starch was gone out of me and would be for some years, but I was able to go about my business with some small effectiveness. The Post had suspended activities for the summer, but now I had a new interest, Skinny. And, I found, Jess was upset. (I remember I was going to bring his marriage into this narrative. Let it go. Maybe some day I'll come back to this study in Western folkways.) As I think I've mentioned, part of our deal with the State Legion was the right to name the Governor's private secretary. We had named an ex-aviator named Nelson, and Nelson had recently sent up from Salt Lake City an anonymous letter that had been addressed to the Governor. Nelson said, here, all unsigned communications go into the wastebasket here, but I thought you might be interested in this. It was many pages long and, in the person of an outraged leader of the community, it announced the defection of Ogden from the Governor's support. I also announced that, secretly, a large band of equally outraged leading citizens had organized a revolt against the Governor and the Governor's appointments, in the name of morality.

(Sorry. We'll have to go from here. I think I can make it in one more installment.)

VI

I fail to make clear the letter to the Governor (his name was Mabey, if I haven't put that on the record, and some years later the present Secretary of War displaced him when the triumphant Democracy achieved this slogan: "We want a Dern good Governor and we don't mean Mabey")—unless I convey its hypothetical plausibility.[45] There ho! such bugs and goblins about Jess's youth, about his wildness, his drinking, his amatory exploits, as would have convinced even me and Charley Torongo.[46] The jeremiad is the easiest of all literary forms, and universally the most successful. This had fire in it. It had righteousness, too, and it instanced certain rulings of the Ogden Juvenile Court as a basis for righteousness. Jess was, God knows, no superior intelligence and certainly no radical, but anyone with brains meant a tremendous innovation in that alcove of our society and Jess really had refused to send fourteen-year-old girls to the reform school on proof that they'd been behind someone's barn. The letter adumbrated a wrought and vindictive personality, affronted beyond toleration by what he conceived to be a slackening of moral standards in his city. And he was Beginning to Move. He had organized some hundreds of others who shared his rebellion in the name of decency. There was a legion of decency forming in Ogden. Already it had doomed Governor Mabey, whose appointment of Judge Holther merely attested his cowardly surrender to the forces of vice and corruption. Let him resign. But first, if he did not want the aroused citizenry to wreck the Republican Party as they had wrecked him, let him denounce and remove this libertine whom he had elevated to custody over the morals of Ogden's youth. And so on. Twenty pages.... You are literate and metropolitan. You know about literary mechanisms but, by those two qualities, you are withheld from knowing about social mechanisms. This was quite fantastic, and altogether plausible. At this moment, dear, the Ku Klux Klan was persuading some five million Americans to pay ten dollars apiece to keep the Pope from establishing the Vatican in Mundelein, Illinois.[47] Just a month or two before there had been—in this citadel of high Mormonry!—a meeting of the Klan in a meadow just to the eastward of the city. One Jerry Roche, a buddy and an Irishman who was our city engineer, happened to be passing that way, highly alcoholized, and, on sight of the burning cross, drove his Cadillac off the road at seventy miles an hour and, at a forced deceleration, through the crowd. There was no prosecution and, a week later, Roche's car was blown to hell with dynamite. Oh, easily, one could take that letter for just what it purported to be.

Jess did and so did Jess's Marie. The bungalow which Torongo ecstatically called The Love Nest was full of alarms and midnight vigils. Well, it was traditionally the kind of predicament I was supposed to cope with and overcome, it was within my jurisdiction, my talents, my reputation. But, confronting it when at last I crawled out of the house and confronted a world crammed full of nameless, formless and undreamed-of perils, I couldn't do much with it. Night after night, after delivering Skinny at her ancestral mansion, I went to The Love Nest and watched with Jess and interrogated him. I finally achieved a solution. During the two months of my strife against God and agoraphobia, there had come a time when the Municipal Judge fell ill of manifold miseries and complaints and Jess had occupied his bench while he sought lenitives at Utah Hot Springs. In the course of that term, he had found against a certain person, of whom I remember nothing except that he was hard-boiled, noisy and blustering. On evidence I cannot now recall, it was possible to make out that this gent had developed a dislike of Jess and had written that letter in pure bravado. If that was so, then Nelson had been right and no attention should be paid to it—and obviously there was no revolt among the citizens. I don't know whether I even believed this myself. Probably I didn't either believe or disbelieve it. One marked characteristic of a neurosis is the way it depersonalizes all suffering but one's own. The tribulations of other people become exactly like propositions in geometry. But at least I convinced Jess and Marie, and presumably nights at The Love Nest were thereafter what they should be in the period of the honeymoon.

So that was over and there was nothing to occupy me but the shapes of my disease and the poignant, warming emotions of the curious relationship I was developing with Skinny. She was eighteen and going away in a few weeks and—very lovely—and I didn't even know the nature of my troubles but only regarded myself as shattered.... From the persistency with which Skinny has been getting into this narrative, I suspect that either I am going to write a chapter about her in these memoirs or she will prove to be a character in a novel that is probably gestating. Well, that lasted only a few weeks. Skinny went away and I had only the shapes I've mentioned to occupy me. A couple of months later at six one bitterly cold morning, breakfasting in a lunch room, I heard, across the partition, two voices which I identified as belonging to a couple of her cousins, who were starting out on a deer hunt. Listening, I heard them casually allude to her approaching death. Three minutes later I had her only resident sister on the phone. Skinny had encephalitis. Six weeks later, she was back in Ogden and not eighteen any longer—the depths discovered and opened up. You may imagine that then there was an even more curious, and more poignant, association of two souls with an iron driven through them.

Balls. Let's get back to the narrative. You will conceive that what is popularly referred to as a nervous breakdown is not the best mood in which to find and keep employment. But life has its simplicities: it was work or starve. I could sleep at the house and possibly keep warm there, but one doesn't eat books or oil paintings of one's uncle's cows. About the middle of October (?) I was back with John Spargo and Fred Scriven in the book store, and just managing to do it. It was about then that the case opened up again.

But first you must understand one characteristic and significant nodule of the Ogden folkways, the penny-ante game at the University Club. Some day I will do a treatise, or even a novel, about the American social mechanisms, groupings and linkages that really count, and why the Republic is impregnable because there are a million-odd such nodules. The University Club, as you may have gathered from its appearance herein was nothing much. But it had one, to sociologists endearing, feature. On Saturday night quite a number of people gathered there. I had gone frequently at one time, to play the rare and almost forgotten game of solo, the only card game I've ever been able to tolerate, with John Junk and Pinky Dawson (recently a supporter of Upton Sinclair in California) and a wizened little shrimp whose name I can't remember.[48] I even looked in these days, say one Saturday in six or eight, just to see that my town was still my town. John Junk was the principal of a sub-high school and he sang bass in St. Joseph's choir. (I have left out the story of how Genevieve, the organist, tried to win me back to Holy Church and how, because Genevieve was sweet and innocent and delightsome, I sometimes went and added my bass to John's. I was once allowed to sing, solo, the Et homo factus est[49] at High Mass, and my Tantum ergo sacramentum was something. Something or other.) After three rounds of the solo game, It was John's custom to join the really significant feature of the Saturday night, the penny-ante game. This has been in existence throughout the two or three years of the club's life, and it had some six or eight regulars and that many more who were occasionals. The small-town, settled husband's escape, the night out, the enduring basis for monogamy. It lasted till four or five o'clock and, when marriage and daring ran high, through to breakfast time. People sometimes won or lost as much as four dollars at such a session, and went home refreshed and at peace with God. Arch Moyes, our deposed Commander, was a regular (and once assaulted me for betraying what I had gleaned from a brother, the secret grips and signals and rites of Beta Theta Pi, a sodality of the bucolic colleges). So was Fitz's sister's husband, Katherine having astounded us all by marrying a Mormon, and she with probably the fourth or fifth best set of legs I ever saw. He taught some science at the high school. So was Karl Hopkins, the Superintendent of Schools. So was Wade Johnson, Ogden's Princeton man, as Art Perkins and Judge Howells and I were Ogden's Harvard men.[50] Wade was city attorney and, some eight or ten years older than I, formerly my model of behavior, my Chesterfield, my Crichton. Also Wade was a member of the School Board—from the Fifth, my ward. I had read his law books, when I was younger, and had endlessly argued his cases with him.... He was also attorney for one Jim Pingree, at the moment one of Ogden's giants, later Ogden's Samuel Insull, and when Jim's financial structure crashed, a year or two later, Wade triumphantly kept him out of jail till diabetes beat the rap for him.[51] There had been an amusing class of loyalties, or retainers, a few months before—before, I mean, the events I am about to chronicle. One of Jim Pingree's sons, a flaming youth, drove his car down Washington Avenue at some outrageous speed, late one night, and at the corner of Twenty-first Street ran into and quite obliterated an elderly woman. Within five minutes Wade was on the spot with a fire hose, flushing the blood off the pavement. Then he went to his office and, as City Attorney, received the regular report of the accident, which he might have to prosecute, from the police.

The temptation is strong to tell you about the others but I've named all I need to and in fact I don't need Arch Moyes.

Well, I came into the University Club one Saturday night, hellridden with anxiety, mourning Skinny, and quite sober—I had avoided alcohol, on no principle but ignorance, since my crash and hadn't yet had the relapse that flung me into rip tides of drinking. And the University Club was very wrong. There was no cube of smoke, no table of solo, no penny-ante game. A couple of unknowns were playing pool. Apart from them there was no one in the club except John Junk, a subdued soul, gloomy, morose, patently apprehensive. I expressed my astonishment. Where was Wade—Karl—Arch—Sam Powell—Fitz's sister's husband—Milnor Jeffries? Where, in God's name, was the penny-ante game? John said there wasn't any penny-ante game. Then he said there wasn't going to be any penny-ante game again. Here, I perceived that he was shaken and scared, and if I'm a bum newspaperman I nevertheless know news when it brings me in the eye. I couldn't get anything from John. I couldn't get anything except the achingly obvious fact that something was up. All he'd say was that they weren't having any games any more—and that it was Karl's idea. So I went away. Monday the boy reporter was going to uncover a beat.

But Monday also Fitz phoned me and said, "Something's happened at the University Club. I can't get it but (oh, God, what was that Mormon's name? It was Al) but Al is worried. See what you can get." And in the course of the morning I went over to the City Hall to get the specifications on some office supplies Scriven was selling to the auditor. The Mayor's door was open and, purely by chance, I went in.... The Mayor was Frank Francis, and sometime I'll send you one of the literary notices he from time to time runs about me in the *Standard-Examiner*. He had been the editor of that sheet when I began to work for it and was still, as mayor, its guiding hand. A queer bird—he'll go into that novel, if there is that novel. He venerates me now, as a literary gent; once he had loved me as the dutiful apprentice; later he raised hell with me and disliked me, in the curious events that marked my departure from the *Standard-Examiner*; at the moment, he was wary of me but had to treat me decently because after all I was a rising politician. I entered and began to chat with him. Now, as I say, he had some wary respect for me and he knew that I knew my town. So when he began to ask me questions about the University Club I knew that he wanted to make use of me. (Oh hell, some day I've got to tell you about his first campaign for Mayor and how some loyal employees, I among them, framed his labor opponent.) So I promptly went into my role as fresh young politician and said, "Oh, hell, I know what's going on. If you want to deal with me, tell me what you know." And it worked. Frank got up and went to the outer office and sent his secretary on an errand (he always made his political deals in an automobile. This, in Ogden.) and closed the door. Then he said, sotto voce, "One of the letters came to me as the Mayor, another went to the *Standard*." I said, "Well, let's see them," and he went to the vault, took out a strong-box and unlocked it, took a bond-box out of it and unlocked that, and handed me two letters. Of about forty manuscript pages each.

I'll have to deal with them all together for I've forgotten what was in them separately (I've got some of them upstairs in an old box still, but somehow not even writing this periodical has moved me to dig them out and re-read them) and in fact I've forgotten just how many there were. I don't know, even, whether I ever heard about the whole sum of them—I imagine that there were some never reported to anyone. But another one I do remember went to the Chairman of the Board of Education, a Mormon physician named Rich (father of the pretty wenches named Cleone, Ortel, Avon, and Myrene), and another one to a Mormon Apostle, and another one to the Presbyterian minister. I think there must have been at least two more that I got hold of, but I can't remember what they were. Anyway, they were all about forty pages long and they were all honeys.

I do remember that the one to the *Standard* was hung on a recent campaign which the paper had been running. Francis's boss—both business and political—was the owner of the *Standard* and one of the owner's perquisites was a tribute from all gambling operations such as the one the Post exacted from carnivals. The proprietor of a resort in Ogden Canyon had objected or asked for a discount or something and quite recently the *Standard* had taken a firm stand against corrupting the youth of Ogden by inducing it to play the paddle games, etc. Whereupon, in prompt response to the *Standard's* moral stand, the Mayor had had the Police Commissioner turn the cops loose on that resort. Our outraged author demanded that the *Standard* operate on the much more vicious conditions he was exposing.

For, behold, vice was rampant in Ogden. A very hellhole of debauchery existed at the University Club, a tony and aristocratic institution that used its false standing to disguise an iniquitous and subtly degenerate activity. Worse, the malefactors, the corrupters, the degenerates were people high in that sacred trust of democracy, the educational hierarchy. There was Al ______, a teacher at the high school, under whose care came tender minds, male and female, of impressionable adolescents; there was John Junk, principal of Washington Junior High, who, notwithstanding his life of evil and excitement and moral filth, ventured to exercise supervision over sincere and earnest teachers, and over some hundreds of Ogden's innocent children. Nay, there was Karl Hopkins, the very apex of the system, a moral leper who dared to prescribe dress and behavior for scores of teachers—yes, there was even Wade Johnson, of the Board of Education, to whom the citizens had solemnly entrusted the supervision even of Hopkins. Here, in all the letters, followed some ten or fifteen pages of perfect ecstasy. It was apocalyptic. I remember phrases about the bloodshot eyes, the quick-drawn breath of hatred and delirium, the pale, sweating foreheads, the oaths of bitter accusation. You had visions of Alexandrian debauchery, of superheated frenzy—and this was just some of the boys. But it sounded like the greatest sinners of all time. I will have to get them out some time and transcribe some specimens.

Then, after drums and thunder, after the University Club's modest rooms reeked like a banquet hall of Caligula, our author went on to describe the uprising of the citizens.[52] This was like the earlier one that had been inflicted on Mabey, but a hundredfold more magnificent. I want to tell you, the armies were forming. Ogden was in revolt. Its hope and faith and trust betrayed, its future menaced, its children corrupted, it was about to rise and rend and destroy. There were secret meetings, secret affiliations, secret pledges. Ogden was ready to act, and when Ogden acted it would act with ruthless finality. If necessary, there would be killings. Certainly, all these evildoers and certainly the recreant officials who permitted their evil and who kept them in office would be tarred and feathered, ridden out of town, their names an offence to all creation thenceforth, and, if need be, their blood smoking to the skies. (Aha, said our sleuth, a touch of Mormon phraseology there, the author is a Saint.) But, depending on who the recipient of the letter was, there was yet once chance to avert wholesale official scandal and possible civil war. The Mayor could throw the gamblers into jail and break up the University Club. The editor of the *Standard-Examiner* could lead a public campaign to that end. The Presbyterian minister could do the same thing, the Apostle could exert the great force of his church on behalf of civic cleanliness. The Chairman of the Board of Education could fire Hopkins, jailed or unjailed, and Wade Johnson—whom the Mayor could also fire from his city attorney's job. Just possibly, our author said, such public action would appease the secret organizations, save the addressee's skins, mollify the public morality, make Ogden wholesome without war.... That about sums up the forty pages.

They were written in the mood of ecstasy. Ezekiel in the valley of the dry bones,[53] Amos coming down from Tekoa. Highly competent denunciation—if you succumbed to it. it was nightmarish, it was inconceivably ridiculous, and yet somehow it was permeated with a righteousness that throbbed and sang. Reading it, I forgot from time to time that it was talking about a half-dozen hometown boys smoking pipes, drinking soda pop and playing cards—I was seeing Dr. Parkhurst and the poor whores and pimps in the Tenderloin and the Tammany sachems buying passage to Paris.[54] But not for long. Whatever else I am, I am primarily a student of literature. As such, I know literature when I see it. Before I finished even the first one I needed all the restraint my platform career had given me in order not to laugh and spoil the fun.

A politician believes everything that scares him. Frank Francis was a shrewd, hardboiled gent, who had grown up in the emerging West and, they do say, had seen his share of gunplay. Oh, not altogether, maybe not more than sixty-five percent, but enough to believe that his job, if not his life, was in danger, that great masses of votes were organizing against him, that maybe, for God's sake, something ought to be done, some public gestures made about the University Club, even a carcass or two thrown to the wolves. Maybe these secret organizations weren't as big as the author claimed, but Frank knew that they existed. Why not? The idea scared him so it must be true.

Well, I integrated myself into something like the working mind at once. I said, look here, you ass, this is just somebody with a grouch against the University Club or maybe just a grouch against Wade Johnson—it may even have been an heir of the poor woman whose evidence Wade washed out with a fire hose, but it certainly isn't any plot to turn you out of office or set up a Kleagle's Kingdom or an Inquisition on Twenty-fifth Street.[55] I talked horse sense for an hour. I didn't in the least convince him, but I did calm him down and persuade him that no action need be taken. I got the names of the other recipients—the deluge had happened about five days before. I counseled him to hold everything while a mastermind got to work on the problem. I took the letters, after he morally abstracted one page that was covered with sexual accusations the most amusing and picturesque but also the most filthy. Then I phoned my boss that I was taking the day off and got to work. I collected all the other letters I'd heard about without any trouble and then I interviewed the accused. Wade Johnson was the sanest but even he was badly scared—I certainly got an eyeful that explains adequately to me the terror of people accused in anonymous letters. Wade felt that he would probably have to resign the city attorneyship and certainly from the School Board. This was just insane to me. Well, it was insane—we were arguing from two completely different sets of logic, where the same syllogism got exactly opposite conclusions. He said he actually had letters of resignation from Junk and Hopkins. He had: he got them out and showed them to me. And he expected the whole thing to blow open publicly at any moment. I don't know just how, and he didn't either, he merely, in such calm as Princeton could confer on him, expected a black and scarlet scandal story to be on everybody's tongue by a quarter to four. He had entirely forgotten that it was just some of the boys playing penny ante at the Club—it was the queen and a stable boy doing the beast with two backs on Washington Avenue at high noon. While I was talking to him Dr. Rich came in—having followed me there after giving up his letter to me. The good Doctor hated my guts—I was a Gentile who had associated with his good Mormon daughters and God knows what I might have done to them—and always had hated my guts, but when Wade told him that I was really working on the problem I think he would have given me the youngest's maidenhead in fee simple. I went on to Junk, who was far worse than Wade, and finally to Hopkins, who was worst of all. Hopkins was a man in desperate anguish. Curiously, the scene is underscored in my memory by his son, a kid of about eight who had lost an eye and who was playing in the front yard where I finally met up with Hopkins, just before sunset. I keep seeing that white, sightless socket while I listened to Karl rave. It was all right for Wade Johnson to resign—after all, the School Board was nothing and the City Attorney's job wasn't much, Wade had his profession and was established in it and was settled in the community. But Hopkins, who had made good in Ogden, he said, and who had looked forward to spending his life there and had bought a house and expected to be a pillar in the community—and he was a busted sucker for keeps if he had to leave this job under a cloud, he couldn't exercise his profession in Pumpkin Corners after that. I want to tell you, Hopkins was scared.

It was grotesque, fantastic, bizarre—what you will. But there it was. Nobody had to tell me that the letters were fake, that they were either insanity or damned foolishness—but nobody could tell that to any of the victims. But I had the nicest job I'd had in a long, long while. I felt almost restored.

I went home and began to study the letters. I studied them for two days and nights of the hardest concentration I've ever put on anything. I slept the clock round and repeated the assignment. My God, I could write Anthony Adverse with less expenditure of intelligence and energy.... They were written in what purported to be three different hands. On three different kinds of paper—one the letterhead of the University Club itself, to show intimate knowledge of the subject, one the letterhead of the Hotel Utah in Salt Lake City, and one on cheap copybook paper, doubtless to indicate the honest poor. They had been mailed from Salt Lake and from waystations between there and Ogden, in various kinds of envelopes. But my guess was that they had all been written in the same ink, with two different pens, at approximately the same time, and I was even, on the experience of a stationery clerk, willing to guess which ink it was. That, however, was nothing. What was something: by the time I finished my study, I was able to establish beyond any doubt whatever that they were all in the same hand.... A pretty good job from an amateur who had never even reported a handwriting expert's testimony. I made out that the three disguises were only sustained for a page or two, not completely through that much space even, and then resumed a different and distinctive penmanship—and that, I found out later, is just what the experts say that any attempt to disguise handwriting does. I demonstrated that the eventual and characteristic handwriting was the same in all the letters. I demonstrated that it had characteristics which were frequently exhibited in each of the disguised passages. Oh, a lovely job. I had some eighty different points which I followed through all the letters, with a table of frequencies for each—letters, capitals, punctuation marks, up-strokes, down-strokes, shadings, word-endings. I proved it up to the hilt. It was the most finished bit of intellectual endeavor I've ever put on. I wrote a long analysis and a long report, with tables and graphs, and I felt much better.

I was able to tell the Mayor, on my word of honor as a former city editor of the *Standard-Examiner*, that he was dealing not with outraged hosts of voters but with only one individual who was probably crazy and could certainly be sent to Leavenworth for ten years if apprehended. I was able to make the same point with the frantic Hopkins. Both were somewhat relieved. But both were scared still, I wasn't ready to show my proof, and the mere proof wouldn't help them anyway. The situation was eased but by no means alleviated. So where was I?

Well, I could now have the resources of the Police Department, guardedly and circumspectly, without revealing to them too much of the show—that is, said the Mayor, if I really wanted them. I said I'd tell him later. Can you imagine the chance of proving up without experts? There wasn't any chance, but I was going to do it, by God, if it took all winter and the rest of my nervous system. I prepared to dig in and become a great detective.

It's an amusing world, especially when it's moving fast. And a bright race, an intelligent race, especially when it's using its brains. In a sudden horror of sleep, a couple of nights later, I dropped into a cheap dance hall where some of the buddies could always be found. I was going to talk the night away with some of them or maybe walk in the foothills till dawn. I didn't see anyone I wanted to talk or walk with, but I did see a girl I'd gone to high school with. By now the common belief was that she was useful for one purpose only, but I danced with her and sat down at a table with her and summoned some ice cream or whatever. We had some reminiscences about the happy high school years and then she said My, I'd got to be an important man, hadn't I, she was always reading about me in the *Standard-Examiner* since I'd been in the Legion, and gee, we put on a swell show last winter didn't we, she'd been thrilled to death. She said she used to know Bob Major and gee, he was a swell fellow wasn't he. So while I gagged and damned her and dozed she told me about her onetime crush on Bob Major. I suddenly became aware that she was telling me how angry Bob had been once about a letter. I said what letter? and she patiently repeated the story about how when she was going with Bob someone, some nasty person who didn't sign her name, had written to her mother a long letter saying the nastiest things about poor Bob, and Bob had simply been furious, why he had even cried.

I got up and went away. There wasn't any mystery, and I was just a God-damned fool. I can only repeat what I remember saying some time ago, the deduction is never made. I took a taxi to Herrick's, got him out of bed and made him go down to his shop and open up the safe and get a lot of records from *The Three Twins*. With some twenty pages of Major's acknowledged handwriting I went home and got to work. And no, there wasn't any mystery.

I didn't know then as I know now that it was paranoia, with all the classic symptoms. Cacoëthes scribendi,[56] sexual irregularities, delusions of grandeur, delusions of persecution, flight of ideas. There appeared to be no hallucinations and no religious mania, but those are less common anyway. I suppose I missed it because, though deeply learned in the Freudian dogmas already, I hadn't ventured into the commoner techniques and ideologies or into the psychoses. By the time I met E. W. Taylor and laid a good foundation in psychopathology it was all clear and simple to me. But it wasn't when I pushed back my notes and knew, with the consummate peace of the poet, that Major was the uprising of our citizenry. I couldn't understand how such magnificent guile and craft and literary effectiveness could exist side by side with such amazing asininity. That combination gives paranoia its charm to the connoisseur and it gave charm to me too but it bewildered me.

Still, I had him now, if I wanted him. Here was scandal, libel, blackmail and threats of force and violence, and all sent through the mail.... I have omitted the part that bore on me, and the truth is I don't remember which letter or letters it came into and what bearing it had on the rest of the logorrhoea. I do remember that it was a charming bit of projection—Major had taken time off to accuse me of scandal, delusions, malicious libel and sexual behavior that exactly duplicated his own, and I wonder what queer urge was behind that, what identification, even, God help me for it may be true, what displacement. Anyway, I can solace myself through life with the reflection that for a while Major thought he was me or I was him.... I also forget just how much I found out at this particular time about his letter-writing. For the next few months I industriously hunted down everything I could about him and I ran into God knows how many episodes—maybe twenty—in which, for purposes of crucifixion and eventual transfiguration and ascension, Major had written anonymous letters about himself, even to himself as in the instances of the Legion and University Club plays. The episode of the tarnished high school virgin was quite common. Bob would write a letter to the mother of every new girl he took up with. I suppose the motivation—the more superficial motivation, the rationalization—was twofold, to get the old lady into a frame of mind which would make her immune to factual gossip if it should arise, and to soften up the girl herself.

Well, I had my ingenious ass. I had him but what did I want to do with him? It suddenly occurred to me that, after all, I didn't want to send even an inconvenient fool to Leavenworth and that I couldn't prevent that if I let the Mayor know the facts. Once freed of his fear, once convinced that the righteous citizens weren't ganging up on him, Francis would get righteous himself, and most indignant. He would turn the city cops loose and prod the City Attorney, Wade probably being in a similar humor himself, and this poor damn fool would find himself weaving cane chair seats in interior Kansas. Whereas the eternal verities demanded that he be allowed to go on making life amusing till some father gave him both barrels for raping a fourteen-year-old. He could make life rich and beauteous for other people a long while yet, as he had given it gaudy colors for me and my gang. As for me, I was content with poetry: it was enough merely to know that I had him, that the probing and superior intelligence had made its way to the facts at last and brought everything into harmony. I practically loved him by now.

After due thought I organized my plan. First I made out a full report on the authorship of the letters marshaling my facts and presenting them graphically. Then I took this and specimen pages for illustration down to Karl Hopkins's office and made the light to shine for him again. He was quite willing to pay my fee for this deliverance: his promise not to do anything about it and to keep the truth to himself. I made the same bargain with Wade Johnson, with greater difficulty. Then, Wade helping me, I made out a series of affidavits covering everything and outlined the hypothetical case—ready for use if need should arise. Wade agreed to tell Junk and Al that there was nothing to be scared of, that they might go on living in Ogden and even playing poker at the University Club, and to withhold the name of their traducer. So fortified, I went down and got dictatorial with the Mayor. I told him the whole story except such parts as might suggest the villain's name. I then announced that the City Attorney and I had a case prepared but weren't going to use it. We were simply going to force the villain out of town with it. Francis kicked like hell but I told him calmly that I had the documents and he didn't, so what was he going to do about that. Finally he gave in and accepted my terms.

It was, I thought, best to get the bastard out of town. After all, I couldn't expect the city to enjoy paranoid blackmail as much as I did. But I was reluctant, too, for I had a curious desire to hold all this long ton of dynamite over his head without his knowing that I had it. Also, I didn't want to let any more people in on the story and I couldn't see any reasonable way of doing the job myself. Finally I hit on the simple solution, aseptic or rather self-limited blackmail. I sought out a young reporter on the *Standard-Examiner* whom, a couple of years before, I had taught to copy names right from hotel registers and court dockets. I gave him a selection of facts from the story, enough to give him plausibility, not enough to let him trump any of my aces. Since he didn't have any of the documents he couldn't use any of the stuff in the paper. The plan was for him to seek out Major and question him suggestively, so that Major would get the idea that the people were rising in a different way—that the forces of the law were at work, that the vengeful University Club and city officials had the hounds loose on his tail. It was a nice idea.

But it didn't work. But that same day before my agent reached him, Major married the latest of his little girls and left for California, where at once he established a school in the art of the cinema and went on into activities beside which any chronicled herein are just primer stuff. God had cooperated with me, but I never found out how far. The shotgun marriage was just a convenient providence and has enormously strengthened my belief in the usefulness of coincidence, whether for fiction or for life. But also I am morally certain that there had been a leak somewhere along the line and that Major had found out something of what was going on. After all, more than ten days had passed since he had mailed the letters, and I had been at work on them for a week at least. And in the course of that time violent emotions had been agitating the ether. Something had got out, I never found out where or how or what, but something—and Major, already involved with an angry father, came sufficiently out of his delusions to act logically. He did. He left for his appropriate environment.

Let's give this the kind of ending that the editors like.... A week or so later I was despondently leaning on a show-case in the bookstore, exercising a feeble control over a dozen mingled impulses to get the hell out and cut my throat. Enter Karl Hopkins, a radiant Karl, an Ogden Lazarus.[57] He marched up to me. "How much does Spargo pay you here?" he said. I told him a hundred a month. He said, "I can't give you the High school job I promised you a year ago—there's no vacancy. But I can give you a hundred and thirty at a junior high school, for five days a week and shorter hours." So the following Monday I was teaching ancient and American history at Mound Fort Junior High.

****

The waters were by no means still but in spite of hell one manages to remember the pastures as green. About all one can say for youth is that it really is anti-evolutionary, it really does exert an instinctive strength against adaptation. In the mews and cloisters of this mingled Boston and Harvard, the one environment I have not fought, I remember the Ogden I grew up in, and more especially the Ogden I finished my adolescence in, with what amounts to incredulity. It is not possible that I lived in that place, that there was such a place, that I was that special kind of ass. Yet I have only to recall the aching hideousness of Washington Avenue in the carmine of an August sunset and my soul retches too realistically for Ogden to be a fantasy, whether of dread or of fulfillment. It was, and so was I. And I'm afraid that my original prescience was correct: I'm probably going to do a novel about it. Whether I do or don't, I have tasted that forbidden liquor, and it's all I've always heard about it—autobiography is fun for the autobiographer. Is it for the ultimate consumer? Do these Ogdenites at all amuse you? If they do, much more can be told.

NOTES

1. Robert S. Forsythe, BDV's colleague at Northwestern, wrote a short biography of him for publicity purposes. See BDV's letter to him of 6 October 1927, *LBDV*, pp. 14–19.
2. "A fortnight ago" would be circa 27 June 1934. If BDV's reckoning by the ecclesiastical calendar is correct, the first installment of *Bucolics* was sent on 13 August 1934.
3. Reference to *These Ten Years*, memoir in *We Accept with Pleasure*.
4. Franklin Roosevelt suffered an attack of poliomyelitis while at his summer home on Campobello Island, New Brunswick, in August 1921. His legs remained partially paralyzed, and he was obliged to use crutches and wheelchairs for the rest of his life.
5. Reed Smoot (1862–1941), Mormon apostle, U.S. senator from Utah.
6. Grand Army of the Republic, or G.A.R.: sons of Union veterans of the Civil War; founded 1866.
7. Charles R. Mabey (1877–1959), governor of Utah, author.
8. Louvain was heavily shelled, with many civilian fatalities, and its incomparable library burned to the ground by the Germans during the earliest days of the Great War. See Barbara Tuchman, *The Guns of August*, 1962.
9. Fabian Franklin, né Frankel (1853–1959), Hungarian-American mathematician, journalist, and author; professor of mathematics, Johns Hopkins; editor, Baltimore *News*; *People and Problems*, 1908; *What Prohibition Has Done to America*, 1922; *Plain Talks on Economics*, 1924. Franklin was co-editor of *The Review*, 1919–1921. Villard (1872–1949), journalist and historian; editorial staff, *The New Republic*. Edwin Gay (1867–1946), editor of the New York *Post*, 1919–1924; professor of economics at Harvard; founder of *Foreign Affairs Quarterly*.
10. (Latin, freely) world without end. The book reviews are not identified.
11. "The Rouge Bouquet" and "Trees," both by Joyce Kilmer (1886–1918), New Jersey poet, 1918.

12. Reed Hotel, built 1891, five stories.
13. The *Tribune* was founded in 1868, C. C. Goodwin, editor; the *Rocky Mountain News* was founded in 1859.
14. Reference to *Godey's Lady's Book*.
15. (Latin) for the sake of honor; often included in inscriptions in honorary degrees, or for degrees awarded posthumously to students killed in the armed services.
16. Christiansen (1868–?), candidate of the National Farmer-Labor Party. Simon Bamberger (1846?–1926), governor of Utah, 1917–1921.
17. Eugene V. Debs (1855–1926), labor organizer, Socialist Party candidate for president in 1912 and 1920, had been convicted of treason under the Espionage Act of 1917 and the Sedition Act of 1918 for denouncing America's entry into the Great War. Even in prison he received nearly one million votes for president, about 3 percent of the total vote cast. The 1917 and 1918 acts expired without renewal in 1921, and that same year, on Christmas Day, President Harding ordered Debs's release from prison. The so-called Lusk Laws, enacted by the state of New York, required teachers to sign a loyalty oath.
18. BDV's memory is flawed here; Joseph Howell (1857–1918) served in Congress from 1903 to 1917.
19. See *Kent Potter Story*.
20. White mule was moonshine.
21. Following the Civil War, the Republican Party regularly blamed the Democratic Party for having caused the war and having sided with the South.
22. Philip Dormer Stanhope, Fourth Earl of Chesterfield (1694–1773), British statesman and author; *Letters to His Son*, 1774.
23. "And so she come tearin' along that night—/The oldest craft on the line—/With a nigger squat on her safety valve,/And her furnace crammed, rosin and pine." John Hay, "Jim Bludso," *Pike County Ballads* (1871).
24. MacNider (1889–1968), appointed National Commander of the American Legion in 1921; he served with distinction in both wars. Roosevelt (1887–1944), son of President Theodore Roosevelt and one of the founders of the American Legion; assistant secretary of the navy, 1921.
25. In the first Battle of the Marne, 5–12 September 1914, French and English forces halted the German advance through northern France and forced a retreat; it was the critical turning point in the first stages of the Great War. In the second Battle of the Marne, summer 1918, the Allied Armies halted the German offensive.
26. Plumed knight, epithet of James G. Blaine (1830–1893), congressman and senator from Maine; Speaker of the House of Representatives, 1868–1872; U.S. secretary of state, 1881, 1889–1892; candidate for president, 1886.
27. See below, Parts V–VI.
28. Kiwanis International, founded 1915; chiefly benefiting children. Lions Clubs International, since 1917. Optimist International, founded 1919, chiefly benefiting children. Engineers, unidentified.
29. W.O.W., unidentified.
30. Lindquist, Larkin and Kirkendall: all three firms were still in business in Ogden as of 2005; Kirkendall is now Kirkendall-Darling.
31. The Plimsoll mark refers to the stripes painted on the hull of a cargo ship, marking the displacement of the ship under load.
32. John Held Jr. (1889–1958), illustrator, renowned for woodcuts in *The New Yorker*.
33. Chopin, Funeral March from the Piano Sonata in B flat minor, op. 35, 1837. Siegfried's Funeral (not burial) Music from Wagner's *Die Götterdämmerung*, 1874.
34. *The Gods of the Mountain*, play by Lord Dunsany (1878–1957), 1911.

35. Olsen (1889–1954), stage and screen actor. Knox (1505–1572), Scottish theologian and historian.
36. A daily newspaper for members of the United States armed services; originally produced during the Civil War and in 1918, and regularly since 1942.
37. In Sinclair Lewis's *Main Street*.
38. Of the John Culley Drug Company; president of the Utah Pharmacists Association in 1911.
39. Bread Loaf Writers' Conference.
40. See 34-50.
41. Fancy suit jackets.
42. (1868–1915), British poet and playwright.
43. Southern Pacific Railroad.
44. Captain John Parker of the Minute Men, before the Battle of Lexington (Massachusetts), 19 April 1775: "Stand your ground. Don't fire unless fired upon, but if they mean to have a war, let it begin here."
45. George Henry Dern (1872–1936), governor of Utah, 1925–1933; Secretary of War, 1933–1936.
46. "With, ho! such bugs and goblins in my life," *Hamlet*, Act V scene 2.
47. Mundelein, Illinois, named after George William Mundelein (1872–1939), Cardinal Archbishop of Chicago, had three previous names.
48. In 1934, Sinclair ran unsuccessfully for governor in California on a platform called EPIC (End Poverty In California).
49. "And was made man," part of the Credo.
50. Arthur Perkins '19 ('20), M.D. '23. Howell was probably James Albert Howell '97, Ll.B. '99.
51. Insull (1859–1938), British-American public utility executive (gas and electricity) and corporate swindler.
52. Gaius Caesar Caligula (12–41 CE), Roman emperor, noted for madness and debauchery.
53. Ezekiel 37.
54. Charles Henry Parkhurst (1842–1933), Presbyterian minister in New York City, denounced and exposed corruption in the city government, 1892. The Tenderloin, a term referring to different parts of New York City at different times, mostly the wide area south of Forty-second Street along Broadway and between Fourth and Seventh Avenues; now chiefly used in reference to the busiest part of downtown San Francisco.
55. Kleagle's Kingdom of the Ku Klux Klan.
56. "an incurable passion for writing or scribbling," Lewis and Short, *A Latin Dictionary*; citing Juvenal.
57. Raised from the dead; see St. John 11.

APPENDIX B

KENT POTTER STORY

Now that I sit down to write this, I suddenly realize that it hasn't much story value as such. I could, by making it very short, give the death scene some of the tremendous impact it had. Or I could write the whole thing at novel length and draw out real values, which are those of interrelationships, like all stories of personality, and of doubt and ambiguity and the unknown and the unknowable. I can't get either virtue into such a narrative as this will have to be. But I'm going ahead with it. You have, in all innocence and defencelessness, habituated me to autobiography. It's a habit-forming stimulant. And I rather want to see how I can set down this particular bit of my past and what I'll make of it once it's set down. I'll keep myself out of it so far as may be.

Let's make some obeisance to the conventions. Toward the end, I'll have to put in a couple of frankly false names, for the real ones are of some moment in the modern world, or rather of some publicity, and since a moral certainty is not a moral proof I can't even be sure of their identity anyway. There's no hope that I'd be able to call Kent anything but Kent very long, so that goes, and I might as well call his brother Elmer by name. Let's call their last name Potter, which is quite a way from the real one, and their sister Pamela, which has something of the flavor of her real name.[1]

The first thing that occurs to me is this. At the moment there is a very English pair of shoes on my feet—heavy as hell, rough, very much mist on the moors and keeping fit. A month ago I saw them in a shop window. Passing it several times, I found myself unaccountably attracted by those shoes, and so one day I went in and bought them. Sometime later I realized they were just like a pair that Kent Potter wore in the fall of 1919.

I came to Harvard in the fall of 1915, after an experimental and hilarious but negligible year at the University of Utah. Memorial Hall made up a number of tables of such transfer students and so chance threw several of us together who remained more or less together—Gordon King from CCNY, Tommy Raysor (the completely mindless man) from the U of Chicago, Dave Snodgrass from the U of California, Kent Potter from the U of Illinois.[2] Gordon King had transferred from motives of the highest intellectuality and idealism, and I for no particular reason; the others were just taking the back door into Harvard. King and I became friends at once, and remained so until he died, two months before his namesake was born. Raysor was inexhaustibly amusing, the way the first phonograph must have been. Snodgrass was an amiable pirate whose destiny as the attorney of a wildcat oil company was predictable the first night I saw him. I can't say that I ever particularly cared for either of them, though I later roomed with them for a year in Fairfax Hall.

Kent was another matter. For some weeks I regarded him as the greatest pest since the Exodus. He had a flipness that offended me, a young sophistication that was beyond my still rural understanding, a faculty for dragging out latent asininities and then ruthlessly trampling on them, and a queer kind of cultural inheritance that it took me a long time to make out. He was a smaller man than I, slightly built, stoop-shouldered with an odd, shambling gait when he walked. Gordon King had the most classically beautiful man's face I've ever seen outside of a Greek frieze, but Kent's face was an assemblage of utterly mediocre and commonplace features—on a bet, you couldn't have brought together such a job-lot of inanities. Yet the queer thing was, the effect was rather humorous and pleasant, and after he came back from the war a kind of sculpture had been accomplished so that something primordially mid-western and fundamental, like the Lincoln in Jackson Park (<u>not</u> the one in Lincoln Park), showed through. He had character in his face, after the war.

He had a brother in the class of 1915. That and the next class, '16, are still referred to as, in the college jargon, big years. Certainly they were, as things go, in the literary business. Dos Passos, cummings, Hillyer, Auslander and a good many more.[3] There was a definite mood and movement in the literary Harvard of those days, and Cowley almost described it in the *New Republic* a couple of years back.[4] I'd do a better—and more honest—job if I set out, but Cowley did suggest something of the Esthetic Years. Well, in that crew, which included a good many no one has ever heard of since, Elmer Potter was easily the best bet. He was as brilliant a young man as ever made a show of dissipation in the Yard. Handsome, handsomely depraved, a mind like a lightning flash, given to the Wilde-ish epigram that young Harvard favored in that happy time, an episodic but sensitive and alert intelligence, great savoir-faire, a baroque imagination. Hillyer ran him a very bad second, and Dos Passos was generally supposed to come considerably behind Hillyer.... Robert was a young man of brilliant promise for years, until it was realized that he used to have great promise.

Understand, I was hardly even a hanger-on of this high-church estheticism. I was an oafish kind of cub, lubberly and stammering and Rocky Mountain. No kind of form was imposed on me until after the war. I knew these great ones, sometimes I was privileged to listen to them, but no more—though sometimes I could carry a sonnet that George Percy had written or listen to some other wisp of the Braithewaite movement describe his soon to be written five act tragedy in perfumed and uncapitalized verse, with some symbols in the stage directions, such as "Utter Darkness," "To be accompanied by a hautboy and a lute," or "The mist lifts and Christ is seen."[5] But, hell, I lacked money to buy peyote, I never saw Pan and never raped a wood nymph, I didn't know about Rosicrucianism and hardly even about tribadism or the higher Urning.[6] I was just a dub and something of a grind.

Kent had nothing of Elmer's brilliance. He wasn't showy. He didn't glitter. He wasn't literary. It took me a long time to realize that he was intelligent as hell, and even longer to make out the curiously deep-rooted individuality and authenticity of his thinking. He was an inattentive student, but something of a chemist. He was sowing his oats, too, drinking outrageously and giving all the town girls a flutter. He was a very conventional person, and I think it was partly conventionality that made him work so hard at sin—he was of an old Springfield family, a rich man's son, and old and wealthy families in the Sangamon country had to behave that way. There were certain fixed things, you understand, precisely as there were two kinds of women, as respect for the law and support of the church were obligatory, as one reproved slights and avenged a sister's honor.

I came to understand that much of him resulted from a couple of injuries he'd had. The sight of one eye was seriously impaired, as a result of a fight with Elmer when they were both boys. Then, at Howe's School for Manly Boys, a midwestern Groton, he had injured his spine in the gymnasium and had spent a year in bed, laced in some fiendish kind of leather corset.[7] Thereafter there was either the threat or the actuality, I don't know which, of tuberculosis in the spine. The year in bed had been a year of uninterrupted agony. He was resolved never to go through it again. With some dread of that sort—I wish to God I had had then the training I've had since in the symptomology of dread—hanging over him constantly, he constantly carried on his person a sizable shot of refined cyanide salt.

Even more of him can be understood only in relation to Springfield, Illinois. These days of gloom and the apprehension of doom, I reject all prophecies of what is to come. For I have seen none that takes the Middle West into account. They are all based on the slum and better than slum alien populations of New York, Philadelphia, the New Jersey factory belt and, very occasionally, Boston. Well, I don't prophesy—largely because I don't know what the Middle West is like these days. But I do know that whatever happens to the Republic, the Middle West will be the final, the determining force. For good or ill, and I can make out a case both ways, the Middle West is America. It is the America of yesterday, as, belatedly, a few thinkers are coming to faintly understand. Even more certainly, it is the America of tomorrow. And that whether Chicago can buy the future, or crush it into shape by mere weight, or has to do some bloodletting. And of the Middle West, past and present but especially past, Illinois is the heart. And of Illinois, the Sangamon country, the Lincoln country, is the heart of hearts. I'll try to make an essay on that theme sometime, explaining it for youse easterners as no middle-westerner has ever been able to do, not even Grierson.[8] Here, you'll have to take it on faith.

The Potters were of that soil. They lived in a big house on a gentleman's farm a few miles from the city. Kent's father was a doctor, and a very brilliant one, as who should know better than I, since he cleared up a job that various talents had made no headway with in Utah and Boston. He practiced with his brother, and they both had big holdings in Illinois farm land, Springfield buildings, Oklahoma oil, etc. Dr. Potter was bred out of Illinois loam, which has the shadow of Lincoln on it always: he had the idealism and sentimentality of that loam, too, with violent colorations of arrogance and stubbornness from his inheritance. There is no gentry like the Springfield gentry. J. Ham Lewis, a lifelong friend of the Potters, is a perfect specimen.[9] Or, move down the social ladder several rungs, and you get much of the same feeling in Edgar Lee Masters, curdled somewhat and made famous by Freud and Bob Ingersoll, or you can even glimpse it, under showmanship and a differently curdled sentimentality, in Clarence Darrow. Masters, I may say, was an acquaintance though definitely not a friend.

There was in both Kent and Elmer, besides this grass-roots Americanism, a distinct and distinctly conflicting anarchy, eccentricity, genius, what you will. It was what produced Elmer's showiness and brilliance. It was less apparent in Kent but I soon felt it, without being able to define it. I leave it to you to find a name, if there is one. Well, this came from their mother. We will take her up later on, and I'll put her into a book sometime, for she is the most interesting, the most fascinating woman I've ever known. As the tale will tell, there was once some thought that I might marry her daughter. I firmly discouraged that, for the prospect did not attract me. But there was never a moment when I would not have married the mother, if I could have. Bear in mind that I saw her only for ten days of one September, ten days of the following Christmas holidays, and corresponded with her from September to April, and for all that I say that no woman I've ever seen influenced me so profoundly, gave me so much or seemed to me so completely magnificent. It is enough, at the moment, to list a few facts. She was not Illinois but Pennsylvania. She was, I have a vague impression, the first woman ever awarded a Ph.D. And her life in Springfield had been one sustained—and hidden—rebellion.

Yes, and I wonder. We who kneel at a Vienna altar rail come to have our ideas about things. A week or so ago, going through a strong box, I found a letter from her. I know it is a letter from a woman nearing fifty to a young man of twenty-five, who had been the best friend of her dead son and who, she desperately hoped, might marry her daughter. You wouldn't know that, if you read the letter. It would be just any love letter. Why, I wonder at the altar rail, was she moved from a lifelong circumspection to influence me to marry Pamela? But let's leave that to its place in the sequence.

I knew Kent only casually, that first half-year at Harvard. He brought Krafft-Ebing and similar works into my life, as the result of a dinner table conversation, taught me all I learned about the day by day Harvard, and argued with Sangamon righteousness against the intellectual anarchism I was learning. (I remember with much pleasure that Freud entered my life at about the same time, by way of a Craig Kennedy story in the *Cosmopolitan*.)[10] But my intimate was Gordon King and so I thus early worked into, through and out of the young intellectual phase. Gordon had built it up out of French novels, the Russian poor-student tradition, Plato and the Utopian socialism that was advanced thought in Little Old New York when the world was drifting towards its end. I submit that a recusant Mormon-Catholic who had grown up in a labor town and had occupied some of the jobs I had already filled cannot long, thoroughly or comfortably exist as a y. i., but such as I could I did, and it fitted me to write MT's A as one having authority.

Toward spring, however, Kent suddenly persuaded me into a small, now extinct, club over which he was shortly to preside—a gang of mostly literary gents under the domination of Elmer.[11] I suppose it was good for me, since I learned how to keep on my feet while the chosen were being brilliant all about, and I lost some of my oafishness, and I met some people I could like, even a few I could admire, as Bill Hewitt, later killed in the war, who was a pianist and, in 1916, had already written a symphony one movement of which was in, well, ragtime.[12] Also it had a bar.

I had also met a dependent of Dave Snodgrass's named Stephenson.[13] He is a story in himself, but I name him now merely to explain that he also held back the development of my friendship with Kent. That ripened steadily but, considering its strength in the post-war year, probably not as much as it would have if I hadn't been so friendly with Steve. Kent and I were friends, even good friends, but our relationship didn't have that timelessness and profundity that came afterward. If, as the church holds, friendship is a homosexual relationship, then certainly that was to be the strongest homosexual influence of my life.

From September 1916 on, the nation was obviously drifting to war. . . . There was a poignant scene as early as January or February, which will last while I do as the moment when the war came out of the picture sections into realization. Gordon King took me to one of those Monday Nights which were, except for the role of Charles Townsend Copeland, Copey's only contribution to our times. He had a guest that night, one whom three or four years later he would hate and fear as a burning Bolshevik, S. K. Ratcliffe, then, I believe, of the Guardian.[14] He sat in the guest's green chair, Copey vis-à-vis, with the yellow light of Copey's oil lamp on him, and a score or two of us young stotes ranged in the brown shadows on the floor. Quite simply and unemotionally, but with a fine art—one then much practiced by visiting Englishmen—he told about seeing the troops march off for Folkstone, singing "Send father and mother, send sister and brother, but for God's sake don't send me," about following them to France, simple, isolated, immensely effective vignettes militaires. Just as simply and inevitably, he from time to time dropped his narrative, looked round at us through great gleaming spectacles, mildly, reflectively, and remarked, "I'll see you young men there in a year or two." It was a perfection of propaganda, of a particular British propaganda that stinks to God, but—it did its job. At least, sitting there with a fire burning on the hearth of Emerson and Thoreau and Everett, looking out to bright moonlight on the snowy roofs of Thayer and Holworthy, I heard the tramp and shuffle of those feet and the hoarse singing overseas. He may have seen some of us over there, too. To my certain knowledge, Gene Galligan was in the room that night, and Gene Galligan got his on the Vesle.[15]

Not that I swallowed it as propaganda. Probably the one fixed reliance of my life is the knowledge that up to April 6, 1917, I did not share the hysteria, and that on that day I decided with logico-experimental dispassionateness that it was going to be more comfortable in the Army than out of it and so I'd get in.... We were, I say, drifting into war, impelled by, among other things, that same propaganda. To Kent it was all very simple. America was going to war. Patriotism waters the roots of prairie grass and that's all there was to it. Gordon King, the intellectual, was forced into rationalization and came out with Aristotle and Plato and the sense of the state, branding me as an anarchist and, though still upholding his late principles of the freedom of individual choice, urging that such an anarchist be allowed to set himself up on an uninhabited isle where there was no state, since the state could tolerate no interference with its sovereign necessity.... It was a shock to the idealists of the Republic when the Spargos, Brookses, Lippmanns and so on took just that road. It was no shock to me. And I imagine the DeVoto repudiation of the soft-minded, which may live to go farther than print has so far taken it, got powerfully stepped up in just those days.... As for me, I was just cutting my intellectual milk teeth. I'd just formulated ideas about the individual. I wasn't going to war, nor could I see any canon of obligation or necessity that could command me to. That was the idealist in me who died, if not on the following April 6, at least no later than the first time I commanded a platoon. There was also the contrary DeVoto, part idealist too maybe, and when the Harvard boys, say about November, began to form societies for the suppression with eggs of the other Harvard boys who were forming societies against war I, who had up till then been too much of an individualist to have any truck with either, joined one of the latter. It sufficed to give me an early conception of economic determinism of applied emotion and to have an enjoyable battle with the to be martyred son of a to be martyred ex-President.[16] I forget what we called ourselves. I know there was no taint of the Nazi-ism or Communism of those days, pro-Germanism. But we got egged. And spat at by Copey, whose class I was then in, and who called me yellow to my face and from the desk. Oh, rich and rambunctious days, very fertilizing for the mind.

My treason was very hard on Kent. He did his best, not to understand it for understanding it was beyond his power, but to allow for it, to consider me, it may be, a lovable and gallant person whose mind had been poisoned or, more likely, quite addled. I have one clear memory—Kent dropping into King's room, where I had taken to spending most of my evenings, *vice* Desperate Jack Desmond who had sailed for France at Copey's expense, late one night. There had been some kind of dinner at the club and he had missed me and his heart had been troubled, so he tucked a couple of bottles of charged Italian wine into his pockets and set out to find me. So there the three of us sat on the top floor of Hollis smoking and yarning before a fire and presently broke off and were talking war. As, I fancy, Harvard boys break off today to talk about revolution or that more universal and deeper dread, the jobs they may not get. I can still feel the sputter of that—oh, spumante or moscato or the like—in my nostrils. And the talk widened out to argument and then Gordon was suddenly denouncing me as a traitor to society who would not take his share of society's obligations, and his voice rose and his cheeks reddened and it was uncomfortable, awkward, with painful feelings of reticences broken up and scattered, of decencies surrendered to the unforeseen calamity. And Kent's face was white—and so damn plain—and he was trying to soothe Gordon down and placate me and bring our minds to meet—and he agreed with every word Gordon said, it being probably the first time he had ever found sense in a theoretical discussion.... That was what it was like in the colleges when Wilson was writing briefer notes and the flags were already out on State Street.

So one day the flags were legal. Snodgrass and Stephenson and I went to *The Tailor Made Man* at the Hollis Street Theater, and at the end of the first intermission people came in with newspapers that had flown the expected heads at last.[17] We saw the show out and then went out to the greatest of Harvard bars, just round the corner. I stood at a ticker, drinking ale from one of those great and now forgotten glasses, and read Wilson's speech... her life, her fortune, and her sacred honor, God helping her, she can do no other.[18] ... it will always have the creaminess of that ale with it, if I read it in hell.

Woodrow Wilson became at once the greatest stylist in Copey's class and one morning Harold Laski said, in History 2, "How many of you are taking the special examination in this class?" and I realized that I'd made up my mind, I was taking it. I was going to be a hero but I was going to be damned if I'd be an enlisted hero. I was just too young for Plattsburg and they caught my perjury, so I went for a while into the Harvard Regiment, about which I'll certainly set down some reminiscences sometimes.[19] For the moment we lingered in Cambridge, being quartered in the Freshman Dormitories, where my barracks was later to be part of Ronald Ferry's Master's lodging in Winthrop House.

The roles had been abruptly reversed. I was, de facto anyway, a patriot—and Kent wasn't. That bad eye and that tortured spine kept him out of every service. Through April and May he lingered on in Cambridge, the unhappiest man in North America, all but in tears whenever he saw olive drab swinging down the street. He tried every branch of every service, he called on all his father's political pull, he offered bribes. He got a few chances at non-combatant, or rather unmilitary, appointments, but he simply could not get into uniform. For the first time, he began to defer to me. He cherished me—I remember his concern, one hot day, lest I might drown swimming across the Charles—he asked my opinion about things—he was rapidly building up an inadequacy that could have destroyed him.... Sudden flash, as I write. I remember shucking my uniform one night and going off to Boston with him for another traditional tour of the bars. The flash shows the two of us standing at one bar near Scollay Square drinking treat and treat with some violent and hairy-chested mechanic who was all for annihilating the Huns and kept showing us how he only had three and a half fingers on his left hand, so them bastardly draft guys would never get him. Kent pointed to me and whispered in the mechanic's ear, with a pride that carried the length of the room, "He's in the infantry."

Then, with an intricate machinery of perjury, bribery, subornation and fraud, the culminating piece of which was a hundred dollars paid to a broken-down Irish M.D., he got himself accepted in the ambulance service. He sailed before the end of May and by June 10th was at the front. I'm not going to identify his S.S.U., though probably you don't know anything about it anyway, but it was a famous.[20] It was attached to the 20me French Division, part of the shock forces. For nine months continuously after Kent reached it, it was in action at Verdun, in the last or holy-horror stage of that endless battle.[21] It was practically continuously in action up to Armistice Day and it was part of the Army of Occupation from that time on. Kent was with it all that time except for a couple of short leaves and about three weeks all told in hospitals. Don't ask me how he stood it—if, in fact, he did stand it. It may have been the flare of a wracked body that ended by consuming itself. He received the Croix de Guerre and had two later citations, one corps, one armée. He was, as I'll show later, probably recommended for the Legion d'Honneur. He had a name for reckless daring. Both his citations mention bringing out wounded under heavy fire. One that didn't get into the books dealt with salvaging an ambulance. He and a chap whom I'm calling Meredith were able, by a fluke and the grace of God, to get hold of some German plans for *coup de main*,[22] and that made quite a big stir.[23] He was several times gassed, in a small way. He got odd bits of shrapnel into him to the number of fifteen or more, but never in any important part of him. He had a ghastly dysentery when the food went bad—it was at the fag-end of 1917 when the poilus were mutinying here and there on that sufficient ground.[24] It was a heroic war record and, considering his physique, it's all but incredible. He was in everything. His war letters, which I have in typescript, are magnificent. He also wrote a couple of studies of Verdun that are cut from the same piece. But I'm not writing about his war record. Let this suffice. Anyway, he led a full and violent life in the French army. So he lived through the war and in due time came home.

II

What of Elmer, in the meantime? Graduating in 1916, he went back to Springfield and began to work on a local paper. I'm not sure whether your near namesake was then in Springfield or not—the Potter-Stern lineup may have been earlier or later.[25] Anyway, Elmer now entered on a dashing if condescending career as a reporter, the vague pre-war prelude to all literary achievement. A young man of fashion and elegance in this midland capital, the phase changing a little, no doubt, from the symbolist mood of Harvard. There would be a tie-up with the seething politics of down-state Illinois. He joined the National Guard, because young men of position were responding to Gen. Wood and the elder Roosevelt, who felt strongly about national defence, and also because those of a certain position in interior America must have a military connection, for show and for the encouragement of the lower orders.[26] And also Romance. A daughter of the well-connected gladdened his heart and the phase lapsed to the Victorian which is—still—a high flavor in some aspects of Mid-America. There were treasured gloves, a rosebud from a corsage given him in a moment of daring and provocative allure, missives scribbled in the late hours and sent to the beloved's home by messenger with three violets—something of the plush years, the era of cravats and padded shoulders, manly sighs and manly honor, triolets, the plucked mustache.

But fair could be false. She up and eloped with someone else. A young blade had no recourse but to dissipate in the grandest manner; so for some time Elmer splendidly ran the range, a limited range, of sin in Springfield. Inevitably, he was called back to his better self, saved from ruin, moved to remake his life, by the humble adoration of a singer in Springfield's primordial night club. A sweet, gallant, pure miss, I promise you, but for all that an entertainer, which was bad, and a Catholic which, in the Spoon River country, was much worse. Once a Valois always a Bourbon to be sure,[27] and he was Elmer Potter still, son of Dr. Potter, great-grandson or grandnephew of President Pierce, heir of The Oaks, the gentry of the prairies. The family was kind but appalled, resolute but heartbroken. And now Wilson sent Black Jack into Mexico on a foray whose thunder had less success than was intended and the National Guard aristocrats were soon using common latrines and washing their faces in water heavily impregnated with alkali.[28] The Guard was still on the Border, frying its tail lean in desert sun, when the symphony for which the raid had been an overture sounded its opening chords. Elmer took examinations for commission from private life and, being a person who passed all examinations, was soon Lt. Potter. At the end of the summer, myself uncommissioned, I wrote to Dr. Potter asking for word of Kent and got it, with a quiet notation that Elmer had "joined his regiment."

Joining it he went on with it to North Carolina and, in due time, to France. About August, 1918, it pushed slowly forward, leapfrogged the supporting forces, lined up and went over. Fifteen minutes later Elmer went down, the military glory for which his Midland inheritance had prepared him lasting just a quarter of an hour. The messenger boy carried the yellow envelope up the winding path of The Oaks and I have no doubt that some ancestral quiver of satisfaction passed along Dr. Potter's spine when he learned that he had given a son for the defence of the fatherland. A week later there was a requiem mass at St. Luke's—the kind of prairie Canterbury that made the archbishop of Chicago feel the superiority of his own simple, Roman rites. It was absolutely true to the Potters that mother, sister, father and the for once welcome widow, arrived at the mass twenty minutes late. A month later a letter came to the bereaved mansion from a hospital in southern France. Elmer wrote that his career had been honorable, that he had a wound stripe, that some ounces of waste matter had been carried away from his thighs and buttocks, and that he was enjoying his convalescence. He came back with his division and that splendid melancholy flared up long enough to promote attempts to enlist in the Polish Legion and several other lost causes. That a man might live with gallantry and by his sword. They failed. Elmer, bearing in mind a wife who would not do and a genius betrayed by the miscellany that were to make a generation Lost some years later, stayed in the Army and became a contented Captain moving in peacetime order from post to post. He troubles this chronicle no longer and has been detailed thus far only to make plain:—that the pitcher was broken at the fountain,[29] that Mrs. Potter had lost her brilliant son, that her vicarious literary career had been cut off.

I had heard nothing whatever from Kent after he sailed for France. I later found plenty of allusions to me in the letters he wrote home, but he wrote none to me. I got back to Harvard on the Saturday before classes began in September, 1919, and met him two hours later at the corner of Dunster and Massachusetts Avenue. I had, to save time and trouble, agreed to share a suite in Fairfax with Dave Snodgrass and Tommy Raysor, veterans both and Tommy, the Texan, noisomely so. I didn't like either of them much and found Tommy, who had the highest summa cum ever granted by Harvard and would eventually get the best Ph.D. but was without trace, vestige or premonition of intelligence, a Goddamned pest. Still, one had to live somewhere and I had lived with much worse than either of them during the late crusade. I met Kent, I say, and at once we were friends of the deepest.

That relationship is practically beyond analysis. Below the censor, the relation of man to man is, I doubt not, ambiguous and dark. Above it, it is infinitely more complex than the relation of man to woman and, sometimes, fully as intense. Anyway, wide apart as our minds and interests and ambitions were, we somehow dovetailed into an offensive and defensive alliance that highly amused and deeply satisfied us both. We ate together, did our work together, drank together, toured Boston together, walked and went to shows and endlessly held bull sessions together. The episodes of John Bakeless, Dicky Quintana, Joe Blickensderfer and the ghost of Wm. James and a good many others I have related to you belong to this period.[30]

A good year. The last year of youth as such. And yet not altogether as such, at that. After all, three hundred of us were back, variously, from the wars. And however inglorious one's military career, it had done something. Me, for example. God knows, the only perils I had faced were those of measles and meningitis in camps where one slept on a mattress every night and had steam heat at one's bunk end and could come in out of the rain. Yet I had spent some sixteen months under sentence of death and though all conscious realization of it vanished about the time I first mixed mush and beans and bacon and maple syrup and molasses in a mess kit for breakfast, it was certainly eating away below the threshold all the time. How much more, then, a man who had spent sixteen months in the actual presence and imminent menace of death. That was one difference. Another, more conscious one, was sixteen months of association with democracy. No anarchism, of course, ever survived a contact with reality: I do not see how any socialism, any faith in the race, could survive an experience of the army. Again, the habit of command. I had been charged with the health, efficiency and preparation for war of as many as four hundred men at a time. I had accepted responsibility for thousands of dollars, for the management and safety of a rifle range, for training on which conceivably the success of an attack might depend. Most of all, I had done handily, even easily, against the odds, what no one had supposed me capable of doing: I had been a practical success.

So a lot of the oaf was gone from me, I was cocky as hell, self-assured, impudent. And I was determined not to slip back. I got more from Harvard in that one year than ever before—or since. One studies well and learns thoroughly after such a break. I became a first-rate student. An examination of Henry Adams's scientific notions which I did for L. J. Henderson's History of Science remains as good a job as I have ever done. We three hundred were pre-eminent throughout Harvard and I unexpectedly found myself a literary figure, heir to Elmer Potter, et al.... I was without knowing it a symbol of the age that was on American lit, reading Anatole France, Aldous Huxley, Mencken, Lawrence, O'Neill, writing in the idiom, scorning the trance-ecstasy-shrine mood of the pre-war Harvard and hilariously attacking and burlesquing its sole survivor, a vestigial dramatist who wrote about boys and arrows in the air, a pallid pansy who has vanished beyond the farthest reach of my memory. The year I graduated, 1920, was the year of *Main Street, Moon Calf, This Side of Paradise, Smoke and Steel, A Few Figs From Thistles, The Sacred Wood*.[31]

Kent was quieter, more subdued, more fixed and purposeful. I've mentioned the refinement of his features. He whored and drank a good deal less, he worked harder, he knew what he wanted to do. He had moods of *cafard*,[32] of hangover from the war, when the nihilism that is the only bit of actuality in the Lost Generation myth attacked him. At such times he would be silent and morose, grouchy, sensitive—would break out in meaningless denunciations of anything at hand. But mostly he was cheerful and stuck to his last. He was suddenly a fine chemist, full of promise, tireless in the laboratory. He was working on an idea for mechanical—electrical—refrigeration, which wasn't bad for the fall of 1919, since his idea had to do with small units to be used in private houses and produced in masses. Once or twice I went to the Boston Public and did patent research for him. He disciplined his sprawling penmanship to a minute copperplate adapted to laboratory records. Having spent seventeen months in the French army, he naturally had some trouble passing French A, in which he had a condition. He worked late into the night and never seemed to get enough sleep. He contrived an attachment for his alarm clock that let down a shelf from his desk square on his head when it went off. He did well in his classes. He was at peace with the Dean.

Pamela was a freshman at Wellesley that year. He didn't introduce me to her for some time. When I finally realized what was eating him, it was a vivid symbol of the change in our relative relationship—it was because he figured that Benny would be bored. Finally he did, and thereafter I saw her occasionally, took her to dinner or a show in Boston or went out to Wellesley and wandered through the woods. She lived with twelve other girls in a house in the Village which was locally known as The Birdcage. She was a rather hefty girl of mediocre intelligence, with Kent's plainness of face and feature. She abjectly worshiped him. She always had, and both abjectness and worship had been stepped up a thousand times by the war, which she was aware had been won by Kent, with some brilliant but unimportant assistance from Elmer. It was the most fervid brother-worship I ever saw—there may be a clue to the whole maze in the fact that all the Potter relationships were fervid, even tropical. Like this, for instance. Dave Snodgrass, in his breezy California way: Where the hell were you all afternoon, Benny? DeV: I took Miss Potter out to City Point and we looked at the fish. Dave, whinnying: Miss Potter! Jesus, you haven't got very far with that girl, have you. So Kent calls Dave aside and blisteringly bawls him out for the familiarity and demands an apology in the name of pure Illinois womanhood, and gets it.... She had the same fervidness and alas the same abjectness in all her emotions. The Christmas vacation I spent at The Oaks, we went down town one day and she told her mother that she'd be back at three. We were delayed some twenty minutes and she shook all over and I had to hire a taxi to transport us some six miles. There was no reason why we need be back at any particular time but she'd told her mother three o'clock.... "Pamela," the Doctor calls, "it's stopped raining, get out and take a walk." She got out—with me—so fast that she was in an agony of embarrassment for ninety minutes because she hadn't had time to put on her garters.... I mentioned my annoyance because the Northwestern Library was so bum; it didn't even have a copy of a well-known history of religions I wanted to refer to. So as soon as she got back to Wellesley, she typed out nearly five hundred pages and sent them to me, to refer to.... And all this concentrated on the sacred image of Kent. Guilt? Yes, but what desire produced the guilt?

Sometimes Kent and I would go out to the Birdcage together and let the Wellesley Inn stare at us as one woman. Sometimes, when he had a check from The Oaks, he'd summon all thirteen of them in for dinner—and once, having loaded them with food, we took them riding on the beautiful but rough Harbor and spilled thirteen dinners overside. An age was vanishing with these college girls. In outside America the Flapper was being born—see an earlier work by the same author—but these were sedate girls, still prim, still proper, still earnest, still devoutly looking forward to the ideal career of the Wilson Age and the New Freedom, romantic service in some cloudy Hull House where they would Inspire and Teach and Save. One spring day Pamela and I had paddled across the Lake and were sitting there smoking—I smoking, for these girls smoked only on a dare, and made a pretty sputter when they did that. Another canoe glided up, and a handsome girl getting out of it exposed a leg on which the stocking was rolled below the knee. This was a novelty and the leg was excellent. Pamela had answered the girl's "Hello," and I asked who she was. She told me reluctantly and added that this rolled stocking notion was Fast.

Pamela had, of course, a fanatical interest in Kent's war record and had it by heart. She told it off to me in detail, from the memorized letters, from everything he had ever said about it at The Oaks. He had been close-mouthed about it with me, and it's a sound rule that people who had any war record to speak of didn't speak of it much.

Pamela's blurting enabled me to kid him a lot and finally to induce him to talk to me. As a white-stripe veteran, with no experience of shellfire, I was absorbed by such narratives and I drew him out in our endless talk, by night, over a little alcohol, some crackers and cheese and jam from the delicatessen, Cambridge and the world shut out. I began to write some short sketches from them for Dean Briggs, and that pleased and delighted Kent, who would send copies of them home.... His mother was telling him that he had a gift for correspondence, that his real destiny was probably as foreign correspondent for some newspaper. So she was getting a literary career for herself, maybe. So, also, word of me got to The Oaks in a more personalized form.

Those were great nights. Life had grain and tissue. A birch log in Fairfax, a gas log in Kent's room on Mass. Avenue, the absurd crackers and cheese, hours of talk, the war behind us, God knew what ahead, but something that, on the whole, sentence of death repealed, didn't seem unattractive.

There was a lot about Meredith in those stories. I'd never known him, he was a couple of years ahead of me at Harvard, but his reputation lingered. An amazing person, suave and letter perfect in a dozen languages, a brilliant mathematician, a brilliant physicist, a brilliant violinist, acquainted with all the great everywhere and by no means the least of them in any company. He had been just as brilliant an ambulancier, and he had been Kent's inseparable companion, refuge, stimulus, support. They had been together when their S.S.U. got caught in the crush when the Germans broke through the British Fifth Army, and the saga of those two weeks drifting free in chaos was something out of Dumas. They had also pulled off the stunt I mentioned in the first installment. Again, they dashed in between converging attacks and pulled out an abandoned car. And so on. Stories like that. Stories of delivering a child in the ambulance, in the Army of Occupation. If you ever got as far as Gordon Abbey's war vignettes, all except the wound were from Kent's yarns. And other people besides Meredith. Men who got killed. Men who got captured. Men who went crazy. Men who got scared. Men who put on a lot of side. One of the last had annoyed Kent a lot by going back home, after a couple of months, and writing a heroic book about the heroic S.S.U., full of omniscience, misinformation, damn lies and egotism.[33] He held forth about that a lot and I later found a seething letter on the subject in the mass Pamela turned over to me. This guy, call him Abernathy, because that has the literary flavor, now began to be reminiscent and informative in an occasional published article, and I could always send Kent into bitter intensities of abuse and obscenity by reading one with exclamations of pleasure.

Before a year had passed, I had occasion to sift everything that happened during these months as finely and as frantically as I could. I never got anything to tie to. Well.... A sudden passion for exercise hit me in midwinter and I took to going to the gymnasium every day and working out with apparatus. One day Kent, always derisive of effort, took a whim to come along. He got out a punching bag and worked on it surprisingly well, but I was appalled to see how slight, how emaciated and insubstantial, his body was. I made the same observation once or twice later. Again—here we come to something that will bother me while I still draw breath. I don't know whether it happened as I remember it, whether it happened at all, or whether it was a mere delusion, a compulsive product, in November 1920 [*sic*], of grief and anxiety and the need to explain, the vital obligation to dispel mystery. I believe it happened and happened as I remember it, but at the same time some fragment of my mind rejects it as delusion. Anyway, somehow, whether in an earlier hint of Kent's or as a deduction from some prattle of Pamela's, who certainly knew nothing, I had got the idea that Kent and Meredith (or just Kent, God knows which) had been recommended for the Legion of Honor, and that the citation had been cancelled as the result of his or their being caught in some infraction of discipline. It may have been the glint of something when he spoke about the sons of bitches who stuck to the rules or used them for purposes of their own. I don't know—I don't know a damn thing. Anyway, one afternoon we had Pamela and one of her friends in town to a matinee. After feeding them we put them on their train and wandered back to Cambridge. We went to Kent's room and settled down to an evening of talk and tobacco and such liquor as, in those days of wartime prohibition in effect and the national drought to come, we could get hold of. Kent had amused himself at dinner making me uncomfortable by telling the girls Paul Bunyan yarns about my literary prowess at Harvard—Pamela, I have no doubt, believed the last syllable of them. As my liquor took hold, I began to want that play back and so I got eloquent about the heroic war service of Kent Potter. I made a sort of home town Fourth of July speech. I magnificently translated the citations for his Croix de Guerre, which Pamela had devoutly given me but which he had no idea I'd ever heard about. That brought him down and he yelled for mercy. But I was started now and I wanted blood, so I went on making my speech. I told how he had been recommended for the Legion of Honor for heroic conduct under fire and how he would have got it if he'd only stayed sober at inspection and hadn't stolen the Commandant's *pinard*.[34] I shut up abruptly. For Kent got out of his chair, his face contorted, grabbed me by the throat and said, "You son of a bitch, if you ever mention that to anyone, I'll kill you." Well, by God! I threw him off easily enough, for I was stronger than he, but he went on threatening to kill me if I ever alluded to it again. We were both, I think, pretty drunk. It didn't seem credible. Pretty soon he quieted down and said that I was crazy as hell, that nothing of that sort happened, that I'd made it up out of the whole cloth, and that he simply couldn't stand being kidded about the war. I was amazed, shaken, but it was an incredible scene and I concluded that he was just drunk. So was I. I forgot about it practically at once.

Now that's that. I don't know whether it ever happened. I think it did, but I'll never know.

As the year ended he began to want to go back to France. He loved a lot of things about it and he longed to see it in time of peace. He worked harder than ever at his studies. Maybe, if for the first time in his life he got good marks, maybe his father would let him go to Paris for a year to study chemistry.

At the end of the year, as I've mentioned, Henderson and Briggs threw a Belgian fellowship my way, but I couldn't take it. Kent was in despair. If I was over there and he was over there—could anything be better? So we drifted into the examination period and the end approached. One day we took Pamela to the train. The next day I took an exam in the morning and left for New York, and eventually Ogden, in the afternoon. Kent went to the South Station with me. We sat in the Waldorf for a last cup of coffee and were silent, finding nothing to say to each other.[35] I got up and held out my hand. I said, "I'll beat it now," and he slouched away, with that queer, shambling gait. It was a rainy day. He was wearing a black topcoat and the crumpled brown hat that Harvard affected in those days. I saw him through glass when he turned the corner and I never saw him again.

When the marks were in at the end of June he wrote that his father consented to a year in Paris and begged me, with strong emotion, to come with him. It was out of the question. I had letters from him through the summer and one or two from Pamela. He sent me copy of "Mont St. Michel and Chartres," to commemorate our discussions of the Education and my paper on Adams's science, which I had talked out with him.[36] I get the book down and find this written in it: "Only the courage lent by distance permits me to sigh for the days of old or regret what might have been—by what price would I have paid for the possibility of you and I together looking on the things herein described. Benny Benny!" Signed with a symbol he had designed for himself—to go, he said, on his shingle when he emerged from the Sorbonne, "K. Potter, Ph.D. Janitor."

He sailed about the middle of September. He wrote to me on the boat and finished the letter on the stationery of the Hotel Normandie on the Left Bank. The letter was wrapped round a little pocket edition of "Aucassin et Nicolette" which he had been reading.[37] A day or two later he sent me, without comment but with reference to my Anatole France period, a copy of "Le Petit Soldat de Plomb."[38] I heard nothing more from him.

I got a couple of letters from Pamela. Just as she got back to Wellesley, The Oaks burned to the ground. That gave her a nervous panic and I heard from her oftener. She began to complain that she wasn't hearing from Kent and the complaints rapidly grew to neurotic desperation. Why hadn't she heard from Kent? What had happened? What was he doing? Was he all right? I wrote the first long letter I'd ever sent her, soothing and fatherly, assuring her that Kent was having too good a time to write to either of us. I talked like a priest and a psychiatrist and, disastrously, like a brother. I got another frantic letter a little later on the same theme. Then a short one: "Benny, I'm worried sick. Why doesn't Kent write to me?" The next day an ink-splotched envelope on which her writing was almost unrecognizable reached me. The letter said, "Kent's dead, Benny. Father just wired me."

Four or five days later, she wrote to me again from Springfield. They did not yet know what he had died of, but the man named Burroughs who had cabled the news had taken charge and her father was trying to get him to bring Kent's body home. A few days later she wrote that Burroughs had agreed to. Then, a couple of days after that, I got a wire: "Benny, we've had a letter from Kent."

III

Either I knew or someone told me that it took time to get clearance papers on the body of a foreigner who had died in France. As soon as I received Pamela's wire I cabled to Melville Smith to look up Kent's death and see this Burroughs, who I assumed would not yet have been able to start back. Melville Smith had been one of our gang at Harvard and was in Paris studying music. More about him in a moment.

(Here's a curious thing, Kate. All the available documents are in a foot locker in an alcove off my study, fifteen feet from this desk. I've been reluctant to get them out and review them, and I'm respecting that reluctance, I'm writing this from memory. Melville and I went over them three or four years ago when he was in Cambridge, being analyzed. That's the only time I've ever gone over them.)

Well, by air mail, I soon had a copy of that letter. Or not air mail.[39] Anyway, within forty-eight hours. I ought to get it out and give it to you word for word. But I couldn't possibly invent one that was more unbelievably phrased. The following isn't word for word, but it's just about:

Dear Father:

Ever since I got back to France, I have been looking for a certain man. He is a man who once—during the war—did me an injury for which only death can atone. I would be no true son of yours and you could have only contempt for me if I permitted that injury to go unavenged. At last I have caught up with him and tomorrow we shall meet. If there is a righteous God in heaven our meeting can end but in one way. But if he should kill me there are others now in Europe who know him for the white-livered cur he is and will take up my job if I fail.

I am writing this to you. You are a man and will understand. You would not have me act otherwise. Also you will be able to prevent Mother and Pamela from worrying if I am forced to disappear for a while without writing to you.

Yours,

Kent.

No, both the filial piety and the resolution were more melodramatically expressed than I have got them. But that's the gist.

The letter was postmarked a day later than the telegram from Burroughs and two days later than the date of Kent's death, as Burroughs reported it.

Now from the way this worked on me I was able to understand something of the way it worked on Pamela. (Her father showed it only to her. No other member of the family had heard of it when I was last conversant with the situation.) True, it did not make me suppose Kent was alive, as she at once concluded. But it did shock me in a way that nothing else has ever done. Coming on top of the shock of his death, it did things to me.

Observe the melodrama of the phrases: righteous God in heaven, white-livered cur, go unavenged, can end in but one way. Phrases that would have made the Kent I had always known roar with derision. Above all, observe the melodrama of the implied situation and of the declared one. It was inconceivable, and yet there it was, a habit inconceivable things have. Pamela was not likely to mistake the handwriting—and any suggestion that it had been counterfeited made the situation more inconceivable still. It seemed to be on the level. But if it was—then, had Kent been murdered?

I at once wrote Melville Smith, copying the letter and instructing him to use every device he could to find out what was behind it. Out of my own turmoil I got no suggestion whatever except the memory I have already set down here. Even at the time I produced it as a single incident out of a crowded year, and one that I had paid little attention to at the time, it was vague at the edges. That vagueness has not diminished in fifteen years. At the time, I thought there was a one in fifty chance that the whole thing might be compulsively produced, a mere fiction conditioned by my desperate need to explain. I'd lower it to one in ten now. Of course my memory today is clear and sharp—but it is a memory of November 1920, of the image I then dredged up.

Probably there are people in the world who know whether or not he was recommended for the Legion of Honor and, if he was, why he didn't get it. Probably there is even some kind of documentary evidence. I have wondered how, given unlimited power and whatever money might be needed, one would go about finding out. I've imagined a thousand steps to take.... It isn't possible. One would need the power and omniscience of God. It is not a thing that, the world being what it is, anyone could settle now. But it makes an amusing exercise in detective fiction.

Suppose you did find out? Nothing but the fact would be established. You would still know nothing whatever about the central mystery.

I at once wrote the memory to Pamela as soon as I had produced it. She was now writing to me, and I to her, every day. I had no motive except to find out what I could, to give some expression to my own grief and bewilderment. And, I suppose, to do what I could to help her out. I knew that she was heartbroken and nerve-shattered. I didn't know how nerve-shattered, though.

She was convinced that Kent was alive. Perhaps he was a murderer but that didn't matter. He had gone into hiding. This cablegram was just part of his plot. He was just covering his tracks. Maybe she wouldn't hear otherwise for years, but some day she would hear. Some day word would be brought to her from him, secretly. Or even some day he would appear in person. I dealt with this as I could, recognizing it as hysteria. After all, she couldn't talk to her mother at all. She was keeping her mother in the dark about the mystery. She couldn't talk to her father, who was scientific and skeptical. So she poured it all out to me. At fifteen hundred miles one can't deal very effectively with that sort of delusion.

Well, that ended. Finally Burroughs and the body arrived. Pamela and her father went down and had the coffin opened. It was Kent, all right.

Burroughs was—well, I don't know. I know nothing about him except through Melville Smith's eyes and Pamela's. Melville had talked to him I soon found out, before he left. Melville's judgment was that he was just what he seemed to be, a salesman of cheap jewelry, rather talkative and hearty, stupid, proud of himself as a traveled man and a devil with women but honest, as honesty goes, quite incapable of managing a profound plot. That squares with everything and I know nothing to impeach it—except a profound belief that Melville has no way of understanding any person on earth. Pamela distrusted him. He frightened her. She thought him sinister and equivocal. She felt he was lying to her and to her father. She built up a nightmare structure of deceit and criminality on that distrust. Nothing in it has ever had any reality for me. I don't know what she believes now. But she believed then that Burroughs was possibly the murderer and certainly in [on] the murderer's secret. Her father, to whom she confided the belief, only fastened it on her tighter by deriding it.

Burroughs presented the official death certificate, which gave the cause as cerebral hemorrhage. That is an extremely rare thing in men so young, unless they are syphilitics, which Kent wasn't. This was Burroughs's story. He had met Kent some four or five weeks before his death. A certain group of students and hangers-on had been formed and Burroughs, who described himself as being in Paris on a buying trip and a vacation, was drawn in. Kent seemed to like him more than the others, came to his rooms a lot, spent evenings with him, drinking and talking and reading. On the evening of Kent's death, they came into Burroughs's room about ten o'clock. It was raining and Kent decided not to go back to his room some distance away. Burroughs, who had been drinking and was tired, said "Okay, stay here if you want, I'm going to bed." Kent sat down by the radiator (there was one—Melville saw it) with a full bottle of cognac and a copy of *Vanity Fair*. (It was his favorite book, and I had often seen this particular copy, a large blue-bound volume from a set. Ronald Levinson has it now.)[40] Burroughs had gone to bed and at once to sleep. When the maid came in, the next morning, she went over to draw the curtains, exclaimed sharply, and said to Burroughs, who was still in bed, "Votr'ami—il est mort." Burroughs got up and found out she was telling the truth. Kent was dead, still sitting with his back to the radiator, on the floor, the *Vanity Fair* on his knees and the empty cognac bottle beside him.

That was substantially all that the Potters got from Burroughs, except that he did tell Dr. Potter that Kent had been drinking pretty heavily all along. I at once wrote his story to Melville. And now I began to get the results of Melville's search.

This was interrupted and delayed by a perfectly characteristic thing. He is the most erratic and unstable man I've ever known. He will go down to the corner to buy a newspaper and come home months later by way of California. He has—or maybe had, for I imagine it was what he was analyzed for—a strong streak of, latent, homosexuality in him. I have no reason for supposing that it ever became overt. Well, at the very beginning of his investigation he met a chap, in fact the one who had mailed Kent's letter, who struck him as having the most beautiful soul he had ever known. So that, mixed up with his account of his search, I would get whole pages, sometimes whole letters, devoted to the exquisite friendship, the rarity of this ape's love for the beautiful, the heart-warming trips they took to look at the daisies at Versailles, etc.

Two weeks before Kent's death, Melville got home one afternoon and found a note from Kent, giving his address and asking him to come round sometime. He hadn't got round to acting on it when my cable came. When it came, he at once got to work. I think he did a pretty good job. I know damned well I'd have done a better one. I don't know that I'd have found out anything more.

He saw Burroughs, who added a little to what he'd told the Potters. For one thing, Kent was due to start on a walking trip, destination unknown to Burroughs, the day after the day on which he died. For another, there was a little more to that last evening. Both Burroughs and Kent had picked up and were living with some little tarts. The four of them went out to dinner and drank quite a bit. Burroughs's tart got abusive and quarreled with B. Kent tried to smooth her down but she wouldn't be smoothed. She declared she wasn't coming home with B, and didn't. She went off with Kent's girl to a cinema—just why Kent's girl abandoned them never came out. Kent and B were pretty drunk when they got to B's hotel. It was B's opinion that Kent had drunk the whole bottle of cognac and that it had killed him.

It well might. But it would kill him by paralyzing his stomach, not by rupturing an artery in his brain.

That was all Melville got from Burroughs. He began to chase down everyone who had known Kent. He went to the physician who had examined the body, who assured him that he had made a very careful examination. The circumstances had suggested to him, he said, that there might have been "un petit drame," and so he had minutely inquired and scrutinized everything. There was no doubt about it, the poor M. Potter had died of a cerebral hemorrhage.... Of course, any opinion whatever could be bought from a Paris police surgeon for, say, 500 francs.... On the other hand, the doctor suggested that M. Smith might, if he wished, have an inquiry made. Melville thought hard and finally decided against it. For my part, I think that was the rockbottom mistake. But—if he had, the body would have had to be held in Paris, the consulate would have been called in, and the whole Potter family would have been apprised that there was something going on. I suppose that Pamela's peace of mind, and her mother's, was worth more, considering Kent, than my certainty.

All of Kent's acquaintances, who were either American or English, knew that he was going off on a walking trip the next day. He had been secretive about its duration and in fact about its location. No one knew where he was going, only that he was going. He had given his girl (Melville was a pure young man in those days and his letter describing her was at an extremity of shock) enough money to run her and her ménage in comfort for at least two months.

No one suspected that Kent was looking for anyone, had any enemies or animosities, or was anything but what he seemed to be. Except Melville's soul mate, who must have been the vaguest man in all Paris. Kent had helped him out with several loans. He had also broken a number of jests over his head which Melville fumed about in his letters. About noon on the day he died he took this chap aside and offered him a hundred francs if he'd do something for him. He turned over a stamped letter addressed to his father. He said, "If anything happens to me, mail this. If I'm not back here in a week, mail it. And don't mention it to anyone." He then paid over a hundred francs and left him. After Kent died the young man didn't know what to do with the letter. Finally someone advised him to mail it, and he did.

Two men were supposed to know Kent better than the rest. One of them declared simply, but with an anger that Melville couldn't explain, that he had drunk like a fool all the time he was in Paris and had died of alcoholism. The other—he was supposed to be the best and brightest of the lot and to have known Kent most intimately—worked for the American Embassy. Melville made an appointment with him and then missed it, having gone off with his boy friend to see some more daisies. When he got back to calling the Embassy again, the man had been sent off with some mission to the Far East.

The girl had nothing to contribute. She wept noisily whenever Melville called on her and divided her time between mourning Kent and letting her kimono fall open with an eye to doing some business with Melville. She too took the walking trip at face value. She hadn't heard or seen anything to suggest that Kent was after anyone or that anyone was after him. She scared and disgusted Melville and he only saw her a couple of times.

All the facts that any of us ever learned are now in. Except one. Kent was never registered at the Sorbonne, or anywhere else.

And two more facts which are certainly facts but may be, except for speculation must be, quite outside the orbit. Meredith went to Europe at about the same time Kent did. There, after a couple of months, he simply vanished. Nothing has ever been heard of or from him. And a few months after Kent's death, Abernathy, the heroic *brancardier*[41] and imaginative writer, came back to America. He had been discharged from the Army in England and had, to the surprise of his friends, refused to come home from that time on.

There you are. It is an odd story but, on the facts, not one which should have agonized my life for a long time, as it did—sleeping as well as waking. In what anguish of mind I turned it over and over I leave you to imagine. Mystery is fascinating when it is impersonal. It is something other than fascinating when it concerns someone who is near to you. This has not, of course, troubled me for many years. But it did trouble me.

The necessity was to have some explanation. And of course there could be none.

I reported to Pamela—only her blind faith in me prevented her from observing that I never sent her Melville's letter—that Melville's researches backed up Burroughs's story of the death and vindicated B. I told her that I accepted Kent's letter at its face value. That I believed he had really intended to kill someone but had died a natural death before he had a chance to. That his war service had unquestionably undermined his all too frail strength and that he had simply died of exhaustion. That for my part I was glad things had turned out as they had—Kent was dead and had not died a murderer. That she must give up her imaginings and accept the simple truth.

Well, that is possible. I have no prejudice one way or another. I see various possibilities and little or nothing to make one a superior hypothesis to the others. None satisfies all the facts.

It is a fact, and probably the bedrock fact, that Kent's strength was gone. Seventeen months of war service had used him up. All right. A return to heavy drinking would have caused death, or could have caused death. There's no need to debate that. But, in the absence of an autopsy, there is no way of knowing that it did.

All right. Did he have an injury which he wanted to avenge? In any event, he was given to queer interpretations of honor, he had this wild prairie romanticism. At his sanest, he could certainly have had that motive. If he had, then the act of reporting an infraction of discipline that cost him his Legion of Honor could have been such an injury. On that hypothesis, I could be morally certain that he fought with Abernathy, whom he considered a liar, a coward and a swine, and that Abernathy, paying him off, made the report that cost him the cross. On the same hypothesis, I could have a lively conviction, but less assurance, that Meredith was involved in the same way Kent was.

There can be no doubt that he told everyone that he was going to take a walking trip or that he named a specific day. It is also inconceivable that Kent would take a walking trip. He never had and never would—he loathed exercise of every kind and in fact, at the time of his death, couldn't take exercise. But a walking trip would provide the best kind of alibi in advance. It would give him priceless time in which to get away. And the evidence of the hundred francs and the letter is very suggestive.

Yes, it is conceivable that the whole thing is simple and straightforward. Kent had an enemy whom he intended to kill. He made arrangements to kill him and to get away. But before he had a chance to kill him, he died of overdrinking.

Or he may have been killed. There was no autopsy. Everyone was aware that he was drinking heavily. What could be more easy than to slip poison into his liquor and suggest that he had died of overdrinking? Burroughs could have done it, on his own behalf or as the agent of someone. Or someone unknown could have done it without Burroughs's knowledge.

Or the whole thing can be a form of delirium tremens. Exhausted, running on his nerve alone, he simply succumbed to alcohol and built up the whole monstrous story out of drunken dreams. On this hypothesis, there was no injury, there was no enemy, there was no reality behind any of the facts we unearthed.

Or—when he got to Paris, he couldn't run on nerve alone and he began to die. As he died he went crazy. The whole thing was a delusion, the product of a mind that faded as his body faded. By a wild poetry, his fantasy reached a climax just as his body wore out. His crazed mind fixed as the day of his mortal test the day after the one when his heart stopped.

Yes, all that and one more, a darker one. Perhaps his body wasn't as far gone as the other hypotheses assume—and perhaps there had been prophecy of what now happened to his mind. Anger, fear, resentment, suspicion—all those were in him in seedtime. The Potter home, I have said, was a tropical place. Emotions rioted there. The family relationships were intense, the most intense I've ever known. All right. He may have been, and now we see why I have always had such a concern about paranoia—he may have been a paranoid. He may have invented, out of his own compulsions, a whole intricate fantasy. Someone had deeply injured him. Someone…there would be no going back to childhood to find out who it was. He must invent someone. He had the Croix de Guerre. Certainly a man like him, a man who could so triumphantly defeat fate, rise above his crippling handicap, live a hero in heroic action for seventeen months—surely such a man was, of right, entitled to the highest cross, that of the Legion of Honor. But he didn't have it. Therefore it must have been unrighteously denied him. Who was responsible? Clearly, someone must have been. So he would invent one. This swine Abernathy, with whom he had had trouble. Yes, Abernathy. Or someone. <u>Someone whom he would find in France.</u> He would go back to France, he would revisit the scene of his heroism, and there, on that heroic soil, he would find the man who had kept him from the highest honor, and, finding him, he would kill him. Find and kill the man who had denied him his highest recognition.… So he did. He went back to France and, one night, he took out the little capsule of cyanide which he always kept on his person, slipped it into the cognac, and presently the man who had most deeply injured Kent Potter was dead on the floor of Burroughs's room.

Well, it is in the dark. With the answers to all other questions. I was a long time reconciling myself to the blackness. You can see why.

So ends the story of the death. I have come, as I come with all human matters, to see that the real story is in the inter-relationships. There is, if you want it, another chapter of them. Hester was dead three-fourths the way through S.G. and the problem of the novelist was to keep the novel running after its high point. Shall I try?

IV

Not explain. The explanations are all in. All I can do is to detail my later experiences and observations, the sum of which supports the fourth—was it four?—at any rate, the last hypothesis. It is not, you understand, the one which, on the whole, I accept—so far as I accept any. The best hypothesis, I should say, if we have to bring in one only, is the first one, the one on the surface, that the thing was as it seems, that he meant to but died naturally. But the truth is, the longer I live, the farther I wander in the dark forest of the proverb, the less I am content with any explanation of human action that cometh from without. The spoiled psychiatrist rebels—and plays, it may be noisomely, with the twisted roots. I have tried to express in fiction, and will probably try again, a conviction that what decides is the impingement of lives on one another, and that the snarl increases as the years do.… The friend of mine who died so needlessly in January was an analyst.[42] He had been deeply interested in S.G. His trade holds, and I think with great reason, that the basis of imaginative art is just the basis of analysis. He had a number of highly interesting things to say about my book. Some of them were obviously true, he convinced me about others with difficulty, and I think he was flatly wrong about still others. We differed about the amount and the directions of conscious, objective invention. He was considerably more liberal than most Freudians but not as liberal as I insisted he should be. Well, he harped on Julian a lot, so I told him as much as need be of this story. That being told, I could not convince him of what I hold to be true, that so far as Julian was not made up to fit the necessities of the book, he was based on a young son of a bitch whom I thoroughly disliked and who achieved martyrdom and commemoration in a Boston square (that last bit ought to have weight) by being shot down. And, in my opinion, the clinching argument is the name. For that name rose of its own will to my pen, and happens to have been borne in my experience by only one person, a man whom I thoroughly dislike, a relative of the heel aforesaid, Julian Coolidge. But no. My analyst friend asked me, the story being told, just what Kent Potter had done to me to make me take such revenge. The answer is: nothing, he was the best friend I ever had, that man I had thought most of in all my life. The analyst shook his head. He wasn't satisfied. Well, so far as the hypotheses for Kent's death go, I'm not satisfied. And like the analyst I keep looking for something deep and instinctive, some drive from the depths. Keep Freud and our last hypothesis in mind from now on.

The next eight or nine months, whose exterior has been covered in the *Memoirs of a Legionnaire*, were a period of deepening gloom and emotional malaise. I have no doubt that Kent's death accelerated the breakdown that finally hit me the next July but certainly it was only an accessory and minor cause. I was drunk a good part of that year and—erratic. And getting more so.

Also I was writing to Pamela with great frequency—she was writing to me every day. She came close to the rocks herself; several times she was actually on the edge of them. And it is quite true, and quite without credit to me, to say that I was what saved her from going over. Natural enough. She simply floundered about and then in the simplest way transferred to Kent's best friend the complicated series of needs she had sustained by means of Kent. I was too dumb to understand what was happening. I merely saw that she had been badly shocked, that her life had been dangerously upset by his death, and felt that [I] could help her work out of it by being friendly. Besides, she was the sister of my best friend.

She poured herself out to me in ink, and I thought it was good for her to do just that. The process by which I became a kind of benevolent dictator was so gradual that I did not notice it.... I'm not that emotionally dumb: if my own emotions hadn't been the obsessive center of my life I wouldn't have missed it and could have stopped it.... But that is just what I became. Every slightest decision that girl had to make was put up to me in the form of a quandary and, without knowing it usually, I told her what to do and she did it. Usually I was telling her by indirection, by expressing opinions on strictly impersonal things, but quite often I was making up her mind by direct appeal. My God, Kate, everything—how many pairs of stockings to buy, whether it was right for her to go to a dance with Dicky Quintana, who was still in Cambridge, whether she could bluff a course in zoology, how she should treat the confidences of Wellesley girls, which train to take out of Chicago to Springfield, how she could reconcile a hope to get married sometime with a religious dedication to Kent, how God and religion came into the matter, whether it was hygienic to go horseback riding at the critical phases of the moon.

Well, this intensified all the way up to September, 1922. Meanwhile, in the late Spring of 1921 my generalized investigation into the Flapper began to specialize on Skinny. A swell kid. She was the sole amusement in Ogden. That spring and early summer, and what part of the year was left after I rounded too from my collapse I saw a good bit of her, impersonally, entertained, above all amused and quieted. I remember the night before she went to Washington to school. Some carnival was in town, under the protection of the Herman Baker Post, and I bucolically swained her through it, collecting the dolls and watches and popcorn balls of the sagebrush culture, and then we swung up into the hills for several hours, strolling and talking about finishing schools and laughing. Almost breathtakingly chaste and uninvolved. I saw her off the next day and remember thinking oddly that after all it was possible to be amused by the young on a non-sexual and even unemotional basis. The emotions of Ogden in her absences were more involved. The story of Jessie that I never got around to telling belongs to that period.[43] And other stories. My nerves ebbed and flowed, from acute phobias and compulsions to a kind of queasy and despairing ease—cut across by alcohol, by Legion upheavals and ultimate defeat, by the alarms of the Mound Fort Junior High, by the eccentric behavior of my blonde cousin. Then Skinny was reported dying but didn't die, and after a while she was back in Ogden—arriving with the earliest Spring the Wasatch had ever seen. She had neurotic sequelae following the encephalitis, I was a profound neurotic and neither one of us understood a damned thing about it. A queer thing happened at once. We became absolutely essential to each other and yet the exterior of it was just an amused friendship. Neither one of us ever told the other, except in rare and momentary oblique allusions, what was wrong with us, but both of us knew damned well—so far as we could know without the vocabulary that I'm now letter-perfect in. And, what was in the circumstances inconceivable, we didn't have an affair, we didn't make love to each other, we didn't even, in the language of the period, neck. Only, if I showed up at the hideous sandstone mansion at the corner of Twenty-seventh and Adams at seven-thirty in the morning, noon, or half past nine at night, Skinny quite unquestioningly grabbed a hat and we were off to walk five or twenty miles or drive twenty or a hundred and fifty. Or I might say good-night to her at midnight and go home and go to bed. After I'd been asleep an indefinite time I'd sit straight up in bed, recognizing the toot of a certain Willys-Knight horn. At whatever time it was I knew that Skinny had had an attack of the horrors, I'd finish dressing in the car, and we'd be off—not saying much, just deriving some odd and intimate and profound stability from each other.

Then, about the time summer came, not so good. One night we'd been to dinner at a summer hotel up in the canyon. The Willys-Knight must have been laid up because, after dancing a little and sitting in the shadows by the river for a while, we started home in one of the roofless trolley cars that are supposed to give you glimpses of the peaks. Summer wear in 1922, I have the best reasons for remembering, had to do with frilly little capes of—oh, tulle, or crêpe de chine, or whatnot. This one was yellow and faintly blue besides. Skinny was looking at the canyon wall and smiling. I was watching her and somehow managed, in a terrific tumult, to ask her what she was smiling at. She blushed and asked if I really wanted to know. I did. She said she'd had a sudden and rather silly thought: how damned nice it was that I could be so much her friend and mean so much to her and not either of us be bothered by falling in love. Which was very lovely, for the reason behind my sudden tumult was quite simple. Looking at her, I had been knocked groggy with a realization that months and events had piled up on me and I was fathomlessly in love with her.

This isn't my love story, much as I seem to want to write it, and all this account really needed was a half-dozen lines summarizing my various emotions. You are free to imagine those that now ensued. I was a young ass of intense ambition and an even intenser inferiority complex, jobless and hopeless. I regarded my disease, whatever it was, as incurable. I thought I was certain to die of it, or kill myself, or go crazy. It seemed inconceivable that I should ever get out of Utah, and still more inconceivable that I should ever be a sound man or ever do anything to justify my existence. And now in love with Skinny who, besides being all the unutterable things that girls are when you are in love with them, was the daughter of the richest man in Utah.[44]

(I'll bet you the DeVoto Collection of American Newspaper Humor and Mormoniana against an A.L.S.[45] from John Chamberlain that my next novel contains a man and a girl who drive endless hours together in defence against the horrors.)

So tumult was now raised to the nth. Three or four weeks later, in a determined effort at rehabilitation, I was off to Tom Keogh's desert ranch in Raft River Valley. The night I left—on a late train—Skinny and I were driving around with Eddie Higman and Flossie Turner. Skinny was very silent. I knew and she knew I knew that the reason was her apprehension of being alone in the difficult hours. The other two would occasionally wail, "Aw, Benny, don't go." After a while, Skinny said it too. She said it out loud two or three times. She was driving and I was beside her. Pretty soon she whispered it, "Aw, Benny, don't go." So I whispered back, "I'll stay, if you'll marry me." She said, "Where can we?" I said, "Try Brigham City." She swung the car round in a sharp arc and speeded up the state road hellbent. The pair of merry souls in the rear seat began to shout and laugh. It was swell stuff. Benny was being kidnapped. Skinny was going to keep Benny from making his train. In the mood I was now experiencing they grated on me. They grated on Skinny too. She said over her shoulder, "Shut up, you damned fools. I'm not kidnapping Benny—I'm marrying him." Brigham City is some twenty-odd miles from Ogden. We made fine time but we got there too late. We found the county clerk's house and got him out of bed. He wouldn't put on his clothes and go down to the office to issue a license. Nothing is flatter than an elopement that doesn't come off. We got back to Ogden in time for me to take my train.

That was the climax of my romance. I stayed at the Keogh ranch just as long as I could force myself to, which was practically not at all. By Jesus Christ, I was engaged to Skinny! By Jesus Christ, if Brigham City had been more than a Mormon village, I'd even be married to her! I tore back to Ogden. But Skinny didn't figure it that way. The simple truth was that she wasn't in love with me. I exerted myself to the utmost, but no go.... She was a darling, Kate. I can remember no other woman out of my adolescence, and there was a God's quantity of them, without shuddering.

I think we can now come back to the story. The offer, through Harvard, of the Northwestern job offered me the first gleam of hope in fourteen months. I spent my last evening with Skinny, mournfully resigned to the immutable, and she and Flossie saw me off on the Overland. I had arranged to go down to Springfield for a couple of weeks with the Potters.

That trip east, and the two weeks at Springfield, marked the nadir of my nerves. This is the condition I was in: I wrote my name and address of my father on a card and kept it in my pocket—I didn't expect to get off the Overland alive. I left my adolescence somewhere east of Thousand Mile Tree, I grew up.[46]

I'd better clarify my last sentence. A neurosis is a psycho-biological adaptation. Ogden, though agonizing, was an amniotic home.[47] When I finally, God knows how, probably by way of Skinny, found resolution to act, to get out, to go about my business—I took the indispensable step. That I'm not pushing up the daisies in Mountain View, or counting them in the Provo home for the mentally incurable, is due to just that. I shed my adolescence on the Overland Limited and with it I made the first step toward shedding my infancy. But the shock was terrific and I had no way of guessing what it meant.... When I finally settled down at Northwestern I found a ~~neurologist~~ psychiatrist. He was eighty percent faith healer, a big, handsome gent who radiated energy, confidence, and hope. His methods were almost childish but I didn't know that and he was the first person I'd met who showed signs of understanding what was wrong with me and enabling me to understand. That was enough to begin the process of restoration. Five years later the job had to be done over, and really done by a scientist and artist at last, in Boston, by E. W. Taylor. But I'd broken free when I left Ogden, I'd got a hand up from Stearns, presently I was writing again, I was holding down a job, and by winter I was in an adult emotional relationship with Avis.[48]

But when I got to The Oaks I was all but dissociated. My neurosis was yelping like a stuck pig. And it was hot—100 at midnight when I reached Chicago, worse than that at Springfield when I got there—and heat was my worst phobia. Nobody noticed—I was able to hold a single thread of control over it—except one afternoon when I had a minor collapse under Mrs. Potter's ministrations. You are to gather that my mind was not exactly clear.

It was clear enough to realize, the moment Pamela met me at the Springfield station at 7 A.M., that I was spang in the middle of a situation. She was in a semi-liquid state and she trembled constantly. Her eyes were big and suffused, she constantly blushed, her voice trembled and ebbed.... I really should have called her Evelina in these pages—she had something of Miss Burney's girls, or better still of the early Victorian heroines, some wide-eyed child from Mrs. Gaskell, something of the young Amelia, even of Dora.[49] The girls who really fluttered, yearned, had shy visions. She had, rioting inside her, a chaos of emotions beside which my own disturbance was relatively clear, simple and tangible. She was expending on me a ferment of unresolved attitudes toward two parents and two brothers—and she had, to express them, only the surface ideas and impulses of some nineteenth-century, convent-bred innocent. The worst stupidity of parents, if I can dare a superlative in that area, is to allow children to grow up ignorant of emotions. A dozen capital crimes had been committed in the rearing of the young Pamela, but that was the worst kind. What she wanted was quite simple: she wanted to sleep with me and so with Kent and so with Dr. Potter, to carry that theme no farther than the doctor, and then to live with me forever as the child Pamela had lived in infantile security in a world limited to Kent and the early Others. And she had, to understand that desire and to give it active expression, only a series of pious mottos, chaste scenes from romantic novels, and stray, horrible fragments of misunderstood conversations at Wellesley, and all of these feeble things tabooed by what she had been taught at home and at church, the taboos given a thousandfold added vigor by the glimpsed frenzy behind them.

I can hardly select instances that will seem credible. I've mentioned, I think, how she typed out a whole book that I'd casually alluded to. Her father had given her a magnificent fire opal—I remember it as shining like a headlight and weighing a couple of ounces. I took her hand, once, to look at it and expressed my admiration. She stripped off the ring and gave it to me, and when I refused it burst into a frenzy of weeping and dashed off into the dark woods, either to be alone, or to be followed, or, it may be, to be followed and laid, though of course she wouldn't have been aware of the last possibility. She had a small photograph of me, a two-inch square duplicate of an application-for-job fifty-cent snapshot. She had put it into a frame that weighed five pounds. She hid it for a few days, then produced it, then confessed—and the question was, was it unmaidenly for her to think so much of that photograph, followed at once by a further question, was it even more unmaidenly to talk it over with me?... I feel the conventional polite shame about telling these things, but I can see no point in telling a story at all without telling it as it happened.... She had no flirtation, she was too early-convent-school to have even that inevitable word, coquetry. She had a few impulses that seem either comic or tragic. I said that a pair of shoes she was wearing one day were charming. So presently we went up to her room to look at her wardrobe, bit by bit, till we were finally looking at drawers full of underclothes, and that was daring and fascinating and charged with a tremulous ecstasy. One afternoon—the heat wave having gone—we were tossing a child's ball on the sloping lawn. Running after it, she stumbled, for she was not a graceful girl, and rolled twenty yards down hill. She was of course agonized. I said, placatingly, "Why, Pam, what nice knees you have." The intermittent tears came to her eyes at once and she was ecstatic but frightened. Thereafter, she several times asked me if her knees were really nice, and several times, at great sacrifice of modesty and idealism, contrived to show one or the other of them for a moment.... If my sleeve touched hers, if I helped her out of chair or over a brook, if I saw her crying in the long evenings on the lawn when her mother was talking about Kent and so reached out and touched her forearm or her shoulder, she quivered like the tuneswept fiddlestring of the poetry that fits her.[50]

And in what a heat of masochism she lived! That was where she ran smack into one of my own fundamental taboos and so cancelled whatever thin possibility may have existed that I could have yielded to my own sentiments about Kent and her mother. The abject woman has ever been poison to something at the base of my unlovely ego. She was in a constant tumult lest she might have innocently displeased her father, her mother, or me. She quivered to be abased and if no one would abase her she had a great faculty of abasing herself. In sudden exasperation, after I'd been there for a couple of days, I said, "For Christ's sake, Pam, don't apologize so much." I saw that I would have done her less service by kissing her, and from then on I had to watch out for that too.

And so on. The details were innumerable, but I saw the whole set-up during the twenty minutes drive from the station to The Oaks. (They had remodeled the carriage house and were living in it, pending architectural solutions of the country house problem that would reconcile the Doctor's ideas with his wife's.) It was a dilemma to be sprung on a man who had been too dumb to get any intimation of it from letters that suddenly told everything in retrospect, and who was holding himself together as a personality by virtue of one very frayed string. A man, too, I add reflectively, who had been accustomed to taking his fun where he found it. I instantaneously adopted a policy of the most extreme decorum.

And at once I was struck amidship. I have already said that Mrs. Potter, whom I now met for the first time, finishing her morning coffee two hours before she would normally be awake, was the most remarkable woman I have ever met. Don't think that that judgment flows from my own necessities: I have never met anyone who had ever met her who did not accept it offhand. She was a personal miracle; there is no other word.

Not that she was beautiful in any way—she wasn't. A small woman, rather plump than not, with a worn face and tired eyes. But she had that quality which has never been satisfactorily described except as magnetism. Polarization might come nearer—she at once focused all one's personality in straight lines...directed at her. She talked with amazing brilliance, she had a great and instinctive and tender kindness, she had (though normally energetic and even nervous in manner) a capacity for the peace of soul that is the rarest of American, especially female American, qualities. There was no moment when you were with her that you weren't aware of a personal force immediate and overwhelming. She was a million volts. And every last volt hit me.

I was there something less than two weeks. For the first half of the stay Pamela's agitation was increased by a terrific conflict which she could not even phrase. I was always talking with her mother, her mother was always talking with me, and though that made us both more resplendent, it was darkly intolerable. Well, it wasn't for me. Such talk I had never listened to and never uttered. She engulfed me. Why shouldn't she? My mother was dead and she had lost her son. Also, she flowed out to me, and that too was—or is now—quite explicable, for I was a literary man and she had never had her literary career. She knew more about me than I had thought. I had assumed that my letters to Pamela would be read forthwith; what I didn't know was that Kent had written home, over two and a half years and especially during our last year, what Benny DeVoto, the literary guy, said and thought and wrote and did about this and that. So it came out that many things written to Kent had been aimed at the literary guy. And I found out about the slow process of trying to convince Kent that he should become a foreign correspondent, size up the world, write books about it. She was quite sure that that was what he would have done eventually. He had exactly as much aptitude for it as I have for research chemistry.... Elmer's failure had gone deep.

Then she suddenly checked herself and thrust Pamela forward. I fail to make this woman clear unless I establish that she was a person of marked analytical power, of brilliant judgment and of complete social mastery. Her judgment was the best, I can say flatly, that I've ever known. And that is what makes so significant the fact of its betrayal, for she did betray it. At first obliquely and tentatively, then explicitly, she told me that she hoped I would marry Pamela. She said that the child was in love with me and had been for a good deal more than two years—she was wrong there, for it did not antedate October, 1920. She said that Pamela was now in a condition of nervous excitement and hope and fear as a result of my presence. She sketched in the precariousness of Pamela's health and personality following Kent's death, she suggested the ambiguity of the future if this new integration should be broken.

That is the heaviest evidence I have.

I bungled things. Not as badly as I might have, considering everything, but badly enough. I was in precarious health myself and my mind was clouded, I had been so long convinced that my life could mean nothing that there was intoxication in the idea it could mean so much to these people and... I had met Mrs. Potter. She was a new experience to me a new world. If she had suggested that we go to Mexico and get married I would have phoned the Pullman office within ten seconds. If I couldn't marry her, I could at least be her son, be with her a great part of the time, submit to her magnificence, drink in power and intelligence and inspiration. And she was Kent's mother. Not, I grant you, lovely sentiments, but just what sentiments are lovely? Well, for once protected instead of betrayed by the hesitation of a neurotic, I temporized. I must say, though, that I quite forgot Pamela, and how she repelled me, whenever I saw or talked to her mother. What I said was, in effect: look here, I've always had some hope that that would work out (a lie—I'd never thought of it), but it would be very wrong to rush into it—Pamela really isn't in love with me, she's just grateful—she doesn't know anything about me, she shouldn't be stormed into anything—I really don't know anything about her—and I'm not going to marry anyone or propose marriage till I'm healed of my disease, whatever it is. And Pamela's mother promptly attacked that last part. What if I was sick? These things could be cured. And Pamela's life could be put on a firm footing forever by three words from me. But I held out. I got rhetorical and said purple things about manly honor—that sort of attitude.

She at once saw that she had blundered and she did some magnificent retrieving from then on though several times before April the same urgency took her into modifications of the same blunder. As for me, I would lie awake at night and think about her and decide that on the whole I'd marry Pamela right after breakfast. Then at breakfast Pamela would flog her shoulders with some imaginary failure to be all I asked or would abjectly apologize for thinking the day pleasant or Shakespeare a great poet when I thought otherwise, and my gorge would rise and all the hidden sources of my own soul would revolt.

I went back to Chicago undeclared and unpledged. And now I began to get letters from Mrs. Potter every few days. Sparkling letters, brilliantly phrased, compact of that curiously mingled wellbeing and unrest, unforced, intimate, affectionate and warm. A strange warmth I can't express. The glib and easy thing to say is what I've already said, that they were love letters, but that profoundly misrepresents them. I have no doubt whatever that one element was just that. A young man of feverish ambition, in grave trouble and great bewilderment, obviously bowled over by her—of course I satisfied some drive backward to her own youth and of course in her own soul he was, in letters and those long talks, the wise and tender elder mistress that we read about. But there was much more than that. There was a wit and wisdom freed as it hadn't been free for a long time, there was the play of a fine mind delighted with its own play, there was even a kind of unaware but fierce gratitude. There was also a shrewd and canny fascination, I wonder how far rationalized. And below that… God knows.

Away from her, I was quite clear that I was not going to marry Pamela. But how keep the mother and make sure of losing the daughter? I made one sidesplitting essay, among a good many. I wrote to her stressing Pamela's innocence and purity and exposing myself as the blacksouled corrupter that I was in the more acid Ogden rumors and Bob Major's frenzies. Not a chance. The worldly Mrs. Potter was enchanted.

I went down for Christmas vacation. I met Pamela's train in Chicago, squired her round Evanston for an afternoon, and went on to Springfield with her. When we reached The Oaks, I kissed Mrs. Potter. She said casually, "Pamela, did he kiss you?" Pamela said I hadn't, and her mother said something about the Christmas spirit. I kissed Pamela. So we came out of the trenches [*handwritten:* went over the top]. Some very queer days followed. Christmas had always been a big festival for the Potters and she was making this one more than ever gala. So there was that; there was also hours of reading to her and talking over with her the first hundred pages of *The Crooked Mile*, which she magnificently criticized; and, through it all, this hard duel of wits. She was bound, and there was now no disguise, that Pamela and I were going to be an engaged pair before I went back to Northwestern. I was quite sure we weren't going to be—but I still wanted to keep the mother. It was, in its way, exhilarating—and I don't doubt to her too—but at the same time it was more than slightly awful.… With comic interludes. I got a blinding nervous headache late on Christmas Eve, when I had been pressed hardest. And, getting unwisely liquored at another party, I felt myself suddenly vindictive and made open and persistent love to some thin-flanked and liquorish brunette and all but raped her, all under Pamela's horrified gaze—the one incident I'm genuinely sorry for.… Then one afternoon, Pamela having to attend to one or another of the charities that the Springfield equivalent of the Junior League managed, her mother and I started out for a walk. We both knew this was the showdown. After a mile or so, wanting to get it over and blindly searching also for some explanatory or justificatory theme, I found myself saying, "I wish to God you'd tell me why Pamela is so abject."

Mrs. Potter didn't say anything for easily five minutes. Then she said, quietly, "I've made a dreadful mistake. I'm not going to try to influence either you or her any more." That was all either of us said. We went home. It was over. She was gay and witty and detached all the rest of my stay. But I was looking at her when she said that and I've never seen so much fatality in anyone's eyes.

Well, I was detached too. I had to go to Northwestern before Pamela went to Wellesley. I promised to meet her train, and didn't. I put the brake on our correspondence. Her mother's letters continued—charming as ever, and quite without warmth. So in April I wrote that I was going to get married in June. The significant thing is that when Mrs. Potter wrote me in answer the last letter I ever got from her, she wrote as flippantly as a finishing school girl and quite unnecessarily told me that a couple of new oil wells had come in on the Doctor's Oklahoma land. And that lapse also has to be triangulated.... So let's, at long last, start to draw the lines. [*handwritten:* I never got round to drawing them]

NOTES

1. "Kent Potter" is BDV's alias for Kent Dunlap Hägler (1897–1920), Harvard '19 ('20), second son of Elmer Ellsworth Hägler and Kent Rolla Dunlap Hägler. The family name was usually printed without the umlaut over the a, but pronounced in the German way with long ā. Kent's older brother, Elmer Ellsworth Hägler Jr. (1894–1939), was Harvard '15. Their sister "Pamela" was actually Clarissa. When BDV says "something of the flavor of her real name" he is thinking of two enormous epistolary novels by Samuel Richardson (British, 1689–1761), *Pamela, or Virtue Rewarded* (1740) and *Clarissa Harlowe* (1747–1748, 3 vols.).
2. Thomas Middleton Raysor (1895–1974), '17, A.M. '20, Ph.D. '22; later professor of English at the University of Nebraska, an expert on Coleridge; in his twenty-fifth anniversary Class Report he mentioned both BDV and Gordon King. David Snodgrass (1894–1963), '17, Ll.B. '21, later professor at the Hastings College of the Law, University of California, San Francisco; Dean, 1940–1963.
3. Joseph Auslander and Robert Hillyer were both in the class of 1917.
4. "The Homeless Generation: I, Mansions in the Air," *New Republic* 72/934 (26 October 1932).
5. Apparently George Almy Percy (1895–?), '18 ('19); alumni records do not indicate that he was ever a poet.
6. A term coined by Karl Ulrichs, German author, in 1864, as a synonym for homosexuality.
7. Now the Howe Military School, in Howe, Indiana; established 1884, coed since 1988.
8. Francis Grierson, author of *The Valley of Shadows*, 1909.
9. James Hamilton Lewis (1863–1939), congressman from Washington, 1897–1899; senator from Illinois, 1917–1919; noted for his flawlessly elegant manner of dress.
10. "Craig Kennedy," sometimes called "the American Sherlock Holmes," is the hero of many short stories by Arthur B. Reeve (1880–1936), including several published in *Cosmopolitan*.
11. Kent Hägler's obituary in his first class report shows him to have been president of a K.G.X. Club (Kappa Gamma Chi?) in 1916–1917.
12. William Noel Hewitt (1891–1918), '14, A.M. '16, organist and composer.
13. Clarence Baker Stephenson (1896–1922), '21; or possibly Philip Edward Stevenson, '19 ('20).

14. Samuel Kerkham (S. K.) Ratcliffe (1868–1958), journalist; the "Guardian" is presumably the Manchester *Guardian*.
15. Eugene Galligan, '17, was killed on 6 September 1918 at Fismes, north of Blanzy.
16. Quentin Roosevelt (1897–1918), Harvard '19, son of former president Theodore Roosevelt, was killed in action in July 1918.
17. *A Tailor-made Man*, play by Harry James Smith, 1917.
18. BDV misquotes from the Declaration of Independence; President Wilson's address to Congress on 2 April 1917, asking for a declaration of war, concludes: "To such a task we can dedicate our lives and our fortunes, everything that we are and everything that we have, with the pride of those who know that the day has come when America is privileged to spend her blood and her might for the principles that gave her birth and happiness and the peace which she has treasured. God helping her, she can do no other."
19. Plattsburgh, city in northeastern New York State, on Lake Champlain; site of present Plattsburgh Air Force Base.
20. S.S.U., Special Service Unit.
21. The prolonged and desperately bloody battle at Verdun on the Meuse River in northeastern France began in February 1916.
22. (French) surprise attack.
23. Meredith is unidentified.
24. The mutiny in the French army of 1917 resulted from the bloody offensive and failed breakthrough of April 1917; order was restored with difficulty in time for the arrival of large numbers of American forces by the end of the year.
25. The near namesake, J. David Stern (1886–1971), newspaper publisher, owned both the Springfield *News* and the Springfield *Record*.
26. Leonard Wood (1860–1927), Spanish-American War general and military governor of Cuba and the Philippines; candidate for the Republican presidential nomination in 1920.
27. The Valois dynasty of French kings, successors to the house of Capet, reigned from 1328 (Philip VI) to 1589 (Henry III), and was succeeded by the first Bourbon king, Henry IV.
28. In 1916 General John J. Pershing ("Black Jack") commanded Army forces on an expedition into Mexico in a failed effort to capture the bandit Francisco ("Pancho") Villa.
29. Reference to Genesis 24.
30. Ricardo Quintana (1898–1989), Harvard '20; professor of English at the University of Wisconsin. Joseph Blickensderfer (1894–1960), A.M. '20, Ph.D. '26; editor, professor at the University of Pittsburgh.
31. *Moon Calf*, by Floyd Dell. *Smoke and Steel*, poems by Carl Sandburg. *A Few Figs from Thistles*, poems by Edna St. Vincent Millay. *The Sacred Wood: Essays on Poetry and Criticism*, by T. S. Eliot.
32. (French) humbug, hypocrisy, sanctimoniousness.
33. The book is unidentified.
34. (French, slang) wine.
35. Waldorf Cafeteria in Harvard Square.
36. *Mont St. Michel and Chartres*, by Henry Adams, 1904.
37. A satirical romance, French, thirteenth century.
38. *The Little Tin Soldier*, 1919.
39. Commercial air mail was first established in the U.S. on a regular basis only in 1926, on a few select routes in the Midwest.
40. (1896–1980), '19 ('20), later professor of philosophy at the University of Maine.
41. (French) stretcher-bearer.

42. Dr. William Herman.
43. See "Bucolics", Preface.
44. John Moses Browning (1855–1926), engineer, manufacturer of firearms, developed the Browning automatic rifle.
45. Autograph letter, signed (an abbreviation from bibliography and documentary studies).
46. In Weber Canyon in Ogden, a thousand miles west of Omaha along the Union Pacific route.
47. "The Amniotic Home" is the title of part I of Stegner's *The Uneasy Chair*.
48. Presumably Harold Edmund Stearns (1891–1943), Harvard '13, newspaperman, social critic, editorial staff of *The New Republic*; editor of *Dial*; *Rediscovering America*, 1934. What assistance he provided to BDV is unexplained.
49. *Evelina, or the History of a Young Lady's Entrance into the World*, by Fanny Burney (1752–1840), British novelist, 1778. Elizabeth Gaskell (1810–1865), British novelist; *Cranford*, 1853. *Amelia*, novel by Fielding, 1751. Dora, possibly Dora Spenlow in Dickens's *David Copperfield*, 1850.
50. "Let me be as a tuneswept fiddlestring/That feels the Master Melody—and snaps." From "Let me live out my years," in *The Quest*, 1916, by John G. Neihardt (1881–1973), Nebraska poet, novelist, and parapsychologist.

REFERENCE WORKS

American Film Institute Catalog. 23 vols. University of California Press, ongoing. (*AFI*).

American National Biography. 24 vols. New York: Oxford University Press, 1999. Published under the auspices of the American Council of Learned Societies (*ANB*).

Annual Obituary. New York: St. Martin's Press, 1980–1982; St. James Press, 1983.

Author Biographies Master Index. 4th ed. Detroit: Gale Research, Inc., 1994 (*ABMI*).

Baseball Encyclopedia. 10th ed. New York: Macmillan, 1996.

Biographical Dictionary of the American Congress, 1774–1996. Alexandria, Va.: Congressional Quarterly Staff Directories, Inc., 1997.

Biography and Genealogy Master Index, database.

Bloom, Ken, ed. *American Song: The Complete Musical Theatre Companion*. 2nd ed. New York: Schirmer Books, 1996.

Brewer's Dictionary of Phrase and Fable. 15th ed. New York: Harper-Collins, 1995.

Butler's Lives of the Saints. New full edition. 12 vols. Revised by Peter Doyle. Collegeville, Minn.: Liturgical Press, 2000.

Chielens, Edward E., ed. *American Literary Magazines: The Twentieth Century*. New York: Greenwood Press, 1992.

Christianson, Stephen G. *Facts about the Congress*. New York: H. W. Wilson Company, 1996.

Columbia Encyclopedia. 3rd ed. New York: Columbia University Press, 1963 (*CE*).

Contemporary Authors: A Bio-bibliographical Guide to Current Writers. New revision series. 104 vols. Detroit: Gale Research Corp., ongoing (*ConAu*).

Contemporary Theatre, Film and Television. 38 vols. through 2001. Detroit: Gale Group.

Dictionary of American Biography. 20 vols. New York: Charles Scribner's Sons, 1928–1936; supplement, 10 vols., 1944–1995 (*DAB*).

Dictionary of American History. Rev. ed. 8 vols. New York: Charles Scribner's Sons, 1976; supplement, 2 vols., 1996.

Dictionary of Literary Biography. Detroit: Gale Research Group, ongoing.

Drabble, Margaret, ed. *The Oxford Companion to English Literature*. Rev. ed. New York: Oxford University Press, 1998 (*OCEL*).

Encyclopedia Judaica. 17 vols. Jerusalem: Encyclopedia Judaica, 1972–1982 (*EJ*).

Encyclopedia of World Biography. 2nd ed. 17 vols. Detroit: Gale Research Group, 1998.

Ewen, David, ed. *American Popular Songs: From the Revolutionary War to the Present*. New York: Random House, 1966.

Grand Dictionnaire encyclopédique Larousse. 10 vols. Paris: Librairie Larousse, 1982.

Hartnoll, Phyllis, ed. *The Oxford Companion to the Theatre*. 4th ed. New York: Oxford University Press, 1983.

Havlice, Patricia Pate. *Index to Artistic Biography*. 2 vols. Metuchen, N.J.: Scarecrow Press, 1973; supplement, 1981.

Historical Register of Harvard University, 1636–1936. Cambridge: Harvard University Press, 1937.

Hogg, Ian. *Twentieth-century Artillery*, New York: Barnes & Noble Books, 2000.

Howard, Philip H. and Michael Neal. *Dictionary of Chemical Names and Synonyms*. Boca Raton, Fla.: Lewis Publishers, 1992.

Jens, Walter, ed. *Kindlers Neues Literatur-Lexikon*. 21 vols. Munich: Kindler-Verlag, 1988–1992; supplement, 1996.

Larkin, Colin, ed. *Encyclopedia of Popular Music*. 3rd ed. 8 vols. London: MUZE UK Ltd., 1998.

Leiter, Samuel R. *The Encyclopedia of the New York Stage, 1930–1940*. New York: Greenwood Press, 1989 (*ENYS*).

Lubbock, Mark. *The Complete Book of Light Opera* London: Putnam & Co., 1962.

Ludlow, Daniel H., ed. *Encyclopedia of Mormonism*. 4 vols. New York: Macmillan, 1992.

Mallegg, Kristin, ed. *Acronyms, Initialisms & Abbreviations Dictionary*. 44th ed. 4 vols. Detroit: Gale CENGAGE Learning, 2011.

Merriam-Webster's Encyclopedia of Literature. Springfield, Mass.: Merriam-Webster, 1995.

New Catholic Encyclopedia. 18 vols. New York: McGraw-Hill, 1967 (*NCE*).

New Century Encyclopedia of Names. 4 vols. New York: Appleton-Century-Crofts, 1954 (*NCEN*).

Peterson, Carolyn Sue, and Ann D. Fenton. *Index to Children's Songs*. New York: H. W. Wilson Company, 1979.

Placzek, Adolf K., ed. *Macmillan Encyclopedia of Architects*. New York: Free Press/Macmillan, 1982.

Sandoval, Annette. *The Directory of Saints: A Concise Guide to Patron Saints*. New York: Dutton/Penguin, 1996.

Sharp, Harold S., and Marjorie Z. Sharp. *Index to Characters in the Performing Arts*. 5 vols. Metuchen, N.J.: Scarecrow Press, 1966–1973.

Smith, G. E. Kidder, and the Museum of Modern Art. *The Architecture of the United States*. 3 vols. Garden City, N.J.: Doubleday/Anchor, 1981.

Tebbel, John, and Mary Ellen Zuckerman. *The Magazine in America, 1741–1990*. New York: Oxford University Press, 1991.

Treasure, Geoffrey, ed. *Who's Who in British History: Beginnings to 1901*. London: Fitzroy Dearborn Publishers, 1998.

Turner, Jane, ed. *The Dictionary of Art*. 34 vols. New York: Grove Press, 1996.

Variety Obituaries. 15 vols. New York: Garland Publishing, 1988, ongoing.

Ward, Roy D., and Betty A. Laird. *A Soviet Lexicon: Important Concepts, Terms and Phrases*. Lexington, Mass.: Lexington Books of D. C. Heath, 1988.

Wearing, J. P. *American and British Theatrical Biography*. Metuchen, N.J.: Scarecrow Press, 1979.

Webster's Ninth New Collegiate Dictionary. Springfield, Mass.: Merriam-Webster, 1991 (*WNCD9*).

Webster's Third New International Dictionary of the English Language, Unabridged. Springfield, Mass.: Merriam-Webster, 1991 (*W3*).

Who Was Who in America, with World Notables. Historical vol. (1607–1896). New Jersey: Marquis Who's Who; 10 vols., 1897–1993 and ongoing.

Who Was Who in the Theatre: 1912–1976. 4 vols. Detroit: Gale Research Group, 1978.

Who's Who in America. Wilmette, Ill.: Marquis Who's Who, 1904 and ongoing.

Wright, Joseph. *The English Dialect Dictionary*. 6 vols. London: H. Frowde, 1898–1905.

OTHER REFERENCES

KJV King James Version

LBDV *The Letters of Bernard DeVoto*, edited by Wallace Stegner

NEQ *New England Quarterly*

OED *Oxford Dictionary of the English Language*

SEP *Saturday Evening Post*

SRL *Saturday Review of Literature*

INDEX